HOUSEHOLDS IN CONTEXT

HOUSEHOLDS IN CONTEXT

DWELLING IN PTOLEMAIC AND ROMAN EGYPT

EDITED BY

Caitlín Eilís Barrett and Jennifer Carrington

CORNELL UNIVERSITY PRESS

Ithaca and London

Publication of this book has been aided by a grant from the von Bothmer Publication Fund of the Archaeological Institute of America.

Publication of this book has been aided by a grant from the Hull Memorial Publication Fund of Cornell University.

First published 2023 by Cornell University Press

Printed in the United States of America

Library of Congress Cataloging-in-Publication Data

Names: "Better to Dwell in Your Own Small House": Households of Ptolemaic and Roman Egypt in Context (Conference) (2018 : Cornell University) | Barrett, Caitlín E., editor. | Carrington, Jennifer, 1987–editor.
Title: Households in context : dwelling in Ptolemaic and Roman Egypt / edited by Caitlín Eilís Barrett and Jennifer Carrington.
Other titles: Dwelling in Ptolemaic and Roman Egypt
Description: Ithaca : Cornell University Press, 2023. | This volume publishes the proceedings of a two-day international conference at Cornell University, "'Better to Dwell in Your Own Small House': Households of Ptolemaic and Roman Egypt in Context" (April 27–April 28, 2018), organized jointly by the current co-editors, Caitlín Barrett and Jennifer Carrington. | Includes bibliographical references and index.
Identifiers: LCCN 2023015808 (print) | LCCN 2023015809 (ebook) | ISBN 9781501771309 (paperback) | ISBN 9781501772597 (epub) | ISBN 9781501772603 (pdf)
Subjects: LCSH: Household archaeology—Egypt—Congresses. | Households—Egypt—History—Congresses. | Social archaeology—Egypt—Congresses. | Dwellings—Egypt—History—Congresses. | Egypt—History—Greco-Roman period, 332 B.C.–640 A.D.—Congresses.
Classification: LCC DT92 .B477 2023 (print) | LCC DT92 (ebook) | DDC 932—dc23/eng/20230523
LC record available at https://lccn.loc.gov/2023015808
LC ebook record available at https://lccn.loc.gov/2023015809

In fond memory of our friend and colleague Ross Iain Thomas

Contents

Preface and Acknowledgments

This volume publishes the proceedings of a two-day international conference at Cornell University, "Better to Dwell in Your Own Small House": Households of Ptolemaic and Roman Egypt in Context (April 27–April 28, 2018), organized jointly by the coeditors of this book, Caitlín Barrett and Jennifer Carrington. Dorothy J. Thompson delivered the keynote presentation (published here as chapter 4). The current volume includes edited and revised versions of all of the papers presented at the conference, as well as two additional papers kindly contributed by Paola Davoli and David Frankfurter. The preparation of all of these papers for publication coincided with the onset of the COVID-19 pandemic, and we are immensely grateful to all of our contributing authors for their dedication, resilience, and patience under the resulting challenging circumstances, which unavoidably lengthened the time between conference and publication.

This conference, and the present volume, could not have taken place without the help of many individuals and institutions. The Department of Classics at Cornell University was the primary institutional sponsor for the conference and provided essential funding. We also received generous grants from a number of cosponsors at Cornell: the Cornell Institute of Archaeology and Material Studies (CIAMS); the Departments of Anthropology and Near Eastern Studies; the Religious Studies Program; the Archaeological Institute of America, Finger Lakes Chapter; the Cornell Society for the Humanities; and the Mario Einaudi Center for International Studies. By enabling us to subsidize the travel expenses of our participants, this funding made it possible for the conference (and resulting volume) to bring together an international group of scholars. We are immensely grateful for this generous support.

We are equally grateful for the help of many individual colleagues. Four colleagues at Cornell agreed to serve as discussants for the panels: Adam Smith (responding to Panel 1, "Households in Spatial Context"), Jonathan Boyarin (responding to Panel 2, "Households in Social Context"), Dana Bardolph (responding to Panel 3, "Households in Practice"), and Astrid Van Oyen (responding to Panel 4, "Expanding the Household"). These four discussants offered thoughtful feedback and insightful observations that, we believe, have materially improved the resulting publication.

The Cornell Classics Department accounts coordinators—first Philip Rusher, then Jessica Smith—coordinated the travel plans and hotel arrangements for all of our speakers. Jessica also went above and beyond in negotiating with hotels, restaurants, and caterers all across Ithaca to ensure that the event would be successful. We thank Classics Department manager Keeley Boerman for overseeing the finances for the event, and undergraduate coordinator Linda Brown for helping with logistics. We are also very grateful to the graduate student volunteers, Salpi Bocchieriyan, Katie Guttman, and Elizabeth Proctor, who helped with registration, setup, and cleanup and generally kept everything running smoothly during the conference.

At Cornell University Press, we are very grateful to Bethany Wasik, the acquisitions editor, for her support of this project and her helpful feedback; to Karen Laun, the assistant managing editor, for shepherding this project to completion; to Jack Rummel, the copy editor, for the keen eye that he brought to the text; to Joyce Goldenstern, for preparing the index; and to Kristen Gregg and the marketing team, for helping put this volume out into the world. We are also immensely thankful to Bradley Ault and to the anonymous reviewers of this volume, both external and on the Cornell University Press editorial board and faculty board, for numerous constructive, thoughtful, and helpful comments on the manuscript.

Financial support for this publication came from grants generously awarded by the Hull Memorial Publication Fund of Cornell University and the von Bothmer Publication Fund of the Archaeological Institute of America. This funding has been put toward lowering the purchase price of the volume, and we are grateful for the opportunity to make this volume more widely accessible to those who wish to read it.

We would like to express our most sincere thanks to all of the authors in this volume for their varied and exciting contributions, which bring new perspectives to bear on households, dwelling, and daily experience in Ptolemaic and Roman Egypt.

As is only fitting—for all publications, really, but especially one on the subject of households and families—we send our warmest thanks and love to our own families, who have supported us in this project as in everything.

Finally, we are deeply saddened to note that Ross Thomas passed away while this volume was in preparation. We thank his wife, Elisabeth O'Connell, for helping to review the text of his chapter and ensure that it is faithful to Ross's wishes. We are honored to be able to include Ross's work in this book, which we dedicate to his memory as a small tribute to a brilliant scholar, generous colleague, and kind friend.

Contributors

Youssri Abdelwahed, Faculty of Tourism and Hotels, Minia University

Richard Alston, Professor of Classics, Royal Holloway, University of London

Caitlín Eilís Barrett, Associate Professor of Classics, Cornell University

Anna Lucille Boozer, Professor of Archaeology and Ancient History, Baruch College and the Graduate Center, City University of New York

Jennifer Carrington, PhD alumna, Department of Classics, Cornell University

Paola Davoli, Professor of Egyptology, University of Salento (Lecce)

David Frankfurter, William Goodwin Aurelio Chair of the Appreciation of Scripture, Department of Religion, Boston University

Jennifer Gates-Foster, Associate Professor of Classical Archaeology, University of North Carolina at Chapel Hill

Melanie Godsey, Visiting Assistant Professor of Classical Archaeology, Texas Tech University

Darlene L. Brooks Hedstrom, Myra and Robert Kraft and Jacob Hiatt Associate Professor of Christian Studies, Department of Near Eastern and Judaic Studies, Brandeis University

Sabine R. Huebner, Professor of Ancient History, University of Basel

Gregory Marouard, Senior Research Scholar and Lecturer, Department of Near Eastern Languages and Civilizations, Yale University

Miriam Müller, University Lecturer in Egyptian Archaeology, Art, and Material Culture, Leiden University

Lisa Nevett, Professor of Classical Archaeology, University of Michigan

Bérangère Redon, Researcher, CNRS (Centre National de la Recherche Scientifique), Laboratoire HiSoMA (Histoire et Sources des Mondes Antiques)

Bethany Simpson, Assistant Professor of Art History, Virginia Commonwealth University

Ross I. Thomas, Curator, Department of Greece and Rome, The British Museum

Dorothy J. Thompson, Newton Trust Lecturer (emerita), Faculty of Classics, University of Cambridge

Figure 0.1. Participants in the 2018 conference "Better to Dwell in Your Own Small House": Households of Ptolemaic and Roman Egypt in Context (Cornell University, April 27–April 28, 2018). Bottom row (from left): Jennifer Carrington, Dorothy J. Thompson, Caitlín Eilís Barrett, Liam Benjamin Zarzycki Barrett (*in utero*), Dana Bardolph, Youssri Abdelwahed. Second row (from left): Gregory Marouard, Bethany Simpson, Anna Lucille Boozer, Lillian Rose Boozer-Velasco (*in utero*), Miriam Müller, Melanie Godsey. Third row (from left): Sabine Huebner, Darlene L. Brooks Hedstrom, Lisa Nevett. Top row (from left): Jennifer Gates-Foster, Ross I. Thomas, Richard Alston. Not pictured: Paola Davoli, David Frankfurter, and Bérangère Redon, who did not participate in the conference, and Jonathan Boyarin, Adam Smith, and Astrid Van Oyen, who participated as discussants. (Photograph by Elizabeth Proctor.)

Note on Abbreviations

In this volume, abbreviations of journals, book series, and standard reference sources follow those used by the *American Journal of Archaeology* wherever possible. Abbreviations of additional standard references in the field of Egyptology follow the conventions published in *Lexikon der Ägyptologie* 7. Abbreviations for Greek or Latin primary sources typically follow those found in the *Oxford Classical Dictionary*, fourth edition.

HOUSEHOLDS IN CONTEXT

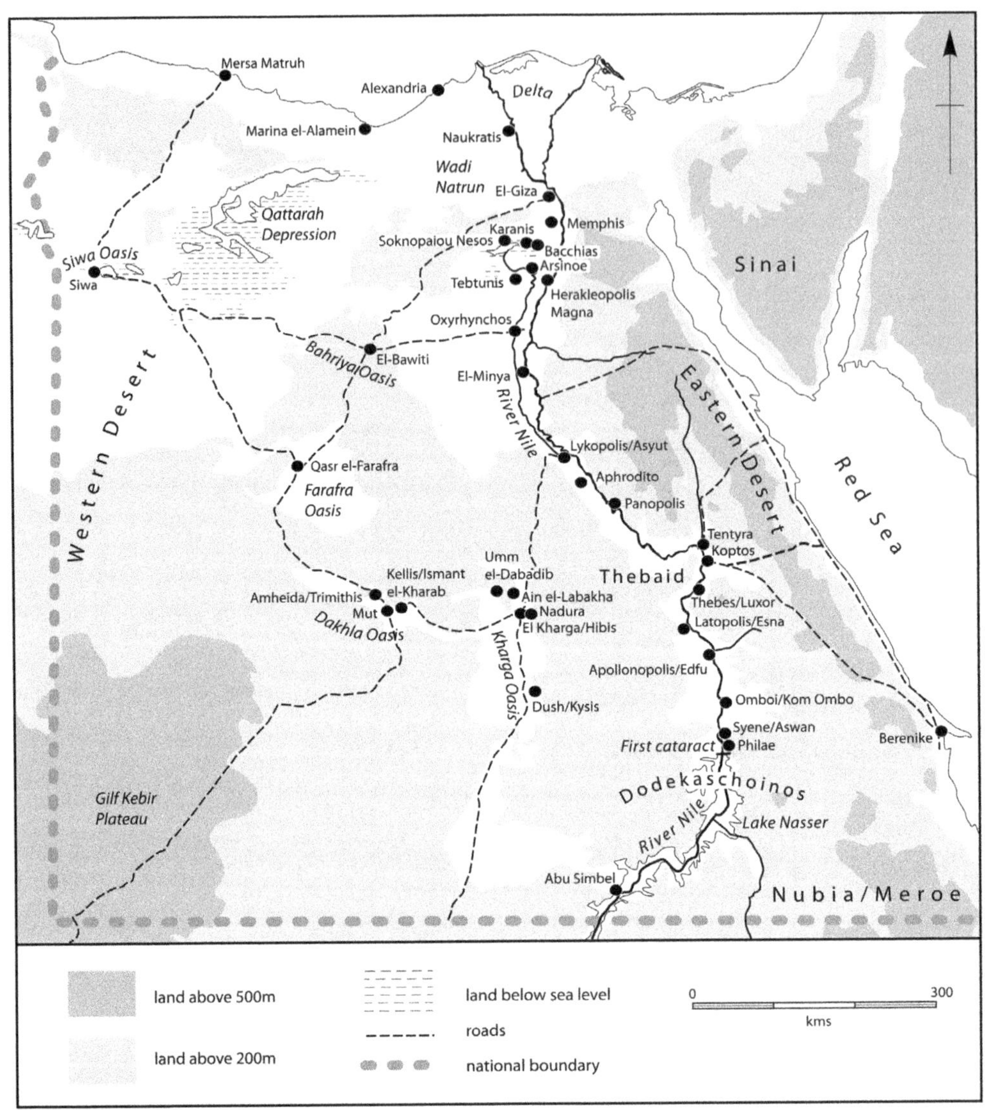

Figure 0.2. Map of Egypt in the Ptolemaic and Roman periods. (Created by Margaret Mathews; originally published as figure 1.1 in A. L. Boozer, *Amheida II: A Late Romano-Egyptian House in the Dakhla Oasis. Amheida House B2*. New York: New York University Press, 2015). CC-BY.

Introduction

Houses, Households, and Homes: Toward an Archaeology of Dwelling

CAITLÍN EILÍS BARRETT

One of the major achievements of late twentieth- through twenty-first-century archaeology has been the growth of theoretically engaged, multidisciplinary research on houses and households.[1] The study of ancient domestic life provides crucial insights into everyday dwelling practices, lived experiences, and the interactions of families and individuals with larger social and cultural structures.[2] Historically, scholars working in Egypt and the ancient Greco-Roman world have often focused more on monumental temples, tombs, and elite material and visual culture. However, an explosion of new research on houses and households is transforming the way that we think about life in ancient Egypt[3] and throughout the Mediterranean.[4] As the first synthetic book-length study of houses and households in Ptolemaic and Roman Egypt, this volume aims to bring together archaeologists, papyrologists, historians, and art historians to offer new perspectives on dwelling and daily practice.

Egypt during the Ptolemaic and Roman Periods provides especially rich material for household studies. Thanks to the extraordinary preservation of both material and textual remains, these eras of Egyptian history offer abundant evidence for ancient households: indeed, in some ways, even more than has survived from Pharaonic Egypt.[5] Egypt at this time also offers an important test case for "big questions" of cross-cultural importance, concerning, for example, the domestic impact of imperialism and colonialism.[6] The Macedonian king Alexander's conquest in 332 BCE initiated a turbulent new period of Egyptian history. After about three centuries as an independent kingdom under a dynasty of Greco-Macedonian origin, the Ptolemies (305–31 BCE), Egypt fell to the Roman warlord Octavian in 31 BCE and became a province of the Roman Empire. These two periods are sometimes categorized together as the "Greco-Roman Period," although as many scholars have pointed out, there were actually major social, political, and economic differences between the Ptolemaic and Roman administrations.[7] Nonetheless, both periods do share some distinctive cultural features, including the existence of a substantial, and in certain ways privileged, element of the population that identified as Hellenes (i.e., Greeks).[8] During the Ptolemaic Period and continuing into Roman rule, Egypt became a multiethnic, multicultural, and multilinguistic society, with multiple (and indeed frequently overlapping) population groups that included not only Egyptians and Greeks, but also Jews, Arabs, Thracians, and many others besides.[9] As a result, Egypt in these periods provides an important case study for investigating cultural entanglement, empire, globalization, and the negotiation of power relations and identities in the household.

Yet, while research on houses and households in Ptolemaic and Roman Egypt has substantially increased over the past two decades,[10] no major synthetic study of household archaeology has yet been published for these complex periods of Egyptian history—a gap that we hope this volume will help address. Some recent contributions provide synthetic analyses of settlements and household architecture in Roman Egypt.[11] However, the only comprehensive monograph on Ptolemaic-period houses is now over fifty years old, and there is a great need for newer synthetic studies of Ptolemaic housing that take account of recent research.[12] A better knowledge of Ptolemaic houses and households would also enrich the study of the Roman-period evidence. By facilitating deeper understanding of the ways in which Ptolemaic and Roman-period practices overlapped and diverged,[13] a diachronic perspective can address ongoing scholarly interest in questions of change and continuity between these two periods of foreign rule in Egypt.[14]

Through a multidisciplinary exploration of households in Ptolemaic and Roman Egypt, we intend this volume to promote further discussion about the interrelationships between domestic material culture and larger social, political, and cultural phenomena. In so doing, we seek to place the study of Greco-Roman Egypt in dialogue with recent theoretical and comparative research on households, dwelling, and daily practice.[15] A Ptolemaic-period text of wisdom literature in demotic Egyptian, *The Instruction of Ankhsheshonq*, advises ancient readers that "it is better to dwell in your own small house than to dwell in the great house of another."[16] While this passage's valorization of autonomy and exhortation to satisfaction with one's lot furnish intriguing evidence for ancient cultural values and social expectations, the emphasis on "dwelling" (Demotic *ḥms*) also provides a link to much more recent intellectual developments. Tim Ingold's so-called dwelling perspective treats buildings not as fixed and immovable containers for human activity, but as dynamic and socially embedded structures whose form and meaning are constituted through daily practice.[17] Viewed in this light, Ankhsheshonq's "small house" may be small in scale, but enormous in its potential to shape the daily experiences and practices of its occupants.

Approaching the Household

So what is it, exactly, that we are purporting to investigate? The modern English word *household* evokes a rather daunting array of meanings and connotations.[18] According to the *Oxford English Dictionary*, "household" can mean "a group of people (esp. a family) living together as a unit"; a "domestic establishment"; or even "the contents or appurtenances of a house considered collectively; household goods or furniture."[19] In other words, depending on context, "household" can evoke everything from people, to institutions, to places and structures, to things themselves: the physical "stuff" of domestic life. Nor are we on much firmer ground with "house," even if that term might initially seem to offer a reassuring solidity.[20] Architectural definitions of the "house" are challenging, because not all dwelling sites involve formal architecture,[21] and even when they do, there is not always a one-to-one relationship between a structure and a dwelling; some homes consist of massive multibuilding estates, while others are single apartments or rented rooms within buildings that are mostly occupied by other people.[22]

One of the most influential efforts to create operational definitions of "household" (and assorted related concepts) is that of the historian Peter Laslett. For Laslett and those who follow him, a *household* is about both people and place: it consists of individuals who both share a residence and act together as a meaningful socioeconomic unit.[23] These individuals may consist of a single *family* (that is, people who are genealogically related through kinship, however kinship may be defined in their society),[24] but this is not always the case. Besides family members, a household can also include dependents, such as enslaved laborers or live-in servants. In this volume, Dorothy Thompson (chapter 4) discusses a Ptolemaic-period demotic Egyptian property contract that refers to two types of servants (*bꜣk.w, šms.w*) as well as enslaved people (*ẖl.w*) as potential members of households. Laslett further distinguishes between household and *houseful*, which is a more comprehensive term for people who share a residence: whereas the members of a household are socially united in some capacity as members of a shared economic and legal unit, a houseful could also incorporate more distantly connected individuals, such as lodgers.[25]

We frequently read that the "household" is a socioeconomic entity, whereas the "house" is a physical entity. Yet if that is the case, the relationship between these two very different sorts of things is by no means straightforward. As Bruce Routledge puts it in a review of several recent publications on household archaeology:

> On reading these books in succession, I was immediately struck by the impression that (1) most scholars begin from the assumption that the household is a fundamental social group; (2) most scholars accept that this group bears some significant relationship to houses as built structures encountered in the archaeological record; and (3) no one presents a clear and coherent argument to explain this relationship; indeed, a number of authors seem to hold rather different views. So, from the beginning, we have a problem with the link between archaeological houses and households.[26]

And Routledge is not wrong to identify a serious issue here. Let's say we dig up a structure that we identify as a "house." If we assume an a priori one-to-one correspondence between this structure and the activities of a single social group that we call a "household," we risk eliding both the predepositional and postdepositional history of the structure. By the time we encounter the physical remains of houses in the archaeological record, they may have been inhabited by not just one household, but a whole series of households over generations.[27] Additionally, their current condition has been shaped not just by their ancient inhabitants, but by all manner of subsequent formation processes.[28] In this volume, Anna Boozer highlights the reuse of abandoned houses as garbage dumps (chapter 8).

Most recently, the "material turn" in the humanities and social sciences has prodded some scholars to problematize the apparent Cartesian dualism of "household" (as social construct) versus "house" (as actual, physical thing). As Julia Hendon expresses the situation:

> [A] certain unease has pervaded household archaeology, precisely because of the assumption that the true focus of interest is a social institution which must be an abstraction or an idea in people's heads, not a material form. Thus, houses become a stand-in that must always be qualified as less than ideal.[29]

Yet is the household really just an abstraction, a ghost in the house's machine?[30] If "household" refers, as per Laslett, to a group of people who live and work together in intimate proximity, then the household is not so much an *abstraction* as it is a *set of relations*. It describes the relationships between real people, whose bodies were just as material as anything else in the house, and whose interactions with each other would have been enacted through, and even constructed by, domestic material culture.[31] In other words, the household is a tiny network, whose participants—if we follow actor-network theory or a range of other "new materialist" approaches—could indeed be said to include objects as well as people.[32] Ultimately, the supposed dichotomy between the household and the house is a red herring. Instead of imagining the house as separate from the household, we may do better to conceive of it as a *member* of the household.

In which case: just as the human members of a household vary widely in their identities and personalities, so too do the material forms that share (and constitute) their living space. And in many cases, that living space may not confine itself neatly within the bounds of a single built architectural structure. As Lynn Rainville asks:

> Is domestic limited to the archaeologically discovered "home" or "house"? If so, would a communal bread oven (visited by neighbors each morning) constitute a "domestic activity area" or is the domestic space only the locale where family members consume the bread? On the other hand, would a local market where shoppers collect ingredients for baking the daily bread (or other meals) be considered part of a domestic activity area? . . . . [Are] the sherds recovered from a men's teahouse part of a domestic assemblage? . . . To pose the question another way, do people have to sleep in a structure for it to be domestic? And, if so, are inns, caravanserai, hotels, and so forth considered domestic residences? Or does sleeping have to co-occur with other domestic activities such as eating, child rearing, and bathing? With [*sic*] the co-occurrence of these two activities, a cemetery could be defined as domestic because it provides eternal rest.[33]

To rephrase Rainville's series of questions: of all the various activities that we associate with "dwelling," which ones are the most essential, why, and to whom? Here we also need to consider the possibility of differences between emic and etic conceptions of "house" and "home." Ancient people's understanding of what made a place into a home, or what made a group of people into a family or household, may often have been different from our own. To this end, the chapters in this volume address a wide range of perspectives on the relationships that connect and separate the English "household," Egyptian *per*, Greek *oikos*, and Coptic *ma nshōpe*.

In fact, let's go back to Rainville's comment about cemeteries as possible domestic spaces. In context, this statement appears to be intended as a rhetorical flourish—a sort of mic drop to prove her point about blurry definitions. Yet there are in fact societies where people speak of tombs as the houses of the ancestors[34] or preserve the bodies of the dead within the houses of the living,[35] and there are places, like the "City of the Dead" in modern Cairo, where living people repurpose tombs as dwellings.[36] The necropolis and the polis are not always categorically separate.

More broadly, many of the activities that take place in houses also take place in other residential or quasi-residential settings. Take, for example, inns, taverns, and brothels, all of which Glazebrook and Tsakirgis call "places of temporary habitation and dining."[37] Such sites are indeed "places of temporary habitation" from the perspective of their customers, but they may well be permanent habitations for the people working there. In the ancient Mediterranean, the proprietors of many small businesses—inns, shops, restaurants, bars, and other places—lived on the premises with their families.[38]

Brothels too were often long-term residences for the individuals who worked there,[39] raising the prospect of a household that is not centered on a family. Discussing one apparent brothel in Building Z of the Athenian Kerameikos, Bradley Ault proposes that the women who lived here should be considered "homeless," because even though they had a roof over their head, they did not have the sort of domestic community that Greeks would have understood as an oikos.[40] Yet the Greek oikos, or household, was (much like the English word) not defined in terms of kinship relations alone.[41] The people who lived and worked in this building may have remained there for a long time, and it is hard to imagine that they did not form any meaningful interpersonal relationships among themselves. Can we be certain that they did not understand themselves to constitute a sort of oikos?[42] We have ancient texts that inform us about how some Classical-period Greeks thought about the oikos, but these are almost entirely written by elite men,[43] whose perspectives might be very different from those of the women in Building Z.[44] When we ask how ancient people conceptualized "house," "home," and "family," it is important to consider differences between emic and etic perceptions—but we can also go farther. Rather than searching for one single homogeneous emic view, we should recall that many different opinions, worldviews, and perceptions can coexist within the same society.

So what actually are the limits of the "domestic"? Yanagisako notes that we typically do not consider as households "institutions like orphanages, boarding schools, men's houses, and army barracks" because their inhabitants do not share what we usually consider domestic activities, by which she means food production, food consumption, sexual reproduction, and childcare.[45] Yet most of these groups do in fact share food together, an activity widely recognized as a powerful generator of fellow-feeling and communal identity.[46] And while "child-bearing and child-rearing" are certainly important activities for many households, they are not necessary ones.[47] In antiquity as today, not all couples had children, and as Dorothy Thompson shows in her analysis of Ptolemaic tax registers (chapter 4), some people lived alone.[48]

By this point, readers would be forgiven for thinking (probably with some dread) that I want to reinterpret essentially every imaginable archaeological site, from tombs to shops to schools, as a sort of "domestic context." I hope it will come as some relief to read that this is not, in fact, my goal! Rather, I want to highlight the extent to which "dwelling" is a *spectrum* rather than an on/off condition, involving a wide range of possible activities and conditions that do not lend themselves well to a simple checklist.

I am skeptical about our ability to generate a universal list of conditions that must always be met before we declare a context to be "domestic." More to the point, even if it were possible to create such a list, I doubt we would learn very much from the exercise. The category of the "domestic" is what cognitive psychologists call a "fuzzy set": that is, a set whose borders are inherently blurry, and within which gradations of membership are possible. Psychologists have demonstrated that many, if not most, of the concepts expressible in human natural languages are fuzzy sets.[49] In other words, the slipperiness of terms like *house*, *household*, or *domestic* is not evidence that we need to work harder to define these categories more perfectly; it is an inevitable result of the way that natural languages work.

As editors of this volume, we choose to foreground the fuzziness of the set(s) that it explores, rather than trying to force the gloriously messy reality of life into artificially neat categories.[50] To that end, we have intentionally taken a hands-off approach to definitional issues, encouraging our contributors to define (or question, or reject, or redefine) "houses and households" as they see fit. The blurry boundaries of the household are perhaps most obvious in part V, "Expanding the Household: Dwelling Practices in Monastic and Military Contexts." These chapters investigate places of residence that are organized around groups other than the family: namely, monastic communities (Brooks Hedstrom, chapter 11) and military fortresses (Gates-Foster, Redon, and Godsey, chapter 12).

Yet in the earlier chapters too, houses, households, and families prove more slippery than one might expect. As Richard Alston shows (chapter 7), families might maintain dense ties across multiple households—and indeed even multiple communities—as well as houses. Household and family organization and composition varied widely (Thompson, chapter 4; Alston, chapter 7). Sabine Huebner's discussion of *habitatio* (chapter 5) explores one of the legal arrangements that might structure an individual's or family's relationship to a dwelling, underlining (among other things) that the resident of a house might not be its legal owner. A Ptolemaic tax register demonstrates that individuals might live not only in architecturally identifiable houses, but also in everything from shrines to gatehouses to bathhouses to shops (Thompson, chapter 4). Many domestic tasks took place outside houses, often in courtyard spaces or streets that might be shared between multiple households (Simpson, chapter 2; Alston, chapter 7). Activities essential to household maintenance might also be conducted farther afield. These could range from practical errands, like the grocery shopping that Rainville mentions above, to making offerings in temples to secure the well-being of family members.

Going further, the status of a given space as "private" or "public" often shifted over time and might be bitterly contested, with people appropriating public streets as personal property (Davoli, chapter 1; Simpson, chapter 2; Marouard, chapter 3) or, on the other hand, allowing neighbors to access routes on their property (Simpson, chapter 2) or converting abandoned houses into neighborhood waste disposal sites (Boozer, chapter 8). Concepts of the "family" were also up for renegotiation and might reach far beyond the common understanding of the family as "a group of people related by descent or marriage."[51] The Coptic monks studied by Darlene Brooks Hedstrom (chapter 11) were not biologically related to each other, but they used kinship terms, like *father* and *son*, to assert both hierarchy and intimacy within their community. Such language suggests a model of family that centers socially constructed relationships rather than biological descent.

Household Studies: From the Rearview Mirror to the Road Ahead

In a themed volume such as this, one of the introduction's traditional functions is surveying the history of research on that theme, so that readers can better appreciate where this intervention has come from and what it aims to do. A comprehensive survey of all previous household studies would be impossibly vast: we would need to cover the disciplinary histories of, at a minimum (and in alphabetical order), anthropology, archaeology, architecture, art history, classics, Egyptology, history, Near Eastern studies, philosophy, sociology, and urban planning.[52] Given the reality of space constraints, this will not be such a behemoth of a treatise. Instead, I will focus primarily on the history of household studies within one of the multiple disciplines represented in this volume: archaeology. Developments in other fields will also be referenced, but largely in relation to their impact on that one. This choice is of course not unrelated to my own specialization as an archaeologist! However, beyond such individual factors, I also believe—as I will discuss below—that household archaeology is especially well placed to contribute to current interdisciplinary dialogues about "posthumanism" and its limits.

The Creation of a "Household Archaeology"

Paradoxically, household archaeology was both a late and an early development within the larger archaeological field. The first explicit call for a "household archaeology" did not appear until 1982, in an article by Richard Wilk and William Rathje. Yet at the same time, archaeology might without much exaggeration be said to *originate* in digging houses; the eighteenth- and nineteenth-century excavations at Pompeii and Herculaneum, which started out as antiquarian treasure grabs and evolved into more rigorous research programs, were early laboratories for the development of archaeology as a serious academic discipline.[53] However, even if those first excavators spent much of their time in domestic contexts, they did not envision themselves as pursuing "household studies" per se. Their interest was initially antiquarian and subsequently culture-historical, and they did not seek to engage with (or generate) a corpus of social theory about families, households, or dwelling. Wilk and Rathje's essay was thus the first *programmatic* call for "household archaeology" as a distinct field of study.[54] This innovation followed, and was made possible by, the earlier development of "settlement archaeology."[55] In the Americas, settlement archaeologists had used house floor assemblages to reconstruct household activities since the 1970s.[56]

Wilk and Rathje's article appeared some years after the initial heyday of the "processualist" or "New Archaeology" but was very much a product of that movement. Setting out the goals for their new subfield, the authors reproduce the aims of the processualist movement as a whole: testing hypotheses in order to generate universal laws for human behavior, generating "middle-range theory," and interpreting human behavior in terms of ecological adaptation.[57] The emphasis on culture as what Lewis Binford called an "extrasomatic means of adaptation for the human organism"[58] led many processualists to treat ideology, ontology, religion, emotion, arts, and essentially everything else classifiable under the heading of "humanities" as epiphenomenal. Skeptical of the possibility of even studying such dubious business, the New Archaeology charge leader Binford scoffed that he was not a "paleo-psychologist."[59]

Processualist archaeology placed more emphasis on the (supposedly) "hard" drivers of history, which in practice meant mostly technological, economic, and sociopolitical factors.[60] And to that end, Wilk and Rathje inform us: "Looking at households cross-culturally, we find that the many activities they perform can be classified into four categories of function: production, distribution, transmission, and reproduction."[61] They go on to clarify these categories as follows: "Production is human activity that procures resources or increases their value,"[62] distribution is "moving resources from producers to consumers,"[63] transmission is "a special form of distribution that involves transferring rights, roles, land, and property between generations,"[64] and reproduction "consists of the rearing and socializing of children. . . . Child care demands constant time and effort, and households can be organized to provide this constant care in different ways. Pooling of labor is a frequent solution to the problem."[65]

In other words, households, as Wilk and Rathje portray them, are fundamentally *economic* institutions. They are about producing resources, moving them around, and transmitting them over generations. Even "reproduction," a category that we might expect to have slightly more emotive charge, turns out to be all about labor management.[66] Archaeologists are not to be concerned here with intimate relationships or family dynamics, but with the organization of child care duties and the question of whether or not "women's labor" is deployable to "play a major productive role" outside of child care.[67]

In fact, early household archaeology was not really about households per se. As Tringham puts it: "Household archaeology in the 1980s implied examining and analyzing social change at a microscale as a complement to analyses of social and economic change at a broader scale. . . . Household archaeology served to provide a richness of detail, but was not an end in itself. The ultimate target was to understand social evolutionary change."[68]

Wilk and Rathje's essay helped to jumpstart the entire subfield of household studies within archaeology, and I do not intend to downplay the importance of their work by pointing out the ways in which it was a product of its time; after all, archaeologists should be the first to affirm that everything is a product of its time. This book, and I, are profoundly indebted to these and other scholars' pioneering work—and to the processualist movement at a whole. The rigorous analysis of find assemblages, formation processes, and the whole rainbow of methodologies and approaches describable as "archaeological science" are dependent on the advances made by the New Archaeology. Nor do I intend to downplay the importance of research on domestic economies. Such work remains vibrant today and continues to produce important and far-reaching conclusions (and is indeed well represented within this volume: many of the contributions address economic concerns among others). Indeed, we might see households as fundamentally baked into economic studies at the level of basic vocabulary; the English word *economy* is derived from Greek *oikonomia*, the management of the oikos![69]

Nonetheless, when most of us think about the role of households and household dynamics in our own lives, it seems safe to say that we are not *exclusively* concerned with economic considerations. Until the 1990s, however, an economically oriented approach dominated the field of household archaeology. In areas where the processualist movement had a strong impact, such as Mesoamerica and (slightly later on) Near Eastern prehistory, Wilk and Rathje's work inspired a proliferation of household studies centering on socioeconomic concerns.[70] The household was seen as fundamentally an economic unit as well as (simultaneously) a spatial one; households could also be described as the smallest "unit of settlement."[71] This conflation of social and spatial was, as we have seen, to be long lasting.[72]

When archaeologists of the 1990s started to question some of these assumptions, they were inspired by developments both within and beyond their own field. The so-called postprocessualist movement had begun to reshape archaeology's dominant goals, questions, and methods. At the same time, archaeologists were also engaging with approaches developed in other disciplines for studying ancient houses and households. Accordingly, let's first take a look at some of those models and methods, and then consider some ways that archaeologists of the late twentieth and early twenty-first centuries have sought to incorporate their insights while also developing new, archaeology-specific approaches.

Models outside Archaeology: Other Twentieth-Century Approaches to Houses and Households

Outside of archaeology, early studies of households and families often looked very different. Anthropologists of the nineteenth and twentieth centuries were deeply interested in kinship rules and residence patterns, which led them to conduct research on households at a much earlier date than within archaeology.[73] If economy was the defining focus of early household archaeology, then kinship played a similar structuring role within early anthropological studies. Importantly, some of this research positioned households and families as sites for making, not just reflecting, "big-picture" history. For example, Jack Goody argued in the 1970s that different kinds of marriage and residence practices produced a series of massively cascading differences in social organization across cultures.[74] Claude Lévi-Strauss's concept of "house societies" similarly positioned households (of a sort) as central structuring principles of social organization, although the "houses" he had in mind were not (just) physical structures but powerful corporate bodies organized around kinship or fictive kinship: say, the House of Windsor, not the house down the road.[75] Additionally, Donald Bender's 1967 definition of the household as a group of coresidents "who together carry out domestic functions"[76]—that is, activities "concerned with the day-to-day necessities of living"[77]—provides an early precedent for an activity-oriented, dwelling-focused perspective on households. Finally, new anthropological and sociological approaches to patterned human behavior, both within and without the household, were developed in the later decades of the twentieth century. Most important here is Pierre Bourdieu's "practice theory," which was rooted in a close examination of activities within Kabyle houses in Algeria and will be discussed further below.[78]

Historians also took an explicit interest in households and families at an earlier date than archaeologists. The twentieth-century move toward social history, which incorporated new interests in everyday life and nonelites, helped to inspire such research.[79] Historians of the Annales school, such as Fernand Braudel, positioned households within the context of larger "multiscalar histories."[80] A central figure in the 1970s was Peter Laslett, whom we've already encountered for his influential definitions of key terms. Reacting against social-evolutionary theories of family structures, Laslett made the case that the nuclear family was commonplace throughout human history rather than being an artifact of the Industrial Revolution.[81] While his arguments have been criticized as going too far in claiming consistency in family structures over time, his work helped to move the discourse away from unilineal, universal evolutionary schemes.[82] He also insisted—decades before such an approach would become widespread in archaeology—on the importance of studying "relationships *within* familial groups," rather than (exclusively) "relationships *between* them."[83]

If anthropologists and historians provided archaeology with models of research on the *people* involved in households, architecture and urban planning provided new ways of thinking about the built space of *houses*. In the second half of the twentieth century, architects and planners developed a range of new theoretical perspectives and methodologies that subsequently proved extremely influential for archaeologists: for example, Hillier and Hanson's space syntax theory, Rapoport's conception of built space as a form of nonverbal communication, or Lynch's work on the perception of urban space.[84] In these approaches, built space emerges not just as a container for human activity, but a shaper of that activity: facilitating some practices or social relations, while rendering others impossible or challenging. Different types of space have what the psychologist James Gibson would call different "affordances," or potentials for facilitating certain outcomes, actions, or behaviors.[85]

"Households with Faces"

In the last decade of the twentieth century, archaeologists began to consider new questions about the individuals who actually populated ancient households. An important pioneer was Ruth Tringham, who in 1991 challenged scholars to envisage "households with faces," that is, to examine the range of identities and social roles available to different individuals in ancient households.[86] Such interventions were closely linked to larger movements within the field: first, the rise of feminist archaeology, and second, the broader postprocessual movement, which placed greater emphasis on subjectivity, identity, ideology, and experiential approaches to the past.[87] While Tringham and other feminist archaeologists were especially interested in gender dynamics within the household, they also called for research on intrahousehold variation more broadly. Members of a single household might differ from each other based not only on gender, but also age, bodily ability or disability, ethnicity, legal status (for example, free versus unfree), socioeconomic status, social roles, and much more besides.

The same period also saw new explorations of symbolism and ideology within the household. This work was often heavily influenced by the broader postprocessualist enthusiasm for structuralism and semiotics. For example, Ian Hodder's early writings placed great emphasis on the house as a *cognitive construct*: a sort of *idea* of domesticity which, placed in structuralist-style opposition to wilderness ("domus" vs. "agrios"), helped shape the development of sedentary farming life in European prehistory.[88] Another, and more architecturally grounded, source of inspiration was Rapoport's work on the communicative functions of built structures.[89] Even Richard Blanton's comparative study of households, which otherwise largely centers processualist concerns and methods, aimed to address such new areas of interest as "gender relations" and "how house form communicates cosmological principles."[90]

It was also around this time that socially oriented studies of ancient households started to make more of an impact, not only in the Americas and at prehistoric sites (i.e., places where processualist archaeologists tended to work), but also in the study of ancient historical states in the Near East, Africa, and southern Europe.[91] In Egypt and the Greco-Roman world, many of the most famous settlements—Deir el-Medina, Amarna, Olynthos, Delos, Pompeii, Herculaneum—had first been excavated long before. However, archaeologists working in these and other Egyptian and Mediterranean sites started asking new questions of their data.[92] Topics of interest to postprocessualist household archaeologists, such as gender dynamics in the household, were frequently central to this work.[93]

At the same time, archaeologists working in these regions sought to take on board many of the methodological advances associated with the processualist movement. While the so-called "great divide" between anthropological archaeology and more text-focused "classical" archaeologies had largely prevented the latter from adopting the "New Archaeology" when it was actually new, household archaeologists sought to make up for lost time.[94] Scholars such as Lisa Nevett, Bradley Ault, and Penelope Allison have advocated forcefully for moving beyond typological and stylistic analysis to contextualize artifacts within larger domestic assemblages; treating "small finds" as seriously as more monumental or beautiful objects; incorporating archaeobotanical and faunal evidence into household studies; and paying attention to formation processes.[95] Microarchaeology is also starting to make inroads today in Near Eastern, Egyptian, and Mediterranean household archaeology, despite some ongoing practical challenges.[96]

Material Households

By the early twenty-first century, Rana Özbal could write that household archaeology was "no longer in its infancy" and "has shed much of its functionalist, adaptive, and ecological foundations" to address a wider range of questions and perspectives.[97] Yet while many of us might no longer endorse Binford's reductive characterization of culture as humans' "extrasomatic means of adaptation" to the environment, that environment—and the material world more generally—made a major reappearance in the scholarship of the new millennium.[98] The "material turn" in the humanities and social sciences has refocused archaeologists' attention on the physical "stuff" of our subject. A broad assortment of theoretical movements, diverse in their details but loosely describable as "new materialist" or (following Ihab Hassan) "posthumanist," have emphasized the agency of the material world: the ability of things to act on humans, not just be acted on, and to make things happen.[99] Scholars associated with these movements also tend to be wary of semiotic or symbolic approaches to material culture.[100] Rather than asking what houses *represent*, the "new materialisms" typically ask what they *do*.

Within household archaeology, this perspective has inspired a range of different research directions. One of these concerns the impact of the natural environment in shaping house forms. For example, Mantha Zarmakoupi shows that the architecture of elite Roman houses should not be understood *solely* as a response to social pressures (e.g., patrons' need for space to receive their clients in style) or competition between rivals. Certainly, these motivations were important, but climate and environmental factors also played major roles in Roman house design.[101] Similarly, in this volume, Paola Davoli and Darlene Brooks Hedstrom explore the impact of the (often harsh) Egyptian physical environment on dwelling structures (chapters 1 and 11). Another line of research concerns the material affordances and dependences of houses' raw materials.[102] The material properties of clay, for example, had profound effects on domestic life at Çatalhöyük. As Susan Gillespie discusses, many of this settlement's distinctive building practices (e.g., the repeated demolishing and rebuilding of mud-brick houses) and architectural features (e.g., the uneven elevations of house roofs) were directly dependent on the physical characteristics of mud bricks.[103] Yet another strand of contemporary household archaeology explores the ways that domestic material culture shapes people's activities, ideologies, and social roles.[104] Along these lines, my own work on Roman wall paintings asks how domestic representations of Egyptian landscapes would have helped to construct, not just represent, ideologies of imperialism.[105] Leire Olabarria similarly portrays Egyptian stelae as creating, not just expressing, kinship relations.[106] And in a recent study of Roman storage practices, Astrid Van Oyen shows that the arrangement of storage facilities around Roman houses had serious social consequences; no single member of the household could possess a complete knowledge of all these decentralized storage facilities, and this limitation on central control created opportunities for women and enslaved people to exercise more agency.[107]

Although we may think of "new materialism" as a recent development, this approach (or, better, collection of approaches) to houses actually has ancient, emic precedents. In a treatise on household management by the Greek writer Xenophon, a character explains that the physical affordances of the rooms determine the activities that people can perform within them: "The rooms themselves invited what was suitable for each of them."[108] Although this observation sounds as though it could come straight out of contemporary theoretical literature, it dates back to the fourth century BCE.

Decidedly not available in Xenophon's day, however, were a variety of new quantitative and digital tools for studying exactly how houses might have impacted, not just reflected, their ancient residents' lives. In order to connect "space" to "people," archaeologists have often drawn on anthropological or sociological theories about the social construction of space[109] or the nature and patterning of human behavior.[110] What has been missing, however, is an effective bridging mechanism between theory and data—what processualist archaeologists called "middle-range theory."[111] While theorists such as Lefebvre or Giddens offer frameworks for conceptualizing space and social interaction, they do not provide concrete tools for analyzing the kind of evidence that archaeologists have to work with.[112] An exciting new way forward comes from computer-based, quantitative analytical approaches to spatial analysis, many of them developed over the past fifteen years by architects and urban planners. These include techniques for studying visibility (e.g., isovist analysis, visual integration analysis, lighting analysis), movement and behavior patterning (agent-based modeling, least-cost path analysis, spatial network analysis), and the creation of immersive virtual environments (3D modeling). Formal spatial analysis has great potential for archaeological research and is increasingly applied at Egyptian and Mediterranean sites;[113] within this volume, Bethany Simpson applies Space Syntax Analysis to Roman-period Karanis (chapter 2). A major recent breakthrough has been the integration of 3D modeling with geographic information systems (GIS) data.[114] Integrated 3D-GIS has exciting capabilities for modeling embodied, sensory experience within built space, potentially incorporating data not only visual but also auditory and tactile.[115]

Today, research on ancient households continues to explore many of the questions that animated earlier processualist and postprocessualist research programs, but in ways that engage seriously with critiques of the earlier approaches. For example, much new work continues to investigate domestic economies, but without seeking to reduce the household to entirely economic concerns.[116] Identity also remains a major focus of interest, but with a greater awareness of the interpretive problems involved. Recent publications increasingly take pains to disavow simplistic "pots = people" approaches that attempted to isolate distinct material signatures for specific identities (ethnic, gender, socioeconomic, and religious, among others).[117] Instead, twenty-first-century scholarship often prefers to explore the impact of domestic material culture on social identities, rather than the other way around. We may not be able to say that a particular pottery type or decoration style proves the presence of people with a particular identity—but we *can* ask, for example, what affordances a particular domestic environment provides for people with different embodied identities: what different experiences would have been possible for people of, say, different genders, ages, or physical conditions?[118]

Contemporary research also seeks to nuance the twentieth-century rejection of overreliance on textual sources. Within Greco-Roman, Egyptian, and Near Eastern archaeology, early research on households tended to center textual sources and treat material evidence as merely illustrative of insights gleaned from the texts.[119] So when archaeologists in these regions embraced household archaeology in the late twentieth century, there was something of a backlash against the (over)use of textual evidence.[120] Indeed, by 2013, a review article on Levantine household archaeology could lament that "it is surprising how little use is made of texts in these books, given the rich sources relating to domestic life available from the ancient Near East."[121] Miriam Müller has recently advocated for the reintegration of material and textual evidence to construct a more holistic understanding of ancient households.[122] This volume allies itself with such a synthetic approach (as most explicitly advocated by Dorothy Thompson, chapter 4).

Today, we find ourselves about two decades into the "material turn"—as a general rule, about the point at which one expects new paradigms to rear their heads. And indeed, some forms of the "new materialisms" are increasingly targets of forceful critique, even alongside ongoing enthusiasm.[123] Recent scholarship questions whether a non-anthropocentric archaeology is genuinely desirable (or indeed possible, given that the research papers are still being written by humans); whether the concept of "agency" still retains sufficient force if separated from intentionality; whether the appropriation of other cultures' ontologies risks patronizing or erasing the people who actually came up with those ideas; and perhaps most compellingly, whether a "flat ontology" lets humans off the hook for the ethical consequences of their own bad actions, and thus damages scholars' ability to produce social critique.[124] This last objection actually also has ancient precedents. Athenian law permitted not only humans, but also inanimate objects and animals, to be tried for murder.[125] However, people could also perceive this symmetry as problematic. For example, we hear of ancient debates over the accidental death of an athlete, and whether he had "really" been killed by a javelin, the person who threw the javelin, the judges who oversaw the contest, or the athletic trainer who called him onto the field.[126] In one account, the dead athlete's father resists all attempts to blame any agent other than the person who threw the weapon.[127] The bereaved father is, effectively, rejecting a flat ontology as ethically unacceptable.

Household archaeology is well positioned to contribute to this debate. As with all archaeologists, our work depends on things: the material objects that have survived from the past. However, houses and households are also sites powerfully charged with human emotional significance. We cannot understand the functioning of domestic artifacts without situating them within this space of powerful, affective, sensory, embodied experience. At the same time, we cannot understand those human experiences without examining the ways that the material conditions of ancient households would have prompted particular sensations, thoughts, and emotions.

Archaeology is inherently oriented around the study of *things*—the *archaia,* or "old things," for which we are supposed to provide a *logos.* As such, this field should occupy the very center of any movement to challenge anthropocentric biases and position things, no less than humans, as historical agents. But at the same time, the study of everyday, domestic experience also orients us toward some of the most profoundly human aspects of the ancient world: the daily activities, interactions, perceptions, feelings, and sensations that actually constituted people's lives. And while archaeology is about *archaia*, it is also about *logos*—which means, among many other things,[128] a story. Humans may not be the only historical actors that matter, but stories do still require people to tell and listen to them. Household archaeology can help us unite the insights of the "new materialisms" with an unapologetic interest in—and empathy for—embodied, sensuous, cognitive, emotive human experience.

New Directions in Household Studies

Different scholars might well choose to emphasize different facets of the contributions to this volume, and the two afterwords provide stimulating examples of such syntheses (Müller, this volume; Nevett, this volume). Here I wish to highlight three major themes that seem to me to emerge from the chapters collected here. One is an understanding of the household as a complex assemblage, which brings together humans, material things, nonhuman animals and plants, and even supernatural entities. The second is a multiscalar perspective on ancient households, which were embedded within a whole range of larger networks that included neighborhoods, cities, states, and international systems of exchange. The third is an emphasis on people's practices of dwelling and homemaking.

Households as Assemblages

Turning first to the household as assemblage (and further developing the theme of material agency),[129] multiple chapters suggest that the important actors in ancient households were not just human beings, but also the material things that shaped those people's lives.[130] Darlene Brooks Hedstrom (chapter 11) advocates most explicitly for a "thing theory" approach to the agency of the physical house itself.[131] Paola Davoli (chapter 1) demonstrates the ways that the physical environments of Egyptian houses constrained and shaped the forms that they could take—and thus also, to a great extent, the activities that were possible within and around them. As she shows, the design of Fayum and Oasean houses responded to the practical necessity of protecting their inhabitants against windblown sand, dust, and strong sunlight. The result was an enclosed, dark, inward-looking house structure that would have afforded privacy and seclusion—but while those affordances might have consequences for the ways people used and conceptualized domestic space, their origins derived at least in part from environmental necessities rather than exclusively cultural values. Gregory Marouard argues for another set of environmental influences on the vertical form of the Ptolemaic tower house, which he sees as originally a response to limited building space in the Delta and Nile Valley (chapter 3). Turning to the material culture within those houses, Ross I. Thomas's contribution (chapter 9) deals with domestic figurines to which ancient people may themselves have attributed agency. While terracotta figurines of gods or other supernatural beings may look small and unimposing today, ancient people sometimes imagined them to possess awesome powers—even to incarnate deities themselves,[132] complete with all those gods' subjectivity, volition, and awareness.[133]

As I have proposed above, a material agency approach can help us overcome the Cartesian dichotomy between "house" and "household," enabling us to see the physical house as a *member* of the household rather than a passive container for it. At the same time, other contributions to this volume point to a role for the *im*material. As Frankfurter's chapter shows, the occupants of ancient houses also included (or, at least, were believed to include) supernatural beings: unseen demonic powers whose visitations were an unwelcome, but widely recognized, feature of domestic life (chapter 10). Yet while these powers were invisible, they were by no means intangible; their presence could cause bodily illness and injury, and protection against their powers often included physical, wearable objects such as amulets. People might also have interpreted interpersonal violence, such as that discussed for unsafe houses in chapter 6 (Abdelwahed) and in the Sakaon archive in chapter 7 (Alston), as a concrete manifestation of supernatural maleficence. Indeed, as Frankfurter observes, some ritual curses explicitly set out to cause domestic discord (chapter 10). Ultimately, the material and immaterial aspects of household life were intertwined to the point of inextricability.

Efforts to recognize the agency of things, as well as people, are sometimes framed as calls for a "symmetrical archaeology."[134] In practice, however, that symmetry usually has its limits. Nonliving things may have agency, in that they can make things happen and shape the trajectories of events, but most archaeologists working within what we (unsatisfactorily) term "Western" ontologies would not attribute intentionality, emotion, or subjectivity to them.[135] Here the "ontological turn" in contemporary archaeology may help us appreciate some of the ways in which ancient individuals would have disagreed with us.[136] For example, the so-called Greek and Demotic Magical Papyri make clear that in Greco-Roman Egypt, people might well have viewed domestic figurines or amulets as possessing thoughts and volition.[137]

As an example of the complex interactions of human and material agency within these domestic spaces, let's consider the interplays between the physical form of the houses and the human activities that took place within and around them. As Davoli shows, the architecture of houses and settlements in arid environments was in large part a response to those environments, not solely cultural values or individual preferences.[138] Nonetheless, that architecture could still have had consequences at both the cultural and individual levels, helping generate the linkage between spatial organization and social behavior that Bethany Simpson explores in her contribution (chapter 2). For example, enclosed houses with high, narrow windows afforded a privacy that might sometimes help facilitate the socially aberrant behavior discussed by Youssri Abdelwahed (chapter 6), as domestic abuse could be kept invisible from neighbors.[139] Such behavior would of course not be *necessitated* by the houses; as per the ethical critiques sometimes launched against the "new materialisms," we can still hold human beings to account for their own destructive choices![140] But the physical affordances of a space can make it easier or harder for people to pursue certain actions. Similarly, the labyrinthine street systems of Fayum and Oasean settlements (Davoli, chapter 1; Simpson, chapter 2; Marouard, chapter 3) might originate in attempts to protect against the elements, but they would also have consequences for human behavior: for example, making it much harder for nonlocals to find their way around a neighborhood, and thus placing a high importance on the embodied, intimate knowledge of urban space that results from long-term dwelling. As Simpson shows (chapter 2), such a context could facilitate complex interpersonal and neighborly relationships. The tall, narrow, towerlike structure of many dwellings (Marouard, chapter 3) could also have had social and cultural motivations and/or consequences, serving "to discourage substantial social interaction and to create a highly controlled, enclosed, and private interior" (Simpson, chapter 2).[141] Environmental factors, sociocultural values, and individual choices were all closely entangled in these dwellings, with none entirely determining the others, but all responsive to each other.

Still other participants in ancient household assemblages were neither humans, nor nonliving things, nor supernatural entities. People in Ptolemaic and Roman Egypt also shared their homes with a wide variety of nonhuman living beings, both animals and plants. Domesticated animals could be kept for economic purposes, like the pigs, chickens, donkeys, and cows who occupied the courtyards and animal pens of houses in Roman Egypt (e.g., Simpson, chapter 2; Alston, chapter 7; Boozer, chapter 8). These creatures provided food, labor, and even waste disposal (Boozer, chapter 8) for their households. Domestic pigeoncotes, like the one referenced in one of the rental agreements that Huebner discusses (chapter 5; see also Simpson, chapter 2), could be sources of fertilizer.[142] Other domesticated animals, like dogs, may have been valued not only as work animals but as companions; iconography from Ptolemaic and Roman Egypt suggests that dogs were sometimes kept as pets.[143] In a society where the gods frequently took animal form, animals (and their images) could also evoke divine powers and protection.[144] Of course, not all of the house's nonhuman residents were welcome. People would also have shared their space with rats, insects, and dangerous pests such as scorpions and snakes. These last are visible in ritual attempts to ward them away from the house (Frankfurter, chapter 10). Plants, too, were essential participants in household well-being; not only were roofs, furniture, and many other domestic objects made with plant matter,[145] but most households were economically dependent in one way or another (whether directly or indirectly) on grain agriculture.[146]

So households included far more participants than just humans alone, and yet for many of us, the main reason to study ancient households is the window that they open onto the human experience. Here the rich evidence from Ptolemaic and Roman Egypt is especially evocative. Thanks to archives of papyri and other textual materials, we can track the whole history of an individual's marriages, divorces, and disputes with their in-laws (Alston, chapter 7); appreciate both the opportunities and restrictions that shaped the lives of widowed women (Huebner, chapter 5);[147] explore the variety of family and household arrangements in a Ptolemaic village (Thompson, chapter 4); and witness a pregnant woman's anxiety that she be able to stay at her own mother's house to give birth, rather than having to go back to her husband (Frankfurter, chapter 10).[148] The material and textual evidence for domestic rituals (Thomas, chapter 9; Frankfurter, chapter 10) also provides vivid testimony to relatable human hopes and anxieties, such as maintaining the favor of the gods, protecting one's children, and preventing sickness. More grimly, as Youssri Abdelwahed's contribution reminds us (chapter 6), home was not only a place of love and protection, but sometimes also violence and abuse. Navigating their way through a world of both tenderness and cruelty, the people who lived in these households were—for both better and worse—vividly human.

There is something deeply affecting about these glimpses into real people's lives, partial and murky though the glimpses are. One of the key sources for Dorothy Thompson's discussion in chapter 4 is a bilingual house-by-house survey from a Ptolemaic village. In addition to painting an amazingly detailed and lively picture of a community where, as Thompson (chapter 4) puts it, "geese honked, children played outside, and courtyards were full of activity," this document also introduces us to specific villagers such as Tharetis, who managed an Isis shrine; her seventy-year-old-husband; and their adult son, a priest of Isis, who still lived with his parents. We know nothing else about this family, but the description is still specific enough that we experience the sudden jolt of the encounter with real, once-living people in their irreducible individuality.

Multiscalar Households

This volume also makes a case for a multiscalar perspective on the household. Multiple contributions address the relationship between microscale and macroscale history (see most explicitly Alston, chapter 7; and Boozer, chapter 8). As we've seen, domestic activities were not just limited to the physical structure of the house, and families could maintain ties across multiple households. Other chapters demonstrate that individual houses were not self-sufficient entities, but enmeshed in the fabric of larger neighborhoods. Important areas for domestic activities, such as courtyards and streets, might be shared between multiple households (Simpson, chapter 2; Alston, chapter 7). The material forms of houses might also wind up shaping the organization of larger neighborhoods; Gregory Marouard (chapter 3) suggests in his conclusion that at the end of the Ptolemaic Period, the preference for multistory houses could have encouraged the development of insulae. The neighborhood, no less than the house, emerges as one of the key units of dwelling.

This volume thus contributes to a growing literature in twenty-first-century household archaeology that emphasizes the theme of access and communication *between* houses.[149] Such approaches have also made an impact within Egyptology, classics, and Near Eastern studies. For example, Miriam Müller has explored neighborhood dynamics at late Middle Kingdom Tell el-Dab'a,[150] and at Amara West, Spencer explores the conjoined "biographies of houses and settlements."[151]

Goldberg proposes that close neighbors in Classical Athens may have viewed each other as "fictive families,"[152] and Tsakirgis notes that multiple houses at Archaic Zagora might share the same open area, outside their doors, as a communal dwelling space.[153] Most recently, Kondyli and Anderson investigate Byzantine neighborhoods as sites of political agency.[154] Much additional scholarship explores the relationship of individual houses to broader settlement-wide dwelling patterns.[155]

If we understand households as tiny networks, as proposed above, then a multiscalar approach may help us understand how those networks connect to other, larger webs of connectivity.[156] At the smallest scale, the household is composed of individuals—who could, as David Frankfurter's chapter shows, themselves sometimes be equated to houses! One amulet refers to a pregnant woman *as* a house, and in so doing, also transforms the woman's (actual) house into an "extension of the maternal body" (chapter 10).[157] Expanding beyond the level of the house or even the neighborhood, households are situated within still larger communities: cities, provinces (or, in Egypt, nomes), states, and beyond. Lehner has argued for conceptualizing all of (Pharaonic-period) Egypt as a massive household,[158] and indeed, the term *Pharaoh* itself literally means "great house," Egyptian *per-aa*. Households can also act as microcosms of international networks: for example, when people purposely display exotic-looking objects in order to perform cultural ideals of cosmopolitanism, or, conversely, use imported forms or styles for entirely local purposes,[159] treating the artifacts' international connections as banal or irrelevant to their value.[160] To quote the historical archaeologist Charles Cobb, "Households mediate the local and the global"[161]—and in Greco-Roman Egypt as elsewhere, globalization seems always already to be glocalization.[162]

Practices of Dwelling and Homemaking

In this volume, the term *dwelling* is regularly employed to describe the practices associated with houses and households. One of my goals in using this particular language is to invoke what Tim Ingold calls the "dwelling perspective" on ancient houses. For Ingold, a "dwelling perspective" presumes that human beings do not enter a world "to which form and meaning have already been attached," but rather, "the world continually comes into being around the inhabitant, and its manifold constituents take on significance through their incorporation into a regular pattern of life activity."[163] For the purposes of household archaeology, this means (among other things) that domestic material culture does not come preprogrammed with a set of meanings and functions that people passively download; instead, people are constantly actively engaged in creating, transforming, and reinterpreting their surroundings. Additionally, as Ruth Tringham points out, a "dwelling perspective" on ancient houses reminds us that those houses may have led long "lives" before they entered the archaeological record, so that their forms, contents, uses, inhabitants, and essentially everything about them may have altered dramatically.[164] Such is certainly the case for many of the dwellings in this volume, whose chapters testify to substantial changes over time to the structures of houses, streets, neighborhoods, and even cities (Simpson, chapter 2; Marouard, chapter 3).

The language of "dwelling" also helps to foreground the *practices* of household life, as opposed to (just) the built structures. So-called practice theory has been central to household studies ever since Pierre Bourdieu's classic study of the Kabyle house, with which Richard Alston engages in this volume (chapter 7).[165] When archaeologists use domestic material culture as evidence for everyday practices, they commonly make reference to Bourdieu's concept of *habitus*: that is, the socially conditioned "systems of durable, transposable *dispositions*" that shape our behavior, causing us to unconsciously reproduce the same social structures that acculturated us into possessing such dispositions.[166]

More broadly, when someone asks what is really at stake in the study of ancient households, most of us probably give an answer that has something to do with practices. We may say that we want to understand how ancient people's lives compared to our own, or the ways that different social identities (socioeconomic, ethnic, cultural, gendered, age-based, or many others) impacted everyday life, or the relationships between the macrohistory of empires and the microhistory of the household, or much more besides. To answer questions like these, we need to move beyond treating houses as static containers for people, and toward a more dynamic understanding of households as living, moving, changing assemblages.

Earlier, I considered some challenges of definition—what actually constitutes a house or a household? One way to respond to those questions, but without attempting to reduce their complexities to a checklist, is through reference to the practices of dwelling. A "house" is a place where people dwell, and a "household" is the collection of people, things, and nonhuman beings that are collectively engaged in that dwelling. Of course, the obvious follow-up question is: All right, so exactly what acts constitute "dwelling"? And the equally obvious answer is that "dwelling activities" are another fuzzy set. Some common examples might include sleeping, eating, cooking, caring for children, having sexual relations, making clothing, urinating and defecating, conducting home repairs, sweeping and cleaning, engaging in personal leisure activities, and socializing with invited guests, but numerous other examples might also be invoked, and there are plenty of domestic or domestic-like contexts from which many of the above are absent.[167] As with the other concepts central to this undertaking, it seems preferable to embrace flexibility rather than to attempt to force life's complexities into the Procrustean bed of a rigid formula.

Another concept closely linked to "dwelling," though not quite interchangeable with it, is "homemaking." In a study of what she calls "homemaking" in antiquity, Meredith Chesson describes homes as spaces deeply imbued with their residents' emotions, thoughts, sensations, and perceptions of meaning.[168] Homemaking, then, is whatever activities turn a house into a home for its residents—and the nature of those activities might vary widely across societies. Exploring the creation of "homespace" as an act of resistance by enslaved Africans on American plantations, Whitney Battle-Baptiste similarly emphasizes the importance of embodied, everyday practice.[169] Here we might also compare Anna Boozer's characterization of "dwelling as place making" (this volume, chapter 8).

One advantage of what we might call the "homemaking perspective" is the emphasis it places on emic, as opposed to etic, conceptions of home. Rather than trying to come up with some universally applicable definition of "home," or (even worse) assuming that whatever evokes "home" for us must automatically also apply in antiquity, this approach provokes us to ask new questions about ancient people's perspectives on "home." What did *they* see as essential or desirable in order to feel "at home" in the places where they dwelled? What practices did they adopt in order to achieve that result? In other words: rather than taking ancient people's experiences of "home" as either an a priori given or an inaccessible "black box" that we have no hope of opening, an archaeology of homemaking challenges us to explicitly investigate the ways that dwelling practices generated affective, sensuous, and emotional experiences.

Many examples emerge from this volume. Domestic rituals, in which people might manipulate figurines (Thomas, chapter 9), light lamps, hold celebratory feasts, or try to compel dangerous spirits (Frankfurter, chapter 10), provide obvious examples of engaging, emotionally charged household practices. Frankfurter even suggests that rituals for safeguarding the house "might be analogized to a kind of therapy" in their emotional and cognitive effects on the people conducting the rituals (chapter 10). And as Boozer shows in this volume, even mundane-seeming tasks such as rubbish disposal could evoke powerful feelings of "guilt, shame, or regret" (chapter 8). This emphasis on domestic emotions and sensations points toward one way in which we might connect household studies to broader calls for a more multisensory, experientially oriented archaeology that takes affect and subjectivity seriously.[170]

I also enjoy—although this is not a point that Chesson herself makes explicitly—the subtle subversion implicit in the language of "homemaking." For many American English speakers, the term *homemaker* evokes a particular image, and associated conservative ideology, of a dutiful wife and mother who adheres to a rigid set of mid-twentieth-century Western gender roles. However, "homemaking," as Chesson defines it, is not specific to any gender; it is something that everyone does, one way or another. Claiming homemaking as a subject for archaeology is thus not only a political choice but also a practical necessity. Since homemaking (of various kinds) occupies such an enormous amount of human beings' time and energy, we will have a very hard time understanding ancient societies if we do not study it.

Household studies—particularly within archaeology—have a long history of holding the more "squishy" aspects of their subject at a wary distance. As we have seen, the first explicit calls for a "household archaeology" positioned the household as above all else an *economic* entity. The resulting portrayals of all domestic activities in economic, instrumentalist terms suggest a household populated exclusively by ancient accountants. And despite the subsequent impact of the postprocessualist and posthumanist movements, this initial starting point continues to shape household archaeology today. As Bruce Routledge observes, most contemporary studies still "explicitly or implicitly opt for the economic definition of households as task groups related to production and consumption."[171] The purposeful embrace of highly emotively charged concepts, such as "home" and "homemaking," is thus a useful corrective to the earlier sidelining of affective and subjective experience within ancient domestic contexts.

All of the chapters in this volume deal, in one way or another, with dwelling. Do they all deal with sites whose inhabitants would have understood them as "homes"? After all, it is possible to dwell in a place without feeling at home there. In her recent work on the lives of young Black women in the early twentieth-century United States, Saidiya Hartman draws a distinction between a residence where one "settles"—essentially, one might say, a dwelling whose inhabitants feel at home within it—and a residence where one simply "stays" (even if that "staying" proves to be long-term).[172]

Chapter 12 in this volume may provide one example of a place where people *stayed*, some potentially for lengthy periods, without necessarily feeling at home. In this contribution, Jennifer Gates-Foster, Bérangère Redon, and Melanie Godsey explore the Ptolemaic fort at B'ir Samut as a "forthold": not a household per se, but a place where soldiers, *phylakites* (police), and other personnel engaged in many of the same dwelling activities (e.g., sleeping, food preparation, eating, storage, bathing) that we find in more prototypically domestic contexts. In the Roman Period, forts might indeed serve as places of long-term residence; at sites elsewhere in the empire, such as Vindolanda, we have clear evidence for the presence of children and families.[173] What then of this earlier, Ptolemaic fort? Would the military personnel stationed at B'ir Samut, or the travelers who found temporary housing in the fort, have considered it to be, on some (or any) level, "home" during their time there? Even if the answer is no—even if some or most of them actively longed to return to their own houses and families—can we find evidence for any practices that might have helped to create a more "homelike" sense of comfort, normalcy, and security, even if its effects could be only partial?[174] Some of the objects found at the fort may be personal possessions of the soldiers, staff, or visitors: for example, the handmade cookpot of possible East African origin, or the faience amulet (Gates-Foster, Redon, and Godsey, this volume). Might the presence of objects from home have helped recall sensations, emotions, and memories associated with "home"?

Turning to a very different context, Darlene Brooks Hedstrom's chapter reveals the existence of ancient tensions regarding what we might call the "homeliness" of monastic dwellings.[175] On the one hand, ancient texts like the *Sayings of the Desert Fathers* idealize the notion of a dwelling place that generates no attachments and provides only the barest minimum of shelter to support life; but on the other hand, both those texts and the material record also demonstrate that many monks sought to create a more personalized "sense of place" within their cells (chapter 11). Ultimately, acts of homemaking turn out to retain their power even in this supposedly ascetic environment: "By stepping into the dwelling place, monks were making a house a home" (Brooks Hedstrom, chapter 11).

Structure of the Volume

The themes chosen for the subdivisions of this volume are explicitly multiscalar. Part I, "Households in Spatial Context: Settlements, Neighborhoods, and Urbanism," examines the relationship of houses to larger neighborhoods and settlements and addresses ongoing debates about the nature of urbanism in Greco-Roman

Egypt. Part II, "Households in Social Context: Families, Individuals, and Communities," focuses on the scale of the individual household. Chapters in this section address the role of domestic space in shaping people's performance of social roles and structuring families and communities. Part III, "Households in Practice: Production, Consumption, and Discard," moves beyond the previous section's focus on the *inhabitants* of domestic space to explore the *activities* that enlivened these spaces. Chapters in this section examine household practices of production, consumption, and discard and explore the ways those practices linked individual households to pan-Mediterranean networks of connectivity and exchange. Part IV, "Households in Cosmic Context: Religion and Ritual," investigates religious, ritual, and magical practices within the household.[176] The evidence and discussions in this section contribute to recent debates about the nature and limits of personal cult, individual religion, and their relationship to state or official cult, while also adding to anthropological and archaeological research on the materiality of religion. Finally, part V, "Expanding the Household: Dwelling Practices in Monastic and Military Contexts," investigates dwelling in contexts other than family residences: for example, monastic communities and military fortresses. Such contexts provoke questions about the nature and definition of "households" and encourage further exploration of the utility of "household" as an analytical construct.

As the contributions to this volume demonstrate, the household is a place where etic categories like "social," "political," "economic," and "religious" become thoroughly blurred in practice. The study of everyday dwelling practices thus provides an opportunity to question the ways we conceptualize and categorize human behavior, whether in antiquity or today. Rather than representing a genuinely separate sphere of activity, households turn out to be inextricable from larger lifeworlds. This entanglement is apparent as early as part I, "Households in Spatial Context," whose chapters consider settlement planning as both a domestic issue and a civic/administrative issue. The blurry boundaries of the "household" are perhaps most visible in part V, "Expanding the Household," which questions standard assumptions about what actually constitutes a house, household, or dwelling. These chapters examine arenas for dwelling that are not based on the biological family. In separating the practice of *dwelling* from the sociocultural unit of the *family*, these chapters demonstrate the profound embeddedness of dwelling within other, seemingly separate spheres.

Collectively, this volume argues that a serious study of households reveals the limitations of some old, but common, assumptions about the location of agency, innovation, and historical change. Traditional historical accounts tend to represent the household—insofar as they represent it at all—as an essentially passive entity, affected *by* important events rather than affecting them. The real action is attributed instead to spaces such as the court, the battlefield, and the temple: these are contexts where we traditionally imagine "serious" history happening. This downplaying of the agency of the domestic undoubtedly derives, at least in part, from the perceived lower status of a space that scholarship has historically (and reductively) associated with "women's work."[177] However, as the contributions to this volume demonstrate, events in the domestic sphere were not just reactions to developments that "really" occurred somewhere else. A focus on households reveals the power of the everyday: the critical role of quotidian experiences, objects, and images in creating the worlds of the people who live with them. The household emerges not as a bystander to history, but as a laboratory for social, political, economic, and religious change.

Introduction: Houses, Households, and Homes. Towards an Archaeology of Dwelling

1 Two sections of this chapter—the introduction and the closing remarks about the structure of the volume—are based on the opening statement to the 2018 conference whose proceedings this volume publishes. I thank Jennifer Carrington for her contributions and feedback on the original opening statement, as well as her helpful comments and keen editorial eye on the present piece. I also thank the students in two of my seminars at Cornell, "Themes in Mediterranean Archaeology" and "The Archaeology of Houses and Households," for many productive and intellectually exciting discussions of problems in household archaeology.

2 For multiregional and comparative approaches to household archaeology, see within the past twenty-five years Allison 1999a; Barile and Brandon 2004; Westgate et al. 2007; Parker and Foster 2012; Madella et al. 2013; Fogle et al. 2015; Müller 2015a; Tringham 2015; Carpenter and Prentiss 2022. On the archaeology of everyday life, see Robin 2002; Mullins 2012; Naum 2012; Overholtzer and Robin 2015; Foxhall 2020.

3 For Pharaonic-period Egypt, see (from the 1990s on) Shaw 1992; von Pilgrim 1996; Meskell 1998, 2002; Spence 2004, 2015; Koltsida 2007; Bietak et al. 2010 (selected contributions on household archaeology); Kemp and Stevens 2010; Moreno Garcia 2012; Müller 2012, 2015d, 2015e; Zarmakoupi 2014, 2015; Di Castro and Hope 2015; Kamel 2015; Moeller 2016; Mazzone 2017; Olabarria 2020; Sigl and Kopp 2020; Sigl 2022. For houses and households in Nubia under Egyptian occupation, see recently Dalton 2013; Spencer 2014a, 2014b; Budka 2017, 2020. On Meroitic houses and households, see Wolf, Nowotnick, and Hof 2014; Baldi 2017.

4 In Greco-Roman (and more generally Mediterranean) studies, see (from the 1990s on): Jameson 1990a, 1990b; Veyne 1992; Clarke 1991, 2003; Ducrey et al. 1993; Hoepfner and Schwandner 1994; Wallace-Hadrill 1994; Walter-Karydi 1994; Bruneau 1995; Pesando 1997; Laurence and Wallace-Hadrill 1997; Siebert 1998; Trümper 1998, 2003, 2005; Zanker 1998; Dickmann 1999; Métraux 1999; Nevett 1999, 2008, 2010, 2015; Ault 2000, 2005a, 2005b; Ellis 2000; Westgate 2000, 2007, 2013; Cahill 2002; Droste and Hoffmann 2003; Hales 2003; Reinders and Prummel 2003; Allison 2004, 2006; Putzeys et al. 2004; Ault and Nevett 2005; Tang 2005; Tsakirgis 2005, 2015, 2016a; Bonini 2006; Westgate et al. 2007; Nanoglou 2008; Souvatzi 2008; Bowes 2010; Ladstätter and Scheibelreiter 2010; Haagsma 2010; Morgan 2010; Anguissola 2012; Baird 2014; Joshel and Petersen 2014, 24–86; Huebner and Nathan 2016; Rathmayr 2017; Baldini and Sfameni 2018; Marín-Aguilera 2018; Berg and Kuivalainen 2019; Stoner 2019; Dardenay and Laubry 2020; Uytterhoeven 2020; Harrington 2021. Baird and Pudsey 2022 was published while this volume was in production and could not be consulted for this contribution.

5 See Müller (afterword 1, this volume), on the greater amount of household-related textual evidence from Greco-Roman Egypt as compared to Pharaonic Egypt.

6 Ptolemaic Egypt differs in many respects from the colonial states of the modern world (Bagnall 1997), but Dietler's general definition of colonization as "imposing political sovereignty over foreign territory and people" (2010, 18) clearly applies to Alexander's conquest of Egypt. Subsequently, the Roman rule of Egypt certainly involved, as per Dietler's (2010, 18) definition of colonialism, "projects and practices of control marshaled in interactions between societies linked in asymmetrical relations of power." On the devastating consequences of Roman imperialism, see Fernández-Götz et al. 2020; Padilla Peralta 2020.

7 Lewis (1995) famously emphasized discontinuity rather than continuity between these periods; see further Barrett 2015a, s.v. "Introduction." Monson (2012) has more recently reexamined the transition from Ptolemaic to Roman rule.

8 Although definitions of "Hellene" were subject to much change over time: see Thompson 2001; Hall 2002; Clarysse 2019.

9 See most recently Thompson 2011; Honigman 2019. The label of "Persian" or "Persian by descent" describes a military category, not an actual group of Persian expatriates (Vandorpe 2008).

10 See, e.g., (since the late 1990s), Alston 1997; Depraetere 2005 (focused primarily on house plans, but wide-ranging in temporal scope); Hadji-Minaglou 2007, 2012; Boozer 2010, 2012, 2015a, 2015b, 2015c, 2019, 2021; Marouard 2010, 2012; Daub and Griesbach 2013, 26–29; Abbas and Abdelwahed 2014; Marchi 2014; Abdelwahed 2015, 75–101; Hudson 2016; Langellotti 2020, 86–101; Cole 2022; Davoli 2022. On domestic cult and "magic," see Frankfurter 1998, 131–42; 2019; Wilburn 2012, 95–168; Grüner 2013; Boutantin 2014; Barrett 2015b; Abdelwahed 2016. See also the growing literature on cities and settlements (Davoli 1998, 2001, 2010; Bowman 2000; Alston 2002a, 2002b, 2006; Mueller 2006; Leclère 2008; Marouard 2008; Müller 2010; Subías et al. 2011; Tacoma 2012; Boozer 2014; Fassbinder et al. 2015; Langellotti 2020) and on families and family structure (e.g., Thompson 2002; Yiftach-Firanko 2003; Alston 2005; Huebner 2007, 2013; Remijsen and Clarysse 2008; Pudsey 2011, 2012, 2013, 2015; Malouta 2012; Bagnall et al. 2016; Rowlandson and Lippert 2019). Baird and Pudsey 2022 was published while this volume was in production and could not be consulted for this contribution.

11 E.g., Alston 1997, 2002a; Abdelwahed 2015, 75–101; and see now Boozer 2021 on domestic life.

12 Nowicka 1969.

13 Husson's (1983) study of the vocabulary of domestic housing takes such a diachronic perspective, covering the third century BCE to the seventh century CE, but focuses on papyrological rather than archaeological evidence.

14 See note 7 above.

15 See note 2 above.

16 Trans. Ritner 2003, 523; for the text edition, see Glanville 1955.

17 Ingold 2000, 172–88, drawing on Heidegger 1971, 145–61. Building on Ingold's work, Ruth Tringham stresses the importance of treating ancient houses as "places," rather than "spaces": "A place is a space that is given meaning by and creates meaning for people who pass through and within it" (2003, 93). See further Tonner 2018.

18 As also discussed by Thompson (chapter 4, this volume).

19 *OED Online*, s.v. "household," accessed July 29, 2021.

20 Note too that "house" need not refer exclusively to a physical location: consider the use of "house" to describe elite family lineages (as in the "house societies" of Lévi-Strauss 1982, 176–87), political entities such as the House of Representatives, clothing designers (e.g., Maison Margiela), or the chosen families of American Black and Latinx LGBTQ ballroom culture. Cf. the similar observations of Birdwell-Pheasant and Lawrence-Zúñiga 1999, 7.

21 See, e.g., Chesson 2012, 49, on caves and campsites as "residential units."

22 Cf. the distinction that Spence draws between "house" and "residential establishment" (2015, 85).

23 See, e.g., Laslett 1972, 23–45, 86; Hammel and Laslett 1974, 75–79. Note, however, much subsequent critique and refining of Laslett's definitions of family, household, and houseful, see references collected by Grey 2011, 36n42.

24 Such relationships need not be limited to biological descent, but could include adoption and other social practices recognized within a society as creating kinship ties. Some scholars treat the term "family" as distinct from "relatives" in that the members of a family must live together (e.g., Alston 2002a, 69), whereas others see the concept of "family" as disconnected from questions of residence (e.g. Bender 1967, 504). On emic and etic concepts of kinship (especially in ancient Egypt), see now Olabarria 2020, 75–95.

25 See note 23 above. The distinction is now fairly widely used in Mediterranean archaeology (e.g., Wallace-Hadrill 1994, 92, 103–17; see also Thompson, chapter 4, this volume).

26 Routledge 2013, 208. He is not the first to point this out; among others, Rani Alexander raised a similar critique almost fifteen years previously (1999, 80–81). For Alexander, "household archaeology is a misnomer. Archaeologists do not actually study households; they study spatial patterns of settlement that include dwellings, compounds, and house lots" (1999, 81). See similarly Allison 1999b, 2.

27 On the temporal depth of houses' occupational history, and household assemblages as potentially multiperiod palimpsests, see (inter alia) Hirth 1993; Smith 1992; Alexander 1999, 81; Tringham 2003, 93–95; Rainville 2015, 17–18; Barrett 2019, 27.

28 On formation processes, see Schiffer 1987 generally, and LaMotta and Schiffer 1999 on house floor assemblages in particular.

29 Hendon 2004, 275.

30 With apologies to Gilbert Ryle, who originally coined the phrase "ghost in the machine" as a dismissive characterization of Cartesian dualism (1949, 15–16).
31 As argued at more length in Barrett 2019; see now also Barrett and Bellucci 2022.
32 On objects as agents (or, in actor-network theory terminology, "actants"), see below, "Material Households."
33 Rainville 2015, 3, 6.
34 E.g., on Roman Italy, Wallace-Hadrill 2008. On house tombs generally: Barrie 2017, 74–89.
35 Flinders Petrie proposed that people in Roman Egypt kept mummies in their houses, although this theory is today much disputed (see overview in Gessler-Löhr 2012, 666–67). More common cross-culturally is the practice of burying the dead underneath house floors: e.g., Gillespie 2000, 140–41 (on Maya practices); Boz and Hager 2013 (on Çatalhöyük).
36 See El Kadi and Bonnamy 2007; El Kadi 2016. Tombs might be repurposed as houses in antiquity as well (Ault 2005b, 140).
37 Glazebrook and Tsakirgis 2016, 7.
38 E.g., for the Greco-Roman world: Pirson 1999, 19–20, 53–55; Trümper 2003, 2005; Flohr 2007; Joshel and Petersen 2014, 121–25.
39 Ault 2005b, 147–50; 2016; Glazebrook 2016; Levin-Richardson 2019, esp. 38–39. On the difficulty of distinguishing find assemblages from brothels and more "standard" houses, see Glazebrook 2016; Lynch 2016.
40 Ault 2005b, 147–50. On the archaeology of "homelessness," see Kiddey 2017 on the experiences of contemporary unhoused individuals.
41 For a discussion of Greek sources on the oikos, see Nevett 1999, 4–20. Besides family members, the oikos could also include enslaved people (Jameson 1990a, 104) as well as the house and other physical possessions (see further *LSJ*, s.v. οἶκος).
42 I am grateful to the students in my 2020 graduate seminar, "Archaeology of the Hellenistic Mediterranean," for a lively and productive discussion on this point. In particular, Quinn Stickley made a strong case for the possibility that Building Z's residents could have viewed themselves as an oikos.
43 E.g., Lys. 1, Xen. *Oec*. See, among others, Nevett (1999) on the limits of these texts as evidence.
44 If indeed they were all women; male prostitutes are also well attested, and the places where they worked were not necessarily architecturally distinct from those of female prostitutes. See Glazebrook 2011, 39–43.
45 Yanagisako 1979, 164–66, 164.
46 Sexual activity, whether reproductive or (usually) otherwise, is also not unknown in most of these settings. Within the vast bibliography on the archaeology of commensality, see Dietler and Hayden 2016; Pollock 2015.
47 Quoting Yanagisako 1979, 166.
48 On singles in antiquity, see Huebner and Laes 2019. Yanagisako recognizes "solitaries (individuals living alone) as constituting households" (1979, 164).
49 Smithson 1987, 1; Rosch 2011.
50 Compare Alston's warning against definitions that artificially "bring a sociological clarity to social practices that were fundamentally messy" (chapter 7, this volume).
51 Quoting Rainville 2012, 142.
52 For previous histories of household studies in (some of) these fields, see Buchli 2010 (anthropology); Tringham 2015 (archaeology); Steadman 2016, 164–68 (archaeology); Barrie 2017, 109–26 (architectural theory).
53 On these excavations' place within the history of archaeology, and on Giuseppe Fiorelli as a pioneer of stratigraphic excavation, see Trigger 1996, 62–63, 290; Dyson 2006, 20–64.
54 Soon followed by additional publications by Wilk and various collaborators: Netting et al. 1984a; Wilk and Netting 1984; Wilk and Ashmore 1988.
55 Which is in some ways traceable back to the politically unsavory figure of Gustaf Kossinna, but came into its own in the mid-to-late twentieth-century Americas (Trigger 1996, 237, 372–82).
56 As discussed by LaMotta and Schiffer 1999, 19; Foster and Parker 2012, 2; Tringham 2012, 83. An important contribution, and immediate precedent for Wilk and Rathje's article, was Flannery 1976 (see especially chapter 2, "Analysis on the Household Level").

57 Wilk and Rathje define the household in ecologically adaptive terms as "the most common social component of subsistence" (1982, 618); declare their goals to be, first, bridging archaeology's "mid-level theory gap" (1982, 617) and, subsequently, constructing a grand theory of "the nature and evolution of household organization" (1982, 620); and propose a list of universal rules of household organization (1982, 631–32). On the processualist movement generally, see Trigger 1996, 386–444. For a critique of the "definition of the household as an adaptive mechanism," see Hendon 1996.
58 Binford 1965, 205 (closely paraphrasing White 2007 [1959], 8).
59 Binford 1965, 204.
60 Thus largely following Christopher Hawkes's famous "ladder of inference" (1954), which ranked technology, subsistence, sociopolitical institutions, and religion in order of increasing difficulty of archaeological study.
61 Wilk and Rathje 1982, 621. Wilk and Netting (1984, 5) reproduce the same list of household functions, with the addition of "coresidence."
62 Wilk and Rathje 1982, 622.
63 Wilk and Rathje 1982, 624.
64 Wilk and Rathje 1982, 627.
65 Wilk and Rathje 1982, 630.
66 And not the procreative kind of "labor," either—although that would appear to be germane to the subject of reproduction!
67 Wilk and Rathje 1982, 631. The role of men's labor in child care is not addressed, even though men did demonstrably contribute to child-rearing in many ancient societies; consider, for example, the male *paidagogoi* who educated elite Greek children. A tendency to project twentieth-century Western gender norms onto past societies was not uncommon in early household studies. Compare, for example, Goody's matter-of-fact assertion that if we want to study domestic production, "Concentrating upon units of production rather than consumption means taking men rather than women as the focus of one's analysis" (1972, 111).
68 Tringham 2015, 218.
69 Though, of course, the ancient word did not have the same meanings as its modern descendant. On oikos and oikonomia, see Ault 2007.
70 See discussions and bibliography in Allison 1999b, 2–3; Steadman 2016, 166.
71 Quoting Alexander 1999, 80.
72 See note 26 above.
73 For surveys of this literature, see Laslett 1972, 1–10; Netting et al. 1984b, xiii–xix; Birdwell-Pheasant and Zúñiga 1999, 1–5; Buchli 2010, 503–9.
74 Goody 1973, 1976.
75 Lévi-Strauss 1982, 176–87; for recent archaeological applications, see inter alia Joyce and Gillespie 2000; Beck 2007; Picardo 2015 (on Egypt); Relaki and Driessen 2020 (on Aegean prehistory).
76 Bender 1967, 495.
77 Bender 1967, 499.
78 Bourdieu 1977, 1979.
79 Yanagisako 1979, 177.
80 Braudel 1972; for the quoted phrase and an analysis of Braudel's influence on household archaeology, see Tringham 2015, 220.
81 Laslett 1972.
82 See the remarks of Netting et al. 1984b, xix.
83 Laslett 1972, 1.
84 Lynch 1960; Hillier and Hanson 1984; Rapoport 1990.
85 Gibson 1986. For archaeological adaptations of the concept of affordances, see Knappett 2004; Costall and Richards 2013; Günther and Fabricius 2021.
86 Tringham 1991. See also Hendon 1996, 2006; Allison 1999b, 2; Robin 2003, 312; Tringham 2012, 85–86; Beaudry 2015, 3–5. Similar lines of questioning emerged earlier in anthropological scholarship on the family: see, e.g., Yanagisako 1979, 190–96.
87 Tringham's paper was a contribution to Gero and Conkey 1991, a landmark in early feminist archaeology; see previously Conkey and Spector 1984. For discussions of these movements more generally, see Trigger 1996, 444–83; Meskell 2007; Whitehouse 2016.

88 Hodder 1990, 38–41, 291; see further Buchli 2010, 508–9.
89 E.g., Rapoport 1990. In this volume, Brooks Hedstrom (chapter 11) applies some of Rapoport's ideas to late antique monastic communities.
90 Blanton 1994, quoting p. vi and p. 79. Blanton (1994, 8–9) explicitly cites Rapoport as his inspiration for studying architecture as communication. However, the chief focus of Blanton's book is economic (he wants to assess the relative wealth of households: see, e.g., p. 186). His central method—the collection of ethnographic analogies—was one heavily promoted by the New Archaeologists (e.g., Binford 1967).
91 See above, notes 3, 4, and 10.
92 Involving not only new excavation, but also what we might call "archival archaeology," revisiting archival data from old excavations in order to draw new conclusions (e.g., Berry 1997; Nevett 1999; Cahill 2002; Allison 2004).
93 See the discussions in Allison 1999b; Nevett 2007; Nevett 2010, 3–9; 2012; Müller 2015e; and see further Nevett, this volume (afterword 2).
94 Quoting the title of Renfrew 1980; see further Morris 1994; Whitley 2001, 42–59; Plantzos 2012.
95 E.g., Ault and Nevett 1999; Allison 2004; Nevett 2008, 2015.
96 E.g., Hodder and Cessford 2004; Matthews 2005; Ullah 2012; Müller 2015a; Pecci et al. 2018; Barrett et al. 2020. On remaining challenges, see further Müller, this volume (afterword 1).
97 Özbal 2012, 322.
98 See note 58 above.
99 For overviews, see, e.g., Hicks 2010; Hodder 2012; Witmore 2014; Webb and Selsvold 2020; Crellin et al. 2021. The pioneering call for "posthumanism" was Hassan 1977. Besides archaeology, posthumanism is also increasingly influential in other disciplines devoted to the study of the ancient world (e.g., Chesi and Spiegel 2020).
100 Cf., in this volume, Richard Alston's critique of symbolic "readings" of domestic space (chapter 7), though see also Frankfurter for a forceful defense of the house as a "symbolic entity" (chapter 10).
101 Zarmakoupi 2023.
102 E.g., Ault 2015; and see further Brooks Hedstrom, chapter 11, this volume. See also Van Oyen 2020 on the ways that Roman storage practices, and their related domestic architecture, depended on physical properties of the raw materials to be stored. For "dependences" as a counterpart to affordances, see Hodder 2012.
103 Gillespie 2021.
104 Precedents for this move can also be found in literature that long predates the "material turn" as we usually think of it. For example, Hillier and Hansen's "space syntax" approach already grants agency to architecture, insofar as it asserts that different spatial layouts facilitate different types of social relationships (Hillier and Hansen 1984; see more recently Fisher 2009).
105 Barrett 2019.
106 Olabarria 2020, 3–23.
107 Van Oyen 2020.
108 Xen. *Oeonomicus* 9.2–5, quoting 9.2 (ed. and trans. Pomeroy 1994, 154–55).
109 Lefebvre 1974; Soja 1996.
110 E.g., Bourdieu 1977; Giddens 1984. Also influential is Foucault (1970, 1977) on the creation of "other" spaces (heterotopias) and the role of space in maintaining regimes of power.
111 On middle-range theory in archaeology, see initially Binford 1977, with subsequent critique (e.g., Raab and Goodyear 1984).
112 Fisher 2009, 440; Paliou 2014, 3–4.
113 E.g., Paliou 2014.
114 Landeschi et al. 2015; Dell'Unto et al. 2016; Landeschi 2018; Campanaro and Landeschi 2022.
115 Landeschi 2018, 9–11.
116 Socioeconomic considerations are relevant, in one way or another, to many of the works cited above, notes 2, 3, 4, and 10.
117 On the perils of assuming such material signatures, see, inter alia, Kramer 1977; Brody 2015, 289–91; Rebillard 2015; Carrington 2019; Van Oyen 2020, 95; Bader 2021, 15–40.
118 Cf. Barrett et al. 2020, 24.

119 See further Nevett (afterword 2, this volume).
120 As discussed by Müller 2015b, xiv–xv.
121 Routledge 2013, 215.
122 E.g., Müller 2015b, xv, xvii–xviii.
123 For critiques of, and debates about, the "new materialisms," see most recently Fernández-Götz et al. 2021a.
124 See generally Fernández-Götz et al. 2021b; for more specific arguments, see most recently Díaz de Liaño and Fernández-Götz 2021; McGuire 2021, esp. the genuinely devastating remarks on pp. 5–6; Ribeiro 2021; Van Dyke 2021. Fowles sees new materialism as a "response to post-coloniality and the politics of representation" that is ultimately self-serving, in that it actually expands rather than decreases the authority claims of "Western anthropologists" (2016, quoting p. 24).
125 *Ath. pol.* 57.4; cf. Plato *Leg.* 9.873E-874A; and see Kindt 2016, 117–22. The foundation myth of the Bouphonia festival involves blaming an axe for the death of an animal; see discussions, with an eye to object agency, in Collins 2003, 38–39; Kindt 2016, 120–21.
126 Plu. *Per.* 36; Antiph. 3; see further Collins 2003, 32–33.
127 Antiph. 3.3.
128 The Greek word can also mean "explanation," "reason," "debate," and much more, but it has particularly close ties to oral accounts (*LSJ*, s.v. λόγος). For *logoi* as stories in Herodotus's *Histories,* see most recently Kirk 2021.
129 On assemblages in archaeology, see Jones and Hamilakis 2017; Jervis 2018; Antczak and Beaudry 2019. On households as assemblages, see also Marín-Aguilera 2018; Salazar et al. 2022.
130 Or "actants," if you prefer the actor-network-theory terminology for entities that do things or make things happen (e.g., Latour 2005, 52–58).
131 Drawing in particular on Brown 2001; see also below, "Material Households."
132 Or perhaps in-*terrate* (if you'll forgive me the coinage), since they are made of clay instead of flesh!
133 On terracotta figurines as agents, see also Barrett, forthcoming.
134 See originally Olsen 2003, followed by a massive subsequent bibliography. Recent contributions include Olsen and Witmore 2015; Witmore 2018.
135 "Unsatisfactorily," in part, because of the extensive history of interconnections across the ancient Mediterranean, Near Eastern, and North African regions. See recently Purcell 2013.
136 See, e.g., Heywood 2017; Crellin et al. 2021. For an Indigenous feminist critique of the "ontological turn," however, see Todd 2016.
137 Barrett, forthcoming.
138 Which is not to say that cultural values and individual preferences were not simultaneously at play; see Simpson, chapter 2, this volume, for a strong argument for the former. Boozer (chapter 8) discusses the role of cultural ideas about cleanliness and dirtiness in shaping discard practices. Thompson (chapter 4) shows that house type might correlate to some degree with "Greek" versus "Egyptian" identity (though, given the often privileged status of the "Greeks" in question, economic factors are difficult to disentangle here from ethnic and cultural ones). Historical factors would also have been at play in shaping the appearance of houses. Marouard (chapter 3) interprets Ptolemaic tower houses as originally a Delta-based architectural form, which was only later introduced to Upper Egypt, the Fayum, and the Oases.
139 This consideration would be relevant for one of the two locations that Abdelwahed associates with domestic violence: namely, the house interior. Violent acts committed at the house façade (Abdelwahed, chapter 6) would have been more visible to the neighborhood.
140 See note 124 above.
141 Note that different contributors use the term *tower house* somewhat differently. Marouard (chapter 3) argues for restricting this term for a particular house form of the Ptolemaic Period, while others use the term for a wider variety of towerlike domestic structures from Greco-Roman Egypt (e.g., Davoli, chapter 1; Simpson, chapter 2).
142 Cf. Husselman 1953.
143 E.g., Boutantin 2014, 217–50.
144 For a useful introduction to religion in Ptolemaic and Roman as well as Pharaonic Egypt, see Dunand and Zivie-Coche 1991.

145 See, e.g., references in the chapters by Boozer, Brooks Hedstrom, Davoli, Marouard, and Thompson (chapters 1, 3, 4, 8, 11, this volume). On the role and agency of plants as agents within the household, see Tally-Schumacher 2020.
146 See, e.g., references to granaries in Alston (chapter 7, this volume); Simpson (chapter 3, this volume).
147 E.g., Huebner's chapter demonstrates that widowed women might retain the right to live in their husband's house, but only on condition that they never remarried (chapter 5, this volume).
148 This last example is actually substantially later than the "Roman Period" as typically defined, dating to the eighth or ninth century CE (Frankfurter, chapter 10), but still provides a vivid example of textual evidence for individual experience.
149 Spencer-Wood questions "whether it is always possible to define the household as distinctly separate from the community" (1999, 162). Precedents for a multiscalar approach to households go back as early as Flannery's 1976 study, which devotes separate chapters to "analysis on the household level," "analysis on the community level," "analysis on the regional level" (this last gets two chapters), and "interregional exchange networks." See further the comments of Tringham 1991, 100; Robin 2002; Foster and Parker 2012, 2.
150 Müller 2015c.
151 Spencer 2015, 200.
152 Goldberg 1999, 156, drawing on previous work by Small (1991, 339).
153 Tsakirgis 2016b, 19.
154 Kondyli and Anderson 2022.
155 E.g., inter alia, Robin 2003, 330–33; many of the contributions to Parker and Foster 2012, especially Nishimura 2012; Beaudry 2015, 2–3; Cobb 2015, 202–3; Steadman 2016, 51–53.
156 Compare Allison's description of the household "not as a unit but as a system of membership" in a larger community (1999b, 2).
157 Compare the characterization of a man's wife as his "house" in some Jewish traditions (Baker 1998; Alston 2007).
158 Lehner 2000. See also Nicholas Picardo (2015) on Middle Kingdom Egypt as a Lévi-Straussian "house society."
159 See, e.g., Barrett 2019; Barrett, forthcoming.
160 E.g., Carrington 2019.
161 Cobb 2015, 189.
162 For globalization in archaeology, especially Mediterranean archaeology, see (inter alia) Pitts and Versluys 2017; Hodos 2017; Belvedere and Bergemann 2021.
163 Ingold 2000, 153; see further note 17 above.
164 Tringham 2003, 94–95.
165 Bourdieu 1977, 1979. On the impact of practice theory within household archaeology, see Tringham 2015, 221; Tsakirgis 2016b, 28–31. Wilk and Rathje's pioneering study already characterizes households as constructed through, among other things, shared activities (1982, 618).
166 Within archaeology, Lynn Meskell's concept of "material *habitus*" has also become influential (Boozer, chapter 8, this volume). While Meskell's concept is indebted to Bourdieu's, she defines "material *habitus*" quite differently, as the "lifeworld" or "enmeshing that combines persons, objects, deities, and all manner of immaterial things together" (2005, 3).
167 For example, in many societies, poorer urban dwellings may lack kitchens, so cooking and eating may be done elsewhere (Svensdotter et al. 2020, 346–47). Sexual relations are often prohibited, at least in theory, at monastic dwelling sites (though see e.g. Wilfong 2002 on both prohibitions and violations). Small apartments, in antiquity as today, often lack space for entertaining.
168 Chesson 2012, 48. On "home" as a site of powerful emotions and perceived meaning, see also Moore 2012; Barrie 2017; and compare earlier explorations of the concept of "home" in Benjamin and Stea 1995. On the concept of "home" in (Greek) antiquity as distinct from a mere place of residence, see Ault 2005b; Westgate 2013.
169 Battle-Baptiste 2011, 73–108.
170 E.g., Hamilakis 2002, 2013; Harris and Sørensen 2010; Tarlow 2012; Skeates and Day 2020.
171 Routledge 2013, 209.
172 Hartman 2019, 3–4.
173 van Driel-Murray 1995; Greene 2013, 2014.

174 Even in the direst extremity, people may assert ways of homemaking; see Battle-Baptiste's work on the creation of "homespace" as a form of resistance among enslaved Africans in the United States (2011, 73–108).
175 On monasteries as domestic contexts, see also Pudsey 2015.
176 On the historical prominence of ritual studies within household archaeology, see Steadman 2016, 16, 249–89.
177 As also critiqued by Hendon 2006, 177.

Works Cited

Abbas, E., and Y.E.H Abdelwahed. 2014. "The Domestic Pylon in the Light of Greek Papyri." *Rosetta* 15: 1–27.

Abdelwahed, Y.E.H. 2015. *Egyptian Cultural Identity in the Architecture of Roman Egypt (30 BC-AD 325)*. Oxford: Archaeopress.

Abdelwahed, Y.E.H. 2016. *Houses in Greco-Roman Egypt: Arenas for Ritual Activity*. Oxford: Archaeopress.

Alexander, R. 1999. "Mesoamerican House Lots and Archaeological Site Structure: Problems of Inference in Yaxcaba, Yucatan, Mexico, 1750–1847." In *The Archaeology of Household Activities*, edited by P. Allison, 78–100. New York: Routledge.

Allison, P.M., ed. 1999a. *The Archaeology of Household Activities*. New York: Routledge.

Allison, P.M., ed. 1999b. "Introduction." In *The Archaeology of Household Activities*, edited by P.M. Allison, 1–18. New York: Routledge.

Allison, P.M. 2004. *Pompeian Households: An Analysis of the Material Culture*. Los Angeles: Cotsen Institute of Archaeology.

Allison, P.M. 2006. *The Insula of the Menander at Pompeii*. Vol. 3. *The Finds: A Contextual Study*. Oxford: Oxford University Press.

Alston, R. 1997. "Houses and Households in Roman Egypt." In *Domestic Space in the Roman World: Pompeii and Beyond*, edited by R. Laurence and A. Wallace-Hadrill, 25–40. Portsmouth, RI: Journal of Roman Archaeology.

Alston, R. 2002a. *The City in Roman and Byzantine Egypt*. London: Routledge.

Alston, R. 2002b. "Reading Augustan Alexandria." In *Ancient West & East*, edited by G.R. Tsetskhladze, 141–61. Leiden: Brill.

Alston, R. 2005. "Searching for the Romano-Egyptian Family." In *The Roman Family in the Empire: Rome, Italy, and Beyond*, edited by M. George, 129–58. Oxford: Oxford University Press.

Alston, R. 2006. "Settlement Dynamics in Third- and Fourth-Century Roman Egypt." In *Settlements and Demography in the Near East in Late Antiquity*, edited by A.S. Lewin and P. Pellegrini, 23–34. Rome: Istituti editoriali e poligrafici internazionali.

Alston, R. 2007. "Some Theoretical Considerations and a Late Antique House from Roman Egypt." In *Building Communities: House, Settlement, and Society in the Aegean and Beyond*, edited by R. Westgate et al., 373–78. Athens: British School at Athens.

Anguissola, A., ed. 2012. *Privata Luxuria. Towards an Archaeology of Intimacy: Pompeii and Beyond*. Munich: Herbert Utz Verlag.

Antczak, K.A., and M.C. Beaudry. 2019. "Assemblages of Practice: A Conceptual Framework for Exploring Human-Thing Relations in Archaeology." *Archaeological Dialogues* 26: 87–110.

Antonaccio, C. 2000. "Architecture and Behavior: Building Gender into Greek Houses." *CW* 93 (5): 517–33.

Ault, B.A. 2000. "Living in the Classical Polis: The Greek House as Microcosm." *CW* 93 (5): 483–96.

Ault, B.A. 2005a. *The Excavations at Ancient Halieis*. Vol. 2. *The Houses: The Organization and Use of Domestic Space*. Bloomington: Indiana University Press.

Ault, B.A. 2005b. "Housing the Poor and the Homeless in Ancient Greece." In *Ancient Greek Houses and Households: Chronological, Regional, and Social Diversity*, edited by B.A. Ault and L.C. Nevett, 140–59. Philadelphia: University of Pennsylvania Press.

Ault, B.A. 2007. "*Oikos* and *Oikonomia*: Greek Houses, Households, and the Domestic Economy." In *Building Communities: House, Settlement, and Society in the Aegean and Beyond*, edited by R. Westgate et al., 259–65. London: British School at Athens.

Ault, B.A. 2015. "ΟΙΚΟΣ ΚΑΛΟΣ: The Environmental Logic of Greek Urban House Forms." In *Housing and Habitat in the Ancient Mediterranean: Cultural and Environmental Responses*, edited by A. Di Castro and C.A. Hope, 123–32. Leuven: Peeters.

Ault, B.A. 2016. "Building Z in the Athenian Kerameikos: House, Tavern, Inn, Brothel?" In *Houses of Ill Repute: The Archaeology of Brothels, Houses, and Taverns in the Greek World*, edited by A. Glazebrook and B. Tsakirgis, 75–102. Philadelphia: University of Pennsylvania Press.

Ault, B.A., and L.C. Nevett. 1999. "Digging Houses: Archaeologies of Classical and Hellenistic Greek Domestic Assemblages." In *The Archaeology of Household Activities*, edited by P. Allison, 43–56. New York: Routledge.

Ault, B.A., and L. Nevett, eds. 2005. *Ancient Greek Houses and Households*. Philadelphia: University of Pennsylvania Press.

Bader, B. 2021. *Material Culture and Identities in Egyptology: Towards a Better Understanding of Cultural Encounters and Their Influence on Material Culture*. Vienna: Austrian Academy of Sciences Press.

Bagnall, R.S. 1989. "Official and Private Violence in Roman Egypt." *Bulletin of the American Society of Papyrologists* 26: 201–16.

Bagnall, R.S. 1997. "Decolonizing Ptolemaic Egypt." In *Hellenistic Constructs: Essays in Culture, History, and Historiography*, edited by P. Cartledge et al., 225–41. Berkeley: University of California Press.

Bagnall, R.S., N. Aravecchia, R. Cribiore, P. Davoli, O.E. Kaper, and S. McFadden. 2016. *An Oasis City*. New York: New York University Press.

Baird, J.A. 2015. *The Inner Life of Ancient Houses: An Archaeology of Dura-Europos*. Oxford: Oxford University Press.

Baird, J.A., and A. Pudsey, eds. 2022. *Housing in the Ancient Mediterranean World: Material and Textual Approaches*. Cambridge: Cambridge University Press.

Baker, C.M. 1998. "'Ordering the House': On the Domestication of Jewish Bodies." In *Parchments of Gender: Deciphering the Bodies of Antiquity*, edited by M. Wyke, 221–42. Oxford: Clarendon Press.

Baldi, M. 2017. "Domestic Architecture and Daily Life in Meroitic Nubia." In *Egypt 2015: Perspectives of Research*, edited by M. Tomorad and J. Popielska-Grzybowska, 77–84. Oxford: Archaeopress.

Baldini, I., and C. Sfameni, eds. 2018. *Abitare nel Mediterraneo tardoantico*. Bari: Edipuglia.

Barile, K.S., and J.C. Brandon, eds. 2004. *Household Chores and Household Choices: Theorizing the Domestic Sphere in Historical Archaeology*. Tuscaloosa: University of Alabama Press.

Barrett, C.E. 2015a. "Hellenistic and Roman Egypt." *Oxford Bibliographies in Classics*. http://www.oxfordbibliographies.com/view/document/obo-9780195389661/obo-9780195389661-0189.xml.

Barrett, C.E. 2015b. "Terracotta Figurines and the Archaeology of Ritual: Domestic Cult in Greco-Roman Egypt." In *Figurines grecques en contexte: Présence muette dans le sanctuaire, la tombe et la maison*, edited by S. Huysecom-Haxhi and A. Muller (editors-in-chief) and C. Aubry, C.E. Barrett, C. Blume, and T. Kopestonsky (collaborating editors), 401–20. Villeneuve d'Ascq: Presses Universitaires du Septentrion.

Barrett, C.E. 2019. *Domesticating Empire: Egyptian Landscapes in Pompeian Gardens*. Oxford: Oxford University Press.

Barrett, C.E. Forthcoming. "The Affordances of Terracotta Figurines in Domestic Contexts: Reconsidering the Gap between Material and Ritual." In *Stuff of the Gods: The Material Aspects of Religion in Ancient Greece*, edited by M. Haysom, M. Mili, and J. Wallensten. Stockholm: Swedish Institute at Athens.

Barrett, C.E., and N. Bellucci. 2022. "A 'New' (Rediscovered) Nilotic Scene from the Casa del Gemmario: Context, Iconography, and Sub-Elite Viewership." *Rivista di Studi Pompeiani* 33: 89–109.

Barrett, C.E., K.L. Gleason, and A. Marzano, with additional contributions by D. Langgut. 2020. "The Casa della Regina Carolina (CRC) Project, Pompeii: Preliminary Report on 2018 and 2019 Field Seasons." *FOLD&R (Fasti OnLine Documents & Research) Italy*. http://www.fastionline.org/docs/FOLDER-it-2020-492.pdf.

Barrie, T. 2017. *House and Home: Cultural Contexts, Ontological Roles*. New York: Routledge.

Battle-Baptiste, W. 2011. *Black Feminist Archaeology*. New York: Routledge.

Beaudry, M.C. 2015. "Households Beyond the House: On the Archaeology and Materiality of Historical Households." In *Beyond the Walls: New Perspectives on the Archaeology of Historical Households*, edited by Fogle et al., 1–22. Gainesville: University Press of Florida.

Beck, R.A., ed. 2007. *The Durable House: House Society Models in Archaeology*. Carbondale: Southern Illinois University.

Belvedere, O., and J. Bergemann, eds. 2021. *Imperium Romanum: Romanization between Colonization and Globalization*. Palermo: Palermo University Press.

Bender, D. 1967. "A Refinement of the Concept of Household: Families, Co-Residence, and Domestic Functions." *American Anthropologist* 69 (5): 493–504.

Benjamin, D.N., assisted by D. Stea. 1995. *The Home: Words, Interpretations, Meanings, and Environments*. Aldershot: Avebury.

Berg, R., and I. Kuivalainen, eds. 2019. *Domus Pompeiana M. Lucretii IX 3, 5.24: The Inscriptions, Works of Art and Finds from the Old and New Excavations*. Vantaa: Finnish Society of Sciences and Letters.

Berry, J. 1997. "Household Artefacts: Re-Interpreting Roman Domestic Space." In *Domestic Space in the Roman World: Pompeii and Beyond*, edited by R. Laurence and A. Wallace-Hadrill, 183–95. Portsmouth, RI: Journal of Roman Archaeology.

Bietak, M., E. Czerny, and I. Forstner-Müller, eds. 2010. *Cities and Urbanism in Ancient Egypt*. Vienna: Verlag der Österreichischen Akademie der Wissenschaften.

Binford, L.R. 1965. "Archaeological Systematics and the Study of Culture Process." *American Antiquity* 31 (2): 203–10.

Binford, L.R. 1967. "Smudge Pits and Hide Smoking: The Use of Analogy in Archaeological Reasoning." *American Antiquity* 32 (1): 1–12.

Binford, L.R. 1977. "Introduction." In *For Theory Building in Archaeology*, edited by L. Binford, 1–13. New York: Academic Press.

Birdwell-Pheasant, D., and D. Lawrence-Zúñiga. 1999. "Introduction: Houses and Families in Europe." In *House Life: Space, Place, and Family in Europe*, edited by D. Birdwell-Pheasant and D. Lawrence-Zúñiga, 1–35. Oxford: Berg.

Bonini, P. 2006. *La Casa nella Grecia romana. Forme e funzioni dello spazio privato fra I e VI secolo*. Rome: Edizioni Quasar.

Boozer, A.L. 2005. "In Search of Lost Memories: Domestic Spheres and Identities in Roman Amheida, Egypt." *ISERP Working Papers 05–07*: 1–28.

Boozer, A.L. 2010. "Memory and Microhistory of an Empire: Domestic Contexts in Roman Amheida, Egypt." In *Archaeology and Memory*, edited by D. Borić, 138–57. Oxford: Oxbow.

Boozer, A.L. 2012. "Globalizing Mediterranean Identities: The Overlapping Spheres of Egyptian, Greek, and Roman Worlds at Trimithis." *JMA* 25: 219–42.

Boozer, A.L. 2014. "Urban Change at Late Roman Trimithis (Dakhleh Oasis, Egypt)." In *Egypt in the First Millennium AD: Perspectives from New Fieldwork*, edited by E.R. O'Connell, 23–42. Leuven: Peeters.

Boozer, A.L. 2015a. *Amheida II: A Late Romano-Egyptian House in the Dakhla Oasis. Amheida House B2*. New York: New York University Press.

Boozer, A.L. 2015b. "Tracing Everyday Life at Trimithis (Dakhleh Oasis, Egypt)." *Archeological Papers of the American Anthropological Association* 26: 122–38.

Boozer, A.L. 2015c. "The Tyranny of Typologies in Romano-Egyptian Domestic Archaeology." In *Material Evidence: Learning from Archaeological Practice*, edited by A. Wylie and R. Chapman, 92–109. Malden: Blackwell.

Boozer, A.L. 2019. "Cultural Identity: Housing and Burial Practices." In *A Companion to Greco-Roman and Late Antique Egypt*, edited by K. Vandorpe, 361–80. Hoboken, NJ: John Wiley & Sons.

Boozer, A.L. 2021. *At Home in Roman Egypt: A Social Archaeology*. Cambridge: Cambridge University Press.

Bourdieu, P. 1977. *Outline of a Theory of Practice*. Translated by R. Nice. Cambridge: Cambridge University Press.

Bourdieu, P. 1979. "The Kabyle House or the World Reversed." In *Algeria 1960*, translated by R. Nice, 133–53. Cambridge: Cambridge University Press. Reprinted in P. Bourdieu. 1990. *The Logic of Practice*, 271–83. Cambridge: Polity Press: Cambridge.

Boutantin, C. 2014. *Terres cuites et culte domestique: Bestiaire de l'Égypte gréco-romaine*. Leiden: Brill.

Bowes, K. 2010. *Houses and Society in the Later Roman Empire*. London: Bloomsbury.

Bowman, A.K. 2000. "Urbanization in Roman Egypt." In *Romanization and the City: Creation, Transformations, and Failure*, edited by E. Fentress, 173–87. Portsmouth, RI: Journal of Roman Archaeology.

Boz, B., and L.D. Hager. 2013. "Living Above the Dead: Intramural Burial Practices at Çatalhöyük." In *Humans and Landscapes of Çatalhöyük: Reports from the 2000–2008 Seasons*, 414–40. London: British Institute at Ankara.

Braudel, F. 1972. *The Mediterranean and the Mediterranean World in the Age of Philip II*. Translated by S. Reynolds. New York: Harper and Row.

Brody, A.J. 2015. "Living in Households, Constructing Identities: Ethnicity, Boundaries, and Empire in Iron II Tell en-Nasbeh." In *Household Studies in Complex Societies: (Micro) Archaeological and Textual Approaches*, edited by M. Müller, 289–306. Chicago: The Oriental Institute.

Brown, B. 2001. "Thing Theory." *Critical Inquiry* 28 (1): 1–22.

Bruneau, P. 1995. "La maison délienne." *Ramage* 12: 77–118.

Buchli, V. 2010. "Households and 'Home Cultures.'" In *The Oxford Handbook of Material Culture Studies*, edited by D. Hicks and M.C. Beaudry, 502–17. Oxford: Oxford University Press.

Budka, J. 2017. "Life in the New Kingdom Town of Sai Island: Some New Perspectives." In *Nubia in the New Kingdom: Lived Experience, Pharaonic Control, and Indigenous Traditions*, edited by N. Spencer, A. Stevens, and M. Binder, 429–47. Leuven: Peeters.

Budka, J. 2020. *AcrossBorders 2: Living in New Kingdom Sai*. Vienna: Austrian Academy of Sciences.

Cahill, N. 2002. *Household and City Organization at Olynthus*. New Haven: Yale University Press.

Campanaro, D., and G. Landeschi. 2022. "Re-Viewing Pompeian Domestic Space through Combined Virtual Reality-Based Eye Tracking and 3D GIS." *Antiquity* 96: 479–86.

Carpenter, L.B., and A.M. Prentiss, eds. 2022. *Archaeology of Households, Kinship, and Social Change*. New York: Routledge.

Carrington, J. 2019. "Striking Similarity: Pottery Features and Their Relations in Ptolemaic Egypt." PhD diss., Cornell University.

Chesi, G.M., and F. Spiegel. 2020. *Classical Literature and Posthumanism*. New York: Bloomsbury Academic.

Chesson, M.S. 2012. "Homemaking in the Early Bronze Age." In *New Perspectives on Household Archaeology*, edited by B.J. Parker and C.P. Foster, 45–80. Winona Lake, IN: Eisenbrauns.

Clarke, J.R. 1991. *The Houses of Roman Italy, 100 B.C.–A.D. 250*. Berkeley: University of California Press.

Clarke, J.R. 2003. *Art in the Lives of Ordinary Romans: Visual Representation and Non-Elite Viewers in Italy, 100 B.C–A.D. 315*. Berkeley: University of California.

Clarysse, W. 2019. "Ethnic Identity: Egyptians, Greeks, and Romans." In *A Companion to Greco-Roman and Late Antique Egypt*, edited by K. Vandorpe, 299–324. Hoboken, NJ: John Wiley & Sons.

Cobb, C.R. 2015. "The Spooky Entanglements of Historical Households." In *Beyond Kinship: Social and Material Reproduction in House Societies*, edited by R.A. Joyce and S.D. Gillespie, 188–207. Philadelphia: University of Pennsylvania Press.

Cole, S.E. 2022. "Negotiating Identity through the Architecture and Interior Decoration of Elite Households in Ptolemaic Egypt." *Arts* 11.3. https://www.mdpi.com/2076-0752/11/1/3.

Collins, D. 2003. "Nature, Cause, and Agency in Greek Magic." *TAPA* 133 (1): 17–49.

Conkey, M.W., and J.D. Spector. 1984. "Archaeology and the Study of Gender." *Advances in Archaeological Method and Theory* 7: 1–38.

Costall, A., and A. Richards. 2013. "Canonical Affordances: The Psychology of Everyday Things." In *The Oxford Handbook of the Archaeology of the Contemporary World*, edited by P. Graves-Brown et al., 82–93. Oxford: Oxford University Press.

Crellin, R.J., et al. 2021. *Archaeological Theory in Dialogue: Situating Relationality, Ontology, Posthumanism, and Indigenous Paradigms*. New York: Routledge.

Dalton, M. 2013. "Reconstructing Lived Experiences of Domestic Space at Amara West: Some Preliminary Interpretations of Floor Deposits Using Ethnoarchaeological and Micromorphological

Analyses." In *Nubia in the New Kingdom: Lived Experience, Pharaonic Control and Indigenous Traditions*, edited by N. Spencer, A. Stevens, and M. Binder, 357–88. Leuven: Peeters.

Dardenay, A., and N. Laubry, eds. 2020. *Anthropology of Roman Housing*. Turnhout: Brepols.

Daub, J., and J. Griesbach. 2013. "Zu den Fundkontexten der Terrakotten und ihrer Bedeutung." In *Griechisch-Ägyptisch. Tonfiguren vom Nil*, edited by Jochen Griesbach, 23–34. Regensburg: Verlag Schnell & Steiner GmbH.

Davoli, P. 1998. *L'archeologia urbana nel Fayyum di età ellenistica e romana*. Naples: Generoso Procaccini Editore.

Davoli, P. 2001. *Saft el-Henna. Archeologia e storia di una città del Delta orientale*. Imola: La Mandragora.

Davoli, P. 2010. "Settlements—Distribution, Structure, Architecture: Graeco-Roman." In *A Companion to Ancient Egypt*, edited by A.B. Lloyd, Vol. 1, 350–69. Malden, MA: Wiley-Blackwell.

Davoli, P., with a contribution by N. Warner. 2022. *The House of Serenos, Part II. Archaeological Report on a Late-Roman Urban House at Trimithis*. New York: ISAW/New York University Press.

Dell'Unto, N., et al. 2016. "Experiencing Ancient Buildings from a 3D GIS Perspective: A Case Drawn from the Swedish Pompeii Project." *Journal of Archaeological Method and Theory* 23: 73–94.

Depraetere, D. 2005. "Archaeological Studies on Graeco-Roman and Late Antique Housing in Egypt." PhD diss., K.U. Leuven.

Díaz de Liaño, G., and M. Fernández-Götz. 2021. "Posthumanism, New Humanism, and Beyond." In *Posthumanism in Archaeology* (special edited section of *Cambridge Archaeological Journal*), edited by M. Fernández-Götz et al. *Cambridge Archaeological Journal* 31 (3): 543–49.

Di Castro, A.A., and C.A. Hope, assisted by B.E. Parr, eds. 2015. *Housing and Habitat in the Ancient Mediterranean: Cultural and Environmental Responses*. Leuven: Peeters.

Dickmann, J.-A. 1999. *Domus frequentata: Anspruchsvolles Wohnen im pompejanischen Stadthaus*. Munich: Pfeil.

Dietler, M. 2010. *Archaeologies of Colonialism: Consumption, Entanglement, and Violence in Ancient Mediterranean France*. Berkeley: University of California Press.

Dietler, M., and B. Hayden. 2016. *Feasts: Archaeological and Ethnographic Perspectives on Food, Politics, and Power*. Washington, DC: Smithsonian Institution Press.

Droste, M., and A. Hoffmann, eds. 2003. *Wohnformen und Lebenswelten im interkulturellen Vergleich*. Frankfurt: Peter Lang.

Ducrey, P., I.R. Metzler, and K. Reber. 1993. *Eretria, fouilles et recherches VIII. Le quartier de la Maison aux mosaïques*. Lausanne: Editions Payot.

Dunand, F., and C. Zivie-Coche. 1991. *Dieux et hommes en Égypte, 3000 av. J.-C.—395 apr. J.-C.: Anthropologie réligieuse*. Paris: Armand Colin.

Dyson, S.L. 2006. *In Pursuit of Ancient Pasts: A History of Classical Archaeology in the Nineteenth and Twentieth Centuries*. New Haven: Yale University Press.

El Kadi, G. 2016. "Vernacular Architecture for the Dead: Cairo's Medieval Necropolis." In *Culture mediterranee dell'abitare. Mediterranean Housing Cultures*, edited by A. Picone, 238–45. Naples: Clean.

El Kadi, G., and A. Bonnamy. 2007. *Architecture for the Dead: Cairo's Medieval Necropolis*. Cairo: American University in Cairo Press.

Ellis, S.P. 2000. *Roman Housing*. London: Duckworth.

Evans, K.G. 1992. "Domestic Violence and Women's Rights in Roman Egypt: The Case of P. Oxy. VI.903." Paper presented at the Annual Meeting of the American Academy of Religion/Society of Biblical Literature, San Francisco, November 1992.

Fassbinder, J., L. Kühne, and M. Flossmann-Schütze. 2015. "The Hellenistic Settlement of Tuna el-Gebel." *Archaeologia Polona* 53: 276–80.

Fernández-Götz, M., A. Gardiner, G. Díaz de Liaño, and O.J.T. Harris, eds. 2021a. *Posthumanism in Archaeology* (special edited section of journal). *Cambridge Archaeological Journal* 31 (1): 455–549.

Fernández-Götz, M., A. Gardiner, G. Díaz de Liaño, and O.J.T. Harris, eds. 2021b. "Posthumanism in Archaeology: An Introduction." In *Posthumanism in Archaeology* (special edited section of *Cambridge Archaeological Journal*), edited by M. Fernández-Götz et al. *Cambridge Archaeological Journal* 31 (3): 455–59.

Fernández-Götz, M., D. Maschek, and N. Roymans. 2020. "The Dark Side of the Empire: Roman Expansionism between Object Agency and Predatory Regime." *Antiquity* 94: 1630–39.

Fisher, K. 2009. "Placing Social Interaction: An Integrative Approach to Analyzing Past Built Environments." *Journal of Anthropological Archaeology* 28: 439–57.

Flannery, K.V., ed. 1976. *The Early Mesoamerican Village*. New York: Academic Press.

Fletcher, R. 1992. "Time Perspectivism, *Annales* and the Potential for Archaeology." In *Archaeology,* Annales*, and Ethnohistory*, edited by A.B. Knapp, 35–49. Cambridge: Cambridge University Press.

Flohr, M. 2007. "Nec quicquam ingenuum habere potest officina? Spatial Contexts of Urban Production at Pompeii, AD 79." *BABesch* 82: 129–48.

Fogle, K.R., J.A. Nyman, and M.C. Beaudry, eds. 2015. *Beyond the Walls: New Perspectives on the Archaeology of Historical Households*. Gainesville: University Press of Florida.

Foster, C.P., and B.J. Parker. 2012. "Introduction: Household Archaeology in the Near East and Beyond." In *New Perspectives on Household Archaeology*, edited by B.J. Parker and C.P. Foster, 1–14. Winona Lake, IN: Eisenbrauns.

Foucault, M. 1970. *The Order of Things: An Archaeology of the Human Sciences*. New York: Pantheon Books.

Foucault, M. 1977. *Discipline and Punish: The Birth of the Prison*. Translated by A. Sheridan. New York: Pantheon Books.

Fowles, S. 2016. "The Perfect Subject (Postcolonial Object Studies)." *Journal of Material Culture* 21 (1): 9–27.

Foxhall, L. 2020. "Everyday Objects." In *A Cultural History of Objects*. Vol. 1. *Classical Antiquity*, edited by R. Osborne. London: Bloomsbury.

Frankfurter, D. 1998. *Religion in Roman Egypt: Assimilation and Resistance*. Princeton: Princeton University Press.

Frankfurter, D., ed. 2019. *Guide to the Study of Ancient Magic*. Leiden: Brill.

Gero, J.M., and M.W. Conkey, eds. 1991. *Engendering Archaeology: Women and Prehistory*. Malden: Blackwell.

Gessler-Löhr, B. 2012. "Mummies and Mummification." In *The Oxford Handbook of Roman Egypt*, edited by C. Riggs, 664–83. Oxford: Oxford University Press.

Gibson, J. 2015 (1986). *The Ecological Approach to Visual Perception*. New York: Taylor & Francis.

Giddens, A. 1984. *The Constitution of Society: Outline of the Theory of Structuration*. Cambridge: Polity Press.

Gillespie, S.D. 2000. "Maya 'Nested Houses': The Ritual Construction of Place." In *Beyond Kinship: Social and Material Reproduction in House Societies*, edited by R.A. Joyce and S.D. Gillespie, 135–60. Philadelphia: University of Pennsylvania Press.

Gillespie, S.D. 2021. "Clay: The Entanglement of Earth in the Age of Clay." In *The Impact of Materials on Society*, edited by S.K. Acord, K.S. Jones, M. Bryant, D. Dauphin-Jones, and P.S. Hupp, 15–43. Gainesville: University of Florida Library Press.

Glanville, S.K. 1939. *Catalogue of Demotic Papyri in the British Museum*. Vol 1. *A Theban Archive of the Reign of Ptolemy I, Soter*. London: Trustees of the British Museum.

Glazebrook, A. 2011. "*Porneion*: Prostitution in Athenian Civic Space." In *Greek Prostitutes in the Ancient Mediterranean, 800 BCE–200 CE*, edited by A. Glazebrook and M.M. Henry, 34–59. Madison: University of Wisconsin Press.

Glazebrook, A. 2016. "Is There an Archaeology of Prostitution?" In *Houses of Ill Repute: The Archaeology of Brothels, Houses, and Taverns in the Greek World,* edited by A. Glazebrook and B. Tsakirgis, 169–96. Philadelphia: University of Pennsylvania Press.

Glazebrook, A., and B. Tsakirgis. 2016. "Introduction." In *Houses of Ill Repute: The Archaeology of Brothels, Houses, and Taverns in the Greek World,* edited by A. Glazebrook and B. Tsakirgis, 1–12. Philadelphia: University of Pennsylvania Press.

Goldberg, M.Y. 1999. "Spatial and Behavioural Negotiation in Classical Athenian City Houses." In *The Archaeology of Household Activities*, edited by P. Allison, 142–61. New York: Routledge.

Goody, J.R. 1972. "The Evolution of the Family." In *Household and Family in Past Time*, edited by P. Laslett and R. Wall, 103–24. Cambridge: Cambridge University Press.

Goody, J.R. 1973. "Bridewealth and Dowry in Africa and Eurasia." In *Bridewealth and Dowry*, edited by J.R. Goody and S.J. Tambiah, 1–58. Cambridge: Cambridge University Press.

Goody, J.R. 1976. *Production and Reproduction: A Comparative Study of the Domestic Domain.* Cambridge: Cambridge University Press.

Greene, E.M. 2013. "Female Networks in Military Communities in the Roman West: A View from the Vindolanda Tablets." In *Women and the Roman City in the Latin West*, edited by E. Hemelrijk and G. Woolf, 369–90. Leiden: Brill.

Greene, E.M. 2014. "If the Shoe Fits: Style and Status in the Assemblage of Children's Shoes from Vindolanda." In *Life in the* Limes, edited by R. Collins and F. McIntosh, 29–36. Oxford: Oxbow.

Grey, C. 2011. *Constructing Communities in the Late Roman Countryside.* Cambridge: Cambridge University Press.

Grüner, C. 2013. "Götter für den Heimbedarf." In *Griechisch-Ägyptisch. Tonfiguren vom Nil*, edited by Jochen Griesbach, 47–55. Regensburg: Verlag Schnell & Steiner GmbH.

Günther, E., and J. Fabricius, eds. 2021. *Mehrdeutigkeiten. Rahmtheorien und Affordanzkonzepte in der archäologischen Bildwissenschaft.* Wiesbaden: Harrassowitz.

Haagsma, M.J. 2010. *Domestic Economy and Social Organization in New Halos.* PhD diss., Rijksuniversiteit Groningen.

Hadji-Minaglou, G. 2007. *Tebtynis IV. Les habitations à l'est du temple de Soknebtynis.* Cairo: IFAO.

Hadji-Minaglou, G. 2012. "L'apport des Grecs dans l'architecture de la *chôra* égyptienne: l'exemple de Tebtynis." In *Grecs et Romains en Égypte: Territoires, espaces de la vie et de la mort, objets de prestige et du quotidien*, edited by P. Ballet, 107–20. Cairo: IFAO.

Hales, S. 2003. *The Roman House and Social Identity.* Cambridge: Cambridge University Press.

Hall, J.M. 2002. *Hellenicity: Between Ethnicity and Culture.* Chicago: University of Chicago Press.

Hamilakis, Y. 2013. *Archaeology and the Senses: Human Experience, Memory, and Affect.* Cambridge: Cambridge University Press.

Hamilakis, Y., M. Pluciennik, and S. Tarlow, eds. 2002. *Thinking through the Body: Archaeologies of Corporeality.* New York: Kluwer.

Hammel, E.A., and P. Laslett. 1974. "Comparing Household Structure over Time and between Cultures." *Comparative Studies in History and Society* 16 (1): 73–109.

Harrington, K.B. 2021. "Housing and the Household." In *The Cambridge Companion to Ancient Athens,* edited by J. Neils and D.K. Rogers, 124–39. Cambridge: Cambridge University Press.

Harris, O.J.T., and T. Flohr Sørensen. 2016. "Rethinking Emotion and Material Culture." *Archaeological Dialogues* 17 (2): 145–63.

Hartman, S. 2019. *Wayward Lives, Beautiful Experiments: Intimate Histories of Social Upheaval.* New York: W.W. Norton.

Hassan, I. 1977. "Prometheus as Performer: Towards a Posthumanist Culture?" *Georgia Review* 31 (4): 830–50.

Hawkes, C. 1954. "Archaeological Theory and Method: Some Suggestions from the Old World." *American Anthropologist* 56: 161–62.

Heidegger, M. 1971. *Poetry, Language, Thought.* Translated by A. Hofstadter. New York: Harper and Row.

Hendon, J.A. 1996. "Archaeological Approaches to the Organization of Domestic Labor: Household Practice and Domestic Relations." *Annual Review of Anthropology* 25: 45–61.

Hendon, J.A. 2004. "Living and Working at Home: The Social Archaeology of Household Production and Social Relations." In *A Companion to Social Archaeology*, edited by L. Meskell and R.W. Preucel, 272–86. Malden: Blackwell.

Hendon, J.A. 2006. "The Engendered Household." In *Handbook of Gender in Archaeology*, edited by S.M. Nelson, 171–98. Lanham: AltaMira Press.

Heywood, P. 2017. "Ontological Turn, The." In *The Cambridge Encyclopedia of Anthropology*, edited by F. Stein et al. https://www.anthroencyclopedia.com. Cambridge: University of Cambridge.

Hicks, D. 2010. "The Material-Cultural Turn: Event and Effect." In *Oxford Handbook of Material Culture Studies*, edited by D. Hicks and M.C. Beaudry, 25–98. Oxford: Oxford University Press.

Hillier, B., and J. Hanson. 1984. *The Social Logic of Space.* Cambridge: Cambridge University Press.

Hirth, K.G. 1993. "The Household as an Analytical Unit: Problems in Method and Theory." In *Prehispanic Domestic Units in Western Mesoamerica. Studies of the Household, Compound, and Residence*, edited by R.S. Santley and K.G. Hirth, 21–36. Boca Raton: CRC Press, Inc.

Hodder, I. 1990. *The Domestication of Europe*. Oxford: Blackwell.
Hodder, I. 2012. *Entangled: An Archaeology of the Relationships between Humans and Things*. Malden, MA: Wiley-Blackwell.
Hodder, I., and C. Cessford. 2004. "Daily Practice and Social Memory at Çatalhöyük." *American Antiquity* 69: 17–40.
Hodos, T., ed. 2017. *The Routledge Handbook of Archaeology and Globalization*. Abindon: Routledge.
Hoepfner, W., and E.-L. Schwandner. 1994. *Haus und Stadt im klassischen Griechenland*. 2nd ed. Munich: Deutscher Kunstverlag.
Honigman, S. 2019. "Ethnic Minority Groups." In *A Companion to Greco-Roman and Late Antique Egypt*, edited by K. Vandorpe, 315–26. Hoboken, NJ: John Wiley & Sons.
Hudson, N. 2016. "A Hellenistic Household Ceramic Assemblage from Tell Timai (Thmuis), Egypt: A Contextual View." *BASOR* 376: 199–244.
Huebner, S.R. 2007. "'Brother-Sister' Marriage in Roman Egypt: A Curiosity of Humankind or a Widespread Family Strategy?" *JRS* 97: 21–49.
Huebner, S.R. 2013. *The Family in Roman Egypt: A Comparative Approach to Intergenerational Solidarity and Conflict*. Cambridge: Cambridge University Press.
Huebner, S.R., and C. Laes, eds. 2019. *The Single Life in the Roman and Later Roman World*. Cambridge: Cambridge University Press.
Huebner, S.R., and G. Nathan, eds. 2016. *Mediterranean Families in Antiquity: Households, Extended Families, and Domestic Space*. Chichester, UK: Wiley-Blackwell.
Husselman, E.M. 1953. "The Dovecotes of Karanis." *TAPA* 84: 81–91.
Husson, G. 1983. *Oikia: La vocabulaire de la maison privée en Égypte d'après les papyrus grecs*. Paris: Publications de la Sorbonne.
Ingold, T. 2000. *The Perception of the Environment: Essays on Livelihood, Dwelling, and Skill*. London: Routledge.
Jameson, M.H. 1990a. "Domestic Space in the Greek City-State." In *Domestic Architecture and the Use of Space: An Interdisciplinary Cross-Cultural Study*, edited by S. Kent, 92–113. Cambridge: Cambridge University Press.
Jameson, M.H. 1990b. "Private Space and the Greek City." In *The Greek City from Homer to Alexander*, edited by O. Murray and S. Price, 171–95. Oxford: Oxford University Press.
Jervis, B. 2018. *Assemblage Thought and Archaeology*. London: Routledge.
Jones, A.M., and Y. Hamilakis. 2017. "Archaeology and Assemblage." *Cambridge Archaeological Journal* 27: 77–84.
Joshel, S., and L. Hackworth Petersen. 2014. *The Material Life of Roman Slaves*. Cambridge: Cambridge University Press.
Joyce, R.A., and S.D. Gillespie, eds. 2000. *Beyond Kinship: Social and Material Reproduction in House Societies*. Philadelphia: University of Pennsylvania Press.
Kamel, M.E. 2015. "The Ground Plan as a Tool for the Identification and Study of Houses in an Old Kingdom Special-Purpose Settlement at Heit el-Ghurab, Giza." PhD diss., University of California, Los Angeles.
Kemp, B.J., and A. Stevens. 2010. *Busy Lives at Amarna: Excavations in the Main City (Grid 12 and the House of Ranefer, N49.18)*. 2 vols. London: Egypt Exploration Society.
Kiddey, R. 2017. *Homeless Heritage: Collaborative Social Archaeology as Therapeutic Practice*. Oxford: Oxford University Press.
Kindt, J. 2016. *Revisiting Delphi: Religion and Storytelling in Ancient Greece*. Cambridge: Cambridge University Press.
Kirk, A. 2021. "Orality and Literacy." In *The Herodotus Encyclopedia*, edited by C. Baron. Hoboken, NJ: John Wiley & Sons.
Koltsida, A. 2007. *Social Aspects of Ancient Egyptian Domestic Architecture*. Oxford: Archaeopress.
Kondyli, F., and B. Anderson, eds. 2022. *The Byzantine Neighbourhood: Urban Space and Political Action*. New York: Routledge.
Knappett, C. 2004. "The Affordances of Things: A Post-Gibsonian Perspective on the Relationality of Mind and Matter." In *Rethinking Materiality*, edited by E. DeMarrais et al., 43–51. Cambridge: McDonald Institute.

Kramer, C. 1977. "Pots and Peoples." In *Mountains and Lowlands: Essays in the Archaeology of Greater Mesopotamia*, edited by L.D. Levine and T.C. Young, 91–112. Malibu: Undena Publications.

Ladstätter, S., and V. Scheibelreiter, eds. 2010. *Städtisches Wohnen im östlichen Mittelmeerraum 4. Jh. v. Chr.—1. Jh. n. Chr.* Vienna: Verlag der Österreichischen Akademie der Wissenschaften.

LaMotta, V.M., and M.B. Schiffer. 1999. "Formation Processes of House Floor Assemblages." In *The Archaeology of Household Activities*, edited by P. Allison, 19–29. New York: Routledge.

Landeschi, G. 2018. "Rethinking GIS, Three-Dimensionality and Space Perception in Archaeology." *World Archaeology* 50: 1–16.

Landeschi, G., et al. 2015. "Enhanced 3D-GIS: Documenting Insula V 1 in Pompeii." In *Proceedings of the 42nd Annual Conference on Computer Applications and Quantitative Methods in Archaeology*, edited by F. Giligny et al., 349–60. Oxford: Archaeopress.

Langellotti, M. 2020. *Village Life in Roman Egypt: Tebtunis in the First Century AD*. Oxford: Oxford University Press.

Laslett, P. 1972. "Introduction: The History of the Family." In *Household and Family in Past Time*, edited by P. Laslett and R. Wall, 1–90. Cambridge: Cambridge University Press.

Latour, B. 2005. *Reassembling the Social: An Introduction to Actor-Network-Theory*. Oxford: Oxford University Press.

Laurence, R., and A. Wallace-Hadrill. 1997. *Domestic Space in the Roman World: Pompeii and Beyond*. Portsmouth, RI: Journal of Roman Archaeology.

Leclère, F. 2008. *Les villes de Basse Égypte au 1er millenaire av. J.-C.: Analyse archéologique et historique de la topographie urbaine*. 2 vols. Cairo: IFAO.

Lefebvre, H. 1974. *La Production de l'espace*. Paris: Anthropos.

Lehner, M. 2000. "The Fractal House of Pharaoh: Ancient Egypt as a Complex Adaptive System, A Trial Formulation." In *Dynamics in Human and Primate Societies: Agent-Based Modeling of Social and Spatial Processes*, edited by T.A. Kohler and G.J. Gumerman, 275–353. Oxford/New York: Oxford University Press.

Levin-Richardson, S. 2019. *The Brothel of Pompeii: Sex, Class, and Gender at the Margins of Roman Society*. Cambridge: Cambridge University Press.

Lévi-Strauss, C. 1982. *The Way of the Masks*. Translated by S. Modelski. Seattle: University of Washington.

Lewis, N. 1995. "Greco-Roman Egypt: Fact or Fiction?" In *On Government and Law in Roman Egypt: Collected Papers of Naphtali Lewis*, edited by Ann Ellis Hanson, 138–49. Atlanta: Scholars Press.

Lynch, K.A. 1960. *The Image of the City*. Cambridge, MA: MIT Press.

Lynch, K.M. 2016. "Can Pottery Help Distinguish a Brothel from a Tavern or a House?" In *Houses of Ill Repute: The Archaeology of Brothels, Houses, and Taverns in the Greek World*, edited by A. Glazebrook and B. Tsakirgis, 36–58. Philadelphia: University of Pennsylvania Press.

Madella, M., G. Kovács, B. Kulcsarne-Berzsenyi, and I. Briz i Godino, eds. 2013. *The Archaeology of Household*. Oxford: Oxbow Books.

Malouta, M. 2012. "Families, Households, and Children." In *The Oxford Handbook of Roman Egypt*, edited by Christina Riggs, 288–304. Oxford: Oxford University Press.

Marchi, S., ed. 2014. *Les maisons-tours en Égypte durant la Basse-Époque, les périodes ptolémaïque et romaine* (special issue of *NeHeT*). *NeHeT* 2.

Marín-Aguilera, B. 2018. "Inhabiting Domestic Space: Becoming Different in the Early Iron Age Western Mediterranean." *JMA* 31 (1): 77–100.

Marouard, G. 2008. "Rues et habitats dans les villages de la *chora* égyptienne à la période gréco-romaine (IIIe s. av.–IVe s. apr. J.-C.): Quelques exemples du Fayoum (nome arsinoïte)." In *La rue dans l'Antiquité: Définition, aménagement et devenir de l'Orient méditerranéen à la Gaule*, edited by P. Ballet, N.Dieudonné-Glad, and C. Saliou, 117–28. Rennes: Presses universitaires de Rennes.

Marouard, G. 2010. "Archéologie, architecture et images de la maison urbaine d'époque hellenistique et romaine dans la chôra égyptienne." PhD diss., Université de Poitiers.

Marouard, G. 2012. "Les données archéologiques et architecturales des quartiers domestiques et des habitats dans les fondations et les refondations lagides de la *chôra* égyptienne. Une révision archéologique." In *Grecs et Romains en Égypte: Territoires, espaces de la vie et de la mort, objets de prestige et du quotidien*, edited by Pascale Ballet, 121–40. Cairo: IFAO.

Matthews, W. 2005. "Micromorphological and Microstratigraphic Traces of Uses and Concepts of Space." In *Inhabiting Çatalhöyük: Reports from the 1995–1999 Seasons*, edited by I. Hodder, 355–98. Ankara: British Institute of Archaeology at Ankara.

Mazzone, D. 2017. "The Dark Side of a Model Community: The 'Ghetto' of el-Lahun." *Journal of Ancient Egyptian Architecture* 2: 19–54.

McGuire, R.H. 2021. "A Relational Marxist Critique of Posthumanism in Archaeology." In *Posthumanism in Archaeology* (special edited section of *Cambridge Archaeological Journal*), edited by M. Fernández-Götz et al. *Cambridge Archaeological Journal* 31 (3): 495–501.

Meskell, L. 1998. "An Archaeology of Social Relations in an Egyptian Village." *Journal of Archaeological Method and Theory* 5: 209–43.

Meskell, L. 2002. *Private Life in New Kingdom Egypt*. Princeton: Princeton University Press.

Meskell, L. 2005. "Introduction: Object Orientations." In *Archaeologies of Materiality*, edited by L. Meskell, 1–17. Oxford: Blackwell.

Meskell, L. 2007. "Archaeologies of Identity." In *The Archaeology of Identities: A Reader*, edited by T. Insoll, 23–43. New York: Routledge.

Métraux, G. 1999. "Ancient Housing: 'Oikos' and 'Domus' in Greece and Rome." *Journal of the Society of Architectural Historians* 58 (3): 392–405.

Moeller, N. 2016. *The Archaeology of Urbanism in Ancient Egypt: From the Predynastic Period to the End of the Middle Kingdom*. Cambridge: Cambridge University Press.

Monson, A. 2012. *From the Ptolemies to the Romans: Political and Economic Change in Egypt*. Cambridge: Cambridge University Press.

Moore, J.D. 2012. *The Prehistory of Home*. Berkeley: University of California Press.

Moreno Garcia, J.C. 2012. "Households." *UCLA Encyclopedia of Egyptology*. http://escholarship.org/uc/item/2bn8c9gz.

Morgan, J. 2010. *The Classical Greek House*. Exeter: Bristol Phoenix Press.

Morris, I. 1994. "Archaeologies of Greece." In *Classical Greece: Ancient Histories and Modern Archaeologies*, edited by I. Morris, 8–47. Cambridge: Cambridge University Press.

Mueller, K. 2006. *Settlements of the Ptolemies: City Foundations and New Settlement in the Hellenistic World*. Leuven: Peeters.

Müller, M. 2012. "Das altägyptische Wohnhaus: Interaktion als Vergleichsmoment?" In *Orte des Geschehens: Interaktionsräume als konstitutive Elemente der antiken Stadt*, edited by C. Rödel-Braune and C. Waschke, 244–63. Berlin: LIT Verlag.

Müller, M., ed. 2015a. *Household Studies in Complex Societies: (Micro) Archaeological and Textual Approaches*. Chicago: The Oriental Institute.

Müller, M. 2015b. "Introduction. Household Studies in Complex Societies: (Micro) Archaeological and Textual Approaches." In *Household Studies in Complex Societies: (Micro) Archaeological and Textual Approaches*, edited by M. Müller, xiii–xlii. Chicago: The Oriental Institute.

Müller, M. 2015c. "Late Middle Kingdom Society in a Neighborhood of Tell el-Dab'a/Avaris." In *Household Studies in Complex Societies: (Micro) Archaeological and Textual Approaches*, edited by M. Müller, 339–70. Chicago: The Oriental Institute.

Müller, M. 2015d. "Modelling Household Identity in a Multi-Ethnic Society." *Archaeological Review from Cambridge* 30: 102–12.

Müller, M. 2015e. "New Approaches to the Study of Households in Middle Kingdom and Second Intermediate Period Egypt." In *The World of Middle Kingdom Egypt (2000–1500 BC): Contributions on Archaeology, Art, Religion, and Written Sources*, edited by W. Grajetzki and G. Miniaci, 237–55. London: Golden House Publications.

Müller, W. 2010. "Urbanism in Graeco-Roman Egypt." In *Cities and Urbanism in Ancient Egypt*, edited by M. Bietak, E. Czerny, and I. Forstner-Müller, 217–56. Vienna: Verlag der Österreichischen Akademie der Wissenschaften.

Mullins, P.R. 2012. "The Importance of Innocuous Things: Prosaic Materiality, Everyday Life, and Historical Archaeology." In *Historical Archaeology and the Importance of Material Things II*, edited by J.M. Schablitsky and M.P. Leone, 31–44. Missoula, MT: Society for Historical Archaeology.

Nanoglou, S. 2008. "Building Biographies and Households: Aspects of Community Life in Neolithic Northern Greece." *Journal of Social Archaeology* 8 (1): 139–60.

Naum, M. 2012. "Ambiguous Pots: Everyday Practice, Migration and Materiality. The Case of Medieval Baltic Ware on the Island of Bornholm (Denmark)." *Journal of Social Archaeology* 12 (1): 92–119.

Netting, R.McC., R.R. Wilk, and E.J. Arnould, eds. 1984a. *Households: Comparative and Historical Studies of the Domestic Group*. Berkeley: University of California Press.

Netting, R.McC., R.R. Wilk, and E.J. Arnould. 1984b. "Introduction." In *Households: Comparative and Historical Studies of the Domestic Group*, xiii–xxxviii. Berkeley: University of California Press.

Nevett, L. 1999. *House and Society in the Ancient Greek World*. Cambridge: Cambridge University Press.

Nevett, L. 2007. "Greek Houses as a Source of Evidence for Social Relations." In *Building Communities: House, Settlement, and Society in the Aegean and Beyond*, edited by R. Westgate et al., 5–10. Athens: British School at Athens.

Nevett, L. 2008. "Artefact Assemblages and Activity Area Analysis: A Comparison from Greek Domestic Contexts." In *Thinking about Space: The Potential of Surface Survey and Contextual Analysis in the Definition of Space in Roman Times*, edited by H. Vanhaverbeke et al., 153–60. Turnhout: Brepols.

Nevett, L. 2010. *Domestic Space in Classical Antiquity*. Cambridge: Cambridge University Press.

Nevett, L. 2012. "Housing and Households in Ancient Greece: The Greek World." In *Classical Archaeology*, edited by S.E. Alcock and R. Osborne, 2nd ed., 209–27. Oxford: Wiley-Blackwell.

Nevett, L. 2015. "Artifact Assemblages in Classical Greek Domestic Contexts: Toward a New Approach." In *Household Studies in Complex Societies: (Micro) Archaeological and Textual Approaches*, edited by Miriam Müller, 101–16. Chicago: The Oriental Institute.

Nishimura, Y. 2012. "The Life of the Majority: A Reconstruction of Household Activities and Residential Neighborhoods at the Late-Third-Millennium Urban Settlement at Titriş Höyük in Northern Mesopotamia." In *New Perspectives on Household Archaeology*, edited by B.J. Parker and C.P. Foster, 347–72. Winona Lake, IN: Eisenbrauns.

Nowicka, M. 1969. *La maison privée dans l'Égypte ptolémaïque*. Wrocław, Poland: Zakład Narodowy Imienia Ossolińskich.

Olabarria, L. 2020. *Kinship and Family in Ancient Egypt: Archaeology and Anthropology in Dialogue*. Cambridge: Cambridge University Press.

Olsen, B. 2003. "Material Culture after Text: Re-Membering Things." *Norwegian Archaeological Review* 36 (2): 87–104.

Olsen, B., and C. Witmore. 2015. "Archaeology, Symmetry, and the Ontology of Things: A Response to Critics." *Archaeological Dialogues* 22 (2): 187–97.

Overholtzer, L., and C. Robin, eds. 2015. *The Materiality of Everyday Life* (special issue of *Archeological Papers of the American Anthropological Association*). *Archeological Papers of the American Anthropological Association* 26.

Özbal, R. 2012. "The Challenge of Identifying Households at Tell Kurdu (Turkey)." In *New Perspectives on Household Archaeology*, edited by B.J. Parker and C.P. Foster, 321–46. Winona Lake, IN: Eisenbrauns.

Padilla Peralta, D. 2020. "Epistemicide: The Roman Case." *Classica* 33 (2): 151–86.

Paliou, E., ed. 2014. *Spatial Analysis and Social Spaces: Interdisciplinary Approaches to the Interpretation of Prehistoric and Historic Built Environments*. Berlin: De Gruyter.

Parca, M. 1997. "Violence by and against Women in Documentary Papyri from Ptolemaic and Roman Egypt." In *Le role et le statut de la femme en Égypte hellénistique, romaine et byzantine*, edited by H. Melaerts and L. Mooren, 283–96. Leuven: Peeters.

Parker, B.J., and C.P. Foster, eds. 2012. *New Perspectives on Household Archaeology*. Winona Lake, IN: Eisenbrauns.

Pecci, A., et al. 2018. "Combining Residue Analysis of Floors and Ceramics for the Study of Activity Areas at the Garum Shop at Pompeii." *Archaeological and Anthropological Sciences* 10: 485–502.

Pesando, F. 1997. *Domus: Edilizia private e società pompeiana fra III e I secolo a.C.* Rome: "L'Erma" di Bretschneider.

Picardo, N. 2015. "Hybrid Households: Institutional Affiliations and Household Identity in the Town of Wah-sut (South Abydos)." In *Household Studies in Complex Societies: (Micro) Archaeological and Textual Approaches*, edited by M. Müller, 243–87. Chicago: The Oriental Institute.

Pirson, F. 1999. *Mietwohnungen in Pompeji und Herkulaneum: Untersuchungen zur Architektur, zum Wohnen und zur Sozial- und Wirtschaftsgeschichte der Vesuvstädte*. Munich: Verlag Dr. F. Pfeil.

Pitts, M., and M.J. Versluys, eds. 2015. *Globalisation and the Roman World*. Cambridge: Cambridge University Press.

Plantzos, D. 2012. "Archaeology after the End of History." *Historein* 12: 68–78.

Pollock, S., ed. 2015. *Between Feasts and Daily Meals: Towards an Archaeology of Commensal Space*. Berlin: Topoi.

Pomeroy, S.B. 1994. *Xenophon, Oeconomicus: A Social and Historical Commentary*. Oxford: Clarendon.

Pudsey, A. 2011. "Nuptiality and the Demographic Life Cycle of Families in Roman Egypt." In *Demography and the Graeco-Roman World: New Insights and Approaches*, edited by C. Holleran and A. Pudsey, 60–98. Cambridge: Cambridge University Press.

Pudsey, A. 2012. "Death and the Family: Widows and Divorcées in Roman Egypt." In *Families in the Imperial and Late Antique Roman Worlds*, edited by L. Larsson Lovén and M. Harlow, 157–80. New York: Continuum.

Pudsey, A. 2013. "Children in Roman Egypt." In *Handbook of Children and Education in the Classical World*, edited by J. Evans Grubbs and T.G. Parkin, with R. Bell, 484–509. Oxford: Oxford University Press.

Pudsey, A. 2015. "Children and Families in Late Roman Egypt: Family and Everyday Life in Monastic Contexts." In *Children and Family in Late Antiquity: Life, Death, and Interaction*, edited by C. Laes, K. Mustakallio, and V. Vuolanto, 215–34. Leuven: Peeters.

Purcell, N. 2013. "On the Significance of East and West in Today's 'Hellenistic' History: Reflections on Symmetrical Worlds, Reflecting through World Symmetries." In *The Hellenistic West: Rethinking the Ancient Mediterranean*, edited by J.R.W. Prag and J.C. Quinn, 367–90. Cambridge: Cambridge University Press.

Putzeys, T., et al. 2004. "Analyzing Domestic Contexts at Sagalassos: Developing a Methodology Using Ceramics and Macro-Botanical Remains." *JMA* 17 (1): 31–57.

Raab, L., and A. Goodyear. 1984. "Middle Range Theory in Archaeology: A Critical Review of Origins and Applications." *American Antiquity* 49: 255–68.

Rainville, L. 2012. "Household Matters: Techniques for Understanding Assyrian Houses." In *New Perspectives on Household Archaeology*, edited by B.J. Parker and C.P. Foster, 139–64. Winona Lake, IN: Eisenbrauns.

Rainville, L. 2015. "Investigating Traces of Everyday Life in Ancient Households: Some Methodological Considerations." In *Household Studies in Complex Societies: (Micro) Archaeological and Textual Approaches*, edited by Miriam Müller, 1–27. Chicago: The Oriental Institute.

Rapoport, A. 1990. *The Meaning of the Built Environment: A Nonverbal Communication Approach*. Tucson: University of Arizona Press.

Rathje, W., and C. Murphy. 2001. *Rubbish! The Archaeology of Garbage*. Tucson: University of Arizona Press.

Rathmayr, E. 2017. "Identity in the Private Sphere: Interpreting Houses as *Loci* Reflecting the Identity of Their Inhabitants." In *Cityscapes and Monuments of Western Asia Minor*, edited by E. Mortensen and B. Poulsen, 109–21. Oxford: Oxbow Books.

Rebillard, E. 2015. "Material Culture and Religious Identity in Late Antiquity." In *A Companion to the Archaeology of Religion in the Ancient World*, edited by R. Raja and J. Rüpke, 427–36. Malden, MA: John Wiley & Sons.

Reinders, H.R., and W. Prummel. 2003. *Housing in New Halos: A Hellenistic Town in Thessaly, Greece*. Lisse: A.A. Balkema.

Relaki, M., and J. Driessen, eds. 2020. *OIKOS. Archaeological Approaches to House Societies in Aegean Prehistory*. Leuven: Presses universitaires de Louvain.

Remijsen, S., and W. Clarysse. 2008. "Incest or Adoption? Brother-Sister Marriage in Roman Egypt Revisited." *JRS* 98: 53–61.

Renfrew, C. 1980. "The Great Tradition versus the Great Divide: Archaeology as Anthropology?" *AJA* 84 (3): 287–98.

Ribeiro, A. 2021. "Revisiting the Chinese Room: Looking for Agency in a World Packed with Archaeological Things." In *Posthumanism in Archaeology* (special edited section of *Cambridge Archaeological Journal*), edited by M. Fernández-Götz et al. *Cambridge Archaeological Journal* 31 (3): 533–41.

Ritner, R.K. 2003. "The Instruction of 'Onchsheshonqy (P. British Museum 10508)." In *The Literature of Ancient Egypt: An Anthology of Stories, Instructions, Stelae, Autobiographies, and Poetry*, edited by W.K. Simpson, 497–529. 3rd ed. New Haven: Yale University Press.

Robin, C. 2002. "Outside of Houses: The Practices of Everyday Life at Chan Nòohol, Belize." *Journal of Social Archaeology* 2 (2): 245–68.

Robin, C. 2003. "New Directions in Classic Maya Household Archaeology." *Journal of Archaeological Research* 11 (4): 307–56.

Rosch, E. 2011. "'Slow Lettuce': Categories, Concepts, Fuzzy Sets, and Logical Deduction." In *Concepts and Fuzzy Logic*, edited by R. Belohlavek and G.J. Klir, 89–120. Cambridge: MIT Press.

Routledge, B. 2013. "Household Archaeology in the Levant." *BASOR* 370: 207–19.

Rowlandson, J., and S. Lippert. 2019. "Family and Life Cycle Transitions." In *A Companion to Greco-Roman and Late Antique Egypt*, edited by K. Vandorpe, 327–46. Hoboken, NJ: John Wiley & Sons.

Ryle, G. 1949. *The Concept of Mind*. New York: University Paperbacks.

Salazar, J., et al. 2022. "Perspectives: Households as Assemblages." In *Archaeology of Households, Kinship, and Social Change*, edited by L.B. Carpenter and A.M. Prentiss, 18–26. New York: Routledge.

Schiffer, M. 1987. *Formation Processes of the Archaeological Record*. Albuquerque: University of New Mexico Press.

Shaw, I. 1992. "Ideal Homes in Ancient Egypt: The Archaeology of Social Aspiration." *CAJ* 2 (2): 147–66.

Siebert, G. 1998. "Vie publique et vie privée dans les maisons hellénistiques de Délos." *Ktema* 23: 171–78.

Sigl, J., ed. 2022. *Daily Life in Ancient Egyptian Settlements*. Wiesbaden: Harrassowitz.

Sigl, J., and P. Kopp. 2020. "Working from Home—Middle Kingdom Daily Life on Elephantine Island, Egypt." In *Approaches to the Analysis of Production Activity at Archaeological Sites*, edited by A.K. Hodgkinson and C.L. Tvetmarken, 8–24. Oxford: Archaeopress.

Silliman, S.W. 2015. "A Requiem for Hybridity? The Problem with Frankensteins, Purées, and Mules." *Journal of Social Archaeology* 15: 277–98.

Silliman, S.W. 2016. "Disentangling the Archaeology of Colonialism and Indigeneity." In *Archaeology of Entanglement*, edited by L. Der and F. Fernandini, 31–48. Walnut Creek: Left Coast Press.

Skeates, R., and J. Day, eds. 2020. *The Routledge Handbook of Sensory Archaeology*. New York: Routledge.

Small, D. 1991. "Initial Study of the Structure of Women's Seclusion in the Archaeological Past." In *The Archaeology of Gender*, edited by D. Walde and N. Willows, 336–42. Calgary: University of Calgary.

Smith, M.E. 1992. "Braudel's Temporal Rhythms and Chronology Theory in Archaeology." In *Archaeology, Annales, and Ethnohistory*, edited by A.B. Knapp, 223–34. Cambridge: Cambridge University Press.

Smithson, M. 1987. *Fuzzy Set Analysis for Behavioral and Social Sciences*. New York: Springer-Verlag.

Soja, E. 1996. *Thirdspace: Journeys to Los Angeles and Other Real-and-Imagined Places*. Malden, MA: Blackwell.

Souvatzi, S.G. 2008. *A Social Archaeology of Households in Neolithic Greece: An Anthropological Approach*. Cambridge: Cambridge University Press.

Spence, K. 2004. "The Three-Dimensional Form of the Amarna House." *JEA* 90: 123–52.

Spence, K. 2015. "Ancient Egyptian Houses and Households: Architecture, Artifacts, Conceptualization, and Interpretation." In *Household Studies in Complex Societies: (Micro) Archaeological and Textual Approaches*, edited by Miriam Müller, 83–100. Chicago: The Oriental Institute.

Spencer, N. 2014a. "Amara West: Considerations on Urban Life in Colonial Kush." In *The Fourth Cataract and Beyond*, edited by J.R. Anderson and D.A Welsby, 457–85. Leuven: Peeters.

Spencer, N. 2014b. "Creating and Re-Shaping Egypt in Kush: Responses at Amara West." *Journal of Ancient Egyptian Interconnections* 6 (1): 42–61.

Spencer, N. 2015. "Creating a Neighborhood within a Changing Town: Household and Other Agencies at Amara West in Nubia." In *Household Studies in Complex Societies: (Micro) Archaeological and Textual Approaches*, edited by M. Müller, 169–210. Chicago: The Oriental Institute.

Spencer-Wood, S.M. 1999. "The World Their Household: Changing Meanings of the Domestic Sphere in the Nineteenth Century." In *The Archaeology of Household Activities*, edited by P. Allison, 162–89. New York: Routledge.

Steadman, S.R. 2016 (2015). *Archaeology of Domestic Architecture and the Human Use of Space.* Paperback ed. New York: Routledge.

Stockhammer, P.W., ed. 2012a. *Conceptualizing Cultural Hybridization: A Transdisciplinary Approach.* Heidelberg: Springer.

Stockhammer, P.W. 2012b. "Entangled Pottery: Phenomena of Appropriation in the Late Bronze Age Eastern Mediterranean." In *Materiality and Social Practice: Transformative Capacities of Intercultural Encounters*, edited by J. Maran and P.W. Stockhammer, 89–103. Oxford: Oxbow Books.

Stockhammer, P.W. 2013. "From Hybridity to Entanglement, from Essentialism to Practice." *Archaeological Review from Cambridge* 28: 11–28.

Stoner, J. 2019. *The Cultural Lives of Domestic Objects in Late Antiquity.* Leiden: Brill.

Subías, E., P. Azara, J. Carruesco, I. Fiz, and R. Cuesta, eds. 2011. *The Space of the City in Graeco-Roman Egypt: Image and Reality.* Tarragona: Institut Català d'Arqueologia Clàssica.

Svensdotter, A., M. Guaralda, and S. Mayere. 2020. "Street Food and Placemaking: A Cultural Review of Urban Practices." In *Routledge Handbook of Street Culture*, edited by J.I. Ross, 346–56. New York: Routledge.

Tacoma, L.E. 2012. "Settlement and Population." In *The Oxford Handbook of Roman Egypt*, edited by Christina Riggs, 122–35. Oxford: Oxford University Press.

Tally-Schumacher, K.J. 2020. "Cultivating Empire in Ancient Roman Gardens: Unearthing the Tangled Relationship between Plants and their Gardeners." PhD diss., Cornell University.

Tang, B. 2005. *Delos, Carthage, Ampurias: The Housing of Three Mediterranean Trading Centres.* Rome: "L'Erma" di Bretschneider.

Tarlow, S. 2012. "The Archaeology of Emotion and Affect." *Annual Review of Anthropology* 41: 169–85.

Thompson, D.J. 2001. "Hellenistic Hellenes: The Case of Ptolemaic Egypt." In *Ancient Perceptions of Greek Ethnicity*, edited by I. Malkin, 301–22. Cambridge: Harvard University Press.

Thompson, D.J. 2002. "Families in Early Ptolemaic Egypt." In *The Hellenistic World: New Perspectives*, edited by D. Ogden, 137–56. London: Classical Press of Wales and Duckworth.

Thompson, D.J. 2011. "Ethnic Minorities in Ptolemaic Egypt." In *Political Culture in the Greek City after the Classical Age*, edited by O. van Nijf and R. Alston, 101–17. Leuven: Peeters.

Todd, Z. 2016. "An Indigenous Feminist's Take on the Ontological Turn: 'Ontology' Is Just Another Word for Colonialism." *Journal of Historical Sociology* 29.1: 4–22.

Tonner, P. 2018. *Dwelling: Heidegger, Archaeology, Mortality.* New York: Routledge.

Trigger, B.G. 1996. *A History of Archaeological Thought.* 2nd ed. Cambridge: Cambridge University Press.

Tringham, R. 1991. "Households with Faces: The Challenge of Gender in Prehistoric Architectural Remains." In *Engendering Archaeology: Women and Prehistory*, edited by J.M. Gero and M.W. Conkey, 93–131. Malden: Blackwell.

Tringham, R. 2003. "(Re)-Digging the Site at the End of the Twentieth Century: Large-Scale Archaeological Fieldwork in a New Millennium." In *Theory and Practice in Mediterranean Archaeology: Old World and New World Perspectives*, edited by J.K. Papadopoulos and R.M. Leventhal, 89–114. Los Angeles: Cotsen Institute of Archaeology.

Tringham, R. 2012. "Households through a Digital Lens." In *New Perspectives on Household Archaeology*, edited by B.J. Parker and C.P. Foster, 81–122. Winona Lake, IN: Eisenbrauns.

Tringham, R. 2015. "Household Archaeology." In *International Encyclopedia of the Social and Behavioral Sciences*, edited by N.J. Smelser and P.B. Baltes, 2nd ed., 219–23. Oxford: Pergamon Press.

Trümper, M. 1998. *Wohnen in Delos: Eine baugeschichtliche Untersuchung zum Wandel der Wohnkultur in hellenistischer Zeit.* Rahden: Marie Leidorf.

Trümper, M. 2003. "Wohnen und Arbeiten im hellenistischen Handelshafen Delos. Kontexte und Verteilung der tabernae." In *Wohnformen und Lebenswelten im interkulturellen Vergleich*, edited by M. Droste and A. Hoffmann, 125–59. Frankfurt: Peter Lang.

Trümper, M. 2005. "Modest Housing in Late Hellenistic Delos." In *Ancient Greek Houses and Households: Chronological, Regional, and Social Diversity*, edited by B.A. Ault and L.C. Nevett, 119–39. Philadelphia: University of Pennsylvania Press.

Tsakirgis, B. 2005. "Living and Working around the Athenian Agora: A Preliminary Case Study of Three Houses." In *Ancient Greek Houses and Households: Chronological, Regional, and Social Diversity*, edited by B.A. Ault and L.C. Nevett, 67–83. Philadelphia: University of Pennsylvania Press.

Tsakirgis, B. 2015. "Tools from the House of Mikion and Menon." In *Autopsy in Athens: Recent Archaeological Research on Athens and Attica*, edited by M.M. Miles, 9–17. Oxford: Oxbow Books.

Tsakirgis, B. 2016a. "The Architecture of Greek Houses." In *A Companion to Greek Architecture*, edited by M.M. Miles, 273–87. Malden: John Wiley & Sons.

Tsakirgis, B. 2016b. "What Is a House? Conceptualizing the Greek House." In *Houses of Ill Repute: The Archaeology of Brothels, Houses, and Taverns in the Greek World*, edited by A. Glazebrook and B. Tsakirgis, 13–35. Philadelphia: University of Pennsylvania Press.

Ullah, I.I.T. 2012. "Particles of the Past: Microarchaeological Spatial Analysis of Ancient House Floors." In *New Perspectives on Household Archaeology*, edited by B.J. Parker and C.P. Foster, 123–38. Winona Lake, IN: Eisenbrauns.

Uytterhoeven, I. 2020. "Following 'Western' Fashion Trends. The Impact of 'Italian' Elements on Private Housing in Roman Imperial Asia Minor." In *Zwischen Bruch und Kontinuität / Continuity and Change*, edited by U. Lohner-Urban and U. Quatember, 453–71. Istanbul: Ege Yayınlan.

Vandorpe, K. 2008. "Persian Soldiers and Persians of the Epigone: Social Mobility of Soldiers-Herdsmen in Upper Egypt." *ArchPF* 54 (1): 87–108.

van Driel-Murray, C. 1995. "Gender in Question." *Theoretical Roman Archaeology: Second Conference Proceedings*, edited by P. Rush, 3–21. Aldershot: Avebury.

Van Dyke, R.M. 2021. "Ethics, Not Objects." In *Posthumanism in Archaeology* (special edited section of *Cambridge Archaeological Journal*), edited by M. Fernández-Götz et al. *Cambridge Archaeological Journal* 31 (3): 487–93.

Van Oyen, A. 2020. *The Socio-Economics of Roman Storage: Agriculture, Trade, and Family*. Cambridge: Cambridge University Press.

Veyne, P., ed. 1992. *A History of Private Life*. Vol. 1. *From Pagan Rome to Byzantium*. Trans. A. Goldhammer. Cambridge, MA: Belknap Press of Harvard University Press.

von Pilgrim, C. 1996. *Elephantine XVIII. Untersuchungen in der Stadt des Mittleren Reichs und der Zweiten Zwischenzeit*. Mainz am Rhein: Philipp von Zabern.

Wallace-Hadrill, A. 1994. *Houses and Society in Pompeii and Herculaneum*. Princeton: Princeton University Press.

Wallace-Hadrill, A. 2008. "Housing the Dead: The Tomb as House in Roman Italy." In *Commemorating the Dead: Texts and Artifacts in Context*, edited by L. Brink and D. Green, 39–78. Berlin: De Gruyter.

Walter-Karydi, E. 1994. *Die Nobilitierung des Wohnhauses: Lebensform und Architektur im spätklassishen Griechenland*. Konstanz: Universitätsverlag Konstanz.

Webb, L., and I. Selsvold. 2020. "Introduction: Posthuman Perspectives in Roman Archaeology." In *Beyond the Romans: Posthuman Perspectives on Roman Archaeology*, edited by I. Selsvold and L. Webb, 1–10. Oxford: Oxbow.

Westgate, R., N. Fisher, and J. Whitley, eds. 2007. *Building Communities: House, Settlement and Society in the Aegean and Beyond*. London: British School at Athens.

Westgate, R. 2000. "Space and Decoration in Hellenistic Houses." *BSA* 95: 391–426.

Westgate, R. 2007. "House and Society in Classical and Hellenistic Crete: A Case Study in Regional Variation." *AJA* 111 (3): 423–57.

Westgate, R. 2013. "Making Yourself at Home in the Hellenistic World." In *Belonging and Isolation in the Hellenistic World*, edited by S.L. Ager and R.A. Faber, 245–67. Toronto: University of Toronto.

White, L. 2007 (1959). *The Evolution of Culture: The Development of Civilization to the Fall of Rome*. Walnut Creek: Left Coast Press.

Whitehouse, R.D. 2016. "Gender Archaeology and Archaeology of Women: Do We Need Both?" In *Archaeology and Women: Ancient and Modern Issues*, edited by S. Hamilton, R.D. Whitehouse, and K.I. Wright, 27–40. Walnut Creek: Left Coast Press.

Whitley, J. 2001. *The Archaeology of Ancient Greece*. Cambridge: Cambridge University Press.

Wilburn, A. 2012. *Materia Magica: The Archaeology of Magic in Roman Egypt, Cyprus and Spain*. Ann Arbor: University of Michigan Press.

Wilfong, T.G. 2002. " 'Friendship and Physical Desire': The Discourse of Female Homoeroticism in Fifth-Century CE Egypt." In *Among Women: From the Homosocial to the Homoerotic in the Ancient World*, edited by N.S. Rabinowitz, 304–30. Austin: University of Texas Press.

Wilk, R.R., and W. Ashmore, eds. 1988. *Household and Community in the Mesoamerican Past*. Albuquerque: University of New Mexico Press.

Wilk, R.R., and R.McC. Netting. 1984. "Households: Changing Forms and Functions." In *Households: Comparative and Historical Studies of the Domestic Group*, edited by R.M. Netting, R.R. Wilk, and E.J. Arnould, 1–28. Berkeley: University of California Press.

Wilk, R.R., and W.L. Rathje. 1982. "Household Archaeology." *American Behavioral Scientist* 25 (6): 617–39.

Witmore, C. 2020. "Symmetrical Archaeology." In *Encyclopedia of Global Archaeology*, edited by C. Smith, 2nd ed. Cham: Springer Nature Switzerland.

Wolf, P., U. Nowotnick, and C. Hof. 2014. "The Meroitic Urban Town of Hamadab in 2010." In *The Fourth Cataract and Beyond*, edited by J.R. Anderson and D.A. Welsby, 719–37. Leuven: Peeters.

Yanagisako, S.J. 1979. "Family and Household: The Analysis of Domestic Groups." *Annual Review of Anthropology* 8: 161–205.

Yiftach-Firanko, U. 2003. *Marriage and Marital Arrangements: A History of the Greek Marriage Document in Egypt, 4th century BCE–4th century CE*. Munich: C.H. Beck.

Zanker, P. 1998. *Pompeii: Public and Private Life*. Translated by Deborah Lucas Schneider. Cambridge, MA: Harvard University Press.

Zarmakoupi, M. 2014. *Designing for Luxury on the Bay of Naples: Villas and Landscapes (c. 100 BCE—79 CE)*. Oxford: Oxford University Press.

Zarmakoupi, M. 2015. "Les maisons des négociants italiens à Délos: structuration de l'espace domestique dans une société en movement." *Cahiers "Mondes anciens"* 7. https://journals.openedition.org/mondesanciens/1588.

Zarmakoupi, M. 2023. *Shaping Roman Landscape: Ecocritical Approaches to Architecture and Wall Painting in Early Imperial Italy*. Los Angeles: Getty Publications.

PART I

Households in Spatial Context

Settlements, Neighborhoods, and Urbanism

1

Egyptian Houses in Their Urban and Environmental Contexts

Some Case Studies of the Roman and Late Roman Periods

PAOLA DAVOLI

Excavations in urban and domestic areas of all periods have increased in recent years in Egypt and are helping to define characters, traditions, habits, and innovations for the different parts of the country. It is well established that we cannot give a single definition or description of Egyptian domestic architecture because it varies according to periods, geographical locations, and social status of the owners. Building technique and materials, on the contrary, are quite uniform across time and space, but still possess regional peculiarities, often determined by the climate and, in general, by the environment and available materials. Urban layouts of villages, towns and cities are also clearly influenced by local geomorphology and climate. This influence is particularly evident in marginal areas, like the oases and the outskirts of the Fayum.[1] Studies of urban layout and domestic architecture in ancient settlements have too often been pursued in isolation, without an integrated analysis of the geographical, geomorphological, and environmental contexts. Here, I present a first attempt to focus the attention on the environmental contexts and constraints in which houses and settlements were built, and aim to add a new perspective to social and cultural interpretative theories on domestic architecture.[2] This environmental perspective helps to clarify the origins of some peculiar features of the spatial organization of local communities.[3] Some characteristics are far from being of Greek or Roman origin: it has been noted that houses in settlements located on the outskirts of cultivated land and close to the desert, such as those in the Fayum and in the oases of the western desert of Egypt, cannot be defined as either Greek or Roman in their structure and are far from having characteristics common to Mediterranean houses with central open-air courtyards. Instead, they constitute relatively small, closed systems and are often inserted into a dense and labyrinthine layout of streets, partly shaded and closed by doors.

Settlements in Arid and Sandy Environments: General Characteristics

Considering the Greco-Roman and Late Roman settlements in arid environments in Egypt, it is immediately evident that the main characteristics of Hellenistic and Roman architecture and urban planning, as they are well established in other regions, are not present, at least in the settlements we know best. One of the main characters of Roman urban plans[4]—the close connection between the public buildings, the public squares, and the space outside the urban perimeter—is not present in extant Egyptian settlements, but it must be noted that none of them are nome capitals or *metropoleis*.[5]

Settlements on the Outskirts of the Fayum

A relevant and monumental feature in the Roman-period Fayum settlements is the main temple with an associated *dromos*, or processional road, which played important religious and social functions. The dromos cannot be considered, however, as a connecting road within the settlement: in some cases, like Tebtynis, the dromos was used as a market area, and therefore as an agora, but in others, like Soknopaiou Nesos (figure 1.1) and Narmouthis, it seems to have been used only to perform rituals.[6]

A compacted and labyrinthine layout, with narrow streets and few open spaces, seems to characterize most of the settlements in arid environments in Egypt. In the Fayum the best-preserved settlements were, and in a few cases still are,[7] located on its fringe. Here the anthropization stopped after the settlements' abandonment, which occurred between the third and the seventh centuries CE, and the desert sand covered the ancient remains, protecting them until the end of the nineteenth century.[8] The Fayum is usually described as the most Hellenized region of Egypt because of the presence of a high number of "Hellenes" as settlers and the impressive Greek documentation on papyri. From the beginning of the Ptolemaic Period, a series of new settlements was founded throughout Egypt, particularly in the less densely populated areas of the *chora* and the Fayum and in the new agricultural lands created by large-scale projects of land reclamation. We do not know much about the urban layout and house types of these new settlements of the Hellenistic Period, because they were enlarged and replaced by those of the Roman Period. The excavations of some multistratified sites (in Arabic *kiman*, artificial hills) demonstrated transformation over time in settlement dimension and number and density of buildings.[9] Identification of different phases in settlements with only one occupation level preserved, like Dionysias, Euhemeria, Theadelphia and Philadelphia, is more difficult to determine and would need new careful, stratigraphic excavations, where still possible. Only in a few cases and in limited areas have archaeological excavations exposed sequences of occupational levels: for example, at Karanis, Soknopaiou Nesos, Bakchias, and Tebtynis.[10] From these cases we can infer that the dimension of towns and the density of buildings started to increase at the end of the Ptolemaic Period and that a significant growth of the urbanized population in the Roman Period, reaching a peak in the first half of the second century CE, caused substantial change in urban layouts.[11] The Hellenistic phase of the oases settlements is still largely unknown and our analysis will be confined to the Roman and Late Roman Periods.

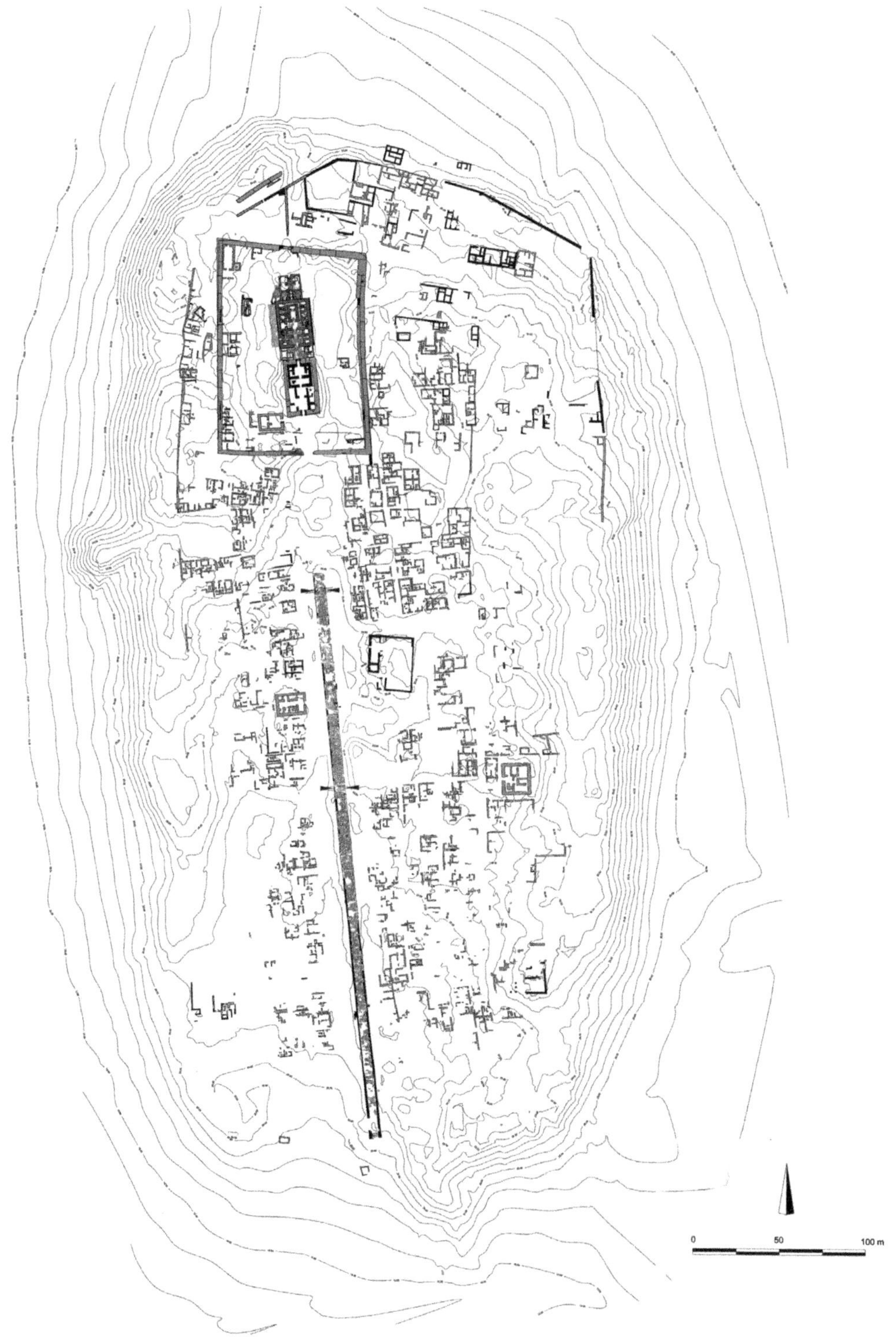

Figure 1.1. Plan of Dime/Soknopaiou Nesos. (Courtesy of Soknopaiou Nesos Project.)

Examining the urban layout of these villages and towns in their evolution, we see the basic "rule" of orthogonal organization holding constant for streets and houses, but it did not necessarily result in chessboard plans.[12] Often the streets are of irregular width, and in the Roman Period the narrowest alleys leading into blocks of houses were often partitioned and became courtyards, serving single families with kitchen facilities and/or pens for animals. The use of what we tend to consider public spaces, like the streets, still requires more analysis in the Egyptian context.[13] Especially in the Roman Period, when houses were built abutting each other on rows separated by narrow alleys, people often modified alleys for private use by constructing transversal walls that enclosed spaces to form courtyards, sometimes equipped with doors or narrow passages to let people pass from one area to the other.[14] Moreover, streets and alleys were closed with walls and/or doors. Examples include the east and west sectors of the University of Michigan excavations at Soknopaiou Nesos, Karanis, and the houses east of the temple at Tebtynis.[15] The use of walls and doors to close all or part of the alleys may suggest a need to protect houses and courtyards from intruders, but it may also be considered as a protection against wind and sand accumulation. In Soknopaiou Nesos, the west excavation sector consists of one block of houses built on the outskirts of the settlement: the west side of the block is a continuous wall composed of a row of houses, forming a sort of barrier against the northwesterly winds. The two east-west oriented streets (I 100 and I 115), bordering the block of houses, were closed by walls on their west end, probably as a protection from wind and sand (figure 1.2). Fences made with stones were built, probably in the

Figure 1.2. Dime. Plan of sector west First Level, excavations of the University of Michigan 1931–32. (Boak 1935, Plan VII.)

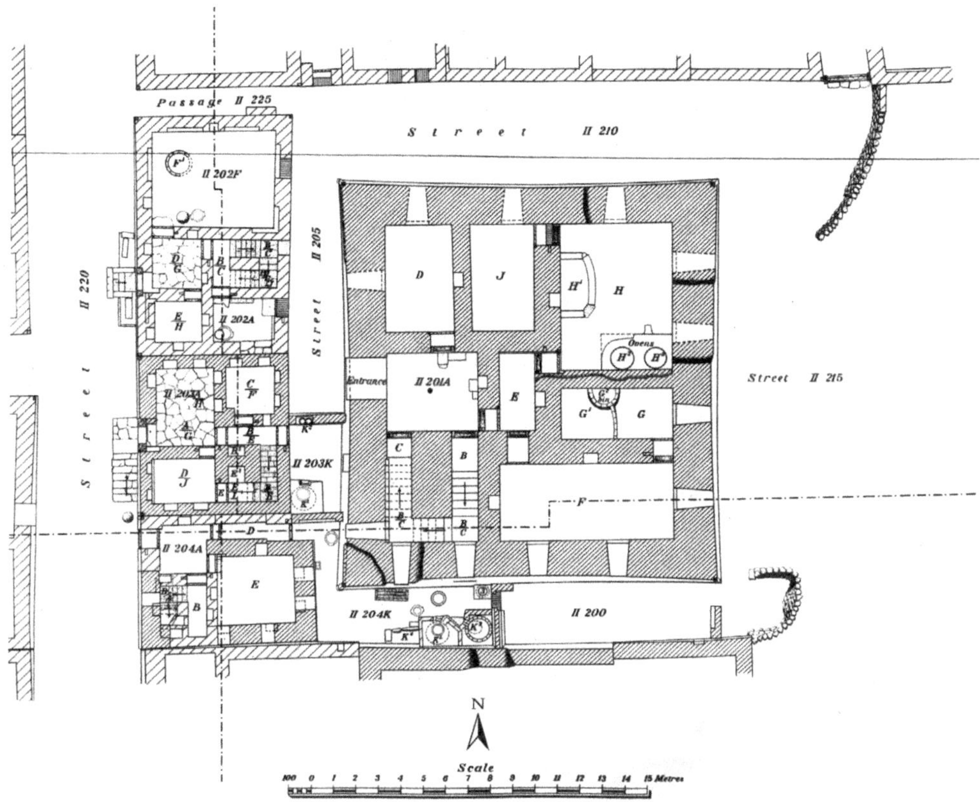

Figure 1.3. Dime. Plan of sector east Late First Level, excavations of the University of Michigan 1931–32. (Boak 1935, Plan III.)

first half of the third century, on the east side of the east excavation sector, to protect the entrance of the east-west running streets (II 200, II 210) (figure 1.3).[16]

At Karanis, windbreak walls also appear in streets and in front of building entrances, and walls with doorways close off alleys to create private courtyards or passages with animals' pens, ovens, or bins.[17] A similar use is attested in Roman-period alleys in Tebtynis, where the partitions became courtyards, usually placed at the rear of houses and directly connected with them.[18]

These doors, walls, and barriers in and at the entrances of streets limited the free circulation of people, and some were presumably intended to prevent accumulation of windblown sand. The climate and environmental conditions in these settlements on the fringe of the Fayum were and are still characterized by wind throughout the year, and accumulation of windblown sand is clearly visible in their stratigraphy.[19] Open spaces like courtyards and streets were exposed to strong sun, winds, and dust and needed simple and pragmatic protection strategies, such as maximally reducing open areas and building barriers. It would also be reasonable to consider some kind of roofing on kitchen facilities to avoid direct exposure to wind and sun. Unfortunately, the evidence of roofing in streets and courtyards is rarely documented in archaeological excavations, because the traces of wooden beams high on walls are not always easily recognizable. In Soknopaiou Nesos, either the University of Michigan expedition did not document these traces, or likely, the perimeter walls of the excavated houses were not preserved to the height of any external roof. However, G. B. Belzoni described the houses and the roofing technique he saw in Dime during his visit in 1819 with a wealth of detail and noticed that the narrow lanes among the houses were also covered.[20]

Settlements in the Western Desert Oases

The private use of streets and the closing of alleys with walls and doors are also common in Roman and Late Roman settlements in the Great Oasis (Dakhla and Kharga) of the western desert of Egypt, including Amheida/Trimithis, Ismant el-Kharab/Kellis, and Douch/Kysis. The presence of different kinds of street roofing has been clearly identified at Amheida in the fourth-century level. The site is under investigation by New York University: the team has documented the buildings visible on the surface and excavated four sectors of the third-fourth century polis, as well as the temple area (figure 1.4).[21]

In Area 2, the two streets east (S 2) and west (S 3) of the rich fourth-century house of the city councilor Serenos (figure 1.5) reveal peculiarities in road organization and use, including a combined use of doors and roofs to divide and protect parts of the open spaces. The conservation of this part of the city is remarkable because three meters of windblown sand covered the buildings soon after their abandonment toward the end of the fourth century CE.[22] Similarly well-preserved settlements are Kellis, in the center of Dakhla Oasis, with quarters of the third and fourth century recently explored,[23] and Kysis in the south of Kharga Oasis.[24]

The urban layout of these settlements cannot be considered as a purely Roman conception: they lack a "city center," thoroughfares, and public buildings clearly connected to each other.[25] None of them were equipped with monumental public buildings, with the exception of the temples;[26] their planning and architecture cannot be compared with higher-ranking cities either in Roman and Late Antique Egypt or in the Roman provinces more generally, a possible sign of the absence of imperial interventions on the urban setting.[27]

The excavation of Serenos's house and part of its neighborhood at Amheida may help us interpret other, still-unexcavated areas of the city, as well as the overall street layout. The buildings bordering Streets 2 and 3 in Area 2 are preserved, like Serenos's house, up to 2.5–3 meters in height; the compacted mud floors in the streets are also well preserved and were excavated according to the stratigraphic method (figure 1.5).[28] Accordingly, we can distinguish several floors and features built and dismantled in different phases and connected to the house's activities. Both streets look like private passages, closed at the south end by walls, and with gates that seem to separate the "properties" and regulate the passage or offer protection.[29] Moreover, Street 2 (6 meters wide, excavated for 17 meters in length), was at a certain point used for private purposes: a *stibadium*, or reclining sigma-shaped seat used for banqueting, was built on the east side of Serenos's house, and the street was closed

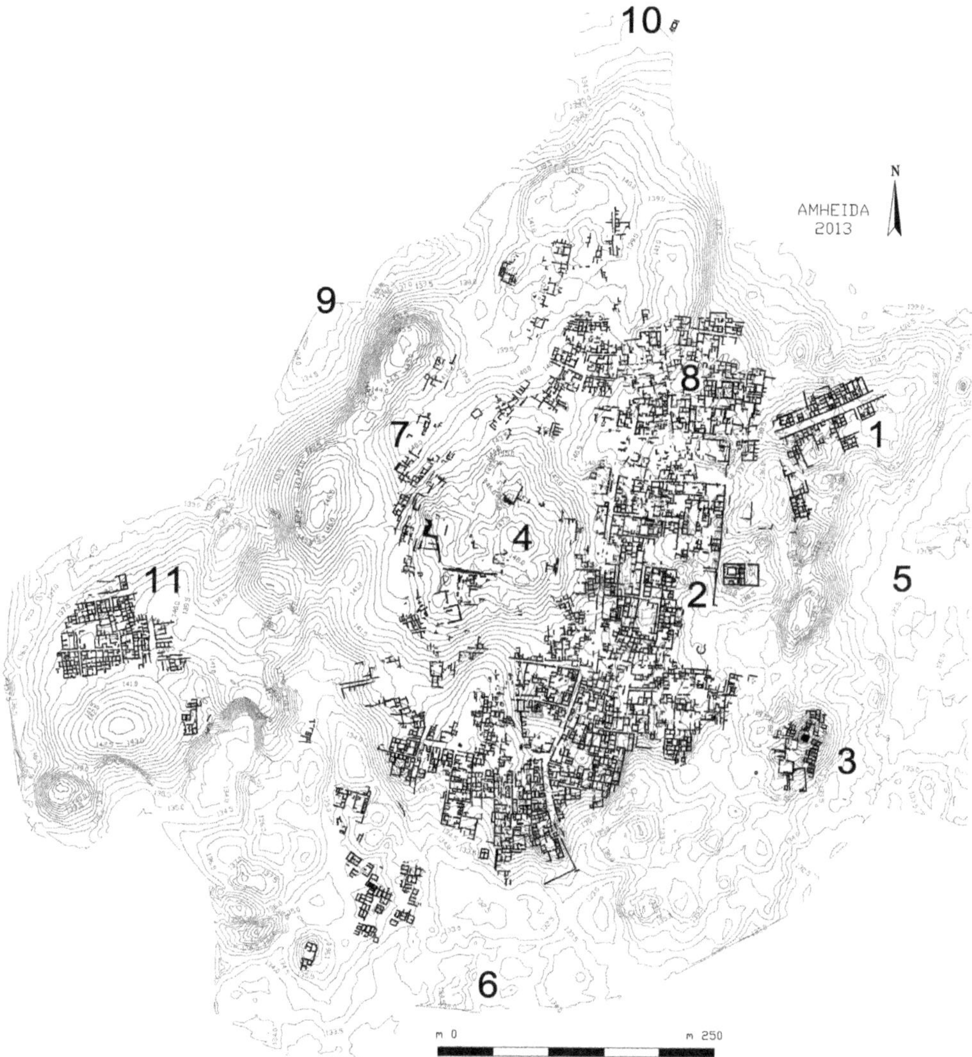

Figure 1.4. Plan of Amheida/Trimithis (Dakhla Oasis) with areas' numbers. (Courtesy of NYU Excavations at Amheida.)

with two doors defining the space "belonging" to the house (figure 1.5). The area with the stibadium was also covered with a flat, light roof supported by two pilasters in the front and by a thin wall on the east. The stibadium seems to have been short-lived: it was demolished down to its first two courses and covered by a new mud floor. However, Street 2 did not return to being a public and open passage, because the small door to its south edge was bricked up.[30]

Street 3 (from 1.8 to 2.40 meters wide, excavated for 25 meters in length) runs north-south in front of the west and main entrance of Serenos's house (figure 1.5). The excavation revealed that the alley was partitioned in two sectors by a door that

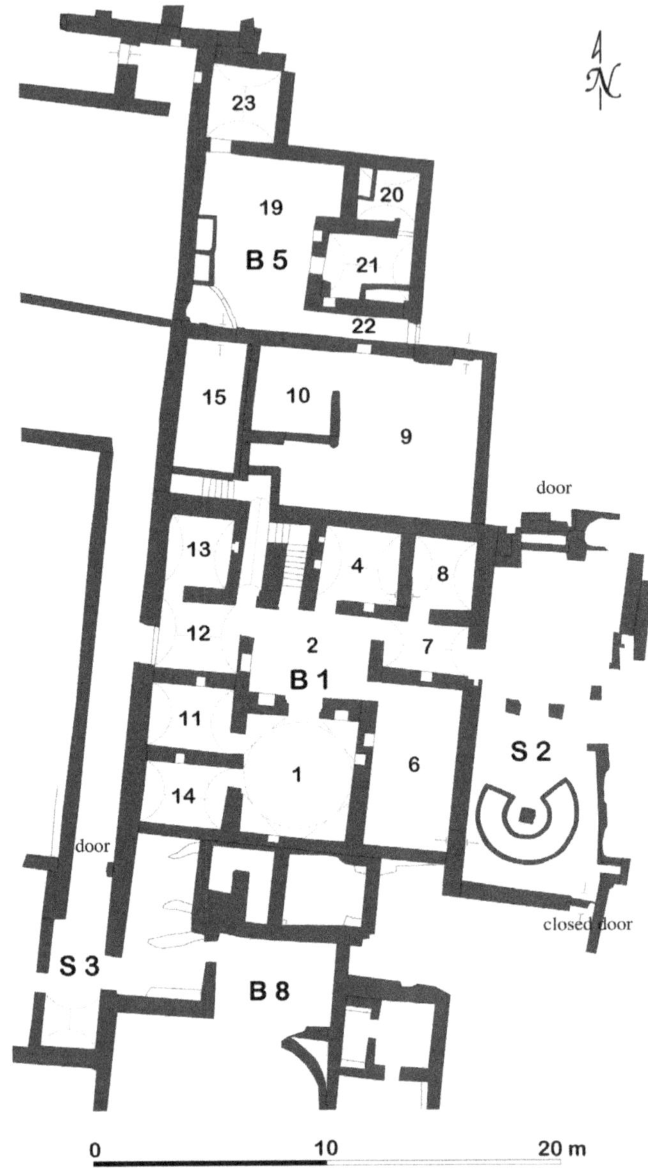

Figure 1.5. Plan of Serenos's house (B1) with streets (S2 and S3) and annexed building to the north. (Courtesy of NYU Excavations at Amheida.)

defined the spaces pertaining to two houses (B1 and B8). The alley was shaded by a flat roof between the doors of the two houses, and by a two-meter-long mud-brick barrel vault at its south end. The space above the entrances to the houses was left uncovered to give light to them.

Kitchen or storage facilities or animal pens did not appear in these two streets. The street surface was fairly clean and the waste from Serenos's house was deposited in a short dead-end alley northeast of the building.[31] Evidence for the partial roofing of these two alleys includes collapsed wooden beams in S2 and still-preserved recesses for beams in the side walls in S3, as well as a posthole for a vertical support for the flat roof in S3. However, the most striking roof in alley S3 was the barrel vault at its southern end, still partly preserved. We can only speculate about its function, because the street surface underneath was perfectly clean and provided no evidence for the use of the space, and the side houses are not yet excavated. The vault seems to have supported a room or passage connecting the two side buildings, and at the same time, it offered a shaded space in the alley.

The fourth-century street layout at Trimithis appears today as a labyrinth formed by narrow alleys that often disappear in the wall network (figure 1.4). This mazelike effect probably derives not only from the irregularity of the street system, but also to the inclusion of partly covered alleys among the visible features. These can be misinterpreted as corridors or internal passages because they are covered by vaults and flat roofs or partitioned by walls and doors.[32] Linking buildings above the roads and supported by vaults, as with S3, are other possible elements of fourth-century domestic architecture. Described in a recent publication, a barrel vault covering a passageway was also found at Ain el-Gedida, a fourth-century rural village near Kellis.[33] Archaeologists in this *epoikion* found a church and a pagan temple among several buildings that constitute a network of rooms connected by narrow passages and clustered in blocks separated by main orthogonal streets.

The street network in the last phase of Trimithis's life has marked characteristics of a closed system, difficult to cross and well protected from winds and sun. The heavy doors that blocked the streets, like the one found in Street 2 (1.6 meters wide and closed by one wooden leaf), may also have been intended as protection from intruders. Streets closed by doors also appear elsewhere in the Late Roman settlements of the oasis. At Kysis, Reddé excavated part of the settlement that featured an irregular layout and narrow streets. Doors and other passageway-blocking features appeared in the explored streets, but the published report does not mention any possible roof. At Kellis, doors closing streets are also common in the compact blocks of densely built buildings; however, no analysis of the street network or the use of "public" spaces has yet been accomplished.[34]

In summary, common characteristics of the Roman and Late Roman settlements in arid environments include a high density of buildings; labyrinthine street layout; narrow alleys closed by doors and in some cases also roofed; and windbreak walls. Settlements of this type must have appeared as extremely compact and closed urban clusters. Even more compact clusters are the fortified settlements of the third to fourth centuries in Kharga. According to Rossi and Ikram, the internal street layout of the Umm el-Dabadib fort consists of narrow alleys covered by vaults in a way very similar to local medieval settlements.[35] The same scholars also recognized other possible alleys and streets protected by vaulted ceilings in Umm al-Qusur.[36]

As already noted, these same practices are present in Byzantine and medieval settlements in the same regions, such as El-Qasr and Balat in Dakhla Oasis, but also in Kharga.[37] Namely, the origin of features like mud-brick architecture; compact organization of built space; high density of buildings; labyrinthine layout with a hierarchy of streets that are mostly narrow, shaded or semi-shaded, and often closed with doors; and a tendency to close spaces to avoid the exposure to sun and winds can thus be traced back to Late Roman and Byzantine urbanism of the Middle East and North Africa, and these features are most probably the result of climatic and security constraints.

Houses in Arid and Sandy Environments

The environmental conditions in the oases and at the fringe of the Fayum in the Roman Period seem to have deeply influenced the urban setting, conferring to the settlements some characteristics that would be further developed, also for social and cultural reasons connected to religious behaviors, in local medieval settlements. In these dry, windy, and sandy environments, built spaces were organized to avoid exposure to the elements as much as possible. Consistently, people built houses as closed systems, taking advantage of local materials and of a deep-rooted building tradition.

Houses in the Fayum Settlements

Built in mud brick, local stone, or stone and mud brick, the houses in the Greco-Roman-period Fayum are rather uniform in their architectural features.[38] Each building differs from the others in several details and disposition of rooms, and typological classification can become very elaborate, depending on what criteria we employ.[39] This study does not aim to create such a typology, but rather to point out some characteristics of domestic architecture that were, in my opinion, deeply influenced by local environment and climate. These characteristics are clearly identifiable where entire blocks of houses and streets were brought to light and where the buildings are preserved at least to the roof of the first floor, as at Karanis, Bakchias, Soknopaiou Nesos, and Tebtynis.

Domestic buildings dated to the Hellenistic and Roman Period have square or rectangular plans, are free standing, and have more than one story, with a staircase generally inside the building. The external shape is that of towers: either built in isolation and surrounded by streets or a courtyard, as is the case for Hellenistic-period houses, or abutting each other to form blocks of houses in the Roman Period. Scholars have debated the origin of this tall building type, its Egyptian or Greek cultural background, and its potential identification with the *pyrgoi* mentioned in papyri.[40]

The University of Michigan excavations at Karanis (1924–34) and at Soknopaiou Nesos (1931–32) discovered several houses, in an excellent state of preservation, in the shape of towers, tapering toward the top, with small windows and with a terrace on the roof (figure 1.6).[41] More recently (1988 to present), the Italian-French Mission at Tebtynis found the same kind of domestic buildings. This type of house was very massive, tapering, and above all, closed; the only open spaces were the annexed external courtyards, as we have seen above, and the terrace on the roof.[42] The interior would have been quite dark, fresh in summer and rather warm in winter. Common features in these houses are the deep foundations (also known as *fondations à*

Figure 1.6. Dime. Sector east, excavations of the University of Michigan 1931–32, the tower house and adjacent buildings in 2018. (Courtesy of Soknopaiou Nesos Project.)

caissons); underground vaulted cellars (to avoid open-air storage); and narrow windows, closed with vertical or horizontal wooden bars, and located directly beneath the ceilings, with sharp, long sills sloping toward the interior. These windows served only for light and air and not as viewpoints.[43] A narrow horizontal opening above the main entrance door was documented for some Karanis houses, suggesting that the door was intended to be closed most of the time and that the entrance room got light and air from this small opening.[44] The walls were mud plastered, and in some rooms at Karanis they were also painted black. The roofs of the aboveground rooms are usually flat in these Fayum houses.

Another, more complex, kind of house is also present in the Fayum settlements.[45] Generally, it did not have deep foundations or underground cellars and was not multistory, even if the presence of a staircase implies at least a terrace on the roof or one upper floor. The appearance of these houses was different from the tower-like houses, with a broader extension at the ground floor. This kind of building has been found in Dionysias, Narmouthis, and Theadelphia, and its rich decorative apparatus of non-Egyptian style suggested to the excavators public or semipublic functions rather than domestic. The main room is generally painted and provided with several niches; it is open on the front side, where two pillars mark a tripartite entrance closed by wooden leaves. The peculiar shape and decoration of these kinds of rooms are well-established markers of a banquet hall in Roman and Late Roman domestic architecture. This room type became popular and widespread in Egypt in particular during the fourth century CE, in houses of mid- to high-status families.[46] In these houses, too, windows must have been located high on walls.[47] In a few cases the central room, which served as a sort of hub connecting the other rooms and the staircase, has been interpreted as an internal open-air courtyard: for instance, in buildings in Medinet Ghoran and Theadelphia, both settlements on the west fringe of the Fayum.[48] Previous debates have discussed whether the internal courtyard was derived from Greek or Egyptian domestic architecture, and it is beyond question that different architectural models or different personal adaptations may have influenced house designs.[49] However, at least in the cases mentioned above, there is insufficient archaeological evidence to conclude that these rooms were open air. The presence of internal courtyards would strongly contrast with the general characteristics of these houses and settlements, generally conceived and organized, as we have seen, to protect the inhabitants from strong sunlight and winds.

Houses in the Oases

The houses in the western desert oases of the Roman and Late Roman Periods do not have a towerlike shape and are not self-standing. Typically, they share their perimeter walls with adjacent houses and have shallow foundations. These building techniques, already well known in Pharaonic-period settlements, saved materials, space, and labor, but limited the load-bearing capacity of the walls. These buildings had one or two stories and no underground rooms or cellars. Rooms could be covered with barrel vaults, rarely with domes, and with flat roofs made of palm beams and mats of palm ribs.[50] In Serenos's house, windows were not preserved, but based on the domestic architecture of Kellis and Kharga Oasis, we can infer that they were narrow vertical openings just below the vault and without sloping sills.[51] The house was built on a square plan (15 x 15 meters), and in a later phase it was expanded northward to incorporate parts of another building, formerly a Greek-language schoolhouse.[52] The building was accessed by three entrances from Streets 2 and 3;[53] the central Room 2 functioned as a hub for the house and was also the antechamber to Room 1, a squared, domed space richly decorated with wall paintings in classical style and with Greek and Roman subjects.[54] This space was certainly used as a reception room and a banquet hall, and it was designed to amaze guests with its particularly complex and colorful decoration, in which geometric panels and figurative registers covered the side walls and a circular, concentric geometric freeze delimited a psychedelic feather motif on the dome. This colorful room occupies a central position in the house and lacks windows; light may have come from Rooms 2, 11 and 14 when their doors were opened, or from an oculus in the dome, for which, however, we do not have any evidence. Room 2 was also placed in the middle of the house, and it got light and air from vertical openings in the flat roof. This air and light system was observed for the first time in this room, thanks to the good vertical preservation of the side walls. The roof of the room was certainly flat, even though its collapsed remains were not found in the fill. Four vertical recesses,

Figure 1.7. Serenos's house Room 2. Detail of the recesses above the doors leading to R6 and R7. (Courtesy of NYU Excavations at Amheida.)

similar to shallow niches, are located above the lintels of the doors entering into R4, R6, and R7, and above the niche on the west wall of R2 (figures 1.5 and 1.7). These vertical shafts reached the flat roof and gave light and air to the room. They were built in the walls according to the length of the underlying doors (95 centimeters) or niche (75 centimeters), with depths respectively of 20 and 10 centimeters.

Even though no material remains of a roof have been found in R2, these vertical openings provide secure evidence that a roof was present. This example should warn archaeologists against automatically interpreting central rooms as open-air courtyards, at least in domestic contexts in arid environments.[55] Furthermore, the presence of ovens and fireplaces in rooms is not necessarily evidence for the lack of a roof, because there may have been vertical openings in the roof itself. Well-preserved evidence for this arrangement comes from Room 4 of Serenos's house, in which a fireplace was built in front of the doorway during the last phase of occupation. Room 4 was barrel vaulted and the walls were blackened by the smoke of the fireplace, whose position in front of the doorway was deliberately chosen because of the presence on top of the door of a vertical shaft in the flat roof of the connected R2. Hearths were also found in Kellis houses, in some cases also in the central rooms, here interpreted as covered rooms.[56]

Open spaces were clearly present in some houses of the Hellenistic and Roman Periods in Egypt, as is demonstrated by the Classical-style houses in Alexandria, Marina el-Alamein, and also Tebtynis, so it is not impossible that people may have reproduced such a feature in other geographic and climatic contexts.[57] In the oasis settlements and on the fringe of the Fayum, however, the widespread adoption of urban and architectural patterns suited to minimizing the environmental hazards of arid and sandy contexts (such as strong winds, sand accumulation, alternating low and high temperatures during the night and day, and strong sunshine) suggests that internal open rooms in domestic architecture would be incoherent. *Aithrion*, usually translated as internal courtyard, is a Greek term attested in papyri of the Roman and Byzantine Periods for a space in Egyptian houses. However, Daniel has demonstrated that in Egyptian contexts such rooms were not open air, but rather central, covered rooms provided with a ventilation system, like the vertical windows found in Room 2 of Serenos's house.[58] Thanks to the good preservation of the building, this room provides unique archaeological evidence in Egypt for the existence of a ventilation system in a central room that served as a hub for the internal circulation of people.

Serenos's house was reproduced in 1:1 scale at the entrance to the site of Amheida to serve as a local tourist information center (figure 1.8). The reconstruction was designed to allow visitors to enter the house and admire the extraordinary paintings that were also reproduced. N. Warner and D. Schulz respectively built and painted the replica with great skill and precision, according to the archaeological remains.[59]

Figure 1.8. Serenos's house replica built at the entrance of the archaeological area. (Courtesy of NYU Excavations at Amheida.)

Figure 1.9. Serenos's house Room 2 replica, with the vertical window above the west niche. (Courtesy of NYU Excavations at Amheida.)

Some interpretations were necessary to fill gaps in the evidence, like the oculus in R1 and narrow windows in the side rooms. This reconstruction gave us the opportunity to quantify materials and labor time, to study building and painting techniques, and to come to a good, realistic understanding of the living space. The reproduction of the house in the same environment as the original (but in isolation) has proved invaluable for our understanding of the interior living environment in the changing weather: the few and narrow windows reproduced in the various rooms according to comparanda elsewhere in the oases, as well as the vertical window in the central Room 2, were more than enough to illuminate and ventilate the whole building while also avoiding the intrusion of sand during sandstorms (figures 1.9 and 1.10).

Adapting to Local Environments

The settlements built in the western desert oases and on the Fayum's fringe had to deal with a sandy desert environment that, as in the medieval period, discouraged the creation of any wide openings, like wide streets and squares. For the same reason, houses were structured to prevent wind, dust, and sun entering abruptly. Reddé has identified certain features of these settlements' layout—the use of doors to close streets, which are often narrow alleys forming a labyrinthine network of passages, sometimes roofed—as typical characteristics of Near Eastern tradition, which was not only Egyptian, and which characterized the oases settlements until premodern

Figure 1.10. Serenos's house Room 1 replica. (Courtesy of NYU Excavations at Amheida.)

times.[60] These settlements appeared compacted and closed, difficult to cross, and well protected.

Greek textual evidence from Egypt, and specifically the vocabulary used to describe houses and their parts, has suggested to several scholars that the domestic architecture of Greco-Roman Egypt was similar to that in other Mediterranean countries. Some Greek and Roman house types certainly were imported and may have been common in Alexandria, Lower Egypt, and most probably the *metropoleis*. However, practical considerations ensured that these house types, with a peristyle or a central open-air courtyard, were certainly not common all over the country—especially in arid contexts, where domestic architecture was designed to drastically separate interior family life from the outside world, in contrast to Greek practice in other parts of the Mediterranean.[61] The adaptation of architecture, especially domestic architecture, to different environments and locally available construction materials is an obvious principle already stressed by Vitruvius (*De Architectura*, VI, 1, 1). Recent discoveries in the western desert of Egypt allow a better understanding of Vitruvius's statements and add an important chapter to the study of ancient domestic architecture. The good state of preservation of several houses allows us to appreciate and evaluate domestic architecture not only on the basis of ground plans preserved at foundation level (as is the case at many archaeological sites), but through standing architecture, which allows us to study the house as a three-dimensional space and to identify the roofing typology and the presence/absence of windows and openings.

Houses are certainly expressions of cultural and social identity,[62] but at the same time, people had to take into consideration practical issues and adapt to local environments.

Notes

1 On our partial knowledge of Egyptian urbanism, see Davoli 2011.
2 Subías 2011. See Nevett 2015; Huebner 2017 on the complex interactions of cultural, social, environmental, and personal needs within domestic buildings. On the social interpretation of Karanis's layout, see Simpson (chapter 2, this volume).
3 I would like to thank N. Aravecchia for having corrected my English and for the helpful discussions about Ain el-Gedida architecture.
4 MacDonald 1986, 30.
5 This analysis will exclude Antinoopolis and Oxyrhynchos, which were located in arid environments: the first because of its Roman foundation according to non-Egyptian traditions, the second because its present condition does not allow a precise evaluation of its layout and kind of domestic architecture. For an overview of Roman monumental settings in the nome capitals see Bowman 2000; Bailey 1990, 2012.
6 On the dromos as a monumental road for processions (*pompé*) in Egypt and in the Hellenistic world, cf. Cavalier and Des Courtils 2008, 90; Davoli 2011, 80–81; and Davoli 2018.
7 These settlements were affected by the activities of the *sebbakhin* in the last two centuries and what is left is at present threatened by continuous expansion of cultivation and villages.
8 Davoli 1998 and 2012.
9 The multistratified sites are those that were originally surrounded by the desert and thus subject to accumulation of sand, which was one of the causes of their growing levels. On multilevel and monolevel settlements in the Fayum see Davoli 2011, 72. The expansion of the settlement from the beginning of the Roman Period is related to the population increase, probably due to good climate conditions (good Nile floods) and to an efficient management of the water within the region. On climate change in the Roman Empire: McCormick et al. 2012, 169–220.
10 See respectively: Husselman 1979; Boak 1935; Davoli 2005, 218–19; Hadji-Minaglou 2007.
11 For plan comparisons see Davoli 2011. For population estimates see Mueller 2011.
12 Davoli 2011. Dionysias and Philadelphia had quite regular grids of streets and house blocks.
13 Marouard 2008; Kaiser 2011, 45; for the hierarchy and terminology of streets, cf. Du Bouchet 2008.
14 This phenomenon appears in the stratigraphic sequence of buildings east of Tebtynis temple: Hadji-Minaglou 2007, figs. 81–83.
15 See respectively: Boak 1935, Pls. III–VII; Husselman 1979, 29–31; Hadji-Minaglou 2007, figs. 81–83. On Karanis see Simpson, chapter 2, this volume.
16 Some other cases in Marouard 2008, 123.
17 Karanis Level C, Husselman 1979, 29–31. No roofs have been noted in Karanis streets, in which presses for oil were also found, together with kitchen facilities and several animal pens; roofs and doors protected the latter. On Karanis, see Simpson, chapter 2, this volume.
18 Tebtynis east of the temple area: Hadji-Minaglou 2007, 197–98. There is no mention of possible roofs in streets or courtyards.
19 Layers of desert sand separate the various levels of buildings: Boak 1935, Pls. XIII–XIV.
20 We cannot say to which level/period the houses and streets excavated by Belzoni belonged to, but most probably they were on the top of the *kom*. Belzoni 1820, 385–86.
21 For an overview, cf. Bagnall et al. 2015; for yearly reports www.Amheida.org. For a detailed analysis of the urban layout, street network, and the environment, cf. Davoli 2019; Bravard et al. 2016; Bagnall and Davoli 2020.
22 The settlement was built on cemented dunes and is covered by sand dunes that move southward from the north escarpment at a speed of ca. 7 meters per year: Davoli 2019; Bagnall et al. 2015, 11.
23 Hope 2015.
24 Reddé 2004.

25 According to MacDonald (1986, 3), "To be truly Roman, towns had to have at least the rudiment of armatures; those of large cities were highly elaborated."
26 On the monumentalization of Late Roman cities and its ceremonial function, see Dey 2015, 65–77, 91–92 and 126, on the case of fourth-fifth century Ephesus. On monumental armatures, Roman architecture, and colonnaded streets in Egypt, see McKenzie 2007, 151–72; Ballet 2008; Bailey 1990; Pensabene 1993.
27 Jacobs 2012. Private euergetism and city councilors' intervention in the cityscape is almost non-existent in the fourth century: Dey 2015, 93.
28 Davoli 2022.
29 The two doors found in S2 and S3 are in phase with the first floor in the streets. They may have been built immediately after the completion of Serenos's house (around 340 CE).
30 Reddé considered the presence of doors closing the roads to be a local oasean feature that continued in subsequent medieval settlements. A small and rough structure built in Kysis's "voie est-ouest 2" can probably be interpreted as a stibadium: Reddé 2004, 16–17, 21–22, fig. 20. The phenomenon of smaller structures encroaching on or usurping public spaces was very common in the late antique Roman empire: cf. Jacobs 2009.
31 Among the waste, several ostraka belonging to Serenos's circle of people were found. This occurrence suggested the provenance of the waste from the house of Serenos.
32 Doorjambs are clearly recognizable in several streets and alleys.
33 Aravecchia 2018, B11 151–56; Bagnall et al. 2015, 157–68.
34 Hope 2015.
35 Rossi and Ikram 2006, 286, 465.
36 Rossi and Ikram 2018, 123.
37 Dabaieh 2011, 61–67, 160–65; Balbo 2006. A similar layout appears at Kafr Samir, a Byzantine village in Israel: Yeivin and Finkelsztejn 2008, 186–87.
38 On the basic typology, cf. Davoli 2015.
39 I will take into consideration those houses for which we have good documentation and a date derived from stratigraphic analysis. For a detailed study of domestic architecture in Greco-Roman Egypt, see Depraetere 2004–05. The author, however, did not discuss the reliability of the dating given by the excavators of single houses or sites. His study concerns mainly the plans of the buildings and the internal disposition of spaces and their connection. It must be noted, however, that internal connections between rooms in a house often changed over time, according to changing needs (see i.e. Davoli 1996, fig. 49; Bagnall et al. 2015, 89–90). Clear evidence comes from the stratigraphy of the walls, in which opening or bricking up of doors is widespread, as well as the building of partitioning walls. It follows that a classification of houses based on internal communication and/or numbers of rooms must be retained with caution. See also Correas-Amador 2013, 74.
40 Representations and remains of New Kingdom urban houses testify to the presence, in Thebes and Amarna, of a similar self-standing and multistory house type. However, the diffusion of this model into rural settlements with urban layouts started probably in the Hellenistic Period. On this topic cf. De Garis Davies 1929; Grimal 1939; Novicka 1975; Marchi 2014; Davoli 2015. Tower houses are well described by Marouard (chapter 3, this volume).
41 Husselman 1979; Boak 1935.
42 Some of these tall houses were bigger than average, and certainly had more stories: several examples are in Marchi 2014.
43 There were no large openings to let people look outside the house, meaning that this kind of architecture completely avoided the dialectic between interior family life and exterior life and landscape. By contrast, in Roman-period Syria, large houses in several cities had wide windows allowing some form of sight into the landscape. Internal courtyards, peristyles, and fountains are common features in these Syrian houses: De Giorgi 2015.
44 Husselman 1979, Pl. 43a.
45 Type 3 in Davoli 2015, 179.
46 Alfarano 2018; Davoli 2015, 181.
47 For a brief description of the windows in houses at Narmouthis, see Bresciani et al. 2006, 234.
48 Davoli 1998, 218; Rubensohn 1905; Nowicka 1969, 118–23.
49 Nowicka 1969, 119–23; Hope 2015, 225.

50 A very representative example of a flat roof was found collapsed in Room 7 in House B/3/1 at Kellis: Hope 2015, 210 fig. 9.
51 In Serenos's house, two windows of this kind (48–50 centimeters high and 17 centimeters wide) are actually still preserved in two walls added in a late phase to close a passage leading to the annexed Room 15.
52 On this school see Cribiore, Davoli, and Ratzan 2008; Cribiore and Davoli 2013.
53 In a second phase, one of the three doors was bricked up.
54 McFadden 2014.
55 In Amheida another house (B2) was completely excavated and the results published (Boozer 2015b). It is located in Area 1 and is preserved for about 50 centimeters in height. The erosion on the north area of the site is very harsh and the buildings are very badly preserved. Walls and their collapses are severely eroded, and the sand cover is very shallow. For this reason, some rooms in B2 contained no traces of collapsed walls and roofs. However, the excavator interpreted the absence of this evidence to testify to the absence of roofs in two rooms (7 and 5) of the house. Personally, I do not think this interpretation is feasible; certainly, it is not proved by the available evidence. The presence of a bread oven and a brazier in these rooms is not enough to assert the absence of a roof. On the contrary, the presence of a brazier (Room 5) testifies to the necessity to heat up the room, which thus was covered. The hypothesis that Room 5 was open air forced Boozer to an unrealistic reconstruction of the flights of the staircase and of its ending on the terraced roof (Boozer 2015b, fig. 6.4).
56 For a synthesis on houses at Kellis and a discussion of the presence of internal courtyards, see Hope 2015, 225–26, who thinks that the presence of a courtyard within the house is not proved by the evidence. On the same topic see Boozer 2015a, 190–92, who thinks the central rooms are to be considered open courtyards. In his analysis of Kellis architecture, Hope stresses the importance of sociocultural and environmental factors in individuals' choice of house type: Hope 2015, 226. On the doubtful interpretation of internal courtyards in ancient mud-brick architecture: Correas-Amador 2013, 78.
57 A peristyle house was found at Tebtynis: Hadji-Minaglou 2008, 125, 132 fig. 4. Another late Roman building with a peristyle was found in Kysis, but Reddé suggests it may have been covered with a flat roof (2004, 74). Peristyle houses are more common in settlements near Alexandria, such as Marina el-Alamein: Daszewski 1995; McKenzie 2007, 163–64. Greek papyri mention Hellenistic-type villas, such as the rich residential mansions of Diotimos, Apollonios, and Artemidoros at Philadelphia, known from Zenon's archive (255 BCE): see Davoli 2015, 181–82, with previous bibliography.
58 Daniel 2010, 128–47. A sort of wind-catcher was already used in Pharaonic architecture and still survives in the architecture of Islamic Egypt (*malqaf*): Spence 2004, 129. In the tower-shaped multistory houses of the Fayum, the rooms were located along the perimeter of the building and could access air and light from windows.
59 Warner 2012, 373–78; Schulz 2015.
60 Similar characteristics are documented for Syrian villages; see Reddé 2004, 17–18n22 and 23.
61 As Ault (2015, 127) explains: "Greek houses offered a sheltered, yet open arrangement for living ideally suited to Mediterranean settings, in which the outdoors was essentially brought indoors, harmoniously integrating exterior and interior spaces."
62 Nevett 2015, 143–49, with previous bibliography.

Works Cited

Alfarano, S. 2018. "Architettura dei riti conviviali nell'Egitto tardoantico." In *Theatroeideis. L'immagine della città, la città delle immagini. Atti del Convegno Internazionale, Bari 15–19 giugno 2016*, edited by M. Livadiotti et al., 469–87. Thiasos Monografie 11, Vol. II. Roma: Edizioni Quasar.

Aravecchia, N. 2018. *ʿAin el-Gedida: 2006–2008 Excavations of a Late Antique Site in Egypt's Western Desert (Amheida IV)*. New York: New York University Press.

Ault, B.A. 2015. "OIKOS KALOS: The Environmental Logic of Greek Urban House Form." In *Housing and Habitat in the Mediterranean World: Cultural and Environmental Responses*, edited by A.A. Di Castro and C.A. Hope, 123–31. Leuven: Peeters.

Bagnall, R.S., and P. Davoli. 2020. "Amheida (Dakhla Oasis): the First Fifteen Years." In *Guardian of Ancient Egypt: Studies in Honor of Zahi Hawass*, edited by J. Kamrin, M. Bárta, S. Ikram, M. Lehner, and M. Megahed, 163–75. Vol. 1. Prague: Charles University.

Bagnall, R.S., et al. 2015. *An Oasis City*. New York: Institute for the Study of the Ancient World and New York University Press. Accessed March 18. http://dlib.nyu.edu/awdl/isaw/oasis-city/.

Bailey, D.M. 1990. "Classical Architecture in Roman Egypt." In *Architecture and Architectural Sculpture in the Roman Empire*, edited by M. Henig, 121–37. Oxford: Oxbow Books.

Bailey, D.M. 2012. "Classical Architecture." In *The Oxford Handbook of Roman Egypt*, edited by C. Riggs, 189–204. Oxford: Oxford University Press.

Balbo, R. 2006. "Shape, Culture, and Environment: A Lesson of Urban Design from Dakhleh Oasis, Egypt." In *PLEA 2006 23rd International Conference on Passive and Low Energy Architecture, Geneva, Switzerland, 6–8 September 2006, Conference proceedings*. Accessed March 18. https://www.semanticscholar.org/paper/Shape%2C-culture-and-environment%3A-a-lesson-of-urban-Balbo/c467a4c2fd5c9228594dd0c9f7e709addb59451c.

Ballet, P. 2008. "D'Alexandrie à Antinoopolis. Fondations égyptiennes et réseau viaire." In *La rue dans l'antiquité: Définition, aménagement et devenir de l'Orient Méditerranéen à la Gaule*, edited by P. Ballet, N. Dieudonné-Glad, and C. Saliou, 151–60. Rennes: Presses universitaires de Rennes.

Belzoni, G.B. 1820. *Narratives of the Operations and Recent Discoveries*. London: Murray.

Boak, A.E.R. 1935. *Soknopaiou Nesos: The University of Michigan Excavations at Dimê in 1931–32*. Ann Arbor: University of Michigan Press.

Boozer, A.L. 2015a. "Inside and Out: Romano-Egyptian Houses from the Fayyum and Dakhla Oasis." In *Housing and Habitat in the Mediterranean World: Cultural and Environmental Responses*, edited by A.A. Di Castro and C.A. Hope, 185–97. Leuven: Peeters.

Boozer, A.L. 2015b. *Amheida II. A Late Romano-Egyptian House in the Dakhla Oasis. Amheida House B2*. New York: New York University Press and Institute for the Study of the Ancient World.

Bowman, A.K. 2000. "Urbanization of Roman Egypt." In *Romanization and the City*, edited by E. Fentress, 173–87. Portsmouth, RI: Journal of Roman Archaeology.

Bravard, J-P., et al. 2016. "Construction and Deflation of Irrigation Soils from the Pharaonic to the Roman Period at Amheida (Trimithis), Dakhla Depression, Egyptian Western Desert." *Géomorphologie* 22 (3): 305–24.

Bresciani, E., et al. 2006. *Medinet Madi: Venti anni di esplorazione archeologica 1984–2005*. Pisa: Università di Pisa.

Cavalier, L., and J. Des Courtils. 2008. "Degrés et gradins en bordure de rue: aménagements pour les pompaï?" In *La rue dans l'antiquité: Définition, aménagement et devenir de l'Orient Méditerranéen à la Gaule*, edited by P. Ballet, N. Dieudonné-Glad, and C. Saliou, 83–91. Rennes: Presses universitaires de Rennes.

Correas-Amador, M. 2013. "Ethnoarchaeology as a Tool for a Holistic Understanding of Mudbrick Domestic Architecture in Ancient Egypt." *Cuadernos de Prehistoria y Arqueología Universidad Autonóma de Madrid* 39: 65–80.

Cribiore, R., and P. Davoli. 2013. "New Literary Texts from Amheida, ancient Trimithis (Dakhleh Oasis, Egypt)." *Zeitschrift für Papyrologie und Epigraphik* 187: 1–14.

Cribiore, R., P. Davoli, and D. Ratzan. 2008. "A Teacher's Dipinto from Trimithis (Dakhleh Oasis)." *Journal of Roman Archaeology* 21: 170–91.

Dabaieh, M. 2011. "A Future for the Past of Desert Vernacular Architecture: Testing a Novel Conservation Model and Applied Methodology in the Town of Balat in Egypt." PhD diss., Lund University.

Daniel, R.W. 2010. *Architectural Orientation in the Papyri*. Papyrologica Coloniensia 34. Paderborn: Schöningh.

Daszewski, W.A. 1995. "Témoignage de l'urbanisation de la côte méditerranéenne de l'Egypte à l'époque hellénistique et romaine à la lumière des fouilles de Marina el Alamein." *Bulletin de la Société française d'egyptologie* 132: 11–29.

Davoli, P. 1996. "Lo scavo 1995. Relazione preliminare." In *Bakchias III*, edited by S. Pernigotti-M. Capasso, 9–78. Pisa: Giardini.

Davoli, P. 1998. *L'archeologia urbana nel Fayyum in età ellenistica e romana*. Napoli: G. Procaccini.

Davoli, P. 2005. "Examples of Town Planning in the Fayyum." *Bulletin of the American Society of Papyrologists* 42: 213–33, pls. 8–18.

Davoli, Paola. 2011. "Reflections on Urbanism in Graeco-Roman Egypt: a Historical and Regional Perspective." In *The Space of the City in Graeco-Roman Egypt: Image and Reality*, edited by E. Subías, P. Azara, J. Carruesco, I. Fiz, and R. Cuesta, 69–92. Tarragona: Institut Català d'Arqueologia Clàssica.

Davoli, P. 2012. "The Archaeology of the Fayum." In *The Oxford Handbook of Roman Egypt*, edited by C. Riggs, 152–70. Oxford: Oxford University Press.

Davoli, P. 2015. "Classical Influences on the Domestic Architecture of the Graeco-Roman Fayyum Sites." In *Housing and Habitat in the Mediterranean World: Cultural and Environmental Responses*, edited by A.A. Di Castro and C.A. Hope, 173–84. Leuven: Peeters.

Davoli, P. 2018. "Soknopaiou Nesos: una città cerimoniale nell'Egitto di epoca greco-romana." In *Theatroeideis. L'immagine della città, la città delle immagini. Atti del Convegno Internazionale, Bari 15–19 giugno 2016*, edited by M. Livadiotti et al., 393–408. Thiasos Monografie 11, Vol. I. Roma: Edizioni Quasar.

Davoli, P. 2019. "Trimithis: A Case Study of Proto-Byzantine Urbanism." In *The Great Oasis of Egypt: Kharga and Dakhla Oases in Antiquity*, edited by R.S. Bagnall and G. Tallet, 46–80. Cambridge: Cambridge University Press.

Davoli, P. 2022. *Amheida VI. The House of Serenos. Part II: Archaeological Report on a Late-Roman Urban House at Trimithis*. New York: Institute for the Study of the Ancient World and New York University Press.

De Garis Davies, N. 1929. "The Town House in Ancient Egypt." *Metropolitan Museum Studies* 1 (2): 233–55.

De Giorgi, A. 2015. "Domestic Architecture in Roman Syria." In *Housing and Habitat in the Mediterranean World: Cultural and Environmental Responses*, edited by A.A. Di Castro and C.A. Hope, 255–64. Leuven: Peeters.

Depraetere, D. 2004–05. "Archaeological Studies on Graeco-Roman and Late Antique Housing in Egypt." PhD diss., Leuven University.

Dey, H.W. 2015. *The Afterlife of the Roman City: Architecture and Ceremony in Late Antiquity and the Early Middle Ages*. New York: Cambridge University Press.

Du Bouchet, J. 2008. "Les nomes de la rue en Grec ancient." In *La rue dans l'antiquité: Définition, aménagement et devenir de l'Orient Méditerranéen à la Gaule*, edited by P. Ballet, N. Dieudonné-Glad and C. Saliou, 57–61. Rennes: Presses universitaires de Rennes.

Grimal, P. 1939. "Les maisons à tour hellénistiques et romaines." *Mélanges d'archéologie et d'histoire* 56: 28–59.

Hadji-Minaglou, G. 2007. *Tebtynis IV. Les habitations à l'est du temple de Soknebtynis*. Fouilles de l'Institut français d'archéologie orientale du Caire 56. Caire: Institut français d'archéologie orientale.

Hadji-Minaglou, G. 2008. "L'habitat à Tebtynis à la lumière des fouilles récentes: Ier s.av-Ier s.apr. J.-C." In *Graeco-Roman Fayum—Texts and Archaeology. Proceedings of the Third International Fayum Symposion, Freudenstadt, May 29-June 1, 2007*, edited by S. Lippert and M. Schentuleit, 123–33. Wiesbaden: Harrassowitz.

Harris, W.V., ed. 2013. *The Ancient Mediterranean Environment between Science and History*. Leiden: Brill.

Hope, C.A. 2015. "The Roman-Period Houses of Kellis in Egypt's Dakhleh Oasis." In *Housing and Habitat in the Mediterranean World: Cultural and Environmental Responses*, edited by A.A. Di Castro and C.A. Hope, 199–229. Leuven: Peeters.

Huebner, S.R. 2017. "Egypt as Part of the Mediterranean? Domestic Space and Household Structures in Roman Egypt." In *Mediterranean Families in Antiquity: Households, Extended Families, and Domestic Space*, edited by S.R. Huebner and G. Nathan, 154–73. Chichester, West Sussex: Wiley-Blackwell.

Husselman, E.M. 1979. *Karanis: Topography and Architecture*. Ann Arbor: University of Michigan Press.

Jacobs, I. 2009. "Encroachment in the Eastern Mediterranean Between the Fourth and the Seventh Century AD." *Ancient Society* 39: 203–43.

Jacobs, I. 2012. "The Creation of the Late Antique city: Constantinople and Asia Minor during the 'Theodosian Renaissance.'" *Byzantion* 82: 113–64.

Kaiser, A. 2011. *Roman Urban Street Networks*. New York: Routledge.

MacDonald, W.L. 1986. *The Architecture of the Roman Empire, II: An Urban Appraisal*. New Haven: Yale University Press.
Marchi, S., ed. 2014. *Les maisons-tours en Egypte durant la Basse Epoque, les périodes Ptolémaïque et Romaine: Actes de la table-ronde de Paris Université Paris-Sorbonne (Paris IV) 29–30 novembre 2012*. NeHet 2. Paris: Revue numérique d'égyptologie.
Marouard, G. 2008. "Rues et habitats dans les villages de la chôra Egyptienne à la période Gréco-Romaine (IIIe S.AV.-IVe S.APR. J.-C.): quelches exemples du Fayoum (Nome Arsinoïte)." In *La rue dans l'antiquité: Définition, aménagement et devenir de l'Orient Méditerranéen à la Gaule*, edited by P. Ballet, N. Dieudonné-Glad, and C. Saliou, 117–28. Rennes: Presses universitaires de Rennes.
McCormick, M., et al. 2012. "Climate Change during and after the Roman Empire: Reconstructing the Past from Scientific and Historical Evidence." *Journal of Interdisciplinary History* 43 (2): 169–220.
McFadden, S. 2014. "Art on the Edge: The Late Roman Wall Painting at Amheida, Egypt." In *Antike Malerei zwischen Lokalstil und Zeitstil. Akten des XI. Internationalen Kolloquiums der AIPMA 13.-17. September 2010 in Ephesos*, edited by N. Zimmermann, 359–70, Taf. CXXV–CXXVII. Wien: Österreichischen Akademie der Wissenschaften.
McKenzie, J. 2007. *The Architecture of Alexandria and Egypt 300 BC-AD 700*. New Haven: Yale University Press.
Mueller, K. 2011. "Past and Present Population Trends in the Fayyum Region." In *The Space of the City in Graeco-Roman Egypt: Image and Reality*, edited by E. Subías, P. Azara, J. Carruesco, I. Fiz, and R. Cuesta, 129–43. Tarragona: Institut Català d'Arqueologia Clàssica.
Nevett, L.C. 2015. "Understanding Variation in Ancient House-Forms: A Preliminary Discussion." In *Housing and Habitat in the Mediterranean World: Cultural and Environmental Responses*, edited by A.A. Di Castro and C.A. Hope, 143–49. Leuven: Peeters.
Nowicka, M. 1969. *La maison privée dans l'Egypte ptolémaïque*. Warzawa: Zakład Narodowy im. Ossolińskich.
Nowicka, M. 1975. *Les maisons à tour dans le monde grec*. Warzawa: Polskiej Akademii Nauk.
Pensabene, P. 1993. *Elementi architettonici di Alessandria e di altri siti egiziani*. Roma: L'Erma di Bretschneider.
Reddé, M. 2004. *Douch III. Kysis. Fouilles de l'ifao à Douch Oasis de Kharga (1985–1990)*. Caire: Institut français d'archéologie orientale.
Rossi, C., and S. Ikram. 2006. "North Kharga Oasis Survey 2003 Preliminary Report: Umm el-Dabadib." *Mitteilungen des Deutschen Archäologischen Instituts Abteilung Kairo* 62: 279–306.
Rossi, C., and S. Ikram. 2018. *North Kharga Oasis Survey: Explorations in Egypt's Western Desert*. Leuven: Peeters.
Rubensohn, O. 1905. "Aus griechisch-römischen Häusern des Fayum." *Jahrbuch des Deutschen Archäologischen Instituts (Berlin)* 20: 1–25.
Schulz, D. 2015. "Colours in the Oasis: The Villa of Serenos." *Egyptian Archaeology* 46: 23–26.
Spence, K. 2004. "The Three-Dimensional Form of the Amarna House." *Journal of Egyptian Archaeology* 90: 123–52.
Subías, E. 2011. "Oxyrhynchos: Metropolis and Landscape." In *The Space of the City in Graeco-Roman Egypt: Image and Reality*, edited by E. Subías, P. Azara, J. Carruesco, I. Fiz, and R. Cuesta, 93–116. Tarragona: Institut Català d'Arqueologia Clàssica.
Yeivin, Z., and G. Finkelsztejn. 2008. "Les rues du bourg byzantin de Kafr Samir ("Castra"; Porphyreion du sud) à Haïfa, Israël." In *La rue dans l'antiquité: Définition, aménagement et devenir de l'Orient Méditerranéen à la Gaule*, edited by P. Ballet, N. Dieudonné-Glad, and C. Saliou, 185–90. Rennes: Presses universitaires de Rennes.
Warner, N. 2012. "Amheida. Architectural Conservation and Site Management, 2004–2009." In *The Oasis Papers 6: Proceedings of the sixth International Conference of the Dakhleh Oasis Project*, edited by R.S. Bagnall, P. Davoli, and C.A. Hope, 363–79. Oxford: Oxbow Books.

2

Neighborhood Networks

The Civic and Social Organization of Accessways in Ancient Karanis

BETHANY SIMPSON

This chapter examines social organization in ancient settlements, as evidenced by archaeological remains. Focusing on the ancient Roman-era Egyptian town of Karanis, it uses space syntax analysis (SSA) to quantify and compare complex systems of access. The results demonstrate that in addition to the public street system, access throughout the town was supplemented and often improved by local access routes across private domestic property. As the use of such routes was monitored and negotiated through interpersonal social agreements, the ancient inhabitants of Karanis were invested in maintaining complex networks of social interaction through permitting access to their property, transcending legal conceptions of "privacy" and property. The strength of this system also helped the town survive and even thrive through periods of administrative uncertainty, throughout the Roman Period into Late Antiquity.

Space Syntax and Analysis of Complex Spatial Environments

Structures are built to give order and organization to human activities: to prescribe boundaries as to what is possible and permissible, in both the physical and sociocultural sense. For example, cultural decorum may require certain household activities to be strictly divided by gender, age, or rank, and as a result the architecture of the house itself reflects some of those culturally explicit considerations.[1] Once constructed, the spatial arrangement of the house reinforces these social norms, as the walls and doorways create physical limitations on the movement of people throughout the spatial system.

The specific spatial organization of ancient architectural remains can therefore be used as evidence of past social practices. Space syntax analysis is an analytical method designed to compare modes of access within a given spatial system "on the basis of social content of spatial patterning and the spatial content of social patterning."[2]

It relies on mathematical probability, calculating the statistical likelihood of anyone entering any given room or space in a system, whether in order to perform an activity in that space or to pass through to another space. This statistical likelihood in turn helps to identify socially prescribed attitudes of privacy. For example, a highly connected room, with many entrances and exits, serves as a major thoroughfare, and any activity occurring in such a space is likely to be seen or even interrupted by those passing through. This results in a relatively public characteristic for the space in question. In contrast, a dead-end room with only one way in and out will be more private, as there will be statistically less chance that anyone will need to enter the space.

Space Syntax values can be local or global measures. While local measures are calculated based only on directly adjacent spaces (i.e., a single room away from the given space), global measures account for the entire spatial system, which often includes a multitude of possible paths through the network. As every space has an effect, great or small, on the global system, the identification and calculation of all the relationships in the system is best accomplished by a computer program.[3] However, there are a few values that are more easily obtained by analyzing maps and justified access plans (see figure 2.1). The major spatial values discussed here are as follows:

Depth: a measure of how many other rooms or distinct spaces must be crossed in order to reach a given space. This measure is often synonymous with "threshold depth," and most commonly is calculated with respect to a single structure and its external environment, such as rooms in a house versus the outdoor world. Justified access plans can visualize depth, showing increasing depth as one proceeds into a house interior. These access plans are perhaps the most simplified and frequently used (though very effective) method for exploring concepts of privacy within ancient houses.[4]

Connectivity: a simple count of how many spaces are directly connected to a given space (i.e., a local measure). High connectivity suggests a space is an important hub of movement throughout the spatial system, and therefore likely to see more public use than private.

Symmetry: a global measure of connectivity, calculated as the average number of thresholds or boundaries that must be crossed to reach a given space from any starting point within the system.[5] The more complex value of *real relative asymmetry*, or RRA, adjusts for the size of the entire system, permitting quantitative comparisons between separate systems.[6] As RRA values increase, a system can be said to be less well-connected overall.

Relative Ringyness: a measure of how many alternative routes exist to reach a specific space, found by counting the number of existing rings that pass through a given space and dividing that number by (p – 1), where p equals the total number of spaces in the system. If there is only one path to a room, as in the "clustered" plan shown above, that space will have a low measure. The relative ringyness of an entire system can be found by counting the total number of rings in the system and dividing by (2p – 5). High levels of ringyness are linked to higher distribution of traffic, lower rates of congestion, and are thus often considered more efficient than linear, non-ringy systems.

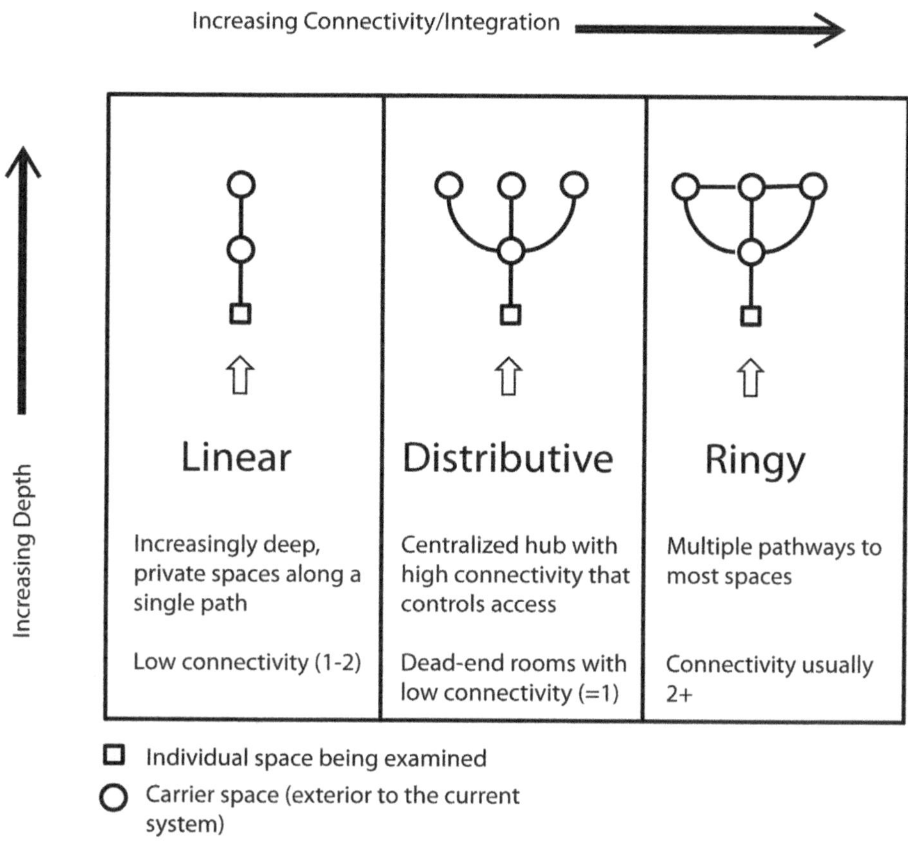

Figure 2.1. Simplified examples of justified access plans, demonstrating different syntactical values.

Interpreting Archaeological Data with SSA

Space syntax analysis originally developed out of studies of modern architecture and urban planning, and therefore relies on the certainty that the dataset in question is completely known.[7] In contrast, archaeological datasets always introduce a degree of uncertainty: ancient structures are rarely perfectly preserved, and any spot of low preservation or uneven excavation/recording would introduce great potential for error in the ensuing calculations. For instance, an area of "missing" wall might indicate the presence of an original doorway, but also might be the result of decay and collapse of the structure following its abandonment. In addition, global studies require large continuous areas: not only individual structures, but also the streets and paths between them. For this reason, studies of larger networks of towns and neighborhood analysis have been largely limited to a few well-preserved and excavated examples, including ancient Pompeii, Herculaneum, and Ostia.[8]

Individual ancient structures have proved better suited for syntactical studies, and houses in particular have proved a popular subject.[9] The syntactical analysis of

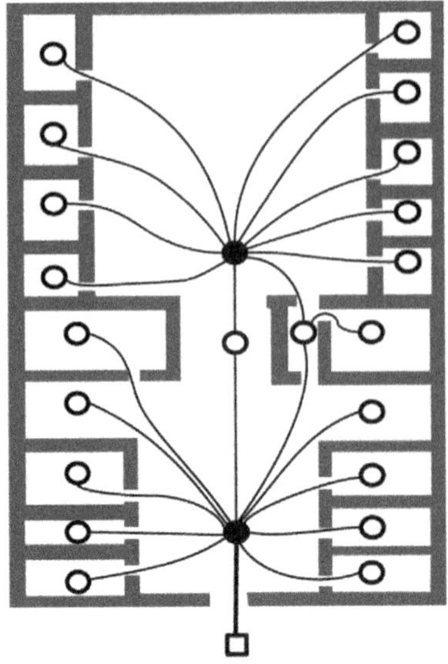

Access routes for a Roman atrium house

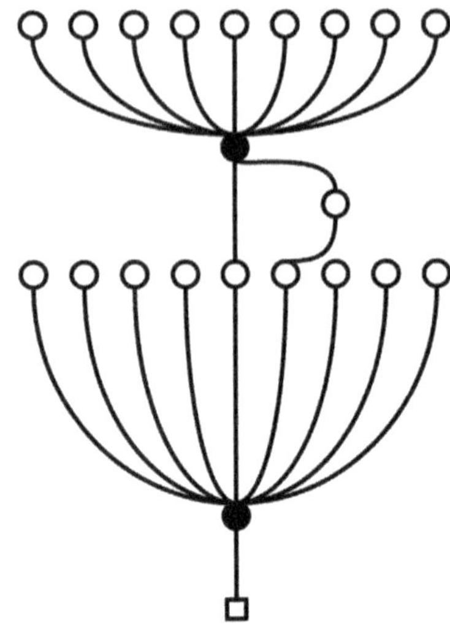

Justified access plan

Figure 2.2. A floor plan of a Roman villa, showing all the access connections between rooms (left). To the right is a justified access plan of the same house, where all rooms are arranged to show increasing step depth as one proceeds "deeper" into the building. Major distributive hubs are shown as blackened circles in the justified plan.

ancient Roman houses has proved particularly important, as it provides comparative evidence for the rich documentary sources of information on Roman cultural attitudes toward domestic space. For example, the Roman *domus* is traditionally interpreted as highlighting the house owner's social status via intentional display of wealth, rank, and cultural taste within the central rooms, the atrium, and peristyle.[10] Syntax analysis of the typical Roman floor plan (see figure 2.2) confirms the importance of these distributive hubs through which most of the household traffic ran.[11]

Space Syntax Analysis of Ancient Karanis

Roman Karanis is well suited to syntax analysis on both local and global levels: the University of Michigan's excavation of the site from 1924 to 1935 uncovered more than 180,000 square meters of domestic neighborhoods dating from the first to late third centuries CE. The major publication, an architectural report by Elinor Husselman, included top plans for most excavated areas, drawn into three major phases according to the stratigraphic levels of the town.[12] This publication provided scholars with the opportunity to begin syntax analysis of the ancient housing.[13]

However, the published information only represented a small percentage of the data recorded by the Michigan team; the architectural report only included detailed plans for thirteen mud-brick structures, representing less than 3 percent of the total

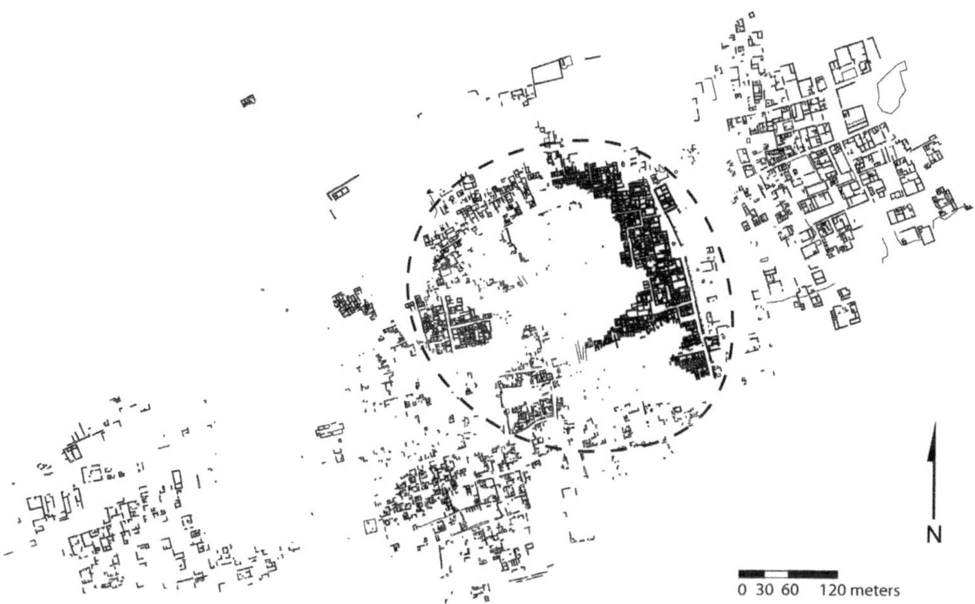

Figure 2.3. The full extent of the ancient settlement, as recorded by the UCLA team in 2007–14, is 1.8 kilometers, east to west. Michigan focused their excavation on the 180,000 square meter area at the center of the town, indicated by the dotted line. The buildings of KAC are shown in bold.

excavated by the Michigan team. In 2002, a joint project between the University of California, Los Angeles; the Rijksuniversiteit Groningen; and the University of Auckland began to survey, excavate, and conserve the site.[14] As the primary investigator of the Karanis Architecture Project since 2008, I have worked to combine published, archival, and modern survey results to create a fully digital spatial database of the ancient site.[15] This work has greatly expanded what is known of the city, including more than one thousand domestic properties from over 524,000 square meters of area—almost tripling what was recorded and published by Michigan (see figure 2.3). In addition, associated pottery and other archaeological finds have firmly expanded the occupation dates for Karanis beyond the third century and into the sixth century CE.[16]

As a result, there are large portions of Karanis that provide a suitable dataset for SSA. One in particular, designated Karanis Central (KAC), includes more than twenty-six thousand square meters of continuously excavated area. The original Michigan excavation identified three distinct phases of occupation: of these, Layer C is the oldest, dating roughly from the late first to early second century CE. Layer B is mid-second to mid-third, after which there was a period of abandonment before the poorly preserved A layer, which probably dates from the late third century until the abandonment of the site sometime in the sixth century.[17]

Each property within KAC is clearly defined by perimeter walls, enclosing the open space of the courtyards as well as any associated structures. More than

84 percent of the properties include a house. This has been used as the major criterion for categorizing them as domestic, as opposed to properties that have a more purely commercial function. In all other respects domestic properties share many similarities with economic structures: granaries and dovecotes can be found in properties with houses as well as those that lack associated dwellings. Houseless commercial properties may have been privately owned, but it is also possible that they were under state control and not private at all.[18]

Houses in Karanis are easy to identify by their construction characteristics, which remain consistent throughout the C and B layers. They are invariably freestanding buildings, with compact floor plans and walls built to support the weight of upper stories. Property C45 is a typical example of a C layer, second-century domestic property at Karanis (see figure 2.4): the lot is only eighty-three meters square, slightly below the average of ninety. The house itself shares no walls with any of the other structures on the lot. The floor plan only has two rooms, each located off the central stairwell structure that leads to the other stories of the house. Even while Karanis houses are not often preserved today above ground-floor level, the ubiquitous staircase proves the existence of additional stories, or at least a flat roof space that could also serve as an activity area. Ptolemaic and Roman-era documents describe mud-brick houses that stood as many as eight or more stories;[19] the highest preserved house at Karanis was at least three stories, including the ground floor. Basements were also common when the bedrock level allowed for them, and were used for storage of domestic and economic goods.[20]

The justified access plan immediately makes clear just how essential the stairway is for all movement throughout the house. Most of the rooms have a connectivity of only 1: that is, they are dead-end spaces. These could be used for either private or social activity with little chance of casual interruption, as they have no

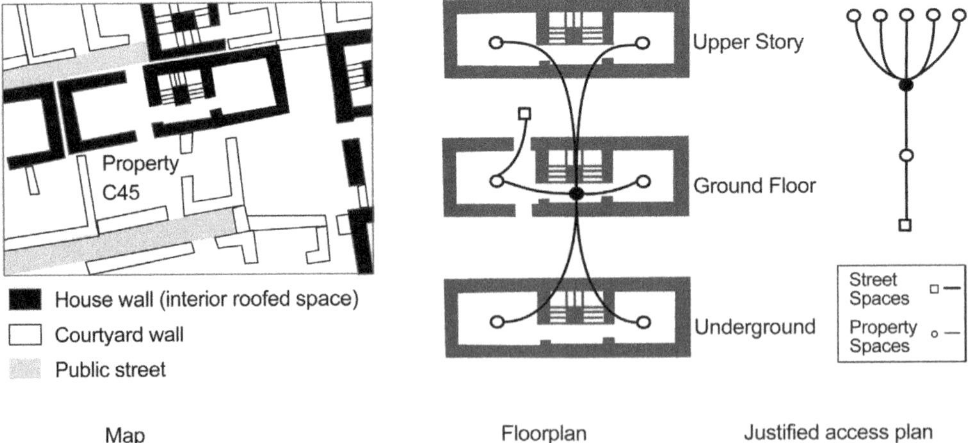

Figure 2.4. To the left, a floor plan of a typical Karanis domestic property surrounded by other structures and public streets. In the center, the house floor plan is shown for the ground floor, basement, and upper story. To the right, the justified access plan shows a central distributive hub (the staircase).

through-access. Even the upper story rooms are separate cells, dependent on the stairway for access. In contrast, the stairway passage is the highly connected, well-integrated hub of the system. This single central space also keeps overall threshold depth low; every room is easy to reach, with no single space being significantly "further" in threshold depth from the others.

At first the Karanis house appears to reflect a similar "clustered" access plan to the Roman domus, which might initially seem to suggest that both house types have similar functions in social display of the homeowner's status. Yet compared to the wide-open atrium at the center of the domus, the Karanis house clusters around the restrictive space of the stairway: a narrow passage that is rarely more than 0.6 meters wide. Two people cannot occupy the space at once, or even pass each other at all in their comings and goings, and yet even important guests would be required to squeeze through this space in order to reach any room suitable for hosting company. The physical limitations of the house, both in terms of scale and in syntax, seem designed to discourage substantial social interaction and to create a highly controlled, enclosed, and private interior.

It is possible that the rationale behind such restrictive house structures is due to more than just social considerations: environmental factors are also at play. An enclosed mud-brick house is uniquely suited to the temperature swings of desert climates, staying cool in the day and releasing heat during the nights.[21] Another serious issue was sand: the Egyptian Fayum towns, lying on the borders of habitable land, faced constant problems from windblown sand and other debris blowing in and filling every possible space.[22]

However, there are other indications that privacy and control were intentional aspects of Karanis house construction: the houses are all completely freestanding, independent buildings. While courtyards frequently share perimeter walls with neighbors, houses are never built adjoining other structures.[23] Documentary papyri from Hellenistic and Roman Egypt demonstrate how the structural autonomy of such houses could be considered crucial and was protected in formal agreements between neighbors in times of construction. For example, British Museum Papyrus 10524 preserves a case from 283 BCE Luxor, where a woman named Tahib swore to her neighbor Pleehe that her construction activities would not alter his walls, even though her own house would abut his own house.[24] The document is a social contract written with formal legal language, including the monetary penalty and a list of sixteen witnesses to the contract. The papyrus and other surviving documents like it emphasize the importance placed on private property rights during the era, and how the autonomy of the house itself was of the utmost importance.

Private Space and Social Interaction: Courtyard and Economic Activities

While Karanis house interiors may have been highly protected and private, they were only a fraction of the total domestic space: every property had some type of unroofed courtyard, its area enclosed and defined by a perimeter wall or series of abutting wall segments. Unlike house walls, these *were* frequently shared with neighboring properties, but as they were not load-bearing they could be altered or repaired quite easily without threatening the structural integrity of either neighbor's buildings.

In many ways courtyard space seems to have taken priority over the house itself, as the average courtyard space is at least half of the total lot area. The Karanis house structure makes this arrangement possible, as the compact building footprint maximizes outdoor space. Even the largest properties maintain these multistory plans instead of the horizontal sprawl of, for example, a Roman villa.

In contrast to the standardized floor plans of the Karanis houses, there seems to be no preferred or consistent layout for courtyard spaces: depending on the size and dimensions of the lot, courtyards can vary from wide, undifferentiated spaces to complex networks of passages and outbuildings. Similarly, while interior doors and passageways are narrow and controlled (0.6 meters wide), connections between courtyard spaces are frequently much wider: see, for example, the pathway between courtyard spaces in figure 2.4. In fact, it can be difficult to distinguish between individual courtyard spaces, as there are few formalized thresholds between areas.

In terms of syntax analysis, the courtyards could be considered an extremely distributive clustered plan: a basic open space with many options for movement to and around other loosely defined activity areas. Perhaps the most important SSA feature of Karanis courtyards is that each one has direct access to the public street system, independent of the house. This feature is obviously practical in allowing traffic to bypass the restricted house interiors, permitting freer movement. This arrangement also increases the public nature of the domestic courtyards, making them accessible not only to household inhabitants but also to neighbors and potentially even strangers. In contrast to the restricted-access house interiors, access to courtyards from the public street was rarely controlled via physical barrier: doors or gates are very rarely attested. Therefore, it seems quite likely that these routes were left intentionally "open," allowing for people outside the immediate household to access the courtyard.

The reason for this accessibility likely lies in the function of the courtyard itself as a space for household economic activity. Excavation of the Karanis courtyards revealed special installations and dedicated activity areas, including threshing floors, flour mills, and cooking stoves.[25] Most common of all are bread ovens: by no means did every property have its own, but they were well-distributed throughout the neighborhoods, so each house at least had potential access to one nearby (see figure 2.5). This distribution pattern strongly suggests that many activities associated with food preparation were highly social. Such an arrangement has ethnographic parallels from Pharaonic Egypt, where baking was commonly shared among households, thus optimizing the use of fuel.[26] Communal food preparation activities are inherently social encounters of some duration, increasing the likelihood that individuals from distinct households will interact while working side by side. This behavior has the ultimate effect of creating close neighborhood ties that would be maintained through repetition over time.

Moreover, many adjacent properties have direct access between their courtyards—that is, *interproperty* access points (figure 2.6). In the mid-second century of Layer C, more than a quarter of all properties shared access with an adjacent neighbor,

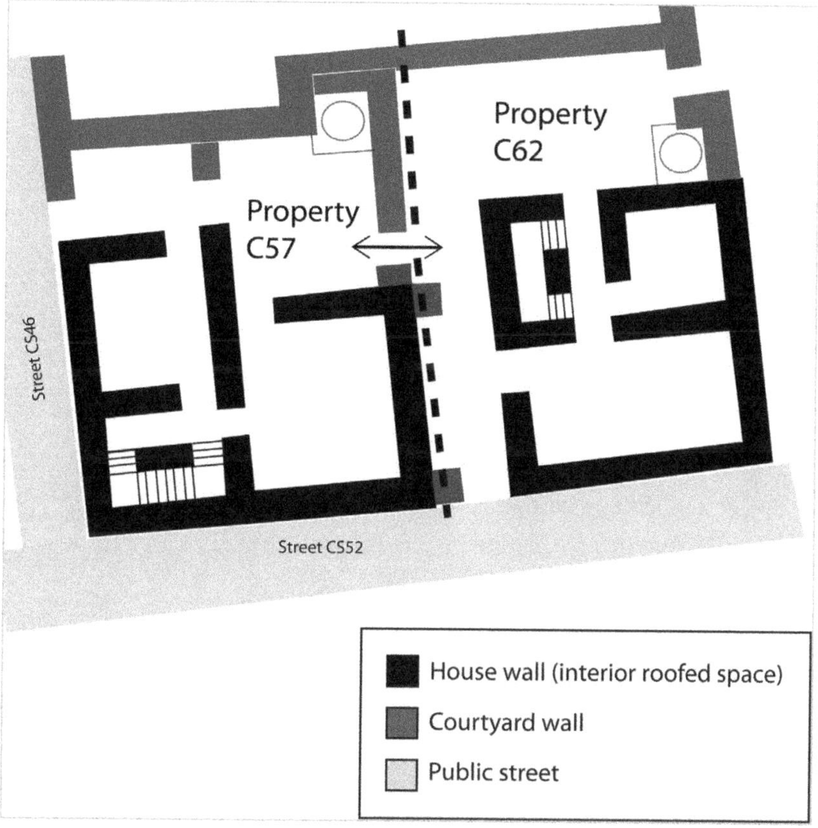

Figure 2.5. Distribution of bread ovens in KAC—first century shown at left, second century at the right.

either through a small gate or a simple opening between the property walls. It is impossible to reconstruct the specific social connections between the inhabitants of such properties—perhaps some represent extended family relationships. However, neighbors who were initially strangers could have grown into both economic and social alliances through sharing activity space. Again, bread ovens provide crucial evidence for specific activities that likely united these partnerships: more than 77 percent of these conjoined properties have oven access.

Private Space in the Public Realm: The Use of Shortcuts to Expand the Street System

So far we have considered access to private properties in order to share workspace for social and economic domestic activities. However, there are also more temporary, transient types of access to consider: How often was private property used for wider, more global access through Karanis? The existence of interproperty routes

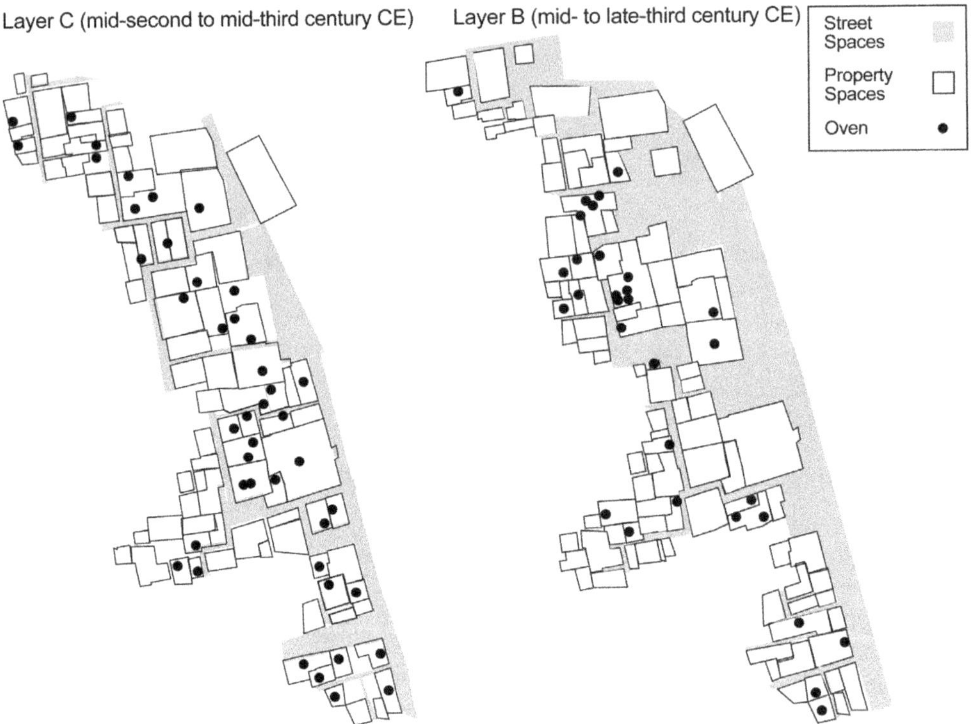

Figure 2.6. Interproperty access point between Property 57, at left, and 62 to the right. Note the presence of bread ovens in the courtyards, shown as black dots.

creates the possibility for through-travel in a way that could provide "shortcut" alternatives to the public street system.

The Karanis street system seems designed to prevent the need for such routes—like many other towns of the Greco-Roman Fayum and indeed the eastern Mediterranean, it was built according to a modified Hippodamian grid.[27] The intersecting Karanis streets created a network of connected paths, with multiple options for travel along syntactic rings. Each ring encircles a block of private properties, each one directly connected to the public street system and therefore independent of its neighbors for free movement through the town. For this sample neighborhood of Karanis, eight complete rings can be identified, with each individual street connecting to an average of roughly eight to ten private properties. The streets are therefore highly connected distributive hubs of access, controlling movement to private properties much as the stairwells controlled movement to other rooms in the domestic house plans.

However, the great freedom of movement and path choice was even further increased when one includes the interproperty access routes. These create even more potential traffic rings: the eight complete traffic rings created by the town streets alone expand to forty-one when the routes through private properties are included (see figure 2.7).

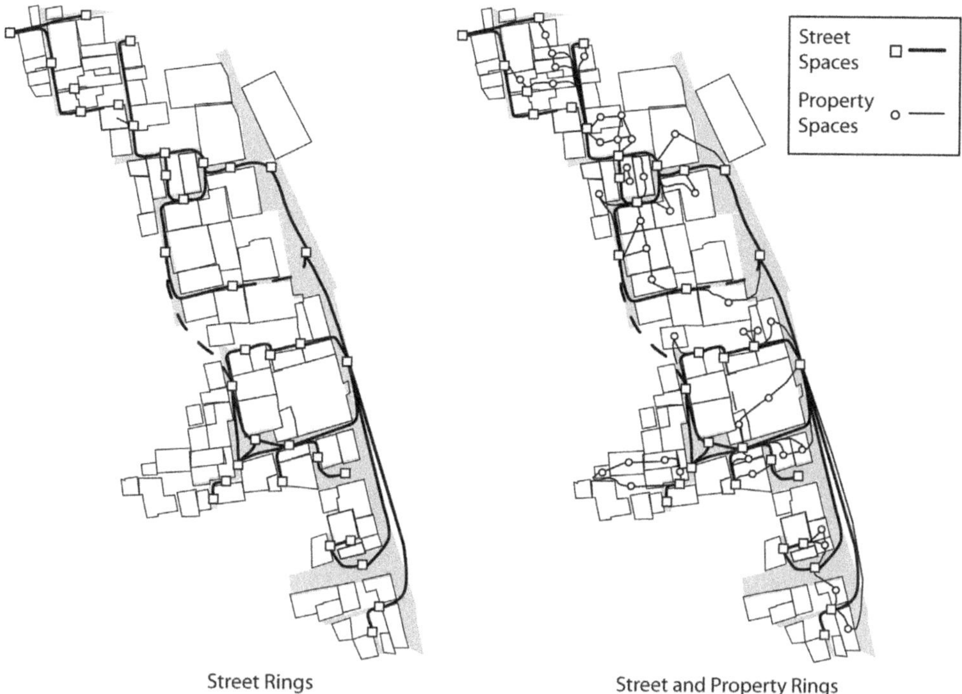

Figure 2.7. Map and simplified access plans of the Karanis street systems. At left, the network created by the official public street system. To the right, the same street network supplemented by routes that go through private properties to create additional access rings.

Obviously, many of these routes are theoretical rather than practical. We can dismiss almost any that run through house interiors: even if the lengths (both metric and syntactically speaking) are "shorter," the physical limitations of narrow passageways make these routes too restrictive for real traffic. However, some domestic courtyards provide legitimate "shortcuts." Property C86 (see figure 2.8) is an excellent example of this: it probably dates to the first century, when the area was the northern edge of Karanis occupation, but successive years of town expansion led to it being surrounded to the north and east.[28] As other properties encroached, public access became restricted and C86 posed a serious obstacle to the flow of traffic between two large blocks. Perhaps because of social pressures to keep traffic circulating within the expanding neighborhood, the owner of C86 seems to have allowed some of the private property to be used as a virtual roadway, running east to west so it joined two major streets. This completes a syntactic ring with the public system and allows a shortcut: an 18-meter trip across instead of the 104-meter southern route along the official streets.

Even though it provided such access, the space remained part of the private courtyard property: instead of optimizing control over the rest of the property by constructing a privacy wall along the south edge of the ersatz street, the area remained open, suggesting trust that users would stick to the shortest path rather than wander

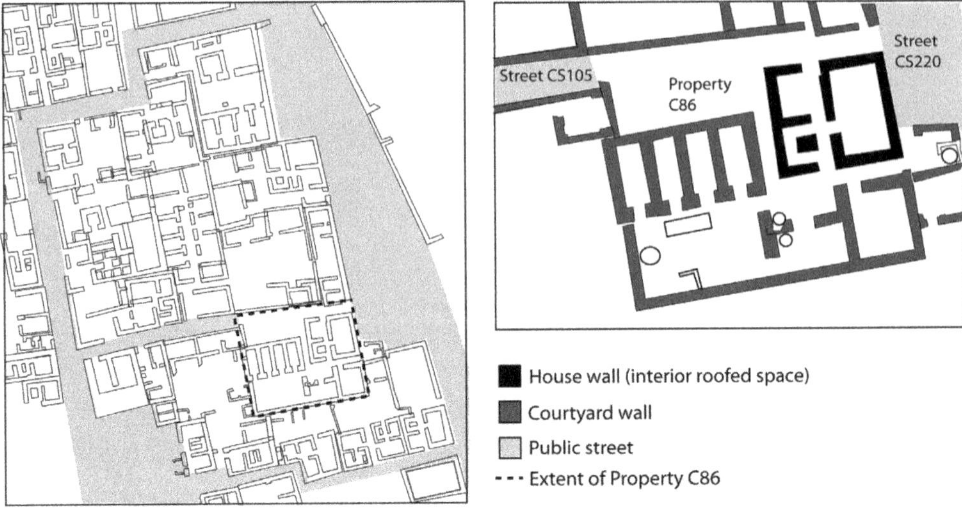

Figure 2.8. Property C86. The northern property limit represents fairly "public" access connecting two major streets—CS105 and CS220. The southern courtyard area is more private, with a controlled route passing close by the house and household storage areas that the occupants may have used.

through the courtyard. This openness is particularly interesting as C86 is one of the largest and most economically complex properties of KAC: courtyard installations include bread ovens, an olive press, and several large stone granary bins. Notably, these are all located away from the "path" portion of the property, kept private and nonaccessible through both physical distance (they are not along the shortest, most expedient route) and by obstacles: actual gates and doors that could be bolted and locked. This arrangement demonstrates the careful negotiation the property owners must have made between social cooperation and protecting their own private interests.

It is crucial to realize that interproperty routes were created and maintained through the agreement of the landowner(s) and only lasted for as long as they were considered beneficial. The archaeology at Karanis indicates that shared property-access arrangements were far from permanent, as the overwhelming trend in third century adaptations of older architecture is to block up shared access points. Thirty percent of the shared interproperty routes from the C layer were in fact blocked by the mid-third century B layer, and by the end of the third century, 62.5 percent of all original routes were blocked.

The decline in shared access seems to coincide with socioeconomic changes, including depopulation and especially economic downturn.[29] The situation may have caused inhabitants of Karanis to change many of their own domestic activities, and to protect private economic interests at the expense of broader social cooperation. Evidence of this can be observed in the change in distribution of bread ovens (see again figure 2.6). In the B layer, fewer households have direct access to an oven, or are even in proximity to an oven, and the ovens that remain are clustered onto properties that seem more like large-production bakeries than domestic courtyards.

These properties often lack traditional house structures entirely, and they have highly controlled access points, emphasizing their economic rather than domestic function. The evidence suggests that food production practices may have undergone a widespread cultural shift away from household cooperation to more focused commercial endeavors.

The closing of a privately owned access route was likely an unpopular move, but the action could not be legally stopped: in ancient property law, occupants had almost complete legal authority over who could access and use their private land, as long as their activities did not obstruct the fair use of the streets or of other people's property.[30] In fact, the right to privacy in domestic space was considered so essential under Roman law that even landlords could be denied access by their tenants.[31] So when occupants exerted these rights, blocking private access, the civic government had no obligation (or even authority) to get involved, unless it was a threat to public access as well.

Instead, the inhabitants of Karanis and other communities of the time would have relied on social agreements to give and receive access to private land. These could have taken many forms and varied widely depending on the relative statuses of those involved. For example, a property owner might have allowed casual foot traffic through his courtyard, but no carts or beasts of burden. Even more likely, access could be limited to known individuals—given explicitly rather than assumed for a broader public.

While many access agreements may have been "handshake deals" between individuals that left no lasting trace, papyri of the time preserve some examples of more formalized arrangements. The Greek-language documents employ the phrase "*eisodos kai exodos*" in referring to access into and out of private property.[32] Such clauses were often included in bills of sale, seen as servitudes on the property in perpetuity—to be honored by later generations of owners.[33] Papyri could also specify individual users, even which paths were to be made available and what areas were off-limits.[34]

These documents were codified forms of social agreements, created with the formalized language of legal documents of the time, some with accompanying witnesses and monetary penalties for infractions.[35] They demonstrate the serious social authority given to interpersonal contracts, and the lengths individuals would go to in order to secure their property rights and their access over time.

The Privatization of Public Space: Encroachment and Annexation

While locals were maneuvering to secure through-access to private land, property owners and occupants were also frequently shoring up their bargaining positions and increasing their own authority, not only over their own land but over adjacent public spaces as well. By the mid-third century CE, the public street system itself was facing serious encroachment from private construction. Most of these B-layer features can be characterized as simple structures attached to the houses like steps and windscreens. These privately built features were often considered necessary for facilitating access to houses, especially as the street level of Karanis rose over the years.[36]

Such encroachments into public street space are not unique to Karanis, of course: studies of Pompeii and Herculaneum show benches, steps, and ramps that restrict street space in the name of providing access to private houses.[37] The frequency of the archaeological finds suggests such encroachments were commonly tolerated. However, they were also obstacles to public movement, narrowing the width of streets to points that could restrict cart- or even foot-traffic and cause serious bottlenecks to the neighborhood systems.[38] As such, they were nuisances to public order, and technically illegal.

In its most extreme form, street encroachment ended through-traffic entirely and effectively annexed public space to private properties. Barriers across whole streets converted the public space of a street into a restricted linear route: a dead end or a cul-de-sac, with higher privacy for the property or properties at the end of the street segment. As the third century progressed, many of the Karanis streets were transformed, at least in part, to private courtyard space, either enhancing existing properties or creating new ones altogether.

Roman law was clear on the subject: public space was protected and must be left available to all. Local laws and settlement charters repeatedly emphasized the importance of maintaining street spaces.[39] Yet despite the law, the archaeological record preserves many examples of street encroachments and obstacles that were allowed to persist, suggesting it was rare to succeed in getting one removed once constructed. Scholars have suggested this is direct evidence of decreasing civic power over time, particularly in the eastern Mediterranean during the later Roman Empire. However, as we have already seen, encroachment was hardly limited to weakly controlled provinces, but could be found in Italian towns during the early imperial period.[40] This suggests that civic authorities had little interest in enforcement, even when their power was strong.[41] It is also possible that certain acts of encroachment or annexation were allowed because of monetary incentives: either to the magistrates themselves, as bribes, or as semilegal "sales" of public land.[42]

For Karanis and the other towns of the Fayum, the Late Roman phases are often said to have "lacked internal political and social structures as much as their villages lacked spatial articulation."[43] However, these arguments often focus on the theory that Karanis and other villages of the Fayum were depopulating and even being abandoned by the late third century. In fact, the archaeological evidence now proves that such villages often survived well into Late Antiquity—Karanis itself until at least the early sixth century.[44] The very persistence of the Fayum towns, despite the lack of ideal syntax plans, proves they were still functional, if not optimal, systems, or else existing legal or social pressures would have rectified them.

It is also possible the lack of heavy administrative oversight was viewed as positive rather than neglectful. It gave individuals and local communities more direct agency in managing their public access systems and their own property. And as the public street system grew more restricted by encroachment and annexation, interproperty access routes became even more important factors for travel within neighborhoods. Occupants of important properties like C86 would have faced huge social pressures to keep them open, at the expense of their own privacy and even potentially their economic security. However, they also stood to benefit socially and economically from strategic negotiation of access rights. In fact, the syntactic design of domestic properties makes this feasible, separating and insulating the private house interiors and economic areas away from the more open, accessible space used by interproperty access.

In fact, as we have seen before with eisodos contracts, social negotiation was potentially even more effective than legal action as a means of managing conflict. Builders of street obstructions were probably seen as defying not only the law, but also social conventions of propriety and fairness, and therefore faced negative opinions and even censure from the public.[45] The power of social pressure and public censure was also recognized within legal codes across the Roman Empire: the Tabula Heracleensis, for example, compelled residents not only to fix roads they damaged, but allowed the charges against them to be posted publicly both in the forum and at the property itself, publicly identifying them as lawbreakers.[46] This implies that public censure and shame may have motivated change more efficiently than pure legal proceedings, effectively picking up the slack caused by negligent aediles and other magistrates. The legal system could also be used as leverage in private negotiation, as the threat of lengthy lawsuits and official interference might have driven more expedient solutions derived by social or interpersonal agreements.

Changes to the Access System of Karanis: Practical and Social Consequences

As a result of all this action by private individuals, the entire public street system of Karanis changed drastically over a period of a hundred years. Routes between large town blocks became impassable, essentially combining and creating huge areas that had to be navigated around (see again figure 2.8, and figure 2.9); the average block perimeter increased eighteen meters by the mid-third century, and by the early fourth century A layer, so many former public routes had been converted to private land that none of the original streets remained wholly intact.[47] A path that had formerly been one long street was replaced by a series of short segments angling around the private architecture; the combined effect was to increase mean depth for the system. In the mid-second century C layer, KAC was composed of thirty-five street spaces; by the mid-third century B layer it had risen to fifty-one.

In comparing SSA values between the two time periods (see figure 2.10), we must therefore consider the different scales of the systems. Of all the calculated values, only RRA and relative ringyness directly account for these differences. The apparent increase in mean depth over time is particularly misleading, because the large increase in total spaces has driven up the average. In comparison, the syntactic length (and therefore mean depth) of the traffic rings has markedly increased by the B layer: C-layer rings were simple, often consisting of only the four or five streets that enclosed a block. In contrast, B-layer rings are oblong paths of many streets (see again figure 2.8), twisting and turning around irregular conglomerations of houses. Relative ringyness of the overall system is in fact one of the major changes in Karanis, decreasing from nearly 30 percent to only 10 percent in a century.

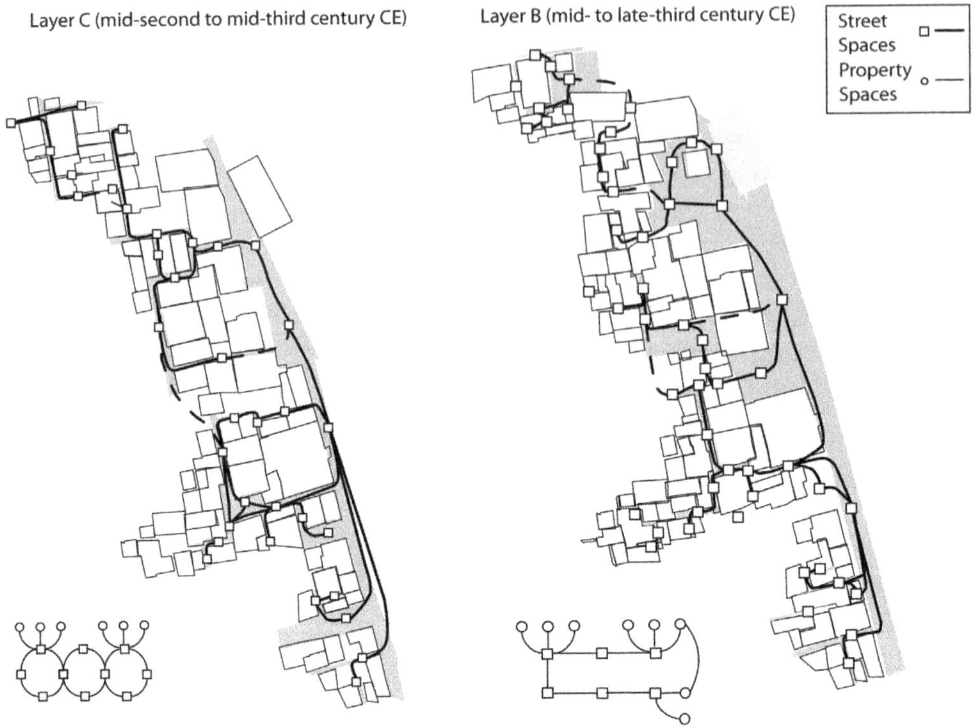

Figure 2.9. The Karanis street system in map and justified access plan form. In the first century (left), short rings utilizing both the streets and private properties were common. By the second century (right), the system changed into longer routes, so that even traffic rings have increased depth.

These changes to access created and, in turn, reinforced changes in the socioeconomic cohesion of Karanis. With fewer ringy options, traffic congestion would have increased on the remaining routes. Quiet neighborhood streets could be transformed into thoroughfares, especially if they were wide enough for carts and commercial traffic. At the same time, the system became more complex in terms of wayfinding, as the complicated, twisting routes might be unfamiliar to infrequent users. Locals would know the way, but outsiders to the neighborhood—even those from other parts of Karanis itself—might have trouble navigating the winding paths. Commercial traffic may therefore have settled on wide and easily traversed routes rather than the shortest paths. The existence of interproperty routes would provide additional options to locals who had permission to use them. As a result, some neighborhoods became even more "private," a modified spatial "domain of the inhabitant," resulting in very localized communities within the larger town.[48]

In space syntax terms, B-layer Karanis was an inefficient system, and one developing further and further away from the ideal. The reliance on interpersonal social negotiation to manage access only operated on a case-by-case basis, with little apparent consideration for the long-term system that stronger civic enforcement could

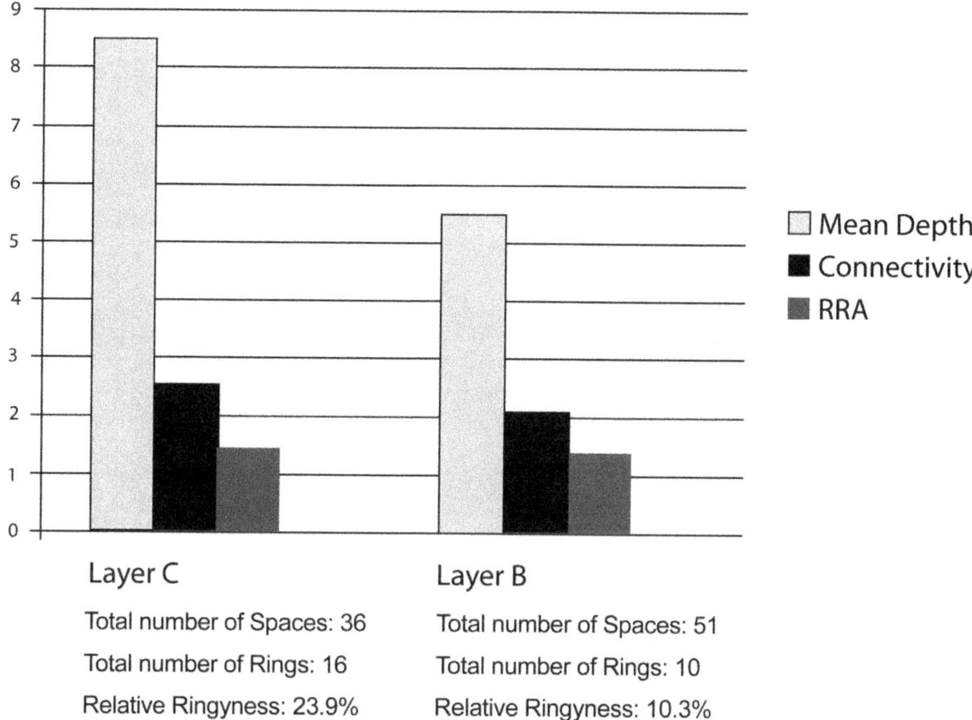

Figure 2.10. Comparison graph of space syntax values for the two major phases of Karanis construction.

have provided. Yet it does not necessarily follow that the ancient inhabitants saw their streets as inherently disorderly or completely dysfunctional. As we have seen throughout the Roman world, maintaining an ideal syntactic system was simply not a priority. While private construction that caused minor restriction to public access was widely tolerated, both legal and social mechanisms existed to effect necessary changes if the system was ever judged to be truly threatened or in need of intervention. The results were a flexible strategy for maintaining public access and a street system that functioned for six centuries: in terms of sheer longevity, it must be termed a success.

While large-scale social organization drove the physical development of the Karanis streets, individuals could work to improve their own access opportunities, by obtaining permission to use private interproperty routes that provided advantageous shortcuts and detours. Strategic inhabitants would carefully manage relationships within their neighborhoods to maintain such access. This in turn strengthened the social cohesion of localized communities within Karanis and assured that the resulting systems of access functioned smoothly. Rather than characterize Karanis as a town on the edge of chaos and abandonment as Late Antiquity approached, it is crucial to recognize the archaeological remains on both private and public property as evidence of a competent system of social organization.

Notes

1 See Bourdieu 1977; Blanton 1994.
2 Hillier and Hanson 1984, xi.
3 See Turner 2004.
4 Grahame 2000; Alston 2002; Spence 2010.
5 Grahame 2000, 34.
6 Hillier and Hanson 1984, 112.
7 Hillier and Hanson 1984.
8 See Perring 1991; Weilguni 2011; Poehler 2017.
9 See Spence 2005; Nevett 1999; Grahame 2000.
10 See Clarke 1991, 9–10; Wallace-Hadrill 1988.
11 See Grahame 2000.
12 Husselman 1979.
13 See Alston 2002, 55–56; Bagnall 1993.
14 See Cappers et al. 2013; Barnard et al. 2015; Wendrich et al. 2013.
15 See Simpson 2014; Wendrich et al. 2013.
16 Simpson 2014; Barnard et al. 2015.
17 These dates were published by the original Michigan team (Boak and Peterson 1931, and especially Husselman 1979), but relied heavily on papyrological and numismatic evidence, without considering any pottery seriation. Efforts to adjust the chronology are ongoing, and include Pollard 1998; Gupta-Agarwal 2011; Cappers et al. 2013; Barnard et al. 2015.
18 See Husselman 1952 and 1953; Tassinari 2009.
19 Nowicka 1969, 108; Husson 1983; Lehman 2013.
20 Husselman 1979.
21 For technical studies of the properties of mud-brick architecture, see Jerome et al. 1999; Kemp 2000. For ethnoarchaeological accounts, including other regions of the Near East, see Oates 1990; Van Beek et al. 2008; Homsher 2012; Correas-Amador 2013; Lehmann 2013; Love 2013.
22 See further Davoli, chapter 1. For the specific effect of windblown debris at Karanis, see Husselman 1979, 8, 29, 67.
23 Cf. Alston 2002, 53, who seems to be describing perimeter walls, which were shared, in contrast to the house itself. Freestanding and independent houses are rare in many crowded Roman cities, and surviving legislation suggests the management of shared constructions was complex (Taubenschlag 1955; Owens 1991, 168). In contrast, houses of the Roman Fayum are usually "self-contained" (Davoli 2011, 81); for Karanis itself, there is only one known example of a house that shared an exterior wall with another property, and this was an alteration made a century after initial construction (Simpson 2014, 187).
24 "And I will build my house from my southern wall to my northern wall up to thy wall, provided that I do not insert any timber in it . . .. If I fail to act according to everything aforesaid I will pay thee 5 silver pieces." P BM 10524; trans S. Glanville 1939.
25 Husselman 1979.
26 Samuel 1999.
27 Owens 1991; Gates 2003; Davoli 2011.
28 Husselman 1979, 12.
29 Boak 1955 and 1959; Geremek 1969; Keenan 2003.
30 Owens 1991, 156–67, 168; Saliou 1994.
31 Taubenschlag 1955, 361.
32 Taubenschlag 1955; Husson 1983, 65–72.
33 Taubenschlag 1955, 259; Kelly 2011.
34 Taubenschlag 1955, 257.
35 For discussion on their status as legal documents, see Taubenschlag 1955; Youtie 1971; Kelly 2011. Kelly 2011, 71, studying the different levels of the courts that petitions reached before being withdrawn or dismissed, suggests that the contracts were equally useful outside the courts as leverage in interpersonal negotiations. See also *PMich* V.226.
36 Husselman 1979, 8, 29.

37 Saliou 1994; Jacobs 2009. Hartnett (2017, 211) notes that many of the encroachments in Pompeii and Herculaneum were in fact not strictly necessary for access, thus throwing into question any legal grounds for their existence.
38 Simpson 2014, 157–61.
39 Lex Coloniae Genetivae Iuliae (FIRA 21) and see Hartnett 2017, 211; Crawford 1996, 393–94. The Tabula Heracleensis ll. 68–67, Lex Iulia Agraria 4 (FIRA 12) in Campania, and Spain's Lex Coloniae Genetivae Iuliae 104 in Spain (FIRA 21) give magistrates the power to intervene in cases of obstruction; see also Hartnett 2017, 211. For details on the limitations on porticoes and benches, see CJ VIII, 11, 20 [AD439] and discussion in Saradi 2006; Jacobs 2009, 205.
40 Saliou 1994.
41 In Rome, public access management was the job of the aedile, but holders of that office were notoriously unmotivated to fulfill their duties. See Cass. Dio 49.43.1 on the astonishing productivity of M. Agrippa's time as aedile as the exception to the general rule.
42 Jacobs (2009, 223) notes that in the case of annexation, the income generated by taxing the new private property could be seen as a benefit for municipal coffers.
43 Bagnall 1993, 114.
44 For third-century depopulation and "abandonment" of Fayum towns, see Boak 1955 and 1959; Van Minnen 1995; cf. Keenan 2003, Cappers et al. 2013, Simpson 2014; and Barnard et al. 2015.
45 Hartnett 2017, 136–37.
46 Tabula Keracleenisis 11.32–45, and see Hartnett 2017, 125–26.
47 Simpson 2014. See also Husselman 1979, 26.
48 Hillier and Hanson 1984, 17.

Works Cited

Alston, R. 2002. *The City in Roman and Byzantine Egypt*. London: Routledge.

Bagnall, R. 1993. *Egypt in Late Antiquity*. Princeton: Princeton University Press.

Barnard, H., W. Wendrich, B. Nigra, B. Simpson, and R. Cappers. 2015. "The Fourth Century CE Expansion of the Graeco-Roman Settlement of Karanis (Kom Aushim) in the Northern Fayum." *Journal of Field Archaeology* 84: 84–100.

Blanton, R. 1994. *Houses and Households: A Comparative Study*. New York: Plenum Press.

Boak, A., and E. Peterson. 1931. *Karanis: Topographical and Architectural Report of Excavations During the Seasons 1924–28*. Ann Arbor: University of Michigan Press.

Boak, A. 1955. "The Population of Roman and Byzantine Karanis." *Historia* 4 (2): 157–62.

Boak, A. 1959. "Egypt and the Plague of Marcus Aurelius." *Historia* 8 (2): 248–50.

Bourdieu, P. 1977. *Outline of a Theory of Practice*. Cambridge: Cambridge University Press.

Cappers, R., E. Cole, D. Jones, S. Holdaway, and W. Wendrich. 2013. "The Fayyûm Desert as an Agricultural Landscape: Recent Research Results." In *Das Fayyûm in Hellenismus und Kaiserzeit: Fallstudien zu multikulturellem Leben in der Anti*ke, edited by C. Arl and M. Stadler, 35–50. Wiesbaden: Harrassowitz Verlag.

Clarke, J.R. 1991. *Houses of Roman Italy 100 B.C.–A.D. 250: Ritual, Space, and Decoration*. Berkeley: University of California Press.

Correas-Amador, M. 2013. "Ethnoarchaeology of Egyptian Mudbrick Houses: Towards a Holistic Understanding of Ancient Egyptian Domestic Architecture." PhD diss., Durham University.

Davoli, P. 2011. "Reflections on Urbanism in Graeco-Roman Egypt: A Historical and Regional Perspective." In *The Space of the City in Graeco-Roman Egypt: Image and Reality*, edited by E. Subias, P. Azara, J. Carrusesco, I. Fiz, and R. Cuesta, 69–92. Tarragona: Institut Calalà d'Arquelogia Clàssica.

Gates, C. 2003. *Ancient Cities: The Archaeology of Urban Life in the Ancient Near East and Egypt, Greece, and Rome*. London: Routledge.

Geremek, H. 1969. *Karanis: Communauté rurale de l'Égypte Romaine au IIe-IIIe siècle de notre ère*. Archiwum Filologiczne, 17. Wrocław: Zakład Narodowy Imienia Ossolińskich Wydawnictwo Polskiej Akademii Nauk.

Glanville, S.K. 1939. *Catalogue of Demotic Papyri in the British Museum*. Vol 1. *A Theban Archive of the Reign of Ptolemy I, Soter*. London: Trustees of the British Museum.

Grahame, M. 2000. *Reading Space: Social Interaction and Identity in the Houses of Roman Pompeii*. Oxford: Archaeopress, British Archaeological Reports.

Gupta-Agarwal, S. 2011. "The Final Curtain Call: The Abandonment of Karanis in Light of Late Roman Amphorae." *Coptica* 10: 6–76.

Hartnett, J. 2017. *The Roman Street: Urban Life and Society*. Cambridge: Cambridge University Press.

Hillier, B., and J. Hanson. 1984. *The Social Logic of Space*. Cambridge: Cambridge University Press.

Homsher, R.S. 2012. "Mud Bricks and the Process of Construction in the Middle Bronze Age Southern Levant." *Bulletin of the American Schools of Oriental Research* 368: 1–27.

Husselman, E. 1952. "The Granaries of Karanis." *Transactions and Proceedings of the American Philological Association* 83: 56–73.

Husselman, E. 1953. "The Dovecotes of Karanis." *Transactions and Proceedings of the American Philological Association* 84: 81–91.

Husselman, E. 1979. *Karanis Excavations of the University of Michigan in Egypt 1928–1935: Topography and Architecture; A Summary of the Reports of the Director, Enoch E. Peterson*. Ann Arbor: University of Michigan Press.

Husson, G. 1983. *Oikia: Le vocabulaire de le maison privée en Egypte d'après les papyrus grecs*. Paris: Publications de la Sorbonne.

Jacobs, I. 2009. "Encroachment in the Eastern Mediterranean Between the Fourth and the Seventh Century AD." *Ancient Society* 39: 203–43.

Jerome, P., G. Chiari, and C. Borelli. 1999. "The Architecture of Mud: Construction and Repair Technology in the Hadhramaut Region of Yemen." *Association for Preservation Technology International Bulletin* 30: 39–48.

Keenan, J. 2003. "Deserted Villages: From the Ancient to the Medieval Fayyum." *Bulletin of the American Society of Papyrologists* 40: 119–39.

Kelly, B. 2011. *Petitions, Litigation, and Social Control in Roman Egypt*. Oxford: Oxford University Press.

Kemp, B.J. 2000. "Soil (including Mud-Brick Architecture)." In *Ancient Egyptian Materials and Technology*, edited by P.T. Nicholson and I. Shaw, 73–103. Cambridge: Cambridge University Press.

Lehmann, M. 2013. "Skylines, Bridges and Mud in the Delta and Elsewhere. A Comparison of Egyptian and Yemeni Tower Houses." Paper presented at the Delta Survey Workshop, Cairo, March 22–23.

Love, S. 2013. "The Performance of Building and Technological Choice Made Visible in Mudbrick Architecture." *Cambridge Archaeological Journal* 23: 263–82.

Nevett, L. 1999. *House and Society in the Ancient Greek World*. Cambridge: Cambridge University Press.

Nowicka, M. 1969. *La maison privée dans l'Égypte ptolémaïque*. Wrocław: Zakład Narodowy im. Ossolińskich.

Oates, D. 1990. "Innovations in Mud-Brick: Decorative and Structural Techniques in Ancient Mesopotamia." *World Archaeology* 21: 388–406.

Owens, E.J. 1991. *The City in the Greek and Roman World*. London: Routledge.

Perring, D. 1991. "Spatial Organization and Social Change in Roman Towns." In *City and Country in the Ancient World*, edited by J. Rich and A. Wallace-Hadrill, 273–93. New York: Routledge.

Poehler, E. 2017. *The Traffic Systems of Pompeii*. New York: Oxford University Press.

Pollard, N. 1998. "The Chronology and Economic Condition of Late Roman Karanis: An Archaeological Reassessment." *Journal of the American Research Center in Egypt* 35: 147–62.

Saliou, C. 1994. *Les lois des bâtiments: Voisinage et habitat urbain dans l'Empire Romain; Recherches sur les rapports entre le droit et la construction privée du siecle d'Auguste au siecle de Justinien*. Beyrouth: Institut Français d'Archeologie du Proche-Orient.

Samuel, D. 1999. "Breadmaking and Social Interaction at the Amarna Workman's Village, Egypt." *World Archaeology* 31 (1): 121–44.

Saradi, H. 2006. *The Byzantine City in the Sixth Century: Literary Images and Historical Reality*. Athens: Society of Messenian Archaeological Studies.

Simpson, B. 2014. "Neighborhood Networks: Social and Spatial Organization of Domestic Architecture in Greco-Roman Karanis, Egypt." PhD diss., University of California, Los Angeles.

Spence, K. 2010. "Settlement Structure and Social Interaction at El-Amarna." In *Cities and Urbanism in Ancient Egypt*, edited by M. Bietak, E. Czerny, and I. Forstner-Müller, 289–98. Vienna: Verlag der Österreichischen Archäologischen Instituts in Kairo.

Tassinari, C. 2009. *Il Thesauros di Bachkias: Rapporto Definitive*. Bologna: La Mandrago Editrice.

Taubenschlag, R. 1955. *The Law of Greco-Roman Egypt in the Light of the Papyri. 332. B.C.–640 A.D.* Warsaw: Panstwowe Wydawnictwo Naukowe.

Turner, A. 2004. *Depthmap 4—A Researcher's Handbook*. London: Barlett School of Graduate Studies.

Van Beek, G.W., and O. Van Beek. 2008. *Glorious Mud! Ancient and Contemporary Earthen Design and Construction in North Africa, Western Europe, the Near East, and Southwest Asia*. Washington, DC: Smithsonian Institute Scholarly.

Van Minnen, P. 1995. "Deserted Villages: Two Late Antique Town Sites in Egypt." *Bulletin of the American Society of Papyrologists* 32 (1): 41–56.

Wallace-Hadrill, A. 1988. "The Social Structure of the Roman House." *Papers of the British School at Rome* 56: 43–97.

Weilguni, M. 2011. *Streets, Spaces, and Places: Three Pompeiian Movement Axes Analysed*. Boreas 33, Uppsala Studies in Ancient Mediterranean and Near Eastern Civilizations. Uppsala: Uppsala Universitet.

Wendrich, W., B. Simpson, and E. el-Gewely. 2014. "Karanis in 3D: Recording, Monitoring, Recontextualizing, and the Representation of Knowledge and Conjecture." *Near Eastern Archaeology* 77 (3): 233–37.

Youtie, H.C. 1971. "Agrammatoi: An Aspect of Greek Society in Egypt." *Harvard Studies in Classical Philology* 75: 161–76.

3

The Tower Houses of the Hellenistic Period

A Solution to the Urban Pressure within Egyptian Towns and Villages

GREGORY MAROUARD

The multistory house is a common feature of the Egyptian settlement landscape, and the urban house had probably incorporated upper levels for a long time before the Hellenistic Period. Archaeology often remains laconic, but iconographic sources attest to one or two stories in elite domestic contexts at least since the early New Kingdom, if not since the Middle Kingdom.[1]

The architectural study of urban settlements and habitats faces strong disparities that are unfortunately ubiquitous in Egyptian archaeology. If this assertion is particularly true for the dynastic phases, it also stands for the Greco-Roman Period in Egypt. Despite hundreds of examples of well-preserved houses and several extensively excavated sites, we face important chronological and geographical inequalities for this period. The Roman Period is far better represented than the Hellenistic Period, and archaeologists unfortunately rarely reach these earlier chronological horizons. There are also important geographical disparities. The peripheral fringes of the Fayum oasis have provided the overwhelming majority of domestic examples, but most were excavated fifty to eighty years ago, often using a hasty methodology. Even with the recent resumption of excavations at Tebtynis, Narmouthis, Philotheris, Karanis, or Dimeh-Soknopaiou Nesos, only the first of these sites has delivered significant excavation results and shed new light on domestic contexts from the Hellenistic phases. During the past two decades, sites in the Delta region have slightly rebalanced this situation by providing new examples about Ptolemaic domestic contexts: for instance, at Buto, Tell el-Dab'a, or Tell el-Balamun. But in these regions, the methodological complexity and limited state of preservation prohibit the opening of sizable excavation areas. Only geomagnetic survey can provide an extensive picture of urban patterns, but its depth is limited, and the distinction between the Ptolemaic, Roman, or earlier and later horizons is often difficult to evaluate. Archaeological projects in the Western Oases since the late 1980s (Kysis-Doush, Kellis, Mut, Amheida) have provided much new data, but are still extremely quiet for the Ptolemaic Period.

Karanis presents one of the most exceptional sets of domestic examples for the Roman Period, and scholars use this site intensively—sometimes inaccurately—to demonstrate an archetype of the domestic sphere or give a form to some of the houses mentioned in textual sources. But Karanis's Roman contexts cannot really support any conclusions about earlier phases, and this site is of little help for studying the Ptolemaic Period. In order to illustrate the Hellenistic house and household, we must thus use a complex patchwork of examples and uneven fragments from various archaeological, iconographic, and textual sources.

In this contribution, I will attempt to define in detail a particular form of habitat—the tower house of the Ptolemaic Period—and the specific urban organization that accompanies it. Both seem inherited from a vernacular Egyptian tradition that dates back at least to the Saite Period and originates in the marshy regions of the Nile Delta. This type of multistory house, which is characterized by a peculiar system of foundations and a strong vertical development, apparently constituted the prevalent form of housing for at least six centuries, starting in the Late Period and covering almost the entire Ptolemaic Period. Those can be found regularly in many urban contexts, from the end of the fourth century to the mid-second century BCE, from the northernmost sites of the Delta to the southern border of Egypt at Aswan, although not yet in the Western Oases regions. Tower houses were the common solution for housing, indifferently used at diverse ranks of settlements (figure 3.1), from the nome capitals (Elephantine, Edfu, Buto) to the secondary agglomerations of the Delta (Tell el-Herr, Tell el-Balamun), as well as in religious communities in Middle Egypt (Tuna el-Gebel) and farming villages at the fringes of the Fayum oasis newly (re)settled by the first Lagid rulers (Tebtynis, Philadelphia, Soknopaiou Nesos, Bakchias, Karanis). This analysis puts the most recent archaeological data in dialogue with limestone or terracotta models, which allow us to attempt a three-dimensional reconstruction of this dwelling type.

Criteria for Identifying Ptolemaic Tower Houses

The predecessors of the tower houses appear to be the so-called casemate foundation buildings found throughout Late Period urban centers in the northern Nile Delta.[2] Since the early 2000s, geomagnetic surveys of Nile Delta sites have revealed large densely urbanized areas: for instance, at Tell el-Fara'in-Buto,[3] Tell el-Balamun,[4] and recently at Naukratis or Tanis.[5] There, dozens of similar units appeared in residential areas located outside the sacred precinct/*temenos* and largely datable to the Late Period (Saite/26th Dynasty and Persian Period).[6] These results, combined with the higher-resolution satellite images,[7] have provided many recent examples and helped identify existing, but previously unrecognized, examples from older excavations (Tell el-Nebesheh-Tell el-Faraon,[8] Tell Atrib,[9] Mendes,[10] Tell el-Muqdam,[11] Tukh el-Qaramus,[12] Tell Tebilla).[13] Old interpretations as exclusively official, administrative, or economic structures are no longer tenable, given the increasing number of new archaeological examples measuring under twenty-five to thirty meters on each side.[14] More properly designated now as "cellular substructures"

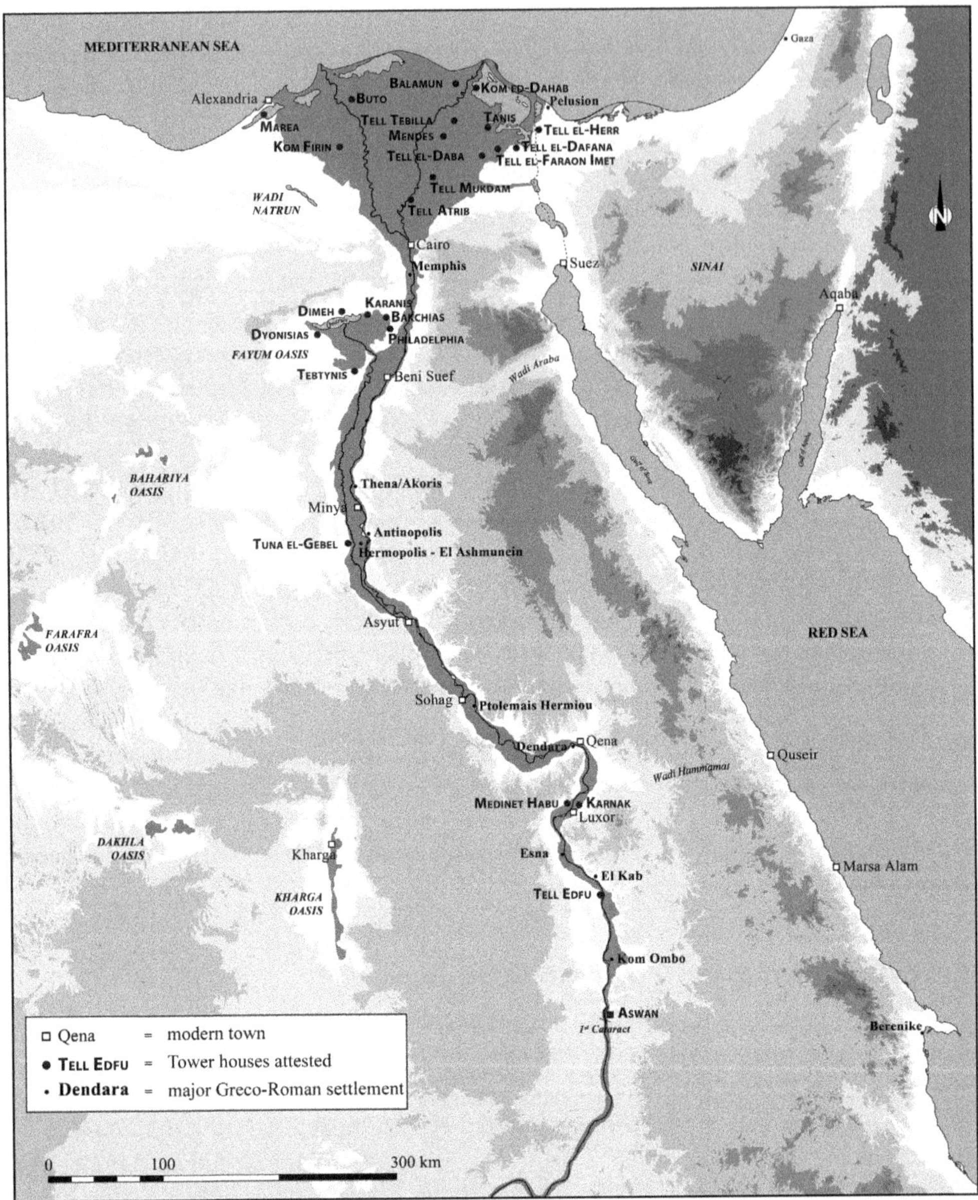

Figure 3.1. Map of Greco-Roman Egypt, showing the locations of tower houses attested by archaeological finds. (Map G. Marouard.)

or "cellular foundations," these constructions are the remains of the foundation level of multistory tower houses.[15] The number and density of these installations, their dimensions, and their very similar plans leave little doubt about their domestic nature, which was clearly demonstrated by recent excavations. Exceptionally, the magnetic map of Kom A at Buto provides more than fifty examples of buildings with comparable layouts that form an extensive domestic neighborhood occupied for at least two centuries.[16]

All these examples should be considered as the original models and prototypes for the Hellenistic-period structures to be described here. The Hellenistic houses are thus clearly inscribed within a continuous Egyptian domestic tradition and its associated organic urban pattern. The known Late Period examples are overwhelmingly located in the northern Nile Delta versus the rest of Egypt. However, even accounting for the random nature of previous research and the unequal geographic distribution of excavations in urban contexts, this ratio seems to change with the beginning of the Ptolemaic Period (figure 3.1). Examples from the Delta are still numerous, as at Buto,[17] Tell el-Herr (figure 3.2),[18] or Tell el-Dab'a,[19] but many other examples appear from the Fayum oasis to Upper Egypt. To date more than thirty-five such structures have been archaeologically identified outside of the Delta region, although recent geomagnetic results suggest that a single site such as Tuna el-Gebel (figure 3.5) could easily triple this number.

Ptolemaic tower houses are well attested within the farming villages on the periphery of the Fayum oasis, such as Karanis, Dimeh/Soknopaiou Nesos, Philadelphia,[20] Bakchias,[21] and Tebtynis (figure 3.3). In the cases of Dimeh,[22] Karanis,[23] or Tebtynis,[24] which are all three (re)foundations undertaken by the first Lagid rulers, the tower house is the only housing form attested for the very first phase of installation (third century BCE or, at Tebtynis, the last quarter of the fourth century BCE) (figure 3.4). The tower houses at those sites appear to belong to the oldest recognized occupation levels and are built directly onto the natural sand substratum. We are confronted here with the pioneer colonization phase at these newly (re)founded settlements.

The diffusion of mud-brick tower houses outside of the Delta obviously occurred at the end of the Late Period or the beginning of the Ptolemaic Period, perhaps because of the practical benefits of this kind of traditional domestic architecture, which was well adapted to Egyptian urban contexts. But the omnipresence of tower houses in the earliest levels of ex nihilo foundations might also possibly reveal the origin of the populations that were settled (maybe sent?) there in connection with the first Lagid rulers' development of the Fayum periphery. This colonization process might have involved populations originally from the Delta regions, who would have pragmatically transposed their own familiar construction techniques and domestic architectural forms to the Fayum. Greek-inspired domestic and urban layouts were therefore perhaps rare or absent in the original landscape of these villages,[25] and a formally planned colony such as Philadelphia, founded to accommodate Greek veterans, stands clearly as an exception.[26]

Tower houses also appear in Middle Egypt, at Tuna el-Gebel, where recent work by the University of Munich confirms the spread of this domestic form throughout Egypt.[27] Geomagnetic survey has revealed about forty examples on both sides of the processional pathway to the animal necropolis (figure 3.5), and at least forty more at the settlement site of Kôm el-Loli (figure 3.5). Several excavated examples date to the early and mid-Ptolemaic Period, with a first phase dating to Ptolemy I–II (first half of the third century) and a second phase in the reign of Ptolemy VI (second quarter of the second century).[28]

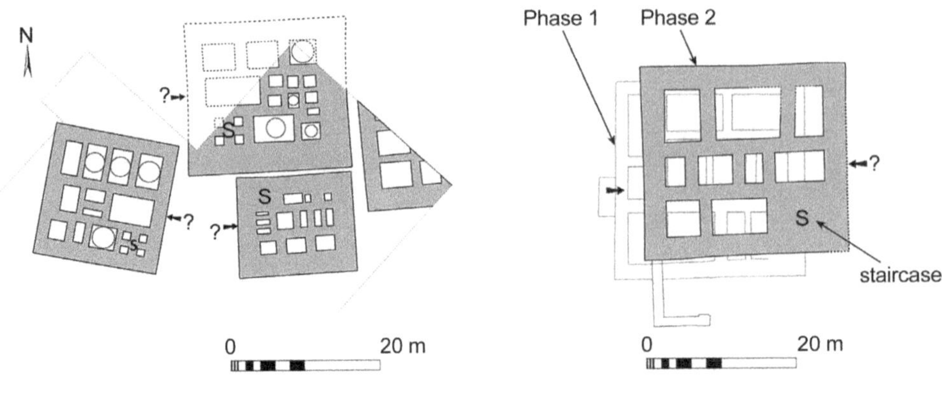

Tell el-Fara`in - Buto
Saite period, 1st half 6th Cent. BCE

Tell el-Herr
Early (Phase 1) and Middle of 4th Cent. BCE (Phase 2)

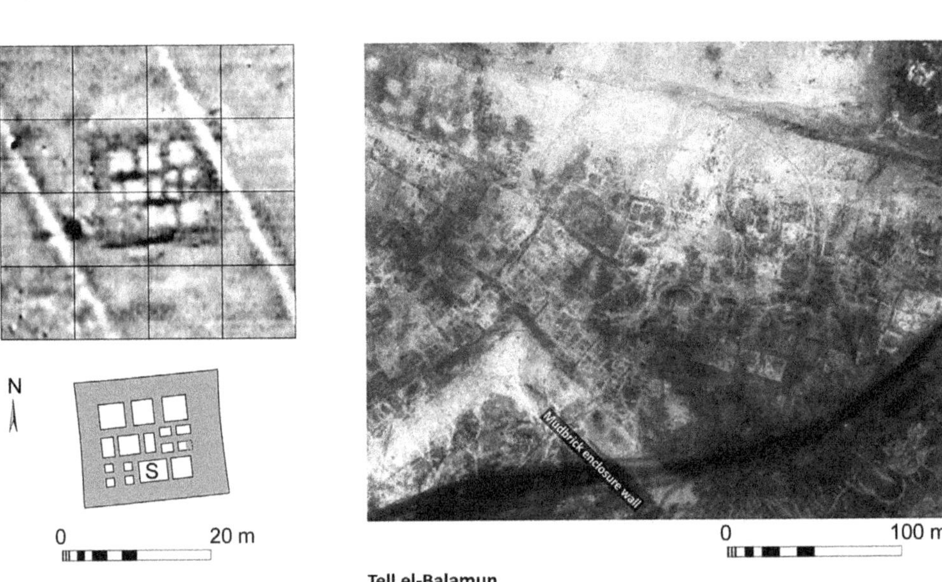

Tell el-Iswed
Saite Period, 6th Cent. BCE ?

Tell el-Balamun
Domestic quarter with aligments of tower-houses North-East of the temple enclosure wall (from the Saite to the Ptolemaic Period ?)

Figure 3.2. Examples of tower house foundations in the Nile Delta region from the Late Period to the early Ptolemaic Period. (Figure by G. Marouard, redrawn from Hartung 2009, fig.3; Marchi 2014, fig. 9; Herbich 2011, Pl. XVII; satellite view courtesy of ©Google Earth.)

Several other examples can be found further south on the Nile, but they often appear as a few scattered units: for instance, at Karnak,[29] Medinet Habu,[30] Tell Edfu,[31] or Elephantine (figure 3.6).[32] Aside from the oasean settlement sites in Kharga (e.g., Kysis) or Dakhla (Amheida), these four sites are the only Greco-Roman-era urban contexts significantly excavated and whose results have been partially published for Upper Egypt. Yet here too, each site has produced several tower houses, datable exclusively to the Ptolemaic Period.

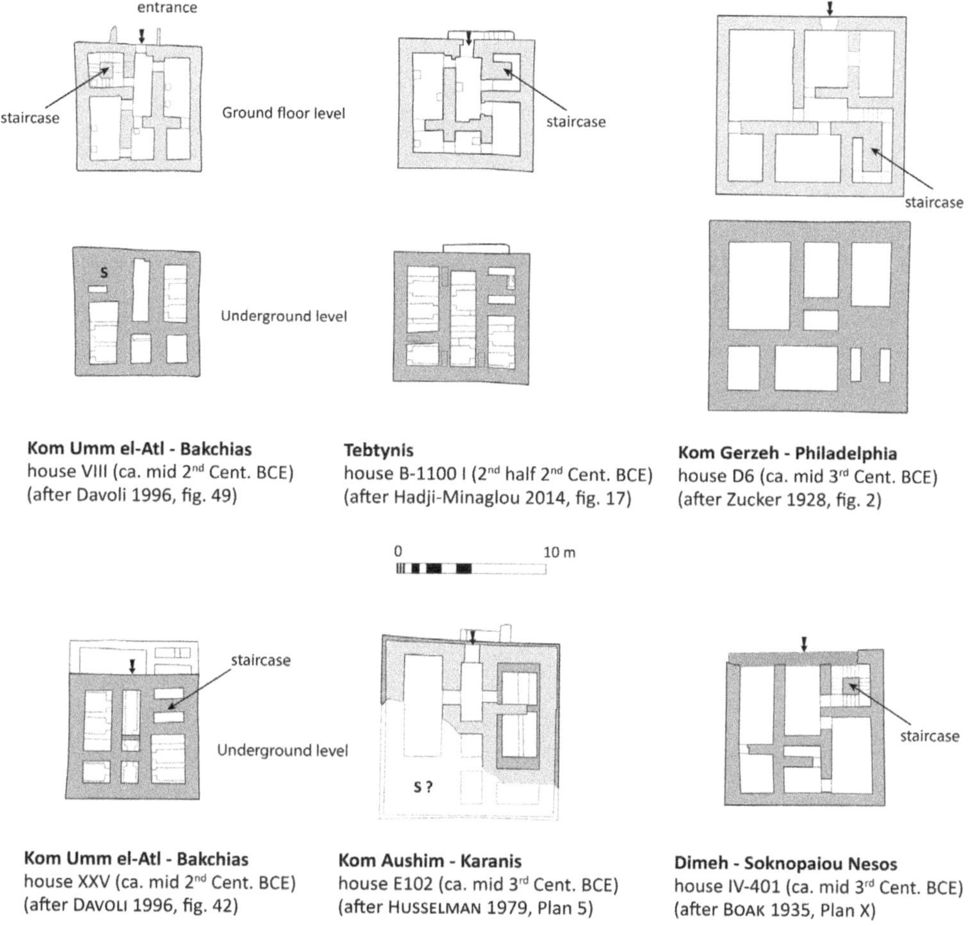

Figure 3.3. Examples of Ptolemaic tower house foundations from the Fayum oasis. (Figure by G. Marouard, redrawn from Davoli 1996, fig. 42 and 49; Hadji-Minaglou 2014, fig. 17; Viereck1928, fig. 2; Husselman 1979, Plan 5; and Boak 1935, Plan X.)

The presence of several floors above the ground level is not a sufficient criterion alone to characterize the morphology of the tower house, which is a very distinctive form within a large and diversified family of Egyptian multistory houses. As Greek textual sources equally emphasize, the tower house should not be confused with other types of multilevel houses.[33]

At all the sites where it has been identified, the Hellenistic tower house is very homogeneous in form, and the examples remain fully within a continuous tradition from the Late Period. Architectural specifics and archaeological characteristics, chronology, even their position in the urban landscape, have been well-defined since a recent conference on these structures.[34]

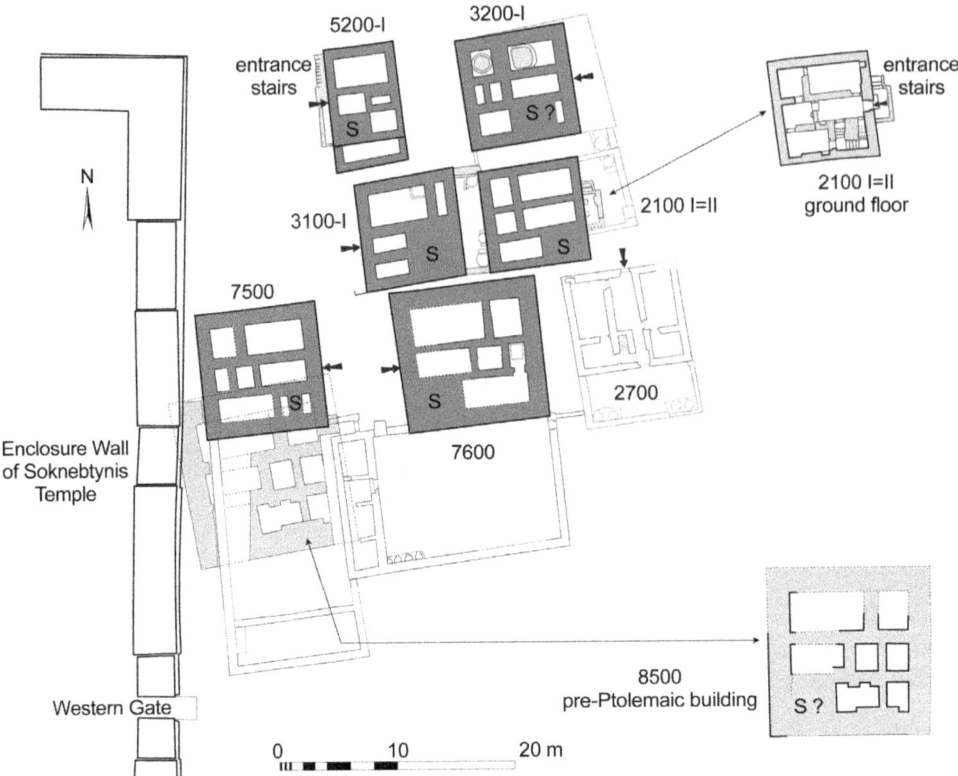

Figure 3.4. Domestic quarter from the late fourth and early third century BCE at Tebtynis, east of Soknebtynis temple. (Figure by G. Marouard, reconstructed after Hadji-Minaglou 2007, fig. 4; and Hadji-Minaglou 2014, fig. 13.)

The criteria for identifying a tower house are as follows:

- A square or near-square plan, with dimensions ranging from 8.50 m to 15 m on each side and a ground surface area from 80 to 200 m². The average length size is about 10 m to 12 m (examples at Tuna el-Gebel and Tebtynis show a consistent length, respectively between 9.30 m to 12.30 m and 8.40 m to 12.00 m) and an average ground surface area of 100 m² to 140 m².[35]
- A high and massive semi-buried foundation infrastructure, about two to three meters in height, of which a part always exceeds the surrounding levels on the exterior, such as the domestic courtyard or the street level (figure 3.9). This foundation is always carefully built with a "cellular" layout characterized by very thick outer walls. The masonry of all outer walls and internal partition walls always ties together at the corners to form a solid, freestanding base of strongly linked walls, in order to support a significant elevation.

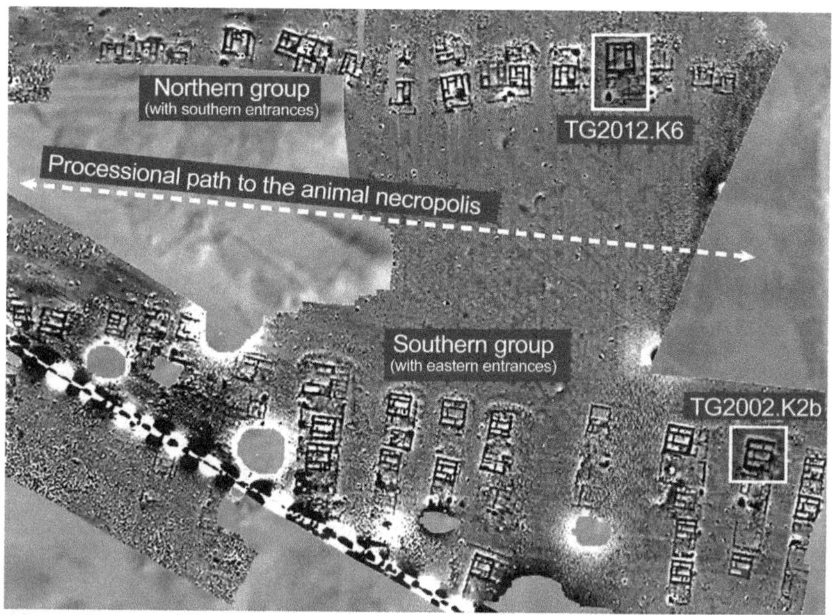

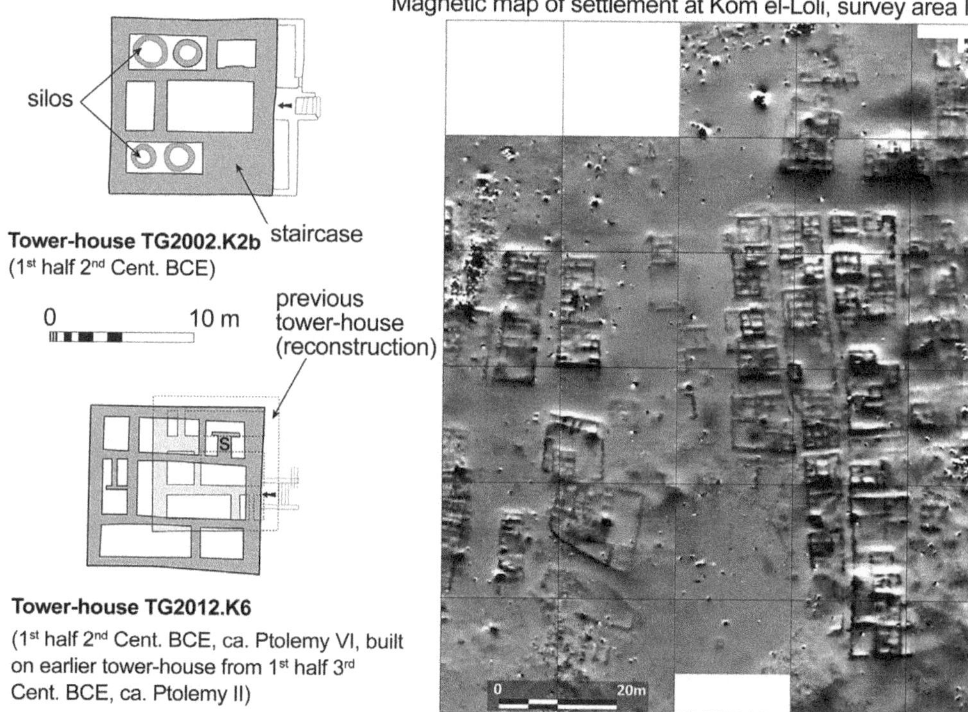

Figure 3.5. Geomagnetic maps of settlement areas and two examples of tower house foundations at Tuna el-Gebel, Middle Egypt. (Geomagnetic maps courtesy of M. Flossmann, LMU excavation project at Tuna el-Gebel.)

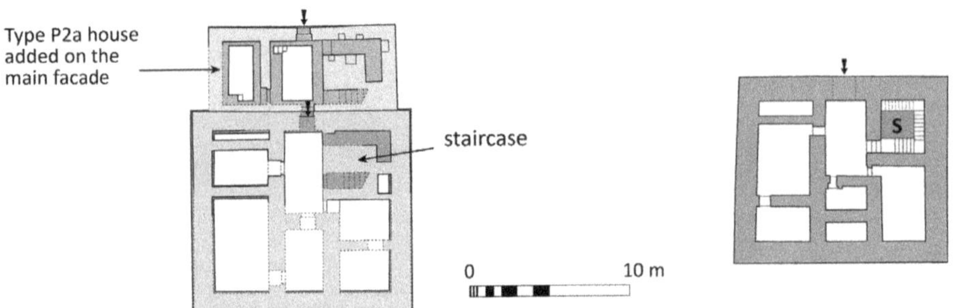

Elephantine
houses K19 and K19A (late 3rd Cent. BCE to Ptolemy VI-VIII)
(after Dreyer et al. 2008, Fig. 4)

Tell Edfou
'maison centrale' (late 3rd Cent. BCE)
(after Bruyere 1937, Plan IV)

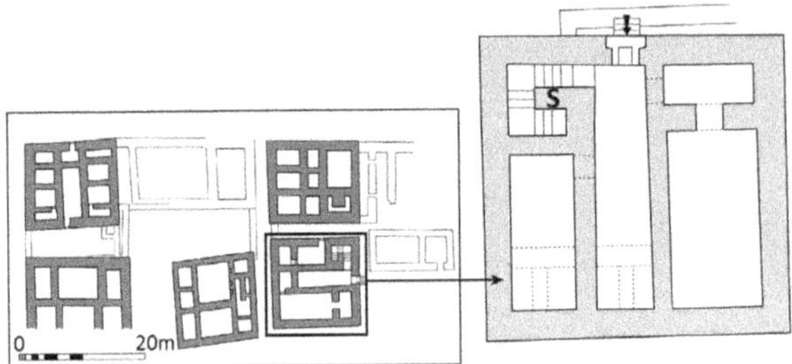

Medinet Habu
Eastern harbor *extra-muros* area (late Ptolemaic period ?)
(after Hölscher 1934, Pl. 10)

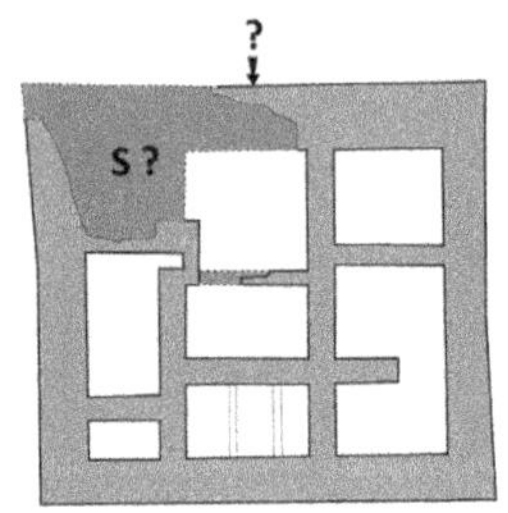

Karnak
'Maison A' (1st half 2nd Cent. BCE)
(after Lauffray 1995, fig. 6)

Figure 3.6. Examples of Ptolemaic tower house foundations from Upper Egypt. (Figure G. Marouard redrawn after Dreyer et al. 2008, fig. 4; Bruyère 1937, Plan IV; Hölscher 1934, Pl. 10; Lauffray 1995, fig. 6.)

- The outer wall thickness never measures under 1.00 meters; usually the walls are up to 1.20–1.50-meters thick and sometimes even 2.00 meters, particularly in the massive foundation.[36] Our data do not currently permit establishing a precise relationship between the width of the walls and the original elevation of the house, which could reach two to three levels above the ground floor (four total floors).[37] There is always a slight slope to the external face of the outer walls, generally more marked at the base of the building (figure 3.7). This external slope, like the wall thickness, decreased at higher elevations in order to lighten the weight of the upper-level masonry.
- At only one known site, Dimeh, the foundations were made of stone slabs (Houses IV-401 and IV-402, figure 3.3); otherwise, they were always mud brick.[38] The mud bricks used for the foundation were sometimes better quality and higher density than those at higher levels. Walls employ a concave courses technique, or a combination of horizontal and concave courses with regular insertion of wooden elements and beds of reeds to limit rising

dampness. This concave arrangement of brick courses helped channel vertical pressure toward the center of the walls and the center of the volume, and it relieved the building corners of stress and weight (figure 3.7). However, this concavity was not maintained continuously in the upper elevation. It was regularly corrected, usually in line with the separation between two floors, by a series of horizontal layers of mud bricks that provided a level surface for the horizontal beams and joists used for the ceiling and the floor above. A new series of curved courses was then mounted above. This construction detail is archaeologically attested at Tell Edfu and also appears on some tower house models (M1, figure 3.10).

- The infrastructure level has two main layout types. The first type is a series of disconnected square or rectangular underground spaces, so-called cellular foundations, which were often filled with construction debris or sand and used as crawl spaces, especially in the Delta. These spaces sometimes held underground silos, covered with a mud-brick dome and accessible from the top by an opening at the ground-floor level (figures 3.2, 3.4, 3.5, and 3.8). Usually, to maximize use of the underground surface, a so-called Nubian vault covered these spaces. All were accessible on one end by a hatch opening at the ground-floor level, thus forming a set of oblong, independent, vaulted cellars (figure 3.8). The second, rarer type of layout features vaulted rooms partly or completely interconnected by doors. This layout produced a basement level directly accessible from the ground floor through the staircase at the corner of the house, as with House IV-401 at Dimeh or the "maison centrale" at Tell Edfu (figures 3.3 and 3.6).
- The arrangement of all underground spaces follows a clear logic: a "tripartite organization" with three series of parallel spaces symmetrically aligned around the center.[39] This symmetry is sometimes perfect but more often inverted, with two larger rectangular spaces/rooms in opposite corners; this latter appears in many examples from the Fayum (figure 3.3). Together with the square plan and the massiveness of the architecture, this tripartite organization is one of the main identifying features of the tower house. Any plan that deviates from this tripartite composition may be a multistory house, but it is no longer strictly speaking a tower house.
- All excavated examples include a massive staircase in one of the corners, covering 12 to 20 percent of the ground-level surface. For the best-preserved examples, we can restore a staircase with three or four flights of steps (figures 3.3, 3.4, and 3.6). In most cases, especially those with the "cellular foundations" arrangement, this staircase is only identifiable at the foundation level as a solid base in one corner (figures 3.2, 3.4, and 3.6) or as a set of small rectangular spaces (either one space, two parallel spaces, or three in a U shape) around a massive core (figures 3.3, 3.4, 3.5, and 3.6). These spaces often served as underground loft cellars, located under the stairs and accessible by hatches on the landing.
- The opening of the house unit onto the outside is limited. When an entrance is preserved, it is always a single, centered door on one side: generally, on

the façade overlooking a street or a courtyard separating the house from the street, as at Tuna el-Gebel (figure 3.5).[40] Because of the height of the massive infrastructure, the ground floor was always significantly raised above the outside surface and the front door is always significantly higher than street or courtyard level, requiring an external stairway (figure 3.9).[41]

- The tripartite layout of the basement spaces reflects the layout of the rooms for all the floors above. The central axis corresponds always to the location of the main entrance, which led to an entrance/reception room, the so-called vestibule.[42] This vestibule typically leads to a narrow corridor and/or an axial room at the end. On either side of the central axis, the two lateral rows of basement spaces underlie in general three rooms: one large and one small room on one side, and a large room and the stairwell on the opposite. The access to the stairwell is always directly to the right or left of the entrance room (figures 3.3, 3.5, and 3.6). This plan forms a homogeneous composition of spaces with a simple circulation from one room to another.[43]

The foregoing descriptions apply to almost all excavated tower houses, although some special cases also exist. At Tuna el-Gebel and Elephantine, a few tower houses also featured a second contiguously attached structure, perhaps of later date (figure 3.6). This lateral addition provided a way to extend the floor space without adding another upper floor. Over time, the standardized plan of these tower houses remained very consistent, but they became progressively smaller: Late Period

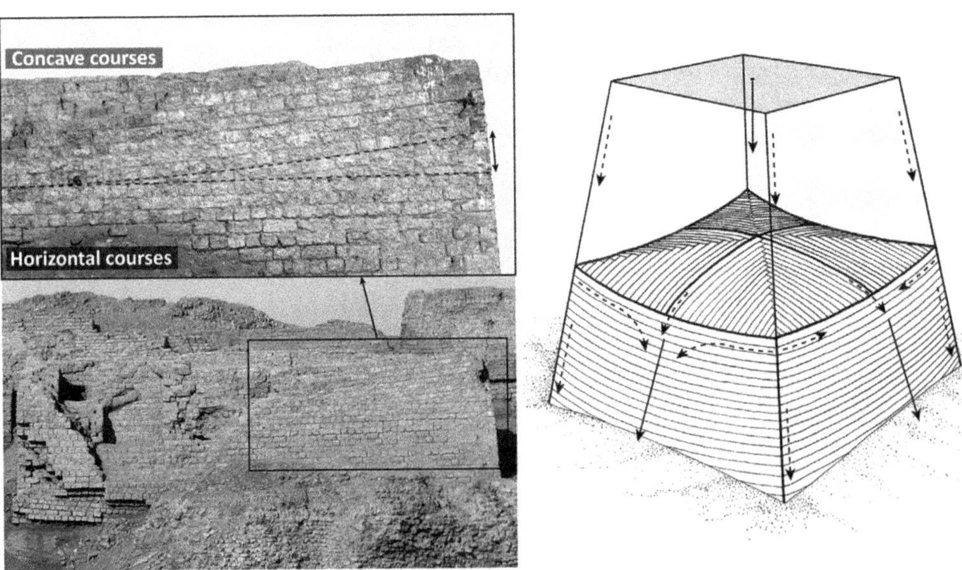

Figure 3.7. Level of adjustment of the concave courses of mud bricks on the "maison centrale" at Tell Edfu and sketch of the distribution of weights and forces in a tower house type structure. (Photos by G. Marouard, sketch modified after Goyon et al. 2004, Fig. 110–3.)

Figure 3.8. Vaulted cellars and domed silos built within the underground spaces of tower house foundation levels. (Drawing by G. Marouard, photos after Davoli 1996, Fig. 47; Husselman 1979, Pl. 35a; Hadji-Minaglou 2007, Photo 117; Bruyère 1937, Pl. XIII-2.)

examples have an average side length of fifteen to thirty meters, compared to ten to twelve meters for Ptolemaic examples. This reduced footprint implies a lower elevation, with accordingly fewer stories.

Of all known Greco-Roman-era tower houses, about 95 percent are from the Ptolemaic Period and built between the late fourth century and the second half of the second century BCE.[44] Gradually, after the end of the second century BCE, significant changes can be seen in urban and domestic traditions, as clearly demonstrated at Tebtynis.[45] After that date, domestic neighborhoods still contained several forms of multistory houses, but these were no longer strictly speaking tower houses according to our criteria: they had significantly smaller footprints and much more varied plans. Settlement plans now featured *insula* patterns with multiple types of multistory dwellings, which made more efficient use of the available urban space. The transition to the Roman era marks the development and the prevalence of a completely new, and much better known, layout for residential neighborhoods, as seen at Tebtynis, Soknopaiou Nesos, and especially Karanis, where the Ptolemaic tower house, as defined above, is totally absent.

The tower house archetype becomes much rarer in the early Roman Period, which provides fewer than 5 percent of all known examples. This form survives only

Figure 3.9. Courtyard, perpendicular staircase, and main entrance to the tower house TG2012.K6 at Tuna el-Gebel. (Images courtesy of M. Flossmann, LMU excavation project at Tuna el-Gebel.)

in a few much larger buildings, whose dimensions are closer to the original Late Period structures. Only three examples are known, all from the Fayum: one at Dimeh (House II-201: 17 m x 19 m)[46] and two at Tebtynis (House 2400-III: 13.50 m x 16 m and house 2800: 17 m x 18.60 m).[47] All three seem to have been constructed during the Augustan Period and were used throughout most of the first century CE. The rareness and atypicality of these structures, their isolated position within settlement landscapes otherwise characterized by small multistory houses, and their close proximity to a sanctuary (Tebtynis) or processional pathway (Dimeh) create considerable doubt about their domestic function. These large Roman tower houses might perhaps have functioned as collective dwellings for multiple families/households (*synoikia*), or might have served nondomestic (administrative or official) purposes.[48]

Outside the House: Access, Domestic Courtyards, and Circulation

As noted above, the front door of the Ptolemaic tower house was never level with the external street or domestic courtyard, and an exterior access stairway with a single flight of steps was necessary. Generally, only the foundation of this stairway survives (figures 3.3, 3.4, and 3.5), but several examples indicate two solutions for its layout: either centered on the main doorway, or offset to its side. This arrangement varied depending on the immediate environment. If the street or courtyard was wide enough, people chose a staircase centered on the doorway, to make a more monumental and ostentatious main entrance (figure 3.9). This option often included two platforms flanking the stairs, creating a sort of high entrance podium on the main façade.[49] More frequently, an offset location was preferred (figures 3.3, 3.4, and 3.6) in order to avoid an overly long or steep stairway and to minimize encroachment onto exterior spaces, especially public or semipublic streets or spaces.

All the structures excavated or recognized by geomagnetic survey have freestanding facades. This is another essential feature of the Ptolemaic tower house. No two examples have contiguous facades, back to back against each other; the tower house is always isolated from the neighboring domestic unit, whether it is another tower house or not (figures 3.4 and 3.5). Only the walls of their own or adjacent domestic courtyards lean against the building.

Because of their subsequent destruction and leveling, excavated tower houses are mostly preserved only at the foundation level, but external domestic courtyards are always the best-preserved parts of these units. These were spaces for daily activities: primarily food processing (grain milling), preparation, and cooking (bread ovens), but also temporary storage (silos and storage bins), agricultural work, small-scale craft production, and small livestock husbandry. The courtyard, whatever its size, has only a small and a single exterior access. Whenever it is not located in front of the main entrance façade but on one side and/or behind the house, this space usually—and curiously—lacks direct access to the house; instead, it has its own unique entrance that opens directly onto the street or exterior space. The courtyard often seems to be used as an intermediate access space. Whenever the house entrance opens onto a courtyard rather than the street, this space—reserved for daily activities, and consequently more exposed to interaction with the outside world or other households—served as a transitional entrance, a buffer zone protecting the more private house interior.[50]

Peripheral courtyards were probably included in the original plan of the house when the urban pressure was still low. At that point, the rule seems to have been "first-come, first-served." In the case of Tuna el-Gebel (figure 3.5) or the first phase of Hellenistic settlement at Tebtynis (figure 3.4), where the built environment initially provided little to no constraint, the courtyard can be large—more than two to three times larger than the footprint of the house itself—multipartite, and multifunctional. These courtyards could encompass not only daily life activities but also many professional and craft activities. They may also reflect attempts to reserve additional building space in order to enlarge or add another unit in the future.

In other cases, such as at Tebtynis[51] or Buto,[52] the courtyard was not part of the original construction, but was opportunistically created at a later time by appropriation of semipublic or public space: often by closing a street, alley, or any kind of empty adjacent space (figure 3.4).[53] This solution, usually associated with denser settlement and higher urban pressure, profoundly changed neighborhood circulation patterns by forcing pedestrians to sometimes bypass a large block of agglutinated buildings and courtyards instead of moving freely between them.

A Typical Organic Urban Organization Associated with Tower Houses

We can analyze the pattern of such residential areas based on multiple Late Period through Ptolemaic sites in the Delta, such as Buto,[54] Tell el-Balamun (figure 3.2),[55] Tell Dafana,[56] and Mendes.[57] More limited evidence also comes from the early Ptolemaic sectors at Tebtynis (figure 3.4) and Tuna el-Gebel (figure 3.5).

These domestic quarters show a very characteristic organization: the pre-Roman tower house never appears alone but within a dense urban landscape of several dozen similar units. Such neighborhoods feature a tight network of vertical buildings, but all are physically separated from each other: either by adjoining domestic courtyards, or by undeveloped spaces whose widths range from two meters to more than five meters. These latter are mostly public or semipublic circulation spaces: streets, small squares, alleys, or dead ends. At least, there is always a very narrow interstitial space, about one meter wide, reserved by the builders: a kind of *ambitus* ensuring that the facades of two houses never touch each other directly. Tower houses are thus freestanding on all four sides. The absence of joint facades would have reduced problems of contiguity and constraints of joint ownership between two neighboring buildings. Geomagnetic surveys in Tuna el-Gebel suggest that tower houses have at least two or even three facades overlooking a street or a circulation area, and one to two facades facing a courtyard (figure 3.5).[58] This freestanding position is an essential feature of Ptolemaic tower houses and a major difference from later multistory houses. With the higher diversity of house forms (with rectangular, I-, L-, or T-shape), especially during the early Roman Period, most of these later multistory houses shared at least one or two contiguous facades with adjacent buildings. This evolution coincides with the development, since the end of the second century and during the course of the first century BCE, of a different urban fabric with several units grouped and imbricated with courtyards into *insulae*. Examples appear at Dimeh, Dionysias, Tebtynis, and Karanis, which is the emblematic example of this later organization.[59]

Tower houses and their typical neighborhood configuration therefore reflect an indigenous Egyptian tradition. In this urban landscape, the lines and perspectives are short, and the directions of streets are often irregular and suddenly changing, producing a dense, complex, and obscure network of alleys and dead ends. Because of the quadrangular shape of the house and surrounding courtyards, the street pattern is generally orthogonal, but it is not orthonormal, nor following any master plan. House facades are often significantly misaligned, confirming that no strict grid has been imposed. Naturally, some larger axes exist to facilitate general circulation within the neighborhood, especially when it is located next to a major religious facility (a *dromos* or a processional path, e.g. at Tuna el-Gebel). But within the residential area itself, no circulation hierarchy is clearly distinguishable. There is no sign of strict division and regulated distribution of buildable land, or any preconceived plot, grid, or standardized insulae. The urban pattern is not prescribed or constrained. Instead, it is the square shape of the house itself—and the progressive, probably rapid accumulation of similar buildings and adjacent courtyards—that created the alignments, loose orthogonality, and organic evolution of the urban network.

Far from the common stereotype of Hellenistic town planning, these neighborhoods, as revealed by the archaeological data, had neither rigorously defined insulae nor networks of preplanned orthogonal streets. Such layouts become more perceptible only later, as we see at Tebtynis, Soknopaiou Nesos, and Karanis in the course of the first century BCE. The colony at Philadelphia, which was built according to a Hippodamian grid, is an exception and should no longer be seen as a norm. It is important to note that the only domestic installation recorded for this site (figure 3.3) corresponds to the plan of a Ptolemaic tower house, suggesting a probable mixture of Egyptian and Greek genres in this foundation.[60]

The omnipresence of such a traditional and organic pattern in the early phases of the new Fayum settlements demonstrates that this Egyptian tradition of housing and settlement layout proved well suited for colonizing previously nonurbanized areas. Rather than precise town planning rules, it is likely that codes of "good neighborliness" governed relationships of proximity and conditioned the establishment of a new house in the existing landscape. By avoiding shared facades and creating freestanding elevations, builders could maximize daylight and air intake on all sides of the house. As the slope of the external walls increased on the higher levels, the gap between the facades of neighboring houses also gradually increased, giving the upper floors better ventilation, better lighting, and more privacy.

The Vertical Development of the Tower House: Which Sources Are Reliable?

Archaeological excavation provides very little information about the upper elevation of the tower house. The majority of examples are preserved only at the basement level. Only fragments of the ground floor survive, such as in Tebtynis, Bakchias, or Dimeh, where we sometimes see in situ entrance elements (thresholds, door sockets, door jamb traces), fragments of floors, or portions of the covers and trap doors of underground cellars and silos.

From an archaeological and architectural point of view, the validity of the Egyptianizing Roman imagery and mosaics showing Nilotic scenes, such as the much-overused example from Palestrina,[61] seems very limited. Attempting any detailed reconstruction of the house and its architecture on the basis of these sources would be problematic and highly speculative.[62] However, models and lanterns depicting tower houses can be considered much more trustworthy sources (table 3.1, figures 3.10 and 3.11).[63] Their iconography provides important data on houses of the Hellenistic and early Roman Periods, sometimes including rare details about the architecture, construction technique, and the aspect of the upper elevation. Many remarkable examples appear in the Cairo Museum,[64] Alexandria Museum, Louvre Museum,[65] British Museum,[66] and UCL Petrie Museum,[67] as well as isolated objects in several German museums.[68] These objects are made of either terracotta or a fine limestone (figures 3.10 and 3.11), and they were all produced and found in Egypt. Because they come from old excavations and lack secure archaeological contexts, the dating of these objects is often vague. Stylistic and technical comparanda suggest two major

Table 3.1. Synthetic descriptive data for a selection of models of tower houses (selection from the catalog in Marouard 2010, vol. 2)

Number	Provenance	Date	Material	Levels (including ground floor)	Mud-bricks	Concave courses	extremity of ceiling joists	Massive base (with no opening)	Facade stairway	Wood entrance door	Stone entrance door	Roof top terrace	construction on roof top	Types of window frames									Collection	Registration number	Bibliography
														T 1	T 2	T 3	T 4	T 5	T 6	T 7	T 8	T 9			
M1	Xoïs	Late Period - early Ptolemaic	Limestone	4+	X	X	X	X	X		X					X			X	X			Egyptian Museum, Cairo	JE 56352	Engelbach 1931, 129-130, Pl. III, fig. 1, 2 ; Marouard 2014, fig. 9
M2	Xoïs	Late Period - early Ptolemaic	Limestone	3+	X		X	X	X		X	?	X			X			X	X	X	X	Egyptian Museum, Cairo	JE 50205	Engelbach 1931, 130, fig. 3 ; Marouard 2014, fig. 9
M3	?	Late Period - early Ptolemaic	Limestone	3+	X	X	X			X		X								X		X	British Museum, London	EA 2462	Garis Davies 1929, fig. 14 ; Pillet 1940, 30, fig. 3 ; Marouard 2014, fig. 8
M4	Tebtynis	Early Ptolemaic	Limestone	2?	X	X	X								X	X			X		X		Onsite magazine, Tebtynis	A 7307	unpublished
M5	?	Late Ptolemaic - early Roman	Terracotta	2	X	X	X			X									X				Greco-Roman Museum, Alexandria	23093	Breccia 1934, 25, Pl. XII/38 ; Nowicka 1969, fig. 86
M6	?	Early Roman	Terracotta	3	X	X	X	X			X	X				X			X				Louvre Museum, Paris	E 11886	Pillet 1940, 29-30, fig. 1, 2 ; Dunand 1990, 333, N° 1009
M8	?	Early Roman	Terracotta	3	X	X	X	X	X		X		X	X					X	X			Berlin, uncertain location	14458	Weber 1914, Pl. 41/467 ; Nowicka 1969, fig. 87
M9	?	Late Ptolemaic - early Roman	Limestone	3						X		X	X	X					X				Louvre Museum, Paris	E 5357	Desroches 1938, Pl. I-II ; Ricke 1966, 121-122
M11	Memphis	Late Period - early Ptolemaic	Limestone	2?	X		X													X	X		Petrie Museum UCL, London	UC 14513	Petrie 1909, Pl. XXXIII

ID	Site	Date	Material		c1	c2	c3	c4	c5	c6	c7	c8	c9	c10	c11	c12	c13	c14	c15	c16	c17	c18	Museum	Inventory	Reference
M13	Memphis	Early Ptolemaic	Limestone	3						X		X		X					X				Petrie Museum UCL, London	UC 33426	Petrie 1910, 44, Pl. XXXVIII/6
M16	Ehnasya	Early Roman	Terracotta	2	X	X	X			?									X				Petrie Museum UCL, London	UC 50613	unpublished
M18	?	Roman	Terracotta	3+	X	X	X	X	X		X	?	X										Petrie Museum UCL, London	UC 50582	unpublished
M19	Naukratis	Late Period - early Ptolemaic	Limestone	2+	X											X							British Museum, London	EA68816	Petrie 1888, 100, Pl. XVIII/1 ; Thomas and Masson 2018, 9, fig. 11
M20	?	Early Ptolemaic	Limestone	3+	X	X	X	X	X		X					X							Louvre Museum, Paris	E 11885	Pillet 1940, 27-28, fig. 1, 6 to 8 Marouard 2012, fig. 2; Marouard 2014, fig. 8
M21	?	Late Ptolemaic - early Roman	Terracotta	4	X	X	X	X	X		X	X		X		X			X			X	Louvre Museum, Paris	E 32572	Marouard 2014, fig. 8
M25	Fayum ?	Early Roman	Terracotta	2	X	X				X				X					X				Egyptian Museum, Cairo British Museum, London	26627-28- 29 EA18324	unpublished
M28	?	Early Roman	Terracotta	2+	X	X	X	X	X		X			X			X			X			Louvre Museum, Paris	E 32571	Marouard 2012, fig. 2 ; Marouard 2014, fig. 8
M30	?	Early Ptolemaic	Limestone	3-				X		X		X	X	X					X				Kestner Museum, Hanover	1935-200-168	Ricke 1966, 120-121, Pl. VII
M33	?	Roman	Terracotta	2+	X	X	X	X	X		X	X	X										Greco-Roman museum, Alexandria	24009	unpublished
19	5 Delta 2 Fayum		10 limestone 9 terracotta	2.8	16	13	14	10	8	6	9	7	6	7	1	7	1	0	12	6	3	3			

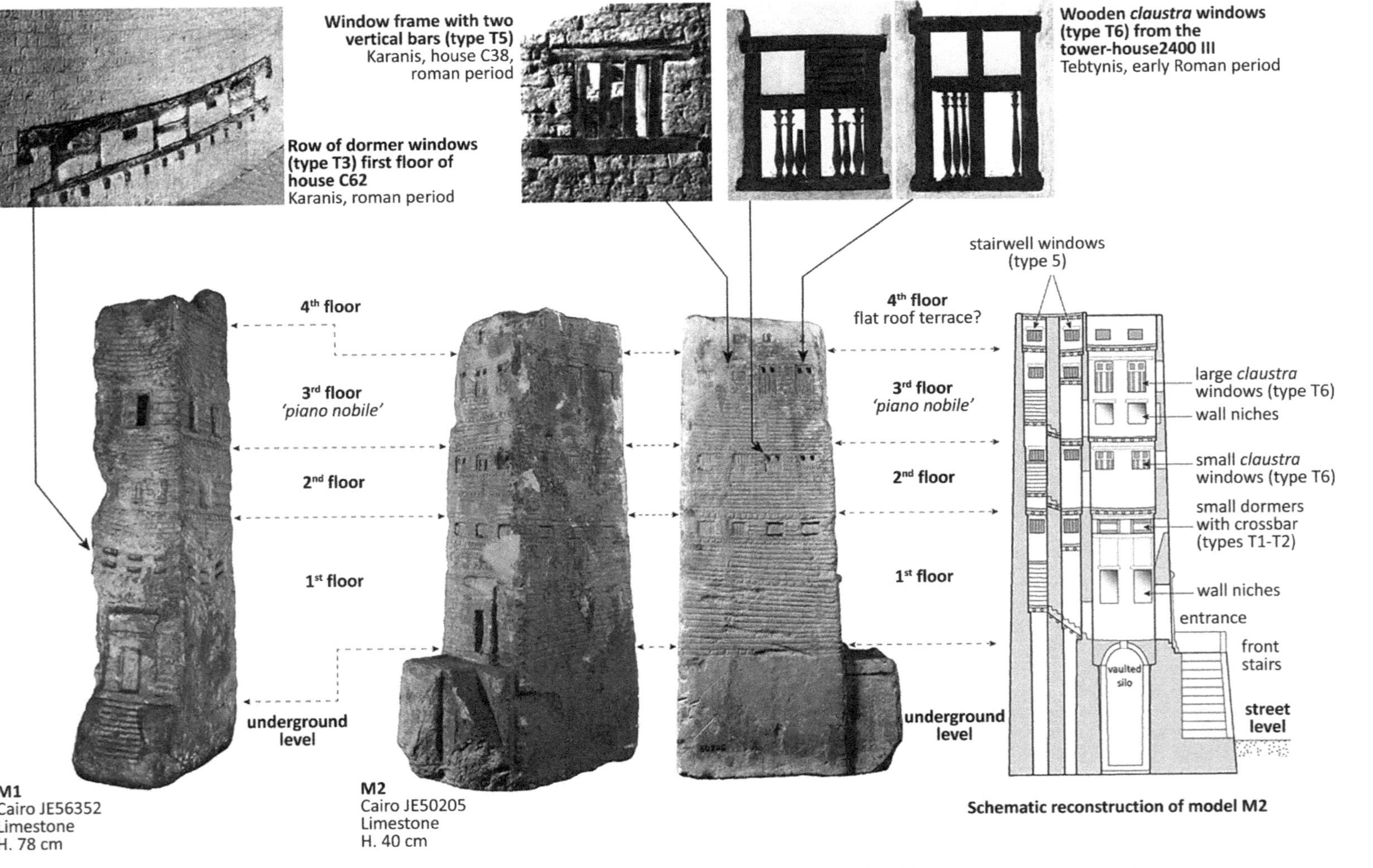

Figure 3.10. Limestone tower house models M1 and M2 from the Egyptian Museum in Cairo, illustrating the different types of windows and a progressive evolution of the openings on the different floors. (Figure by G. Marouard, lower images by the author, upper images after Husselman 1979, Pl. 12a; Husselman 1979, Pl. 61b; Hadji-Minaglou 2007, Photos 124–25.)

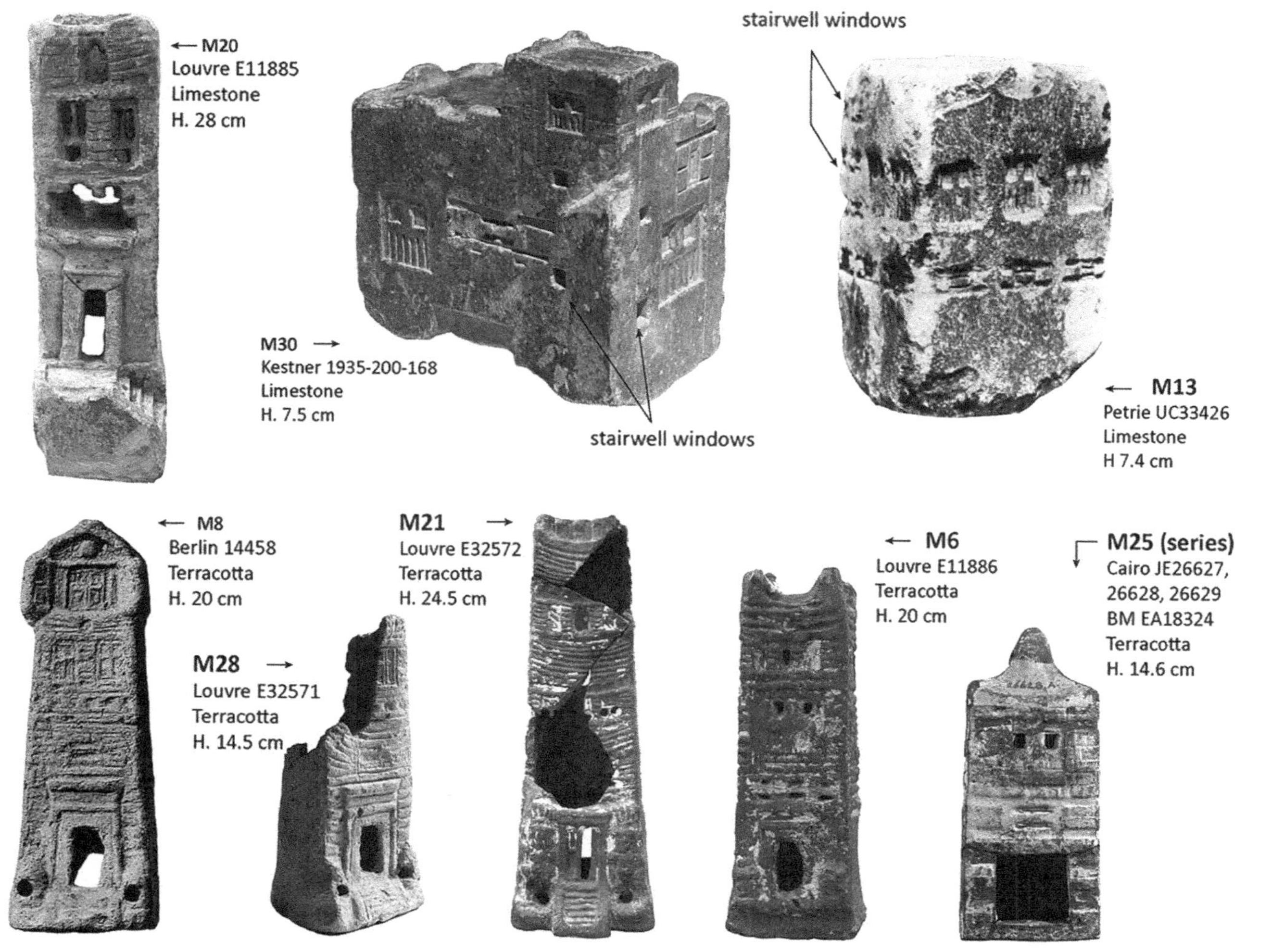

Figure 3.11. Selection of tower house models in limestone or terracotta from the Ptolemaic and early Roman Periods. (Photos by G. Marouard, models M8 after Weber 1914, Pl. 41/467, and M13 after Petrie 1910, Pl. XXXVIII/6.)

chronological phases. Carved limestone models seem to belong to the end of the Late Period and the early Ptolemaic Period, while the terracotta models are attributable to the late Hellenistic and early Roman Periods. These clay models were mass-produced in molds that could have created several dozen to hundreds of individual objects. But as it stands now, only two terracotta mold series have been identified (figure 11, M25 series and M8–M28 series).[69]

Their dominant function, accounting for nearly 60 percent of the examples, was as lanterns or lamp holders. An empty space in the center or at the base would have held a small oil lamp, as evidenced by residual traces of lampblack on the terracotta models or reddened spots on the limestone examples. The internal cavity was accessible from the rear of the model (e.g. M1, M2, M6, M8, M20, M21, M28) or through an opening in the front door on the main face of the object (e.g. M5, M25). Openings at the doors and windows animated the interiors of these representations and, when lit, would have created the impression of human activity. These models were probably not used as a conventional means of lighting. Are they then purely decorative; amuletic objects that protected the house and household; or objects of domestic cult, which we might call "lamp shrines" or "portable altars"?[70] It is premature to assign them any apotropaic function. However, the anachronistic hypothesis that they served as models for architects on house building projects is certainly to be discarded; in this context of vernacular construction, "an architecture without architect," domestic structures were built according to a popular, common knowledge that did not need such support.

Unlike Pharaonic house models, especially the so-called soul houses or the Middle Kingdom wooden models that illustrated recurring activities within the house, the Greco-Roman-era examples are exclusively external, three-dimensional representations of the main façade or all four sides of the house. In their exclusive focus on architectural details, these images likely provide a direct, firsthand testimony and a primary local source for filling the gaps in our archaeological data. Indeed, several models show a relative fidelity to the original mud-brick domestic structures—which certainly surrounded their producers—and many architectural comparisons are possible with the Ptolemaic and Roman houses discovered at several archaeological sites, in particular those from the Fayum. These models are particularly valuable for understanding the vertical development of urban tower houses, enabling us to restore the upper parts of these structures and to question the organization of the summit parts and the upper terraces. They answer problems relating to the facades' elevation, the treatment and organization of openings (either doors or windows), and the "ascending hierarchy" of floor levels.

We can summarize the chief recurring elements of these models as follows:

- The base regularly shows a high foundation level without an opening (e.g. M1, M2, M20, M21).
- Most examples have a square plan, rarely rectangular; only one example shows a L-shaped plan (M13).
- An average of 2.2 upper stories above the ground floor for complete examples.

- A single, axial entrance door, centered on the main façade, with door frames either in wood (often enhanced with red—an apotropaic color—to imitate the material) or stone, often featuring traditional Egyptian architectural features such as a cornice for the door lintel (similar to archaeological examples at Karanis or Narmouthis).[71]
- The entrance door is often elevated with a straight flight of steps positioned perpendicular (e.g. M1, M8, M18, M21, M28, M33) or parallel (e.g. M2, M20) to the main façade.
- When an internal staircase is present, it is positioned at an angle and usually indicated by the presence of very small windows (e.g. M2, M13, M30).
- A construction method with concave courses of mud bricks in the great majority of cases. Alternating courses of bricks can sometimes be identified as headers and stretchers (e.g. M1, M2, M3, M4, M5, M6, M19, M20, M21, M25, M28, M33).
- The ends of the through joists and beams that mark the floor location of the different levels can be often identified (e.g. M1, M2, M3, M6, M19, M20, M25).
- Types of openings, lower dormer windows to high *claustra* windows, are very close to those found in excavation, and the typology of openings on the models matches the typology of excavated examples (figure 3.10).
- More than half the models illustrate windows of T1 to T3 (small dormers with a horizontal crossbar, a very common type at Karanis),[72] always located at the first floor (e.g. M1, M2, M6, M8, M9, M13, M19, M20, M21, M25, M28), just below the ceiling level, indicating its significant height on the walls of the first floor.
- The largest windows—mullion and brace, claustra, or trellis[73]—are invariably situated on the highest levels of the models (e.g. M1, M2, M3, M4, M5, M6, M8, M9, M13, M18, M20, M21, M25, M28, M30, M33).[74]
- The top is flat-roofed or partly occupied by a terrace surrounded by a wall (e.g. M2, M3, M6, M21), sometimes with a small room (M30) that may correspond to the landing level at the top of the staircase, which had to be protected and roofed.

All these models give us valuable indications of what is undoubtedly the essence of the tower house: its vertical development, with functions and destinations that probably changed gradually on the different floors. In contrast to the introverted ground floor, closed and dark with small dormer windows placed high in the walls, are the more open upper floors, much better lit, better ventilated, and less constrained by the opening easements with the surrounding houses.[75] The upper parts of the models also reveal a more generally open top floor, a sort of piano nobile with the largest windows, even ornamental, usually high rectangular windows with claustra or trellis (figure 3.10).

This vertical development can be compared to contemporary domestic examples from Yemen, as in Shabwa.[76] In parallel with the gradual opening of the floors, we may wonder about a possible vertical shift in the function of the Egyptian tower house, the comfort or hierarchy of the spaces, and even a possible social gradation toward the higher levels. Although caution is needed when comparing multistory Egyptian and South Arabian houses, the piano nobile which marks the upper part of the Egyptian tower house models could be equivalent to the main rooms, such as the *mafraj* (floor of the men) or the *diwān* (stateroom and reception room of the head of the family), which always crown the top of the Yemenite tower houses.

Based on the examples available, vertical domestic structures appear in many different settlement types: not only major urban sites such as provincial capitals, but also secondary agglomerations or small agricultural villages in the Delta and Fayum. The original impetus for this phenomenon was likely the urban density and the hydrological determinism that especially affected settlements in Lower Egypt and the Nile Valley. There, the multiplication of upper floors represented a solution to an urban perimeter whose boundaries were naturally restricted, and regularly threatened, by the annual Nile flood. The area of buildable land was not expandable unless it was drained and artificially reclaimed—by polderization of the marshes—from the outskirts of the original, natural limits of the *tell* and *gezira*.

The process of verticalization also rapidly amplified under pressure from an urban population that exploded in some regions over the second half of the first millennium BCE (both from demographic increase and/or the consequences of exceptional floods). This building type then became more geographically widespread with the founding of new settlements—such as on the Fayum fringes—in connection with the agricultural expansion of the early Ptolemaic Period. In these new settlements, the use of traditional tower houses and their distinctive associated urban layout provided an effective response to the necessity (or requirement) to save the maximum of available building space and land. This choice also helped prevent, at least for a while, settlements' encroachment onto surrounding agricultural areas, a problem that could pose a significant threat on the periphery of the oasis, where the maximal extension of cultivable land and agricultural profitability was probably a higher priority than urban expansion.

If the peripheral courtyard often seems to mark the thin line between the household sphere and the outside, the house itself also seems to illustrate—especially according to the evidence of model tower houses—a bipartite opposition between a lower part that was closed, folded back into itself, and more protected from the outside, and an upper part that was much more private and relatively inaccessible, but paradoxically more open to the outside. Therefore, it is likely in the missing upper levels of the Egyptian tower house that we must imagine some of the most comfortable, important, and private living spaces, perhaps differentiated according to position/rank in the family unit or gender.

With more than half or even two-thirds of the house missing, we should not expect archaeological excavation to answer these questions of the functions of the upper floors. They must have housed those functions that we generally do not see in the lower and basement areas, which are dominated by everyday life household activities pertaining to the kitchen, storage, and storerooms, as well as perhaps reception. On the first floor, the small dormer windows placed high in the walls—at the level of the ceiling, a location higher than a man's height—preserved household intimacy, maintained cool daytime temperatures, attenuated external nuisances (noise, prying eyes, heat from the street, smoke from the courtyard), deterred thieves, and prevented for some time at least the consequences of sand accumulation and gradual rise of street levels.[77] Conversely, the higher parts—which were much more open, conveying more daylight and views during the day and more freshness and ventilation at night—were a priori better as sleeping areas and private spaces for social events, meetings, and reception of guests. We may see here a vertical hierarchization, in which the most private spaces occupied the upper parts, the farthest from the ground, whereas on the ground the public-private border remained quite thin. In Greek papyri, multiple references locate the *symposion*, the *andron*, or the bedrooms (*akkubiton*, *koiton*) in the tower or the upper floors of the house, just below the roof terrace or even on the terrace itself.[78] In the Zenon archives, bedrooms also appear as very neat rooms, well-lit with elaborate and painted windows or lattice windows, which the models only locate in the highest parts of the house.[79]

Archaeology suggests that the tower house, a very characteristic type of multistory dwelling, remained the preferred form throughout much of the Hellenistic Period, with significant long-term changes in size but only small variations in plan. However, in the organic urban pattern that resulted from the use of this house type, the house footprint was generally inextensible. If no wide courtyard space existed next to a house, or if that space was insufficient, the only way to expand was to add another floor or to invest in open areas and adjacent streets—an extension into public space that was made possible by a very thin border between the external collective sphere and the internal private domain. Although these houses initially proved well adapted for colonization, as the early Fayum examples suggest, they seem to have become much rarer and then to dramatically disappear after the end of the second century BCE. Replacing them are more modest, although still multistory, houses that gradually lead their neighborhoods into a new organization around insulae. The tower house subsequently appears only in very isolated cases in early Roman urban contexts, in the form of large constructions, perhaps for collective use.

Notes

1 House of Djehutynefer in TT104, various representations in TT23 or TT254, on Nakht papyrus (BM10411), and several fragmentary Amarna-period *talatat* at Karnak (Spence 2004).

2 This terminology is borrowed from the "casemate foundation-platform" buildings regularly described since the 1970s (Spencer 1979; Spencer 1999; Leclère 2008, 645–54; Malecka-Drozd 2014, 76–80).

3 Hartung et al. 2003, 263–66, fig. 1, Pl. 42; Hartung et al. 2007, 160–62, fig. 1, Pl. 20; Hartung et al. 2009, 170–72, fig. 1, 35, Pl. 30.

4 Herbich and Spencer 2006, 16; Spencer 2008, 104–9, fig. 11.1. Another group of houses was recently discovered at Tell el-Iswed (Herbich 2011, 235, fig. 4; Midant-Reynes and Buchez 2014, 30–34, fig. 24).

5 See Thomas (chapter 9, this volume) and current work by the British Museum team available online: https://www.britishmuseum.org/research/online_research_catalogues/ng/naukratis_greeks_in_egypt.aspx

6 Leclère 2008, 645–54.
7 Leclère and Spencer 2014, Pls. 10–14; Spencer 2016; Marouard 2012, fig. 5.
8 Petrie 1888, Pl. XVII; Marouard 2012, fig. 5–3.
9 Adam 1958, Pl. X.
10 Wilson 1982, Pl. II; Marouard 2012, 129, fig. 5–1; Marouard 2014, fig. 5.
11 Redmount and Friedman 1995, 70–76, Figs. 14–16; Morgenstein and Redmount 1998, 133, fig. 2.
12 Edgar 1906, 209, fig. 2; Marouard 2014, fig. 5.
13 Mumford 2002, 19–21; Marouard 2014, fig. 5.
14 Leclère 2008, 211.
15 It seems preferable to privilege the term *cellular foundation*, Marouard 2014, 106n3. A "casemate" designation should not be used for civil installations, as it derives from the technical vocabulary of military architecture and from the erroneous interpretation as fortresses of the large cellular constructions excavated within several sanctuaries in the Delta at Tanis, Naukratis, Tell Dafana, and Tell el-Balamun: Leclère 2008, 630–40.
16 Marouard 2014, 106–8, fig. 2.
17 Ballet et al. 2011, 80–82; Marouard 2014, 113–16, fig. 6.
18 Marchi 2014, 85–104.
19 Lehmann 2012, 29–31; Lehmann 2014, 57–68; Marouard 2014, 121, fig. 11.
20 Marouard 2012, 130–31, fig. 6.
21 Piacentini 1995, 11–23, fig. 1–15; Davoli 1996, 41–49, 54–58, figs. 1, 2, 32–54 (Houses VIII and XXV).
22 Boak 1935, 17–18, 19–20, Pl. XII/fig. 23, Plans X, XIII, XIV (Houses IV-401 et IV-402).
23 Husselman 1979, 10, 13, 22, 33, 40, Maps 5, 8 (Houses E102 et D313).
24 Hadji-Minaglou 2007, 168–70, Figs. 78–80; Hadji-Minaglou 2014; Marouard 2012, 128, fig. 3; Marouard 2014, 115, 116, 123, fig. 11–4.
25 Marouard 2012, 131–32; Marouard 2014, 116.
26 See the archaeological reevaluation proposed in Marouard 2017.
27 Flossmann-Schütze 2013, 4–11; Flossmann-Schütze 2014, 9–31; Fassbinder, Khüne and Flossmann 2015; Flossmann 2020.
28 Flossmann-Schütze 2014, 14.
29 Lauffray 1995, 311–13, 321–26, fig. 6–8, 18 (House A and house D, ca. mid-second century BCE)
30 Hölscher 1934, Pl. 9–10; Marouard 2014, 116, fig. 7.
31 Bruyère et al. 1937, 5–11, 87–92, fig. 4–9, 40, Plan IV; Michalowski et al. 1950, 114, 152–54, Plans IV–V; Marouard 2012, 125, figs. 1–12/13; Marouard 2014, 116, fig. 7.
32 Dreyer et al. 2008, 78–86, fig. 4–6 (House K19, ca. late third century BCE to Ptolemy VI-VII). For observations on tower houses at Elephantine, Arnold 2003, 172–75.
33 Husson 1983, 248–52, 257–67. According to Husson, the term *pyrgos* as used for a tower house—if this term really describes a domestic construction on a regular basis, and not only a high and narrow tower with various possible functions in addition to a domestic one—has to be differentiated from the house with a tower (or two) and from the multistory house with two or maybe three levels.
34 Marchi 2014.
35 Flossmann-Schütze 2014, 16; Hadji-Minaglou 2014, 50, table 1.
36 E.g., house 7500 at Tebtynis, whose walls are 1.80 meters thick at the foundation level and 1.40 meters thick at the ground floor, Hadji-Minaglou 2014, 48.
37 Arnold 2003, 166–68, Table 11; Hadji-Minaglou 2014, 38.
38 Boak 1935, 18, Pl. XII/fig. 23, Plans X, XIII, XIV.
39 Marouard 2010, 350–61; Marouard 2012, 125, 127; Marouard 2014, 117, 119; Flossmann-Schütze 2014, 18.
40 Flossmann-Schütze 2014, 14; Fassbinder, Kühne and Flossmann 2015, 279, fig. 2. At Tuna el-Gebel, all entrances are located on the south or the east side of the houses, avoiding the prevailing winds from north and west.
41 E.g., house B-1100 at Tebtynis: Hadji-Minaglou 2014, 44.

42 Axiality of the entrance space is a characteristic of the Hellenistic-period houses at Tebtynis: Hadji-Minaglou 2014, 50.
43 For parallels and ethnographic comparisons, see examples of tower houses from Yemen: Darles 1998; Breton 1998a; Breton 1998b.
44 Marouard 2010, 361–63, Figs. III-25–III-27. Data collected before 2010 indicated 85 percent but excavations conducted since that date take this estimate to at least 95 percent.
45 Hadji-Minaglou 2007, 170, Figs. 78 and 79.
46 Boak 1935, 10–13, Figs. 2–3, 8–12, Plans III, IV, V, XI.
47 Hadji-Minaglou 2007, 139–47, 179–82, Figs. 66–68; Hadji-Minaglou 2014, 36–40, fig. 2–9. Compared to the Ptolemaic tower houses, these larger Roman examples could correspond to the *pyrgos* from contemporary Greek papyri: seemingly a habitable urban tower, if indeed a purely domestic function can be attributed to this term (Nowicka 1970, 53–61; Husson 1983, 248–51; Hadji-Minaglou 2007, 182; Hadji-Minaglou 2014, 35).
48 Husson 1983, 263, 265, 271–75. About *synoikia*, Husson mentions a "rental house divided into several apartments."
49 Fassbinder, Kühne and Flossmann 2015, 279, fig. 2.
50 See further Davoli (chapter 1) and Simpson (chapter 2).
51 Hadji-Minaglou 2007, 95, 99, 104, 170, Figs. 46, 47, 81, 82; Marouard 2014, 124. On encroachment and interaction between the house/courtyard/private sphere and public realm, see Marouard 2008, 125–26, fig. 4.
52 Marouard 2014, 123–24, fig. 12.
53 See also Davoli (chapter 1) and Simpson (chapter 2). We have no information about the solutions and the location (inside the house or on the rooftop terrace?) that these households used for performing daily domestic activities before the late addition of a domestic courtyard.
54 Marouard 2012, 129, fig. 4; Marouard 2014, 106–8, 121, fig. 2.
55 Spencer 2016.
56 Leclère and Spencer 2014, Pls. 10 and 12.
57 Marouard 2012, fig. 5/1.
58 Flossmann-Schütze 2014, 14, Figs. 9–10.
59 See in particular the evolution of the area east of Soknebtynis Temple: Hadji-Minaglou 2007, Figs. 78–79.
60 Marouard 2012, 129–31, fig. 6; Marouard 2014, 116, fig. 7.
61 For a study of the Nile mosaic of Palestrina at Praeneste, see Meyboom 1994. For comprehensive studies on Nilotic scenes, see Versluys 2002 and Barrett 2019.
62 See e.g. Nowicka 1969, 17–20; Lehmann 2021, 6.
63 This chapter presents only a selection of nineteen of the most interesting pieces from my unpublished dissertation: Marouard 2010, Vol.2, Annexe 2, 2–44.
64 Engelbach 1931, 129–30, Pl. III; Marouard 2014, fig. 9.
65 Dunand 1990, 333, #1009; Pillet 1940, 27–30; Marouard 2014, fig. 8. Since 2020, the four models from the Louvre Museum discussed in this paper are available in the online catalogue:
M6 = E11886 (terracotta, https://collections.louvre.fr/en/ark:/53355/cl010007912),
M20 = E11885 (limestone, https://collections.louvre.fr/en/ark:/53355/cl010007911),
M21 = E32572 (terracotta, https://collections.louvre.fr/en/ark:/53355/cl010036099).
66 M28 = E32571 (terracotta, https://collections.louvre.fr/en/ark:/53355/cl010036098).
Limestone models M3 = EA2462 (https://www.britishmuseum.org/collection/image/505780001) and M19 = EA 68816 (fragmented, from Naukratis, https://www.britishmuseum.org/collection/image/1329992001).
67 Several house models made of limestone, M11 = UC14513 (https://collections.ucl.ac.uk/Details/collect/20069) and M13 = UC33426, or made of terracotta, M16 = UC50613 (https://collections.ucl.ac.uk/Details/petrie/56218) and M18 = UC50582 (https://www.ucl.ac.uk/museums-static/digitalegypt/house/roman.html).
68 Weber 1914, 255, Pl. 41/467; Ricke 1966, 119–23, Pl. VII; Marouard 2014, fig. 10; Fischer 1994, 433, Pl. 125, # 1187.
69 M25 models have been identified in Cairo (JE 26627, 26628, 26629), Alexandria (registration number unknown) and at the British Museum (EA18324). Model M8 from Berlin

(14458) and M28 from the Louvre Museum (E32571, fragmented, not in exhibit) form another series.
70 Thomas and Masson 2018, 10–11, fig. 12.
71 Husselman 1979, Pl. 37b, Plan 8.
72 T1, T2 and T3 from windows typology in Marouard 2010, 256–64, Figs. II-191–II-201.
73 T6, T7 and T9 from windows typology in Marouard 2010, 267–75, Figs. II-214–II-227.
74 Hadji-Minaglou 2007, 145, Photos 122–28, illustrate the only archaeological examples of such *claustra* windows found in the cellar B' of early Roman tower house 2400-III at Tebtynis
75 Marouard 2008, 123; Marouard 2012, 128; Marouard 2014, 124–25.
76 Darles 1998, 20–21, n. 38; Breton 1998a, 67–68, 71.
77 On sand and other environmental considerations, see further Davoli (chapter 1).
78 Husson 1983, 36–37, 151–54, 268.
79 Husson 1983, 153 (PSI 547, 9–21; P. Cairo. Zen. 59847, 48–54; P. Mich. Zen. 38, 18).

Works Cited

Adam, S. 1958. "Recent Discoveries in the Eastern Delta (Dec. 1950–May 1955)." *Annales du Service des Antiquites de l'Egypt* 55: 301–24.

Arnold, F. 2003. *Elephantine XXX: Die Nachnutzung des Chnumtempelbezirks*. Archäologische Veröffentlichungen 116. Mainz am Rhein: Verlag Philipp von Zabern.

Ballet, P., G. Lecuyot, G. Marouard, M. Pithon, and B. Redon. 2011. "Et la Bouto tardive?" *Bulletin de l'Institut Français d'Archéologie Orientale* 111: 75–100.

Barrett, C.E. 2019. *Domesticating Empire: Egyptian Landscapes in Pompeian Gardens*. Oxford: Oxford University Press.

Boak, A.E.R. 1935. *Soknopaiou Nesos: The University of Michigan Excavations at Dime in 1931–1932*. University of Michigan Studies Humanistic Series XXXIX. Ann Arbor: University of Michigan Press.

Breccia, E. 1933. "Fouilles d'Oxyrhynchos." *Le musée gréco-romain d'Alexandrie Volume II* 1931–1932: 36–47.

Breton, J.-F. 1998a. "L'habitat à Shabwa: originalité et traditions régionales." In *Fouilles de Shabwa III, Architecture et techniques de construction*, edited by J.-F. Breton, 467–73. Bibliothèque archéologique et historique 154. Beirut: Institut français d'archéologie du Proche-Orient.

Breton, J.-F. 1998b. "Les établissements antiques." In *Une vallée aride du Yémen antique. Le wâdî Bayhân*, edited by J.-F. Breton, J.-C. Arramond, B. Coque-Delhuille and P. Gentelle., 127–94. Paris: Recherche sur les civilisations.

Bruyère, B., J. Manteuffel, K. Michalowski, and J. Ste Fare Garnot. 1937. *Fouilles Franco-Polonaises Rapport I, Fouilles Franco-Polonaises de Tell Edfou* I. Caire: Institut Français d'Archéologie Orientale.

Busch-Sperveslage, A. 1999. "Hausmodelle im ptolemäisch-römischen Ägypten." In *Architektur, Struktur, Symbol: Streifzüge durch die Architekturgeschichte von der Antike bis zur Gegenwart*, edited by M. Kozok, 11–26. Festschrift für Cord Meckseper zum 65. Petersberg: Imhof.

Darles, C. 1998. "Étude typologique de l'architecture civile intra-muros." In *Fouilles de Shabwa III, Architecture et techniques de construction*, edited by J.-F. Breton, 3–25. Bibliothèque archéologique et historique 154. Beirut: Institut français d'archéologie du Proche-Orient.

Davoli, P. 1996. "Lo scavo 1995." In *Bakchias III. Rapporto preliminare della campagna de scavo del 1995*, edited by S. Pernigotti and M. Capasso, 9–78. Pisa: Giardini.

De Garis Davies, N. 1929. "The Town House in Ancient Egypt." *Metropolitan Museum Studies* 1 (2): 233–55.

Desroches-Noblecourt, Chr. 1938. "Un modèle de maison citadine du Nouvel Empire (Musée du Louvre: n° E. 5357)." *Revue d'Égyptologie* 3: 17–25.

Dreyer, G., F. Arnold, J. Budka, D. Franke, F. Hoffmann, D. Keller, P. Kopp, S. Lippert, B. von Pilgrim, C. von Pilgrim, and D. Raue. 2008. "Stadt und Tempel von Elephantine 33/34/35. Grabungsbericht." *Mitteilungen des Deutschen Archaologischen Instituts Abteilung Kairo* 64: 63–151.

Dunand, F. 1990. *Catalogue des terres cuites gréco-romaines d'Égypte, Musée du Louvre, département des Antiquités Égyptiennes*. Paris: Réunion des Musées nationaux.

Edgar, M. 1906. "Report on an Excavation at Toukh el-Qaramous." *Annales du Service des antiquités de l'Égypte* 7: 205–12.

Engelbach, R. 1931. "Recent Acquisitions in the Cairo Museum." *Annales du Service des antiquités de l'Égypte* 31: 126–31.

Fassbinder, J.W.E., L. Kühne, and M. Flossmann. 2015. "The Hellenistic Settlement of Tuna el-Gebel, Egypt." *Archaeologia Polona* 53: 276–80.

Fischer, J. 1994. *Griechisch-romische Terrakotten aus Ägypten. Die Sammlungen Sieglin und Schreiber, Dresden-Leipzig-Stuttgart-Tübingen*. Berlin: Wasmuth & Zohlen.

Flossmann-Schütze, M. 2013. "Manhattan in der Wüste, Tierkult und Towerhäuser in Tuna el-Gebel." *aMun* 46: 4–11.

Flossmann-Schütze, M. 2014. "Les maisons-tours de l'association religieuse de Touna el-Gebel." In *Les maisons-tours en Égypte durant la Basse Époque, les périodes ptolémaïque et romaine* (Actes de la table ronde de Paris-Sorbonne, 29–30 Nov. 2012), edited by S. Marchi, 9–31. NeHet 2. Paris: Revue Numérique d'Égyptologie.

Flossmann-Schütze, M. 2020. "Die Siedlung am Ibiotapheion: Untersuchungen zur Lebenswelt einer Kultgemeinschaft im griechisch-römischen Tuna el-Gebel." In *Tuna el-Gebel—eine ferne Welt: Tagungsband zur Konferenz der Graduade School "Distant Worlds" vom 16. bis 19.1.2014 in München*, edited by M. Flossmann-Schütze, F. Hoffmann, and A. Schütze, 189–208. Vaterstetten: Patrick Brose.

Goyon, J.-C., J.-C. Golvin, C. Simon-Boidot, and G. Martinet. 2004. *La construction Pharaonique du Moyen Empire à l'époque gréco-romaine: Contexte et principes technologiques*. Paris: Picard.

Hadji-Minaglou, G. 2007. *Tebtynis IV. Les habitations à l'est du temple de Soknebtynis*. Fouilles de l'Institut français d'archéologie orientale du Caire 56. Cairo: Institut français d'archéologie orientale.

Hadji-Minaglou, G. 2014. "Les maisons-tours de Tebtynis." In *Les maisons-tours en Égypte durant la Basse Époque, les périodes ptolémaïque et romaine* (Actes de la table ronde de Paris-Sorbonne, 29–30 Nov. 2012), edited by S. Marchi, 33–56. NeHet 2. Paris: Revue Numérique d'Égyptologie.

Hartung, U., P. Ballet, F. Béguin, J. Bourriau, P. French, T. Herbich, P. Kopp, G. Lecuyot, and A. Schimtt. 2003. "Tell el-Fara'in—Buto 8. Vorbericht." *Mitteilungen des Deutschen Archaologischen Instituts Abteilung Kairo* 59: 199–267.

Hartung, U., P. Ballet, F. Béguin, J. Bourriau, D. Dixneuf, A. Von den Driesch, P. French, R. Hartmann, T. Herbich, C. Kitagawa, P. Kopp, G. Lecuyot, M.-D. Nenna, A. Schimtt, G. Cankardeş-Şenol, and A. Şenol. 2007. "Tell el-Fara'in—Buto 9. Vorbericht." *Mitteilungen des Deutschen Archaologischen Instituts Abteilung Kairo* 63: 69–165.

Hartung, U., P. Ballet, A. Effland, P. French, R. Hartmann, T. Herbich, H. Hoffmann, E. Hower-Tilmann, C. Kitagawa, P. Kopp, W. Kreibig, G. Lecuyot, S. Lösch, G. Marouard, A. Ner-Kopp, M. Pithon, and A. Zink. 2009. "Tell el-Fara'in—Buto 10. Vorbericht." *Mitteilungen des Deutschen Archaologischen Instituts Abteilung Kairo* 65: 83–190.

Herbich, T. 2011. "Geophysical Surveying in Egypt: Periodic Report for 2009–2011." In *Archaeological Prospection: 9th International Conference on Archaeological Prospection (Izmir September 19–24)*, edited by M.G. Drahor and M.A. Berge, 234–39. Istanbul: Archaeology and Art Publications.

Herbich, T. and A.J. Spencer. 2006. "Geophysical Survey at Tell el-Balamun." *Egyptian Archaeology* 29: 16–19.

Hölscher, U. 1934. *The Excavation of Medinet Habu*. Vol. 1. *General Plans and Views*. Oriental Institute Publications 21. Chicago: University of Chicago Press.

Husselman, E. 1979. *Karanis. Excavations of the University of Michigan in Egypt 1928–1935, Topography and Architecture, Kelsey Museum of Archaeology Studies* 5. Ann Arbor, MI: Bell & Howell Information & Lea.

Husson, G. 1983. *Oikia, le vocabulaire de la maison privée en Egypte d'après les papyrus grecs, Université Paris IV—Sorbonne Série papyrologie* 2. Paris: Publication de la Sorbonne.

Lauffray, J. 1995. "Maisons et ostraca ptolémaïques à l'Est du Lac Sacré." *Cahier de Karnak* X: 301–41.

Leclère, F. 2008. *Les villes de Basse Égypte au 1er millénaire av. J.-C., BdE* 144. Cairo: Institut français d'archéologie orientale.

Leclère, F. and A.J. Spencer. 2014. *Tell Dafana Reconsidered: The Archaeology of an Egyptian Frontier Town*. London: The British Museum.

Lehmann, M. 2012. "The City of Avaris after the New Kingdom." *Egyptian Archaeology* 40: 29–31.

Lehmann, M. 2014. "Tower Houses in Tell el-Dab'a. The Late and Ptolemaic Period." In *Les maisons-tours en Égypte durant la Basse Époque, les périodes ptolémaïque et romaine* (Actes de la table ronde de Paris-Sorbonne, 29–30 Nov. 2012), edited by S. Marchi, 57–68. NeHet 2. Paris: Revue Numérique d'Égyptologie.

Lehmann, M. 2021. "Tower Houses." In *UCLA Encyclopedia of Egyptology*, edited by W. Wendrich. Los Angeles: University of California, Los Angeles, Department of Near Eastern Languages and Cultures. https://escholarship.org/content/qt6c57f675/qt6c57f675.pdf?t=qxvbxq.

Lewis, N. 1933. "*'Η Πρώτη Στέγη* in Houses of Several stories." *Classical Weekly* 26: 171–72.

Malecka-Drozd, N. 2014. "The Emergence and Development of Architecture on Casemate Foundation Platforms in the Nile Delta." *Recherches Archeologiques* 4: 69–96.

Marchi, S. 2014. "Les maisons-tours et édifices sur soubassement à caissons de Tell el-Herr." In *Les maisons-tours en Égypte durant la Basse Époque, les périodes ptolémaïque et romaine* (Actes de la table ronde de Paris-Sorbonne, 29–30 Nov. 2012), edited by S. Marchi, 85–104. NeHet 2. Paris: Revue Numérique d'Égyptologie.

Marouard, G. 2008. "Rues et habitats dans les villes et villages de la chôra égyptienne à la période gréco-romaine (IIIe S. av.—IVe S. apr. J.-C.): quelques exemples du Fayoum." In *La rue dans l'antiquité. Définition, aménagement devenir (Actes du colloque de Poitiers, 2006)*, edited by P. Ballet, N. Dieudonné-Glad and C. Saliou, 117–28. Rennes: Press Universitaire de Rennes.

Marouard, G. 2010. "Archéologie, architecture et images de la maison urbaine d'époque hellénistique et romaine dans la chôra égyptienne." PhD diss., University of Poitiers.

Marouard, G. 2012. "Les quartiers d'habitat dans les fondations et refondations lagides de la *chôra* égyptienne. Une révision archéologique." In *Grecs et romains d'Egypte. Territoires, espaces de la vie et de la mort, objets de prestiges et du quotidien (colloque SFAC, Paris, 2008)*, edited by P. Ballet, 121–40. Bibliothèque d'étude 157. Cairo: Institut français d'archéologie orientale.

Marouard, G. 2014. "Maisons-tours et organisation des quartiers domestiques dans les agglomérations du Delta: l'exemple de Bouto de la Basse Époque aux premiers Lagides." In *Les maisons-tours en Égypte durant la Basse Époque, les périodes ptolémaïque et romaine* (Actes de la table ronde de Paris-Sorbonne, 29–30 Nov. 2012), edited by S. Marchi, 105–33. NeHet 2. Paris: Revue Numérique d'Égyptologie.

Marouard, G. 2017. "Completamente distrutte: Réévaluation archéologique de Philadelphie du Fayoum, Égypte." In *Essays for the Library of Seshat: Studies Presented to Janet H. Johnson on the Occasion of her 70th Birthday*, edited by R.K. Ritner, 121–54. Studies in Ancient Oriental Civilization 70. Chicago: Oriental Institute of the University of Chicago

Meyboom, P.G.P. 1994. *The Nile Mosaic of Palestrina. Early Evidence of Egyptian Religion in Italy*. Religions in the Graeco-Roman World 121. Leiden: Brill.

Michalowski, K., C. Desroches, J., De Linage, and J. Manteuffel. 1950. *Tell Edfou 1939, Fouilles Franco-Polonaises de Tell Edfou* III. Le Caire: Institut français d'archéologie orientale.

Midant-Reynes, B., N. Buchez, A. Baher, G. Bréand, F. Briois, J. Cavero, A.-S. Coupey, M. De Dapper, N. Delhopital, R. el Hajaoui, A. Emery-Barbier, B. Fabry, S. Guérin, F. Guyot, C. Hochstrasser-Petit, J. Lesur, S. Marchand, M. Minotti, M. Ownby, I. Regulski, J. Robitaille, L. Torchy, Y. Tristant, F. Vinolas, and M. Wuttmann. 2014. *Tell el-Iswid: 2006–2009*. Fouilles de l'Institut français d'archéologie orientale du Caire 73. Cairo: Institut français d'archéologie orientale.

Morgenstein, M., and C. Redmount. 1998. "Mudbrick Typology, Sources, and Sedimentological Composition: A Case Study from Tell el-Muqdam, Egyptian Delta." *Journal of the American Research Center in Egypt* 35: 131–33.

Mumford, G. 2002. "Reconstructing the Ancient Settlement at Tell Tebilla." *Bulletin of the American Research Center in Egypt* 182: 18–23.

Nowicka, M. 1969. *La maison privée dans l'Égypte ptolémaïque*. Académie Polonaise des Sciences Bibliotheca Antiqua 9. Wrocław: Zakład Narodowy im. Ossolińskich.

Nowicka, M. 1970. "À propos des tours—πυργοι dans les papyrus grecs." *Archeologia* 21: 53–62.

Petrie, W.M.F. 1888. *Tanis. Part II: Nebesheh (Am)and Defenneh (Tahpanhes)*. Egypt Exploration Society Excavation Memoirs 4. London: Trubner & Co.

Petrie, W.M.F. 1909. *Memphis I*. British School of Archaeology in Egypt and the Egyptian Research Account 15. London: School of Archaeology in Egypt.

Petrie, W.M.F. 1910. *Meydum and Memphis III*. British School of Archaeology in Egypt and the Egyptian Research Account 18. London: School of Archaeology in Egypt.

Piacentini, P. 1995. "Lo scavo 1994." In *Bakchias II. Rapporto preliminare della campagna de scavo del 1994*, edited by S. Pernigotti and M. Capasso, 11–27. Pise: Giardini.

Pillet, M. 1940. "Des verrous égyptiens modèles de maisons." *Revue d'Egyptologie* 4: 27–43.

Redford, D. 1994. *The Akhenaten Temple Project*. Vol. 3. *The Excavation of Kom el-Ahmar and Environs*. Toronto: Akhenaten Temple Project.

Redmount, A., and R. Friedman. 1997. "Tales of a Delta Site: The 1995 Field Season at Tell el-Muqdam." *Journal of the American Research Center in Egypt* 34: 57–83.

Ricke, H. 1966. "Ein Hausmodell im Kestnermuseum zu Hannover." *Zeitschrift für Ägyptische Sprache und Altertumskunde* 93: 119–23.

Rondot, V. 2004. *Tebtynis II. Le temple de Soknebtynis et son dromos, Fouilles Franco-Italiennes* II. Cairo: Institut français d'archéologie orientale.

Spence, K. 2004. "The Three-Dimensional Form of the Amarna House." *Journal of Egyptian Archaeology* 90: 123–52.

Spencer, A.J. 1979. "The Brick Foundations of Late Period Peripteral Temples and Their Mythological Origins." In *Orbis Aegyptiorum Speculum. Glimpses of Ancient Egypt: Studies in honor of H. W. Fairman* (Festschrift Fairman), edited by J. Ruffle, G.A. Gaballa, and K. Kitchen, 132–37. Warminster: Aris & Philipps.

Spencer, A.J. 1999. "Casemate Foundations Once Again." In *Studies on Ancient Egypt in Honour of H. S. Smith*, edited by A. Leahy and J. Tait, 295–300. Egypt Exploration Society Occasional Publications 13. London: The Egypt Exploration Society.

Spencer, A.J. 2008. *Excavations at Tell Balamun 2003–2008*. British Museum online report. http://www.britishmuseum.org/research/research_projects/excavation_in_egypt/reports_in_detail.aspx.

Spencer, A.J. 2016. "Tell Balamun: Outside the Temple Enclosure." Unpublished, available online. https://www.academia.edu/38092394/Tell_el-Balamun_outside_the_temple_enclosure.

Thomas, R., and A. Masson. 2018. "Altars, Sundials, Minor Architectural Objects and Models." In *Naukratis: Greeks in Egypt*, edited by A. Villing, M. Bergeron, G. Bourogiannis, A. Johnston, F. Leclère, A. Masson, and R. Thomas. The British Museum online website. https://www.britishmuseum.org/pdf/Thomas_and_Masson_Altars_sundials_models_architecture.pdf.

Versluys, M.J. 2002. *Aegyptiaca Romana. Nilotic Scenes and the Roman Views of Egypt*. Religions in the Graeco-Roman World 144. Leiden: Brill.

Viereck, P., and F. Zucker. 1926. *Papyri, Ostraka und Wachstafelen aus Philadelphia im Fayum*. Ägyptische Urkunden aus den königlichen Museen zu Berlin, Griechischen Urkunden 7. Berlin: Weidmannsche Buchhandlung.

Viereck, P. 1928. *Philadelpheia, Die Gründung einer Hellenistischen Militärkolonie in Ägypten*. Morgenland Beihefte zum Alten Orient 16. Leipzig: J.C. Hinrichs'sche Buchhandlung.

Weber, W. 1914. *Die ägyptisch-griechischen Terrakotten*. Berlin: Curtius.

Wilson, K. 1982. *Cities of the Delta Part II: Mendes. Preliminary Report on the 1979 and 1980 Seasons*. American Research Center in Egyptian Reports 5. Malibu, CA: Undena.

PART II

Households in Social Context

Families, Individuals, and Communities

4

The Papyrus Trail

Houses and Households in Ptolemaic and Roman Egypt

DOROTHY J. THOMPSON

This chapter aims to assess the contribution of the documentary record to our understanding of houses and households in Ptolemaic and Roman Egypt. Exploring different forms of text, I will focus on what these tell us about definitions, household size and makeup, and the relationship of households to houses.

I shall suggest that in the Ptolemaic Period, household size and composition reflect differences in society that correlate with the ethnic divide found also in the nomenclature (Egyptian or Greek) of the householders named in our texts. And although the broader question of what was involved in being Greek or Egyptian at this date is outside the main scope of this investigation,[1] the material considered here clearly demonstrates how, in a land then ruled by an immigrant dynasty from Macedon (the Ptolemies), Greek nomenclature tended to go along with economic and social privilege. Greeks are shown, on the whole, to have had larger households, often including enslaved and other dependent workers. Egyptians, in contrast, lived in smaller households, and the jobs they held were traditional ones. In both groups, marriage was regularly virilocal, where the wife moves into her husband's home; just occasionally, uxorilocal examples can be found. Marriage, however, was rarely important in household formation. In both Ptolemaic and Roman Egypt conjugal households predominated; other households of different degrees of complexity are of course also documented. Such generalizations are only possible when individuals are suppressed in favor of numbers and the problematic of defining any ethnic identity is ignored.[2] In some cases, however, I shall attempt in what follows to reintroduce the individual aspect.

Most of my material is from the early Ptolemaic Period, but at the end of the chapter I briefly discuss the nature of change in the Roman Period, when texts deriving from a broader time period and geographical cover suggest an increase in the size of both households and houses that coincides with an overall increase in population figures. Despite these and other differences, when the data are considered as a whole, the picture provided by the papyri is of family and household structures similar to what earlier demographers have termed a Mediterranean pattern.[3] Throughout my investigation, I am concerned to explore the relationship of what we know from texts to the material record, since it is only through the integration of archaeology and texts that we can even begin to understand the experience of daily life at the time.[4]

Right at the start, however, it is important to stress how hard it is, even when all available evidence is taken into account, to reach any general conclusions. Variety, in both time and place, is the most striking feature that obtrudes, with differences too according to the background and identity of those whose households and houses are recorded. The carefully planned houses of the new Egyptian capital of Alexandria (founded in 331 BCE) and the mud-brick structures of traditional Egyptian villages up along the Nile were very different both in their architecture and in how they functioned. And although certain features may be identified in particular places and circumstances, in making generalizations on this subject, we have always to recognize the particularities of location and period. Nevertheless, in the hope of reaching some general conclusions, I aim to introduce documentary material to set beside the evidence from archaeology.

We may start with the written evidence itself. Below is an extract from one of the more unusual sources to survive from the dry sands of Egypt—a papyrus record of potential mummies that formed part of the property passed down through at least eleven generations of a family of mortuary priests from Memphis.[5] In Egypt it was important to preserve all relevant records and, as with other such collections of family papers, it is possible to reconstitute much of this particular archive, now scattered among at least ten different museums, by the identification of individuals named in these texts and through consideration of acquisition inventories in what papyrologists call "museum archaeology."[6] In putting records together again, we gain a sense of changes over time in the houses and other property belonging to the family. Assets moved, contracted, or grew as family members divided property among their offspring, either during life or on death, and through marriage reconstituted elements earlier scattered through partition. We thus gain a sense of change in the life cycle of both family members and the different elements of the property they owned.[7] This extract comes from a long contract written in demotic Egyptian and dated May/June 197 BCE.[8] It records a division of property made between a certain Imouthes, a mortuary priest from the sixth generation of the family, and Smithis, his half-sister on their mother's side, in which they recognized each other's rights over various of their extensive family assets.[9] Here Imouthes recognizes Smithis's share of property, which is listed house by house—dwellings, that is, together with their inhabitants over whom, as potential mummies, the family held exclusive rights after their death:

> Your part of the house of Tegesa, the workshop . . .
> and equally that of Har[. . .] his brother,
> and your part of the house of the goldsmith *Pꜣ-ỉbrn*
> and equally that of Peteimouthes his brother,

and your part of the house of Paouteres his brother,
and your part of the house of the shepherd Horos,
and your part of the house of Samous with the same profession,
and your part of the house of the resin-seller Teos son of . . .
and your part of the house of Teos-the-Syrian with the same profession,
. . . (another fifty-five entries) . . .
and your part of the house of Harimouthes son of Kelbi (?) of the Settlement of the Crocodile Tail,
and your part of the house of Pasis son of Harchebis of the same settlement,
and your part of their husbands, their wives, their children, their brothers, their parents-in-law, their nurses, their domestic servants (*šms.w*), their slaves (*ḫl.w*), their servants (*bꜣk.w*)

The final portmanteau listing of husbands, wives, children, brothers, parents-in-law, nurses, domestic servants, slaves, and other dependent servants illustrates a generalized rather than any actual household. It is striking, nonetheless, how the full complement of household members mattered as much after death as it did in life. For a mortuary priest, as for a tax collector, households of potential mummies were as important an asset as were the houses in which a household lived.

It is clear from this and many other documents written in both Greek and demotic Egyptian that in Greco-Roman Egypt, records were kept of both houses and households. Such records might, like this one, be private, but there were also similar and still more detailed records preserved by those at different levels of the administration, concerned to collect taxes on property and on those who lived there. Such papyrus texts have been preserved in various ways. Those in collections of family papers, like that just quoted, are likely to have been preserved and found together, in a jar, box, or alcove; more often, texts have been dispersed through the antiquities trade.[10] Some groups of papyri have been excavated intact, but far more, illegally excavated, survive only in part. Many from the Roman Period derive from ancient rubbish dumps—those from Oxyrhynchus are particularly memorable—or from excavated sites of habitation. For the Ptolemaic Period, in contrast, cartonnage is the source of many of our texts.[11] Cartonnage is the papier mâché material used to make mummy casing; discarded texts were mixed with lime and recycled for this purpose. Other papyri were wrapped round sacred animals in the process of mummification, as with the late second century BCE land surveys from the sacred crocodiles at Tebtynis in the South Fayum (see the map of Egypt, front matter, this volume), but most such Ptolemaic documents, like most cartonnage, derive from human mummy casing. We thus possess a wealth of scattered texts in different states of preservation on which to base our research.

Households

What then can we learn from these texts about the size and different features of the households of Ptolemaic and Roman Egypt? First, we need to be clear what it is that we are looking at. For *household* can be a somewhat slippery category and, whereas in a demographic context the distinction between the terms *family* and *household* is a relatively easy one to grasp, what precisely is involved in the term *household* is less clear (on the complexity of this issue, see the Introduction by Barrett in this volume). *Family*, as I understand it here, is the group of those closely related—of kith and kin or those with fictive kinship ties—and in the documentary record, this generally means coresident family members. A *household*, in contrast, is the unit of people who live together, both members of the wider family and other non-kin members, whether dependents, such as both free and unfree household servants, or simply others unrelated who came under a household head. We can think of households in locational terms but also in terms of function—as those who lived, ate, and slept together, or as those coresidents who joined in daily activities, whether in the rearing of children, the preparation of food, or more generally in production and reproduction. Aristotle, for example, was particularly keen on eating together as the base of the household unit (the *oikos*), whereas in the Florentine census of 1427 CE the hearth (*fuoco*) was used to designate a household.[12]

In some contexts, however, a household is not coterminous with a house. For instance, for purposes of taxation, when multiple families lived together within one house, these were sometimes treated as a single household but not always so. This is why, for this latter, composite group of families within a house, demographers have adopted the term *houseful*.[13] Whether or not different family or household groups living within the same physical space functioned together under a single household head for official purposes, or whether they functioned as separate units (perhaps even with their own closed door), presumably mattered as much to those concerned as it did to those who collected their dues. Distinctions like this, important as they are, are not easy to trace in either the documentary or the archaeological record, but they do need bearing in mind.

So how large were households in Greco-Roman Egypt? To answer this question we need to consider the best datasets that we have. From Roman Egypt there are the census returns, drawn up for the payment of taxes and studied by Bagnall and Frier.[14] There are also registers compiled for the payment of different taxes that can be used for household reconstruction. Earlier, from Ptolemaic Egypt, we have more than fifty household registers compiled for the levy of the salt tax which, at least in the third century BCE, functioned as a poll tax paid by men and women alike.[15] Given their purpose, these Ptolemaic registers list only those liable to tax—so adults only, no children.[16] This is a real limitation when set besides the Roman census returns, which not only have children but also often the ages of individuals listed. In both sets of data, however, households are primarily recorded not as residential but as fiscal units, where a named household head was, we assume, responsible for the payment of taxes for all of his or her household.

In the early Ptolemaic Period the salt tax registers that can be used to look at family and household size take various forms. They were compiled by scribes who were often bilingual (in both Greek, the language of the new rulers, and demotic Egyptian, the majority language of the population). Individuals were registered under the name of the household head. Household information was regularly organized by occupational groupings which, termed *ethnē*, formed a convenient means of accessing such information. For in Egypt occupations tended to be inherited through the generations, with sons following their fathers in a trade and, as with the mortuary priests above, marrying within the group. Starting at village level, this information was transmitted to the levels of district, tax area, and finally to the level of the nome before being forwarded to Alexandria. At the upper levels names turned into numbers, so it is only from the detailed registers at the lower levels that we gain the information that we need for household analysis.

The following short extract is from a bilingual tax register excavated at Ghoran in the South Fayum and now in Paris. This section, written in demotic, records small occupational groups in one particular village:[17]

bearers of the gods of Thoeris
Paues (?) son of Peteesis
Tbokonesis his wife, total 2, of whom 1 (male)
Pasis son of - -, total 1
total 3, of who 2 (male)
man of Anubis
Patous son of- - -
Tꜣ-by his wife
total 2, of whom 1 (male)
pastophoros of Atum
Petesouchos son of- - -
Thasos his wife, total 2, of whom 1 (male)
pastophoros of pharaoh Marres
Ḥy-ỉw son of Teos, total 1
servants of the ibises
Pa-nfr-ỉw son of Phibis
Ta-nfr-ỉy.ṯ daughter of Phibis
total 2, of whom 1 (male)
wine merchant (?)
Agathokles (?)
Tꜣ-mỉṯ (?) his wife, total 2, of whom 1 (male)

Two features are striking here. First is the small number recorded both in each family and occupation. In this section, only the bearers of the gods of Thoeris (the hippopotamus goddess Taweret, whom Greeks identified as Athene) have more than one family registered. Second, not surprisingly, is the predominance of Egyptian names among the minor cult officiants listed. It is only with the wine merchant Agathokles that a householder carries a Greek name, but, since wine rather than beer was the beverage of choice for the immigrants to Hellenistic Egypt, this too is not at all surprising. This coincidence, between type of occupation and Greek or

Egyptian name, is one found throughout these registers. It is a feature to which we shall return.

Based on this and other such registers comes a dataset of 427 households, containing 1,271 individuals, that we can use to answer some of our questions on houses and households.[18] These data, however, are limited in geographical scope. Most registers are from Middle Egypt, from the Arsinoite and Oxyrhynchite nomes. Nothing comparable survives from the Thebaid, from the Delta, or from Alexandria, where the climate has not favored the survival of papyri. In terms of geographical coverage, the scope of archaeological material is far wider.

In seeking to assess the size of different houses and their constituent households, in an ideal world, we would set the documentary record against what survives on the ground. The numbers and names of inhabitants (as recorded in documents) would match the excavated dwellings (as measured on the ground). But we do not live in an ideal world, and as yet, to the best of my knowledge, we nowhere have the combination of a household record and excavated area for the same place.[19] What we do have is both forms of evidence in relative abundance, and as persuasively argued by Lisa Nevett, if we consider both together, even if they are not from exactly the same location, each still sheds light on the other, helping us to frame our questions.[20]

So what do the data from tax registers of the mid-third century BCE tell of Ptolemaic households in Middle Egypt? When Ankhsheshonq, languishing in jail, used broken sherds of pottery to record his maxims, he wrote that "it is better to dwell in your own small house than in the large house of another."[21] While decrying dependence, this priest well knew that houses came in different sizes with different forms of household (on Ankhsheshonq, see Barrett, Introduction). So, what do we know of households in the early Ptolemaic Period?

Figure 4.1 shows the percentage of households according to the number of adults, first for all 427 households in the dataset described above, then for the Greek households (163 units), and finally the Egyptian households (256 units) for which we have details. As already indicated above, the distinction made here between Greeks and Egyptians depends on the names of the household heads; and in just eight cases this is not known. At first sight, such a straightforward correlation between name and ethnicity might seem a simplistic one to adopt. After all, in a mixed society where marriage between immigrant males and local women was quite regular and not a few people had both Greek and Egyptian names that they used in different contexts, ethnicity was a malleable category and names formed just one possible aspect of how individuals chose to present themselves or their offspring.[22] Settlers, however, military men more generally, and those in the upper echelons of the administration or certain other professions (or at least the males among them) generally carry Greek names; officiants in local cults (as just noted), brewers, and donkey-drivers all have Egyptian names. There is no one-to-one correlation between name and ethnicity; we must always be aware of exceptions. When dealing with larger groups, however, the criterion appears a reasonably meaningful one. Names can usefully serve as a convenient shorthand for designation of the two major groups within Ptolemaic society.

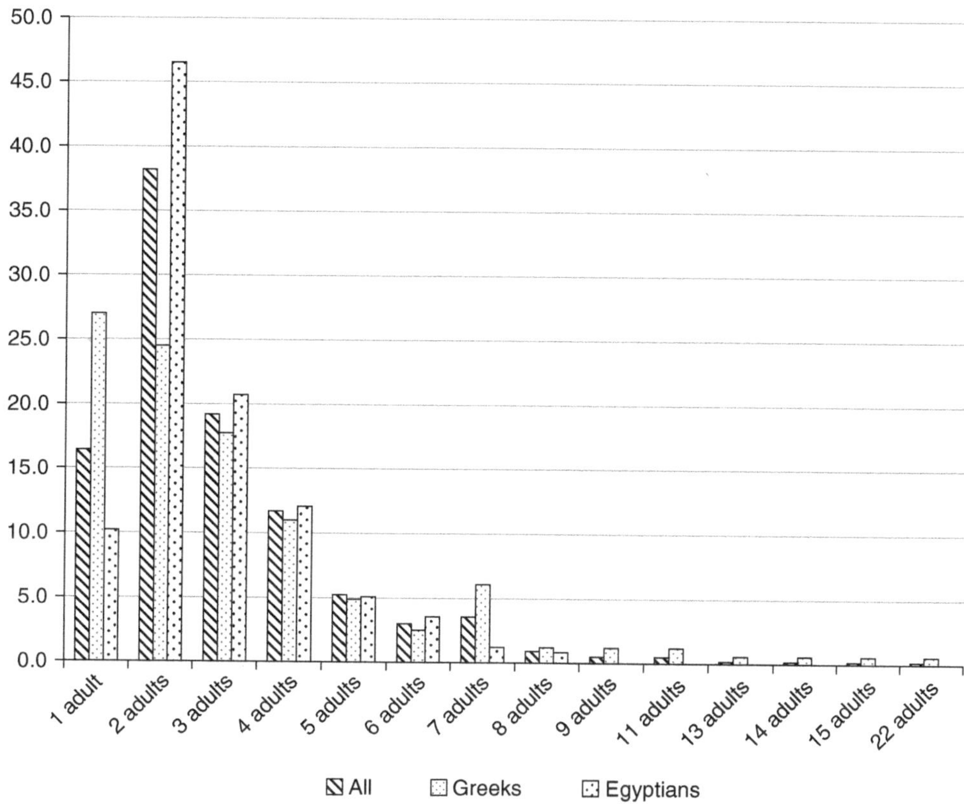

Figure 4.1. Ptolemaic households in the mid-third century BCE (as percent).

And if we look at the household size of these two groups, we find interesting differences that show up in figure 4.1. So, whereas in their analysis of Roman-period census returns, Bagnall and Frier found their material split according to metropolitan and rural inhabitants, here the ethnic divide obtrudes.[23]

Some features are immediately obvious. Overall, two-adult families were the norm. Some 38 percent of households were of this type, and of these, 75 percent were conjugal units of married couples.[24] Many of these of course will also have included children, who are missing from our record. If, then, as was not always the case, a household is taken as coterminous with a house, Ankhsheshonq's small house would indeed be the norm. Second, it is striking that the larger households of nine adults or more were all Greek, with the four largest represented by just a single example. And this pattern leads us to further considerations.

Continuing to exploit nomenclature as an ethnic denominator and exploring the detail of individual registers, we can learn still more of the early Hellenistic households in Middle Egypt. At the upper end of the scale, Greeks—those with Greek names—tended to live in far larger households than did Egyptians. These were military settler households with more family members, often with slaves and other dependents, and substantial holdings of livestock. Autoboulos, listed in a group of cavalry cleruchs, may serve as an example:[25]

Autoboulos son of Autonoos
Ammonia his wife
Kratesippos his son
[M]lyꜣsws his son
Dionysios his son
Ammonios his servant
[. . .]*gyn* his nurse
Eubiote his maidservant
Daphnis his maidservant, total 9, of whom 5 (male)
540 sheep, 170 lambs, 4 goats,
4 kids, 3 *še*-pigs, 10 *delphakes* (i.e. different pigs)

His resident sons, still living at home, were all of an age liable for the salt tax; a one-obol tax was charged on each of the animals. Like the livestock, the presence of three servants (slaves) implies a ménage that was well-off; a nurse, probably a wetnurse, suggests that there were more, younger, children in the family. Other households were larger still. For Greeks overall, 16 percent of adults lived in households of over ten.

In marked contrast, no Egyptian household consisted of more than eight coresident adults; 46.5 percent of households had just two adults in them, and those with one to three adults accounted for 77.5 percent of all households. Furthermore, most Egyptian households were just family groups. The only non-kin dependents that occur in our data are for families that most probably come from an urban context—two were nurses (likely to be free Egyptian employees) and just four were slaves.[26] In contrast to the situation for Greeks, in this sector of the community, slaveholding was not at all widespread. We may thus conclude from our data that household size serves to indicate the economic standing of the two main population groups in the early Ptolemaic Period.

At the same time as charting difference between groups in Ptolemaic Egypt, we can use the same dataset to calculate mean household size. For this, however, the inclusion of children is needed. In their study of the Roman census data, Bagnall and Frier adopted a multiplier of 2.909 applied to adult males to give a total that included children.[27] If the same multiplier is used for the Ptolemaic data, we reach an overall average household size of 4.5, or, broken down by sector, 4.0 for Egyptian households and 5.0 for Greeks.[28]

The composition of households can be further analyzed to investigate Ptolemaic norms of family structure. What, according to the categories of the so-called Cambridge family typology, developed by the Population Group of Tony Wrigley and Peter Laslett, was the percentage of solitaries, of simple conjugal families, of those extended through the presence of coresident kin, or to what degree were households made up of multiple families? The use of this typology enables us to compare and contrast our data over time, look at differences between the Ptolemaic and the

Roman Periods, and make comparisons with later data. Since, however, others have elaborated this approach elsewhere with the addition of further comparanda, and since my concern in this chapter is rather with variety, I shall not repeat it here.[29] Suffice it to comment once more that whereas the most striking differences are those found between the two ethnic groups in third century BCE Egypt, on the whole both Ptolemaic and Roman data fit into a general Mediterranean pattern that apparently changed little over time.

Houses

In archaeology, one of the more interesting recent developments has been a concern with the identification of the cultural preferences of different social groups through the houses they chose to live in and the artifacts and other remains associated with them. On the Red Sea coast, for instance, the different peoples who lived and worked in the ports of Berenike and Myos Hormos—the nomads of the Eastern Desert, the local *Ichthyophagoi* or Fish-eaters, or those coming in from the Nile Valley—may be distinguished through the faunal and ceramic remains uncovered in excavation, from the technologies they used, or traces of their varying diets.[30] In the Dakhla Oasis settlement of Roman Trimithis (Amheida), the different types of housing excavated reflect different social as possibly also ethnic status.[31] The architecture and plans of excavated houses show regional differences and changes over time, which may on occasion point to the identity of their inhabitants or at least to their lifestyle choices or imperatives.[32] Greek influence, for instance, has been identified in the architecture of early buildings at Tebtynis (South Fayum) and elsewhere, though the implications of this for those whose houses these were remain unclear.[33]

Turning now to houses in the documentary record, we find the same contrast between Greeks and Egyptians for Ptolemaic households. Two letters from the mid-third century BCE Zenon papers well illustrate this divide. The first records one of the grand country homes built for Alexandrians in the new town of Philadelpheia in the Fayum. The Alexandrian painter Theophilos sent his estimate for the decoration of rooms in the up-country home of Diotimos:[34]

> Memorandum from the workman Theophilos to Zenon on work for the property of Diotimos.
>
> For the vestibule: to decorate the cornice with deep red edging, upper wall with a multicolor dappled effect, dado the color of vetch, the lower course with a veined effect. Providing all materials myself: 30 drachmas.
>
> For the room with seven couches: to make the vaulted ceiling on the pattern you saw, to paint the dado and the Lesbian frieze with your desired color. Providing all materials myself: 20 drachmas.
>
> For the five-couched rooms, I shall decorate the cornices providing my own materials: 3 drachmas.
>
> Total as outlined: 53 drachmas.
>
> If you provide all materials, I shall do this for 30 drachmas.
>
> Farewell.

The decor was in keeping with the fashion of the time, and measuring rooms by the number of couches they held was the contemporary Greek standard of measurement. The most elaborate description of Ptolemaic interior decoration is that preserved in Athenaeus of the elaborate catamaran barge—a form of floating palace—of Ptolemy IV Philopator.[35] In this, the main reception room was a columned hall of twenty couches, while a dining room had nine couches and a bedroom five. On such a comparison, the country residences of prominent Alexandrians like Diotimos were substantial, but simply that. Zenon himself had a house in Philadelpheia, of which we learn only when one night burglars got in, forced up the trap door to the cellars, removed nineteen jars of wine, and escaped with their loot through the courtyard gate.[36]

At the other end of the scale come the small mud-brick village houses, like that of Paapis, constructed at a total cost of just under twenty-six drachmas. Paapis too sent his account to Zenon:[37]

Expenditure for the mud-brick house:

5,500 bricks @ 15 dr. for 10,000	8 dr. 1 ½ ob.
Donkeys @ 15 dr. for 10,000 bricks	8 dr. 1 ½ ob.
Builders @ 7 dr. for 10,000 bricks	3 dr. 5 ob.
Carriers @ 6 dr. for 10,000 bricks	3 dr.
[Woodwork?]	2 dr.
One window	1 ½ ob.
[ ]	½ ob.
Reed	1 ½ ob.
Total	25 dr. 5 ½ ob.

This was clearly a simple structure with a window and roof, probably covered by reeds, while the use of mud brick rather than any other building material was standard. These two early Ptolemaic examples can be multiplied from elsewhere. It is such individual homes that add up to make the statistics presented above.

All forms of evidence bring their own problems, which need confronting and negotiating as we seek to reconstruct the village scene or understand the backdrop to urban life. A household registered for tax cannot always be equated with "a houseful." Owners did not always live in the houses they owned, and fractional ownership is a well-documented phenomenon.[38] In the documentary material there is little that allows us to distinguish between households and houses. Among the Ptolemaic salt tax registers, for instance, there is only one demotic register where the house (demotic *pꜣʿ.wy*) is listed as the main unit, and within this, households are separately enumerated with their different household heads. The following extract illustrates this phenomenon:[39]

1 [ ]. . . .
The shrine of Anubis
< Hetpanoubis son of Teos, the man of Anubis, 41 (years)
< *Tꜣy-ỉr=w* his wife, 46 (years)

exact Tamounis his daughter, 20 (years), total 3, of whom 1 (male), through(?) Inaros(?)
The house of Andromachos the 25-(aroura) man
Taues his wife, (total) 2, of whom 1 (male)
The house of Ptolemaios, the 100-(aroura) man
Mys (?), the one without (?) fields
Tasis his wife
Dorion his son
< Tasis his wife, total 4, of whom 2 (male)
exact The house of Philippos, the one without (?) fields . . .
Kallo (?) his wife
Dionysodotos his son, total 3, of whom 2 (male)
< The house of Imouthes son of Marres, [the scribe] of the army, 36 (years)
< Senyris his wife, 31 (years), total 2, of whom 1 (male)
< Tryphon (?), the veteran, Year 35
< Philotera his daughter
Demetrios his son, - - [total 3, of whom 2 (male)]

This particular village register is also unusual in recording the ages of some of the homeowners. It further provides a glimpse of varying forms of housing in a Ptolemaic village. Shrines (l. 2) might serve as homes to those responsible for them, as elsewhere could the gatehouse to a courtyard or other structures—bathhouses, for instance, or shops.[40] As suggested elsewhere in this volume, dwelling places came in many different forms (chapters 11 and 12). Normally owners lived in their own homes, as did 75 percent of owners in this register but, as in the house of Ptolemaios (l. 8), this was not always the case. Ptolemaios was a cavalry settler granted 100 arouras by the crown (i.e. 27.5 hectares or 68 acres) as a form of pension or retaining fee. He himself was nonresident; his house was let out to Mys, a man without land, who lived there with his wife, his son, and his son's wife. This household also illustrates the regular Ptolemaic (and later Roman) practice of virilocal marriage. Further down, the house of Imouthes son of Marres is an example of a split dwelling with two separate households in it. Imouthes and his wife inhabit part of the house while the veteran Tryphon and his two children inhabit a separate part. Just how the division worked on the ground is—as so often—unclear.[41]

The separate listing of constituent households in this particular register allows us to appreciate the complexity of composite units of habitation. Recorded in this one register, as shown in figure 4.2, are details for just sixteen houses containing twenty-three households, a very small sector of just one Fayum village:

It is immediately clear from these data that for those living in units of two to four adults (four with two adults, three with three adults and five with four), house and household were the same—with just one household to each house. Five-adult houses were not like this: each of the three examples contains two households. And finally, the one house with 10 adults was made up of five different—and

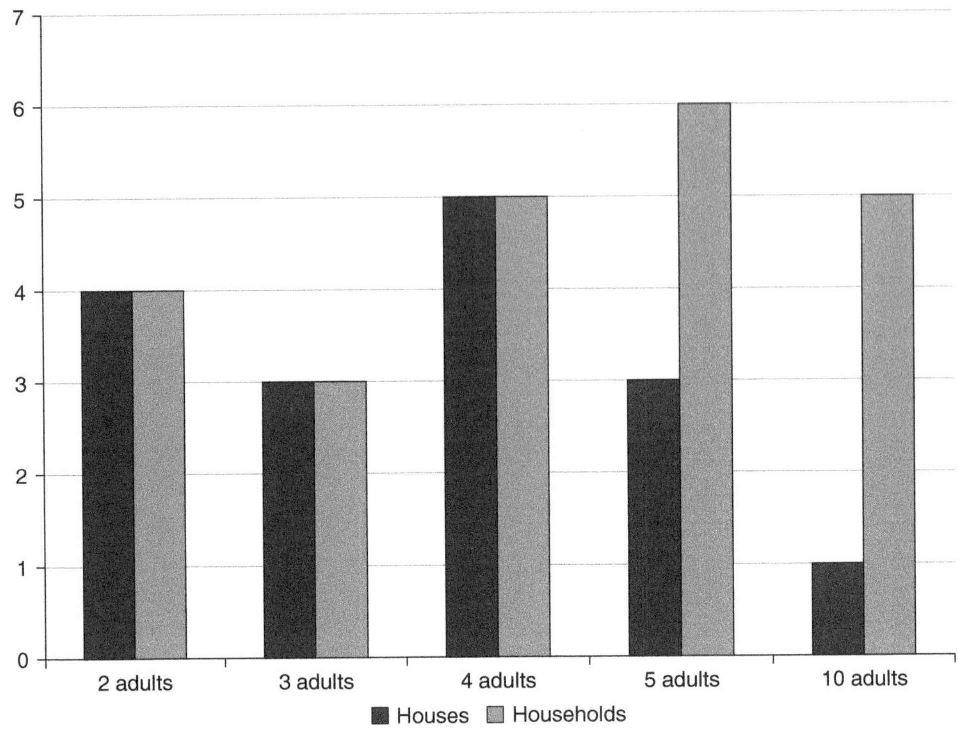

Figure 4.2. Houses and households compared in *P.Count* 9 (251/250 BCE).

very disparate—households. Here, then, for houses with five adults or more—i.e., 25 percent of the total—multihousehold occupancy was standard. But how these different groups actually divided the living space up between them, unfortunately, remains a matter simply for speculation. This is a very small sample indeed, but similar varieties of living arrangements can be documented elsewhere, and it is clear that multifamily occupancy was reasonably common in the villages of both Ptolemaic and Roman Egypt.

A bilingual survey of the second century BCE from the South Fayum may be used to fill in further details.[42] This house-by-house survey is still unpublished and is of a type more common from the Roman Period. The interest of the scribe who drew it up was to register houses and their inhabitants according to their location. As in contemporary land surveys with plots of land, in this register we can follow the scribe from house to house, with items regularly preceded by directions: "lying to the west," "off to the south," "opposite," "with a road running between," and so on. At times the directions get quite chatty—*ēlthes*, "you have reached . . . " (xi.32)—and the text takes us right into an Egyptian village, though its fragmentary state causes problems when we try to draw up a village plan. Its details bring a Ptolemaic village streetscape back to life, telling much about family and household arrangements and different modes of dwelling.

The most common unit recorded is the house (*oikia*), but sometimes this is described as private (*oikia idia*), with one described as a private dower house (viii.6–8, *en phernēi*). Twenty percent of houses were *distegos*, with two stories, and of these 64 percent were inhabited by Greeks. A courtyard (*aulē*) was regularly appended, though sometimes this was small (*aulidion*); storehouses (*tamieia*) and mills (*mylaia*) are recorded, as too are palm trees. Houses might contain several *oikēmata*, with nine recorded in one two-story house that also had two mills (iii.13). *Oikēma* could signify an independent structure off the main house or courtyard, or it could be a separate room, perhaps even a separate apartment within the house, as probably here.[43] As in the text analyzed above (figure 4.2), this register likewise gives no indication of how houses were physically divided up between coresident households, though sometimes this can be guessed from the family groupings.

Interspersed with houses came other structures. A goose farm (iv.22, *chēnoboskion*) lay along one street; connected to the bathhouse were a couple of stores run by families living on the premises; this was an area where many greengrocers had their homes (xii.31–36). A two-story barber's shop specifically for cavalrymen (xvi.33–34, *koureion*) lay empty elsewhere. The royal brewery was home to two brewers and their families (xi.17–22). Nearby, a shrine of Isis was managed by a certain Tharetis; her seventy-year old husband lived there also, together with their son, who—described as an Isis priest—now served as household head (xi.23–27). Shrines and altars formed a standard part of the village streetscape, where they doubled up as dwelling places. The great god Phemroeris, a crocodile deity of the South Fayum, held property here (ii.18–20).

A couple of extracts from this text demonstrate its potential for illustrating different living arrangements and patterns of inheritance: the changing lives, as it were, of dwellings. First (ix.19–36):

19 / lying to the west belonging to Tathoutis daughter of Thesenouphis
20 and Terous her sister and
21 . . . ris a house and courtyard in which
22 4 oikēmata:
23 / Simon son of Ioannes, a Jew
24 [NN daughter of. .]lenynis (his) wife
25 . . . son of Hestieios, a Jew
26 . . .
27 Jos[ephos son of. .]llodotos, a Jew
28 . . . (his) wife
29 / Olympios son of Eudios, a Jew
30 / Sala . . . (his) wife
31 Ani[ketos]. [son of . . .] oures, a Jew
32 / lying next a private house of Di . . . son of Teos:
33 Di . . . himself, an Arab
34 Tages (his) wife
35 aged 70 / Teos son of Teos (his) father, shepherd
36 Thauges (his) wife

Here we first meet a house with four oikēmata belonging to two nonresident sisters and an illegible third. It is inhabited by a group of apparently unrelated Jews: five men with wives for three or possibly four of them. The final individual in the list (l. 31) must have shared an oikēma with one of the married couples. Then next door comes a two-generation family of Arabs. The son is registered as owner of this private house, but his mother and seventy-year-old father, a shepherd (like so many Arabs in Ptolemaic Egypt), still live with their son. Although not all houses were inhabited by their owners, they regularly passed down through the family. Here, as was normal, Tages had moved into her husband's home on marriage. It seems clear that Ankhsheshonq's admonition, "Do not dwell in a house with your in-laws" (9.12), was composed for a male readership.

Yet despite Ankhsheshonq some marriages were uxorilocal, with husbands coming to live in the home of their wives. Uxorilocal marriages were exceptional but occur in both Greek and Egyptian families. There are four such cases in the text under consideration, as illustrated in the following extract (vii.5–9):[44]

5 / lying next, belonging to Tkonnos daughter of Polemon:
6 Pasis son of Nephoreis, *allophylos*
7 Tkonnos (his) wife
8 Harmiysis also known as Hera[kleides]
9 son of Kaikos, *allophylos*

Here Tkonnos owns the house, though interestingly her husband Pasis comes first as household head. It is probably relevant that, contrary to normal practice in this period, Pasis is known only by his mother's name without mention of his father. Such fatherless individuals might be disadvantaged, and Nephoreis's son was perhaps fortunate to find a propertied wife.

As often noted, patterns of habitation were fluid. Over time, as perhaps in the case of Tkonnos, a daughter inherits and the young couple supplants an older generation. Elsewhere, elderly parents continue living in the family home for the remainder of their lives. Just occasionally, the son takes over even when a father is still alive, as in the case of the son of the shepherd Teos.[45] More often, fathers continue to act as household head until their death; dependent mothers figure more frequently, with ten such in this particular register.

We have only had a glimpse of the South Fayum village recorded in this survey. Here dwellings came in different forms and size, both large and small, geese honked, children played outside, and courtyards were full of activity. On either side of the street lay houses made of mud brick, reinforced no doubt with wood, with palms and reeds to form their roofs.[46] Close by, in the early Ptolemaic village of Talei (along the canal west of Tebtynis), houses were built on stone foundations of bedrock in housing blocks of thirty by nineteen meters, laid out on a grid plan reminiscent perhaps of Alexandria. The streets of Talei were four meters wide with stone-covered drainage channels.[47] The impression of *this* village, in contrast, is of a more higgledy-piggledy mix of house sizes interspersed with shops and shrines. The smallest house contained just two adults, the largest twenty-three. The variety found by archaeologists is here in the documents too.

Households and Houses under Rome

Moving on to the Roman Period, figures are comparable but at the same time imply an overall increase in size of both houses and households. The record of archaeology also shows a growth in the size of settlements and the density of village housing.[48] Roman census returns give an average household size of 4.8 in the villages compared with 5.3 in the *metropoleis*, where urban families were more often joined by slaves and other dependents.[49] One recalls the earlier averages of 5.00 for Greek and 4.00 for Egyptian households.

If, however, the Roman tax registers that record taxpayers by both house and household are subjected to scrutiny, a somewhat different picture emerges. These were first analyzed by Deborah Hobson in her lively, innovative study of 1985. There, alongside much else, she was concerned to make the distinction between house and household and to set the documentary evidence against that of excavation. The changing pattern of families and households took place in a physical context that Hobson vividly portrays. Her figures have since been challenged, but this study remains important.[50] More recently, the same registers, with others added, have been scrutinized by Richard Alston. His adjusted averages are somewhat more conservative, but again higher than those from the census returns, and higher still than those from the early Ptolemaic Period.[51] Distinguishing between urban and rural, Alston calculates 4.02–4.11 persons for urban households and 5.58–5.70 for rural; for urban housefuls he has 5.66–5.78 and for rural housefuls 7.86–8.04, somewhat lower than the figures of Hobson but strikingly higher and different from than those obtained from census records only. The discrepancy between these different calculations simply highlights the problems involved in extrapolation from very different forms of data from different periods. And in this respect the census data, scattered in both provenance and period, differ from those provided by house-by-house registers, more closely grouped by period and place.[52] As Alston and others have observed, unlike the Ptolemaic evidence, which comes from a limited period and area, the Roman data derive sporadically from a far broader period and more disparate regions. Studies of demographic data from elsewhere show how fast change can happen even within a decade.[53] Noteworthy under the Romans, however, is the population increase shown in the multiplicity of registers from these later centuries.

Questions remain. What are we to make of the apparent longer-term change from the Ptolemaic to the Roman Period? Was this a real change, seen in the development of larger houses with more people living in them, both in the countryside and in the cities? Or are we, as so often, just the victims of differences in data—the different contexts from which our documents come? It is generally agreed that over time, based on immigration, land reclamation, and improved irrigation, the Ptolemaic Period saw a growth in population, especially in the capital Alexandria but also in the countryside. Of course this was not a consistent development. There were periods of internal dissension and revolt that affected the population, and periods too of low Niles, but on the whole numbers were growing, particularly in urban centers which developed still further under the Romans with a preferential status granted to the metropoleis.[54] The picture was not static and averages should always be treated with caution. Nevertheless, the population does appear to have grown overall; families were larger and houses too. What else can have lain behind such a change is too large a question to answer here, but we may at least chart this change in the context of houses and households. And here, as elsewhere, papyri both corroborate the archaeological record and, at the same time—by preserving details of house building, decoration and ownership, of household numbers, makeup, and so on—they illuminate further aspects of what was a multifaceted and ever-changing scene.

In this chapter, we have seen both the potential and the limitations of the documentary record for our study of Greco-Roman Egypt. As already noted, the main limitation to the papyrological record derives from the pattern of survival. The damper coastal climate of the Mediterranean coastline is hostile to the preservation of papyri. On the whole, Alexandria and the Delta remain undocumented areas. Modern habitation has covered most ancient cities and what has survived from the valley is sporadic in both time and place. Our knowledge of urban and rural differences is therefore limited, though better in some periods than others. And since so often the evidence from texts is for life lived in a local context, larger-scale, comparative questions are harder to treat. Variety constantly obtrudes. Questions of general settlement patterns, town planning, or architecture are difficult to answer from papyri, except in a few specific cases. In questions of ethnicity, religion, or lifestyle choices, what we can chart is also limited, sometimes puzzling, and not easy to integrate within broader patterns.

Nevertheless, the broader picture demands our attention, and the questions asked in this volume may lead us to adopt new approaches to our texts and to begin to place the houses and households of Greco-Roman Egypt in a wider Mediterranean context.[55] So on the more positive side, for some periods and places it has been possible to subject the data to demographic analysis and to reach conclusions on the form and scale of household makeup. Marriage patterns and household formation are illuminated in the official registers and census data that have survived. Like their inhabitants, houses and other property—both moveable and immoveable—were subject to tax, and therefore recorded, under the closely controlled administrative regimes of Ptolemaic and Roman Egypt. On occasion, the evidence of papyri allows a glimpse of the different sorts of home where these households were located; details of construction and decoration may be recorded. In no case, however, can we unite these details with known houses on the ground. Compared to that provided through archaeology, this is a limited and patchy picture. Nevertheless, through looking at the papyri, we have been able to provide a picture of the complexity of households, if not of dwelling practices, that is unparalleled elsewhere in the ancient world.

Notes

1 See Hall 2002, 220–24, stressing the replacement of descent as the defining feature of Greekness (Hellenicity) by a broader emphasis on the adoption of Greek culture and language. In third-century BCE Egypt, those termed Hellenes (including Jews, Thracians and even some with Egyptian names) enjoyed a privileged tax status: Clarysse and Thompson 2006, 2:124–86.
2 For this, see Thompson 2001; Clarysse 2019.
3 See Bagnall and Frier 1994, 171–73, on Peter Laslett's earlier work; Huebner 2013, 19–28; Huebner and Nathan 2017, 1–26.
4 Uytterhoeven 2022.
5 Thompson 2012, 144–76, 260–61. For papyrus citations, see the web-based version of Oates et al. 2001 at www.papyri.info.
6 Vandorpe 1994.
7 For similar studies, see Muhs 2002, on marrying the girl next door; Muhs 2008; 2015, 329–34.
8 *P.Louvre dem.* E 3266.5.L–7.O (197 BCE), ed. de Cenival 1972, 22–24, 38–41.
9 For full family tree, see Thompson 2012, 147.
10 Vandorpe 2009.
11 Cuvigny 2009.
12 Aristotle, *Pol.* I 1.6 (1252b); Herlihy and Klapisch-Zuber 1985, 280–336.
13 Hammel and Laslett 1974, 78.
14 Bagnall and Frier 1994.
15 Clarysse and Thompson 2006; cf. Huebner 2013, 17–46.
16 Children with ages are exceptionally recorded in *W.Chrest.* 198 (240 BCE), a household declaration not a tax register; ages (often rounded) are provided for just some adults in *P.Count* 9 (after 251/250 BCE) and P.Mon.Gr.inv. 344 + 346 (ca. 180 BCE). Consistency was not overly important in such record keeping.
17 *P.Count* 2.67–87 (229 BCE). For new fragments of this text that affect the occupational analysis based on it, see Clarysse and Thompson 2018.
18 Clarysse and Thompson 2006, 2:226–317.
19 Even the case of family papers from Karanis house B17 is problematic: Nevett 2011, 18–19; so too in the case of the disparate texts from granary C123, edited and discussed in *P.Mich.* XXI.
20 Nevett 2011, 29–30.
21 Robert K. Ritner in Simpson 2003, 523, for translation; *editio princeps,* Glanville 1955.
22 Cf. note 2 above.
23 Bagnall and Frier 1994, 66–67.
24 In comparison, the lower 24.5 percent for Greeks is the result of a large number of Greek singletons in one anomalous register, *P.Count* 47 (230 BC). What lay behind this abnormal pattern must be left to the imagination.
25 *P.Count* 2.331–341 (229 BCE). Autoboulos may be the same as the homonymous one hundred-aroura settler recorded in *P.Enteux*. 91 (221 BCE).
26 See Clarysse and Thompson 2006, 2:267–72.
27 Bagnall and Frier 1994, 103n35, as standardly used in calculating local populations from tax statistics.
28 See Clarysse and Thompson 2006, 2:244–46, for further details.
29 Clarysse and Thompson 2006, 2:246–60 with table 7:12 at 255; cf. Bagnall and Frier 1994, 66–67; Huebner 2013, 46, adding Tang China, eighteenth-century Piedmont, nineteenth-century Russia, and more.
30 Thomas 2012, 174–80.
31 Boozer 2012; 2015a, 420–22; cf. Gates-Foster, Redon, and Godsey, chapter 12 this volume, on Bi'r Samut.
32 Marouard 2008, 118; 2012, on Ptolemaic housing; Spence 2015; Boozer 2015a, 178–80, 407–8, regional differences.
33 Hadji-Minaglou 2012, 108–12; Davoli 2015; Langellotti 2020, 19–23, with table 1.1.

34 *P.Cairo Zen.* III 59445; cf. *PSI* IV 407, at the end of the job he was without funds, unable to return home to the capital. Cf. Whitehouse 2010, 1026, on decoration; Orrieux 1985, 133, other such urban structures.
35 Ath. V 204d–206c; Thompson 2013, 190–93.
36 *PSI* IV 396 (241 BCE).
37 *P.Cairo Zen.* III 59480.5–15. See Nowicka 1969, 36 (on reeds), 116.
38 See Muhs 2008.
39 *P.Count* 9.1–20 (after 251/250 BCE). *P.Count* 4 and 18 (third century BCE) also record houses but without constituent households. Figure 4.2 with discussion of *P.Count* 9 updates Clarysse and Thompson 2006, 2:286–87.
40 P.Mon.Gr.inv. 344 + 346 (ca. 180 BCE).
41 Cf. *P.Enteux.* 13 (222 BCE), in which a widow complains that Pooris, on whom her husband had been billeted, is preventing the completion of a wall planned to divide off their billet and protect her.
42 P.Mon.Gr.inv. 344 + 346 (ca. 180 BCE), to be edited in a volume of Munich papyri by Willy Clarysse and myself together with Thomas Kruse.
43 Novicka 1969, 113–14; Husson 1983: 183–85.
44 vii.5–9; xiii.36–40; xvi.6–10; xvii.36–37.
45 ix.35, cf. xi.27.
46 Davoli 2015; Boozer 2015b, on houses.
47 Kirby and Rathbone 1996, Talei; cf. Viereck 1928, Philadelpheia; Davoli 2005, Bacchias and Soknopaiou Nesos; Mueller 2006, 112–21, Ptolemaic planning and its antecedents; McKenzie 2007, 19–30, Alexandria.
48 Alston 1997, 26–32; Hadji-Minaglou 2007, 178; Marouard 2008, 119–25; Bowman 2011, 335; Huebner 2013, 39–41.
49 Bagnall and Frier 1994, 68–69; Huebner 2013, 39.
50 Hobson 1985.
51 Alston 2002, 72–73 with table 3.3 (where in line 1 for 4.58 read 4.82); cf. Hobson 1985, 220–21, an average of 7.34 to a household and 11.27 to a house.
52 See Alston 2002, 73.
53 Cuno 2005 provides a salutary caution.
54 Bagnall 2009b, 109–11, discusses scale.
55 See Huebner and Nathan 2017.

Works Cited

Alston, R. 1997. "Houses and Households in Roman Egypt." In *Domestic Space in the Roman World: Pompeii and Beyond*, edited by R. Laurence and A. Wallace-Hadrill, 25–39. Portsmouth, RI: Journal of Roman Archaeology.

Alston, R. 2002. *The City in Roman and Byzantine Egypt*. London: Routledge.

Bagnall, R.S., ed. 2009a. *The Oxford Handbook of Papyrology*. New York: Oxford University Press.

Bagnall, R.S. 2009b. "Response to Elio Lo Cascio." In *Quantifying the Roman Economy: Methods and Problems*, edited by A. Bowman and A. Wilson, 107–12. Oxford: Oxford University Press.

Bagnall, R S., and B.W. Frier. 1994. *The Demography of Roman Egypt*. Cambridge: Cambridge University Press.

Ballet, P., ed. 2012. *Grecs et romains en Égypte: territoires, espaces de la vie et de la mort, objects du prestige et du quotidien*. Cairo: Institut français d'archéologie orientale.

Boozer, A.L. 2012. "Globalizing Mediterranean Identities: The Overlapping Spheres of Egyptian, Greek and Roman Worlds at Trimithis." *Journal of Mediterranean Archaeology* 25: 93–116.

Boozer, A.L. 2015a. *Amheida II. A Late Romano-Egyptian House in the Dakhla Oasis. Amheida House B2*. New York: New York University Press and Institute for the Study of the Ancient World.

Boozer, A.L. 2015b. "Inside and Out: Romano-Egyptian Houses from the Fayyum and Dakhleh Oasis." In *Housing and Habitat in the Ancient Mediterranean. Cultural and Environmental Responses*, edited by A.A. Di Castro and C.A. Hope, 185–97. BABESCH Supplement 26. Leuven: Peeters.

Bowman, A. 2011. "Ptolemaic and Roman Egypt. Population and Settlement." In *Settlement, Urbanization, and Population*, edited by A. Bowman and A. Wilson, 317–58. Oxford: Oxford University Press.

Clarysse, W. 2019. "Ethnic Identity: Egyptians, Greeks, and Romans." In *A Companion to Greco-Roman and Late Antique Egypt*, edited by K. Vandorpe, 299–313. Hoboken, NJ: Wiley-Blackwell.

Clarysse, W., and D.J. Thompson. 2006. *Counting the People in Hellenistic Egypt*. 2 vols. Cambridge: Cambridge University Press.

Clarysse, W., and D.J. Thompson. 2018. "P. Count 2 Continued: A Ptolemaic Population Register from the Arsinoite Nome." In *Hieratic, Demotic and Greek Studies and Text Editions. Of the Making of Many Books There is No End: Festschrift in Honour of Sven P. Vleeming* (P. L. Bat. 34), edited by K. Donker van Heel, F.A. Hoogendijk and C.J. Martin, 162–89. Leiden: Brill.

Cuno, K. 2005. "Demography, Household Formation, and Marriage in Three Egyptian Villages During the Mid-nineteenth Century." In *Sociétés rurales onation/Ottoman Rural Societies*. Cahier des Annales islamologiques 25, edited by M. Afifi et al., 105–17. Cairo: Institut français d'archéologie orientale.

Cuvigny, H. 2009. "The Finds of Papyri: The Archaeology of Papyrology." In *The Oxford Handbook of Papyrology*, edited by R.S. Bagnall, 30–58. New York: Oxford University Press.

Davoli, P. 2005. "Examples of Town Planning in the Fayyum." *Bulletin of the American Society of Papyrologists* 42: 213–34.

Davoli, P. 2015. "Classical Influences on the Domestic Architecture of the Graeco-Roman Fayyum." In *Housing and Habitat in the Ancient Mediterranean. Cultural and Environmental Responses*, edited by A.A. Di Castro and C.A. Hope, 173–84. BABESCH Supplement 26. Leuven: Peeters.

de Cenival, F. 1972. "Un acte de renonciation consécutif à un partage de revenus liturgiques Memphites (*P. Louvre* E 3266)." *Bulletin de l'Institut français d'archéologie orientale* 71: 11–65.

Di Castro, A.A., and C.A. Hope, eds. 2015. *Housing and Habitat in the Ancient Mediterranean: Cultural and Environmental Responses*. BABESCH Supplement 26. Leuven: Peeters.

Glanville, S.R.K. 1955. *Catalogue of Demotic Papyri in the British Museum*. Vol. 2. *The Instructions of 'Onchsheshonqy (British Museum Papyrus 10508). Part 1*. London: British Museum Publications.

Hadji-Minaglou, G. 2007. *Tebtynis IV. Les habitatations à l'est du temple de Soknebtynis*. Cairo: Institut français d'archéologie orientale.

Hadji-Minaglou, G. 2012. "L'apport des Grecs dans l'architecture de la *chôra* égptienne: l'example de Tebtynis." In *Grecs et romains en Égypte: territoires, espaces de la vie et de la mort, objects du prestige et du quotidien*, edited by P. Ballet, 107–20. Cairo: Institut français d'archéologie orientale.

Hall, J.M. 2002. *Hellenicity: Between Ethnicity and Culture*. Chicago: University of Chicago Press.

Hammel, E.A., and P. Laslett. 1974. "Comparing Household Structures Over Time and Between Cultures." *Comparative Studies in Society and History* 16: 73–103.

Herlihy, D. and C. Klapisch-Zuber. 1985. *Tuscans and their Families: A Study of the Florentine Catasto of 1427*. New Haven: Yale University Press.

Hobson, D.W. 1985. "House and Household in Roman Egypt." *Yale Classical Studies* 28: 211–29.

Huebner, S.R. 2013. *The Family in Roman Egypt: A Comparative Approach to Intergenerational Solidarity and Conflict*. Cambridge: Cambridge University Press.

Huebner, S.R., and G. Nathan, eds. 2017. *Mediterranean Families in Antiquity: Households, Extended Families, and Domestic Space*. Chichester, West Sussex: Wiley-Blackwell.

Husson, G. 1983. *Oikia: le vocabulaire de la maison privée en Égypte d'après les papyrus grecs*. Paris: Publications de la Sorbonne.

Kirby, C., and D. Rathbone. 1996. "Kom Talit: The Rise and Fall of a Greek Town in the Faiyum." *Egyptian Archaeology* 8: 29–31.

Langellotti, M. 2020. *Village Life in Roman Egypt*. Oxford: Oxford University Press.

Marouard, G. 2008. "Rues et habitats dans les villages de la *chôra* égyptienne à la période gréco-romaine (IIIe s. av.–IVe s. apr. J.-C.): quelques exemples du Fayoum (nome Arsinoite)." In *La rue dans l'Antiquité: Définition, aménagement et devenir de l'Orient méditerranéen à la Gaule*, edited by P. Ballet, N. Dieudonné-Glad, and C. Saliou, 117–28. Rennes: Presses universitaires de Rennes.

Marouard, G. 2012. "Les quartiers d'habitat dans les fondations et refondations lagides de la *chôra* égyptienne. Une revision archéologique." In *Grecs et romains en Égypte: territoires, espaces de la vie et de la mort, objects du prestige et du quotidien*, edited by P. Ballet, 121–40. Cairo: Institut français d'archéologie orientale.

McKenzie, J. 2007. *The Architecture of Alexandria and Egypt, 300 BC—AD 700*. New Haven: Yale University Press.

Mueller, K. 2006. *Settlements of the Ptolemies: City Foundations and New Settlement in the Hellenistic World*. Studia Hellenistica 43. Leuven: Peeters.

Muhs, B.P. 2002. "The Girls Next Door: Marriage Patterns Among the Mortuary Priests in Early Ptolemaic Egypt." *Journal of Juristic Papyrology* 35: 169–94.

Muhs, B.P. 2008. "Fractions of Houses in Ptolemaic Hawara." In *Graeco-Roman Fayum—Texts and Archaeology*, edited by S. Lippert and M. Schentuleit, 187–95. Wiesbaden: Harrassowitz.

Muhs, B.P. 2015. "Property Title, Domestic Architecture, and Household Lifecycles in Egypt." In *Household Studies in Complex Societies: (Micro) Archaeological and Textual Approaches*, edited by M. Müller, 321–37. The Oriental Institute Seminars 10. Chicago: Oriental Institute of the University of Chicago.

Müller, M., ed. 2015. *Household Studies in Complex Societies. (Micro) Archaeological and Textual Approaches*. The Oriental Institute Seminars 10. Chicago: Oriental Institute of the University of Chicago.

Nevett, L. 2011. "Family and Household, Ancient History and Archaeology: a Case Study from Roman Egypt." In *A Companion to Families in the Greek and Roman Worlds*, edited by B. Rawson, 15–31. Chichester, UK: Wiley-Blackwell.

Novicka, M. 1969. *La maison privée à l'époque ptolémaïque*. Wrocław: Zakład Narodowy Imienia Ossolińskich Wydawnictwo Polskiej Akademii Nauk.

Oates, J.F., R.S. Bagnall, S.J. Clackson, A.A. O'Brien, J.D. Sosin, T.G. Wilfong, and K.A. Worp. 2001. *Checklist of Editions of Greek, Latin, Demotic and Coptic Papyri, Ostraca, and Tablets*. 5th ed. Bulletin of the American Society of Papyrologists Supplement 9. Exeter, UK: ASP. Ongoing at http://www.papyri.info/docs/checklist.

Orrieux, C. 1985. *Zénon de Caunos*, parépidêmos, *et le destin grec*. Annales Littéraires de l'Université de Besançon 320. Paris: Les Belles Lettres.

Simpson, W.K. 2003. *The Literature of Ancient Egypt: An Anthology of Stories, Instructions, Stelae, Autobiographies, and Poetry*. 3rd ed. New Haven: Yale University Press.

Spence, K. 2015. "Ancient Egyptian Houses and Households: Architecture, Artifacts, Conceptualization and Interpretation." In *Household Studies in Complex Societies. (Micro) Archaeological and Textual Approaches*, edited by M. Müller, 83–99. The Oriental Institute Seminars 10. Chicago: Oriental Institute of the University of Chicago.

Thomas, R.I. 2012. "Port Communities and the Erythraean Sea Trade." In *British Museum Studies in Egypt and Sudan* 18: 169–99.

Thompson, D.J. 2001. "Hellenistic Hellenes: The Case of Ptolemaic Egypt." In *Ancient Perceptions of Greek Ethnicity*, edited by I. Malkin, 301–22. Cambridge, MA: Harvard University Press.

Thompson, D.J. 2012. *Memphis under the Ptolemies*. 2nd ed. Princeton: Princeton University Press.

Thompson, D.J. 2013. "Hellenistic Royal Barges." In *The Ptolemies, the Sea, and the Nile: Studies in Waterborne Power*, edited by K. Buraselis, M. Stefanou and D. J. Thompson, 185–96. Cambridge: Cambridge University Press.

Uytterhoeven, I. 2022. "Mudbricks and Papyri from the Desert Sand: Housing in the Ptolemaic and Roman Fayum." In *Housing in the Ancient Mediterranean World: Material and Textual Approaches*, edited by J.A. Baird and A. Pudsey, 261–99. Cambridge: Cambridge University Press.

Vandorpe, K. 1994. "Museum Archaeology or How to Reconstruct Pathyris Archives." In *Acta Demotica. Acts of the Fifth International Conference for Demotists. Pisa, 4th-8th September 1993*, 289–300. Egitto e Vicino Oriente 17. Pisa: Giardini.

Vandorpe, K. 2009. "Archives and Dossiers." In *The Oxford Handbook of Papyrology*, edited by R.S. Bagnall, 216–55. New York: Oxford University Press.

Viereck, P. 1928. *Philadelpheia: die Gründung einer hellenistischen Militärkolonie*. Leipzig: J. C. Hinrichs.

Whitehouse, H. 2010. "Mosaics and Painting in Graeco-Roman Egypt." In *A Companion to Ancient Egypt*, edited by A.B. Lloyd, 1008–31. 2 vols. Oxford: Wiley-Blackwell.

5

Habitatio

Transfer of Houses and Rights of Residence in Roman Egypt

SABINE R. HUEBNER

Succession and inheritance law provide rich evidence for the ways that people in Greco-Roman Egypt thought about domestic space.[1] Since spouses did not inherit according to Roman law and local Egyptian legal traditions, they were often granted a *habitatio*, a lifelong right of residence in the familial home. The domestic space and living arrangements, as items of negotiation between family members, therefore provide us with information about everyday life interactions of individuals in Greco-Roman society.

This chapter examines the transfer of houses upon the death of the head of the household from the perspective of the deceased's widow (or widower) and the children. The rich documentary evidence on the sharing of domestic space will be set against ancient legal texts and literary sources about ideal constructs of households in the case of inheritance. We see the power relations within the household: the ways that gender, marital status, age, and class wound up affecting legal practice concerning household ownership.

Habitatio

According to classical Roman law, habitatio was the right to reside in someone else's house usually free of rent. The right of habitatio was usually granted by will, strictly personal, and could not be transferred to another person. But habitatio could be granted also inter vivos in exchange for money, in one or several payments. What defines habitatio in Roman law and distinguishes it from lease is that the *habitator* had a "right in rem" (real property right) and therefore a claim that was not restricted to the person who granted him/her the right, but could be raised against anyone.

Habitatio was usually granted for a certain period of time or for life. The imperial Roman jurists such as Gaius, Paulus, and Ulpian understood habitatio as a limited right of *usus*, not to be confused with usufruct.[2] Usus and usufruct, according to the Roman jurists, were personal use rights which, however, never turned into ownership of the property. In Roman law usufruct was the right to use or enjoy a thing and without altering or alienating it. It included, however, the right to derive profit from it, for instance, by renting out an apartment, leasing a piece of land, selling the crops, etc. without impairing the substance. Usus was defined as the right to use or enjoy a thing and its fruits, without, however, the right to renting or leasing it out or selling the fruits.[3]

Habitatio in Roman law followed thus the limited right of usus: The legatee, man or woman, could live in the house together with other persons, be they family members, enslaved household members, workmen, or even a new spouse, for as long as the recipient of the habitatio remained the main resident. But the beneficiary could not rent the property: "Parties who have a right to use cannot lease the premises and give up their residence there, nor can they sell the use of the same."[4]

While habitatio was originally a personal privilege, Justinian later responded to preexisting practice and extended the legal right of habitatio and assimilated it to usufruct, following an opinion that the second-century Roman jurist Marcellus had already expressed in disputes about the construction of habitatio. From then on, Roman law permitted the grantee either to live in the house, or to let it as a place of residence to someone else: "By a constitution which we have published in accordance with the opinion of Marcellus, and in the interests of utility, we have permitted persons possessed of this right not only to live in the building themselves, but also to let it out to others."[5] This constitution published in 530 CE said:

> Emperor Justinian to Julian, Praetorian Prefect: As a doubt arose in ancient times, when the usufruct of a house was bequeathed, in the first place (as the instances are similar), whether the right of lodging referred to the use and usufruct or to neither of them, that is to say, to a peculiar right and a special privilege, and whether the person to whom the right of lodging had been bequeathed could afterwards lease the same, or claim for himself the ownership of the property, We, for the purpose of disposing of the disputes of litigants, have removed all such doubts by the following concise opinion. Where anyone has bequeathed a lodging, it appears to Us to be the more humane opinion to also grant to the legatee the right to lease it, for what difference does it make whether the legatee himself remains there, or gives it up to another for the purpose of receiving compensation? This is much more apparent if he left the usufruct of the dwelling, as it gives rise to greater difficulty where the name usufruct is added, for We do not desire that the lodging should take precedence of the usufruct. The legatee should not expect to obtain the ownership of the right of residence, unless he can prove by the clearest evidence that the ownership of the house was also left to him, for then the will of the testator must in every respect be obeyed. We decree that this decision shall apply to all places in which a right of habitation can be established.[6]

Habitatio in Greco-Roman Egypt

The house in Roman Egypt was the center of everyday family life, a location of production and reproduction, and therefore held central symbolic and literal meaning for the social functions of the village and urban family unit.[7] The guarantee of a right of residence for those members of the family who did not have a proper right of possession of the family home was therefore of the utmost importance. In the Roman papyri, the right of habitatio—or in Greek, *enoikēsis*—was often granted by will in the form of a legacy from which widows, in particular, profited. While children—daughters as well as sons—were the main heirs and inherited equally in Roman and Greco-Egyptian law, a widow did not inherit from her deceased husband. To protect the widow and give her the option of not having to return to her natal family or remarry, a testator could grant a right of residence in the familial house to his widow. Habitatio did not necessarily encompass the entire house, but could also be limited just to a part or even just a room of a house. This right could extend either for a certain number of years until the children reached majority, or for as long as the widow lived.[8] Widowhood was a common fate for women in Greco-Roman Egypt, and many experienced it for the first time as early as their twenties.[9] It was only the demographic transition in the nineteenth century that reduced the numbers of young widows and created the association between widowhood and old age.[10] When children were still minors, widows were even granted an extended usufruct of their late husbands' estates on condition that they took responsibility for the administration of the property for the benefit of their common children until they came of age.[11] In such a situation, the widowed mother stepped into her late husband's role as the head of the household and experienced a degree of independence usually not granted to women in Greco-Hellenistic and Roman times.

This arrangement, leaving everything to the children with the widow only inheriting a right of residence in the family house, was meant to protect the family house and land from alienation. The same pattern has been described for many other premodern patriarchal societies.[12] The restricted nature of the right of habitatio, that is, the impossibility of leasing or selling the right, makes sense in this context: a widow who wanted to lease or sell her right of residence would introduce a complete stranger into the home that she shared with her children and with other family members from her husband's side of the family.[13]

Furthermore, if these widows remarried, they lost this privilege.[14] Some widows, particularly those with small children, found themselves in a quandary as a result of this condition: they needed to remarry for financial reasons in order to be able to feed and clothe their children, but if they did, they were no longer entitled to retain their right of residence and to remain the guardians of their own children. The care and guardianship would then regularly go to the father's closest relatives.[15]

The testator leaving his widow a habitatio had in mind—apart from the latter's well-being—also the interest of his heirs in the family estate. Under Roman law as well as local legal traditions, widows were entitled to receive back the dowry that they had brought with them into the marriage. Since the dowry had often been invested by the husband into the family estate, the heirs were obligated to liquidate enough of their patrimony to return the widow's portion to her. Assigning to the widow a habitatio, with or without usufruct, made it possible to avoid the liquidation of the family estate. However, had the couple been living in a multigenerational patrilocal household with the husband's parents, such an arrangement was not sought. The widow received back her dowry, left her children in their paternal family's care, and returned to her own natal household—often to remarry in due course.[16]

For the widow to be able to enjoy the right of habitatio and to manage the patrimony for her underage children, particular living arrangements had to be in place as a precondition for such a legal arrangement to make sense. The deceased husband needed to have been the head of the household, since only in this case would he have been able to grant these rights to his wife. If the family had been part of an extended household, and the husband's father or his brothers were still alive and all property was held in common,[17] this arrangement would not have been possible.[18] Neither was there a place for an unattached woman in a household consisting of several couples and their children, or a role for such a woman as manager of part of the household's property.[19]

A Right of Residence for the Widow Cleopatra

Let us have a look at a few cases in more detail.[20] The first case is a *donatio mortis causa*, a gift made with a view to the donor's impending death. The papyrus text was drawn up during the reign of Hadrian in the village of Tebtunis in the Fayum. Anticipating his death, the fifty-year old testator, whose name is lost, promises to his two sons, Ammonios and Herakleides, his estate in two equal shares. His property consisted of one *aroura* of vineyard and a half share of a house and courtyard held in joint ownership with the testator's brother, Moschion. The testator wishes:

> [N.N.] the elder, son of Didas son of Didymos, his mother being Dioskorous, daughter of Moschion, from the metropolis . . . fifty years old, with a scar on his upper lip on the left, acknowledges that he has agreed that after his death there shall belong to his two sons, Ammonios and Herakleides, born of his wife Kleopatra, daughter of Dionysios, to be shared by each of them equally, the one aroura of vineyard of the class paying one-sixth, that belongs to him near . . . formerly belonging to [?] . . . also called Areios, of the Archistratian tribe and the Althean deme, and also the half share of the house and courtyard that belongs to him and to his brother Moschion in common and undivided; and also whatever else he shall leave . . . or anything else, together with what shall come to him from any source whatsoever, as well as the household goods that shall be left by him . . . and the furnishings and what is owed to him in any way whatsoever.

To his widow, the testator left the right to reside on the property for as long as she lived on condition that she did not remarry. She was also to enjoy the services of the enslaved persons in their household and the harvest. His widow, in turn, was under the obligation to manage his property for their sons and to feed and clothe them until they reached majority.

> Their aforesaid mother, Cleopatra, daughter of Dionysios . . . shall from the year in which he dies for as long as she lives and remains unmarried . . . to reside on the property and be served by the slaves that he shall leave . . . the said Cleopatra, she feeding and clothing their said children . . . and the said children shall not have the power on the strength of this document to manage anything . . . of their mother, so that there shall remain to her the crop and the residence and the service.

Further down in the text we read: "And she [i.e. Cleopatra, his widow] has agreed to all these conditions, as aforesaid, and I shall seal with the seal."

While the widow Cleopatra seems to have enjoyed the right of residence in the entire house of her deceased husband, another widow received merely the right to reside in one of the rooms of a house whose ownership went to her sons.[21] In a will dated to 117 CE, Diogenis, wife of Dionysius from Oxyrhynchus, is said to be entitled to choose one of the rooms in the house for herself (ἐνοίκησιν καὶ χρῆσιν χωρὶς ἐνοικίου οἴκο[υ] ἑ̣ν̣ός). She could also enjoy the furniture of the entire house and the service of the enslaved persons in their household as long as she fed and clothed the latter properly. The property itself was vested in their children, who would receive it after their mother's death (μετὰ δὲ καὶ τὴν αὐτῆς τελευτὴν εἶναι τὰ πάντα μου [μόνων τῶν ἐξ ἀλλήλων τέκν]ω̣ν).

The Right of Residence for the Widower Hatres

It was, however, not just widows who could enjoy habitatio in a deceased person's house. The fact that women inherited equally with their brothers from their parents meant that a considerable share of the land and houses in the Egyptian *chora* was in the hands of women.[22] And commonly enough, it was the wife's house in which a married couple lived and raised their children. If a woman did not have brothers, she would inherit the paternal estate. In the absence of sons of their own, her parents would make sure to search for a husband for her who would move into their home to take care of them in their old age and to continue the family line.[23] Such an arrangement was particularly interesting for a young man from an impoverished family background or with many siblings at home. If his wife died before him, however, he was left with nothing. Just as widows did not inherit from their husbands, widowers did not inherit from their wives. Everything went to the couple's children, or to the natal family of the deceased if the couple was childless. So it comes as no surprise that women contemplating death also made sure that their husbands could remain in the family home.

A case like this comes from Oxyrhynchus from during the reign of Domitian.[24] Soeris, daughter of Harpochras, leaves to her son Hareotes—or to the latter's heirs, in case he dies before her—her house and all its appurtenances. Soeris describes Hareotes quite simply as "my son." No patronymic is given; he is apparently a "fatherless" child, legally designated simply by his mother's name (l. 10: τοῦ υ[ἱ]οῦ μου Ἀρεώτου χρηματίζοντος μητρὸς ἐμ̣α̣υ̣τῆς τῆς Σοήριος).[25] Soeris further includes the condition that her current husband Hatres retains the right of residence for life and receives from his stepson, Soeris's son, a yearly payment of forty-eight drachmas in silver until three hundred drachmas in silver are reached.[26] Soeris also makes provision for her daughter Tnepheros, her child with her husband Hatres. Her daughter was already married and seems to have received her share of the inheritance already in the form of a dowry. On the death of their father, Soeris's son from a previous union, Hareotes, was to pay an additional forty silver drachmas to his half-sister within thirty days. Furthermore, should Soeris's daughter separate from her husband and wish to return home, the testatrix made sure to include a right of residence, free of rent, for her daughter in a ground-floor single room at the gatehouse for this eventuality. Widowed or divorced women usually enjoyed a place of recourse in the form of their natal homes.[27] Soeris makes sure to consider both of her children from different unions and also grants her current life partner the right to remain in the familial home. A similar case comes from the same city, Oxyrhynchus, a few decades later. Here the testatrix, named Taharpaesis Isidora, leaves all her property to her three children and grants her partner and probably father of her children, among other things, a lifelong right of residence in her home.[28]

Habitatio for the Mother-in-law

In late summer of 136 CE, the widow Aphrodite married off her daughter Aphroditous and gave her as dowry not only jewelry and clothes, but also a half share of a house in the metropolis Arsinoe and three arouras of land.[29] Aphrodite, however, reserves for herself—stipulated in the marriage contract—a right of residence in the house and the usufruct of half of the land as long as she lived. The widowed mother-in-law concluded the marriage contract with her son-in-law. Her daughter already owned the other half of that same house, which she had inherited from her father. The contract now stipulated that the mother of the bride had a right of residence in the entire house. Most likely it was the house the daughter Aphroditous had grown up in, and the mother asked for the right to stay where she had lived during her married life with her husband and raised her children. The mother also reserved for herself the usufruct of half of the three arouras she left her daughter as dowry in the village of Metrodoros.

> l. 8–20: Aphrodite declares to have given to her daughter irrevocably as dowry 3 *arouras* of katoecic land in the village of Metrodoros which belong to her, as proven by two official documents; in addition, the half share of a house with courtyard that belongs as well to her on the main street (plateia street) of the metropolis Arsinoe. . . . The mother declares to have given this dowry under the condition that she keeps for her remaining lifetime a right of residence and usufruct of the entire house with courtyard on the main street and furthermore the usufruct of half of the three katoecic arouras in the village of Metrodoros. In return the mother of the bride will deliver 4 artabas of wheat for the running year to the couple in Arsinoe.

The marriage contract Aphrodite drew up with her son-in-law thus formed for her some kind of retirement contract for her old age. While she already transferred the ownership of the entire house and the land to her daughter, she reserves herself the usufruct of both.[30] Retirement contracts in Greek and Roman Egypt could take on different forms; they could be—as in the case above—part of a marriage contract, a deed of gift, or part of a will. Many old parents would not have felt very comfortable relinquishing all their power and property to their children during their lifetime, since such an act left them with little security by making them dependent on their children's goodwill and sense of moral obligation. For these reasons, Aphrodite reserves herself the usufruct of house and land and warns her daughter not to contest her mother's rights.[31]

Habitatio for a Creditor

We also find another form of habitatio recorded among the papyri from Hellenistic, Roman, and Byzantine Egypt that did involve a right of residence, but not granted by will, and not necessarily to a family member.[32] A loan contract from Arsinoe, the capital of the Arsinoite nome, dating to the first half of the third century, provides an example.[33] This contract, housed today in the papyrus collection of Princeton University, reads as follows:

> In the third year of the Emperor Pius Felix Augustus, Pauni, at Ptolemais Euergetis in the Arsinoite nome. Aurelios Diogenes, aged about seventy and with a scar, acknowledges to Aurelios Serenos, also called Isidoros, son of Olympos, that he has received from him a loan of two hundred drachmas in silver, and in lieu of interest Serenos has the right to inhabit the half part of a house belonging to Diogenes near the village of Philadelphia . . . from the current month Epeiph of the current year. If the aforesaid sum is not paid back . . . Serenos will have the ownership of the aforesaid half portion of the house . . . nor shall Diogenes alienate this property until he pays back the aforesaid loan. Whenever he wishes, Serenos may register this contract in the record-office of Apollinarios . . . Aurelios Serenos has the right of exaction from Aurelios Diogenes in person and from the half part of the house and from all his possessions as if legal decision had been given. Aurelios Diogenes, veteran, . . . acknowledges that he has borrowed two hundred drachmas with the right of habitation in lieu of interest on the aforesaid principal as stated above.

Aurelius Diogenes received a loan of two hundred silver drachmas from Aurelius Serenus. Instead of interest rates payable by Aurelius Diogenes, Serenus was allowed to claim the right to take up residence in the half of the house that Diogenes owned near the village of Philadelphia. If Diogenes failed to repay the loan, the ownership of this half house would fall to Serenus. This habitatio arrangement most closely resembles a mortgage agreement, a temporary transfer of an interest in real estate to a lender as a security on a loan of money. If the borrower failed to meet his payment obligations, the property was foreclosed and went to the lender. The amount paid by Serenus to Diogenes can hardly be interpreted as a down payment on purchasing the house. Nor should we see this loan as a kind of security for any damage incurred over the rental period, since the amount borrowed vastly exceeded the price of any interior furnishings. Nonetheless, in our modern understanding of a mortgage, the lender would not move into the house himself, nor would he be in a position to rent the house to someone else. In most cases, it is the debtor himself who lives in the property he has borrowed the money to purchase in the first place.

Habitatio in this form resembles an antichretic loan. Antichresis under Roman law was a contract whereby a debtor pledged real property to a creditor. Instead of receiving interest on the loan, the creditor was allowed to use the pledged property. Even though it conveyed possession but not title, such an arrangement was subject to a property transfer tax.[34] However, we might rightly ask why a creditor would be interested in such an arrangement. If he had the money, why would he not buy the house in which he wanted to live? In an antichretic loan arrangement, he even had to pay the property transfer tax without becoming the owner. If he had just rented the place, no property transfer tax would have been due. The reason might be that the Roman authorities in Roman Egypt had limited the amount of interest rates that could be charged to 12 percent per year. The maximum the borrower could exact on a loan of 200 drachmas was thus 24 drachmas per year.[35] Moreover, Roman law specified that the total of the interest payable could never exceed the capital borrowed. The right to habitatio for a certain period of time thus allowed circumvention of this restriction.

Let us look at rent prices, which varied, of course, depending on the time, location, and size of the rented property. While a house somewhere in the Arsinoite at the end of the first century was rented for 40 drachmas a year,[36] a house with all its appurtenances in the village of Tebtunis was rented in 141 CE for an annual rent of 25 drachmas.[37] Rental agreements for houses in the *metropoleis* speak of considerably higher prices, however. A house in Oxyrhynchus was rented for an annual payment of 200 drachmas in 164 CE,[38] and just one upper room with a pigeon-cote was rented in 183 CE at an annual rent of 60 drachmas.[39] Another house in Oxyrhynchus was rented in 274 CE at a yearly rent of 400 drachmas.[40] In 280 CE, another house in Oxyrhynchus was rented for an annual rent of 1,000 drachmas.[41] In 323 CE, a share of the house in Oxyrhynchus was rented for the annual payment of 3,000 silver drachmas.[42] Twenty-four drachmas as annual rent in the early third century for a house in the metropolis Arsinoe thus seems ridiculously low. The creditor therefore secured a rental deal far below market value, probably at one-tenth of the amount he could have legally enacted on his loan of 200 drachmas. The creditor was probably able to strike this sensational deal because the debtor was in urgent need of cash. Furthermore, if the borrower was not able to repay the loan within the agreed-on time period, the lender even became the owner of the house. For a mere 200 drachmas he would have acquired a house in the metropolis whose actual worth by far exceeded this amount.

Most of the loans were "peer to peer" loans; professional pawnbrokers and lenders played an insignificant role in these transactions. The aim behind these antichretic loans involving a right of residence might be thus to circumvent the law, exacting considerably higher interest rates or even acquiring a house far below market level.[43]

However, since the recipient of habitatio had to live in the house himself, the creditor could not enter into several loans of this kind. It remains unknown which considerations led late antique lawgivers to change the regulations for previously inalienable habitatio in order to allow the possibility of selling or leasing habitatio rights, but it was certainly creditors who profited from these antichretic loans. Papyrological evidence from the early seventh century CE shows that the recipient of habitatio under a loan was then also allowed to let someone else live in the house and at times even entered into the arrangement with the intention of immediately leasing out the acquired right to a third party. A certain Aurelia Maria rents out an entire house, which she calls her own, to a purple dyer.[44] The truth was that she just owned two-thirds of it. Just the day before, on October 31, she had received the habitatio of the remaining one-third of the house under an antichretic pledge from her sister. This kind of arrangement had only become possible after the change in the law concerning habitatio.

Synthesizing the Evidence on Habitatio

The overview of the documentary evidence shows that habitatio in Roman and late antique Egypt was a limited right, basically the right of usus but not usufruct. The holders of the right could occupy the house alone or with their dependents. The holders of a habitatio could only live there themselves; they could not lease or sell their right—the right of habitatio was inalienable. Widows did not inherit from their deceased husbands, but were often granted a habitatio, a lifelong right of residence in the familial home. The husband regularly added a condition to the effect that his widow was not allowed to remarry if she wanted to retain this right for the duration of her lifetime. As long as the children were not yet of age, the widowed mother was given the task of administering her deceased husband's estate until her children reached the age of majority. This arrangement—with the widow remaining in the family home and functioning as the trustee of the conjugal financial resources—was, however, only possible if her late husband and his brothers had already divided up their parents' estate and the couple had thus already established their own household. If the couple had still resided in the husband's family home when he died, the widow often simply received her dowry back and was then faced with the choice of either remarrying or returning, at least temporarily, to her own natal family. According to the view of the time, her children belonged to the paternal family and also remained with the father's family when the mother moved out.

Since sons and daughters had the same inheritance entitlements, a considerable share of the land and real estate in Roman Egypt was in female hands. It thus occurred not rarely that a couple lived in a house that belonged to the wife. These women sometimes granted their widowers a right to remain living in the family home after their deaths. The woman's heirs, however, were her children. It is understandable that this form of habitatio was designed to be inalienable, since otherwise a complete stranger could have been introduced into a family home.

Some elderly parents also included a right of residence in intergenerational contracts concluded with their children. These contracts enabled the parents to secure a place of residence for their old age while already transferring the property rights to their children during their own lifetime—thereby probably avoiding the payment of the inheritance tax.

In parallel to these situations, however, habitatio, the right of residence, was also used in creditor-debtor arrangements in Ptolemaic, Roman, and later Roman Egypt, a practice that is otherwise not attested in the legal writings on Roman law. The earliest example from the papyri dates to 133 BCE, the latest one to 607 CE. Instead of receiving interest, some creditors preferred to receive a house or apartment rent-free for a fixed period of time from their debtors, with this right of residence ending when the debtor had repaid the loan.

Notes

1 I am grateful to José Luis Alonso (Zurich) for his revisions and advice in Roman legal matters.

2 *Dig.* 7.8, concerning use and habitation. Cf. *Dig.* 39 tit. 5.27 and 32. However, this matter was under discussion among the Roman jurists, where the question was whether habitatio is to be taken as comprising only usus or the entire usufruct.

3 E.g. *Inst.* 2.5.1–2 from 533 CE (transl. J. B. Moyle, *The Institutes of Justinian*, 5th ed. Oxford: 1913): "A use is a less right than a usufruct; for if a man has a bare use of an estate, he is deemed entitled to use the vegetables, fruit, flowers, hay, straw, and wood upon it only so far as his daily needs require: he may remain on the land only so long as he does not inconvenience its owner, or impede those who are engaged in its cultivation; but he cannot let or sell or give away his right to a third person, whereas a usufructuary may. Again, a man who has the use of a house is deemed entitled only to live in it himself; he cannot transfer his right to a third person, and it scarcely seems to be agreed that he may take in a guest; but besides himself he may lodge there his wife, children, and freedmen, and other free persons who form as regular a part of his establishment as his slaves. Similarly, if a woman has the use of a house, her husband may dwell there with her." Again, however, this was not undisputed among the classical jurists; it was even discussed whether the usuary could be completely excluded from the fruits.

4 *Dig.* 7.8.8.

5 *Inst.* 2.5.5 from 533 CE (transl. J. B. Moyle, *The Institutes of Justinian*, 5th ed. Oxford: 1913).

6 *Given on the eighteenth of the Kalends of October, during the fifth Consulate of Lampadius and Orestes, 530.* (*CIust.* 3.33.13 from 530 CE, trans. S. P. Scott, *The Civil Law, XII.* Cincinnati: 1932).

7 See the contribution of Alston, chapter 7, this volume.

8 Cic. *Caec.* 11; *Dig.* 22.1.48; 33.2.32.2–4 (house and all contents), 33.2.35 (villa for five years), 33.2.37 (goods until daughter reaches age eighteen). See for usus: *Dig.* 7.9.11 (house); for *fructus Dig* 33.2.24 pr.; 33.2.25. Cf. Kreller 1919, 18–19.

9 For widows in the Roman Egyptian census returns see Bagnall and Frier 2006, 33-Ar-2 (mother acts as declarant of the entire household for the census officials); 103-Ar-9 (mother is declarant); 117-Ar-1 (lodgers); 117-Ar-5 (mother is declarant); 117-Ar-6 (son is declarant); 117-Ar-7 (son is declarant); 117-Ar-12 (mother is declarant); 131-Ar-12 (mother is declarant); 131-Ar-13 (mother is declarant); 131-He-2 (son is declarant); 145-Ar-1 (mother is declarant); 145-Ar-2 (mother is declarant); 145-Ar-3 (mother and daughter; daughter is declarant); (145-Ar-20: son is declarant); 145-Ar-22 (mother is declarant); 145-Ly-1 (mother is declarant); 159-Ar-10 (son is declarant); 173-Ar-9 (two apparently unrelated widows with children; one widow's son is declarant); 173-Ar-11 (mother and daughter; daughter is declarant); 173-Pr-4 (son is declarant); 173-Pr-11 (son is declarant); 173-Pr-14 (mother is declarant); 173-Pr-15 (mother is declarant); 173-Pr-17 (son is declarant); 187-Ar-29 (mother is declarant); 187-Ar-34 (mother is declarant); 187-Ar-39 (mother is declarant); 187-Me-1 (mother is declarant); 187-Ox-4 (mother is declarant); 201-Ar-1 (mother is declarant); 201-Ar-8 (mother is declarant); 201-Ar-9 (mother is declarant); 215-Ar-1 (son is declarant); 215-Ar-5 (son is declarant); 243-Ar-1 (mother is declarant); 243-Ar-3 (mother is declarant); 243-Ar-4 (mother is declarant); 257-Ar-1 (mother is declarant); ???-Ar-2 (mother

is declarant); *P.Oxy.Census* (Bagnall et al. 1997): 89-Pt-27 (son is declarant); 89-Pt-28? (son is declarant); 89-Pt-36 (son is declarant); 89-Pt-37 (son is declarant); 89-Pt-42 (son is declarant); 89-Pt-51 (son is declarant). Whether a widow acted as head of a household obviously did not depend on the age of her children or whether or not she had sons. We have widows in their seventies with sons in their fifties who nevertheless filed their census returns as household heads (e.g., Bagnall and Frier 2006, 201-Ar-9). Cf. Huebner 2009; Huebner 2013, chap. 4.

10 The census records from fifteenth-century Florence show that one-fourth of the adult female population above the age of twelve was widowed. The model life tables that Richard Saller adduces for Roman society certainly err on the positive side when they claim a rate of more than 90 percent for women between the ages of twenty-five to fifty-five (Saller 1994, 49, table 3.1.b: Female, "ordinary," Level 3 West).

11 Cf. *P.Cair.Masp.* 2.67156 (570 CE); Yiftach-Firanko 2006. Cf. *Dig.* 7.2.8 (Ulpian); 33.2.37 (Scaevola). For mothers in the Greek East serving as guardians of their minor children, cf. Evans Grubbs 2002: 248, 254–60. Yiftach-Firanko sees in this arrangement not a new entity after the husband's death but a continuation of the wife's rights as "mistress" (*kyrieuousa*) of the family estate, which she had already enjoyed during her husband's lifetime (Yiftach-Firanko 2003, 122–23, 242–43).

12 Agmon 2006, 162, for late Ottoman Palestine; Fridell 2003, 156, for twentieth-century Iran; Mann 1987, 44, for ancient China (Qing dynasty); Sommer 2000, 191, for late Imperial China; Wolf 1981, 140; and Holmgren 1985, 2, for nineteenth- and twentieth-century China. Cf. in general Palmore 1987, 101–2; Goody 1990, 202–3.

13 Huebner 2013, chaps. 4 and 5.

14 *CPR* 6.1 (125 CE); *P.Diog.* 9 (186–224 CE); *SB* 8.9642 (11–38 CE); *Chr.Mitt.* 306 (155 CE); cf. *Dig.* 35.1.62.2 (Clementius).

15 Huebner 2009.

16 Huebner 2009; Huebner 2013, 93–106.

17 Cf. *P.Oxy.* 34.2713 (297 CE): "For all that was left to us by the foregoing inheritance—being one household and one family—was in that very house in which they lived in partnership, I mean because the slaves and lands and household and moveable goods were all held in common."

18 Cuno (1995, 491) notes for instance for nineteenth-century Egypt that households were managed by a widow only when the couple had been living in a nuclear household before the husband's death and no other male adult was available within the household to take over the headship. Likewise in traditional India, a wife could only be entrusted with managing her late husband's household when her husband did not own property in common with his joint family (Altekar 1959, 261). Breschi comes to the same conclusion for nineteenth-century Italian sharecropping families who lived predominantly in joint households: if a couple was still living with the husband's family, the likelihood that his widow would remarry after his death was significantly higher than if the couple had been living on their own (Breschi, Manfredini, and Fornasin 2007).

19 Cf. Huebner 2013, 102–3.

20 *SB* VIII 9642 = *P.Mich.inv.* 5579 from 117/118 CE.

21 *P.Oxy.* 3.489.

22 Cf. Rowlandson 1998. For Roman Republican times, see Bannon 1998, 29–30; on late Republican and early Imperial Italy, Garnsey 2004, 112–13; Huebner 2013, 50–53. For later Roman society, see Tate 2008, 1–36; for inheritance rights of Roman daughters to an equal share, see Thomas 1991, 134. For Roman Egypt, see Huebner 2013, 123–24.

23 Huebner 2007; Huebner 2013.

24 *P.Oxy.* 1.104 from 96 CE. See for a detailed discussion, Steinsky 2004, 281–94.

25 On "fatherless" children in Roman Egypt, see Malouta 2009, 120–38.

26 Soeris owed her husband Hatres six hundred silver drachmas and Hareotes was supposed to repay to her husband half the money, i.e., three hundred drachmas (l. 17–22).

27 Huebner 2013, 100–103.

28 *P.Köln* 2.100 after 24. Aug. 133 CE. See for a discussion, Klamp 1968, 81–150; Rowlandson, 1998, no. 170.

29 *SPP* 20.5 = *CPR* 1.24 from 136 CE.

30 Cf. for intergenerational contracts Kreller 1919, 204–7; Pestman 1995, 80–81; Huebner 2013, chap. 5.

31 We find multiple parallels among the surviving papyri from the Roman Period. In a comparable case, a certain Hermione from early second-century Oxyrhynchus bestowed on her daughter her property in exchange for a pension until her death (ἡ δ' ἵνα μὴ καὶ ζῶσα ἡ μήτηρ τούτων στερῆται δίδωσι ἀντὶ τόκου κατ' ἐνιαυτὸν τὴν χορηγίαν ταύτην καὶ τοῦτο αὐτὸ γέγραπται κατὰ τὸ κοινὸν ὁμολόγημα.) (*P.Oxy.* 3.472 from ca. 130 CE; cf. Kreller 1919, 365). In another document from 244–48 CE, a father during his lifetime transfers his complete property to his two sons. The relevant part of the document is heavily destroyed and not readable, but Kreller assumes that we have here similar provisions for the father's maintenance during the last years of his life (Grenf. 2.71 from 244–48 CE; cf. Kreller 1919, 212–13). In a very late sixth-century papyrus, a mother transfers to her son the right of property over some land but stipulates that she would retain the usufruct as long as she was alive (*P.Lond.* 1044; cf. Kreller 1919, 214).

32 *BGU* 4.1115 (from 133 BCE); *P.Lond.* 3.1168 (from 44 CE); *P.Oxy.* 14.1641 (from 68 CE); *P.Mich.* 12.635 (from 71 CE); *P.Mich.inv.* 87 (from 74 CE); *P.Mich.* 10.585 (87 CE); *P.Hamb.* 1.30 (from 89 CE); *P.Oxy.* 8.1105 (81–96 CE); *BGU* 1.260 (from 90 CE); *P.Oxy.* 1.104 (from 96 CE); *SB* 5.7664 (from 109 CE); *P.Oslo* 3.118 (from 111–112 CE); *P.Mich.* 11.605 (from 117 CE); *P.Mich.* 11.625 (from 121 CE); *SB* 22.15849 (from 121 CE); *SB* 28.17056 (from 126 CE); *P.Cair.Masp.* 2.67131 (from 566/7 CE); *SB* 1.5285 (607 CE). Cf. Taubenschlag 1944, 172; 316; Claytor 2013.

33 *P.Princ.* 3.144 from 219/20 CE or 239/40 CE.

34 *SB* 28.17056; *SB* 22.15849; *P.Oslo* 3.118; *P.Mich.* 11.625. Cf. Manigk 1910; Taubenschlag 1944, 216–20; Kupiszewski 1974, 133–49; Rupprecht 1992, 271–89. Antichretic loans were also popular in ancient Mesopotamia, but there they usually involved enslaved people or land rather than a right of residence (Westbrook 2001, 329–33; Lipiński 2000, 587).

35 Bogaert 2000, 135–269.

36 *P.Mich.* 14 678.

37 *P.Tebt.* 2.372.

38 *P.Oxy.* 3.502.

39 *P.Oxy.* 8 1127.

40 *P.Oxy.* 7.1036.

41 *P.Oxy.* 14.1694.

42 *P.Oslo* 3.138.

43 Cf. Modrzejewski 1997, 118.

44 *SB* 1.5286. See also Urbanik 2013, 167–68.

Works Cited

Agmon, I. 2006. *Family and Court: Legal Culture and Modernity in Late Ottoman Palestine*. Syracuse, NY: Syracuse University Press.

Altekar, A.S. 1959. *The Position of Women in Hindu Civilization, from Prehistoric Times to the Present Day*. Delhi: Motilal Banarsidass.

Bagnall, R.S., and B.W. Frier. 2006. *The Demography of Roman Egypt*. 2nd ed. Cambridge: Cambridge University Press.

Bagnall, R.S., B.W. Frier, and I.C. Rutherford. 1997. *The Census Register P.Oxy. 984: The Reverse of Pindar's Paeans*. Papyrologica Bruxellensia 29. Brussels: Fondation Égyptologique Reine Élisabeth.

Bannon, C.J. 1998. *The Brothers of Romulus: Fraternal 'Pietas' in Roman Law, Literature, and Society*. Princeton: Princeton University Press.

Bogaert, R. 2000. "Les opérations des banques de l'Égypte romaine." *Ancient Society* 30: 135–269.

Breschi, M., M. Manfredini, and A. Fornasin. 2007. "Remarriage in a Pretransitional Italian Community." *Continuity and Change* 22: 407–28.

Claytor, W.G. 2013. "Loan of Wheat with Antichresis." *Archiv für Papyrusforschung und verwandte Gebiete* 59: 138–42.

Cuno, K.M. 1995. "Joint Family Households and Rural Notables in Nineteenth-Century Egypt." *International Journal of Middle East Studies* 27: 485–502.

Evans Grubbs, J. 2002. *Women and Law in the Roman Empire. A Sourcebook on Marriage, Divorce and Widowhood.* London: Psychology Press.

Fridell, E. 2003. "Tribal Enterprises and Marriage Issues in Twentieth-Century Iran." In *Family History in the Middle East: Household, Property, and Gender,* edited by B. Doumani, 151–71. Albany, NY: SUNY Press:

Garnsey, P. 2004. *Cities, Peasants, and Food in Classical Antiquity: Essays in Social and Economic History.* Cambridge: Cambridge University Press.

Goody, J. 1990. *The Oriental, the Ancient, and the Primitive.* Cambridge: Cambridge University Press.

Holmgren, J. 1985. "The Economic Foundations of Virtue: Widow-Remarriage in Early and Modern China." *Australian Journal of Chinese Affairs* 13: 1–27.

Huebner, S.R. 2007. "Brother-Sister Marriage in Roman Egypt: a Curiosity of Humankind or a Widespread Family Strategy." *Journal of Roman Studies* 97: 21–49.

Huebner, S.R. 2009. "Callirhoe's Dilemma: Remarriage and Stepfathers in the Graeco-Roman East." In *Growing up Fatherless in Antiquity,* edited by S.R Huebner and D.M. Ratzan, 61–82. Cambridge: Cambridge University Press.

Huebner, S.R. 2013. *The Family in Roman Egypt. A Comparative Approach to Intergenerational Solidarity and Conflict.* Cambridge: Cambridge University Press.

Huebner, S.R. 2014. " 'It is a difficult matter to be wronged by strangers, but to be wronged by kin is worst of all'—Inheritance and Conflict in Graeco-Roman Egypt." In *Inheritance, Law and Religion in the Ancient and Medieval Worlds,* edited by S.R. Huebner and B. Caseau, 99–108. Paris: Peeters.

Justel, J.J. 2015. "An Unpublished Nuzi-Type Antichretic Loan Contract in the British Museum." *Iraq* 77: 129–42.

Klamp, D. 1968. "Das Testament der Taharpaesis: Eröffnungsprotokoll eines griechischen Testaments: P. Colon. inv. 2382." *Zeitschrift für Papyrologie und Epigraphik* 2: 81–150.

Kreller, H. 1919. *Erbrechtliche Untersuchungen auf Grund der graeco-ägyptischen Papyrusurkunden.* Leipzig: B. G. Teubner.

Kupiszewski, H. 1974. "Quelques remarques sur les vocabula ἀντιχρῆσις, ἄρρα, παραφῆρνα dans le Digeste." *Journal of Juristic Papyrology* 18: 133–49.

Lipiński, E. 2000. *The Aramaeans: Their Ancient History, Culture, Religion.* Leuven: Peeters.

Malouta, M. 2009. "Fatherlessness and Formal Identification in Roman Egypt." In *Growing Up Fatherless in Antiquity,* edited by S.R. Huebner and D. M. Ratzan, 120–38. Cambridge: Cambridge University Press.

Manigk, A. 1910. *Gläubigerbefriedigung durch Nutzung: ein Institut der antiken Rechte.* Berlin: Vahlen.

Mann, S. 1987. "Widows in the Kinship, Class, and Community Structures of Qing Dynasty China." *Journal of Asian Studies* 46: 37–56.

Modrzejewski, J.M. 1997. *The Jews of Egypt: From Rameses II to Emperor Hadrian.* Princeton: Princeton University Press.

Palmore, E. 1987. "Cross-Cultural Perspectives on Widowhood." *Journal of Cross-Cultural Gerontology* 2: 93–105.

Pestman, P.W. 1995. "Appearance and Reality in Written Contracts: Evidence from Bilingual Family Archives." In *Legal Documents of the Hellenistic World,* edited by M. Geller, H. Maehler, and A. Lewis, 79–87. London: Warburg Institute.

Rowlandson, J. 1998. *Women and Society in Greek and Roman Egypt: A Sourcebook.* Cambridge: Cambridge University Press.

Rupprecht, H.-A. 1992. "Zur Antichrese in den griechischen Papyri bis Diokletian." In *Proceedings of the XIXth International Congress of Papyrology,* edited by S.H.S. El-Mosalamy, 271–89. Cairo: Center of Papyrological Studies, Ain Shams University.

Saller, R.P. 1994. *Patriarchy, Property and Death in the Roman Family.* Cambridge: Cambridge University Press.

Sommer, M.H. 2000. *Sex, Law, and Society in Late Imperial China.* Stanford, CA: Stanford University Press.

Steinsky, P. 2004. "Ein Beitrag zum Erbrecht des Mannes nach seiner Ehegattin." *Revue Internationale des droits de l'Antiquité* 51: 281–94.

Tate, J.C. 2008. "Inheritance Rights of Nonmarital Children in Late Roman Law." *Roman Legal Tradition* 4: 1–36.

Taubenschlag, R. 1944. *The Law of Graeco-Roman Egypt in Light of the Papyri*. New York: Herald Square Press.

Thomas, Y. 1991. "The Division of the Sexes in Roman Law." In *A History of Women from Ancient Goddesses to Christian Saints*, edited by P. Schmitt Pantel, 83–137. Cambridge, MA: Harvard University Press.

Urbanik, J. 2013. "Tapia's Banquet Hall and Eulogios' Cell: Transfer of Ownership as a Security in Some Late Byzantine Papyri." In *New Frontiers: Law and Society in the Roman World*, edited by P. J. du Plessis, 151–74. Edinburgh: Edinburgh University Press.

Westbrook, R. 2001. "Conclusions." In *Security for Debt in Ancient Near Eastern Law*, edited by R. Jasnow and R. Westbrook, 327–40. Leiden: Brill.

Wolf, A.P. 1981. "Women, Widowhood and Fertility in Pre-Modern China." In *Marriage and Remarriage in Populations of the Past*, edited by J. Dupâquier, E. Hélin, P. Laslett, M. Livi-Bacci, and S. Sogner, 139–47. London: Academic Press.

Yiftach-Firanko, U. 2003. *Marriage and Marital Arrangements. A History of the Greek Marriage Document in Egypt. 4th Century BCE—4th Century CE*. Munich: C.H. Beck.

Yiftach-Firanko, U. 2006. "Spouses in Wills: A Diachronic Survey (III BC-IV AD)." *Journal of Juristic Papyrology* 36: 153–66.

6

Unsafe Houses in Greco-Roman Egypt

Forms and Locations of Violence

YOUSSRI ABDELWAHED

"Cornelius to his sweetest son, Hierax, greeting. . . . Take care not to offend any of the persons at home" (*P.Oxy*. 3.531, second century CE).

As indicated in ancient Egyptian texts, the house was viewed as a place of peace, rest, fortune, and safety for all members of the household,[1] and this notion persisted into the Greco-Roman Period,[2] and as Frankfurter discusses in this volume, into Late Antiquity.[3] In second-century CE Oxyrhynchus, Cornelius instructed his son Hierax "not to offend any of the persons at home,"[4] reflecting the paterfamilias's concern about the peaceful environment that was desirable for a household in Roman Egypt, but that was sometimes disturbed by violent behavior. This chapter attempts to identify and locate different forms of violent behavior committed by or against the house occupants in the light of papyrus petitions uncovered from Greco-Roman Egypt. I simply argue that the house was not a safe place in Greco-Roman Egypt, where violence was one available expression of social interaction between the house occupants and their partners or other inhabitants.

Over the past two decades, scholars interested in material and visual culture in the Greco-Roman world have approached houses from different perspectives. Using archaeology and papyri, scholars have focused on the social dimension of the house,[5] the expression of cultural identity through material culture,[6] the dynamics of the everyday family life of the common people,[7] and the ritual practices of houses in Greco-Roman Egypt.[8] Much valuable work in recent years has highlighted "violence" in Pharaonic and Greco-Roman Egypt. Based on textual and pictorial sources, Matić presented the first monographic study connecting violence and gender in ancient Egypt.[9] Hue-Arcé followed a comparative approach to highlight the characteristics and similarities of this social phenomenon in the New Kingdom and the Greco-Roman Periods. She focused on the mechanisms of expression and treatment of interpersonal physical violence.[10]

Many scholars have called attention to the social and legal dimensions of the problematic concept of violence in Greco-Roman Egypt.[11] Bagnall explored examples in which individuals complained of violence that cut across social hierarchies. He distinguished between violence committed between approximate equals, violence of high-status persons against low-status ones, and official use of force against individuals.[12] There is less evidence of violence of low-status persons against high-status ones, however. In 113 BCE at Kerkeosiris, the oil-smugglers Sisois son of Senapynchis and his wife Tausiris belabored Trychambos, the agent of the oikonomos, and Apollodoros, the contractor for the distribution of and the tax on oil, with blows in the smugglers' house.[13] Recently, Bagnall has also considered public violence and revolts from the reigns of Hadrian to Diocletian. Dramatic public acts of violence committed or experienced by the inhabitants severely damaged some cities, particularly Alexandria, and occasional revolts disturbed the peace within the community and led to the depopulation of many villages.[14]

Parca considered violence committed by and against women in Greco-Roman Egypt, although without fully taking into account the identification and location of violent acts.[15] Evans highlighted the legal protection that women in fourth century CE Egypt enjoyed from household violence.[16] Exploring more than a hundred papyrus petitions, Bryen presented the most detailed study on contemporary perspectives on violence from a legal anthropology and social theory approach.[17] So far, however, no study has fully addressed the issue of the identification and location of different forms of violent behavior committed by or against the house occupants in papyrus petitions from Greco-Roman Egypt. The present contribution is meant to widen our knowledge and understanding of daily practice and social interaction around and within houses in post-Pharaonic Egypt.

Accordingly, I seek to identify different forms of household violence in petitions and to locate these forms in relation to the physical arrangement of the house. I primarily focus on legal petitions from Oxyrhynchus and Tebtynis, highlighting forms and locations of household violence.[18] Yet this is not a comparative study on domestic violence in urban and rural sites. Other corpuses of papyri are also used whenever relevant. The time span of the chapter extends from the foundation of the Ptolemaic Dynasty in 305 BCE to the official recognition of Christianity in 325 CE.

Forms of Domestic Violence in Legal Petitions

From a terminological perspective, violence has been subject to varying definitions and scholarly debates. Based on the agents, victims, and impacts of violence in mass media, Berger has identified nearly seventy types of violence, reflecting the complexity of the concept of violence and the diversity of its aspects.[19] Indeed, the definition of "violence" varies widely depending on individual scholarly usage. For Abelson, "violence connotes illegitimate or excessive force."[20] Similarly, Graham and Gurr define violence as "behavior designed to inflict physical injury to people or damage to property."[21] These narrow explanations agree that violence only conveys physical harm to individuals and their properties. However, I adopt Lawrence's definition of violence to mean "the entire class of actions which result, or are intended to result, in serious injury to life or its material conditions. Serious injury must include the ideas of biological damage, severe physical restraints or property destruction and psychological impairment."[22]

In that sense, violence covers a variety of corporeal and incorporeal behavior intended to threaten human safety, damage property, or debase self-esteem. Yet there are potential differences between ancient and modern perceptions of violence. In legal petitions, the victims of household violence expressed that they were legally wronged by acts that violated the norms of their society. Not only do modern observers agree that these acts are problematic, but the ancient petitioners thought so too. However, households of Greco-Roman Egypt also witnessed other acts that we would today regard as "violent," but that would not have been considered problematic in antiquity. There are certain kinds of physically, verbally, and emotionally harmful acts that would not have risen to the level of illegality or social stigmatization in Greco-Roman Egypt. In 1 BCE, Hilarion writes from Alexandria to his wife Alis, telling her that if "you bear a child and it is male, let it be; if it is female, cast it out."[23] Similarly, ancient teachers used to physically punish students and apprentices for misbehavior and failure to learn.[24] The exposure of unwanted infants and the beating of schoolchildren and apprentices strike us as heartless, abhorrent, and highly violent. However, such acts were viewed as acceptable and tolerated within ancient social norms in Greco-Roman Egypt.[25]

Despite osteological evidence of child abuse on a two- to three-year-old child's skeleton uncovered from Kellis 2, a Romano-Christian cemetery in the Dakhla Oasis,[26] legal petitions from Oxyrhynchus and Tebtynis remain our main source of information about the forms and locations of domestic violence. Violence was a complex social phenomenon in Greco-Roman Egypt, and the inhabitants used a variety of Greek terms to denote different types of household violence. The preference of one appellation over another depended not only on the formalities of the language of legal appeal and scribal tradition, but also on the form of violence inflicted on petitioners.

Greek papyri employ three different terms: *bia*, *loidoria*, and *hybris*. In 150–54 CE, Stotoetis of Soknopaiou Nesos petitioned Demetrios *alias* Harpokratios, the *strategos* of the divisions of Themistes and Polemon, concerning a specific act of bia: namely, he had been forced by Sotas Theonos and his son Amonios to sign away his rights to a sum of money. Bia here refers to the use of violence against property. The culprits forced him to do this "with hybris and *plēgē* [blows]."[27] Although bia and hybris here coexist in a single document, they refer to different violent actions. In a fourth century CE petition, a gamekeeper claims that a hunter repulsed him "with hybris and loidoria" when he attempted to claim a judgment against him, similarly suggesting two different offenses.[28] Three forms of violence can be identified in Greco-Roman Egypt. Bia is physical violence against individuals and properties, loidoria is verbal abuse, and hybris is emotional abuse designed to humiliate or dishonor the victim. These are discussed in the following sections.

Bia (Physical/Bodily Violence)

Bia literally means an act of violence using bodily strength or force.[29] It designates acts of bodily violence committed by or against the house occupants with intentions to harm somebody.[30] Bia also included violent acts directed against the house and household (parents, children, and enslaved persons).[31] Acts of physical/bodily violence included, but are not limited to, blows (*plēgē*),[32] beating (*pugmē*), and trampling on the victim's body (*laktisma*).[33] Petitioners use a broad range of verbs to report incidents of physical violence. The verb employed at the heading of legal complaints is *adikoumai*, meaning 'I am wronged'.[34] Various verbs expressed bodily assaults, notably *katakoptō* (knock down), *prosballō* (offend), *epipherō* (assault), and *eperchomai* (to attack).[35]

In Greek papyri, bia denotes violent behavior against individuals and their properties. Injurious bodily treatment of enslaved laborers, who were counted as property, was thus also called bia. In the fourth century CE, a woman complains of an attack against her household; she complains that the accused's enslaved persons and her enslaved girl were subject to bodily attack (bia) and insolence (hybris), denoting different violent actions.[36] The adjectival or adverbial form of bia (*biaios, biaiōs*) appears in one papyrus petition to designate the individual who commits corporeal violence or harm to property (bia).[37] *Biaioi* are also the persons who died in an untimely manner and whose spirits dwelled somewhere in the neighborhood of their graves until the predetermined time of their death.[38] In magical papyri, the word *biaioi* designates those who died violently and whose spirits were consigned to this world and thus were accessible spiritual agents for love charms.[39]

In Greco-Roman Egypt, neither the inhabitants nor the social order tolerated household violence using bodily strength or weapons. In many cases, the victims addressed their petitions to the Ptolemaic king, demanding the arrest of the aggressor. The Ptolemaic king forwarded the case to the strategos, asking the seizure of the perpetrator by the *epistates* or *archiphylaketes*. In 221 BCE, Hediste complained to Ptolemy IV that she and her husband Philonous were "attacked and beaten in their house and received life-threatening injuries."[40] In the same year, Eutychos, a water-carrier in Aliatos of the Arsinoite, petitioned Ptolemy IV to denounce the son of Apollonios who had "struck my wife and laid his hands on me" in what appears to be a domestic context.[41] In 215 BCE in Lagis of the Arsinoite, a petitioner complained to Ptolemy IV that Horos, the devotee of the god Harpaesis, "broke into the house and gave me many strikes and blows on different parts of my body."[42]

Bodily assaults are the most common and dangerous type of complaint in documents concerning violence, since they endangered the victim's life. Though references to being "half-killed" (*apokteinas*) or "half-dead" (*hemithanēs*) occur in a few late Roman petitions,[43] none of the petitions I surveyed from Oxyrhynchus and Tebtynis concerning domestic violence ended in the death of the petitioner, though in the course of a domestic robbery three individuals (a guard, his brother, and a nurse) were killed at Theadelphia in 167–68 CE,[44] and a pregnant woman claimed that she gave birth to a dead child when she was beaten at Areos Kome.[45] Physical injury of the victim is frequently attested, however. In 305 CE, Hierax appeals to the *logistēs* of Oxyrhynchus to send a public doctor to investigate his wife, who was involved in an altercation whose location is not specified. The wife was subject to bodily harm that necessitated medical examination and, probably, treatment.[46] Similarly, Aurelia

Senpatus complained that thieves invaded their house, robbed it, and attacked her husband Titoes and son Pseces with swords. Pseces was wounded in the head and Titoes in the arm. She asks that a public doctor be sent to the house to investigate their condition so that "they can receive the necessary treatment."[47]

Most petitions concerning corporeal violence are similar in form and language, though the cause and narrative of the assault and the agents differ from one document to another. These petitions normally give the cause of hostility and the full narrative of violence. In 296 CE, Aurelia Taesis of Karanis petitioned Aurelius Gordianus, *beneficiarius*, stating that she suffered bia and unlawful assaults from her father's brother Chairemon, whose wife and daughters "attacked me with blows, dragged[?] me around by the hair, tore my clothing to pieces, and left me prostrate on the ground in the presence of Ol and Casius, officials of the same village, who rescued me from the women."[48] Here, the narrative of the assault did not only include the beating itself, but also the tearing of clothes and the presence of eyewitnesses.

Petitioners claimed monetary compensation on grounds of physical violence. In 218 BCE, Hermogenes, son of Phil[---], a "Persian of the *epigonē*" who lived in Lagis, complained to Ptolemy III against Petosiris, who "placed his hands upon me . . . with beatings and stompings upon whatever part of my body he might strike."[49] Hermogenes requested that if the things he writes prove to be true, "Petosiris may be forced to pay 200 drachmas for the blows."[50] In the fourth century CE, Aurelius Sarapion from Philadelphia was subject to physical assault, verbal abuse, and property destruction by Arios, the son of Agammon. In his petition, Aurelius Sarapion asked that Arios and his father be brought to justice and pay the proper amount "on account of his safety [*sōterias*]."[51] The plaintiff asked for financial compensation for physical assaults (bia), beatings (*plēgai*), and property damage. He also requested that the attackers be brought to court. Perhaps the arrest of the assailants and their appearance in a courtroom was itself partial recompense for the victim of corporeal violence. Yet the victim also claimed financial reimbursement for bodily and property damage. Inhabitants of Greco-Roman Egypt considered money a compensation for physical violence inflicted on them or their property.

Domestic physical violence could also be committed through agents. In 145–47 CE, Ptolemaios son of Diodoros, a tenant on the imperial estates in the Arsinoite, petitioned Lucius Proculus, prefect of Egypt, that Isidoros, a sailor-diver "made an attack on me [*epēlthen*] through one of his suborned agents, a certain Ammonios, also called Kaboi, a culpable fellow who had been proscribed on account of his lawless life . . . he refused to let me enjoy my lease and even excluded me from my house and insulted me (hybris) until he extorted money from me."[52] The otherwise unattested Greek term for sailor-divers, that is, *nautokolymbētai*, is odd. According to the papyrus, these are "public officers and in the service of the water administration and in attendance on the shore-guards and cultivation inspectors."[53] Ptolemaios was subject to violence in his house, where he was not only beaten and insulted, but was forced to leave his house and pay money. Isidoros used a thug to do illegal acts on his behalf in the hope of escaping unpunished. Ammonios was perhaps bribed to commit all these unlawful acts against Ptolemaios.

Loidoria (Verbal/Oral Violence)

In Greek petitions, loidoria (and its cognates) is the most common term used to describe oral abuse committed by or against the household.[54] Roman law understood language as an integral part of *iniuria*.[55] Loidoria appears with bia and hybris, suggesting that the inhabitants understood these words as describing different violent actions. Loidoria appears in connection with bia in a petition of the early Roman Period.[56] It also appears in a personal letter from the third or fourth century CE, in which the writer complains to an associate about the behavior of a particular enslaved person, who treated him "with hybris as well."[57] Petitioners used the verb *loidoreō* when they complained about shameful abuse (*aischita*) uttered against them. In 222 BCE at Ghoran, Pappos complained to Ptolemy III of his son Strouthos that "whenever he meets me, he reviles me [*loidorei*] most shamefully, and abusing me physically [*apobiazom*(*enos*)] . . . into my house."[58]

While the difference between bia (physical assault) and loidoria (verbal abuse) is understood, the difference between loidoria and hybris when they refer to verbal abuse is not fully clear. It seems that loidoria is used to refer to oral abuse, which intends to inflict some sort of emotional burden, while hybris stresses the shame that it seeks to create. This is why both loidoria and hybris sometimes appear in the same document. Given the silence of the papyri on this point, we cannot distinguish many of the specific nuances of loidoria and hybris when they come respectively to designate oral abuse or shameful verbal assault. Unfortunately, petitioners did not record the specific verbal offenses uttered against them in petitions. The emotional impact of oral insult and verbal offense on victims would have differed from one person to another.

Hybris (Emotional Violence)

The concept of "domestic violence" should not be restricted to cases of bodily injury (bia) or verbal offense (loidoria). In fact, there are many acts of violent behavior committed with intentions to distress the soul, offend the dignity, and damage the victim's honor/reputation. In petitions, these acts of hybris are equally important as forms of human injury. Hybris designates shameful acts of insult that place an emotional burden on petitioners.[59] Fisher defines hybris as "the deliberate infliction of shame and dishonor,"[60] and petitions illustrate that hybris denotes bodily or verbal as well as emotional assault with intentions to dishonor somebody.

Hybris covers a variety of offensive conducts against a person's body, honor, or reputation. In petitions, the verb *hybrizō* designates acts of shame. The act of dishonoring someone's social standing was called hybris in the local law. In Roman law, the Latin term *iniuria* seems to cover a much broader range of insults than hybris. *Iniuria* can describe essentially any injustice or insult,[61] while hybris has a much more specific implication since it included physical acts and verbal offenses that showed personal contempt for another person. Hybris conveys all forms of insolence or attempts to inflict humiliation. In his studies on hybris, Fisher demonstrated that the essence of hybris is behavior intended to dishonor people, that is, it refers to moral transgression designed to humiliate and dishonor the victim.[62]

In Greco-Roman Egypt, insolence or attempts to humiliate somebody involved a variety of behavior that carried cultural and symbolic significance. In 218 BCE, the pouring of urine on Herakleides, from Alexandrou Nesos in Krokodilopolis, is called an act of hybris. Herakleides complained to Ptolemy III:

> A certain Egyptian woman, whose name is said to be Psenobastis, leaned over and poured urine down upon my clothing, with the result that they were dripping [with urine]. I was vexed and upbraided her, and she abused me. Psenobastis, with her right hand, yanked the part of my cloak that lay upon my shoulder—the himation I was wearing—and ripped and struck it with the result that my chest was laid bare in the presence of some bystanders whom I called to witness. The things of which I accuse her she did out of hybris and she herself put her hands on me first. . . . She was upbraided by some of those present for the things which she had done to me, and as a result, she left me behind there and went inside [her house], from where she had poured the urine on me. I need you, king, if it seems best to you, to not overlook me, having been treated with hybris so outrageously by an Egyptian woman—I, being a Greek and a foreigner.[63]

Herakleides was subject to a mixture of hybris acts by Psenobastis. He was physically beaten, verbally abused, and emotionally insulted. Hybris can thus overlap with both bia and loidoria. In CE 20–50 at Oxyrhynchus, Syras, daughter of Theonos, similarly complained to Herakleides, priest and chief judge, against her husband Sarapion, who treated her with hybris and laid his hands on her in their dwelling place.[64] In the ordering of the petition, the pouring of urine comes before other physical and verbal engagement, though in reality it occurred at the end of the fight between Herakleides and Psenobastis. In this case, the maintenance of self-esteem is given preference over other physical and verbal well-being. Here, the emotional violence was more insulting to Herakleides than the physical and oral harm hurled at him. Pouring urine was probably meant to cause injury to Herakleides's honor and reputation in the community, a consideration that surely weighed on him.

One may wonder why Psenobastis chose urine in particular. I would like to suggest that the use of urine was not a coincidence, and that she intentionally used urine for the symbolic connotation it carried in an Egyptian context.[65] Although urine was used for different purposes in the ancient world, it was often regarded as a waste discharge and disgusting substance. In Rome, urine was used by the first century CE in hair dyeing and as a teeth therapy.[66] Roman fullers similarly used urine to bleach and stiffen clothing.[67] Galen expressed his abhorrence of using human effluvia such as urine, excrement, sweat, or menstrual blood as remedies.[68] In Greco-Roman Egypt, urine continued to be used in pregnancy tests and for determining fetal sex.[69] In the first century CE, Apollonios Mys, a doctor who worked in Alexandria, listed camel urine as a remedy for dandruff and hot donkey urine for a sore throat.[70] In Egyptian funerary literature, however, urine is a disgusting substance, which is drunk only by the impure dead.[71]

Although pouring urine on somebody is not a dangerous act of somatic violence, it was an effective way to compound an insult to dignity and honor in ancient Egypt. The earliest reference to urine is Pyramid Texts 210, where urine is an abomination of the deceased.[72] In chapter 53 of the Book of the Dead, which is titled "spell for not eating excretion nor drinking urine in the god's domain," urine appears as an abomination and punishment for the sinful deceased during the passage into the afterlife.[73] At this time, the deceased underwent a stage of purification, in which many texts show that he/she sought to protect himself/herself from eating excretion and drinking urine.[74] In an Egyptian context, drinking, and by extension touching, urine was a punishment that transformed a pure into an impure individual. Being impure further meant that the individual would not enjoy an afterlife. Pouring urine on Herakleides could be understood as a way of contaminating him. The association between urine, humiliation, and loss of dignity also explains why the well-known execration texts, which were magical tools for the destruction of the enemies of the Egyptian state, Pharaoh, and personal enemies, were often saturated with urine.[75] Wax figurines of Seth and Apophis, the archenemies of Osiris and the archetypes of chaos, were also pounded, trampled, spit on, stabbed, burnt, and boiled in urine.[76]

In a domestic context, pouring urine on Herakleides was thus meant to defile him and scorn his dignity in public. Bryen argued that "the ordering and highlighting of facts in a legal complaint is a cultural product as it draws on a specific vocabulary of insult, presenting images that have a symbolic resonance in a given community."[77] Bryen's ideas about petition ordering are very useful here. My interpretation of urine symbolism may explain why, in the ordering of his petition, Herakleides gave priority to urine-pouring before other physical and verbal offenses. This example suggests a synthesis of Greek and Egyptian conceptions of personal insult: in presenting Psenobastis's urine-pouring as an act of hybris, Herakleides shows that he recognizes the Egyptian cultural context of urine-pouring, and he translates those Egyptian ideas into the Greek concept of hybris. If an attacker wanted to damage a victim's reputation in the local community and inflict an act of hybris, the front of the house would be a good place to do this because it was so visible.[78] The stripping of honor and damage to individual dignity, the visibility of injury and insult, and exposure to public view are central concerns in petitions.[79]

The stripping of someone's clothing also falls under the category of hybris, entailing the utmost insult to human dignity and reputation. In 103 BCE, Theotimos from Theadelphia petitioned Cleopatra III and Ptolemy X against Diokleos son of Alexander, a "Persian of the *epigonē*." Theotimos "was beaten in his house and then was taken away by force in the street, in which he was oppressed . . . shamefully abused, beaten, and stripped of his himation and clothing."[80] Here, Theotimos was the victim of household violence, in that he was first beaten somewhere inside his house. Then, he was taken or perhaps dragged into the street, where he was beaten again and stripped of his clothing in front of passers-by. In the fourth century CE, a Christian woman similarly complained against her husband for committing violence against the accused's enslaved laborers, agent, and son and her own enslaved laborers and foster daughters for seven days in the cellars of his house. She accused him of committing different acts of hybris, including stripping her foster daughters completely naked, "which is contrary to the laws."[81] In Greco-Roman Egypt, it was illegal to strip off somebody's clothing since it was a visible example of debasing dignity and honor.

Petitioners also used hybris when they complained about shameful reproach (*aischita*)[82] or vulgar abuse (*aselgēmata*)[83] uttered against them. In the fourth century CE, a petitioner claims that an enslaved woman "had come to his house . . . and used uncommon hybris against my wife and unmarried daughter by means of foul and inappropriate language."[84] The Christian woman mentioned above similarly complains against her husband, who, among other acts of hybris, "said cruel things to her face and through his nose."[85] Although the Christian plaintiff gives a detailed description of every other act of violence committed by her husband, she does not mention the content of the cruel statements directed against her. To my knowledge, there are no specific examples of the content of verbal assaults delivered in domestic contexts. This absence may be explained by the desire of the victim to show his/her prudishness, which might win the favor of the responsible official. Perhaps the content was also too rude to be repeated in an official document. In 115 BCE, one individual, Artemidoros, was described as "the hated of heaven" in a private letter.[86] This is probably an example of oral abuse in a nondomestic context.

Verbal abuse frequently co-occurs with physical assaults. In the third century CE, Aurelius A[---] alias Aphynchis, former exhibitor of games in Oxyrhynchus, petitioned to Aurelius Alexander, of the police magistrates:

> Yesterday evening a certain Didyme, the wife of Agathos Daimon, the cook, passing my house and finding me standing there with our family, treated us with insolence [*exhybrizen*], using speakable and unspeakable expressions. . . . Thereupon, when I stopped her, advising her to keep off from us, she leapt upon me, and, being distracted in her senses, even stretched out her hands and smote me, and railed furiously at some of my daughter's sons, whom I called to witness, and not only at them, but even at a public official who was present.[87]

Didyme, "a woman abundantly furnished with the utmost shamelessness and effrontery" as the papyrus describes her, came to Aurelius's house and committed a large number of aggressive behaviors. Not only did she breach the privacy of the household, but she also bombarded the paterfamilias, his household, and a public official with physical and verbal assaults, both of which actions constitute hybris. Rather than a spontaneous confrontation, one suspects that this was a planned assault that had some background, which cannot be reconstructed out of the document.

Additionally, "snorting" and "speaking through the nose" appear in petitions as contemptuous acts of hybris.[88] In 381 CE, Aurelia Eirene complained about a dispute over an empty building lot, in the course of which one of her fellow villagers was "speaking to my face through his nose [*legōn eis prosōpon mou dia tēs eautos rhinos*], wishing to end my life, and if I had not obtained help from Pamoun my fellow villager, he would long since have reached (the end) of my life."[89]

Since Eirene emphasized that she was in danger of losing her life, she might have been subject to or at least threatened by physical violence. Maybe Pamoun held the accused villager back before he could harm her. Yet Eirene stressed the arrogant verbal insult, even though it was certainly coupled with bodily assault. The aforementioned Christian woman similarly charges her husband that he "spoke offensively to me at my face and through his nose."[90] Similarly, a tax collector claims that a villager in Karanis "snorted his contempt for me [*perierronchasen moi*] and wanted to attack me."[91] In all these cases, oral insult is paired with physical assault.

All sorts of pressure also fall into the category of hybris. Our Christian female petitioner also complains that her husband:

> persisted in distressing my soul [*thlibōn tēn psychēn mou*] about his enslaved Anilla, both at Antinoopolis and here, saying, "Get rid of this enslaved girl because she knows equally well how to get what she wants," wishing to confuse me, and on this pretext to take away whatever I possess. However, I refused to get rid of her, and he continued to say, "In the course of a month I will take a mistress for myself." God knows these things.[92]

Here, the husband upset the emotions of his wife by asking her to discard his enslaved female and threatening that he would take a concubine for himself. Although it is unknown whether the husband fulfilled his threat and took a mistress, his threat was sufficient to alter his wife's emotions, annoy her, put her under stress, and displease her soul.

Exclusion from the house was also an act of hybris. The verb *exelaunō,* "knock out" or "expel from," is used in reference to acts of exclusion from houses.[93] The above-mentioned Ptolemaios son of Diodoros petitioned the prefect that Isidoros

> refused to let me enjoy my lease and even excluded me from my house and insulted me until he extorted money from me. . . . I can bring proofs on the spot concerning my being insulted [hybris] and subjected to extortion [*diaseisma*], so that I may be able to live unmolested in my home during the happiest times of our exalted emperor, and your delightful prefecture, and may obtain relief.[94]

These acts of shameful abuse and suppression threatened the safety and property of Ptolemaios, whose goal, the papyrus tells, is to be able to live in peace at home.

Hybris also included forcible entry into houses for the purpose of extortion. The verb *eisbiazomai*, "force one's way into," is used to complain about intrusion into houses. It refers to the violation of private possessions, either in a private house[95] or on royal land.[96] In the mid-second century BCE, Petesouchos son of Petos, a royal farmer from Oxyrhyncha, petitioned Ptolemy VI and Cleopatra II against Stratonike daughter of Ptolemaios of Krokodilopolis. He claimed that Stratonike, "mischievously wishing to practice extortion [*diasisein*] on me, coming with other persons against my house, forces her way in before any judgement has been given."[97] In the third century CE, one person similarly complains to an official, perhaps the strategos, that his son-in-law Polydeukes committed hybris by "rushing into his house."[98] Although these complaints do not report any physical harm befalling the occupants or their property, house encroachment was viewed as an act of hybris because of its violation of household privacy.

Other forms of hybris could entail bodily harm, as in the case of wife beating, which was also regarded as an act of hybris. In a fragmentary petition of the first/second century CE, a woman complained: "My husband Julius, son of Diogenes, together with a girl with two children by him, having unlawfully cast me out of the house with my children and carried off everything in the house, not only . . . but beating me unlawfully."[99]

While some Greek authors condemned wife beating as a shameful spousal behavior, some Latin authors portrayed it as good family discipline.[100] According to John Chrysostom, it was the height of insult (hybris) for a man to beat his wife, because it treated her like an enslaved person.[101] The Roman practice of *patria potestas*, which gave a husband power to chastise members of his household, was not applied in Egypt, where, as Evans noticed, women were historically "equal partners with their husbands in marriage." To be sure, it was illegal for a man to beat a freeborn wife in Egypt by the time of Justinian.[102]

Some petitions place particular emphasis on legal and social status. Petitioners emphasize their legal status and social rank when they were subject to acts of hybris. In 222 BCE at Magdola, Crateuas, a "Macedonian" steward of *klēroi*, was beaten (*plēgas*) and insulted (hybris) by some shepherds, because he was accusing them of pasturing their flock unauthorized on a plot of land which was under his supervision.[103] The already-mentioned "Greek" Herakleides complained that he was outrageously treated with hybris "by an Egyptian woman."[104] In a petition of 163 CE, Gaius Iulius Niger, a Roman veteran, complains that he suffered insolence (hybris) "at the hands of an Egyptian fellow," Isidoros, son of Achillas, scribe of the superintendents of sequestered property of Karanis.[105] The emphasis on ethno-cultural identity (Greek, Macedonian, Roman, and Egyptian) was probably a tactic to ensure that official authorities would take up petitions seriously. Although the treatment of petitioners differed on the basis of their legal/social status, they all could approach local, royal, and imperial officials for redress. For at least some petitioners, legal or ethnic status was a pressing concern in petitions about domestic violence. Yet most petitioners did not try to play up their legal or ethnic status.

Apart from domestic contexts, examples of physical (bia) and oral (loidoria) assault are also confirmed in temples, baths, or barges. In 200 BCE, Poregebthis, priest and warden of the temple of Isis at Berenikis Thesmophorou, petitioned the archiphylaketes that "Perutis, son of Perutis, whipped [me?] . . . and took . . . and when I cried out for help, Papontos, my . . . but they removed by force from the . . . [and] planted many blows [*plēgai*] on me, and wounded my shin, and beat me in my face and took off in possession of my honey and a linen garment worth 2000 drachmas, and a bag containing 328 bronze drachmas, and a bronze altar and a drinking vessel."[106] In the second century BCE, Asklepiades, sitologos for cavalry dues in the division of Polemon, similarly petitioned Petosiris, komogrammateus of Oxyrhyncha, that when he was bathing in the bath, Pasis son of Aretion and other attendants at the bath "with no regard for decency having beaten me [*diarapisantes*] and kicked me [*laktisantes*] in the stomach."[107]

In 164 BCE, the temple of Ammon at Moeris witnessed violent attacks by the Egyptian rebels, who had "not only thrown down parts of the temple but split the stone-work of the shrine and carried off the door-fixtures and other doors to the number of more than 110 and also torn down some of the boarding."[108] In 135 BCE, Paalas son of Harmais, ship's guard of the barge of Apollonios, complained to Demetrios, one of the *diadochoi*, *hipparchēs* over men, and *epistatēs*, that certain persons "leapt on board with unseemly shouts [*phōnas aprepeis*] and gave me many blows [*plēgai*]."[109] In 114 BCE, Haryotes son of Phaesis, royal farmer of Kerkeosiris, also petitioned Menches, komogrammateus, that "while I was in the great temple of Isis here for devotional purposes on account of the sickness from which I am suffering . . . Horos son of Haryotes, a resident in the aforesaid temple of Isis, picked a quarrel with me, and beginning with abuse [*eloidorēsen*] and unseemly behavior [*aschēmonei*] he at last fell upon me and gave me many blows [*plēgai*] with the staff which he was carrying."[110] Robbery was a motivation behind bodily and verbal attacks in religious and public buildings. Emotional violence (hybris) is also attested in a vineyard at Talei, when Petsiris, son of Phoulemis, petitioned the strategos against Patynion, son of Herakleides, and his son, who "heaped unseemly insults upon me and in addition beat me unmercifully on any part of my body that they could, and struck me on the side with their fists, so that now I am confined to bed and am in danger of my life."[111]

Locating Domestic Violence

Having considered forms of household violence, let us now examine their location in relation to the house. In legal petitions, there is a strong association between bia, loidoria, and hybris and two basic architectural/spatial elements of the house: the house front and the house interior. Yet we cannot identify bia with any different location than loidoria or hybris. Almost all acts of bodily, oral, and emotional violence are committed at the house façade and within the house. As liminal zones between the private sphere (the house) and the public sphere (the street), the front door and the domestic pylon were physical settings of violent behavior committed by or against the household.[112]

Women appear in petitions as the doers of violence at the house façade.[113] In 218 BCE, the house façade of Psenobastis witnessed acts of hybris against Herakleides, where Psenobastis abused him and tore a part of his cloak in the presence of bystanders before she went inside her house, from which she poured urine on him.[114] In 183 BCE at Tebtynis, bloody violence occurred at the street door of the house of Dorion (*pros tēi thyrai)*, a desert guard, in the street opposite the Boubastis-shrine of Patsontis. Hesiodos son of Didymos, Thracian, hundred-arouras-holder of the fifth hipparchy, came on a quarrel in which "Dorion . . . the nose of the aforesaid Hesiodos [slitting?] the nostril and cut [?] his lip; and Hesiodos cut the right ear of Dorion clean off."[115] As Davoli and Alston argue in this volume, the boundaries between the "public" and "private" spheres were not clearly marked or experienced in an Egyptian context.[116] The house frontage can be viewed as a private, semipublic, and public space, where violent acts committed in the front of the house were highly visible, particularly in the presence of the house inhabitants, neighbors, passers-by, and other eyewitnesses.[117]

Women similarly appear as the victims of violence at the house façade.[118] It was common for women to stand at the front door of the house to chat with neighbors or watch what was happening on the street. Yet they were sometimes subject to harassment or violent behavior by drunken pedestrians, especially cleruchs. In 110–12 CE, Heraklas Pauseirion from Oxyrhynchus petitions Archias, the strategos, that Apollos Herakleides, being drunken, "attacked his wife Taamois, while she was standing at the front door of the house [*pro tēs thyras*]."[119]

In Greek papyri and Classical literature on Egypt, *thyra* is the normal word for doorway, including the front door of the house.[120] However, there were different ways of referring to the street door of the house. One is the *parodios thyra*, that is, the traversing door.[121] The parodios thyra is mentioned in two petitions from Tebtynis, in which Demas son of Sentheus and other royal farmers at Kerkeosiris complain about a gang of intruders who "crushed the street door of their houses" and stole many valuable items listed in the petitions.[122] Another word for the front door is *exōtera thyra*, that is, the exterior door,[123] as we see in a papyrus from Oxyrhynchus that testifies to the lease of a workshop with its front door.[124] The third phrase designated the front door is *auleia thyra*.[125] Whether followed by thyra or not, the *auleios* or *auleia* can refer to the main entrance.[126]

Men equally appear as the aggressors and victims of violence at the façade of the house. The aforementioned Aurelius Sarapion petitioned:

> When I was going to a wedding at my sister's house, I do not know why Arios the son of Agammon from the same town of Philadelphia was lying in wait for me when I was going out from my house to the town of Kerkeosiris, and he tried to attack me with swords, having with him a group of people whom I can name—the *archephodoi* of the village can also testify to this, as can the inhabitants of the house. He attacked me, speaking many obscenities at my face. Furthermore, last year this same Arios and his father Agammon attacked my house maliciously, setting it on fire and burning it to the ground. . . . I hand in my petition and ask that the aforementioned Arion and his father be brought before you and that you secure them, and that they be required to pay the proper amount on account of my safety.[127]

This was a planned conflict, since Arios and his company were waiting for Aurelius until he left his house. Victims of violent behavior frequently emphasize the location of violence when it was committed in front of the house. In this case, the assaults were committed in the presence of the household and the archephodoi. The visibility of bodily and oral assaults committed in front of the house and the presence of eyewitnesses were considered important to stress in legal petitions.

As it shaped the house façade, the domestic pylon was similarly a fitting space for violent behavior. In 221 BCE, Antigenes, a "Persian of the *epigonē*" and cleruch in Berenikis Thesmophorou, complained to Ptolemy III that Pythiades, cleruch, "hit me before the pylon of the house in the village and verbally abused me most shamefully."[128] In 131 CE, Akous son of Herakleos from Tebtynis similarly petitioned Andromachos, strategos of the division of Polemon, concerning a gang of intruders who "made a bold attack upon my house in the village . . . in the pylon."[129] The house façade was a locus of religious and social practices and a marker of social status in Greco-Roman Egypt.[130] The front door is neither inside nor outside the house. Rather, it is a liminal zone between the house and the street. Domestic properties also included physical forms located before the front door like the *prothyron*, *propylon*, and *eisodos kai exodos* (entry and exit).[131] For these reasons, violent acts were committed by or against the house occupants at structures that shaped the house façade, whether the front door or the pylon.

By contrast, when violence is committed inside a house, papyrus petitioners often do not identify the specific interior part of the house.[132] In 222 BCE at Ghoran, Pappos complained that he was continuously subject to oral and physical violence in his house by his son Strouthos, suggesting that the assault was conducted in different interior parts of the house.[133] In 103 BCE at Theadelphia, Theotimos was similarly beaten somewhere in his village house.[134] In the third century CE, a petitioner similarly complained that his son-in-law Polydeukes committed an outrage (hybris) on him by rushing into his house.[135] In complaints of robbery, petitioners placed emphasis on giving a list of the stolen items for redress without identifying the domestic interior structure being violated. Thus in 176 CE, Soterichos of Tebtynis complained that some persons made a thieving incursion into his village house.[136] In 190 CE, Nechthenebis similarly complained to the strategos concerning a group of thieves who entered into his house at Oxyrhynchus for robbery.[137]

When violence occurred within the house, there were fewer eyewitnesses. It is possible, but uncertain, that the resulting invisibility of this violence is one reason for not specifying the interior element of the house (e.g., *aithrion*, *aulē*) in which violence was committed. The only case I know where a papyrus identifies the specific location of violence within a house is *P.Oxy.* 6.903, in which a Christian woman complains against her husband for committing different acts of hybris against her and members of his and her household for seven days "in the cellars of the house."[138] From the frequency of petitions concerning violence committed within houses, it can be inferred that petitioners were more concerned with reporting violence committed against them within the house rather than with identifying their specific locations, unless violent acts lasted for several days and were life threatening, as in the case of the Christian woman.[139]

The house was a dynamic space in Greco-Roman Egypt, and social interaction between the house occupants and their partners or other inhabitants took many different forms. One such form was violence, a term that I understand to reflect a wide variety of injuries from which individuals might suffer. The practice of offensive acts by or against the house occupants was an unacceptable and illegal behavior that necessitated the submission of legal petitions to official authorities, demanding that they take prompt and serious measures. In legal petitions, the requested actions of the officials included the punishment of the perpetrator; the return of stolen property; and less frequently, claims to financial reimbursement.

Violence appears in legal petitions from Greco-Roman Egypt as a complex and pervasive social concept. Violent behavior might include three different, yet sometimes coincident acts: physical (bia), verbal (loidoria), and emotional (hybris) assault. Family members, coresidents, business visitors, state officials, and pedestrians are all involved in household violence. Almost all forms of corporeal and incorporeal violence are attested at the house façade, either at the front door or the domestic pylon, and in the house interior. There is a strong association between particular forms of violence (bia, loidoria, hybris) and two basic architectural/spatial elements of the house: the house front and the house interior. Victims of violence at the house façade stress this location because it implies a high visibility of violence and exposure to eyewitnesses. By contrast, petitioners complaining about violence committed within the house only focus on the narrative of the assault itself. Although the house occupants stressed their desire to relax and enjoy a peaceful life at home, as the examples of Cornelius and Ptolemaios quoted above show, the house was not always a safe place in Greco-Roman Egypt.

Notes

1 Parlebas 1977. For a discussion of the various, yet often blurry, definitions of the term "household," see Barrett, Introduction, this volume. The household did not necessarily rely on the nuclear family or kinship (Brooks Hedstrom, chapter 11, this volume; Gates-Foster, Redon, and Godsey, chapter 12, this volume).
2 See *P.Mich.* 3.174, in which the petitioner's goal was "to be able to live unmolested in his home."
3 Drawing on a variety of ritual practices, Frankfurter (chapter 10, this volume) stresses that the house protected and materialized the safety and fortune of the family in Late Antique Egypt.
4 *P.Oxy.* 3.531.
5 Alston 2001.
6 Boozer 2005.
7 Huebner 2013.
8 Abdelwahed 2016.
9 Matić 2021.
10 Hue-Arcé 2020.
11 Baldwin 1963; Alston 1994; Bryen 2013.
12 Bagnall 1989.
13 *P.Tebt.* 1.39.
14 Bagnall 2021.
15 Parca 2002.
16 Evans 1992.
17 Byren 2013.
18 Throughout the chapter, I use the texts and translations of papyri as they appear in the Duke Databank of Documentary Papyri. If I use a different text than that of the DDbDP, I record this in the footnote.
19 Berger 1994–95.
20 Abelson 1969.
21 Graham and Gurr 1969, xxx.
22 Lawrence 1970, 35.
23 *P.Oxy.* 4.744.8–10. Cf. West 1998.
24 Cribiore 2001, 65–73; Fischer-Elfert 2001, 439; Lazaridis 2010, 3.
25 Cf. Gai. *Inst.* 3.222.
26 Wheeler et al 2013.
27 *Chr.Mitt.* 52.5–10.
28 *PSI* 3.222.12–15.
29 *P.Wisc.* 1.33.11.

30 *P.Oxy*. 6.903.
31 Taubenschlag 1955, 442–47; Evans 1992, 4.
32 *P.Oxy*. 6.903.6.
33 *P.Enteux* 72.5.
34 E.g. *P.Enteux* 25.1.
35 *P.*Oxy. 3.489.11.
36 *P.*Oxy. 8.1120; cf. Bryen 2008, 192.
37 *BGU* I.45.
38 Németh 2012, 146.
39 Daniel 1975, 255.
40 *P.Enteux* 81.
41 *P.Enteux* 78.5–6.
42 *P.Enteux* 77.
43 *P.Oxy*. 6.301.6; *Chr.Mitt*. 126 = *P.Amh*. 141; *Chr.Mitt*. 126.13, *P.Lips*. 1.37.22.
44 *P.Hamb*. I.10
45 *P.Mich*. 5.228.
46 *P.Oxy*. 61.4122.
47 *P.Oxy*. 58.3926.
48 *P.Cair.Isid*. 63. Ol is variant of Horos.
49 Vandorpe 2008.
50 *P.Enteux* 72.
51 *BGU* 3.909 = *Chr.Wilck*. 382.
52 *P.Mich*. 3.174.
53 *P.Mich*. 3.174.5–6. See Bryen 2013, 13.
54 *P.Oxy*. 6.903.1; *P.Enteux*. 25, 74, 79, 86; *P.Tebt*. 3.765; *SB* 12.11130.15–17.
55 Bryen 2008, 66; Gai. *Inst*. 3.220.
56 *SB* 14.11274.9–10.
57 *SB* 12.11130.15–17.
58 *P.Enteux* 25.8.
59 *P.Wisc*. 1.33.12–13.
60 Fisher 1992, 493.
61 Evans 1992, 4–5.
62 Fisher 1995.
63 *P.Enteux* 79.
64 *P.Oxy*. 2.281.17–18.
65 In ancient Egypt, urine was used in black magic and pregnancy tests (Shokeir and Hussein 1999). In the first century CE, the Romans recognized many uses for urine, including cleaning and whitening teeth and cleaning clothes. For the chemistry of urine in ancient Rome, see Witty 2016.
66 Witty 2016.
67 Plin. *HN* 9.39.
68 "But drinking sweat and urine and a woman's menstrual blood is outrageous and disgusting, and so are feces, no less than these." (Gal. *De temperamentis* or *The Temperaments and Powers of Simple Drugs* 10.1 (translation: Lang 2012, 165).
69 In Pharaonic Egypt, Halioua and Ziskind 2005; Ghalioungui, Khalil, and Ammar 1963. In Greco-Roman Egypt, Frankfurter 2006.
70 Apollonios Mys, *Euporista* or *Common Remedies* (translation: Lang 2012, 166).
71 Allen 1974, 91, 187 (Spells 116, 178)
72 "Unas's abomination is excrement, Unas rejects urine. Unas abominates his abomination. Unas's abomination is these two: he does not eat the abomination of these two." (translation: Allen 2005, 30).
73 "My abomination is my abomination; I will not eat dung, I will not drink urine, nor walk upside down." (translation: Allen 1974, 52).
74 Allen 1974, spells 116 and 178, 91, 187.
75 Ritner 1993, 150.
76 Ritner 1993, 150.
77 Bryen 2008, 185.

78 *P.Enteux* 79; *P.Fay*. 12.12–13.
79 Bryen 2008, 183–84.
80 *P.Fay*. 12.12–20 (author's translation).
81 *P.Oxy*. 6.903.7.
82 *P.Flor*. 3.309 = *P.Lond*. 3.983.
83 *P.Oxy*. 6.903.1, 21.
84 *P.Flor*. 3.309.1–4 = *P.Lond*. 3.983.
85 *P.Oxy*. 6.903.21–22.
86 *P.Tebt*. 3.1.768.
87 *SB* 6.9421.8–11, 13–25.
88 Bryen 2008, 194; Gow 1951.
89 *P.Mich*. 18.793.2–5.
90 *P.Oxy*. 6.903.
91 *P.Col*. 8.242.45.
92 *P.Oxy*. 6.903.32–7.
93 *P.Tebt*. 2.283.9–10.
94 *P.Mich*. 3.174.
95 *P.Tebt*. 3.1.771.
96 *P.Tebt*. 3.2.958.
97 *P.Tebt*. 3.1.771.
98 *P.Oxy*. 8.1120.
99 Coles 1974, 184–85; Evans 1992, 5.
100 Dossey 2008.
101 John Chrys., *In Epistulam I ad Corinthios Homiliae*, xxvi.7.
102 Evans 1992, 5.
103 *P.Enteux* 75.
104 *P.Enteux* 79.
105 *SB* 24.16252.5.29–30.
106 *P.Tebt*. 3.1.797.11–22.
107 *P.Tebt*. 3.1.798.15–16.
108 *P.Tebt*. 3.1.781.7–13.
109 *P.Tebt*. 3.1.802.
110 *P.Tebt*. 1.44.
111 *P.Mich*. 5.229.
112 On the front door and domestic pylon, see Abdelwahed and Abbas 2015.
113 Evans 1992; Parca 2002.
114 *P.Enteux* 79.
115 *P.Tebt*. 3.1.793.11.1–15.
116 Davoli, chapter 1, this volume; Alston, chapter 7, this volume.
117 Cf. *BGU* 3.909 = *Chr.Wilck*. 382 (359 CE), where many eyewitnesses of a domestic act of violence at the house frontage were present.
118 Evans 1992; Parca 2002.
119 *P.Oxy*. 36.2758.
120 *P.Oxy*. 36.2758.10; Hdt. 2.48; Plut. *De Is. et Os*. 7. See Husson 1983: 93–107.
121 Husson 1983: 98–99.
122 *P.Tebt*. 1.45.21–22; *P.Tebt*. 1.47.13–14.
123 Husson 1983: 99. In *P.Oxy*. 6.903.20, it occurs as *tas exō thyras*.
124 *P.Oxy*. 16.1966.14–15 (505 CE).
125 *P.Tebt*. 3.795.7.
126 Husson 1983, 99–100. This term should be distinguished from the *aule* (courtyard), which was the primary domestic space for food storage, preparation, and consumption, and household daily activities in the Roman Egyptian house (Alston, chapter 7, this volume).
127 *BGU* 3.909 = *Chr.Wilck*. 382 (359 CE).
128 *P.Enteux* 74.3–4.
129 *P.Tebt*. 2.331.7–9.
130 Abdelwahed 2016, 17–25.

131 Husson 1983, 65–72.
132 *P.Enteux* 25; *P.Fay*. 12.12–13; *P.Mich*. 3.174.21.
133 *P.Enteux* 25.8.
134 *P.Fay*. 12.12–13.
135 *P.Oxy*. 8.1120.
136 *P.Tebt*. 2.332.
137 *P.Oxy*. 1.69.
138 *P.Oxy*. 6.903.
139 *P.Oxy*. 6.903.

Works Cited

Abbas, E., and Y.E.H Abdelwahed. 2015. "The Domestic Pylon in the Light of Greek Papyri." *Rosetta* 15: 1–27. http://www.rosetta.bham.ac.uk/issue15/abbasandabdelwahed.pdf.

Abdelwahed, Y.E.H. 2016. *Houses in Graeco-Roman Egypt: Arenas for Ritual Activity*. Oxford: Archaeopress.

Abelson, R. 1969. "Letters." *New York Review of Books* 12 (12): 38.

Allen, T.J. 1974. *The Book of the Dead or Going Forth by Day*. Chicago: Oriental Institute of the University of Chicago.

Allen, T.J. 2005. *Writings from the Ancient World: The Ancient Egyptian Pyramid Texts*. Atlanta: Society of Biblical Literature.

Alston, R. 1994. "Violence and Social Control in Roman Egypt." In *Proceedings of the 20th International Congress of Papyrologists, Copenhagen, 23–29 August, 1992*, collected by A. Bülow-Jacobsen, 517–21. Copenhagen: Museum Tusculanum.

Alston, R. 2001. *The City in Roman and Byzantine Egypt*. London: Routledge.

Bagnall, R.S. 1989. "Official and Private Violence in Roman Egypt." *Bulletin of the American Society of Papyrologists* 26: 201–16.

Bagnall, R.S. 2021. "Violence from Inside, Above, and Outside." In *Roman Egypt: A History*, edited by R.S. Bagnall, 130–36. Cambridge: Cambridge University Press.

Baldwin, B. 1963. "Crime and Criminals in Graeco-Roman Egypt." *Aegyptus* 43: 256–63.

Berger, A.A. 1994–95. "Violence." *ETC: A Review of General Semantics* 51 (4): 453–55.

Boozer, A.L. 2005. "In Search of Lost Memories: Domestic Spheres and Identities in Roman Amheida, Egypt." Institute for Social and Economic Research and Policy, Working Paper 05–07, 1–36.

Bryen, A.Z. 2008. "Visibility and Violence in Petitions from Roman Egypt." *Greek, Roman, and Byzantine Studies* 48: 181–200.

Bryen, A.Z. 2013. *Violence in Roman Egypt: A Study in Legal Interpretation*. Philadelphia: University of Pennsylvania Press.

Coles, R. 1974. "New Documentary Papyri from the Fayum." *Journal of Juristic Papyrology* 18: 177–87.

Cribiore, R. 2001. *Gymnastics of the Mind: Greek Education in Hellenistic and Roman Egypt*. Princeton: Princeton University Press.

Daniel, R. 1975. "Two Love-Charms." *Zeitschrift für Papyrologie und Epigraphik* 19: 249–64.

Dossey, L. 2008. "Wife Beating and Manliness in Late Antiquity." *Past & Present* 199: 3–40.

Eichholz, D.E. 1962. *Pliny, Natural History XIII*. Loeb Classical Library. Cambridge, MA: Harvard University Press.

Evans, K.G. 1992. "Domestic Violence and Women's Right in Roman Egypt: The Case of P.Oxy. VI.903." Paper presented at the Annual Meeting of the American Academy of Religion/Society of Biblical Literature, San Francisco, California, November 21–24.

Fischer-Elfert, H.-W. 2001. "Education." In *The Oxford Encyclopedia of Ancient Egypt*, Vol. 1, edited by D.B. Redford, 438–42. Oxford: Oxford University Press.

Fisher, N.R.E. 1992. *Hybris: A Study in the Values of Honour and Shame in Ancient Greece*. Warminster: Aris & Phillips.

Fisher, N.R.E. 1995. "*Hybris*, Status, and Slavery." In *The Greek World*, edited by A. Powell, 44–84. London: Routledge.

Frankfurter, D. 2006. "Fetus Magic and Sorcery Fears in Roman Egypt." *Greek, Roman, and Byzantine Studies* 46: 37–62.

Ghalioungui, P., S. Khalil, and A.R. Ammar. 1963. "On an Ancient Egyptian Method of Diagnosing Pregnancy and Determining Foetal Sex." *Medical Historian* 7: 241–46.

Godley, A.D. 1926. *Herodotus*. The Loeb Classical Library. London: Heinemann.

Gow, A.S.F. 1951. "Notes on Noses." *Journal of Hellenic Studies* 71: 81–84.

Graham, H.D., and T.R. Gurr. 1969. *The History of Violence in America*. New York: F.A. Praeger.

Griffiths, J.G. 1970. *Plutarch's De Iside et Osiride*. Cardiff: University of Wales.

Halioua, B., and B. Ziskind. 2005. *Medicine in the Days of the Pharaohs*. Cambridge, MA: Belknap Press.

Hue-Arcé, C. 2020. *La violence interpersonnelle en Égypte au Nouvel Empire et à l'époque gréco-romaine*. New Brighton, UK: Abercromby.

Huebner, S.R. 2013. *The Family in Roman Egypt: A Comparative Approach to Intergenerational Solidarity and Conflict*. Cambridge: Cambridge University Press.

Husson, G. 1983. *Oikia. Le vocabulaire de la maison privée en Égypte d'après les papyrus grecs*. Paris: Publications de la Sorbonne.

Keller, H. 2013. "Culture and Development: Developmental Pathways to Psychological Autonomy and Hierarchical Relatedness (2)." *Online Readings in Psychology and Culture* 6 (1): 1–14. https://doi.org/10.9707/2307-0919.1052.

Lang, P. 2012. *Medicine and Society in Ptolemaic Egypt*. Leiden: Brill.

Lawrence, J. 1970. "Violence." *Social Theory and Practice* 1 (2): 31–49.

Lazaridis, N. 2010. "Education and Apprenticeship." *UCLA Encyclopedia of Egyptology* 1 (1): 1–14. https://escholarship.org/uc/item/1026h44g.

Matić, U. 2021. *Violence and Gender in Ancient Egypt: Archaeology of Gender and Sexuality*. Abingdon, UK: Routledge.

Németh, G. 2012. "The Corpse Daemon Antinoos." *Archiv für Religionsgeschichte* 14: 145–54.

Parca, M. 2002. "Violence by and against Women in Documentary Papyri from Ptolemaic and Roman Egypt." In *Le role et le statut de la femme en Égypte hellénistique, romaine er buzantine. Actes du collogue international*, edited by H. Melaerts and L. Mooren, 283–96. Leuven: Peeters.

Parlebas, J. 1977. "Les Égyptiens et la ville d'après les sources littéraires et archéologiques." *Ktema* 2: 49–57.

Poste, E. 1904. *Gai Institvtiones or Institutes of Roman Law by Gaius*. Oxford: Clarendon Press.

Ritner, R.K. 1993. *The Mechanics of Ancient Egyptian Magical Practice*. Chicago: Oriental Institute of the University of Chicago.

Schaff, P. 1978. *Saint Chrysostom: Homilies on the Epistles of Paul to the Corinthians*. Grand Rapids, MI: Eerdmans.

Shokeir, A.A., and M.I. Hussein.1999. "Historical Review: The Urology of Pharaonic Egypt." *British Journal Urology International* 84: 755–61.

Taubenschlag, R. 1955. *The Law of Greco-Roman Egypt in the Light of the Papyri: 332 B.C.–640 A.D.* 2nd ed. Warszawa: Państwowe Wydawnictwo Naukowe.

Vandorpe, K. 2008. "Persian Soldiers and Persians of the Epigone: Social Mobility of Soldiers-Herdsmen in Upper Egypt." *Archiv für Papyrusforschung und verwandte Gebiete* 54: 87–108.

West, S. 1998. "Whose Baby? A Note on P.Oxy. 744." *Zeitschrift für Papyrologie und Epigraphik* 121: 167–72.

Wheeler, S.M., P. Beauchesne, L. Williams, and J.E. Molto. 2013. "Shattered Lives and Broken Childhoods: Evidence of Physical Child Abuse in Ancient Egypt." *International Journal of Pelopathology* 3: 71–82.

Witty, M. 2016. "Ancient Roman Urine Chemistry." *Acta Archaeologica* 87 (1): 179–91.

PART III

Households in Practice

Production, Consumption, and Discard

7

Modes of Production and Reproduction in Roman-Era Egyptian Villages

RICHARD ALSTON

This study considers the rural Romano-Egyptian house in its social functions. I begin from the premise that houses provided the material environment for the social practices of the everyday, which ensured social production and reproduction over the short and long term. I approach the problem as one of microhistory, making the ideological assumption that society is generated in multiple engagements through which social power is manifested. The house allows us access to some of those processes.

I approach the problem in four main segments. In a short preliminary part, I focus on methodological issues, discussing primarily the house as a symbol. In the second section, I turn to the house as an everyday location of production. In the third section, I discuss the Egyptian family, working through the archive of Sakaon as an example. In the fourth section, I segue into a discussion of the tenurial division of houses and the clustering of property owned by members of a single family. I argue against any neat conjunction between house and the base sociological units of social reproduction. Those units of family and household extended beyond the walls of the house. This affects our sociological translation of the shapes on the ground to shapes in society. It also allows us to question several of the core anthropological conceptions applied to familial structure (exogamy/endogamy/household/family) in ways which, I suggest, have implications beyond our focus on the Egyptian house. Part of the argument here is that there was a fluidity in social relations that cannot be precisely categorized and the terminology we use to describe those social relations must have a similar fluidity. Definitions are unhelpful since they bring a sociological clarity to social practices that were fundamentally messy, though clearly understood by participants.

House as Symbol

As Anna Boozer remarks:

> Roman domestic spaces provide an ideal nucleus for exploring identities and memories because the Roman house served as a vessel for the cultural identity and memory practices of its inhabitants. Although Roman houses differed architecturally to varying degrees across the Empire, they retained a similar cultural role.[1]

Boozer's summary is a prelude to her discussions of house B1 at Trimithis with its suite of wall paintings, including scenes of dining, a personification of the *Polis*, and an Odyssean scene. Although seeing them as "Roman," Boozer sets the paintings within the cultural complexity of a postconquest society, in which Greek, Roman, and Egyptian elements were all present.[2] Boozer's use of the ethnic marker is subtle, pointing to the microhistorical concern with immediate contexts that will here be adopted. In the same way, the cities of Egypt in this period were Roman, not because they were identical with cities of other regions (they exhibit strong local and regional cultural markers), but because they were constructed within an imperial culture which, in one way or another, they reflect at a local and immediate level.[3]

As Jen Baird notes, much of the historiography and archaeology of the Hellenistic and Roman East has focused on the ethnic labeling of cultures.[4] This obsession is in part historiographical, connected to the hegemonic narratives of Hellenization and Romanization. But cultural markers can also be shorthand for a variety of other social, political, and economic characteristics.[5] Colonial discourses have tended to regard social behaviors as dependent on ethnicity and thus to reflect cultural values with deep histories. Such a separation between the colonized and the colonizer is, of course, highly tendentious and ideological: it suits colonial discourses to emphasize cultural differences so as to maintain political and economic inequalities and justify imperial endeavors. Although one might be able to imagine a colonial society in which there were cultural-ethnic groups who experienced entirely differently the everyday, it seems more likely, certainly in ancient societies, that colonial divisions were highly porous, with multiple shared experiences and repeated traversals of cultural difference, as Boozer's examples would seem to show.[6] Ethnic indicators may have been important as references for identity and consequently have influenced behavior, but the significance of such influences, especially when considered alongside the other constraints operative on the household community (economic, social, cultural, and political), must be open to doubt.[7] Rather than take ethnic markers as a symbolic manifestation of socioeconomic practices of production and reproduction, I see those practices as the context in which those markers appear, as will be explored in the final paragraph.

Such an approach diverges from anthropological-phenomenological methodologies, such as Pierre Bourdieu's 1960 (1979) influential rendition of the Kabyle house. His interpretation uncovers such rich layers in the traditional Kabyle house that we are encouraged to "read" it as a microcosm of the Kabyle cosmos. Bourdieu was likely influenced by Bachelard's 1958 *La Poétique de l'Espace* and stressed the phenomenological over the sociohistorical context. As critics have shown, by 1960, the traditional Kabyle house was an anachronism that functioned as a symbol of national identity.[8] In a complex and multifocal society, it was no longer, if it ever had been, the structuring structure, the Kabyle world in microcosm. Instead, the house was invested in a nostalgia which was counterpoised to modernity.

The poetics of such descriptions feed into our preferences as anthropologists and archaeologists for the visual.[9] Yet, the house was not primarily a symbolic space: it was a functional space, existing within a social dynamic that cannot be disengaged from social production and reproduction.[10] Any symbolic value of the house was generated in the everyday experience of the inhabiting community, and since that everyday was varied and engaged in wider contexts, the habitus could not be an unchanging essence.[11] Bourdieu's poetics played into the view of cultures as "deep structures," embedded in historical time.[12] Reading the domestic as the microsite of the cultural macrocosm makes it a primary location of acculturation and the cultural *origo* of the nation. In modernity, it operates in relation to changes in the nature of public space, seen as susceptible to capitalistic or imperial transformations, so as to create a dichotomy between public and private. Consequently, there often follows a discursive focus on women as guardians of a cultural tradition that needs to be secured within the domestic sphere. The dichotomous readings of public and private therefore can reinforce a particular and conservative gender politics.[13] Any modification in domestic space then can be seen as having increased significance as symbolic of transformation in the "deep structures" of a society.

Such attitudes seem very different from those visible in the documentation from Romano-Egyptian rural communities, but we can see similar attitudes in Philo's discussion of the "Jewish house." In *Special Laws* 3.173–75, Philo argues for the exclusion of women from markets, courts, crowds, and their limitation to the domestic sphere. Men could not confine themselves, but in a hostile public environment, the safety of the house and the confinement of women therein becomes a way of preserving Jewish traditional values.[14] Philo's example seems necessarily and consciously exceptional and points us to a norm in which the functioning of the domestic was freighted differently with symbolic value and in which the boundaries of public and private were more permeable.

The House as a Location of Production

In rural Egypt, a house provided the technology required for survival. This involved shelter; food storage, preparation, and consumption; and community. The primary productive space within the domestic complex appears to have been the *aule* (the courtyard).[15]

Spatially, the house and aule were distinct, and an aule could be sold separately from its neighboring house. Yet, judging from the excavations in Karanis, every house required access to such a yard. The court might be peripheral and bordering another house and with a separate entrance.[16] In the tiny houses excavated at Tebtynis the courts were in a corner (Maison 5300) or at the back (Maisons 4200, 5200, 6300).[17] In her discussion of courtyards uncovered in the recent archaeological investigations at Karanis, Simpson (chapter 2, this volume) shows that courtyards were often transitional places, open to the street to the extent that they seem to have operated as passageways between residences. Many were not, it seems, gated. As Davoli (chapter 1, this volume) also shows, in the Fayum villages, the differences between street, alley, and court appear to have been negotiable, and if these areas were fully or partially roofed, within a labyrinthine village structure, distinctions between public and private were not clearly marked or, as seems likely, experienced.

The equipment and detritus of everyday production have been found in the courtyards. They were equipped with bins and storage facilities. Cooking took place in the aule. Some had ovens, perhaps for the baking of bread, though bread baking may have progressively moved from a domestic to a more commercial provision (Simpson, chapter 2, this volume). Small mills have been found, both rotary and Theban. It looks very much as though the preparation of food was a communal activity, and since the spaces of the aule were not rendered fully private and court spaces could be shared, the community performing this everyday task was not necessarily confined to a particular house. Such activities were performed alongside other productive economic activities. There were animal pens and feeding troughs in many courts. Some houses had dovecotes.[18] Weaving equipment was found in the yards at Tebtynis.[19] It is evident that courts were of central importance to domestic production.

Houses varied.[20] Taking the ground plan area of the houses at Karanis as an indicator, some houses were tiny, with a ground plan area of under 20m^2 (houses C55; C75; C5036; C5034), with the bulk of houses at under 100m^2, with some larger examples. The excavated Tebtynis houses were also small (C5300 is under 60m^2; C6300 about 70m^2; C3100 about 72m^2), though the cluster of excavated houses is not necessarily typical of the village as a whole. Boozer's figures for the Dakhla Oasis suggest a range of 99.2m^2 and 415m^2, so larger than those at Karanis. At Trimithis, House B2 is 121m^2 and would appear to have contained a very different household than the elaborate B1 at 225m^2.[21] Considering variations in the number of stories, the balance between built and open space, and complexity of layout, we are evidently looking at a range of houses, which also seems apparent from the surviving house prices.[22]

At Karanis, this range was limited: we do not have elite residences. The houses were centers of small-scale agricultural production with some differentiation in function and scale of activity within that agricultural economy, as reflected in size and decor. The relative sizes and decoration of the houses suggest a level of economic differentiation, and the presumption must be that the variety of houses was a reflection of differing status. One presumes that in a community as small as Karanis, the population of which was likely under 3,500 in the second century CE,[23] everyone must have known everyone else and all inhabitants would have been aware of micro-differentials that are for us, as outsiders, difficult to map.

The documents allow a degree of resolution unique for the Roman Mediterranean in our understanding of the house and its community. Yet the understanding that can be gleaned from those documents is often fragmentary.[24] Papyri found in house C123, for example, show that it belonged in successive periods to the family of Satabous and that of Gaii Iulii Sabinus and Apollinarius.[25] The structure consisted of two distinct but clearly related elements: a domestic structure which was typologically little different from the neighboring house and a large granary. The granary was clearly far too large to be for production by the associated household and must have provided grain storage and perhaps other administrative services for a significant number of other villagers. The granary was thus embedded within the modes of production of the village. The documents, however, tell us nothing about the operation of the granary. This is in spite of the richness of the record. For the Iulii, the documents attest to multiple economic activities, including farming and military service. They show that the house functioned as one location within a network of partially documented economic and social relations. To these activities, we ought to add the management of the granary. Consequently, any reconstruction of the economic and social activities of a residential group needs to be aware of probable evidentiary gaps and to deploy anthropological and economic models, and considerable imagination, to bridge those gaps.

Census returns show that the coresidential family was a social organization that existed in multiple varied forms.[26] Evidently, those forms were neither ideal nor planned: families were subject to the vagaries of fertility and mortality.[27] Nevertheless, families had agency. As a primary requirement, the families of the Egyptian villages had to deploy their resources to meet their subsistence requirements. The family needed to match resources, labor requirements, and organization. The complex structures attested within the census returns suggest the predominance of a strategy of avoiding the breakup of familial units on the formation of new conjugal couples or on the death of older family members. The most obvious instances of such arrangements are the *frérèches*. One presumes that these came into being when brothers decided not to break up a property holding on the death of a parent. Other extended and complex familial groups fulfilled similar functions, even if the processes of their formation are more difficult to reconstruct. The prevalence of complex familial groups suggests that people tended to be kept in rather than sent out to form new residential and household units.[28]

The advantages of large familial structures are numerous, notably in the pooling of labor and other productive resources. Even if the available labor outran the landholding of the domestic unit, it could be employed in day labor or in renting or in even in diversifying income.[29] Keeping males in the familial unit after marriage likely allowed earlier male marriage since the setup costs for a new conjugal unit were minimized: indeed, costs were shifted primarily to the bridal side in the requirement for a dowry (though the man's family had to provide "gifts").[30] A larger unit allowed access to broader support networks, which gave the household more economic and political muscle.[31] Multiple sources of labor equate to multiple sources of income, and that effectively is a means of spreading risk in a preindustrial society.

In contemporary impoverished environments, managing illness, mortality, and economic fluctuations become easier in larger social units that allow diversification of income sources.[32] Labor is a resource that can be deployed in a variety of locales, sometimes distant from the home, as part of the livelihood strategies of familial units in order to manage risk, increase familial income, and diversify the microeconomies of such groups.[33] Consequently, rather than studying coresidential households of impoverished groups, contemporary analyses tend to focus on livelihood strategies that encompass such factors as remittances sent from family members residing at some distances from the primary familial residence.[34]

There were not the same opportunities for diversification within Roman Egypt as there are in contemporary African communities. Yet the ample if unquantifiable evidence for the movement of young males[35] may reflect such strategies. We might identify regional migration in the fluctuations in registered male population by age category in the census records or in those who went "missing" in tax records.[36] Tax records suggest that mobility was relatively normal for members of village households.[37] Although it has been suggested that some of that mobility was "crisis-mobility" and, in particular, tax avoidance, records that list males of a village having a known residence elsewhere show that not all migration was covert or crisis induced.[38] Those moving to other villages or to the cities were presumably primarily economic migrants, and it seems likely that they maintained close ties to their home village that went beyond issues of tax liability.[39]

Similarly, the letters that flowed between the Nilotic communities also attest the dispersal of communities. One of the characteristics of the epistolary form in Roman Egypt is the extensive list of persons to be greeted: it is evident that such lists do not make sense in the strictly familial terms in which the relations were frequently expressed (addressing people as brothers and sisters, mothers and fathers), but do attest a social need to use the mechanism of the letter to reinforce an extensive network of relationships within the home community.[40] In the Karanis documentation, the connectivity of military families, which encompassed military and civilian spheres, may have been more diversified and extensive, but was similar in kind to that of civilian families. Such networks frequently operated with what seems to have been more than one familial base.[41] Strong social links were maintained between topographically distant members of a home community and meant that a unit effectively had "branches" in different locations.

A livelihood approach moves analytical focus from a particular location to the multiple locations across which a family unit might operate. Locational diversification required a more complex structuring of power relations so as to maintain a group's coherence and renders yet more imprecise the sociological terminology we might want to apply to such groups. Our scholarly terminologies of family, household, and houseful represent complexities in residential relations, but do not necessarily map onto the various multiple strategies employed in historical societies.[42] Although ownership of economic resources was a major source of power, it seems likely that the dependency of the individual on the family unit for their everyday needs and the networks of support that maintained the family went far beyond issues around the possession of property.[43]

Houses and Familial Power

The operation of authority within a familial unit can be seen in archival collections such as that associated with Sakaon of Theadelphia in the Fayum. In a petition of

312, preserved in Sakaon's papers, Aurelius Melas petitioned the authorities about Taues, a girl Sakaon had abducted.[44] Taues was the daughter of Melas's aunt. This aunt had been married to Sakaon, and one presumes that Taues was Sakaon's daughter. Sakaon took a new wife, Kamoution, who supposedly expelled Taues. Taues went to live with Melas. After keeping her in his house for some time, Melas married her to his son Zoilos, who was *sitologos* (administrator of the grain tax) of the village. Supposedly at the behest of Kamoution, Sakaon abducted Taues and demanded bridal gifts. As a consequence Melas went to the authorities (figure 7.1 for the familial relations).

He was not entirely successful. Sakaon's claims on the girl were supported, and Melas was instructed to provide gifts before the girl could be restored to Melas and Zoilos. But Sakaon took the gifts and retained the girl, supposedly because Kamoution intended the girl for her nephew, Sarmates. So Melas went to law again. Again, he had mixed success, since the ruling stressed the importance of the girl's views in deciding where she resided and to whom she was married.

The families clashed again thirty years later.[45] In 343, Zoilos, now a deacon, complained once more of Sakaon. Zoilos had married his son, Gerontios, to Nonna, daughter of Annous. When Gerontios was dying, Sakaon, his brothers, and Annous broke into the house and abducted Nonna. There followed an assault on Melas. Pasis, another son of Zoilos, intervened and was also assaulted. Animals were carried off. It was the assaults and the theft rather than the abduction that led Zoilos to resort to law.[46]

These conflicts allow us to trace familial relations across two generations. Taues was transferred from the Sakaon residence to that of Melas with a view to her marriage to Zoilos. The export of Taues to the family of Melas was a limited transference since Taues's mother had been Melas's aunt. Her marriage became an issue when Kamoution, Sakaon's second wife, sought her for her nephew. Thus, Taues was to be used to reinforce preexisting social links in different branches of the family, but could not be used both to cement relations with Kamoution's relatives and those of Melas. A decision had to be made and conflict resulted.

We see similar issues in the marriage of Nonna. Nonna's relationship to Sakaon was, in modern terms, remote. She was, however, part of Kamoution's family (figure 7.2). In marrying Sakaon, Kamoution had married her maternal cousin. Her relationship to Nonna, was through her father, Kaet. Kaet's sister was Annous whose daughter was Nonna.[47] One might speculate that the marriage of Nonna

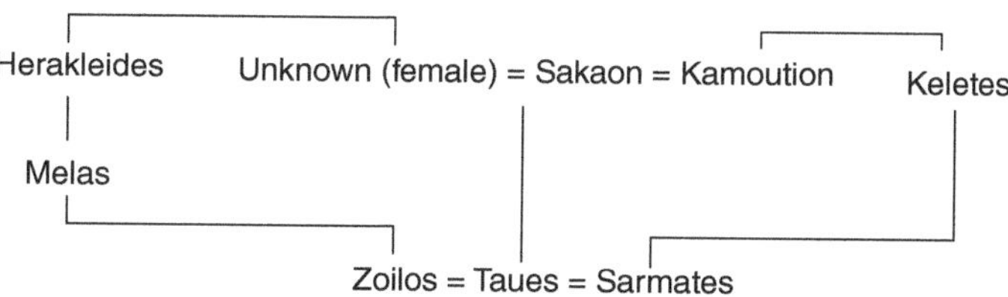

Figure 7.1. The marriages of Taues.

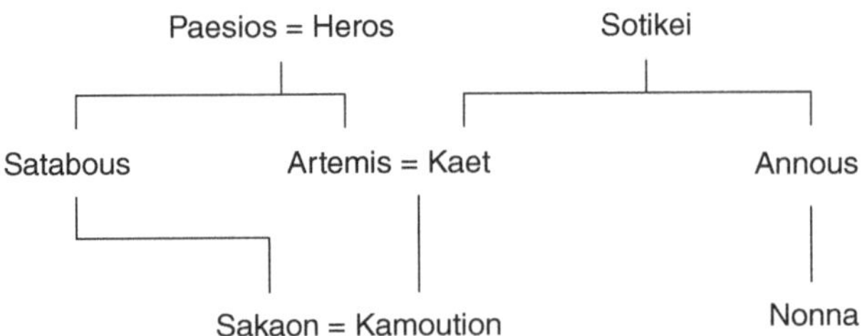

Figure 7.2. The relationship of Kamoution and Nonna.

accomplished the social task that the marriage of Taues and Zoilos had been intended to perform in bringing together these two families. Over the generations, there were five marriages through which the families of Sakaon, Kamoution, and Melas were united (that of Sakaon and his unnamed first wife, Sakaon and Kamoution, Taues and Zoilos, Taues and Sarmates, and Nonna and Gerontios). But these relationships also repeatedly dissolved, two by deaths and one by abduction. On the death of Gerontios, Sakaon and Kamoution were anxious to secure Nonna, and it was that desire to bring back a woman and probably her assets (which would account for the seizure of property) into the Kamoution-Sakaon household that sparked conflict.

Although the marriage of Taues and Zoilos was not brother-sister, it showed similar characteristics. Taues was made a member of the household before her marriage.[48] The other marital relationships in the archive show a strong preference for close-kin marriage. The marriage of Taues and Zoilos was one of cousins, as was that of Kamoution and Sakaon. The abducted Taues was intended for Sarmates, and although their relationship defies English familial vocabulary, the proposed marriage was endogamous to the household. Such marriages reinforced the familial community. Some instances display a strategy for social reproduction which, rather than reproducing the family in another location, maintained this particular household into the next generation. Other instances involved women joining households to which they were already tied through familial connections.

Endogamy potentially established high boundaries between the household and the external world, minimizing the export and import of familial members.[49] In circumstances of cultural endogamy, a new member of a household (perhaps especially a woman) might face difficulties negotiating relationships. But in the Sakaon archive, the two cases of the export of women were to the same household and reversed a prior conjugal export when Sakaon received his unnamed first wife. To describe such marriages as exogamous seems inappropriate. Endogamy and exogamy are modern anthropological categories, and in the relatively small village communities of Roman Egypt, one wonders at the extent to which anyone married "outside." The original household retained a claim on the exported person, as we can see with both Taues and Nonna, and presumably that claim was mutual: a woman exported to another household retained a financial and social interest in the original household.

Although the microhistory attested in the Sakaon archive conforms in some regards to a patriarchal operation of social and familial power, and the legal structures of Romano-Egyptian society tended to reinforce patriarchal structures, particularly through the distribution of property, the character of those households seems to have been more complex than a simple manifestation of patriarchal authority.[50] *P. Sakaon* 1, a census return of CE 310, reflects an official focus on the men, but the attested household would appear to be the product of nonpatriarchal processes. Sakaon registered his male coresidents, who included himself (aged forty-five), his son Aeil (aged sixteen), his brother Paesis (aged fifty-five), Ammonios the son of Pasesis (nineteen), another brother Aunes (aged forty-eight), Keletes son of Kaet and the brother of Kamoution (aged fifty), his son Sarmates (aged sixteen, and the intended spouse of Taues), Alupios son of Herodes (aged thirty-five and the nephew of Kamoution), and his son Heron (aged twelve). The presence of Kamoution's family provides the context in which Sakaon acted as the violent defender of interests that were defined by this coresidential group. The axis around which these disputes turned appears, in fact, to have been Kamoution and her genealogical family. In the context of this household, we can understand Melas's complaint in *P. Sakaon* 38 that Kamoution was the source of discord as more than an instance of the standard misogynistic trope of blaming the wife. Women were both the "assets" transferred and the agents of household strategies. This might contradict patriarchal predilections, but on an everyday basis, women were major contributors to the domestic economy (through labor and assets), reliant on their conjugal house-community, and committed to the longer-term success of their households.

The everyday workings of social and economic relationships necessary for social reproduction likely encouraged social agents to maintain the relationships within and between households that marriages were intended to reinforce. The point of marital strategies was to produce long-lasting social relationships, and in this sense the "gifting" of women should not necessarily be seen as a transfer of property, but of embedding a social agent within a household. The functioning of the familial relationships thus likely depended on a continuity of social intercourse between the familial units, focusing on the women as the point of communication. But such strategies carried within them a considerable potential for clashes of authority between familial units.

Such clashes are at the heart of the petition of Dionysia (*P.Oxy*. 2.237) against her father. It is a complex case that began with a dispute between Dionysia and her father Chaeremon over land that was contracted to her as part of her marriage settlement. Chaeremon had mortgaged this land and got into difficulties with the repayment. Dionysia demanded the land. Chaeremon responded by demanding return of all assets that he had bestowed on her in her marriage contract. This failed (unsurprisingly), but Chaeremon's next move was to attempt to dissolve the marriage (which would entail the property returning to him). Dionysia successfully resisted this, arguing that there was no provision in law for a father to extract an adult daughter from a contracted marriage against her will and that this was an attempt to pervert the prior legal decision. Dionysia quoted a similar case that came before the Prefect Flavius Titianus resulting from a Sempronius abducting his daughter from her husband, Antonius. Sempronius alleged that Antonius had accused him of incest (presumably with the daughter) and that he was within his rights in dissolving the marriage. Antonius responded by claiming that a father had no rights over the dowry or the woman whom he had given in marriage, a position the prefect supported.

Even if they failed to break up their daughters' marriages, these fathers, like Sakaon, felt that they had rights over their daughters that extended into other households. Such claims were not necessarily patriarchal (the household of Sakaon was also the household of Kamoution), but the requirement to control social and economic resources and preserve the integrity of the familial unit on which all depended necessitated adherence to familial hierarchies, the offense to which led to conflict in these cases.

The adventures of the women of the Sakaon-Kamoution family suggest the need for nuance in understanding the social and symbolic significance of the house. The perceived need to abduct the women and the use of violence in so doing attests to the importance of location in controlling resources and protecting individuals. Sakaon's seizure of the women gave him control over the key "assets" in the dispute with Melas. Within the physical space of the house, the household was able to exercise authority over and protection of its members.

The everyday productive activities by which the household maintained itself likely reinforced the household's dense social bonds and further integrated the women. The fact that familial authority extended beyond the boundaries of a particular house did not render those boundaries insignificant. The house remained the location of everyday productive activity and intense social interaction. As the scene of production and reproduction of the family, it must have carried powerful symbolic value within the village, providing identity for its residents. Nevertheless, it was but the primary spatial location of a family's social and economic activity.

Houses as Property

The Sakaon archive suggests a desire to integrate the household and maintain the house as a place of control. That social pressure was in some tension with inheritance practices that fragmented property ownership. In the Sakaon case, even though the family had various properties in the metropolis and the village, the residence of Kamoution and her family was in the busy village house of Sakaon.[51] In other instances, a house might be divided into multiple, sometimes very small fractions.[52] Sales were sometimes used to consolidate property within the family.[53] Other sales were between neighbors who might also have been relatives.[54] In some instances, jointly inherited property was sold, perhaps to simplify the family's property holdings.[55]

House sale documents show that families often owned multiple houses and clustered those houses together in a way that offset any property divisions. To take two examples, *P.Mich.* 5.277 documents the sale of a house in Tebtynis in which the seller co-owned a neighboring house with the buyer and another neighbor was the vendor's brother. In *P.Mich.* 5.276 five siblings sold a seventh share and a half share of a house and aule, which they had inherited from their father, to someone who looks from his patronymic to have been a relative. Two of the siblings owned a neighboring house and aule. The very fact that we have sales documents for transactions within extended families suggests that fragmented ownership could cause tensions, but they also point us away from the house as an insular unit, representing the family.

We can see the familial management of a cluster of houses in a small archive from Oxyrhynchus. The weaver Tryphon bought a half share of a house from his cousin Pnepheros. The house had been divided between Thamounis, Tryphon's mother, and her unnamed sister. In the next generation, the half share passed to the sister's son, Pnepheros. Thamounis was living, but it is a safe assumption that Tryphon expected to inherit her share, so that the house would, at the point of her death, once more be united. Neighboring lots were owned by Thamounis and Tausiris, sister of Pnepheros.[56] The original arrangement, then, seems to have been a plot of three houses, owned by a single family, which became tenurially divided between siblings and cousins and which the familial unit cooperated to maintain control over.

A further example comes in a census declaration (*P.Oxy.* 12.1547) from early second-century Oxyrhynchus from a family of stone cutters. Petosiris, son of Dionusios, grandson of Petosiris, registered a half of a house. Of the remaining half share, two-thirds (one-third of the total house) belonged to his wife Tetoeus daughter of Thoonis, one-third inherited from her father, one further third from her brother Petosiris. The final sixth of the house was owned by Papontos, a third sibling. Thirteen people were registered in the declaration, including a son of the late Petosiris, brother of Tetoeus. It seems clear that a single house belonging to a Petosiris was inherited by Dionusios and Thoonis. It was then passed onto the next generation when one half share was inherited by Petosiris and the other by Tetoeus, Petosiris, and Papontos. The marriage of the cousins Thoonis and Tetoeus brought some tenurial consolidation, which was furthered by the death of the second Petosiris. But the entire family were coresident and all the men were stone cutters. It seems probable that they operated together commercially and as a single domestic unit.

Such tenurial divisions were probably not reflective of living arrangements. Husselman reports some interior doors with bolts and bars, though predictably most lockable doors were to the street. She has also has plates showing bricked-up doorways.[57] Small houses, with single points of entry, single staircases, and seemingly one route of access round the house, could not easily have been separated into multiple units. The same considerations applied in the tiny Tebtynis houses.[58] There may have been tensions, but houses required the occupants to use the communal space of the aule, and it seems likely that such communal living was a social and economic necessity.

The fundamental question I seek to answer is, What are we looking at when we look at a rural house in Roman Egypt? The first part of my answer begins with theory. I argue that anthropological views of the house have embedded within them certain features of a colonial viewpoint. The house is seen in contrast to public space. It is valued primarily as a culture-producing machine. As the scene of family life, the house is portrayed as a deep social structure, the defender and inculcator of tradition. Such views make the house a site of nostalgia and cultural resistance, marginal to the "real history" of cultural and economic development that was taking place in the public spaces. By contrast, I argue that the Romano-Egyptian village house operated not as a point of symbolic resistance, but as the primary location of everyday production and consumption, by which the familial unit survived from day to day, and of social and biological reproduction, by which the familial unit survived from generation to generation.

Our historical analyses are attracted to the relative clarity of visible spaces. When we look at a house, we are tempted to believe that we are looking at the familial unit. It is an expectation that works quite well for modern bourgeois society. In the villages of Egypt, there was a link between the space on the ground (the house) and the familial unit, but that association was imprecise. The house operated as a central point, but there was fuzziness in the relationship of spatial and social boundaries. The meaningful familial unit extended beyond the coresidential group. The economic requirements to generate livelihoods carried individuals to distant places, but they remained members of a topographically concentrated community. Women transferred from one residence to another, but retained ties to the original familial unit.

The administrative process of registering a coresidential group tells us very little about the dynamic process by which that group operated.[59] For the household, there was no clear rule as to who belonged and who did not. The endogamous practices of the Romano-Egyptians knitted families and households into complex structures that show little affinity with, for instance, the simpler patriarchal structures of the Roman family.[60] When the extended family lives next door; when endogamous practices are used strategically to maintain the integrity of localized property holding; when the export of women to other households (if it happens) does not break their tie to the natal household; when such transfers are repeated interchanges between the same familial groups over generations; when men might be expected to work in distant locations so as to diversify and maximize the livelihood of the familial unit; when the boundaries between public and private, between courtyard, house, and street, are ill-defined; when familial units use house sales to consolidate and rationalize property holding within topographically concentrated familial blocks, then the boundaries of house, family, and community lose clarity and the family appears more communal than domestic. A house might represent a concentration of the hierarchically organized power of the household, dominated by its leading figures, but the membership, interests and boundaries of that social unit extended beyond any particular architectural structure.

The house was the scene of the economic, social, and biological processes by which the familial unit was reproduced day to day, year to year, and generation to generation. In circumstances of poverty, close control over familial resources (people and property) was essential. The functional importance of familial units accounts for their social power. Any individual (male or female) required a familial unit.[61] The familial unit was productive of livelihoods and social relationships, established social status, and defended individuals in the competitive environment of the village. The power structure of the familial unit looked inward and outward. On the inside, it managed social relationships and took the decisions, working within economic, demographic, and cultural constraints to give shape to the household. On the outside, the unit was competitive with other similar units and necessarily had to engage with political and administrative structures. The house was a topographical center for the functioning of a familial unit, but it was not a boundary that limited and contained those activities.

My argument has tended to downplay the house as a signifier of cultural identity. Although the macronarratives of acculturation and political identity place considerable emphasis on ethnic markers, it is only if we assume that such markers were signifiers of modes of social reproduction that we would associate their adoption with fundamental economic and social change. The basic challenge that faced the inhabitants of these rural communities was not whether they were Roman, but how to manage everyday issues of production and reproduction and how to protect and advance the interests of their familial units. In such a context, it becomes easier to understand why new ethnic markers might be adopted in local competitions for status and power. These houses were Roman since they sat within the spatial and cultural frames of the Roman Empire, but there is no reason to think that the adoption of non-Egyptian artifacts had much effect on the everyday practices of village society. First and foremost, the rural houses of the Fayum were machines for living and nodal points in the social, economic, and cultural production and reproduction of the familial units.

Notes

1 Boozer 2010, 138.
2 See also Boozer 2011; Boozer 2014.
3 In Alston 2002a, I avoided the issue of Romanization, since it is not a question that can usefully be asked of the complex documentation.
4 Baird 2014, 32–33.
5 This issue has an almost endless bibliography, but see, indicatively, Mattingly 1997, 2013, especially 43–72; Keay and Terrenato 2001; Cooper and Webster 1996.
6 A characteristic of the colonial situation is ambivalence, a being in-between state in which the categories of the colonial never quite fit. See, for example, Bhabha 1990; 2012; Said 1999; Chakrabarty 2000. For a discussion of ambivalence in a Roman text and related bibliography, see Alston 2018.
7 In Alston 2022, I emphasize the complexity of individual and group agency in the production of houses.
8 See Silverstein 2004; Herzfeld 1987, 8.
9 For the visual in archaeology, see the essays in Edwards, Gosden, and Phillips 2006. Mitchell (1991, 19–31) argues that the act of observation is wrapped up in the power dynamics of the colonial situation.
10 Lefebvre (1991, *passim*, but especially 7, 27, 33, 94, 14) argued that an emphasis on poetics of space (codes of interpretation) blinds us to processes of production and the lived experience of space.
11 For the notion of the everyday, see Highmore 2002. Whereas notions of the everyday can become a structural anthropology of advanced cultures, emphasizing system above agency, the everyday also contains within it an element of contingency and *praxis*, as expressed in De Certeau 1988.
12 See Smith 2004, 16–19, on the continuous process of national reinvention, the development of a uniform public culture, and the historical roots on which the nation feeds. Augé (1995) argues that spaces of (inter)national consumption are seen as empty spaces or non-spaces in contrast to the spaces of deeper meaning and cultural resonance.

13 See the summary in Levine 2007; for the link between gender and cultural value, see Wilson 2003, 1–12; Chakrabarty 1997.
14 In *Quaestiones in Genesim* 4.15 the house is a metaphor for the soul, which is divided between male (reasonable, rational) and the female (emotional) parts. There is a similar passage in the *Legum Allegoriae* 4.238–40. In *In Flaccum* 86–91, the Roman raid on Jewish housing leads to an explanation of the confinement of women to the inner quarters. For the Jewish house in Alexandria, see Alston 1997, 2002b. For a recent discussion of the ethnic conflict, see Atkinson 2006.
15 See Husselman 1979, 49–54.
16 Good examples from Karanis in Husselman 1979 at House C45 (plan. 29), House C51 (plan 35), House C56 (plan 38), House C62 (plan 40), House C57 (plan 42).
17 Hadji-Minaglou 2007.
18 Husselman 1953.
19 Hadji-Minaglou 2007, 47–68.
20 Egyptian villages contrast with the more uniform housing at places like Olynthus or Priene. See Robinson and Graham 1938; Hoepfner and Schwandner 1994. For critical discussions see Morgan 2010; Nevett 1999, 74–78.
21 See Boozer 2012. Some elements are, of course similar: B2 has a clustered plan around room R7 which is not very different from that for B1, around room 2 for example. Yet rooms 1/11/14 provide "luxury" space, which is not evidently part of the design of other houses.
22 Alston 2002a, 63–67.
23 Alston 1995, 121.
24 Van Minnen 1994.
25 Claytor 2013; Husselman 1952; Husselman 1963.
26 Bagnall and Frier 1994, 53–74; see also Huebner 2013 for the dynamics of family.
27 Pudsey (2011) shows that the attested structures within the census returns are not the products of ideological preferences but of particular familial events. The approach undermines the macrohistorical approaches, such as Goody 1983.
28 Bagnall and Frier 1994, 57–67.
29 For land rentals, see Rowlandson 1996.
30 Marriage provided an influx of wealth and labor. For marriage gifts, see *P. Sakaon* 38. For the relationship of familial structure to early male marriage, see Huebner 2013, 48–50.
31 Sen (1982) sees a lack of social capital as a root cause of extreme poverty.
32 For modern parallels, see Sen 1994; and Bledsoe 1994. Ismail (2006) argues that the operation of extensive social networks was essential for poorer households. It is only with the development of a middle class that large family-based networks have ceased to be crucial, a change that has resulted in shifts in family structure and changes in age of first marriage: see Singerman 2007; Engelen and Puschmann 2011.
33 Kaag 2004; de Haan 2007.
34 For a contemporary ethnographic account of the importance of remittances, see Ghosh 1998.
35 As surveyed in Braunert 1964; Adams 2016.
36 Bagnall and Frier (1994, 91–94) show an underrepresentation of young adult males, precisely the population who might be "exported" for economic reasons.
37 As Adams (2016, 258) concludes: "Migration was an everyday feature of Roman Egypt, a society that, by any historical standard, was a mobile one."
38 Bell 1938 argues that "going-up" reflected a crisis situation, relying heavily on the Nemesion archive for evidence. Yet "those who have gone up" may have been seeking work elsewhere: see *SB* 4.7462; *P. Ryl. Gr.* 4.595. For a more nuanced approach to the Nemesion archive, see Hanson 1979; 1988; 1989.
39 In *SB* 16.12632, Nemesion registers those away from the village in Hiera, Ptolemais Nea, Ptolemais Euergetis, Babylon, and in Alexandria and associated districts. *SB* 14.11481 is a list of persons resident in Alexandria. The fragmentary *P.XV Congr.* 14 lists men in Ptolemais Neas, the villages of the Boukoloi(?), the villages of Haryotos, in Syron and Ptolemais Hormou, in the metropolis (Ptolemais Eueregetis), and five in Magdolon. These men were not in hiding.
40 See Alston 2005 for discussion and further references.
41 Adams 1977; Pighi 1964; Alston 1995, 127–38; Alston 1999.

42 See Hammel 1984 for a succinct discussion of the problems. For variation within a single society, see Hammel 1980.
43 This continues the argument of Alston 2005, which suggests that the documentation is skewed toward direct ascendants and descendants by the legal processes of inheritance and property registration, but that the social workings of family encompassed a wide grouping, including matrilineal relatives. Looking at familial economics primarily through issues around the ownership of real estate might better suit modern economies than the premodern.
44 *P. Sakaon* 38.
45 These were two of the more prominent families in the village of Theadelphia. See *P. Sakaon* 52 for Pennis son of Sakaon and Zoilos serving as *komarchs* (village leaders) in 326.
46 *P. Sakaon* 48.
47 The family can be reconstructed through *P. Sakaon* 37; 40; 59; 94.
48 See Huebner 2007 for a suggestion that a considerable proportion of sibling marriages fell into this pattern. For *sim-pua* marriages in China as a parallel instance, see Wolf and Gates 1998; Wolf 1995.
49 Huebner 2013, 141–61.
50 Alston 2005.
51 *P. Sakaon* 1; 59; 60.
52 For small fractions in Fayumic documents, see, for example, *P.Petaus* 10; 11; *CPR* 1.223; *P.Lond.* 2.334 (p.224); *P.Mich.* 10.583; *P. Hamb.* 1.15; *P. Gen.* 1.44.
53 See likely examples, *SB* 1.5117; *BGU* 15.2476; *P.Stras.* 4.208; *P. Ryl.* 2.161; *P. Mich.* 5.253; *P.Mich.* 5.285–86; *CPR* 1 223 (probably), *P.Ryl.* 2.160(b); *P. Ryl.* 2.160(d).
54 *P. Mich.* 10.583; *SB* 14.11895; *SB* 1.5246; *SB* 1.5247; *P. Vind. Tand.* 25; *P.Mich.* 5.241; *P.Stras.* 4.602; *PSI* 8.908 (though the neighboring property also seems to have been sold); *PSI* 8.910; *BGU* 1.350; *P. Mich.* 6.428; *P.Ryl* 2.162; *P. Petaus* 14; *P.Ryl.* 2.160(d).
55 *PSI* 8.909; *P.Ryl.* 2.289.
56 *P.Oxy.* 1.99. For the archive, see Biscottini 1966; Brewster 1927.
57 Husselman 1979, 41–44 (doorways and doors), Pl. 45–50 (bolts and bars), Pls. 57, 58 (blocked doorways).
58 Hadji-Minaglou 2007.
59 As argued by Wilk and Netting 1984. See also Cooper and Donald 1995 for the prosopographic methodologies required to go from census returns to kin relations.
60 Although in law and in practice, the *pater* exercised considerable authority in the household (Shaw 1987), lived experience was undoubtedly more varied than legal theory (Saller 1986; 1987; 1994).
61 Huebner 2019 looks for the single person in the pre-Christian Roman Egyptian census records and identifies a surprisingly high percentage of single adults over the age of fifteen (just under 42 percent). Her definition of single relates to those persons who were not obviously in a conjugal relationship. They were not, however, solitary and tended to cohabit with children or other close relatives. Boozer 2019 looks for singles in the archaeological record. She finds evidence of singles in particular residential structures, military sites, field houses, and artisanal workshops. These examples would seem to confirm the argument in the second section of this chapter that individuals might spend some considerable time away from a particular familial unit, but that does not mean that those individuals did not belong to that familial unit.

Works Cited

Adams, C. 2016. "Migration in Roman Egypt: Problems and Possibilities." In *Migration and Mobility in the Early Roman Empire* (*Studies in Global Social History/Studies in Global Migration History*), edited by L. de Ligt and L.E. Tacoma, 264–84. Leiden: Brill.

Adams, J.N. 1977. *The Vulgar Latin of the Letters of Claudius Terentianus* (*P.Mich.VIII, 467–72*). University of Manchester. Faculty of Arts, No. 23. Manchester: Manchester University Press.

Alston, R. 1995. *Soldier and Society in Roman Egypt: A Social History*. London: Routledge.

Alston, R. 1997. "Philo's *In Flaccum*: Ethnicity and Social Space in Roman Alexandria." *Greece & Rome* 44: 165–75.

Alston, R. 1999. "The Ties that Bind: Soldiers and Societies." In *The Roman Army as a Community* (*Journal of Roman Archaeology* Suppl. 34), edited by A. Goldsworthy and I. Haynes, 175–95. Portsmouth, RI: Journal of Roman Archaeology.

Alston, R. 2002a. *The City in Roman and Byzantine Egypt*. London: Routledge.

Alston, R. 2002b. "Reading Augustan Alexandria." *Ancient West and East* 1: 141–61.

Alston, R. 2005. "Searching for the Romano-Egyptian family." In *The Roman Family in the Roman Empire: Rome, Italy, and Beyond*, edited by M. George, 129–57. Oxford: Oxford University Press.

Alston, R. 2018. "The Utopian City in Tacitus' *Agricola*." In *The Production of Space in Latin Literature*, edited by W. Fitzgerald and E. Spentzou, 235–59. Oxford: Oxford University Press.

Alston, R. 2022. "Spaces of Desire: Houses, Households, and Social Reproduction in the Roman World." In *Housing in the Ancient Mediterranean World: Material and Textual Approaches*, edited by J. Baird and A. Pudsey, 442–69. Cambridge: Cambridge University Press.

Atkinson, J. 2006. "Ethnic Cleansing in Roman Alexandria in 38." *Acta Classica* 49, 31–54.

Augé, M. 1995. *Non-places: Introduction to an Anthropology of Supermodernity*. London: Verso.

Bachelard, G. 1958. *La Poétique de l'Espace*. Paris: Presses Universitaires de France.

Bagnall, R.S., and B.W. Frier. 1994. *The Demography of Roman Egypt*. Cambridge Studies in Population, Economy and Society in Past Time 3. Cambridge: Cambridge University Press.

Baird, J.A. 2014. *The Inner Lives of Ancient Houses: An Archaeology of Dura-Europos*. Oxford: Oxford University Press.

Bell, H.I. 1938. "The Economic Crisis in Egypt under Nero." *Journal of Roman Studies* 28: 1–8.

Bhabha, H.K. 1990. "DissemiNation: Time, Narrative, and the Origins of the Modern Nation." In *Nation and Narration*, edited by H.K. Bhabha, 291–322. London: Routledge.

Bhabha, H.K. 2012. *The Location of Culture*. London: Routledge.

Biscottini, M.V. 1966. "L'archivio di Tryphon, tessitore di Oxyrhynchos." *Aegyptus* 46: 60–90; 186–292.

Bledsoe, C.H. 1994. "'Children Are Like Young Bamboo Trees': Potentiality and Reproduction in Sub-Saharan Africa." In *Population, Economic Development, and the Environment* edited by K.L. Kiessling and H. Landberg, 105–38. Oxford: Oxford University Press.

Boozer, A.L. 2010. "Memory and Microhistory of an Empire: Domestic Contexts in Roman Amheida, Egypt." In *Archaeology and Memory*, edited by D. Borić, 138–57. Oxford: Oxbow Books.

Boozer, A.L. 2011. "Forgetting to Remember in the Dakleh Oasis, Egypt." In *Cultural Memory and Identity in Ancient Societies*, edited by M. Bommas, 109–26. London: Continuum.

Boozer, A.L. 2012. "Globalizing Mediterranean Identities: The Overlapping Spheres of Egyptian, Greek and Roman Worlds at Trimithis." *Journal of Mediterranean Archaeology* 25 (2): 219–42.

Boozer, A.L. 2014. *Amheida II: A Late Romano-Egyptian House in the Dakhla Oasis: Amheida House B2*. New York: New York Library. http://dlib.nyu.edu/awdl/isaw/amheida-ii-house-b2/.

Boozer, A.L. 2019. "Looking for Singles in the Archaeological Record of Roman Egypt." In *The Single Life in the Roman and Later Roman World*, edited by S.R. Huebner and C. Laes, 57–84. Cambridge: Cambridge University Press.

Bourdieu, P. 1979. "The Kabyle House or the World Reversed." In *Algeria 1960*, translated by R. Nice, 133–53. Cambridge: Cambridge University Press. Reprinted in P. Bourdieu, *The Logic of Practice*, 271–83. Cambridge: Polity Press, 1990.

Braunert, H. 1964. *Die Binnenwanderung: Studien zur Sozialgeschichte Ägyptens in der Ptolemäer und Kaiserzeit*. Bonn: L. Röhrscheid.

Brewster, E.H. 1927. "A Weaver of Oxyrhynchus: Sketch of a Humble Life in Roman Egypt." *Transactions of the American Philological Association* (1927): 132–54.

Chakrabarty, D. 1997. "The Difference—Deferral of a Colonial Modernity: Public Debates on Domesticity in British Bengal." In *Tensions of Empire: Colonial Cultures in a Bourgeois World*, edited by F. Cooper and A.L. Stoler, 373–405. Berkeley: University of California Press.

Chakrabarty, D. 2000. *Provincializing Europe: Postcolonial Thought and Historical Difference*. Princeton: Princeton University Press.

Claytor, W. 2013. "Penthemeros Certificates from the Granary C123, Karanis." *Bulletin of the American Society of Papyrologists* 50: 49–75.

Cooper, D., and M. Donald. 1995. "Households and 'Hidden' Kin in Early-Nineteenth-Century England: Four Case Studies in Suburban Exeter, 1821–61." *Continuity and Change* 10 (2): 257–78.

Cooper, N.J., and J. Webster, eds, 1996. *Roman Imperialism: Post-Colonial Perspectives: Proceedings of a Symposium Held at Leicester University in November 1994*. Leicester Archaeology Monographs 3. Leicester: University of Leicester.

De Certeau, M. 1988. *The Practice of Everyday Life*. Berkeley: University of California Press.
de Haan, L. 2007. "Studies in African Livelihoods: Current Issues and Future Prospects." In *African Alternatives*, edited by P. Chabal, U. Engel, and L. de Haan, 59–72. Leiden: Brill.
Edwards, E., C. Gosden, and R.B. Phillips, eds, 2006. *Sensible Objects: Colonialism, Museums, and Material Culture*. Oxford: Berg.
Engelen, T., and P. Puschmann. 2011. "How Unique is the Western European Marriage Pattern? A Comparison of Nuptiality in Historical Europe and the Contemporary Arab World." *History of the Family* 16 (4): 387–400.
Ghosh, A. 1998. *In an Antique Land*. London: Granta.
Goody, J. 1983. *The Development of the Family and Marriage in Europe*. Cambridge: Cambridge University Press.
Hadji-Minaglou, G. 2007. *Tebtynis IV: Les habitations à l'Est du temple de Soknebtynis*. Cairo: Institut français d'archéologie orientale.
Hammel, E.A. 1984. "On the *** of Studying Household Form and Function." In *Households: Comparative and Historical Studies of the Domestic Group*, edited by R. McC. Netting, R.W. Wilk, and E.J. Arnold, 29–43. Berkeley: University of California Press.
Hammel, E.A. 1990. "Household Structure in Fourteenth-Century Macedonia." *Journal of Family History* 5: 242–73.
Hanson, A.E. 1979. "Documents from Philadelphia Drawn from the Census Register'." In *Actes du XVe Congrès international de papyrologie, [Bruxelles--Louvain, 29 août-3 septembre 1977]*, edited by J. Bingen and G. Nachtergael, 60–62. Brussels: Fondation égyptologique Reine Élisabeth.
Hanson, A.E. 1988. "The Keeping of Records at Philadelphia in the Julio-Claudian Period and the 'Economic Crisis under Nero.'" In *Proceedings of the XVIII International Congress of Papyrology: Athens, 25–31 May 1986*, edited by B.G. Mandilaris, 261–77. Athens: Greek Papyrological Society.
Hanson, A.E. 1989. "Village Officials at Philadelphia: A Model of Romanization in the Julio-Claudian Period." In *Egitto e storia antica dall'ellenismo all'età araba: Bilancio di un confronto: Atti del colloquio internazionale, Bologna, 31 agosto-2 settembre 1987*, edited by L. Criscuolo and G. Geraci, 429–40. Bologna: CLUEB.
Herzfeld, M. 1987. *Anthropology through the Looking-Glass: Critical Ethnography in the Margins of Europe*. Cambridge: Cambridge University Press.
Highmore, B. 2002. "Introduction: Questioning Everyday Life." In *The Everyday Life Reader*, edited by B. Highmore, 1–36. London: Routledge.
Hoepfner, W., and E.-L. Schwandner. 1994. *Haus und Stadt im klassischen Griechenland*. München: Deutscher Kunstverlag.
Huebner, S.R. 2007. "'Brother-Sister' Marriage in Roman Egypt: A Curiosity of Humankind or a Widespread Family Strategy?" *Journal of Roman Studies* 97: 21–49.
Huebner, S.R. 2013. *The Family in Roman Egypt: A Comparative Approach to Intergenerational Solidarity and Conflict*. Cambridge: Cambridge University Press.
Huebner, S.R. 2019. "Single Men and Women in Pagan Society: The Case of Roman Egypt." In *The Single Life in the Roman and Later Roman World*, edited by S.R. Huebner and C. Laes, 37–56. Cambridge: Cambridge University Press.
Husselman, E.M. 1952. "The Granaries of Karanis." *Transactions and Proceedings of the American Philological Society* 83: 56–73.
Husselman, E.M. 1953. "The Dovecotes of Karanis." *Transactions and Proceedings of the American Philological Association* 84: 81–91.
Husselman, E.M. 1963. "Texts Discussed at the Annual Meeting, 28 December 1962: Two Archives from Karanis." *Bulletin of the American Society of Papyrologists* 1: 3–5.
Husselman, E.M. 1979. *Karanis: Excavations of the University of Michigan in Egypt, 1928–1935: Topography and Architecture: A Summary of the Reports of the Director, Enoch E. Peterson*. Kelsey Museum of Archaeology Studies 5. Ann Arbor: University of Michigan Press.
Ismail, S. 2006. *Political Life in Cairo's New Quarters: Encountering the Everyday State*. Minneapolis: University of Minnesota Press.
Kaag, M. 2004. "Ways Forward in Livelihood Research." In *Globalization and Development: Themes and Concepts in Current Research*, edited by D. Kalb, W. Pansters, and H. Siebers, 49–74. Dordrecht: Kluwer Academic Publishers.
Keay S.J., and N. Terrenato, eds. 2001. *Italy and the West: Comparative Issues in Romanization*. Oxford: Oxbow.

Lefebvre, H. 1991. *The Production of Space*. Translated by D. Nicholson-Smith. Oxford: Blackwell.

Levine, P. 2007. "Introduction: Why Gender and Empire?" In *Gender and Empire*, edited by P. Levine, 1–12. Oxford: Oxford University Press.

Mattingly, D.J., ed. 1997. *Dialogues in Roman Imperialism: Power, Discourse and Discrepant Experience in the Roman Empire*. Journal of Roman Archaeology Supplementary Series 23. Ann Arbor, MI: Journal of Roman Archaeology.

Mattingly, D.J. 2013. *Imperialism, Power, and Identity: Experiencing the Roman Empire*. Princeton: Princeton University Press.

Mitchell, T. 1991. *Colonising Egypt*. Berkeley: University of California Press.

Morgan, J. 2010. *The Classical Greek House*. Exeter: Bristol Phoenix Press.

Nevett, L.C. 1999. *House and Society in the Ancient Greek World*. New Studies in Archaeology. Cambridge: Cambridge University Press.

Pighi, G.B. 1964. *Lettere latine d'un soldato di Traiano, P. Mich. 467–472*. Bologna: Zabichelli.

Pudsey, A. 2011. "Nuptiality and the Demographic Life-Cycle of the Family in Roman Egypt." In *Demography and the Graeco-Roman World New Insights and Approaches*, edited by C. Holleran and A. Pudsey. 60–98. Cambridge: Cambridge University Press.

Robinson, D.M., and J.W. Graham. 1938. *The Hellenic House: A Study of the Houses Found at Olynthus, with a Detailed Account of Those Excavated in 1931 and 1934 (Excavations at Olynthus Pt. 8)*. Johns Hopkins University Studies in Archaeology No. 25. Baltimore: Johns Hopkins University.

Rowlandson, J. 1996. *Landowners and Tenants in Roman Egypt: The Social Relations of Agriculture in the Oxyrhynchite Nome*. Oxford Classical Monographs. Oxford: Clarendon Press.

Said, E.W. 1999. *Out of Place: A Memoir*. London: Granta Books.

Saller, R. 1986. "*Patria potestas* and the Stereotype of the Roman Family." *Continuity and Change* 1: 7–22.

Saller, R.P. 1987. "Men's Age at Marriage and Its Consequences for the Roman Family." *Classical Philology* 82: 21–34.

Saller, R.P. 1994. *Patriarchy, Property, and Death in the Roman Family*. Cambridge: Cambridge University Press.

Sen, A. 1982. *Poverty and Famines: An Essay on Entitlement and Deprivation*. Oxford: Oxford University Press.

Sen, A. 1994. "Population and Reasoned Agency: Food, Fertility, and Economic Development." In *Population, Economic Development, and the Environment*, edited by K.L. Kiessling and H. Landberg, 51–78. Oxford: Oxford University Press.

Shaw, B.D. 1987. "The Family of Late Antiquity: The Experience of Augustine." *Past and Present* 115: 3–51.

Silverstein, P.A. 2004. "Of Rooting and Uprooting: Kabyle Habitus, Domesticity, and Structural Nostalgia." *Ethnography* 5: 553–78.

Singerman, D. 2007. *The Economic Imperatives of Marriage: Emerging Practices and Identities among Youth in the Middle East*. The Middle East Youth Initiative Working Paper 6. Dubai: Wolfensohn Center for Development, Dubai School of Government. http://www.meyi.org/publications.html.

Smith, A.D. 2004. *The Antiquity of Nations*. Cambridge: Polity.

Van Minnen, P. 1994. "House-to-House Enquiries: An Interdisciplinary Approach to Roman Karanis." *Zeitschrift für Papyrologie und Epigraphik* 100: 227–51.

Wilk, R.W., and R. McC. Netting. 1984. "Households: Changing Forms and Functions." In *Households: Comparative and Historical Studies of the Domestic Group*, edited by R. McC. Netting, R.W. Wilk, and E.J. Arnold, 1–28. Berkeley: University of California Press.

Wilson, K. 2003. *The Island Race: Englishness, Empire, and Gender in the Eighteenth Century*. London: Routledge.

Wolf, A.P. 1995. *Sexual Attraction and Childhood Association: A Chinese Brief for Edward Westermarck*. Stanford: Stanford University Press.

Wolf, A.P., and H. Gates. 1998. "Modelling Chinese Marriage Regimes." *Journal of Family History* 23: 90–99.

8

Domestic Discard

The Making and Unmaking of Romano-Egyptian Houses

ANNA LUCILLE BOOZER

We can better understand the everyday practice of living within and beyond the walls of Romano-Egyptian houses by examining activities of cleaning, disposing, and scavenging.[1] These activities are critical components of domestic life and create a substantial portion of the archaeological record. Unlike most other household activities, evidence of rubbish disposal has great longevity and is readily accessible to the archaeologist.[2] Close attention to rubbish and discard behavior also helps us to understand how people related to the material goods and places that once made up their object worlds. For example, sometimes rubbish deposits are associated with "household clearances," which might be due to the rapid abandonment of a house or a transitional event in the household, such as a death or marriage.[3] Other depositions, such as ash from domestic hearths, might be more habitual and part of everyday practice over a long period of time. Thus, a close examination of rubbish depositions and the discarded items themselves might be able to tell us how households refashioned themselves and their dwellings over time, as well as how households related to the spaces and materials around them. Careful analyses of site formation processes are key to understanding these events and the enmeshed relationships that develop between people and objects.

To address this issue, I investigate an individual case study of domestic discard that fits into larger social processes at work on local, regional, and global scales. I privilege neither the microscale nor the macroscale by limiting myself only to the study of houses and their courtyards.[4] Instead, I explore the linkages between households and broader society over time through the act of domestic discard. To this end, I explore cleanliness, rubbish disposal, and scavenging in House B2 and Courtyard C2 from Trimithis (Roman Amheida), compare this case study to aggregated rubbish data from other Romano-Egyptian sites, and situate these disposal practices within the broader global context of domestic discard. This multiscalar analysis demonstrates that rubbish can reveal an enormous amount about identity construction, the maintenance of family and communal traditions, hygiene, and dwelling as place making.

Discard Behavior

Disposal practices are not simple, dispassionate events. They can be imbued with strong emotions and deep convictions. Disasters, such as an earthquake, a fire, or a building collapse, are events that suddenly change the fortunes of a household. Such events result in substantial debris that must be sorted, removed, repaired, or discarded. As one might expect, dealing with the refuse created by such scenarios often carries strong emotional components.[5] I suggest that mundane rubbish disposal, such as the material that archaeologists find in pits, privies, middens, or in public areas, might also be imbued with strong emotion.[6] For example, rubbish disposal can be associated with death, marriage, abandonment, and even routine daily habits, such as housekeeping. People often dispose of objects that can no longer be repaired with great reluctance. On other occasions, individuals empty their secrets into middens, privies, or pits. These individuals were potentially ridden with sentiments of guilt, shame, or regret. Infants are the most heart-rending of these disposals, but there are other poignant items as well, such as letters, contracts, and mementos from past relationships.

The ways that households deal with rubbish on a consistent basis reveal deep convictions about how to manage hygiene, health, time management, and changes in the household structure over time. There are cultural rules about what constitutes cleanliness and what constitutes rubbish.[7] These concepts are usually grounded in concepts of purity, pollution, and even ethics.[8] The philosophical underpinnings behind Romano-Egyptian rubbish disposal are tantalizing, and many topics remain to be explored. Even without this philosophical foundation, we can deduce the resultant rules by carefully studying discard behaviors. Together, all of these reasons suggest that close attention to rubbish and discard behavior helps to reveal the enmeshed relationships between objects, activities, and households.

Understanding Rubbish: Terminology and Past Studies

Terminology

While contemporary society uses the terms *garbage*, *trash*, *refuse*, and *rubbish* synonymously in casual speech, these terms have different meanings.[9] "Trash" refers specifically to dry discards such as papyri, figurines, ceramics, and so on. "Garbage" technically refers to wet discards such as food and agricultural remains. Human and animal waste are a special subset of garbage in most societies; animal waste is often used as fertilizer or for fuel, while human waste is typically deposited away from settlement areas, because it contains pathogens that can be quite dangerous to human health. "Refuse" includes both wet and dry discards, while "rubbish" includes these discards and even construction and demolition debris. I employ the term *rubbish* throughout this discussion to speak about discard in a general sense, even though most (but not all) of the discarded items I describe were trash. When it is quite clear that there were only dry discards within the assemblage, I use the term *trash*.

Just as there are specific terms associated with rubbish, there is also terminology to describe the act of rubbish disposal. Michael Schiffer was the first archaeologist to discuss the impact of rubbish disposal on the archaeological record.[10] In his 1976 study, Schiffer distinguished between three categories of disposal:

(1) "*de facto* refuse," which he defines as tools and items that are still usable left behind at an activity area;
(2) "primary refuse," which is the intentional discard of items at or near the end of their use life, but still in the area where they were being used; and
(3) "secondary refuse," which is the disposal of items in areas other than where they were used.

Nearly forty years after Schiffer's initial study, Ian Hodder added a fourth category to this list:

(4) "tertiary refuse," which he defines as "all the items of refuse that become incorporated into deposits as background constituents of the deposit matrix."[11]

To put all of this terminology into plain language, rubbish is material deemed to be of no present or future value to an individual or to society, so it is taken out of circulation. Rubbish can be found in de facto, primary, secondary, and informal disposals. De facto and primary refuse disposal are found away from high-density accumulations, such as at water sources, in agricultural fields, along paths, and in courtyards or on house floors. Secondary refuse disposal can be found in intentional rubbish depositions, such as middens. Middens are deliberate and sequentially accumulated rubbish deposits. Landfills occupy this category in the contemporary world. In Roman Egypt, archaeologists often find middens on the edges of settlements or—as I argue here—in abandoned houses. Most of the materials discarded into middens, either in antiquity or in the contemporary world, are household items and waste from household activities. In Roman Egypt, these items might include broken ceramics, figurines, bone, basketry, papyri and other dry discards that were either not reused or could not be reused in a manner close to their primary function. Specialized activities, such as house construction and feasting, rarely contribute to middens cross-culturally. Informal rubbish disposal occurs in single events and produces a low-density scatter of rubbish, which can include in-transit primary or secondary refuse. We usually refer to such informal refuse disposals as litter. Secondary refuse disposal areas are usually richer than either primary or informal refuse disposals, but we lose the household specificity that we find when dealing with de facto and primary domestic rubbish.

A Multiscalar Approach to Rubbish Disposal

A multiscalar approach to rubbish disposal reveals the links between specific households and broader society. While connectivity is always important in the study of households, it is particularly important for the study of rubbish. For example, the main conclusion reached by Hayden and Cannon in their influential case study of Mayan rubbish is that it is not sufficient to examine a single deposit from a household and its immediate surrounding area: ideally, the whole of the surviving rubbish from a specific household should be tracked down and examined if the picture of the inhabitants' behavior is to be accurately reconstructed.[12] This and other studies demonstrate above all that secondary rubbish exists in a multitude of different forms of deposit and results from a series of decisions which vary according to special cultural and environmental conditions.[13]

It is difficult, if not impossible, to achieve the ideal suggested by Hayden and Cannon; how can one identify with certitude which household was responsible for rubbish depositions in the absence of ethnographic data? Even so, it is worthwhile to explore surrounding contexts in order to postulate likely household deposition scenarios. Schiffer points out that "artifact diversity is a strong line of evidence that can be used in many cases to differentiate various refuse sources."[14] In other words, even when we cannot connect rubbish with specific sources, we may be able to suggest a range of sources and patterns of disposal (e.g., for a specific neighborhood) on the basis of the artifact assemblage recovered.

As described here, addressing de facto and primary rubbish disposal as well as secondary disposal is essential to provide the full context of domestic discard in Roman Egypt. In other words, I examine the rubbish that usually accumulates in low densities in houses, courtyards, and streets, as well as the rubbish that accumulates in high densities in middens. At the microscale, I explore House B2 from Trimithis in Egypt's Dakhla Oasis, as well as take a brief glimpse into rubbish disposal elsewhere at Trimithis. At the mesoscale, I compare the results from this house with rubbish disposal practices from other areas of Roman Egypt, namely Karanis and Oxyrhynchus. Finally, on the macroscale, I return to the topic of rubbish disposal in a global context, because people have similar approaches toward rubbish, even though they are filtered through cultural specificity. These macroscale insights help to provide insights into the microscale of House B2 at Trimithis.

Case Study: House B2, Courtyard CS, and Street S1 (Trimithis, Egypt)

Trimithis in the Dakhla Oasis

Amheida, known as Trimithis during the Roman Period, is located on the western end of Egypt's Dakhla Oasis (see the map of Egypt in the introduction to this volume). Trimithis was occupied for a very long time prior to Roman rule, as can be seen by material remains that are distributed both horizontally and vertically on the site of Amheida and that date from the predynastic era all the way to the late Roman Period, with a few gaps of evidence in between.

By at least the second century CE, Trimithis was a large urban center whose core consisted of mixed-use architecture: a large temple mound, workshops, houses of different sizes, and courtyards. This urban core was surrounded by tombs, industrial complexes, agricultural fields, and dovecotes (figure 8.1). Archaeologists have not identified any middens with certitude in surface surveys. The city seems to have been

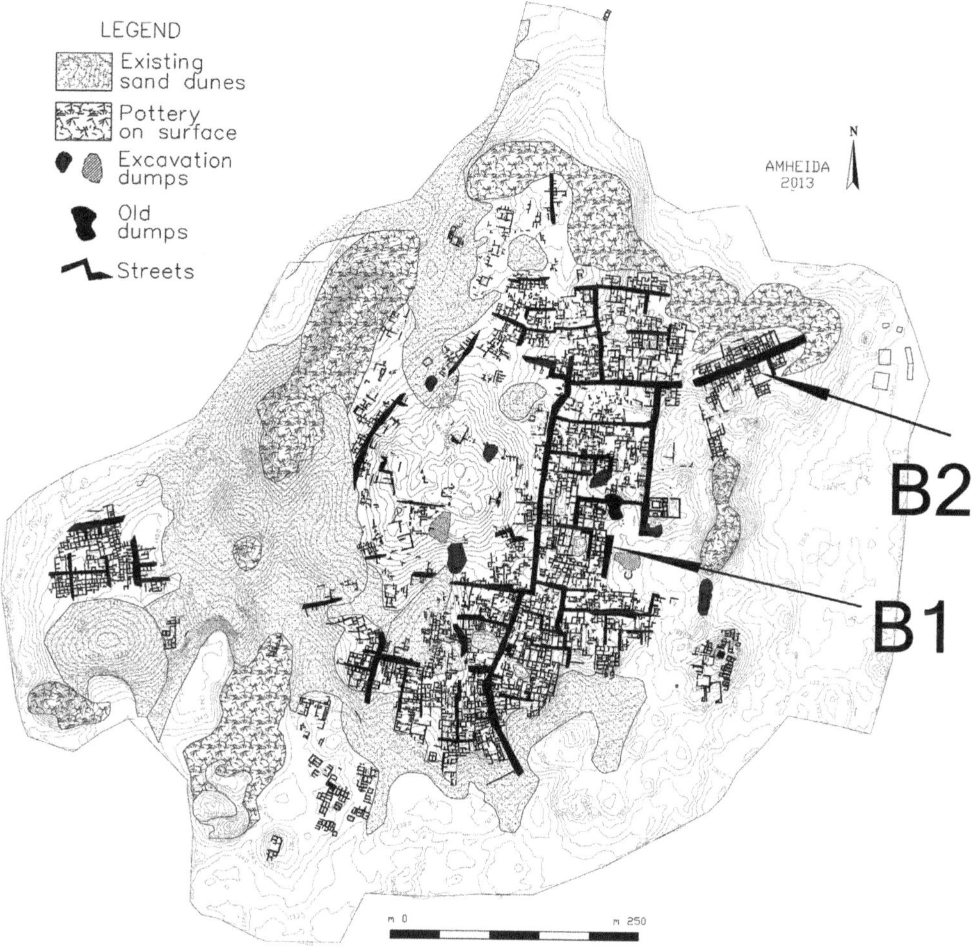

Figure 8.1. Plan of Amheida (Roman Trimithis). (Courtesy of the Amheida Project; CC-BY.)

completely abandoned during the fourth century. This case study will focus on a particular area of the city that appears to have been abandoned in the late third or early fourth century; this area is known as Area 1.

Trimithis: Area 1 and House B2

Area 1 is slightly off-axis from the rest of the city (figure 8.2). The structures in this area consist of modest houses and workshops. The predominant surface sherds date to the late third century CE, as do those that were recovered from excavation and surface scraping. House B2, the focus of our case study, is located immediately opposite a ceramics workshop that was built into what was probably once a house. House B2 is laid out on a simple clustered plan, a design it seems to share with many

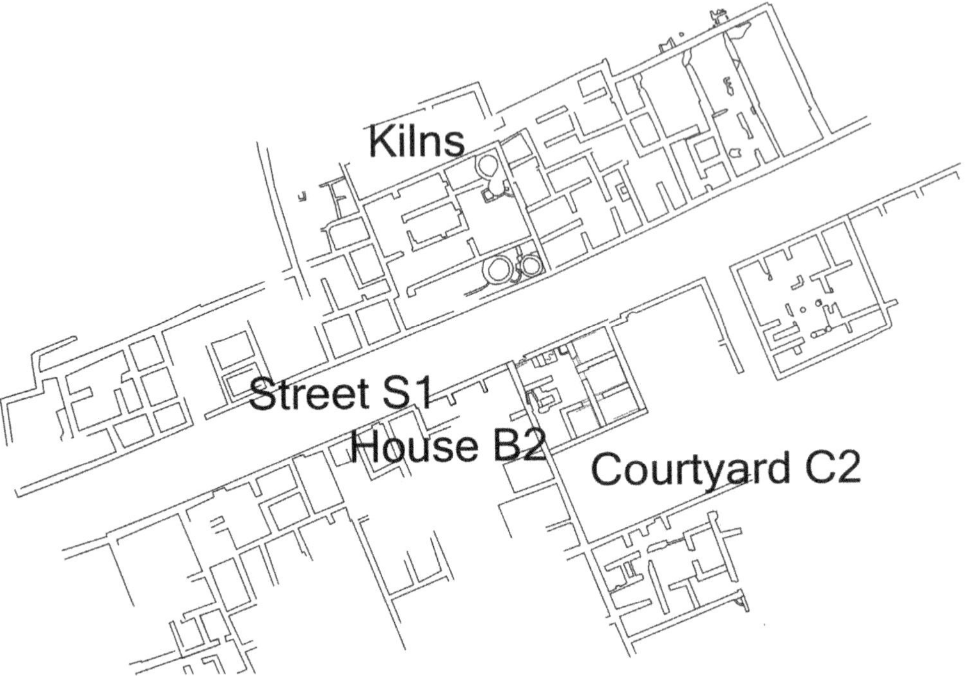

Figure 8.2. Trimithis Area 1. (Courtesy of the Amheida Project; CC-BY.)

of the neighboring houses (figure 8.3). While we were unable to generate a refined occupational history of this structure, the ceramics and ostraka suggest that it was occupied in the late third century with an abandonment sometime around the start of the fourth century. This abandonment date appears to be consistent with the surface data for the rest of Area 1.

The B2 house itself consists mostly of barrel-vaulted rooms surrounding a large room that was either very lightly roofed or open to the skies. This same arrangement can be found in contemporaneous houses from Kellis (Ismant el-Kharab), which is located in eastern Dakhla. Daily tasks and sleeping mostly took place in the four rooms surrounding the central room. The fifth room, in the southwest corner of the structure, was used for food preparation and appears to have had a flat roof. The central room had a bread oven positioned along its northern end with its draft hole opposite the prevailing wind, so we know that this central courtyard was also used for food production. It is the presence of this bread oven that suggests the central room was either lightly roofed or open to the skies. This interpretation contrasts to Davoli's description of such central rooms in the oases (chapter 1, this volume). David Depraetere's comprehensive study of Greco-Roman bread ovens demonstrated that people always positioned them in a room that was open to the skies and with the draft hole located opposite to the prevailing wind (see also Simpson, chapter 2, this volume).[15] Davoli described a hearth located within an enclosed domestic space in her chapter in this volume but could not provide examples of roofed rooms

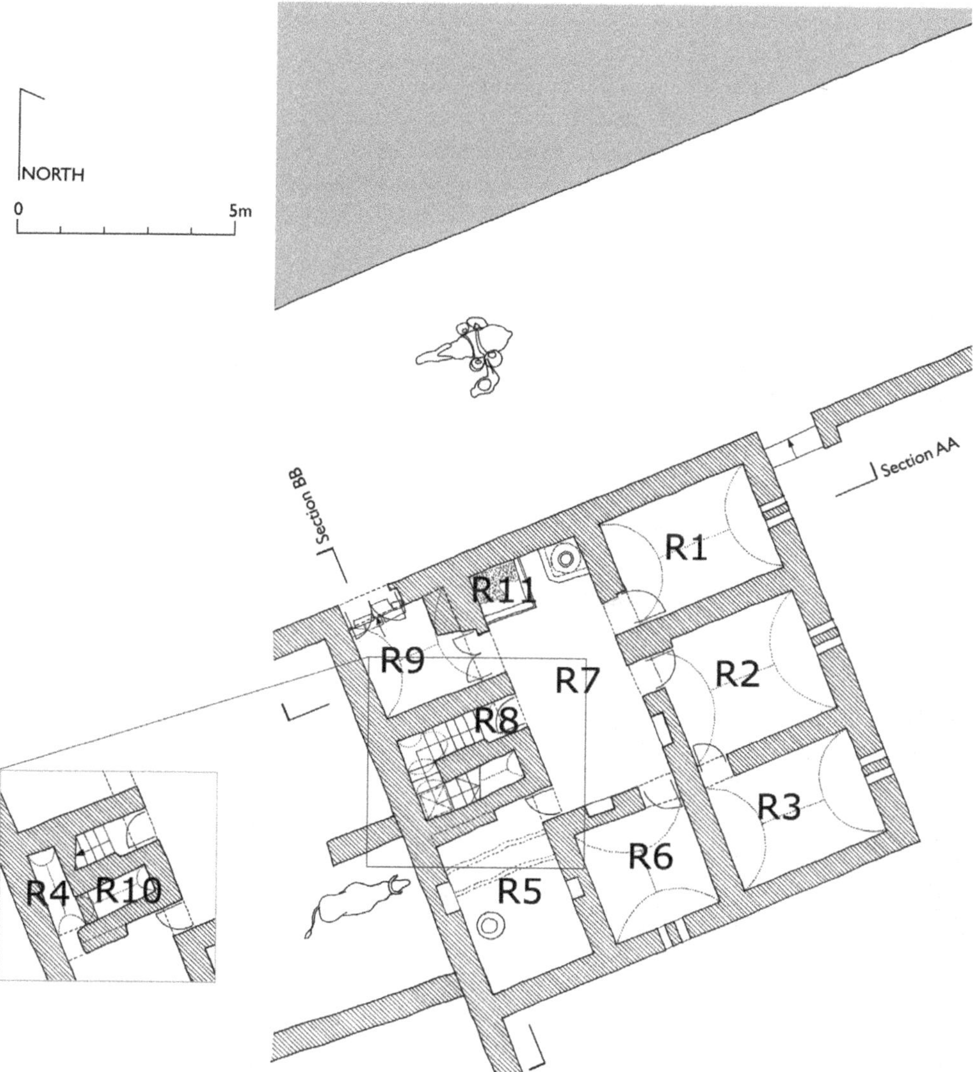

Figure 8.3. Trimithis House B2. (Courtesy of the Amheida Project; CC-BY.)

with bread ovens. Hearths, unlike bread ovens, can be found in a wide variety of architectural spaces. Indeed, many hearths were portable. Bread ovens, however, were specialized and unmovable cooking features that appear to have required certain conditions to function appropriately.

In previous studies of House B2, I have explored entanglements between local Egyptian, Greek, and Roman traditions,[16] but here I shift our focus to the topics of construction, cleanliness, renovation, and abandonment *within* this same structure. Specifically, radically different levels of cleanliness have been observed within the different rooms of the structure, suggesting that there might be a gendered component to this disparity. While this assessment still holds, much more can be said about disparities in cleanliness as well as rubbish disposal, renovation, and scavenging. Rooms 1, 5, and 7 best illustrate this cleanliness disparity, but I refer to other rooms for comparisons. The street (S1) in front of House B2 and the courtyard (C2) behind House B2 provide further information about how the Area 1 inhabitants dealt with rubbish.

Trimithis House B2: The Occupational History as Told by Rubbish

The history of rubbish in House B2 begins with the material used for the construction of the house itself. Rubbish was used to level the site surface on which B2 was built. Demotic ostraka were found within this rubbish,[17] suggesting that at least some of this material was recovered from a midden that was probably several hundred years old when it was reused as leveling material for House B2. We do not know the origins of this midden, as no formal middens have been identified anywhere at Trimithis. But of course, that does not mean that middens did not exist at Trimithis.

During the occupational history of House B2, cleanliness tells us quite a bit about how individuals prioritized their time and presented domestic space to household members and visitors.[18] Although House B2 was found to be fairly clean, it was not completely cleared upon its abandonment. There were some objects that appear to be the result of de facto refuse disposal, such a jar stoppers embedded into floor surfaces (e.g., Room 1), complete jars stacked into corners of rooms (Room 3), a clay tablet (e.g., Room 7), and other items found lying flat on floor surfaces. Only Room 5, the room used for food preparation, had significant accumulations of rubbish, which appeared to be the result of primary refuse disposal. This room was completely full of ash, which was particularly concentrated in the corners of the room. Broken ceramics were used to informally repair a wall that seems to have suffered from being close to a hearth. These ceramics were pouring out of the wall. Even in the best of times, this wall would not have presented a tidy appearance. The substantial quantities of ash and debris in Room 5 remind us that houses were not simply locations of consumption, but also of production.[19]

The ample finds of ash and rubbish in Room 5 contrast sharply with Room 7, which was kept quite clean even though it, too, was used for food production. Even the area immediately around the bread oven was free from ash debris. The disparity in cleanliness between these two rooms demonstrates that individuals prioritized cleaning the central room, through which anyone entering the house would travel, over a room that appears to have been only used for cooking. I also suggest that there was a gendered component to this cleanliness. Women surely spent considerably more time in Room 5 than men, while all household members and visitors used Room 7. As I have argued previously, women may have prioritized saving time over cleanliness when they left Room 5 less clean than the other rooms of the house.[20]

The maintenance of Room 7 also suggests that this room was a focal point for domestic renovations. The floor in this room was well-maintained throughout the occupational history of this structure. The floor was patched repeatedly, and then,

Figure 8.4. Trimithis House B2, Room 7, rubbish reused to level floor surfaces. (Courtesy of the Amheida Project; CC-BY.)

when patching no longer sufficed, it was leveled with a layer of rubbish and then another floor layer was put into place. This process was repeated four times over the occupational history of House B2. Other rooms had repairs and floor resurfacing done, but not nearly so frequently or as carefully as appears to be the case in Room 7. As with the foundation of the house, an assortment of rubbish was used to level each of the floor levels between repairs (figure 8.4).

The abandonment of B2 also tells us something about the inhabitants. There was no complete clearance of this structure when it was abandoned. We found numerous items in apparent de facto depositions, such as storage jars embedded in subfloor storage areas (Room 6), jars clustered in groups in the corner of one room (Room 3), objects in good repair in most rooms, and so on. It may be meaningful that no terracottas or unfired clay figurines were found inside of the house (compare to Thomas, chapter 9, this volume).[21]

House B2: Its Post-Abandonment Reuse

There is another possibility to consider in the story of the House B2 abandonment, and it centers upon post-abandonment reuse. When a house is abandoned and not reoccupied, neighbors and passers-by often take advantage of the empty structure to look for items that may be of use and to throw away their own items rather than transport them to a more distant midden. Scavenging and secondary refuse disposal in abandoned houses are common practices in many cities both ancient and contemporary.[22]

In Cairo since the 1940s, for example, the *zabbaleen* (English: "garbage people") have scavenged and recycled some 80 percent of the rubbish they pick up.[23] Like other professional scavengers, the *zabbaleen* tend to specialize: one family deals in rags, another in glass, and yet another in plastics. Pigs once served as an integral part of the *zabbaleen*'s recycling process. This tradition has come under threat since pigs were culled in Egypt after the H1N1 influenza outbreak.[24] The case of the *zabbaleen* demonstrates how lives and bodies, as much as technical elements, serve as part of a city's infrastructure.[25] The material practices of cleaning, scavenging, and recycling are interwoven with the material and moral aspects of cities. Waste makes clear how governing regimes—and the messy possibilities for their disruption—are constituted through the particularities of discard and filth, as well as their obverse, cleanliness and purity.[26]

Scavengers also abounded in antiquity. They took portable objects as well as building materials. Wood from doors, thresholds, and shelving was especially prized; we find the scars of such removals within many Romano-Egyptian houses. While the walls of House B2 were not preserved to a sufficient height to be able to find evidence of wood scavenging, we do find such scars in House B1 (figures 8.5 and 8.6). We can safely presume that this practice was widespread at Trimithis, just as it was at other Romano-Egyptian sites. As with twentieth-century Cairo, pigs may have served an important role in the recycling process in order to prevent garbage from rotting in the urban space. While most households probably had pigs in "private" and "semi-private" courtyards, we can also imagine that some pigs helped scavenge garbage that might have been left in more "public" areas (on courtyards, see also Simpson, chapter 2, this volume).[27]

The practice of dumping rubbish in abandoned houses also has great longevity and provided ancient scavengers with additional material. Some of this dumping occurred when individuals in the neighborhood wanted to remove rubbish from their own dwelling and did not wish to walk to an officially designated midden. Other rubbish may have accumulated when squatters occupied a structure for a short period of time. We have tantalizing evidence of a possible brief squatter occupation in House B2. Room 1 had a burn mark on a wall above floor level (figure 8.7). This stain may be the result of a fire lit on top of accumulated windblown sand by someone taking shelter in the abandoned house. It is difficult to conjecture further about the possibilities of this ephemeral usage. At the very least, it reminds us that abandoned houses were not as pristine as we might imagine them to be. Items found by archaeologists may well have belonged to the inhabitants, but they also may have belonged to passers-by or squatters who came into the structure after the household had moved on to another locale.

Street S1

The street in front of House B2 also informs our understanding of rubbish disposal in House B2 and the Area 1 neighborhood. We excavated a trench immediately in

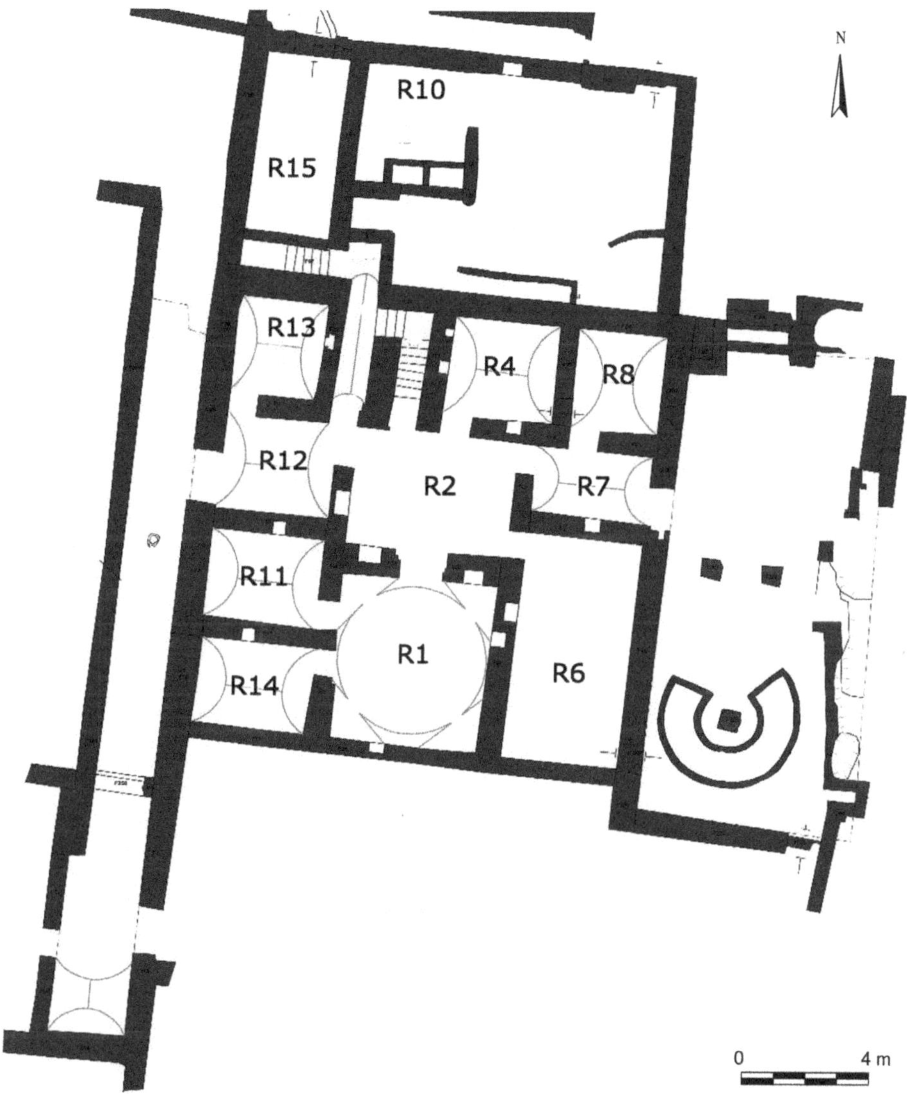

Figure 8.5. Trimithis House B1. (Courtesy of the Amheida Project; CC-BY.)

front of House B2 in order to compare the stratigraphy of the house with that of its immediate surroundings. While we found multiple surface levels for the street, each one with finely broken sherds pressed into its surface, there was very little additional rubbish. Most of the additional rubbish that we found consisted of broken figurines and wasters that presumably originated from the kilns across the street from House B2.[28] Most of these larger items were pushed up against the B2 house walls. There were no faunal remains or garbage strewn about. The cleanliness of the street suggests that there might have been a city mandate against dumping rubbish into public streets. Such mandates were common in Roman cities, and we have evidence of

Figure 8.6. Trimithis House B1, Room 2, scavenging scars visible in wall niche. (Courtesy of the Amheida Project; CC-BY.)

such civic regulation in ancient Egypt, Greece, and Mesopotamia.[29] Street S1, the widest we have identified at Trimithis, was probably monitored by authorities with particular vigilance. Even if there was not an ordinance against dumping garbage in the street, it is highly likely that pigs and other animals were deployed to scavenge this useful organic waste.

Figure 8.7. Trimithis House B2, Room 1, burn mark above floor surface from a possible squatter occupation. (Courtesy of the Amheida Project; CC-BY.)

Courtyard C2

Courtyard C2 is located behind House B2 and its neighbor to the east (House B9). Since a doorway led directly from House B9 into Courtyard C2, it certainly belonged to this house rather than House B2 (see Simpson, chapter 2, this volume, for a description of courtyard types). Like the street in front of B2, Courtyard C2 informs us about rubbish disposal in the Area 1 neighborhood. This courtyard appears to have been used to stable animals, cook food, and weave cloth, among other activities. Among the animals usually kept in courtyards, pigs and chickens were the most common. Larger animals, such as cows and donkeys, may also have resided here, as indicated by their coprolites. Although a wide range of tasks appear to have taken place in the courtyard, the informal floor surface was kept relatively clean during its occupational history. The animals probably contributed to this cleanliness. The pigs and chickens consumed garbage, and the pigs might even have consumed human waste, converting it into a protein safe for human consumption.[30] Donkey dung and cow dung served as crucial fuel for ovens, so they did not accumulate as waste.

Figure 8.8. Trimithis Courtyard C2, DSU 86 rubbish deposition. (Courtesy of the Amheida Project; CC-BY.)

Of particular interest for the present study is the accumulation of rubbish in the eastern half of the courtyard. This rubbish appears in small circular mounds of mixed debris that consisted of statuette fragments, cloth scraps, broken ceramics, ostraka, and so on (figure 8.8). There were few faunal remains among these deposits. The rare plant remains mostly derived from plant fiber objects, such as baskets. Figurines, chiefly made out of unfired mud, were evident in high densities compared with the house (compare to Thomas, chapter 9, this volume).[31] Because of the disparity between these depositions and the mostly clean courtyard surface, I suggest that these rounded depositions come from locals dumping basketfuls of trash into the courtyard after it was abandoned. This practice suggests that neighbors continued to live in Area 1 for some time after this courtyard was abandoned and that they used this area to dispose of items that were no longer wanted or that were in disrepair. This informal discard of rubbish does not appear to have gone on for very long, as the accumulation of dumped material is not substantial. This history appears to be consistent with the abandonment of Area 1 as a whole, which was probably in the early fourth century, at approximately the same time that House B2 was abandoned. Taken together, a picture begins to emerge of a neighborhood that was abandoned within a fairly short time frame. Of course, only additional excavation can verify or deny this suggestion.

House B1

These de facto and primary deposits found in House B2 contrast to the finds from another house from Trimithis, House B1, which is a more elite house located in a central area of the city (see Davoli, chapter 1, this volume). House B1 (figure 8.5) appears to have been more diligently cleared of items upon its abandonment than House B2. Scavengers, or even the occupants themselves, appear to have removed all of the attainable wood from within the structure. Additionally, valuable goods, such as an elaborate lamp and a container, were hidden below floor level in House B1, suggesting that the occupants or neighbors intended to come back for additional items. There is no clear evidence of squatters in B1, perhaps because it was abandoned at the same time as the rest of Trimithis or because it was less accessible to people traveling through the area than B2, which was located on the edge of the settlement.

Despite these contrasts, some practices were the same as with House B2. For example, rubbish served an important role in the construction of House B1. Trash was used to fill in a bath house underneath the house, and potsherds served as chinking for the vaults covering rooms. Bricks from the bathhouse were also reused for constructing House B1. To the north of B1, an open area also shows signs of rubbish depositions, similar to Courtyard C2.

The street, S2, however, has a different history of usage from Street S1 (on streets, see Davoli, chapter 1, this volume). Immediately prior to the abandonment of House B1, a *stibadium*, a type of reclining seat used for dining in the later Roman Period, was constructed in S2, next to House B1. It seems to have been used for a single-use feasting event, as evidenced by faunal remains that were left in the street.[32] This street usage is intriguing, since one of the occupants of House B1, Serenos, was a city councilor. Part of his role would have included ensuring that such misuse of public spaces did not occur. It is entirely possible that this feasting event marked the end of the usage of this area of the site.

Comparisons between House B2 and House B1

There are many possible reasons for the different histories of abandonment, scavenging, disposal, and squatting between House B2 and House B1. The items left behind in House B2 might have been involuntary depositions of items that people would have liked to keep using, but that they did not consider to be worth the effort and cost of moving to a new residence. Removal costs and difficulties grew with distance, and so it may be that the individuals who abandoned B2 did not make a simple local move. The discard of these items also might be able to tell us something about the refashioning of selves and households. The items most crucial to self-identity among the B2 household, such as figurines and jewelry, appear to have been taken away with the residents, while replaceable items, such as jars, baskets, and loom weights, were left behind. The inhabitants of House B1, which was a larger, more architecturally complex, and decorated structure, may have had more objects with meaning and economic value to take with them. It is also probable that the House B1 household had the economic means to take objects with them, or perhaps to organize a planned move to a nearby location. Those objects that they did not take along might have been more appealing to scavengers, as the buried items suggest. Meanwhile, House B1 may have been missed by squatters and people looking for a place to dump rubbish, because it was abandoned at the end of the occupational history of Trimithis as a whole. Based on the current state of evidence, Trimithis shows no signs of being occupied after this structure was abandoned. More excavations are necessary to clarify the abandonment history of this neighborhood and Trimithis more generally.

The House B2 case study provides us with a fine-grained perspective on rubbish disposal within a house and its surroundings. It seems that the B2 inhabitants kept their dwelling clean, removing most rubbish from the house and depositing it elsewhere. We do not know where this "elsewhere" might be located. The inhabitants were less fastidious about cleanliness when it came to keeping their primary food preparation area clean, although it is notable that ample faunal remains were not left behind in that room either. The B2 inhabitants appear to have had easy access to older middens, from which they acquired material to level floor surfaces when they renovated their floors and to fill in a wall when it became undermined. When the household abandoned the structure, they appear to have taken valuable items with them, leaving behind things that they could easily replace. Scavengers, or the inhabitants themselves, cleared the structure of all useful wood. A squatter might have inhabited the house for a brief period of time, perhaps also scavenging it for useful items.

Excavations around the house suggest that neighbors were in the habit of dumping rubbish in abandoned buildings and courtyards, but left streets clean. Since neighbors had no issues with dumping material in houses, there might have been a civic mandate to keep thoroughfares cleared of rubbish. Together, this evidence suggests that the "missing middens" of Trimithis may be found in the houses and courtyards themselves. A comparison with other Romano-Egyptian sites complements this suggestion.

Romano-Egyptian Comparanda

The House B2 case study illuminates domestic discard within one household and neighborhood. How does this case study compare with other areas of Egypt?

Houses as Middens at Karanis and Soknopaiou Nesos

Karanis, in the Fayum, provides us with a large number of structures that were excavated chiefly in the early twentieth century. While these excavations were not recorded and published to the modern standard, the abundance of domestic data helps to provide a broad view of rubbish disposal from a single town. For example, the Karanis reports do not disaggregate rubbish disposal practices from the rest of the data. Publications mention rubbish disposal only incidentally as part of the description of excavations within the Karanis houses.

Karanis was a densely built town that was occupied for more than five hundred years. During periods of this occupational history, abandoned houses could be found located next to occupied ones. It seems that inhabitants took advantage of the changing fortunes of surrounding houses in order to offload items that were no longer wanted. Houses that appear to have been abandoned were found to contain large dumps of material that most likely originated from structures nearby.[33] Additionally, much of the southern portion of Karanis was built on deflated ceramic depositions (figure 8.9). Bethany Simpson, who leads the current UCLA mission at Karanis, suggests that inhabitants intentionally used this rubbish to level the ground surface prior to construction, much like I have suggested for Trimithis.[34] The disposal and reuse of rubbish at Karanis added horizontal stratigraphy to the vertical stratigraphy commonly encountered at archaeological sites. It is perhaps because of this horizontal stratigraphy that the University of Michigan team found it so difficult to decipher temporal horizons.[35]

Inhabitants of the nearby site of Soknopaiou Nesos also seem to have used rubbish as a leveling agent before new construction.[36] Abandoned houses also resided next to occupied ones and seem to have been used advantageously as neighborhood middens.[37] The excavators do not supply great detail about the contents of these middens, but the unpublished records at the Kelsey Museum may be able to reveal something of them if consultation access is provided. For now, we can say that the

Figure 8.9. Photograph from 2014 of deflated ceramic depositions reused to level construction surfaces at Karanis. (Bethany Simpson; courtesy of the URU Fayum Project, now the Northeast Fayum Lakeshore Project.)

disposal of household rubbish in an abandoned house appears to have been commonplace at several sites in the Fayum. These same middens also provided a ready source of leveling material for house construction and renovation. This reuse of material suggests that the rubbish disposal may have been perceived as a sort of "cold storage" of goods that might be reused at some, as yet undefined, moment.

The Middens of Oxyrhynchus

Oxyrhynchus, a large urban site with dense occupation, illustrates a different type of rubbish disposal in Roman Egypt (figure 8.10). The inhabitants used the edge of the desert to dispose of their rubbish. These rubbish mounds accumulated substantial quantities of debris over the long occupational history of Oxyrhynchus. The excavations of Grenfell and Hunt exposed the enormous quantities of papyri that accumulated in this area. Often the baskets in which these papyri were transported to the dump were found dumped along with the papyri they contained.[38] These papyri inform us that these mounds themselves were subject to episodic usage; those on the outskirts of the site produced first- to early fourth-century papyri, while those near the village dated to the medieval period, and the intermediate mounds dated to the Byzantine Period through to the eighth or ninth centuries.[39] One large rubbish

Figure 8.10. Oxyrhynchus in 1903. (A.S. Hunt [?]; Courtesy of the Egypt Exploration Society.)

mound, Kôm Gamman (K 20), was used for approximately six hundred years. It is unfortunate that we do not have comparative data from excavations within the Oxyrhynchus houses themselves that can inform us whether rubbish disposal also took place within abandoned houses. Because of the way that the town was looted, excavated, and recorded, we do not know about depositions within the houses themselves. In the absence of such evidence, I suggest that such depositions probably did occur.

Global Rubbish Disposal: Comparative Case Studies

Although archaeologists have considered rubbish disposal to be an important component of the archaeological record and site formation processes since the publication of Schiffer's influential work, they have studied it only rarely. While many archaeologists acknowledge the need to differentiate between Schiffer's deposition categories, few published reports record data with sufficient rigor to make it possible to do so. This weakness is particularly evident in excavation reports produced prior to the mid-late twentieth century.

Two projects—the "garbology" project run by the University of Arizona[40] and an ethnoarchaeology study within the Kalinga Province of the Philippines[41]—are among the few to suggest broad theories about rubbish disposal practices, how people manage disposal, and what rubbish disposal reveals about society. In addition to these overarching anthropological perspectives, a range of specific case studies have provided insights into regional rubbish disposal practices.[42] Together, these studies suggest that people are willing to travel only limited distances to dispose of their rubbish, unless there is a civic mandate requiring them to use distant middens.

Among these regional case studies, there are a few studies of rubbish disposal in Pharaonic Egypt that help to illuminate the *longue durée* of rubbish disposal in this region. Dixon introduced the earliest study of Pharaonic Egyptian rubbish disposal with a brief survey from the prehistoric era to the New Kingdom.[43] He argued that the first evidence for organized sanitary conditions and human bodily waste disposal took place in the Archaic Period, although this development was primarily among the elite. Later on, Dixon suggested that domestic and civic rubbish was dumped into the Nile, streets, deserted buildings, and pits, citing Twelfth Dynasty Kahun and Eighteenth Dynasty Tell el-Amarna as examples of these practices.[44] Eighteenth Dynasty Deir el-Medina, which was occupied for four hundred years without floor levels being raised, served as a counterexample.[45] Consequently, Dixon suggested that there was strong civic control over building, planning, and rubbish disposal at Deir el-Medina. This suggestion is reasonable given that the state supplied and closely monitored the settlement.

There have been few studies of rubbish disposal in Pharaonic Egypt since Dixon's pioneering article. Most mentions of rubbish depositions have been brief and were focused on a select number of sites. For example, quite a few scholars have mentioned the small pits that households used to dispose of their rubbish at New Kingdom sites such as Tell el-Amarna,[46] Gurob,[47] and Memphis.[48] These brief mentions of rubbish disposal rarely dwell at length on the content of the depositions, the implications of such practices, or how people recycled or reused rubbish. These studies also did not use terms in a consistent manner to discuss the various types of rubbish that people deposited. The confusion between "garbage," "trash," "waste," "refuse," and "rubbish," when used synonymously, makes it difficult to understand what type of material was deposited and whether there were disparities between various waste disposal areas. The end result is that one has to agree with Kemp and Stevens that "the management of waste is an aspect of ancient Egyptian society that is not well understood . . . and it is difficult to get a measure of the impact this had on the quality of life."[49]

Two recent articles provide lengthier explorations of rubbish in Pharaonic Egypt. Shaw simulated diversity among artifact types in his study of rubbish deposits at New Kingdom Akhetaten (Tell el-Amarna).[50] He followed Schiffer's terminology and distinguished between de facto, primary, and secondary refuse, although he did not use the Garbology Project terminology to classify the various types of rubbish he discussed. Adherence to this terminology would have clarified Shaw's argument, since he determined that rubbish disposal varied according to the particular activity and types of material involved. Shaw also differentiated between "communal dumping," such as in the "palace rubbish heaps,"[51] and the individual burial of household refuse in pits beneath these same houses, as reported by past excavators. Significantly, Shaw cautioned that rubbish deposits at el-Amarna were probably unusual compared to other contemporaneous urban sites (e.g., Memphis and Elephantine); they were the product of a short period of human activity, and the most recent period of deposition was less likely to have been disturbed by later activity. Anna K. Hodgkinson built on Shaw's earlier work in her recent article on waste management at Amarna.[52] She employed Schiffer and Hodder's terminology in her work, arguing that further study of the diverse methods of waste disposal in the Central City could be highly informative.

Felix Arnold explored the evolution of rubbish disposal by taking a diachronic perspective on the large number of houses excavated by the joint German-Swiss Mission at Elephantine and dating from 330 BCE to 900 CE.[53] Arnold did not draw from anthropological perspectives on rubbish, and he used the terms *garbage*, *waste*, and *refuse* interchangeably. He argued that the act of deposition itself was the only domestic activity to which archaeological evidence can attest accurately, be that deposition intentional, incidental, or accidental. Arnold did not draw on Schiffer's terminology to disaggregate these acts of deposition, which partially obscured his argument. Even so, I agree with his assessment that rubbish deposition reveals how inhabitants perceived different spaces within the house and its courtyard. For example, he cited an example of long-term ash accumulation (ca. 2100–1950 BCE) in a courtyard that people used primarily for baking, but also for other activities.[54] Meanwhile, contemporaneous houses seem to have been kept much cleaner, suggesting that households maintained systems for removing and reusing ash accumulations. Arnold argued that people were inclined to keep a space clean if it was used for multiple activities that would have been disrupted by rubbish. Arnold further argued that the distinction between a "clean" house proper and an "unclean" auxiliary space appears to have become increasingly formalized over time.[55] This suggestion complements Dixon's arguments.

These Pharaonic Egyptian and regional case studies indicate that there are cultural rules that govern the appropriate distance between living areas and waste disposal areas. Since garbage produces an unpleasant odor and can serve as a health hazard, people appear to have kept it outside of habited areas for most of Egyptian history. Pigs, which were prevalent in most Egyptian settlements in antiquity, served as an efficient means of converting food waste into eatable protein.[56] These animals, among others, may help to explain the absence of garbage in most settlements.

Waste material that did not produce an odor seems to have been subject to more change over time. Typically, people make a division between human and animal bodily waste and trash consisting of objects, such as broken ceramics, glass, figurines, and objects of personal adornment. In most ancient societies, people or animals consumed all food before it could be thrown away.[57] Likewise, people often used papyrus items, such as textual papyri and baskets, as fuel rather than throw them away. Obviously, however, this rule does not always apply, as Oxyrhynchus so clearly illustrates with its mounds of papyri found within middens. Additionally, some materials, such as religious paraphernalia, carry sufficient meaning that they are discarded separately from other materials. Some apparently "ordinary" materials may also be invested with meaning because of religious context and are also disposed of in distinct ways.[58]

The results of these prior studies of rubbish suggest a few common human behaviors, regardless of locality or time period. First, efficiency has an enduring influence on rubbish disposal. A study in the Kalinga Province of the Philippines argued that individuals are only willing to walk short distances to throw away rubbish on a frequent basis.[59] We find that efficiency guided the habits of Romano-Egyptians also; inhabitants commonly dumped household rubbish in abandoned houses and streets unless there was a civic mandate to send rubbish elsewhere.

For example, the rubbish deposits found at Memphis (Kom Rabi'a), mentioned above, include examples from a disused silo and an open courtyard.[60] It thus seems that disused functional areas such as these were prime locales for rubbish deposition. It is clearly important to understand the mechanisms of refuse distribution in such areas, since they are closely entwined with the organization of production and consumption. Indeed, evidence from current and recent excavations at El-Amarna confirms that much of the craftwork actually took place in courtyards and open areas, which are precisely the areas that tended to be neglected by the 1907–37 excavators.[61] As more well-published courtyard excavations come to light, we can expect to understand more about production, consumption, and discard.

Second, there are cultural ideas about what is considered to be "dirty." The concept of cleanliness appears to have evolved over time in Egypt, as the diachronic studies by Dixon and Arnold demonstrate. The act of rubbish deposition is also a culturally constructed judgment of cleanliness. In Roman Egypt, the location of middens and the probable creation of civic mandates relating to rubbish disposal developed over time and according to settlement type. The division between garbage, which produces unpleasant olfactory sensations, and trash, which produces no such smells because it is inorganic, appears to be the most enduring of these evolving cultural practices. Visual disturbances created by rubbish might also have been a concern. While trash depositions in abandoned houses and courtyards may not initially appear to be motivated by aesthetics, these depositions are not readily visible from the street or other houses. By contrast, large middens on the edges of settlements, such as at Oxyrhynchus, were highly visible due to their enormous size. Inhabitants may have preferred local depositions of rubbish because they were easy to deposit items there and because it prevented rubbish from being highly visible in the surrounding landscape.

Third, cultural ideas about utility also may have shaped rubbish disposal. It seems to have been common to reuse rubbish for construction and renovation projects in Roman Egypt. Rubbish was useful for leveling, constructing floor layers, repairing walls, creating vaulted roofs, and even for making mud bricks. For this reason, Romano-Egyptians may have viewed the trash deposited in abandoned buildings as a form of communal "cold storage" for later reuse. Certainly, this type of rubbish reuse is not uncommon in the ancient Mediterranean. For example, the main harbor zone of Hellenistic Delos was developed from 217 BCE onward through the reuse of refuse to fill in the waterfront to the west of the sanctuary of Apollo. Other regions of the city, such as the southern extent of Delos, also experienced massive landfilling through the reuse of rubbish.[62] Even modern cities, such as New York City, have been known to reclaim land through the use of rubbish. Battery Park City in the southwest of Manhattan Island was created by dumping rubbish on the edge of the island in order to create more land. Since such reuse was so common, it is entirely possible that the rubbish deposited within unoccupied space was understood as communal building material.

Fourth, cross-cultural studies reveal counterintuitive results that require more exploration. For example, the Garbology Project demonstrates that people tend to hoard in times of scarcity. This hoarding may result in the wastage of precious goods; organic goods have a limited shelf life, and even inorganic goods may lose value over time. This form of wastefulness is surprising and could change our interpretation of wasted materials in other global contexts. Instead of interpreting waste as evidence of bounty, perhaps we should interpret it as an example of stockpiling gone awry in times of scarcity.

Revisiting House B2

With these larger global insights in mind, I suggest that the rubbish in and around Trimithis House B2 reflects some of these global trends. First, the inhabitants prioritized their time by finding the shortest path to discard. There was probably a Ptolemaic/Early Roman midden nearby, which people reused in order to level the site surface before building House B2. We also see this expediency reflected in the reuse of Courtyard C2 for rubbish disposal by neighbors after it was abandoned.

Second, there are cultural ideas about cleanliness and discard. We see this cultural influence in the selection process by which inhabitants kept some rooms clean (Room 7) while allowing others to grow messy (Room 5). People also seem to have kept Street S1 clean, in front of House B2. This cleanliness of a public space was probably due to a city mandate, since people tend to throw rubbish in streets if not forbidden to do so. Such civic mandates appear to have been in place at other settlements in earlier phases of Egyptian history. For example, the streets of Elephantine appeared to have been kept clear of refuse, only rising because of the accumulation of windblown sand rather than the deposition of rubbish.[63] Arnold suggested that donkeys transported rubbish to the limits of the city and deposited it at the shores of the island.[64]

We also see selectivity in the types of rubbish that were found in and around House B2. Faunal remains were minimal, suggesting that they were reused or that there were laws about how faunal remains could be discarded within the city. Meanwhile, other garbage was also missing. Inhabitants may have fed this organic material to pigs in order to safely convert it into a consumable protein. Finally, it seems probable that inhabitants removed figurines from B2 on abandonment; we did not find them within the house walls, although they were common in the courtyard and the street. Comparisons with mesoscale data in Roman Egypt, such as Thomas's study (chapter 9, this volume), suggest that there may have been cultural guidelines about how to dispose of figurines. This hypothesis would be worth exploring in more detail in future studies.[65]

Finally, I suggest that the "missing middens" at Trimithis probably can be found in abandoned houses and courtyards on the basis of comparisons to other Romano-Egyptian sites (e.g., Karanis, Soknopaiou Nesos), the cross-cultural tendency to dispose of rubbish as quickly as possible, and the evidence from Courtyard C2 itself, which shows signs of post-abandonment dumping.

Rubbish and Material Habitus

As shown here, an individual house and neighborhood, as well as surveyed rubbish disposal at three other sites, can provide essential insights into Romano-Egyptian domestic life. This research also demonstrates the advantages of studying domestic discard within a multiscalar framework.

Rubbish disposal is a profoundly cultural practice, but there are certain commonalities that cut across cultures. People are typically efficient about disposing of items that they intend to discard, throwing them away as quickly and with as little effort as possible. This tendency explains why littering remains a problem in contemporary cultures and why so many people struggle to change their own rubbish disposal practices. Cultural specificities emerge from within this general behavior. People within specific groups formulate different ideas about what constitutes "dirt," what disposal practices are "wasteful," and which items need to be disposed of with particular care and consideration.

The term *material habitus* refers to this life world of choices. It can be defined as "an enmeshing that combines persons, objects, deities, and all manner of immaterial things together in ways that cannot easily be disentangled or separated taxonomically."[66] The materiality of houses involves the objects that households create for themselves and the material habitus that develops based on the object world, the ways in which objects in those worlds affect household members in terms of their sense of self and their presentation of self to others within and beyond the household, and the sentiments and attachments that people form with their belongings.[67] A careful study of domestic rubbish reveals cultural habits, the many forms of agency involved in domestic activities, and emotions, not just consumption.

The approach described here, exploring the material habitus of the B2 household by examining rubbish disposal, cleanliness, construction, scavenging, and abandonment, is somewhat different from how archaeologists typically explore household identities. Archaeologists, including myself, usually examine the material left behind within houses as their way of accessing the identities of individuals who once lived in those spaces. While I still believe in such interpretations, I suggest that we extend our conception of material habitus to include domestic discard practices.

There are many advantages to studying discard. Discard practices help to explain the creation of the archaeological record. To do so, we need to think of depositions such as dirt and ash accumulations as key elements of how individuals present themselves to others. We need to think about repaired and recycled items, as well as renovated architecture, to consider what things people valued preserving and reusing. We also need to consider the items that we do not find within houses: the voids in the material record. These items occupy two extremes in people's emotions: objects that people wanted to discard from their lives, and those that they wanted to keep with them. The most precious materials of all, the ones that individuals took with them, are more difficult to locate. These items may be found in mortuary contexts, but not necessarily, and their identification is a topic worthy of future exploration. However, when we peruse the aggregated household middens found in abandoned houses and on the edges of settlements, we gain a greater sense of what may have constituted the voids of household assemblages—the material that people no longer wanted.

Notes

1 Acknowledgments: Gregory Marouard and Miriam Müller kindly provided me with additional references on rubbish. Bethany Simpson shared her in-progress research at Karanis with me along with a photograph of rubbish reused for leveling material. The editors, as well as additional conference participants, shared helpful thoughts and ideas with me during the conference, which helped me to revise this chapter for the volume. All errors remain, of course, my own.

2 Rathje and Murphy 2001.

3 Beaudry 2015.

4 See Fletcher 1992.

5 E.g., on post-Katrina New Orleans, see Dawdy 2006a; 2006b.

6 *Contra* Beaudry 2015.

7 Lagerspetz 2018, 7.

8 Cf. Bataille 1991; Douglas 1966; Lagerspetz 2018.

9 Cf. Rathje and Murphy 2001, 9fn.

10 Schiffer 1976; 1987.

11 Hodder 2012, 73.
12 Hayden and Cannon 1983.
13 Such as Hammond and Hammond 1981.
14 Schiffer 1987, 282.
15 Depraetere 2002.
16 E.g., Boozer 2012a; 2010; 2015b.
17 Ruffini 2015.
18 Barile and Brandon 2004.
19 On discard and ash, see Hodder 1987.
20 Boozer 2015c.
21 Boozer 2015a.
22 Rathje and Murphy 2001, 192–95.
23 Rathje and Murphy 2001, 193.
24 Fahmi and Sutton 2010.
25 Cf. Simone 2004.
26 Compare to Fredericks 2018.
27 Cf. Miller 1990.
28 Boozer 2015a; Dixneuf 2015.
29 Boozer 2016; Dixon 1972b.
30 Miller 1990; 2013.
31 Boozer 2012b; 2013; 2015a.
32 Boozer 2007; 2010; 2019; Bagnall et al. 2016, 86–104.
33 E.g., Husselman 1979, 15, 25, 29.
34 Bethany Simpson, personal communication.
35 The dating of Karanis layers is notoriously difficult. Various chronological revisions have been suggested over the years (e.g. Husselman 1979; Pollard 1998), and more can be anticipated.
36 Boak, Peterson, and Haatveldt 1935, 5ff.
37 Boak, Peterson, and Haatveldt 1935, 5ff; Boozer 2017.
38 Grenfell and Hunt 2007, 349.
39 Grenfell and Hunt 2007, 349.
40 Rathje and Murphy 2001.
41 Beck and Hill 2004; Beck 2006.
42 E.g., Hodder 1987; Rothschild 1994; Needham and Spence 1997; Cordier and Dieudonné-Glad 2003; Shillito et al. 2011; Aja 2018.
43 Dixon 1972a.
44 Cf. Petrie 1890; 1894.
45 Cf. Bruyère 1939.
46 Pendlebury 1951, 233; James 1984, 229; Kemp and Stevens, 2010, I, 499–503.
47 Thomas 1981, 13–14.
48 Jeffreys 1985.
49 Kemp and Stevens 2010, I, 501.
50 Shaw 2012.
51 Cf. Petrie 1894.
52 Hodgkinson 2021.
53 Arnold 2015.
54 Arnold 2015, 152–53.
55 Dixon 1972.
56 Miller 1990.
57 Dixon 1989.
58 Halstead, Hooder, and Jones 1978; Needham and Spence 1997.
59 Beck 2006.
60 Jeffreys 1985.
61 See Stevens and Eccleston 2007, 153.
62 Zarmakoupi 2018, 34.
63 von Pilgrim 1996, 219.
64 Arnold 2015, 158.

65 On figurines in domestic religious practice, see Boozer 2021, chap. 7. On rubbish depositions primarily of ceramics from cultic contexts during the early dynastic era, see Müller 2017.
66 Meskell 2005, 3.
67 Beaudry 2015, 7.

Works Cited

Aja, A.J. 2018. "What a Waste: Disposal in the Iron Age Near East." *Eretz Israel, Festschrift Lawrence Stager* 33: 1–8.

Arnold, D. 2012. "Pottery Use and Disposal in a "Priest's House" at Dahshur." In *Handbook of Pottery of the Egyptian Middle Kingdom*, Vol. 2, *The Regional Volume*, edited by A. Seiler and R. Schiestl, 161–83. Vienna: Verlag der Österreichischen Akademie der Wissenschaften.

Arnold, F. 2015. "Clean and Unclean Space: Domestic Waste Management at Elephantine." In *Household Studies in Complex Societies: (Micro) Archaeological and Textual Approaches*, edited by M. Müller, 151–68. Chicago: Oriental Institute.

Bagnall, R.S., N. Aravecchia, R. Cribiore, P. Davoli, O.E. Kaper, and S. McFadden. 2016. *An Oasis City*. New York: New York University Press.

Barile, K.S., and J.C. Brandon. 2004. *Household Chores and Household Choices: Theorizing the Domestic Sphere in Historical Archaeology*. Tuscaloosa: University of Alabama Press.

Bataille, G. 1991. *The Accursed Share: An Essay on General Economy*. Vols. 2 and 3. New York: Zone Books.

Beaudry, M.C. 2015. "Households Beyond the House: On the Archaeology and Materiality of Historical Households." In *Beyond the Walls: New Perspectives on the Archaeology of Historical Households*, edited by K.R. Fogle, J.A. Nyman and M.C. Beaudry, 1–22. Gainesville: University Press of Florida.

Beck, M.E. 2006. "Midden Ceramic Assemblage Formation: A Case Study from Kalinga, Philippines." *American Antiquity* 71 (1): 27–51.

Beck, M.E, and M.E. Hill. 2004. "Rubbish, Relatives, and Residence: The Family Use of Middens." *Journal of Archaeological Method and Theory* 11 (3): 297–333.

Boak, A.E.R., E.E. Peterson, and R.A. Haatveldt. 1935. *Soknopaiou Nesos: The University of Michigan Excavations at Dimê in 1931–32, Humanistic Series*. Ann Arbor: University of Michigan Press.

Boozer, A.L. 2007. "Housing Empire: The Archaeology of Daily Life in Roman Amheida, Egypt." PhD diss., Columbia University.

Boozer, A.L. 2010. "Memory and Microhistory of an Empire: Domestic Contexts in Roman Amheida, Egypt." In *Archaeology and Memory*, edited by D. Borić, 138–57. Oxford: Oxbow Books.

Boozer, A.L. 2012a. "Globalizing Mediterranean Identities: The Overlapping Spheres of Egyptian, Greek and Roman Worlds at Trimithis." *Journal of Mediterranean Archaeology* 25 (2): 93–116.

Boozer, A.L. 2012b. "A Preliminary Report on Courtyard C2." In *Excavations at Amheida in Area 1*, edited by A.L. Boozer. http://www.learn.columbia.edu/amheida/html/field_reports.html.

Boozer, A.L. 2013. "A Preliminary Report on Courtyard C2C." In *Excavations at Amheida in Area 1*, edited by A.L. Boozer. http://www.learn.columbia.edu/amheida/html/field_reports.html.

Boozer, A.L. 2015a. "Figurines." In *A Late Romano-Egyptian House in the Dakhleh Oasis: Amheida House B2*, edited by A.L. Boozer, 291–307. New York: New York University Press.

Boozer, A.L. 2015b. *A Late Romano-Egyptian House in the Dakhla Oasis: Amheida House B2*. Edited by R.S. Bagnall, *Amheida II*. New York: New York University Press

Boozer, A.L. 2015c. "Tracing Everyday Life at Trimithis (Dakhleh Oasis, Egypt)." In *The Materiality of Everyday Life*, edited by C. Robin and L. Overholtzer, 122–38. Archaeological Papers of the American Anthropological Association 26. Hoboken, NJ: John Wiley & Sons.

Boozer, A.L. 2016. "Garbage." In *Blackwell's Encyclopedia of Ancient History: Social History*, edited by R.S. Bagnall, K. Brodersen, C. Champlin, A. Erskine, and S.R. Huebner, Oxford: Blackwell, https://onlinelibrary.wiley.com/doi/abs/10.1002/9781444338386.wbeah30207.

Boozer, A.L. 2017. "Towards an Archaeology of Household Relationships in Roman Egypt." In *Mediterranean families in Antiquity: Households, Extended Families, and Domestic Space*, edited by S. Huebner and G. Nathan, 174–203. Hoboken, NJ: Wiley-Blackwell.

Boozer, A. L. 2019. "The Archaeology of Amheida (Egypt)." In *The Encyclopedia of Global Archaeology*, edited by C. Smith, New York: Springer, https://link.springer.com/referenceworkentry/10.1007/978-3-319-51726-1_1108-2.

Boozer, A.L. 2021. *At Home in Roman Egypt: A Social Archaeology*. Cambridge: Cambridge University Press.

Bruyère, B. 1939. *Rapport sur les Fouilles de Deir el Médineh (1934–1935), Troisème Partie FIFAO 16*. Cairo: Institut français d'archéologie orientale.

Cordier, P., and N. Dieudonné-Glad, eds. 2003. *La Ville et ses déchets dans le monde romain: rebuts et recyclages. Actes du Coll. de Poitiers, 19–20 sept. 2002*: EPUISE. Montagnac: Monique Mergoil.

Dawdy, S.L. 2006a. "In Katrina's Wake." *Archaeology* 59 (4): 16–21.

Dawdy, S.L. 2006b. "The Taphonomy of Disaster and the (Re)Formation of New Orleans." *American Anthropologist* 108: 719–30.

Depraetere, D.D.E. 2002. "A Comparative Study on the Construction and the Use of the Domestic Bread Oven in Egypt during the Graeco-Roman and Late Antique/Early Byzantine Period." *Mitteilungen des Deutschen Archäologischen Institutes Abteilung Kairo* 58, 119–56, Plates 115–16.

Dixneuf, D. 2015. "La céramique de la maison B2." In *A Late Romano Egyptian House in the Dakhleh Oasis: Amheida House B2*, edited by A.L. Boozer, 201–80. New York: New York University Press.

Dixon, D.M. 1972a. "The Disposal of Certain Personal, Household and Town Waste in Ancient Egypt." In *Man, Settlement, and Urbanism*, edited by P.J. Ucko, R. Tringham, and G.W. Dimbleby, 647–50. Hertfordshire, UK: Garden City Press.

Dixon, D.M. 1972b. "Population, Pollution, and Health in Ancient Egypt." In *Population and Pollution*, edited by P. R. Cox and J. Peel, 29–36. London: Academic Press.

Dixon, D.M. 1989. "A Note on Some Scavengers of Ancient Egypt." *World Archaeology* 21 (2): 193–97.

Douglas, M. 1966. *Purity and Danger: An Analysis of the Concepts of Pollution and Taboo*. London: Routledge.

Dublin, Susan A., and N. Rothschild. 1994. "Deep Trash: A Tale of Two Middens." In *Exploring Social, Political and Economic Organization in the Zuni Region*, edited by T.L Howell and T. Stone, 91–102. Arizona: Arizona State University Anthropology Research Papers.

Fahmi, W., and K. Sutton. 2010. "Cairo's Contested Garbage: Sustainable Solid Waste Management and the Zabaleen's Right to the City." *Sustainability* 2: 1765–83.

Fletcher, R. 1992. "Time Perspectivism, *Annales*, and the Potential for Archaeology." In *Archaeology, Annales, and Ethnohistory*, edited by A.B. Knapp, 35–49. Cambridge: Cambridge University Press.

Fredericks, R. 2018. *Garbage Citizenship: Vital Infrastructures of Labor in Dakar, Senegal*. Durham, NC: Duke University Press.

Grenfell, B.P., and A.S. Hunt. 2007. "Excavations at Oxyrhynchus (1896–1907)." In *Oxyrhynchus: A City and its Texts*, edited by A K. Bowman, R.A. Coles, N. Gonis, D. Obbink, and P.J. Parsons, 345–68. London: Egypt Exploration Society.

Halstead, P., I. Hooder, and G. Jones. 1978. "Behavioral Archaeology and Refuse Patterns: A Case Study." *Norwegian Archaeological Review* 11: 118–31.

Hammond, G., and N. Hammond. 1981. "Child's Play: A Distorting Factor in Archaeological Distribution." *American Antiquity* 46: 634–36.

Hayden, B., and A. Cannon. 1983. "Where the Garbage Goes: Refuse Disposal in the Maya Highlands." *Journal of Anthropological Archaeology* 2 (2): 117–63.

Hodder, I. 1987. "The Meaning of Discard: Ash and Domestic Space in Baringo." In *Method and Theory for Activity Area Research: An Ethnoarchaeological Approach*, edited by S. Kent, 424–48. New York: Columbia University Press.

Hodder, I. 2012. *Entangled: An Archaeology of the Relationships between Humans and Things*. Hoboken, NJ: Wiley-Blackwell.

Hodgkinson, A.K. 2021. "Waste Management at Amarna." *Horizon* 21: 22–26.

Husselman, E.M. 1979. *Karanis Excavations of the University of Michigan in Egypt, 1928–1935: Topography and Architecture: A Summary of the Reports of the Director, Enoch E. Peterson, Monograph publishing: Imprint series; Studies (Kelsey Museum of Archaeology), 5*. Ann Arbor: University of Michigan.

James, T.G.H. 1984. *Pharaoh's People: Scenes from Life in Imperial Egypt*. Oxford: Oxford University Press.
Jeffreys, D.G. 1985. *The Survey of Memphis*. London: Egypt Exploration Society.
Kemp, B.J., and A. Stevens. 2010. *Busy Lives at Amarna*. 2 vols. London: Egypt Exploration Society.
Lagerspetz, O. 2018. *A Philosophy of Dirt*. London: Reaktion Books.
Meskell, L.M. 2005. "Introduction: Object Orientations." In *Archaeologies of Materiality*, edited by L.M. Meskell, 1–17. Oxford: Blackwell.
Miller, R. 1987. "Appendix: Ash as Insecticide." In *Amarna Reports IV*, edited by B.J. Kemp, 14–116. London: Egypt Exploration Society.
Miller, R.L. 1990. "Hogs and Hygiene." *Journal of Egyptian Archaeology* 76: 125–40.
Miller, R.L. 2013. "Hygiene, Pharaonic Egypt." In *Encyclopedia of Ancient History*, 1st ed., edited by R.S. Bagnall, K. Brodersen, C.B. Champion, A. Erskine, and S.R. Huebner, 3354–56. Oxford: Blackwell.
Müller, V. 2017. "Waste, Offerings or Cultic Depositions? An Insight into the Varieties of Depositional Practices in Ancient Egypt." *Ägypten und Levante* 27: 159–81
Needham, S., and T. Spence. 1997. "Refuse and Formation of Middens." *Antiquity* 71: 77–90.
Pendlebury, J.D.S. 1951. *City of Akhenaten III*. 2 vols. London: Egypt Exploration Society.
Petrie, W.M.F. 1890. *Kahun, Gurob, and Hawara*. London: British School of Archaeology.
Petrie, W.M.F. 1894. *Tell el-Amarna*. London: Methuen & Co.
Pfälzner, P. 2001. *Haus und Haushalt: Wohnformen des dritten Jahrtausends vor Christus in Nordmesopotamien*. Mainz am Rhein: Philipp von Zabern.
Pollard, N. 1998. "The Chronology and Economic Condition of Late Roman Karanis: An Archaeological Reassessment." *Journal of the American Research Center in Egypt* 35: 147–62.
Rathje, W.L., and C. Murphy. 2001. *Rubbish! The Archaeology of Garbage*. Tucson: University of Arizona Press.
Ruffini, G.R. 2015. "Ostraka from Area 1." In *A Late Romano-Egyptian House in the Dakhleh Oasis: Amheida House B2*, edited by A.L. Boozer, 353–67. New York: New York University Press.
Schiffer, M.B. 1976. *Behavioral Archeology*. New York: Academic Press.
Schiffer, M.B. 1987. *Formation Process of the Archaeological Record*. Salt Lake City: University of Utah Press.
Shaw, I. 2012. "The Archaeology of Refuse Disposal in New Kingdom Egypt: Patterns of Production and Consumption at el-Amarna." *Talanta* (*Proceedings of the Dutch Archaeological and Historical Society*) 44 (Special Research Issue): 315–33.
Shillito, L.-M., W. Matthews, M.J. Almond, and I.D. Bull. 2011. "The Microstratigraphy of Middens: Capturing Daily Routine in Rubbish at Neolithic Catalhhyük, Turkey." *Antiquity* 85: 1024–38.
Simone, A. 2004. "People as Infrastructure: People as Intersecting Fragments in Johannesburg." *Public Culture* 16 (3): 407–29.
Stevens, A., and M. Eccleston. 2007. "Craft Production and Technology." In *The Egyptian World*, edited by T. Wilkinson, 146–59. London: Routledge.
Thomas, A.P. 1981. *Gurob: A New Kingdom Town*. 2 vols. Warminster, UK: Aris & Phillips.
von Pilgrim, C. 1996. *Elephantine XVIII. Untersuchungen in der Stadt des Mittleren Reiches und der Zweiten Zwischenzeit, Archäologische Veröffentlichungen 91*. Mainz am Rhein: Philipp von Zabern.
Zarmakoupi, M. 2018. "The Urban Development of Late Hellenistic Delos." In *Ancient Urban Planning in the Mediterranean: New Research Directions*, edited by D. Millette and S. Martin-McAuliffe, 28–49. London: Ashgate.

PART IV

Households in Cosmic Context

Religion and Ritual

9

Figurines and the Material Culture of Domestic Religion

ROSS I. THOMAS

In his groundbreaking catalogue on figurines from Ptolemaic and Roman Egypt,[1] British Museum curator D.M. Bailey (1931–2014) recognized that the study of figurines was hindered by a lack of contextual information.[2] He (and other authors) succeeded in resolving chronological issues caused by the previous overreliance on unprovenanced museum collections. Bailey assessed their function, whom they depicted, what they mean, how and where they were used, and how these factors changed over time. Because figurines are commonly found within houses and domestic refuse contexts, and rarely in tombs and temples, they are a useful artifact group to understand ritual (and other) activities within households in Ptolemaic and Roman Egypt.

The prevailing interpretation is that such figurines were primarily designed for protection and to promote fertility, possibly specifically childbirth, and were part of popular religion or private domestic ritual or religious practices within households.[3] Further references to domestic rituals from historical, epigraphic, or papyrological sources are scarce, as these sources instead focus on the temple or on the unusual, changed, or alien.[4] This scarcity of textual evidence makes the figurines themselves perhaps the best source of information as to how they were used, although the scarcity of good archaeological, contextual data has hindered our understanding to date.

To provide insight into the purpose and function of figurines, this chapter focuses on a corpus of figurines from recently excavated sites comprising the port of Naukratis, a kiln in Memphis, the quarry settlement at Mons Claudianus, and the Red Sea port of Myos Hormos (figure 9.1). These sites have been selected because of the detailed contextual information available from them. However, the findspot of figurines rarely relates to the specific room location of their use.[5] The resolution may be limited to the refuse dumps of a particular area of a settlement, or the courtyard of the house where they were used.[6] For this reason, this chapter considers the broad-scale chronological and spatial distribution patterns of the assemblages from the settlements in order to understand the broader social context that influenced or

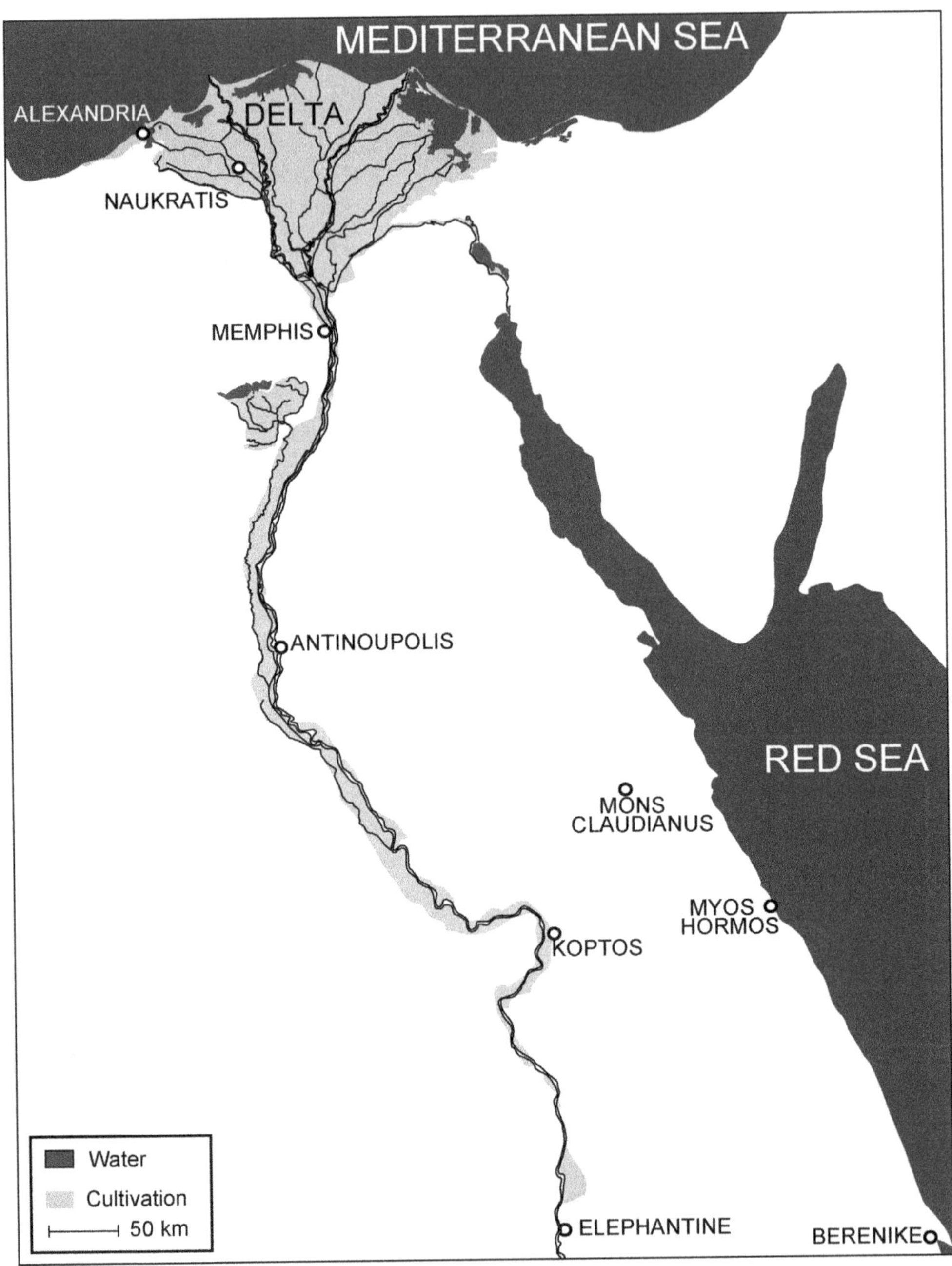

Figure 9.1. Map of Egypt. (By Ross I. Thomas, © Trustees of the British Museum.)

restricted the uses of, and activities associated with, figurines within specific households. Although this study concentrates on the period 175 BCE to CE 175, we will start around 620 BCE to track the unbroken, if modified, traditions of Egyptian figurine production and figurine use in Egyptian houses.

Figurine Use in Late Period Naukratis

The ancient riverport town of Naukratis was established at the end of the seventh century BCE on the Canopic branch of the Nile and has the archaeological signature of different populations. Naukratis provides a large corpus for understanding figurine production and use in Egyptian houses from the Late Period to the Roman Period, and for distinguishing those practices from foreign traditions (mainly Greek and Cypriot). Rediscovered and excavated by Petrie,[7] then others,[8] Naukratis is now the subject of a major reassessment[9] and renewed excavations by the British Museum.[10] Recent excavations and geophysics have enabled the reconstruction of this more than sixty hectare settlement, which accommodated industry, multistory mud-brick tower houses, and a population of more than sixteen thousand people. Naukratis stretched along a kilometer-long riverbank lined from north to south with Greek and Egyptian sanctuaries, the largest of which was that of Amun-Ra and associated deities (figure 9.2).

Context can now be reconstructed for many of the ca. 2,500 figurines of terracotta, stone, metal, faience, and bone found during the old excavations, complemented by recent excavation data. The typological study and analysis of the large Late Period stone and terracotta figure assemblage revealed two distinct patterns at Naukratis:[11]

1. Cypriot and Greek figurines of terracotta and stone were placed within Greek sanctuaries (alongside other votives), but were never found in secure contexts outside of these structures. These were dedicated by foreign visitors to Naukratis, from East Greece, mainland Greece, and Cyprus. They represent primarily either human figurines (probably representing the dedicators), or objects or animals (perhaps representing votives or sacrifices), and rarely depict deities. Regional and chronological patterns were recognized in the sanctuaries, which were frequented by different foreign communities.
2. Egyptian figurines of terracotta and limestone were found in Egyptian houses, but could also be found in domestic dumps, down wells, and on the riverbank. Most represent the Egyptian deities Horus-the-child, Isis-Hathor,[12] or Bes. They were rarely found within Egyptian sanctuaries (where most types were entirely absent, and where most Egyptians had limited or no access), within Egyptian chapels,[13] or adjacent to sanctuaries (where faience and bronze objects were apparently more suitable offerings).[14] They were rarely found within Greek sanctuaries (where most forms were entirely absent).[15]

This distinct patterning is significant, for it records the presence and practices of different groups, with the Egyptian terracotta and limestone figurines almost exclusively being found within houses and refuse deposits within the town, or on the riverbank. This Late Period Egyptian figurine assemblage (figure 9.3) was dominated by figurines representing the god Horus-the-child, Hor-pa-khered (Hellenized as Harpocrates, which is used henceforth), who usually appears as macrophallic; he was sometimes depicted on horseback, with or without macrophallus. Some of these

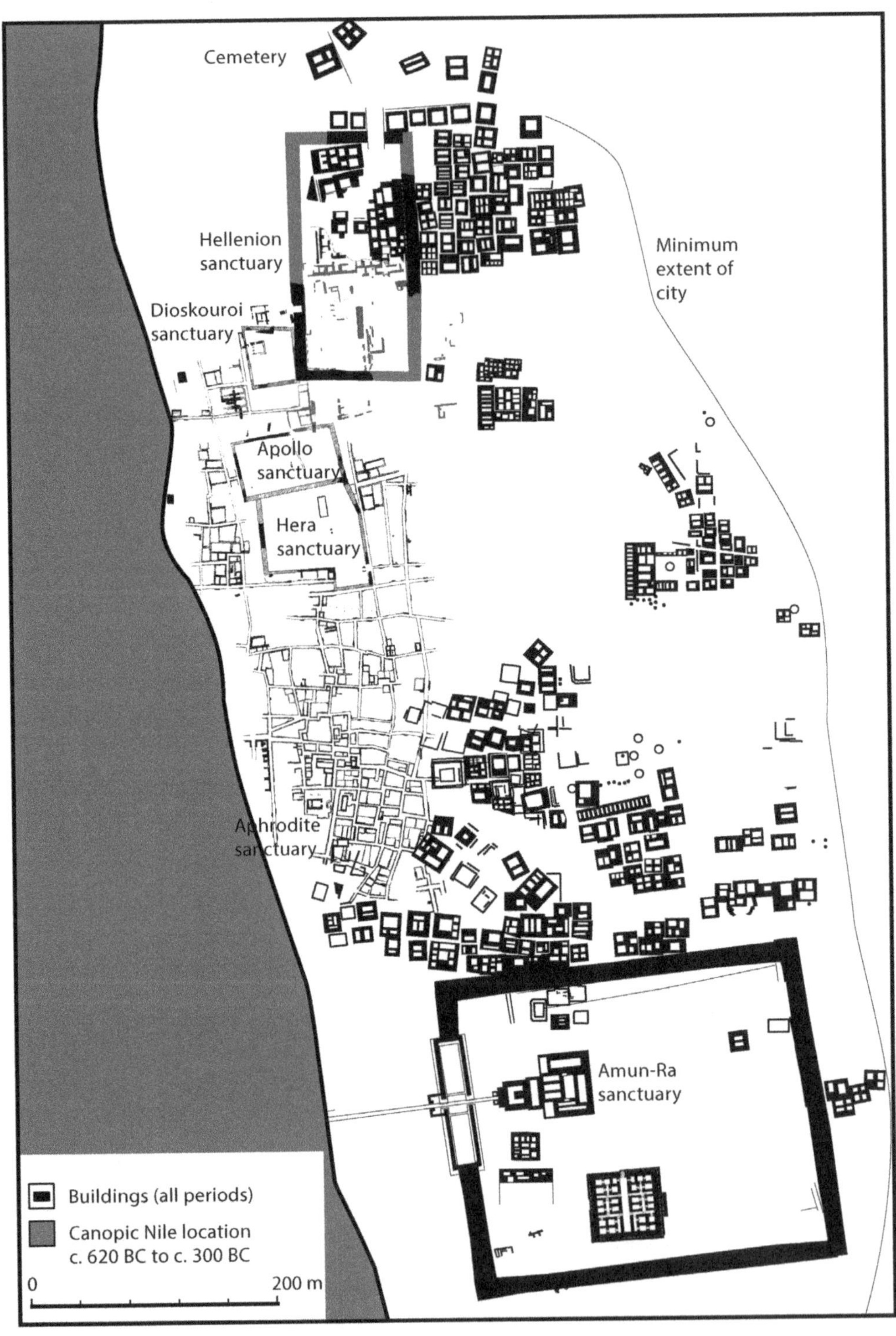

Figure 9.2. Map of Naukratis incorporating all previous fieldwork and preliminary geophysics results from the British Museum excavations at Naukratis. (Ross I. Thomas © Trustees of the British Museum.)

Figure 9.3. Late Period Egyptian figurines from Naukratis comprising top row, left to right: a. Musician (Ashmolean Museum, Oxford, AN1896–1908-G.71); b. Isis-Hathor limestone figure (British Museum, EA 68814); c. Isis-Hathor in the mammisi (British Museum, 1885,1010.28); d–e. birth figures (British Museum, 1965,0930.954; Fitzwilliam Museum, Cambridge, E.191.1899). Second row, from left f–h: Macrophallic Harpocrates figures (British Museum 1965,0930.953, 1965,0930.929, 1965,0930.928); i. Harpocrates rider (British Museum 1900,0214.27); j. Bes fragment from a phallophoric procession (Museum of Classical Archaeology, Cambridge NA581). (Composite by the author based on photographs by British Museum staff. © Trustees of the British Museum, © The Fitzwilliam Museum, Cambridge, © Museum of Classical Archaeology, Cambridge or © Ashmolean Museum, University of Oxford respectively.)

macrophallic child god figurines are depicted enthroned and wearing the crown of Upper and Lower Egypt, clearly identifying the subject as Horus the pharaoh, the god of kingship and one of the Egyptian theological justifications for kingship. Other figurines do not depict such clear features, making their identification as Harpocrates unclear, unless one considers the clearly related group together.[16] When there was a Greek pharaoh during the Macedonian and Ptolemaic Periods, Harpocrates was sometimes depicted in Macedonian dress.[17] Nude "Hathoric" female figurines were also popular.[18] They depict Isis-Hathor nude, sometimes emerging from a *mammisi* or "chapel/house of birth"[19] (identifiable by its distinctive Bes or papyriform columns), sometimes with a child (Harpocrates), or sometimes giving birth. Erroneously named "erotic" figurines show the conception of Harpocrates.[20] Other characters include Bes (protector of Harpocrates), who is often depicted within or next to the mammisi, but also priests and cultists celebrating festivals and involved in phallophoric processions.[21] Collectively, these figurines depict the return of Isis-Hathor, the conception of Horus, the birth of Horus, and the festivals (such as the Festival of Drunkenness) that celebrate these religious events, which occurred during the period of the Nile inundation following the Egyptian New Year.[22] Although Osiris is rarely depicted, these important events in the Egyptian calendar connect the success of the harvest to the cult of the Osirian triad, and ultimately, through Horus, to the ruling dynasty. This is because Horus was the patron of the royal family and the pharaoh was recognized as the living embodiment of Horus in Egyptian theology. The abundance of these cheap local figurines in limestone and terracotta suggests a significant proportion of the Naukratis population followed this cult at home, as was the practice in Memphis and across the Nile Delta.[23]

Ptolemaic Figurines and Related Objects in Naukratis

Following the founding of Alexandria and the establishment of the Ptolemaic dynasty, significant changes are apparent within the figurine assemblage from Naukratis. An abrupt drop in imported figurines from Greece, East Greece, Cyprus, and other parts of Egypt followed. Workshops in Naukratis produced terracotta figurines, supplying the popular demand from Naukratite households. There was a significant change in technology, design, style, and decoration, including the introduction of Hellenistic-style hollow mold-made and brightly painted figurines like those commonly found across the various Hellenistic kingdoms. The figurines look more "Greek,"[24] and there is the introduction of new "Greek" types, depicting characters from Greek theater and Tanagra-style women.[25] However, depictions of Greek deities were rare (1.9 percent), while depictions of Egyptian gods and demigods (41 percent) and their followers (based largely on Late Period precedents) continued to dominate the assemblage (figure 9.4).[26] Harpocrates remained the most popular representation, followed by Isis/Hathor, Bes, and (rarely) Osiris/Apis/Serapis.[27] The two distinct groups—one depicting "Greek" "secular" subjects, while the more common other depicts Egyptian deities and rituals—both use the same visual language. They were produced in the same way, using the same materials, in the same style, in the same workshops,[28] and possibly had the same distributors and consumers. They may have held different (and multiple) meanings or significances that are more complicated than the strict binary categories of religious/ritual or secular/decorative.[29] But the "Greek" and the "Egyptian" objects were distinguished from each other, as evidenced by their distribution across houses and archaeological sites. The shared style, or visual language, is the medium through which the two groups of objects were used to communicate different things, perhaps signaling identity and membership in (or at least knowledge and appreciation of) Egyptian and Greek religious and/or cultural institutions. Unlike with Late Period Naukratis, discussed above, the Greek and the Egyptian figurines are sometimes, but not always, found together (see below).

Egyptian figurines have much in common with molded pottery, lamps, stoves, coffin-fittings, and faience vessels. These were all produced using the same Hellenistic innovation of hollow mold-made terracotta production, and were probably made in the same workshop(s).[30] The full range of molded terracotta artifacts can help explain the meaning of these figurines. The mass production of mold-made lamps depicting Egyptian deities and other symbols of the New Year inundation festivities (such as frogs, or Sothis) continued into the Roman Period, when they were replicated on Roman-style discus lamps (figure 9.5).[31] The popularity of lamps

Figure 9.4. Ptolemaic Egyptian figures from Naukratis. First row, a–c Isis-Hathor, birth and Isis with Harpocrates (British Museum 1888,0601.110, 1886,0401.1452, 1888,0601.107–8). Second row, d–f macrophallic Harpocrates (Leonard 1997, MC#65), Harpocrates rider (Fitzwilliam Museum, Cambridge E.233.1899), Bes (British Museum 1888,0601.96). (Composite by the author based on photographs by British Museum staff. © Trustees of the British Museum, © Volos University [Coulson and Leonard archive, specifically Leonard 1997, MC#65], or © The Fitzwilliam Museum, Cambridge respectively.)

incorporating the same Egyptian religious imagery also found on figurines made them suitable for use in religious contexts, be they domestic, temple, or cemetery, as well as in "magical" contexts, to complement or as an alternative to figurines.[32]

A group of goblets with molded decoration celebrating festivals and possibly used as drinking sets found in Naukratis (figure 9.6),[33] can help explain the relationship

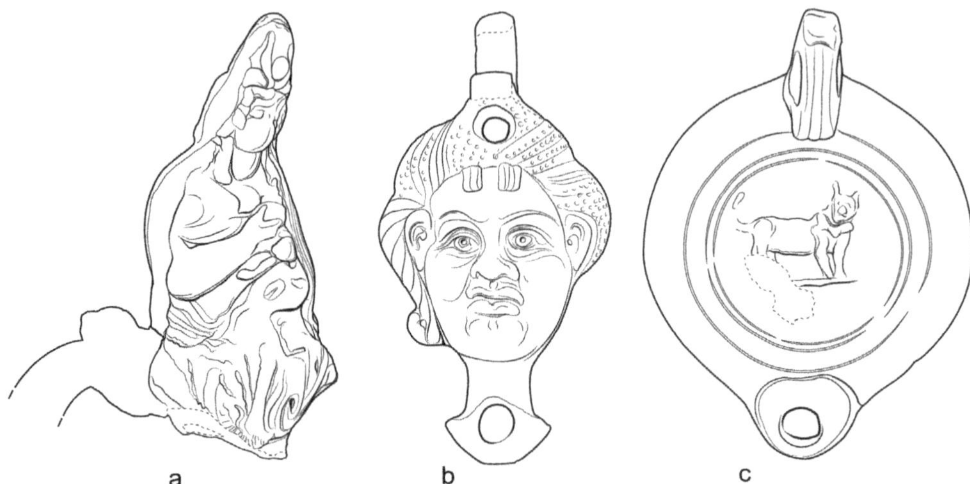

Figure 9.5. Ptolemaic and Roman lamps depicting Isis and Harpocrates: (a) Isis with Harpocrates lamp handle (British Museum 1888,0601.123), (b) Harpocrates head lamp (Egyptian Museum, Cairo JE27198), (c) Sothis discus lamp (Museum of Fine Arts, Boston RES.86.123). (Drawing by Kate Morton based on photography by British Museum staff. © Trustees of the British Museum.)

between Egyptian characters depicted individually on figurines and lamps and as part of a group sequence on these goblets.[34] Made in Naukratis and Alexandria during the second century BCE to the first century BCE, these depict a series of mold-made figures that are often also common figurine forms, creating a sequence of scenes around the wheel-made goblets.[35] Collectively, the scenes record the inundation myth and were intended to be read in sequence: the return of Isis, the conception of Harpocrates, and his birth. These events were celebrated after the New Year and over the season of the Nile inundation, and were particularly associated with mammisi chapels. The scenes depict the following three events (figure 9.6):

1. Isis is depicted reclining accompanied by Sothis (the Dog Star, figure 9.6e), represented as a dog, whose heliacal rising (on the 1st of Thoth) marks the New Year and was associated with the return of Isis.[36] Followers of Isis celebrate her return and the Festival of Drunkenness (20th of Thoth). They are carrying wine amphorae, drinking, playing music, and dancing (figures 9.6a–d). The characters depicted are often Nubians, possibly representing Isis's retinue of followers when she returns from the south.[37] Occasionally the followers are represented as satyrs and maenads, representing the syncretic association of Greek Dionysos with Egyptian Osiris since the Late Period.
2. A male rider (his horse is in the background) and a woman have sex (figures 9.6f–g).[38] This represents the conception of Harpocrates, celebrated as the *hieros gamos* (or holy union) of Isis and Osiris in the "place of drunkenness."[39] Putti/erotes are depicted with cornucopia signifying erotic love and the fertility imbued on the world by hierogamies.

Figure 9.6. Ptolemaic mold-made goblets depicting three events. First, a–d, the return of Isis with her followers (Museum of Fine Art, Boston 88.897; British Museum 1886,0401.1581, 1886,0401.1544); e, Isis reclining with Sothis in dog form (British Museum 2002,0419.1). Second, f–g, the conception of Harpocrates (British Museum 1886,0401.1580; 1965,0930.964); and h putti/erotes (Museum of Classical Archaeology, Cambridge NA639). Third, h–k, the birth of Harpocrates (Antikenmuseum, Heidelberg I.97; Museum of Fine Art, Boston 86.471; British Museum 2002,0419.5; Leonard 1997, MC#85). Fourth row shows the complete profile of a goblet with birth scene (British Museum 1886,0401.1583). (Drawing by Kate Morton based on photography by British Museum staff. © Trustees of the British Museum.)

3. The birth of Harpocrates (1st of Pachons) is depicted with Isis-Hathor shown as pregnant and/or giving birth within a birth chapel (mammisi) (figures 9.6i, 9.6l); the structure is identifiable by its distinctive papyriform columns (figure 9.6i). Sometimes Isis is clearly depicted with her headdress.[40] Harpocrates is depicted emerging from this chapel with his distinctive side lock, carrying a goblet, his macrophallus partially concealed by his long red tunic (figure 9.6j), or wearing the double crown and carrying a cornucopia (figure 9.6.k). He is protected by Bes (figure 9.6m), who is depicted dancing (figure 9.6l).

The representation of Isis giving birth within the mammisi, and the emergence of Harpocrates from this chapel, may explain the long-lived tradition of figurines representing a nude woman giving birth (figures 9.3d, 9.3e, 9.4b, 9.6i, 9.6l), and raises doubts about other interpretations of these figurines.[41] Represented from the Late Period to the Roman Period, these are often cited as evidence of the role of Egyptian figurines in the promotion of fertility and protection during childbirth. Yet the figurines are given different labels and interpretations in the academic literature depending on the period when they were produced (Baubo or pseudo-Baubo, fertility-promoting or fecundity beings, fertility demons, beneficent demons, *orans* figurines and female saints).[42] Some Ptolemaic examples have been identified as Isis-Demeter or Isis-Bast, but many may depict the birth of Harpocrates.[43]

These goblets also suggest a close relationship between seemingly separate figurines as well as between objects in multiple media (figurines, lamps, and vessels), all of which may have been used together to celebrate specific annual events concerning the New Year inundation festivities.[44] If this is the case, then the majority of figurines (as well as certain other objects) found within Ptolemaic and Roman houses across Egypt were conception and nativity sets that were used to celebrate the New Year within the house. Although this distinctive material culture is highly visible archaeologically, we do not know the form of these rituals or whether these objects were temporarily or permanently on display (for example, in wall niches).[45]

Ptolemaic and Roman Figurine Use in Egyptian Houses

The frequency and diversity of figurine production and use changed gradually over the course of the second century BCE through to the second century CE, as we can see from the examples of Naukratis, Memphis, Mons Claudianus, and Myos Hormos, discussed below.

At Naukratis, two excavated late Ptolemaic and early Roman houses revealed a range of Egyptian terracotta figurines.[46] While archaeological contexts were faithfully recorded for these objects, this does not tell us which room they were used in, as all were fragmentary and found with domestic refuse redeposited inside the courtyard (and occasionally redeposited within the house, possibly after abandonment).[47] The first house was on Kom Hadid at the eastern end of the settlement next to an industrial area, the second on the South Mound (figure 9.2). Of the eighteen figurines found in Kom Hadid, all were associated with the substantial inner wall of a high-status building that once had a paved floor, cut stone veneers and molded painted plaster decoration on its walls.[48] Nine figurines date to the period of occupation of this building, 150 BCE–1 BCE; of these nine, five were found within domestic refuse layers disturbed by the collapse from the destruction of the building during the first century BCE. The four remaining Ptolemaic figurines were residual finds within the subsequent Roman refuse layers, where they were found alongside nine Roman figurines, as well as domestic and industrial kiln refuse dating to the period 50 BCE–100 CE. It is interesting to note that the Egyptian figurines of Harpocrates and Isis were concentrated north of the wall, while Greek theater masks were found to the south, or (on one case) as a residual find above the wall.

The Northwest Building on the South Mound can now be identified as the courtyard and outbuildings abutting the west of a large tower house within the southwestern corner of the *temenos* (boundary) wall of the Amun-Ra sanctuary of Naukratis (thanks to new excavations by the British Museum).[49] This was once the house of a priest serving that sanctuary. Of the eleven figurines found there, nine are Ptolemaic and two are Roman Period.[50]

The two areas are superficially similar in figurine composition, both being dominated by representations of Harpocrates and Isis-Hathor (found in close proximity to molded lamps and goblets).[51] However, three distinct differences can be noted. First, the Kom Hadid pieces include Greek theater mask fragments (possibly displaying an appreciation of Greek theater); these are not represented within the Egyptian priest's house, which instead contained a pink painted fragment of a priest's Bes mask.[52] Second, the Ptolemaic material has more representations of Harpocrates (or a priest dressed as Harpocrates), who in three brightly painted examples from the South Mound is represented as macrophallic (providing us with a clear link with earlier Late Period representations) and performing a ritual next to a yellow horned altar (figure 9.4d). Third, the Roman material from Kom Hadid includes more Isis-Hathor figurines, which seem to be part of a general chronological trend toward more female figurines in Roman Egypt (see below). The broad-scale analysis of figurines from Naukratis allows us to see how households are constrained within chronological social trends, but this detailed analysis of two contemporary households in Naukratis also enables us to distinguish some minor but significant differences between the assemblages that betray the different priorities of the two households.

South of Memphis, the thriving ancient capital, cult center, and redistribution node, a Roman-period faience kiln within the industrial zone of Kom Helul produced popular tableware vessels that were distributed across Egypt.[53] Seventy-five second century CE figurine fragments, possibly from a warehouse collapse, had been dumped over this kiln, providing a useful dataset for the range of figurines produced at this time.[54] The assemblage is dominated by Isis and Isis-Hathor figurines, with female figurines accounting for more than 60 percent of the assemblage.[55] Harpocrates, Sothis, Bes, and rarely Serapis are also represented. The limited range is a feature of Roman terracotta production across Egypt. It is distinct from the diverse Ptolemaic production and is very similar in range to the contemporary Naukratis, Mons Claudianus, and Myos Hormos assemblages (figure 9.7).

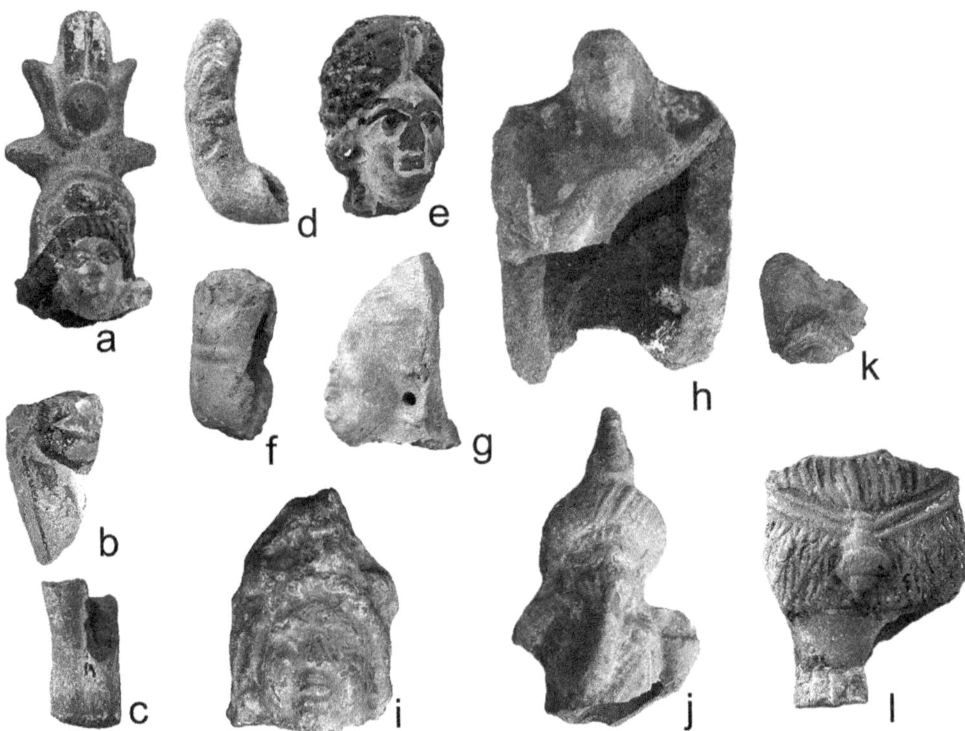

Figure 9.7. Roman Egyptian figurine fragments from Naukratis, Memphis, and Myos Hormos: a–c, Isis-Hathor (Myos Hormos C285; C210; C258); d–g, birth figures (Myos Hormos C248; C257; Memphis P-62; P-110); h, Isis with Harpocrates (Myos Hormos C265); i, Harpocrates (Memphis P-54); j, Harpocrates from Kom Hadid (Leonard 2001, MC#62, Egyptian Museum, Cairo JE97809); k–l, Sothis in dog form (Memphis P-58; Myos Hormos C214). (Composite by the author based on photographs © Southampton University [Myos Hormos], © Courtesy of The Egypt Exploration Society [Memphis], or © Volos University [Kom Hadid] respectively.)

The Roman quarry of Mons Claudianus supplied fine granodiorite from the Eastern Desert for prestige imperial building projects from 40–235 CE. A fortified administrative settlement was founded in 85–86 CE, and suburbs to the west, south, and north housed any overflow of civilians. The soldiers and civilians of Mons Claudianus were occasionally joined by their families, at least in the earliest periods.[56] The abundance of Greek texts listing Egyptian and Greek names (and the scarcity of Latin texts) confirms the workforce and administration was composed of people who grew up in Egypt, who were ethnically Egyptian and/or Greek.

The settlement and its extensive refuse dumps to the south have produced eighty figurines, most of which can be dated to 106–154 CE. Other objects that may have been used during cultic activity within the house comprise five horned altars used for making burnt offerings and 815 lamps.[57] While the horned altars were all found within rooms, most of the lamps and figurines were found broken within refuse deposits outside the fort and settlement (while some are fragmentary figurines found within rooms, most were transported after they were broken to refuse dumps with other domestic rubbish).[58] The settlement was served by a Serapis temple that contained figurine and cult statue fragments of Serapis and Isis. Despite the temple, Serapis figurines were rare (with only six examples), with Isis-Hathor and nude female figurines dominating (57 percent), followed by Harpocrates and Sothis figurines.

The Roman port and naval station of Myos Hormos was of great importance to the Indo-Roman trade from ca. 30 BCE to ca. 250 CE. The excellent preservation at this settlement has left traces of a diverse population of predominantly Roman subjects (both Egyptian and Greek), but also a wide range of other indigenous groups as well as Sabaean, Indian, Nabataean, Palmyran, and East African visitors. Distinct quarters have been identified at Myos Hormos (and also Berenike),[59] associated with certain indigenous ethnic groups (the "Ichthyophagi" fishermen[60] and nomadic "Trogodytes" or Blemmyes).[61] Each had a distinctive diet (almost exclusively Red Sea fish, or Eastern Desert sheep/goat, respectively) and different tablewares (almost exclusively bowls, sometimes made of shell, or Eastern Desert ware globular bowls, respectively).

The earliest figurines from Myos Hormos are dated to 30 BCE–50 CE, while the latest date to 125–175 CE, although the majority are from mid-first to mid-second century CE contexts.[62] Figurines were rare within the harbor (only a gilded Isis headdress fragment and the fragment of a terracotta Sothis),[63] and absent from an area of local fishermen's huts (associated with the fishing boat permit of one Pakubis Ichthyophagos).[64] Egyptian figurines were more frequent finds within the two-story houses of the main town area, populated (based on the evidence available to date) by Greek-speaking traders, and associated refuse dumps to the north. The small figurine assemblage contained exclusively Egyptian figurines and amulets of Isis-Hathor, birth figurines, and Harpocrates (figures 9.7a–c, d–e, h, l). One ca. 100 CE concentration of Isis, Isis-Hathor, birth, and Harpocrates figurines was found inside a defensive wall tower alongside illegible (the words appear to have no semantic meaning), possibly "magical" texts. On the contemporary floor surface on the outside sat a mobile that had fallen from the wall. It was made from string strung with sheep's jaws and the long bones, ribs, jaws, and crania of two young adult males who had been dispatched with sword blows to the head.[65] Gnawed by rodents while they were displayed on the wall, the sheep mandibles signaled the diet and economy of the eastern desert tribes, some of whom were in revolt at this time.[66] Collectively, the figurine assemblage from Myos Hormos consists almost exclusively of representations of Egyptian deities, with just two exceptions.[67] Isis-Hathor and birth figurines dominate the assemblage (66 percent), followed by Harpocrates and a single Sothis figure, making this a similar assemblage to those of contemporary Naukratis, Memphis, and Mons Claudianus (figure 9.8). The Egyptian figurines found to date in Myos Hormos houses and refuse dumps were found exclusively in areas populated by Greco-Egyptian traders, where the faunal and tableware assemblages had more in common with Naukratis and Mons Claudianus than with other parts of the same port populated by indigenous groups (such as the "Ichthyophagi").

Comparison, Distinction, and Consumption

Egyptian figurines during the Ptolemaic and Roman Periods continued to depict a small range of Egyptian deities: specifically, the Osirian triad of Isis, Horus, and (rarely) Osiris, plus their protector Bes and followers.[68] Such images were already produced on a large scale during the Late Period and found predominantly within the house in all periods (see first section above). The significance of the figurine forms (their stance, posture, and dress) and their collective relevance as a group can be explained by the narrative depicted on the Ptolemaic molded ware pottery, which records the return of Isis, the conception of Horus, and the nativity of Horus (second section above). This sequence of events was associated with the New Year that coincided with the rising of the dog star (personified as Sothis, who is depicted as the dog companion of Isis) and the inundation of the Nile. This was celebrated in the religious calendar of Egypt with festivals, such as the Festival of Drunkenness (which was depicted on objects in the form of Isis's followers, depicted carrying wine amphorae, playing music, and dancing).

Although the production techniques, decoration, and style changed considerably at the beginning of the Ptolemaic Period and continued to develop after that,[69] the consistency of themes across time and across Egypt, until the Roman Period, is significant (third section above). One major shift during the Roman Period, recognizable through the quantification of this material, is a shift from the dominance of male (Harpocrates) to female (Isis-Hathor) figurine production and use. During the Late Period, more than half of the figurines depict Harpocrates. During the early Roman Period, more than half the figurines depict Isis-Hathor or birth figurines (figure 9.8). It is possible that this represents a shift from celebrating the conception of Horus toward celebrating the birth of Horus, although this seems unlikely, as both events are depicted together on the Ptolemaic molded goblets discussed above, and it was a standard Egyptian iconographic tradition to depict the birth of the divine baby on objects associated with that child's conception.[70]

The function(s) of the figurines, the "rituals" they represent, and how all of the above changed over time are all intimately linked to the question of who used these figurines. They represent one highly visible aspect of an evolving practice that used a range of ingredients comprising objects as well as actions, most of which do not survive (either the ingredients or any trace of the actions) in the archaeological record. Although overwhelmingly found within domestic contexts, figurines were also found down wells and at the boundaries between places (for example, the wall at Myos Hormos), where they can be found in different states (broken or whole). Aspects of the use-lives of these figurines may be reconstructed, specifically their production, acquisition, display, breakage, and the choice of disposal location.[71] Some parts of this use-life may have been associated with the New Year inundation festivities, particularly those that relate to the conception of Horus and the rising of Sothis. While their significance may have been tied to specific events, such as festivals, and specific deities, they may have had multiple roles in worship, protection, and displaying (to visitors) the performance or observance of Egyptian religion throughout the year.

The use of figurines apparently declines over the course of the late Ptolemaic and Roman Periods, long before the rise of Christianity (which is commonly described

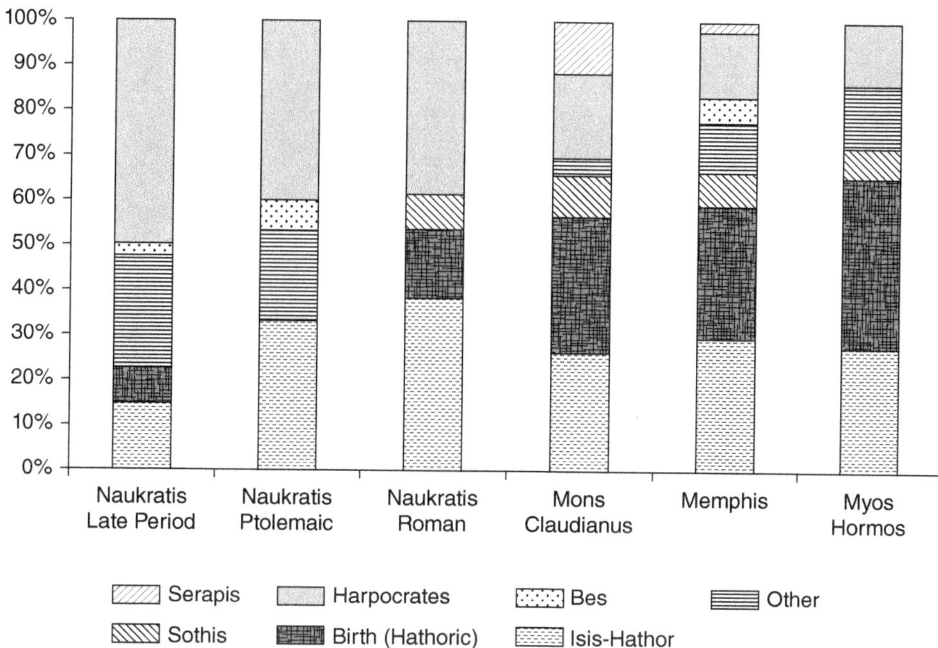

Figure 9.8. Graph showing range of Egyptian figurine depictions from Late Period, Ptolemaic and Roman Naukratis, Mons Claudianus, Memphis, and Myos Hormos. Note all macrophallic child god figures are included within the Harpocrates category.

as causing this decline).[72] There is a significant drop in the absolute number of figurines at Naukratis during the Roman Period, despite this being a period when other objects are abundant and the settlement is apparently thriving.[73] Measuring the popularity of figurines compared with other small finds (excluding industrial and building materials, vessels, and ecofacts) within reliable contexts can add further information (figure 9.9).[74] At Naukratis, in Kom Hadid, and the South Mound, the Ptolemaic and Roman contexts had a relatively high, if declining, occurrence of figurines (56 percent and 50 percent of all the small finds respectively, figure 9.9).[75] An even higher occurrence was recorded at the second century CE kiln at Memphis (63 percent).[76] The unusually high frequency experienced at Kom Hadid and Kom Helul may relate to industrial production associated with both areas. The data from Mons Claudianus and Myos Hormos suggest a significantly lower use of figurines (4.6 percent and 0.5 percent respectively), with the majority of the Myos Hormos examples coming from a single area (11 percent of finds within trench 6P). There are many possible explanations for this: better preservation of small finds (which do not usually survive),[77] the dominance of finds associated with quarrying and trading, the identities (be they ethnic, cultural, gender, or vocational) of the inhabitants, or the possibility that figurines were simply less popular within these (mainly) second-century-CE contexts. The answer is likely to be a combination of these factors. However, it is worth considering that both Myos Hormos and Mons Claudianus had mainly male demographics. One possible explanation for the exceptionally rare

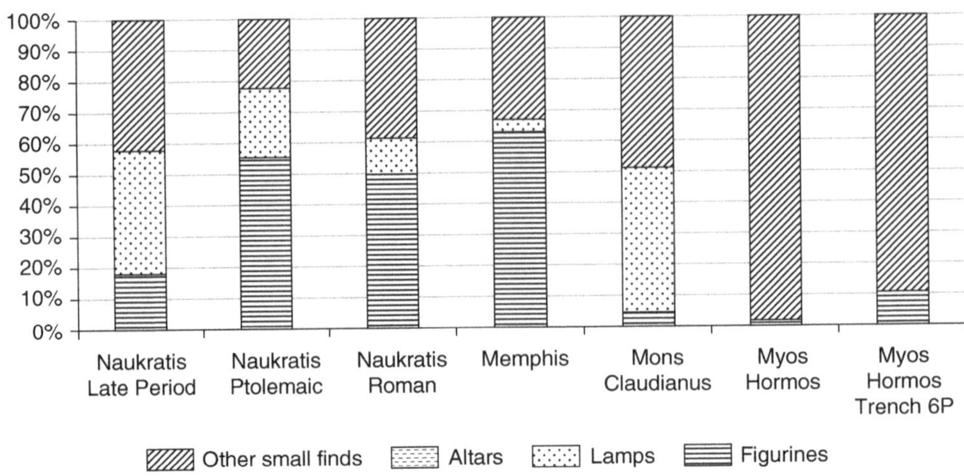

Figure 9.9. Graph showing the proportion of small finds that are figurines, lamps, and altars from Late Period, Ptolemaic and Roman Naukratis, Memphis, Mons Claudianus, Myos Hormos (whole site), and Myos Hormos Trench 6P (only). Altars represent less than 1 percent of finds in the Late Period and Mons Claudianus columns only and are not visible on the graph.

figurine use at these sites could be that figurine ownership was higher among women or family units, as represented by the more gender-balanced demographies expected in Naukratis.

Egyptian religious performance could use different ingredients and objects in different places and at different times. It is clear that lamps were not used exclusively for practical lighting purposes, because they were often deposited within sanctuaries and graves, and their use in rituals is described in texts.[78] Looking at the broad chronological trend at Naukratis, while figurine use declined over the Roman Period, lamp use did not. At this time molded lamps frequently depicted Egyptian deities (figure 9.5) and frogs, which were another symbol of the inundation and New Year festivities.[79] Perhaps lamps were increasingly being used instead of figurines for religious rituals. The multifunctional affordances of lamps and vessels (with representations of Egyptian deities on them), as opposed to figurines, may have impacted (or been determined by) changes in both household activities and ritual practice, concerning where and how they were used. We do not know what changes in ritual practice occurred, but a decline in figurine use and potential rise in lamp use are the archaeological signatures of the physical form of changing ritual practices.

Regional differences may also be significant. Lamps were abundant in Mons Claudianus (accounting for 46.5 percent of all small finds), but were relatively rare at Myos Hormos (where they represent only 1.3 percent of all small finds). Unfortunately, it is not possible to distinguish specific religious ritual contexts for any of these lamps, as they are largely redeposited. Despite the apparent similarities between the types of figurines found, the popularity of figurine and lamp use was quite different between these contemporary sites. The patterns are context specific, relating to either the frequency with which such figurines were acquired and used, or the proportion of the population that followed such practices.

The people who used these figurines are distinctive within the archaeological record. It is not surprising that the majority of the population represented within the papyri and ostraka preserved at Myos Hormos and Mons Claudianus have Egyptian or Greek names, and that the majority of these documents are written in Greek. These populations are also distinctive in what and how they eat, specifically regarding their faunal diet and what tablewares they chose to use.[80] Egyptian figurines were found in domestic areas or their adjacent dumps, both of which also record a mixed diet and an Egyptian tableware service (heavily influenced by Hellenistic and Roman fashions). The diet comprised fish and domesticates (pig,[81] sheep/goat, and cattle) from the Nile Valley, supplemented in the Eastern Desert with locally sourced fauna (sheep and goats) and Red Sea fish and occasionally transport animals (donkey, horse, and camel, as confirmed by butchering marks, papyri, and the presence of their disarticulated remains within domestic refuse). The Egyptian tableware service comprised a range of bowls, dishes, plates, and cups that developed out of Ptolemaic forms and were supplemented by Roman fashions.

While a larger sample of figurines would be necessary to prove through statistical analysis a clear association between Egyptian figurines and specific diet and tableware assemblages, it is clear that the Egyptian figurines found to date in Myos Hormos came exclusively from areas populated by Greco-Egyptian traders, and never indigenous ethnic groups (the "Ichthyophagi," "Trogodytes," or Blemmyes). This pattern can be contrasted with Naukratis, where the ceramic assemblage is indistinguishable—and the Egyptian figurine assemblage is very similar—for the Egyptian priests resident in the South Mound of the Amun-Ra sanctuary and the inhabitants of Kom Hadid, except for the presence of Greek theater masks in the latter and the absence of pig in the diet of the former.[82]

Clear patterns emerge when the types of Egyptian figurine are quantified. First, Greek deities were rarely depicted, even in the Greek city of Naukratis. Second, Egyptian figurines consistently depicted Harpocrates and Isis-Hathor as they had since the Late Period (although it is not always clear from the iconography of Late Period representations of macrophallic child gods whether they represent Harpocrates specifically). Third, Isis-Hathor became a more popular subject than Harpocrates over the course of the Roman Period. Fourth, a long, steady decline in figurine production[83] and use coincided with a rise in lamp use,[84] although this may have been complicated by regional practices.

Egyptian figurines were made and acquired to celebrate the conception and nativity of Horus, the former being associated with the New Year and the Nile inundation. Their acquisition, use, and deposition may relate to rituals associated with specific festivals within the Egyptian religious calendar. However, figurines may have held multiple meanings and numerous functions over their use-life. The owners may have believed the figurines, being associated with divine conception and nativity events, were imbued with the fertile power that hierogamies were thought to bestow on the world.[85] Displaying Isis and Harpocrates figurines clearly communicated to visitors that the household observed Egyptian traditions, but this did not exclude the inhabitants from possessing Greek names, language, legal ethnic status, or also displaying figurine characters from Greek theater. Thus the function of a figurine as either decorative or religious (or both) could vary significantly depending on the context and audience.

These figurines record the constant popularity of Egyptian religious rituals and beliefs over a long period of time and across geographical, class, language, and ethnic boundaries. The presence (or absence) of these common objects within houses is then significant for understanding which people lived (and how they lived) in different areas of multicultural ports, quarries, and urban centers. It is thus important that figurines are not considered alone, but that a correlation is made between contexts, figurine uses, and other ways in which people signaled (or distinguished) their identity. The multifunctional role of figurines should be considered, and the patterning of use across different finds groups could be rewarding for further study. These objects were powerful, as illustrated by their presence marking the boundary wall of a naval base at the limits of the Roman Empire alongside the bound and exposed remains of Rome's enemies. Can there be a clearer distinction, signaled more vigorously, of who belongs and who is excluded?

Notes

1 *Editors' note:* We are deeply saddened to write that Ross I. Thomas passed away while this volume was in preparation. Aside from minor formatting changes and occasional extremely light edits to punctuation or wording, we have kept the text as Ross left it after his initial round of edits. We thank his wife, Elisabeth O'Connell, for conducting a final review of the copy-edited text to ensure that it represents Ross's vision for the chapter. We are honored to be able to include Ross Thomas's work in this volume, as a testament to the insights and achievements of a brilliant scholar, colleague, and friend.

2 Bailey 2008, 1–3.

3 Dunand 1979; Dunand and Zivie-Coche 2004; Frankfurter 1998, 136; 2014; 2017, 34–36. See Frankfurter, chapter 10, this volume, on the use of figurines as routine apotropaia against domestic threats to pregnancies or children, such as child-killing *daimones* or disease. Frankfurter also notes the difficulty in distinguishing between apotropaic/fecundity and binding/curse figurines.

4 See particularly the discussion of the Ptolemaic priestly decrees of Memphis and Philae in Barrett (2015, 408) and the special case of magic (Barrett forthcoming, 14–15).

5 Studying the context of hundreds of Egyptian figurines (see note 10 below) revealed that in the majority of cases, the last phase in the use-lives of these objects was deposition within a domestic refuse context after fragmentation.

6 See Boozer, chapter 8, this volume, who also recognizes that (broken) figurines are commonly found in the courtyard or among trash, but rarely within the house.

7 Petrie 1886.

8 Gardner 1888; Hogarth et al. 1898–1899; Hogarth et al. 1905; Coulson 1996; Leonard 1997; Leonard 2001.

9 Villing et al. 2013–2019.

10 Thomas and Villing 2012; Thomas and Villing forthcoming; Thomas 2015h.

11 Thomas 2015a; 2015b; 2015c; 2015d; 2015e; 2019a; 2019b; Möller 2000; Nick 2006.

12 The syncretism of Egyptian goddesses Isis and Hathor developed during the Late Period, when Isis increasingly acquired the iconography and functions of Hathor. Both were worshipped as versions of the solar eye goddess.

13 Chapels are small subsidiary or ancillary structures, distinct from larger temples. Both are found within sanctuary precincts bounded by *temenos* walls.

14 Masson 2018; Masson-Berghoff 2019.

15 Rare exceptions found in Greek sanctuaries comprise cow figurines within the Aphrodite sanctuary (possibly representations of the Egyptian goddess Hathor who was associated with Aphrodite) and limestone Harpocrates rider figurines found within the Hellenion sanctuary (one has a Greek inscription). Rarely the local Nile silt fabric was used to produce Greek-style terracotta figurines, such as the female protome busts found in the Hellenion (Thomas 2015d, 14).

16 The range of (frequently, but not exclusively macrophallic) child gods may not always have been understood as Harpocrates, as local variants in Egyptian religion had regional triads (Sandri 2006; Ballet and Galliano 2010, 197–220). However, over the course of the Hellenistic and Roman Period, representations of Harpocrates acquired iconography from other deities through a process of syncretism, which is why the name Harpocrates is used below.

17 Thomas 2015b, 60.

18 Specifically identifying these Late Period "Hathoric" nude figures is problematic (Thomas 2015b, 54), as many Egyptian "Eye of Re goddesses" (Hathor, Tefnut, Mut, Isis, Sakhmet, Bastet, and Anuket) were associated with local variants of the inundation myth, rituals, festivals and the associated prosperity and fertility (Fazzini 1988, 8–14; Barrett 2011, 136). Ptolemaic and Roman examples more clearly display symbols consistent with Isis, Hathor, or a syncretic deity incorporating both (which is why the name Isis-Hathor is used within this text). The same regional reception of such deities applies as with "Harpocrates," above.

19 The *pr-mst* (Arnold 2003, 33; Knoblauch and Gill 2012, 9–13).

20 While most figurines reference the standard mythology of Harpocrates' conception, broader sexual themes associated with inundation festivals can also be depicted on material culture (Barrett 2019).

21 On phallophoric processions of Osiris and Dionysos and their possible association with Pamylia, see Herodotus 2.48; Plutarch, *De Iside et Osiride*, 36.365B; Montserrat 1996, 174; Myśliwiec 1997, 126; Coulon 2013, 182–83; Meyboom and Versluys 2006; Thomas 2015, 58–59.

22 See bibliography in Barrett 2011; 2019; Thomas 2015b.

23 Thomas 2015b, 72, 78.

24 The technology and style of these figurines borrows from Hellenistic figurines found across Greece and the Hellenistic kingdoms. These comprise "naturalistic" representation (an idealized form drawn from Greek statuary repertoire), following figurine forms from the Greek world.

25 The term *Tanagra style* is often used to describe the production of various centers, not just the famous center of Tanagra itself, because it has become synonymous with a specific style of early Hellenistic figurine (Burn and Higgins 2001, 26; Kassab Tezgör 2010, 186).

26 Dionysos, Eros, Athena and Aphrodite and Priapus are the non-Egyptian deities represented (although they may have been viewed as equivalents to certain Egyptian deities in antiquity).

27 The cult of the syncretistic deity Serapis is commonly attributed to Ptolemy I in the third century BC, although it derived from the Memphite cult of Osiris-Apis (Osiris and Apis).

28 On Naukratis workshop(s) see Thomas 2015e, 3.

29 Barrett 2019, 317; forthcoming.

30 Thomas 2015f; 2015g; 2017; 2018.

31 The Dog Star (Sirius) was personified by the Egyptian goddess Sothis, depicted as a "spitz-type" dog wearing a bulla pendant, and is found in association with representations of Isis and Harpocrates (Dunand 1990, nos 867–76; Montserrat 1996, 170; Bailey 2008, 175; Barrett 2011, 187). Boutantin's interpretation that these may have been multivalent symbols, also representing pets (2014, 217–50), is unlikely in this context.

32 Thomas 2015f, 10–13, 15–16.

33 A group of 76 catalogued sherds (49 from Naukratis, 22 from Alexandria and 5 from "Egypt") comprise 39 fragments of goblets with molded decoration, 19 table-amphorae, 2 plate or bowl fragments, and 16 unidentified body sherds. They represent at least three different forms of goblet and can be found in two different fabrics (possibly from Naukratis and Alexandria).

34 See Thomas 2018, 12.

35 Bailey 2011, 71–93; Thomas 2018, 11–12. Fine mold-made pottery and faience vessels made at Athribis and Memphis appear during the mid to late third century BCE (Thomas 2017, 4–6; Thomas 2018, 11–12; Myśliwiec 1996, 35–36; Welc 2011, 244, 253). Stratified examples from Naukratis were found within deposits redated (Thomas 2018) to 175–50 BCE (Leonard 1997,

MC#85 from South Mound Locus 2019 phase NW3a) and (with abundant residual material dating 150–1 BCE) from a 50 BCE—CE 100 context in Kom Hadid (Leonard 2001, 193, no.33, MC#29; Egyptian Museum JE97814.1–2).

36 See British Museum 2002,0419.1.

37 Barrett 2011, 260–62; Thomas 2015b, 62.

38 While the woman depicted having sex is wearing a wig with Isis locks, it is not certain that these images always depict Isis herself, who (when dressed) elsewhere on these vessels is clearly depicted in full regalia, including her crown (figs. 6e, 6i, 6l).

39 The place of drunkenness was a chapel structure where the conception of Harpocrates was commemorated. It was also known as "columned porch of drunkenness" or "hall of roaming the marches" (Jasnow and Smith 2010–2011, 42–43). The Bes Chambers in Saqqara is one possible archaeologically attested example (Quibell 1907, 13; Martin 1981, 27–89; Jeffreys et al. 1988, 33–63; Klotz 2012, 395) as is Queen Hatshepsut's earlier limestone gate at the Mut precinct (Bryan 2014). On the rituals associated with the "festival of drunkenness," see Darnell 1995; DePauw and Smith 2004; Jasnow and Smith 2010–11, 42–43; Bryan 2014.

40 On these goblets, Isis wears the Hathoric crown with horns and sun disk above a wreath with lotuses atop a wig of Isis locks (figs. 6i, 6l, see also 6e for wreath, lotus buds, and an unclear sun disk). She also wears a fringed shawl tied across her chest with an Isis knot (fig. 6e), carries a sistrum in her right hand, and carries a small globular pot with an everted rim in her left (figs. 6e and 6i). Harpocrates also carries this small pot in his left hand (fig. 6j), similar to the goblets which depict these scenes (see fig. 6l). These goblets may be a Ptolemaic variant of what are commonly called Bes jars (named so because they frequently depict Bes).

41 The figurines are vulvate, depicted squatting (sometimes as though on a birthing stool, Bailey 2008, 47), appear pregnant, or are depicted resting after birth alongside a baby (fig. 3e). The birth scene on these goblets is depicted within the mammisi, and the appearance of Harpocrates from the mammisi on the same vessels confirms that they commemorate the birth of that deity.

42 Hellenistic and earlier figurines are often called "Baubo," or female fertility demons, while Roman Period examples are assumed to be beneficent demons (Bailey 2008, 43, nos 3112–43). These in turn influenced the Byzantine Period "female saint" figurines (Bailey 2008, 3387–400). The Byzantine examples are clothed and not obviously pregnant, but they are often depicted holding babies or praying in the same pose as earlier examples. See also Frankfurter, chapter 10, this volume.

43 Török 1995, 132–33; Bailey 2008, 46–47.

44 Barrett 2015, 408.

45 Frankfurter 1998, 134, 140. See Boozer, chapter 8, this volume, fig. 8.6, for an example of a robbed niche within a house (although its original function is unclear).

46 The dating of the material from both areas has now been reappraised on the basis of the ceramics, which require some adjustments for the dating of the Ptolemaic and Roman levels (Thomas 2018, 5).

47 See Boozer, chapter 8, this volume.

48 Leonard 2001, trenches 52, 63, and 76. Recorded finds from Kom Hadid comprise: pottery (1003); faience vessels (27); stone vessels (1); building materials (24); figurines (18); lamps (5); glass (1).

49 Leonard 1997, "Northwest Building" trenches 1, 2, 482, 490, 491, 492. Recorded finds from Leonard's excavations of this building comprise: pottery vessels (1015); stone vessels (2); faience vessels (30); faience beads (4) and amulets (2); lamps (5); stone tools (4); and a fish hook.

50 Five figurines were found in 175–50 BCE deposits (phases 3–4) in the northwest corner of the courtyard; two were found in 150–50 BCE deposits (phases 6–8) in Rooms 4 and 1 respectively. One has no findspot recorded, and one was found in Roman deposits above Rooms 3 and 4 (phase 10). Two figurines found during British Museum excavations comprise a Harpocrates head, found immediately to the north of Room 1 from a disturbed Roman context, and a Ptolemaic Bes mask fragment, found in a disturbed late Ptolemaic context potentially belonging to the neighboring house to the southeast of this building, but still within the *temenos* of Amun-Ra.

51 One lamp, a goblet depicting Bes (Fig. 6m), and five figurines (of macrophallic Harpocrates, Fig. 4d, and Isis) were all found within two to four meters of each other in the northwestern corner of the ca. 175–50 BCE courtyard (phases 2B to 4), under and just to the south of where Room 4 was subsequently built. Two figurines of Harpocrates and Isis (in Rooms 4 and 1) and three

lamps (two in Room 1 and one in fire pit Room 2) were found in ca. 150–50 BCE phases 6 to 8. One figurine was found above Rooms 3 and 4 and a lamp in room 1 within Roman deposits (phase 10).

52 This mask is reminiscent of a figurine found 130 years earlier at Naukratis, which may represent how this was used. It depicts a macrophallic priest wearing a Bes mask, carrying a cult statue of Harpocrates (Bailey 2008, no.3154, British Museum 1888,0601.95).

53 Nicholson 2013.

54 Thomas and Nicholson 2013, 201.

55 Including the nude female figurines, often called "beneficent demons," discussed above as putative Isis-Hathor birth figurines.

56 Maxfield and Peacock 2001, 450–52.

57 Bailey 1998, 21–30; 2006, 261–70.1751, small finds were catalogued from the site, although this excludes the large quantities of ceramics also found at Mons Claudianus.

58 See the discussion in Boozer, chapter 8, this volume, on the categories of domestic rubbish disposal.

59 See Thomas 2012, 172 and bibliography.

60 While the ethnonyms Ichthyophagi and Trogodytes are Greek exonyms applied to these indigenous groups, there is evidence that members of those groups used these ethnonyms in Myos Hormos.

61 Tomber 2005; Van Rengen and Thomas 2006; Thomas 2007, 149–60.

62 Thomas 2011, 79–84. Some previously unidentified or misinterpreted fragments have since been reidentified by the author.

63 Although associated with Isis, the New Year, and the Nile flood, the heliacal rising of Sothis was also used to time the start of the sailing season to Arabia (Thomas 2011, 79).

64 Van Rengen 2002, 53–54; *O.Myos*, 512; Thomas 2007, 149–60; Thomas 2012, 174.

65 Van Rengen and Thomas 2006.

66 De Romanis 2003, 118.

67 A bronze Herakles and an unidentified steatite plaque are the only clear exceptions. An acrolithic marble arm from a female figure may be from either an Aphrodite or Isis figurine.

68 The Nubian retinue of the solar eye goddess, and occasionally Dionysiac figures (Barrett 2011; 2019).

69 Thomas 2015e, 5.

70 Barrett 2011, 127.

71 See Boozer, chapter 8, this volume.

72 Thomas 2015a, 9, fig.17.

73 Thomas 2014, 201, fig. 5; 2015a, 9.

74 This is not to say that such classes of finds are not relevant to understanding figurine use. However, assessing their relationship with figurines is difficult, because of their differential preservation, recording, publication, and the volume of the objects.

75 These were more frequent than the preceding Late Period secondary deposits (18 percent) that the British Museum excavated on the riverfront at Naukratis.

76 That was dominated by industrial waste from faience vessel production, which has been excluded from these figurines. While the nonindustrial waste comprises material that could have been redeposited from a domestic context, this corpus is most useful for comparing similarities and differences between production and consumption patterns.

77 The desiccated deposits at Myos Hormos and Mons Claudianus preserved a wide variety of organic artifacts not usually preserved at other sites.

78 See Thomas 2015f for examples and bibliography.

79 Thomas 2015f, 11–12, 17.

80 Thomas 2012, 178–80.

81 An exception being the priests from the Amun-Ra sanctuary at Naukratis, whose observations of ritual purity meant they avoided consuming pig, as suggested by the faunal remains found there (Thomas and Bertini 2019).

82 Thomas and Bertini 2019.

83 Thomas 2015a, 9, fig.17; 2015e, 9, fig. 24.

84 Thomas 2015f, 15, fig. 37.

85 Montserrat 1996, 166.

Works Cited

Arnold, D. 2003. *The Encyclopedia of Ancient Egyptian Architecture*. Princeton: Princeton University Press.

Bailey, D.M. 1998. "Terracotta Figures in Mons Claudius." In *Life on the Fringe: Living in the Southern Egyptian Deserts during the Roman and Early Byzantine Periods. Proceedings of a Colloquium held in Cairo, 9–12 December 1996*, edited by O.E. Kaper, 21–30. Leiden: Research School CNWS.

Bailey, D.M. 2006. "Terracotta and Plaster Figurines, Sealings, and a Stone Group." In *Mons Claudianus III: Survey and Excavation*, edited by V.A. Maxfield and D.P.S. Peacock, 261–88. Fouilles de l'Institut français d'archéologie orientale du Caire 54. Cairo: Institut français d'archéologie orientale.

Bailey, D.M. 2008. *Catalogue of the Terracottas in the British Museum 4: Ptolemaic and Roman Terracottas from Egypt*. London: British Museum.

Bailey, D.M. 2011. "Drinking-Goblets and Table-Amphorae Groups of Ptolemaic Painted Pottery." *Cahiers de la Céramique Égyptienne* 9: 71–93.

Ballet, P., and G. Galliano. 2010, "Les Isiaques et la petite plastique dans l'Égypte Hellénistique et Romaine." In *Isis on the Nile: Egyptian Gods in Hellenistic and Roman Egypt, Proceedings of the IVth International Conference of Isis Studies, Liège, November 27–29, 2008*, Michel Malaise in honorem, edited by L. Bricault and M.J. Verluys, 197–220. Religions in the Graeco-Roman World 171. Leiden: Brill.

Barrett, C.E. 2011. *Egyptianizing Figurines from Delos: A Study in Hellenistic Religion*. Leiden: Brill.

Barrett, C.E. 2015. "Terracotta Figurines and the Archaeology of Ritual: Domestic Cult in Greco-Roman Egypt." In *Figurines grecques en contexte: Présence muette dans le sanctuaire, la tombe et la maison*, edited by S. Huysecom-Haxhi and A. Muller (editors-in-chief) and C. Aubry, C.E. Barrett, C. Blume and T. Kopestonsky (collaborating editors), 401–20. Villeneuve d'Ascq: Presses Universitaires du Septentrion.

Barrett, C.E. 2019. *Domesticating Empire: Egyptian Landscapes in Pompeian Gardens*. Oxford: Oxford University Press.

Barrett, C.E. Forthcoming. "The Affordances of Terracotta Figurines in Domestic Contexts: Reconsidering the Gap between Material and Ritual." In *Stuff of the Gods: The Material Aspects of Religion in Ancient Greece*, edited by M. Haysom, M. Mili, and J. Wallensten. Acta Instituti Atheniensis Regni Sueciae. Stockholm.

Boutantin, C. 2014. *Terres cuites et culte domestique: Bestiaire de l'Égypte gréco-romaine*. Religions in the Graeco-World 179. Leiden: Brill.

Bryan, B. 2014. "Hatshepsut and Cultic Revelries in the New Kingdom." In *Creativity and Innovation in the Reign of Hatshepsut*, edited by J.M. Galán, B.M. Bryan, and P.F. Dorman, 93–124. Studies in Ancient Oriental Civilization 69. Chicago: Oriental Institute of the University of Chicago.

Burn, L., and R. Higgins. 2001. *Catalogue of Greek Terracottas in the British Museum III*. London: British Museum.

Coulon, L. 2013. "Osiris chez Hérodote." In *Hérodite et l'Égypte regards croisés sur le livre II de l'enquête d'Hérodote*, edited by L. Coulon, P. Giovannell-Jouanna and F. Kimmel-Clauzet, 167–90. Lyon: Maison de l'Orient et de la Méditerrané.

Coulson, W.D.E. 1996. *Ancient Naukratis, II/1: The Survey at Naukratis*. Oxford: Oxbow Books.

Darnell, J.C. 1995. "Hathor Returns to Medamûd." *Studien zur Altägyptischen Kultur* 22: 47–94.

DePauw, M., and M.J. Smith. 2004. "Visions of Ecstasy: Cultic Revelry before the Goddess Ai/Nehemanit. Ostraca Faculteit Letteren (K.U.Leuven) dem. 1–2." In *Res Severa Verum Gaudium*, edited by F. Hoffmann and H.J. Thissen, 67–94. Leuven: Peeters.

Dunand, F. 1979. *Religion populaire en Égypte Romaine*. Leiden: Brill.

Dunand, F. 1990. *Catalogue des terres cuites Gréco-Romaines d'Egypte*. Paris: Réunion des musées nationaux.

Dunand, F., and C. Zivie-Coche. 2004. *Gods and Men in Egypt: 3000 BCE to 395 CE*. Ithaca, NY: Cornell University Press.

De Romanis, F. 2003. "Between the Nile and the Red Sea: Imperial Trade and Barbarians." In *Arid Lands in Roman Times: Papers from the International Conference in Rome, July 9th–10th, 2001*, edited by M. Liverani, 117–22. Arid Zone Archaeology Monographs 4. Florence: All'insegna del giglio.

Fazzini, R.A. 1988. *Egypt Dynasty XXII–XXIV*. Leiden: Brill.

Frankfurter, D. 1998. *Religion in Roman Egypt: Assimilation and Resistance*. Princeton: Princeton University Press.

Frankfurter, D. 2014. "Terracotta Figurines and Popular Religion in Late Antique Egypt: Issues of Continuity and 'Survival.'" In *Le myrte et la rose: Mélanges offerts à Françoise Dunand par ses élèves, collègues et amis*, edited by C. Zivie-Coche and G. Tallet, 129–41. Montpellier: Équipe Égypte nilotique et méditerranéenne.

Frankfurter, D. 2017. *Christianizing Egypt: Syncretism and Local Worlds in Late Antiquity*. The Martin Classical Lectures. Princeton: Princeton University Press.

Gardner, E.A. 1888. *Naukratis. Part II*. Sixth Memoir of the Egypt Exploration Fund. London: Egypt Exploration Fund.

Hogarth, D.G., C.C. Edgar, and C. Gutch. 1898–99. "Excavations at Naukratis." *Annual of the British School at Athens* 5: 26–97.

Hogarth, D.G., H.L. Lorimer, and C.C. Edgar. 1905. "Naukratis 1903." *Journal of Hellenic Studies* 25: 105–36.

Jasnow, R., and M. Smith. 2010–11. "'As For Those Who Have Called Me Evil, Mut Will Call Them Evil': Orgiastic Cultic Behaviour and Its Critics in Ancient Egypt (PSI Inv. [provv.] D 114a + PSI Inv. 3056 verso)." *Enchoria* 32: 9–53.

Jeffreys, D.G., H.S. Smith, M. Price, and L.L. Giddy. 1988. *The Anubieion at Saqqâra*. Egypt Exploration Society Excavation Memoir 54. London: Egypt Exploration Society.

Kassab Tezgör, D.K. 2010. "The Production of Tanagra Figurines at Myrina and Alexandria." In *Tanagras: Figurines for Life and Eternity. The Musée du Louvre's Collection of Greek Figurines*, edited by V. Jeammet, 186–94. Valencia: Fundación Bancaja.

Klotz, D. 2012. "The Lecherous Pseudo-Anubis of Josephus and the 'Tomb of 1897' at Akhmim." In *Et in Ægypto et ad Ægyptum: Recueil d'études dédiées à Jean-Claude Grenier*, edited by A. Gasse, F. Servajean and C. Thiers, 383–96. Montpellier: Équipe Égypte nilotique et méditerranéenne.

Knoblauch, C.M., and J.C. Gill. 2012. "Antecedents to the Ptolemaic Mammisis." In *Australasian Conference for Young Egyptologists, 4–6 September 2009, Melbourne*, edited by C.M. Knoblauch and J.C. Gill, 9–13. British Archaeological Reports International Series 2355. Oxford: Archaeopress.

Leonard Jr., A. 1997. *Ancient Naukratis: Excavations at a Greek Emporium in Egypt I. The Excavations at Kom Ge'if*. The Annual of the American Schools of Oriental Research 54. Boston: American Schools of Oriental Research.

Leonard Jr., A. 2001. *Ancient Naukratis: Excavations at a Greek Emporium in Egypt II. The Excavations at Kom Hadid*. The Annual of the American Schools of Oriental Research 55. Boston: American Schools of Oriental Research.

Martin, G.T. 1981. *The Sacred Animal Necropolis at North Saqqâra, the Southern Dependencies of the Main Temple Complex*. Egypt Exploration Society Excavation Memoir 50. London: Egypt Exploration Society.

Masson, A. 2018. "Scarabs, Scaraboids and Amulets." In *Naukratis: Greeks in Egypt*, edited by A. Villing, M. Bergeron, G. Bourogiannis, A. Johnston, F. Leclère, A. Masson and R.I. Thomas. The British Museum, Online Research Catalogue. https://webarchive.nationalarchives.gov.uk/ukgwa/20190801123440mp_/https://www.britishmuseum.org/pdf/Masson_Scarabs_and_amulets.pdf.

Masson-Berghoff, A. 2019. "Naukratis: Egyptian Offerings in Context." In *Naukratis in Context I and II: Proceedings of the First and Second Naukratis Workshops held at The British Museum, 16–17 December 2011 and 22–23 June 2013*, edited by A. Masson-Berghoff and R.I. Thomas. A special issue of *British Museum Studies in Ancient Egypt and Sudan* 24: 127–58. https://webarchive.nationalarchives.gov.uk/ukgwa/20190801105854mp_/https://www.britishmuseum.org/pdf/BMSAES/Issue%2024/Masson-Berghoff_24.pdf.

Maxfield, V.A., and D.P.S. Peacock, eds. 2001. *Mons Claudianus II: Excavations Part I*. Fouilles de l'Institut français d'archéologie orientale du Caire 43. Cairo: Institut français d'archéologie orientale.

Meyboom, P.G.P, and M.J. Versluys. 2006. "The Meaning of Dwarfs in Nilotic Scenes." In *Nile into Tiber: Egypt in the Roman World. Proceedings of the 3rd International Conference of Isis Studies*, edited by L. Bricault, M.J. Versluys, and P.G.P. Meyboom, 170–208. Religions in the Graeco-Roman World 159. Leiden: Brill.

Möller, A. 2000. *Naukratis: Trade in Archaic Greece*. Oxford: Oxford University Press.

Montserrat, D. 1996. *Sex and Society in Graeco-Roman Egypt*. London: Kegan Paul.

Myśliwiec, K. 1996. "Les ateliers d'Athribis ptolémaïque." *Archeologia* (Warsaw) 47: 7–20.

Myśliwiec, K. 1997. "Phallic Figurines from Tell Atrib." *Aksamit* 1997: 119–37.

Nick, G. 2006. *Zypro-ionische Kleinplastik aus Kalkstein und Alabaster*. Archäologische Studien zu Naukratis I. Möhnesee: Bibliopolis.

Nicholson, P.T., ed. 2013. *Working in Memphis: The Production of Faience at Roman Period Kom Helul*. Egypt Exploration Society Excavation Memoir 105. London: Egypt Exploration Society.

Petrie, W.M.F. 1886. *Naukratis. Part I, 1884–5*. Third Memoir of the Egypt Exploration Fund. London: Trubner.

Quibell, J.E. 1907. *Excavations at Saqqâra 1905–1906*. Cairo: Institut français d'archéologie orientale.

Sandri, S. 2006. *Har-pa-chered (Harpokrates): Die Genese eines ägyptischen Götterkindes*. Leuven: Peeters.

Tomber, R. 2005. "Trogodytes and Troglodytes: Exploring Interaction on the Red Sea during the Roman Period." In *People of the Red Sea: Proceedings of Red Sea Project II Held in the British Museum October 2004*, edited by J.C.M. Starkey, 41–50. British Archaeological Reports International Series 1395. Oxford: Archaeopress.

Thomas, R.I. 2007. "The Arabaegypti Ichthyophagi: Cultural Connections with Egypt and the Maintenance of Identity." In *Natural Resources and Cultural Connections of the Red Sea*, edited by J.C.M. Starkey, P. Starkey and T. Wilkinson, 149–60. British Archaeological Reports International Series 1661. Oxford: Archaeopress.

Thomas, R.I. 2011. "Terracotta Figurines." In *Myos Hormos—Quseir al-Qadim: Roman and Islamic Ports on the Red Sea 2. The Finds from the 1999–2003 Excavation*, edited by D.P.S. Peacock and L. Blue, 79–84. British Archaeological Reports International Series 2286. Oxford: Archaeopress.

Thomas, R.I. 2012. "Port Communities and the Erythraean Sea Trade." *British Museum Studies in Ancient Egypt and Sudan* 18: 169–99. https://webarchive.nationalarchives.gov.uk/ukgwa/20190801105904mp_/https://www.britishmuseum.org/PDF/Thomas.pdf.

Thomas, R.I. 2014. "Roman Naukratis and its Alexandrian Context." *British Museum Studies in Ancient Egypt and Sudan* 21: 193–218. https://webarchive.nationalarchives.gov.uk/ukgwa/20190801105730mp_/https://www.britishmuseum.org/pdf/Thomas2014_B.pdf.

Thomas, R.I. 2015a. "Stone and Terracotta Figures from Naukratis: An Introduction." In *Naukratis: Greeks in Egypt*, edited by A. Villing, M. Bergeron, G. Bourogiannis, A. Johnston, F. Leclère, A. Masson and R.I. Thomas. The British Museum, Online Research Catalogue. https://webarchive.nationalarchives.gov.uk/ukgwa/20190801123901mp_/https://www.britishmuseum.org/pdf/Thomas_Figurines_SF_AV.pdf.

Thomas, R.I. 2015b. "Egyptian Late Period Figures in Terracotta and Limestone." In *Naukratis: Greeks in Egypt*, edited by A. Villing, M. Bergeron, G. Bourogiannis, A. Johnston, F. Leclère, A. Masson, and R.I. Thomas. The British Museum, Online Research Catalogue. https://webarchive.nationalarchives.gov.uk/ukgwa/20190801123428mp_/http://www.britishmuseum.org/pdf/Thomas_Egyptian_figures_final.pdf.

Thomas, R.I. 2015c. "Cypriot Figures in Terracotta and Limestone." In *Naukratis: Greeks in Egypt*, edited by A. Villing, M. Bergeron, G. Bourogiannis, A. Johnston, F. Leclère, A. Masson, and R.I. Thomas. The British Museum, Online Research Catalogue. https://webarchive.nationalarchives.gov.uk/ukgwa/20190801125419mp_/https://www.britishmuseum.org/pdf/Thomas_Cypriot_Figures.pdf.

Thomas, R.I. 2015d. "Greek Terracotta Figures." In *Naukratis: Greeks in Egypt*, edited by A. Villing, M. Bergeron, G. Bourogiannis, A. Johnston, F. Leclère, A. Masson, and R.I. Thomas. The British Museum, Online Research Catalogue. https://webarchive.nationalarchives.gov.uk/ukgwa/20190801123855mp_/https://www.britishmuseum.org/pdf/Thomas_Greek_Figures.pdf.

Thomas, R.I. 2015e. "Ptolemaic and Roman Figures, Models and Coffin-Fittings in Terracotta." In *Naukratis: Greeks in Egypt*, edited by A. Villing, M. Bergeron, G. Bourogiannis, A. Johnston, F.

Leclère, A. Masson, and R.I. Thomas. The British Museum, Online Research Catalogue. https://webarchive.nationalarchives.gov.uk/ukgwa/20190801123425mp_/https://www.britishmuseum.org/pdf/Thomas_Ptolemaic_figures.pdf.

Thomas, R.I. 2015f. "Lamps in Terracotta and Bronze." In *Naukratis: Greeks in Egypt*, edited by A. Villing, M. Bergeron, G. Bourogiannis, A. Johnston, F. Leclère, A. Masson, and R.I. Thomas. The British Museum, Online Research Catalogue. https://webarchive.nationalarchives.gov.uk/ukgwa/20190801123856mp_/https://www.britishmuseum.org/pdf/Thomas_Lamps.pdf.

Thomas, R.I. 2015g. "Portable Stoves and Braziers in Terracotta." In *Naukratis: Greeks in Egypt*, edited by A. Villing, M. Bergeron, G. Bourogiannis, A. Johnston, F. Leclère, A. Masson, and R.I. Thomas. The British Museum, Online Research Catalogue. https://webarchive.nationalarchives.gov.uk/ukgwa/20190801125424mp_/https://www.britishmuseum.org/pdf/Thomas_Stoves.pdf.

Thomas, R.I. 2015h. "Naukratis, 'Mistress of Ships', in Context." In *Thonis-Heracleion in Context*, edited by D. Robinson and F. Goddio, 247–65. Oxford Centre for Maritime Archaeology Monograph 8. Oxford: Oxford Centre for Maritime Archaeology.

Thomas, R.I. 2017. "Ptolemaic and Roman Faience Vessels." In *Naukratis: Greeks in Egypt*, edited by A. Villing, M. Bergeron, G. Bourogiannis, A. Johnston, F. Leclère, A. Masson, and R.I. Thomas. The British Museum, Online Research Catalogue. https://webarchive.nationalarchives.gov.uk/ukgwa/20190801123904mp_/https://www.britishmuseum.org/pdf/Thomas_Ptolemaic_and_Roman_faience.pdf.

Thomas, R.I. 2018. "Ptolemaic, Roman and Byzantine Pottery." In *Naukratis: Greeks in Egypt*, edited by A. Villing, M. Bergeron, G. Bourogiannis, A. Johnston, F. Leclère, A. Masson, and R.I. Thomas. The British Museum, Online Research Catalogue. https://webarchive.nationalarchives.gov.uk/ukgwa/20190801123911mp_/https://www.britishmuseum.org/pdf/Thomas_Ptolemaic_and_Roman_pottery.pdf.

Thomas, R.I. 2019a. "Terracotta and Stone Figurines from Naukratis." In *Naukratis in Context I and II: Proceedings of the First and Second Naukratis Workshops Held at The British Museum, 16–17 December 2011 and 22–23 June 2013*, edited by A. Masson-Berghoff and R.I. Thomas. Special issue of *British Museum Studies in Ancient Egypt and Sudan* 24: 175–203. https://webarchive.nationalarchives.gov.uk/ukgwa/20190801105854mp_/https://www.britishmuseum.org/pdf/BMSAES/Issue%2024/Thomas_24.pdf.

Thomas, R.I. 2019b. "Egyptian and Cypriot Stone Statuettes in Context at Late Period Naukratis." In *Statues in Context: Production, Meaning and (Re)uses*, edited by A. Masson-Berghoff, 159–80. British Museum Publications on Egypt and Sudan 10. Leuven: Peeters.

Thomas, R.I., and L. Bertini. 2019. "Shell and Bone Artefacts and Faunal Remains." In *Naukratis: Greeks in Egypt*, edited by A. Villing, M. Bergeron, G. Bourogiannis, A. Johnston, F. Leclère, A. Masson and R.I. Thomas. The British Museum, Online Research Catalogue. https://webarchive.nationalarchives.gov.uk/ukgwa/20190801105436/https://www.britishmuseum.org/research/online_research_catalogues/ng/naukratis_greeks_in_egypt.aspx.

Thomas, R.I., and P.T. Nicholson. 2013. "Figurines." In *Working in Memphis: The Production of Faience at Roman Period Kom Helul*, edited by P.T. Nicholson, 201–35. Egypt Exploration Society Excavation Memoir 105. London: Egypt Exploration Society.

Thomas, R.I., and A. Villing. 2013. "Naukratis Revisited 2012: Integrating New Fieldwork and Old Research." *British Museum Studies in Ancient Egypt and Sudan* 20: 81–125. https://webarchive.nationalarchives.gov.uk/ukgwa/20190801110637mp_/https://www.britishmuseum.org/PDF/ThomasAndVilling.pdf.

Thomas, R.I., and A. Villing. Forthcoming. "Return to Naukratis: New Fieldwork at Kom Geif, 2012–2014." *Annales du Service des Antiquités de l'Égypte*.

Török, L. 1995. *Hellenistic and Roman Terracottas from Egypt*. Rome: "L'Erma" di Bretschneider.

Van Rengen, W. 2002. "Sebakh Excavations and the Written Material." In *Myos Hormos—Quseir al-Qadim: A Roman and Islamic Port on the Red Sea Coast of Egypt*, edited by D.P.S. Peacock, L. Blue and S. Moser, 53–54. Southampton: University of Southampton.

Van Rengen, W., and R.I. Thomas. 2006. "The Sebakh Excavations." In *Myos Hormos—Quseir al-Qadim: Roman and Islamic Ports on the Red Sea 1. Survey and Excavations 1999–2003*, edited by D.P.S. Peacock and L. Blue, 146–54. Oxford: Oxbow Books.

Villing, A., M. Bergeron, G. Bourogiannis, A. Johnston, F. Leclère, A. Masson, and R.I. Thomas, eds. 2013–19. *Naukratis: Greeks in Egypt*. The British Museum, Online Research Catalogue. https://webarchive.nationalarchives.gov.uk/ukgwa/20190801105436/https://www.britishmuseum.org/research/online_research_catalogues/ng/naukratis_greeks_in_egypt.aspx.

Welc, F. 2011. "Decorated Ptolemaic Faience Bowls from Athribis (Tell Atrib, Nile Delta)." *Études et Travaux* 24: 244–69.

10

The Supernatural Vulnerabilities of Domestic Space in Late Antique Egypt

Perspectives from the "Magical" Corpus

DAVID FRANKFURTER

Chapters in this volume discuss the Greco-Roman Egyptian house as an architectural entity and as a social site whose groups often extended across several houses.[1] Yet the house was also a symbolic entity, materializing and locating family concord and fortune, the safety of its members, and the success of marriages. Take, for example, the scenario depicted in one of two oracle tickets submitted to St. Leontius of Tripolis at one of his Egyptian shrines during the eighth or ninth century CE: "O God of St. Leontius! If I (should) stay at this house where I am and remain inside with [my] mother, my heart will be at rest and shall bear a living child . . . [then return to me this ticket]."[2] Presumably the corresponding ticket with the woman's alternative path involved her return to her husband's house somewhere else, an often uncomfortable situation for a young wife in Roman Egypt, since—as Sabine Huebner has discussed—the virilocal arrangement kept her under the repressive control of the husband's mother.[3] So here the supplicant reflects the benefits of returning home in the wording of her oracle request: to remain in the house with her mother would bring peace and a hopeful childbirth. And it is not only her mother's house that is credited with powers of safety; here it is St. Leontius who will guarantee those powers through his answer.

Houses and the Conceptualization of Domestic Vulnerability and Misfortune

The house, then, is a place in which one *pays attention to* spaces, entrances, and exits. More than the theater, the shop, the agora, or the baths, the house protects and materializes the fortune of the family. It thus becomes a place of ritual focus, from formally invoking St. Leontius's blessing on staying put, to the multiple ways that inhabitants engage in domestic ritual practices: lamp lighting, the hanging of apotropaic symbols, feasting, and all the verbal and gestural expressions through which dwellers forged festal bonds with neighbors, cultivated beneficial spirits and ancestors, and repelled negative spirits. These are all *ritual* expressions, not because they involve repetition or sacred structures, but in the sense that they involve focused attention to spaces, activities, and calendar.[4]

There is a sizable record of these domestic ritual expressions in archaeological remains like figurines, lamps, and the occasional documentary papyrus.[5] But one can also see these expressions and gestures in the protective amulets, incantation manuals, and binding spells preserved in Greek and Coptic from the fourth through about the tenth centuries. Generally, these texts function to convey material efficacy in situ—through their deposit or their verbal performance (gesture, incantation) in a particular place. And in this chapter, I use these texts to look at the conceptualization of supernatural danger to the domestic sphere: to houses and households. How do "magical" texts imagine demonic and malevolent human access to the house and its inhabitants?[6] And how is the domestic sphere itself imagined spatially in relationship to the apotropaic—and also subversive—goals of such texts?

The magical texts of the Christian Period cumulatively represent the craft services of literate specialists within the broad penumbra of the Christian institution: monks, scribes, shrine attendants, and the occasional bishop. But their actual compositions represent a negotiation between the liturgically imbued scribal world of monks and scribes and the particular demands and feelings of lay clients. In this way we model ritual expertise—the providing of various ad hoc ritual services in the local milieu as well as to outsiders in a more exotic vein—not as the pretentious deceptions of self-appointed, freelance wizards, but rather in terms of preexisting social roles. As Egyptian priests had once served primarily in this role, mediating the symbolic (including writing) systems of the temples for practical, often healing purposes,[7] so in the Christian Period it was predominantly monks and clergy who did so, likewise conveying the material efficacy of the religious institution in practical assemblages for everyday use.[8] This model obviously cannot exclude the activity of *independent* ritual experts, unaffiliated in any sense with a religious institution or status, but it recognizes the deep affiliation of the media and language of magic, especially in the Christian Period, with those of the Christian institution, its liturgical expressions, and its charismatic roles.[9] In addition, one can detect influences from prevailing oral traditions as well as traditions of conveying verbal power maintained in scribal subcultures (e.g., ancient priestly milieux) over the *longue durée*.

The materials I will be discussing concern in the broadest sense the "demonic": a broad, *un*systematized category for what afflicts the domestic sphere from the outside, disrupts fortune, and occasions popular diagnosis and discussion.[10] A common formula used in erotic binding spells, for example, charges a *daimon*, often the restless spirit of a local corpse, to "go into every place, into every quarter, into every house, and bind" a particular woman with lust only for the spell's client, suggesting that restless, ambiguous spirits were regularly shooting through neighborhoods and into homes, chaotically inflaming women.[11] But even in these cases, the demons are directed by nefarious conspirators in the community. Thus the "demonic" should properly cover not only supernatural beings but also the evil eye, the focus of many domestic *apotropaia* in ancient Rome, as well as sorcery—that is, aggressive or malevolent ritual acts, whether real or imagined in social (not supernatural) terms, and of course various dangerous fauna, like serpents.[12] The demonic is not a system of thought—a "demonology"—but a tradition of conceptualizing vulnerability, misfortune, and the potencies of the liminal in consultation with a ritual specialist, such as a monk or shrine attendant.[13] Both the deployment of routine apotropaia (like Bes heads or figurines) and the placement of exorcistic or protective devices in the event of particular concerns (such as many of the Babylonian incantation bowls) involve extensive consultation and craft strategies to identify demonic forces, portals of domestic vulnerability, and the best ritual assemblage to resolve concerns and allay anxieties.[14] During such consultations, a ritual specialist will express his authority in naming demons and developing the precise language to keep them away. For example, two amulets prepared to protect individuals from headless demons—in one case, a headless dog—likely follow such individual consultations as well as the independent (and innovative) discernment of a particular ritual specialist, who may have drawn on earlier Egyptian traditions of epithets for Osiris.[15]

My basic assumption here is that, unlike (e.g.) Babylonian incantation bowls, there was no established demonology surrounding domestic misfortunes and afflictions in late antique Egypt, but rather, flexible traditions that could be drawn into an appearance of precision and certainty through the authority of a ritual specialist.[16] At the same time, as we will see, the house itself, its boundaries and portals, provided a relatively consistent framework for conceptualizing threat, protection, and the ritual performances to express them both. For example, as Sabine Huebner has found, the wooden doors used to close off the typical mud-brick houses were of such value for their locks and general craftsmanship that they were occasionally stolen themselves. We should thus presume these doors' material potency extended in many ways beyond the practical function of opening and closing spaces, to signifying—even conveying agency in the guarantee of—safety and security within.[17]

Conceptualizing Vulnerability in the Late Antique Egyptian Home

The Aramaic incantation bowls from late antique Babylonia provide a rich and essential comparison to the amulets and spells considered in this chapter, since they are meant to be placed on the floor in one or more particular rooms in the house, and they draw on an extensive tradition of naming demonic beings: *shed* spirits, *dev* spirits, idol spirits, male and female liliths, Ashtarot, Satans, and so on.[18] Moreover, when they mention interior spaces of vulnerability, they focus on the nature of the spaces rather than points of entry, protecting "his house, with its four b[orders and with] its f[ou]r c[orn]ers" or listing the demons "who reside in the inner room, and in the vaulted chamber, and in the hall, and in the whole dwelling."[19] By comparison, most of the late antique Egyptian protective amulets focus predominantly on points of access to the people within. In the following text, from the sixth century, the demons are already within the house, lurking in the shadows:

> I adjure [you], unclean spirits, who do wrong to the Lord: Do not injure the one who wears these adjurations. Depart from him. Do not hide down here in the

> ground; do not lurk under a bed, nor under a window, nor under a door, nor under beams, nor under utensils, nor below a pit.
>
> . . .
>
> And now I adjure all of you spirits who weep, or laugh frightfully, [or] make a person have bad dreams or terror, or make eyesight dim, or teach confusion or guile of mind in sleep and out of sleep.[20]

These demons afflict sleep itself, a sensitive condition in the course of the day, although usefully receptive for divination when performed at one of the many incubation shrines in late antique Egypt.[21] The interior of the house is imagined as harboring demons in crevices and corners—demons as, virtually, coresidents in the house with the family. The demonic is likened to vermin—dangerous insects and creatures that invade the house—except the affliction lies not in bites but in dreams and general anxiety. The elision of dangerous vermin and the demonic emerges more vividly in two amulets meant to protect the interior of a house from the "Artemisian scorpion":[22]

> (O) door Aphrodite[23]
> phrodite, rodite odite
> dite ite te te e ōrōr
> phōrphōr Iao Sabaoth Adone
> I bind you, Artemisian scorpion!
> Free this house
> from every evil reptile
> [and] action quickly quickly!
> St. Phocas is here!
> Phamenoth 13, third indiction.[24]

> Hor hor Phor Phor, Iao Sabaoth Adonai, Elōe Salaman Tarchi
> I bind you, Artemisian scorpion, 315 times! Preserve this house
> with its occupants, from all evil, from all sorcery [*baskosunēs*]
> of spirits of the air and human [evil] eye
> and terrible pain [and] sting of scorpion and snake, through the
> name of the highest god . . .
> . . . Be on guard, O Lord, son of
> David according to the flesh, the one born of the holy virgin
> Mary, O holy one, highest god, from the holy spirit. Glory to you,
> O heavenly king, Amen. [*nomina sacra* and Christian insignia][25]

Both texts are conscious of the house as a human enclosure into which venomous beings can enter, yet both imagine the demonic object of the charm, the Artemisian scorpion, as encompassing both reptiles and broader dangers—in the second, sorcery as well: that is, the harm that nefarious and jealous humans might bring against the occupants. It is the literate expert's ingenuity to combine various evils in the repelling of the Artemisian scorpion.

Among the most elaborate protective invocations is a large amulet (136 lines; 37.5 x 23 cm) directed at a pregnant woman:

> Watch and protect the 4 sides of the body and the soul and the spirit and the entire house of N daughter of N and her child who is in her womb, as well as every child born to her. Bring them to life [or keep them alive] yearly without any disease.[26] Cast from her every evil force [*energia*]. Never allow them to approach her or any of her children until she bears them. Cast forth from her every doom and every devil and every Apalaf and every Aberselia and every chill and every fever and every trembling. Restrain them all. Cast them away from her and away from all her children until she bears them and away from all her dwellings, immediately and quickly! Do not permit them ever to visit her or the child with whom she is pregnant for approximately two hundred miles around [*na-shēt milion ep-kōti*].[27]

This adjuration is repeated several more times in slight variation throughout this extensive amulet. The key features in every case consist, first, of the *listing* of esoteric demonic powers that might afflict an infant. Many amulet texts (especially those among the Jewish corpora) strive for a comprehensiveness in covering afflictions and their agents, a comprehensiveness achieved through the form of the list. As scholars of early writing systems have noted, the list is one of the most basic and most distinctive uses of writing, insofar as it extracts items from their contextual environments and collects them according to class or purpose.[28] Thus an Aberselia demon, as above, may well be imagined or adjured only in the context of children's illness, but here it is listed along with chills and with devils to make a comprehensive list of dangers to mothers and infants. In other texts, we will see, the list is used to collect parts of the house—walkways, doors, thresholds—rarely imagined together, but enumerated in such a way as to "fix" each component as protected. Indeed, listing in these contexts carries an *illocutionary* function, in the sense that the writing of the list and its comprehensive picture of coverage ritually effects that very comprehensive coverage.[29]

The second key feature of this last amulet, perhaps most importantly for the conceptualization of domestic space, lies in the elision this adjuration makes between the mother's body and the house in which she dwells. She is imagined, in a way, both *in* and *as* a house. That is, the language of spatial protection applied to this woman's body comes from the language of domestic apotropaia—"4 sides of the body . . . and the entire house of"—yet also conceptualizes maternity in terms of the house it should fill. As a model of vulnerability, the domestic structure is thus an extension of the maternal body itself, and the amulet extends the zone of domestic safety to "two hundred miles around."

A different construction of domestic spatial boundaries emerges in a Coptic handbook for apotropaic ritual (fourth to sixth centuries CE). Like several other such handbooks, this one opens with a long invocation to heavenly powers and then lists a variety of material applications of this invocation, for healing specific ailments, for resolving social crises, and

> For your house, and your sheep enclosures, and all that belongs to you: recite [the formula] over some water and sprinkle your house and every place that belongs to you, [and] no evil will overtake you.
>
> . . .
>
> For the safety of your house and the walkways by your door: recite it over some torrential water and sprinkle your house and the walkways by your door, and it will guard you from every *pharmakia*, and [will] heal every disease, and [guard you from] every demon and every evil eye; and it also will not allow estrangement to occur in your house, nor [any] trouble [at all].[30]

This manual not only shows the imaginative elision of demonic and social threats (evil eye, *pharmakia*) to the domestic sphere, it expands the sites of invasion and zones of domestic vulnerability to walkways and sheep enclosures. Another Coptic codex (sixth century CE), a compendium of different kinds of formulae and spells, employs the list form to detail the full range of interior and exterior vulnerabilities—indeed, one might say, the very components of the late antique house (or at least a large one):

> You must guard the entrance and the exit,[31] and all his dwelling places, and his windows, and his courtyards [*aulē*], and his bedrooms, and his open rooms [*ma etčolep*], and the lands which belong to him, and his foundations, and his orchards, and his wells, and his trees that bear fruit, and those that do not bear fruit.[32]

The dangers envisioned here for the intended (and presumably wealthy) client—one with extensive lands and multiple courtyards—come not from the realm of demonic spirits but from social threats: sorcery, especially foreign-borne sorcery:[33]

> I invoke you, God of Gods, king of all powers, the one who sits over the cherubim [and] the seraphim, that you do away with all violent deeds [that] are directed against [every] place where this prayer will be uttered, . . . if someone has bound a place by having put bonds of deceit in it, hidden in its foundations, or in its open places, . . .
>
> You violent deeds, all that have happened or are destined to happen, I adjure you . . . that you be undone and withdraw from every one near whom this prayer shall be recited, or every place where it will be deposited and all those who belong to it, and each of you descend upon the head of the one who sent you to perform these abominations . . . whether the person is a stranger or a boss of those belonging to him, or is one who leads, or is a servant, or is a free person or is a *magos* or a female *magos*, or is a male Persian or a female Persian, or is a Chaldean or a female Chaldean, or is a Hebrew or a female Hebrew, or is an Egyptian or a female Egyptian, in general, whoever it is.[34]

Danger—that is, sorcery, subversion of the domestic sphere—is enumerated in list form in an effort to be comprehensive and "complete," as we saw above with the listing of demons; but here the multiplicity of threats is imagined in terms of foreigners and their ambiguous powers. This is also a common theme in the social mapping of danger, perhaps making more sense for a client whose domestic spaces include "open rooms," courtyards, and orchards, and who might thus fear the envy and malevolence of others most of all.[35] In other cases, we have seen, demonic and social agents of misfortune are combined or elided: "If someone writes these glorious . . . words upon the gates of his house: [series of numerical cryptograms], no temptation of the Adversary will enter that house nor will plots of evil men be able to prevail over it."[36] We might say that the popular conceptualization of threats to the domestic sphere in late antique Egypt was as acutely conscious of social dangers as it was of the range of demons—scorpion- and snake-shaped, dream-entering, child-killing.

And yet it is important not to ascribe this conceptualization simply to general "beliefs" in the culture as a whole. The move to cast danger in terms of demons, evil eye, and specific constructions of social threat and sorcery—or to stress one type to the exclusion of others—must be attributed to the scribal expert, the composer of the incantation or charm, who draws on local consultations as well as local (monastic?) traditions and personal intuition into social tensions and human nature.[37] Variations may reflect the class of the client, the type of domestic structure or holdings, and gender (what types of dangers might preoccupy men versus women?), but generally it is the scribal expert who lays out in potent written formulae a conceptualization of domestic threats.

In this way the process of securing the house through apotropaia might be analogized to a kind of therapy, although externalized to specific threats deemed concrete and resolvable through ritual, material methods. Furthermore, while in many cases such protection is deployed as a pro forma response to vulnerable or anxious states of family members—pregnancies, infants—anthropologists have noted that in some cases the very mobilization against demonic powers that family members undertake can have stabilizing, empowering corollary benefits, as those individuals rise up to defend themselves.[38]

Conceptualizing Vulnerability: Targets and Access Points for Sorcery

It is not just protective charms that reveal the sense of the domestic sphere as vulnerable, but also the instructions for and artifacts of sorcery[39] and binding spells: that is, ritual acts designed to afflict, subvert, or manipulate members of households.[40] For example, a lengthy incantation in the Macquarie University collection (seventh to eighth century CE) is followed by a list of ways to direct the powers the incantation constructs: for instance, to bind someone annoyed at you, bury the inscribed formula at his door; to keep a "brother [*pson*]" (presumably a monk) from coming into your house, inscribe the angelic name Eremiel and put it on the door-hinge; to bind someone, speak the incantation over two nails and drive them into the victim's doorpost; while a charm to protect a business requires that angelic names be written on potsherds and buried in each corner of the interior and exterior, and then the incantation is spoken over water and splashed "inside and outside and in front of you."[41] Likewise, an inscribed erotic charm (sixth century CE) in the Ashmolean

Museum begins with the formula "that just as I take you [i.e., the written charm] and put you at the door and the pathway of P-Hello son of Maure, (so also) you must take his heart and his mind; you must dominate his entire body."[42] Such texts reveal the corners, pathways, and doors of people's houses to be actively targeted for purposes of erotic desire and control, not just protection.

But what misfortunes did people in late antique Egypt imagine might transpire as the result of such malicious ritual? P-Hello, son of Maure, so the Ashmolean charm above goes on to describe, might suffer insomnia and restlessness (to be soothed only in the presence of the ritual agent, Papapolo, son of Noe). But other protective charms show a greater range of domestic experience that sorcery might threaten. A parchment codex from Heidelberg addresses the situations of "one who is bound so he is unable to have sex with his wife" and "a herd of cattle, when sorcery has been performed against you" (i.e., the cattle owner).[43] The Michigan codex quoted earlier promises that its protective rites "will not allow estrangement [*p-ōrj*(?)] to occur in your house, nor any trouble [*shtortr*] at all."[44] The late Byzantine Testament of Solomon attributes "divisions among men" and the subversion of households to the demon Lix Tetrax (7.5), and the desertion of houses to the demon Rhyx Miamet (who is repelled by inscribing the words "Melto Ardad Anaath" on the front entrance of the house, 18.40).[45] Thus multiple domestic conflicts, tensions, and disasters could be owed to supernatural interference.

Youssri Abdelwahed's chapter in this volume (chapter 6) covers a range of violent and stress-inducing domestic situations that might well have been attributed to outsiders' curses. In many cases the cause of domestic crisis is someone's *hybris*, "insolence"; but why would someone develop *hybris* in the first place? An inscribed ostracon from second-century Oxyrhynchus designed to inflame a wife erotically, such that she leaves her husband for the client, actually specifies that she should gain *hybris* (as well as hatred and obnoxiousness) "until she departs the *oikias* of Apollonius!"[46]

Other such curse spells imagine more elaborate misfortune in the homes of their victims: for instance, that two named women and a man "and their children, and everyone who resides with them—Amen!—[are hit] with any evil grief and every suffering and every unhealing pain";[47] that there "be a great distress and outcry on [the victim's] house and his wife";[48] that the heavenly powers should afflict someone and "turn [?] the favor of his dwelling-place [*charis epebma-nhe-maas*] around with destruction, with hatred, with scattering, with reversal. The people among all these [who] dwell in it must not be able to look at him in any way." This latter curse is meant to be materially enacted by means of wax dolls buried at the victim's door.[49] A domestic division charm sent to a man in late fourth-century Kellis (at his request) invokes God to make a married couple's "heart be black for each other . . . [to] wash (away) the desire which is between them for each other. . . . The house in which I place [this charm], do not come out of it without having instigated a dispute and a quarrel with thundering."[50]

Likewise, a number of curses focus on extensions of household property, much as some of the protective amulets above invoke protection over properties and fields well beyond the house. One elaborate assemblage, recommended in a fourth-century manual, consists of a frog, a lead lamella, and bat's blood and is meant to cause the wasting of the victim; the manual instructs that this assemblage be placed "at the east of the property [*tou chōriou*]."[51] A similar attack on a man's property as the economic extension of his household is the subject of an official complaint in a farmer's second-century letter to the Roman *strategos*. Twice, this farmer claims, his neighbor (along with the neighbor's wife and friend) had approached him or his chief cultivator during the harvest and tossed a fetus (*brephos*) at him—doubtless a stillborn fetus prepared in some kind of nefarious assemblage—in order to "surround him with malice." The farmer hopes that the strategos will intervene in this flagrant case of public sorcery.[52] For us, the letter demonstrates that sorcery really did take place on the edges, not only the interiors, of domestic property. (A carefully wrapped stillborn fetus found in the roof-rubble of a late fourth-century house in Kellis suggests that the same malign "throwing-assemblage" could be used against central domestic spaces as well).[53]

Thus a variety of social situations might be attributed to—or sought through—sorcery or unnamed demonic threats: mental stresses (insomnia, restlessness), domestic discord, sexual dysfunction, and—in the Heidelberg text cited above with the wax poppets—an individual's humiliation in his own home.[54] As extensions of the household, cattle too (and sheep, in a protective charm quoted earlier) might fall victim to such threats. The house itself and its satellite buildings are imagined as structures that both enclose social actors and yet are riven with portals, access points, where hostile (or envious) people can place objects that bind or curse and through which the evil powers of demons and the evil eye can pass.

Ritual, Religion, and Agency

To the extent that the late antique (or, for that matter, Greco-Roman) Egyptian house was fundamentally a site of social and generative reproduction regardless of the specific relationships of the occupants, then it was also a site culturally attentive to the vicissitudes of fortune.[55] In one sense, the house could be a sanctuary secure from public gossip and the malevolent spirits of the landscape.[56] But in another sense we see that walls, especially exterior walls, and doorways could be points of supernatural vulnerability for a social site seeking a minimization of marital discord, the maintenance of hierarchy, the prosperity of infants, and the assurance of female fecundity. (Of course, these concerns may be perennial to premodern homes.) Liminal areas were also clearly points of attack when others sought to inflict sorcery: for instance, thresholds, walkways, and even fields.[57]

The media by which aggressors attacked these sites consisted of magical assemblages, whose invariably weird and impure components (like fetuses) conveyed—at least to the perpetrator, whether or not they were found by the householder—a malevolent material agency. But the protection of the home from sorcery as well as demons involved such material assemblages as well—figurines, nails, eggs, among other things—and it can be difficult for the modern archaeologist to distinguish an apotropaic or fecundity assemblage left in a domestic site from one meant to bind or curse.[58]

Much as Richard Alston has observed of the archaeology of the house itself, the primary texts used in this chapter cannot reflect on matters of socialization or of identity, generally vital to domestic life; however, they do reflect on domestic reproduction and on domestic economy, extending as this does to spaces beyond the house itself.[59] They reflect on the house as a materialization of domestic anxieties about procreation and harmonious hierarchy, and on the house and its portals as material extensions of the vulnerable bodies within. Although we may speak of these anxieties generally in terms of the demonic, the range of apotropaic and binding spells we have seen demonstrate a common perspective that supernatural beings might be "sent" by enemies, that the nefarious agency entering the house may well be sorcery of one kind or another, and that evils must be enumerated and repelled in all their forms, from scorpions to malevolent Persians.

Furthermore, these texts show not only the experience and exploitation of domestic vulnerability to supernatural threats; they also show the active and creative integration of Christian idioms, names, and liturgical phrases to lend authority to protective ritual or even curses. In fact, this integration of Christian elements is the only indication of historical development apparent among these materials, and then only as a development from the very different inscribed ritual corpora of an earlier period, like the so-called Greek Magical Papyri.[60] Domestic religion, broadly conceived, is remarkably consistent in its values and fears—certainly by the evidence of the texts in this study, which range over several centuries.[61] While the Christianization of magical *texts* has been associated with a greater attention to the protective, the amuletic, and the therapeutic than in earlier times, the materials I have explored here reflect a wide range of aggressive *as well as* protective rituals, both oral and inscribed, which were apparently purveyed by the same types of specialists.[62] These specialists were experts in liturgical and ecclesiastical lore, sometimes on the margins of institutional religious life and sometimes closely affiliated. Indeed, the very use of Christian symbols in these materials required the active mediation of such a literate ritual specialist, quite likely a monk, who was regarded (and regarded himself) principally as a master of the magic of the written word. We can see the agency of such experts in improvising liturgy, composing demonologies (with or without attention to social threats like evil eye), conveying the authority of comprehensive protection through writing, and editing charms into and out of codex collections.

But we must also infer the agency of members of households in appealing to such experts as representatives of Christian authority and efficacy, as well as in accepting the imaginative constructions of domestic vulnerability produced in consultation.[63] That is, people in their domestic spheres were clearly ready to think about demons, evil eye, and sorcery in ways that reflected Christian traditions. Likewise, the scribal agents behind the writing of these texts clearly respected the particular fears and zones brought to them by agents of the domestic sphere. The Christianization of responses to domestic vulnerability corresponds to broader Christian currents in Egypt, like the promotion of the cross itself as an apotropaic (as opposed to redemptive or narrative) symbol.[64]

Notes

1 Abbreviations: *ACM* = Meyer and Smith 1994; *AKZ* = Kropp 1931; *PGM*= Preisendanz 1973; *CTBS* = Gager 1992; *GMPT* = Betz 1986. This paper was presented at Ewa Wipsycka's Late Antique Seminar, University of Warsaw, May 19, 2022.
2 P. Ryl. Copt. 100 = *ACM* #65, tr. *ACM*, 125. On the cult of St. Leontius, see Papaconstantinou 2001, 137–38. On the ticket oracle tradition in Egypt, see Frankfurter 1998, chap. 4; 2005; 2017, 130–38.
3 Huebner 2013, chap. 6
4 On conceptualizing "domestic religion" in Roman Egypt, see Frankfurter 1998, 131–44; 2008; 2016, 2017, chap. 2, drawing on theoretical models by Bell 1992; Smith 2004; Hodder 2003. See now Abdelwahed 2016; Wilburn 2018.
5 On figurines from the Christian Period as evidence for domestic ritual, see Frankfurter 2015a.
6 For the purposes of this chapter, "magic" will signify areas of ritual that involve the materialization of power and the creation of material (including inscribed) assemblages, as well as texts that instruct in the preparation of such materials. See in general Frankfurter 2019a.
7 See Koenig 1994; Frankfurter 1998, chap. 5; Dieleman 2005, 2019.
8 See Richter 1997; Van der Vliet 2011; De Bruyn 2017; Frankfurter 2017, 189–211; Frankfurter 2019b.
9 An alternative model of freelance (nonecclesiastic or temple-affiliated) *literati* is offered in Love 2016, 278–82. Van Minnen (1998) associates literary collecting and production in the earlier Roman Period also with temple priests. See also Frankfurter 1998, chap. 6.
10 Frankfurter 2006a, chap. 2; see in general Stewart 1991.
11 *Suppl. Mag.* ##47 (= *CTBS* #28), 6–7, 18–19; 48, J-K, 6, 20, 32; 49, 17–18; 50, 17–51.
12 Evil eye: see Bailliot 2010; Dunbabin and Dickie 1983; Elliott 2016. Sorcery thus comprises acts of binding and cursing based on ritual expertise or consultation with ritual experts. Margaret Mitchell (2022, 135–39) offers an incisive analysis of a sermon by John Chrysostom in which the fourth-century Antiochene bishop recommends placing scripture amulets throughout the Christian house to protect inhabitants from malicious *pornai.*
13 On demonology as the conceptualization of liminality, see Smith 1978. On the integral function of ritual specialists in assembling demonologies, see Frankfurter 2006a, chap. 2.
14 On such external iconographic apotropaia see Mitchell 2007; Wilburn 2019, 572–84.
15 Frankfurter 2018. Zellmann-Rohrer (2020) makes a compelling case that these amulets reflect a more elaborate mythology of fever healing in antiquity.
16 Frankfurter 2017, 218–26; cf. Frankfurter 2007.
17 Huebner 2016, 162–64; on the magic of portals in general, Wilburn 2019, 585–89.
18 See the compilation of Naveh and Shaked 1985; Levene 2012; and, on the ritual use of these bowls, Frankfurter 2015b.
19 JBA 57, 59, ed./tr. (Shaked, Ford, and Bhayro 2013, 254, 260). A parallel study to this one has been initiated by Mokhtarian 2022.
20 Vienna G337 (Rainer 1) = *ACM* #20, ed. PGM P10, tr. *ACM*, 45.
21 Cf. Michigan 593 = *ACM* 133, which includes an application "to cause a revelation to be given to you in a dream."
22 I have arranged the following two translations according to the line breaks in the original artifacts.
23 *tēn thuran tēn Aphroditēn*, most likely an accusative of invocation (cf. Smyth, *Greek Grammar* §1596), where Aphrodite is associated with the door. I thank Fritz Graf for consultation (12/2018) on this odd phrase.
24 P. Oxy VII.1060 = *PGM* P2 = *ACM* #25, tr. *ACM*, 49, translation emended. While I have reproduced the lines of the text the way they appear on the papyrus, it is clear that the receding letters of the name Aphrodite in the first lines—if laid out in a triangle—would produce a triangular *klima* design (as both PGM and ACM publications show). But the purpose of the *klima* is not clear: is the sacred name Aphrodite being *expanded* to gain graphic powers (see Frankfurter 2019c) or, conversely, is a nefarious name meant to be *dissipated* through the disappearing letters (Faraone 2012)?
25 P. Oslo I.5 = *PGM* P3 = *ACM* #26, tr. *ACM*, 50, translation emended.

26 *neshēli tērou shasjpaou; touōnah ralamp ajen laouei shōni*, implying that the amulet is meant to protect her for subsequent children, who (b1) should be kept alive as they arrive, or (b2) subsequent children should hopefully arrive yearly [*ralamp*, from *rompe*].
27 Lond. Or. 5525 = *ACM* #64, ed. *AKZ* 1: 15–16, tr. *ACM*, 120–21. See also Crum 1905, 253.
28 Goody 1977, 74–111.
29 On the magical power of listing, see Gordon 1999; Frankfurter 2006a, 14–20.
30 Michigan 593, 8–9, 10–11, ed. Worrell 1930, 248, 249 = *ACM* #133, tr. *ACM*, 306–7. See also Mirecki 1994.
31 Cf. Ps 121: 8, a popular apotropaic phrase in late antiquity represented on lintel inscriptions in Syria.
32 Leiden Anastasi 9, 1r-v = *ACM* #134; ed. Pleyte and Boeser 1897, tr. *ACM*, 314.
33 See Boozer 2017, 178, on the status and location of the *aulē* in the Egyptian house.
34 Leiden, Anastasi 9, 1v-3r = *ACM* #134, ed. Pleyte and Boeser 1897, tr. *ACM*, 315.
35 See Brown 1970.
36 British Library Or. 7029, f. 73a-b, ed. Budge 1915, 519–20; cf. Dongola Burial Vault T28, in Łajtar and Van der Vliet 2017, 72–74.
37 Frankfurter 2017, 76–87; Brakke 2009.
38 Favret-Saada and Cullen 1989; Favret-Saada 2015.
39 Since some scholars of antiquity eschew "sorcery" for the term *malign magic* (see Eidinow 2019; *Magic, Ritual, and Witchcraft* 14, 2 [2019]), I will define it here as deliberate, historical efforts through ritual performance and material assemblage to subvert the agency, fortune, or life of another, often under the direction or expertise of a ritual specialist.
40 See in general Wilburn 2019, 597–98.
41 P. Macquarie 1, 1, ##3, 9, 12, 5, ed. Choat and Gardner 2013.
42 Ashmolean Museum 1981.940 = *ACM* #84, ed. (Smither 1939), tr. *ACM*, 177.
43 Heidelberg copt. 686, 15: #5; 16: #20 = *ACM* 135.
44 Michigan 593, 11, ed. Worrell 1930, 249 = *ACM* #133, tr. *ACM*, 307.
45 Lix tetrax: (McCown 1922, 29*; Duling 1983, 969); Rhyx Miameth: (McCown 1922, 59*)
46 PGM no. O2 (2: 233–34) = *CTBS* #35.
47 Oxford, Bodleian coptic ms. C.(P) 4 = *ACM* #91, tr. *ACM*, 192.
48 Michigan 1523, ed. Worrell 1935, 3–4 = *ACM* #108, tr. *ACM*, 218
49 Heidelberg copt. 679 (perhaps eleventh century CE), ed. Bilabel and Grohmann 1934, 410–14 = *ACM* #110, tr. *ACM*, 222.
50 P. Kellis copt 35, ed./tr. Mirecki, Gardner, and Alcock 1997.
51 *PGM* XXXVI. 240, tr. *GMPT*, 275.
52 P. Mich. VI. 423–24; see Frankfurter 2006b; Wilburn 2012, 95–102.
53 Frankfurter 2006b, 42–45.
54 On the range of problems that afflict households in Roman Egypt, see Abdelwahed, chapter 6, this volume.
55 See Alston, chapter 7, this volume.
56 Pearce 2020, 484. In Apuleius's *Metamorphoses,* the witch Meroe is imagined as impervious to all such domestic boundaries, breaking into tightly secured rooms (I.11) and, on the other hand, using the security of doors and windows to shut in a whole village (I.10). Thus she is a nightmare beyond the capacity of any *apotropaion* to repel.
57 Wilburn (2018, 105–8) interprets a small female figurine found in the basement of a house in Karanis as part of an erotic binding assemblage, but it may equally be a protective or fecundity object.
58 See again Wilburn 2018; and especially on the archaeology of domestic magical assemblages, Hutton 2016.
59 Alston 2007, 373–74.
60 On the wide differences in genre and scribality between the two corpora see Dieleman 2019; Van der Vliet 2019.
61 Features of domestic religion in Roman and late antique Egypt, see Frankfurter 1998, 131–42; 2017, 38–54.

62 On the development of "magic" in Egypt as a function of Christianization, see Shandruk 2012 and now, especially, De Bruyn 2017.
63 Frankfurter 2017.
64 See Frankfurter 2004.

Works Cited

Abdelwahed, Y.E.H. 2016. *Houses in Graeco-Roman Egypt: Arenas for Ritual Activity*. Oxford: Archaeopress.

Alston, R. 2007. "Some Theoretical Considerations and a Late Antique House from Roman Egypt." *British School at Athens Studies* 15: 373–78.

Bailliot, M. 2010. *Magie et sortilèges dans l'Antiquité romaine: archéologie des rituels et des images*. Paris: Hermann Éditeurs.

Bell, C.M. 1992. *Ritual Theory, Ritual Practice*. New York: Oxford University Press.

Betz, H.D. 1986. *The Greek Magical Papyri in Translation*. Chicago: University of Chicago Press.

Bilabel, F., and A. Grohmann. 1934. *Griechische, Koptische und Arabische Texte zur Religion und Religiösen Literature in Ägyptens Spätzeit*. Veröffentlichungen Aus Den Badischen Papyrus-Sammlungen 5. Heidelberg: Verlag der Universitätsbibliothek.

Boozer, A.L. 2017. "Towards an Archaeology of Household Relationships in Roman Egypt." In *Mediterranean Families in Antiquity Households, Extended Families, and Domestic Space*, edited by S. R. Huebner and G. Nathan, 174–203. Hoboken, NJ: John Wiley.

Brakke, D. 2009. *Demons and the Making of the Monk: Spiritual Combat in Early Christianity*. Cambridge: Harvard University Press.

Brown, P. 1970. "Sorcery, Demons, and the Rise of Christianity from Late Antiquity into the Middle Ages." In *Witchcraft Confessions and Accusations*, edited by M. Douglas, 17–45. London: Tavistock.

Budge, E.A.W. 1915. *Miscellaneous Coptic Texts in the Dialect of Upper Egypt*. Coptic Texts 5. London: British Museum.

Choat, M., and I. Gardner, eds. 2013. *A Coptic Handbook of Ritual Power (P. Macq. I 1)*. Macquarie Papyri 1. Brepols: Turnhout.

Crum, W.E. 1905. *Catalogue of the Coptic Manuscripts in the British Museum*. London: British Museum.

De Bruyn, T. 2017. *Making Amulets Christian: Artefacts, Scribes, and Contexts*. Oxford: Oxford University Press.

Dieleman, J. 2005. *Priests, Tongues, and Rites: The London-Leiden Magical Manuscripts and Translation in Egyptian Ritual, 100–300 CE*. Religions in the Graeco-Roman World 153. Leiden: Brill Academic Pub.

Dieleman, J. 2019. "The Greco-Egyptian Magical Papyri." In *Guide to the Study of Ancient Magic*, edited by D. Frankfurter, 283–321. Religions in the Graeco-Roman World 189. Leiden: Brill.

Duling, D.C. 1983. "Testament of Solomon." In *Old Testament Pseudepigrapha*, edited by J.H. Charlesworth, 935–87. Vol. 1. Garden City, NY: Doubleday.

Dunbabin, K.M.D., and M.W. Dickie. 1983. "Invida Rumpantur Pectora: The Iconography of Phthonos/Invidia in Graeco-Roman Art." *Jahrbuch für Antike und Christentum* 26: 7–37.

Eidinow, E. 2019. "Magic and Social Tension." In *Guide to the Study of Ancient Magic*, edited by D. Frankfurter, 746–74. Religions in the Graeco-Roman World. Leiden: Brill.

Elliott, J.H. 2016. *Beware the Evil Eye: The Evil Eye in the Bible and the Ancient World: Greece and Rome*. Vol. 2. Eugene, OR: Cascade Books.

Faraone, C. 2012. *Vanishing Acts on Ancient Greek Amulets: From Oral Performance to Visual Design*. London: Institute of Classical Studies.

Favret-Saada, J. 2015. *The Anti-Witch*. Translated by Matthew Carey. Chicago: Hau Books.

Favret-Saada, J., and C. Cullen. 1989. "Unbewitching as Therapy." *American Ethnologist* 16 (1): 40–56.

Frankfurter, D. 1998. *Religion in Roman Egypt*. Princeton: Princeton University Press.

Frankfurter, D. 2004. "The Binding of Antelopes: A Coptic Frieze and Its Egyptian Religious Context." *Journal of Near Eastern Studies* 63 (2): 97–109.

Frankfurter, D. 2005. "Voices, Books, and Dreams: The Diversification of Divination Media in Late Antique Egypt." In *Mantikê: Studies in Ancient Divination*, edited by S.I. Johnston and P.T. Struck, 233–54. Leiden: Brill.

Frankfurter, D. 2006a. *Evil Incarnate: Rumors of Demonic Conspiracy and Ritual Abuse in History*. Princeton: Princeton University Press.

Frankfurter, D. 2006b. "Fetus Magic and Sorcery Fears in Roman Egypt." *Greek, Roman, and Byzantine Studies* 46: 37–62.

Frankfurter, D. 2007. "Demon Invocations in the Coptic Magic Spells." In *Actes Du Huitième Congrès International d'Études Coptes*, edited by N. Bosson and A. Boud'hors, 453–66. Vol. 2. Leuven: Peeters.

Frankfurter, D. 2008. "The Interpenetration of Ritual Spaces in Late Antique Religions: An Overview." *Archiv für Religionsgeschichte* 10: 211–22.

Frankfurter, D. 2015a. "Female Figurines in Early Christian Egypt: Reconstructing Lost Practices and Meanings." *Material Religion* 11 (2): 190–223.

Frankfurter, D. 2015b. "Scorpion/Demon: On the Origin of the Mesopotamian Apotropaic Bowl." *Journal of Near Eastern Studies* 74 (1): 9–18.

Frankfurter, D. 2016. "The Spaces of Domestic Religion in Late Antique Egypt." *Archiv Für Religionsgeschichte* 18/19: 7–23.

Frankfurter, D. 2017. *Christianizing Egypt: Syncretism and Local Worlds in Late Antiquity*. Princeton: Princeton University Press.

Frankfurter, D. 2018. "The Threat of Headless Beings: Constructing the Demonic in Christian Egypt." In *Fairies, Demons, and Nature Spirits: "Small Gods" at the Margins of Christendom*, edited by M. Ostling, 57–78. Palgrave Historical Studies in Witchcraft and Magic. London: Palgrave Macmillan.

Frankfurter, D., ed. 2019a. *Guide to the Study of Ancient Magic*. Religions in the Graeco-Roman World 189. Leiden: Brill.

Frankfurter, D. 2019b. "Sortes, Scribality, and Syncretism: Ritual Experts and the Great Tradition in Byzantine Egypt." In *My Lots Are in Thy Hands: Sortilege and Its Practitioners in Late Antiquity*, edited by A.-M. Luijendijk and W.E. Klingshirn, 211–31. Religions in the Graeco-Roman World 188. Leiden: Brill.

Frankfurter, D. 2019c. "The Magic of Writing in Mediterranean Antiquity." In *Guide to the Study of Ancient Magic*, edited by D. Frankfurter, 626–58. Religions in the Graeco-Roman World 189. Leiden: Brill.

Gager, J.G., ed. 1992. *Curse Tablets and Binding Spells from the Ancient World*. New York: Oxford University Press.

Goody, J. 1977. *The Domestication of the Savage Mind*. Cambridge: Cambridge University Press.

Gordon, R.L. 1999. " 'What's in a List?' Listing in Greek and Graeco-Roman Malign Magical Texts." In *The World of Ancient Magic: Papers from the First International Samson Eitrem Seminar*, edited by D.R. Jordan, H. Montgomery, and E. Thomassen, 239–77. Papers from the Norwegian Institute at Athens 4. Bergen: Norwegian Institute at Athens.

Hodder, I. 2003. "The Domus: Some Problems Reconsidered." In *Archaeology Beyond Dialogue*, edited by I. Hodder, 99–109. Salt Lake City: University of Utah Press.

Huebner, S.R. 2013. *The Family in Roman Egypt: A Comparative Approach to Intergenerational Solidarity and Conflict*. Cambridge: Cambridge University Press.

Huebner, S.R. 2016. "Egypt as Part of the Mediterranean? Domestic Space and Household Structures in Roman Egypt." In *Mediterranean Families in Antiquity: Households, Extended Families, and Domestic Space*, edited by S.R. Huebner and G. Nathan, 154–73. Oxford: Blackwell.

Hutton, R., ed. 2016. *Physical Evidence for Ritual Acts, Sorcery and Witchcraft in Christian Britain: A Feeling for Magic*. Houndmills: Palgrave Macmillan.

Koenig, Y. 1994. *Magie et magiciens dans l'Egypte ancienne*. Bibliothèque de l'Egypte ancienne. Paris: Pygmalion.

Kropp, A. 1931. *Ausgewählte Koptische Zaubertexte*. 3 vols. Bruxelles: Édition de la Fondation égyptologique reine Élisabeth.

Łajtar, A., and J. Van der Vliet. 2017. *Empowering the Dead in Christian Nubia: The Texts from a Medieval Funerary Complex in Dongola*. Journal of Juristic Papyrology Supplements 32. Warsaw: Journal of Juristic Papyrology.

Levene, D. 2012. *A Corpus of Magic Bowls: Incantation Texts in Jewish Aramaic from Late Antiquity*. 2nd ed. Southampton: Dan Levene.

Love, E.O.D. 2016. *Code-Switching with the Gods: The Bilingual (Old Coptic-Greek) Spells of PGM IV and Their Linguistic, Religious, and Socio-Cultural Context in Late Roman Egypt*. Zeitschrift für Ägyptische Sprache und Altertumskunde, Beihefte 4. Berlin: De Gruyter.

McCown, C.C 1922. *The Testament of Solomon*. Leipzig: Hinrichs.

Meyer, M.W., and R. Smith, eds. 1994. *Ancient Christian Magic: Coptic Texts of Ritual Power*. San Francisco: Harper.

Minnen, P. van. 1998. "Boorish or Bookish? Literature in Egyptian Villages in the Fayum in the Graeco-Roman Period." *Journal of Juristic Papyrology* 27: 99–184.

Mirecki, P.A. 1994. "The Coptic Wizard's Horde." *Harvard Theological Review* 87 (4): 435–60.

Mirecki, P.A, I. Gardner, and A. Alcock. 1997. "Magical Spell, Manichaean Letter." In *Emerging from Darkness: Studies in the Recovery of Manichaean Sources*, edited by P.A. Mirecki and J. BeDuhn, 1–32. Leiden: Brill.

Mitchell, J. 2007. "Keeping the Demons Out of the House: The Archaeology of Apotropaic Strategy and Practice in Late Antique Butrint and Antigoneia." In *Objects in Context, Objects in Use: Material Spatiality in Late Antiquity*, edited by L. Lavan, E. Swift, and T. Putzeys, 273–310. Leiden: Brill.

Mitchell, M.M. 2022. "John Chrysostom and Christian Love Magic: A Spellbinding Moment in the History of Interpretation of 1 Cor 7.2–4." *New Testament Studies* 68: 119–43.

Mokhtarian, J. 2022. "Families in the Incantation Bowls." Paper presented at Aramaic Incantation Bowls in Their Late Antique Jewish Context, Yale University/Zoom, April 4–5.

Naveh, J., and S. Shaked. 1985. *Amulets and Magic Bowls: Aramaic Incantations of Late Antiquity*. Jerusalem: Magnes Press.

Papaconstantinou, A. 2001. *Le culte des saints en Égypte, des Byzantins aux Abbassides: l'apport des inscriptions et des papyrus grecs et coptes*. Monde byzantin. Paris: CNRS Editions.

Pearce, C. 2020. "The Night-Side of Zangskar: Spirits, Landscape, and the Uncanny." *Material Religion* 16 (4): 471–90.

Pleyte, W., and P.A.A. Boeser. 1897. *Manuscrits Coptes Du Musée d'antiquités Des Pays-Bas à Leide*. Leiden: Brill.

Preisendanz, K. 1973. *Papyri Graecae Magicae: Die Griechischen Zauberpapyri*, edited by Albert Henrichs. 2 vols. Stuttgart: Teubner.

Richter, S.G. 1997. "Bemerkungen zu magischen Elementen koptischer Zaubertexte." In *Akten des 21. Internationalen Papyrologenkongresses*, edited by B. Kramer, 835–46. Stuttgart: Teubner.

Shaked, S., J.N. Ford, and S. Bhayro. 2013. *Aramaic Bowl Spells: Jewish Babylonian Aramaic Bowls*. Vol. 1. Magical and Religious Literature of Late Antiquity 1. Leiden: Brill.

Shandruk, W.M. 2012. "Christian Use of Magic in Late Antique Egypt." *Journal of Early Christian Studies* 20 (1): 31–57.

Smith, J.Z. 1978. "Towards Interpreting Demonic Powers in Hellenistic and Roman Antiquity." *Aufstieg und Niedergang der Römischen Welt* 2 16 (1): 425–39.

Smith, J.Z. 2004. "Here, There, and Anywhere." In *Relating Religion: Essays in the Study of Religion*, edited by J.Z Smith, 323–39. Chicago: University of Chicago Press.

Smither, P.C. 1939. "A Coptic Love-Charm." *Journal of Egyptian Archaeology* 25: 173–74.

Stewart, C. 1991. *Demons and the Devil: Moral Imagination in Modern Greek Culture*. Princeton: Princeton University Press.

Van der Vliet, J. 2011. "Literature, Liturgy, Magic: A Dynamic Continuum." In *Christianity in Egypt: Literary Production and Intellectual Trends in Late Antiquity: Studies in Honor of Tito Orlandi*, edited by P. Buzi and A. Camplani, 555–74. Rome: Institutum Patristicum Augustinianum.

Van der Vliet, J. 2019. "Christian Spells and Manuals from Egypt." In *Guide to the Study of Ancient Magic*, edited by D. Frankfurter, 322–50. Religions in the Graeco-Roman World 189. Leiden: Brill.

Wilburn, A.T. 2012. *Materia Magica: The Archaeology of Magic in Roman Egypt, Cyprus, and Spain*. Ann Arbor: University of Michigan Press.

Wilburn, A.T. 2018. "The Archaeology of Ritual in the Domestic Sphere: Case Studies from Karanis and Pompeii." In *Material Approaches to Roman Magic: Occult Objects and Supernatural Substances*, edited by A. Parker and S. Mckie, 103–14. TRAC Themes in Roman Archaeology 2. Oxford: Oxbow Books.

Wilburn, A.T. 2019. "Building Ritual Agency: Foundations, Floors, Doors, and Walls." In *Guide to the Study of Ancient Magic*, edited by D. Frankfurter, 555–602. Religions in the Graeco-Roman World 189. Leiden: Brill.

Worrell, W.H. 1930. "A Coptic Wizard's Hoard." *American Journal of Semitic Languages and Literatures* 46 (4): 239–62.

Worrell, W.H. 1935. "Coptic Magical and Medical Texts." *Orientalia* 4: 1–37, 184–94.

Zellmann-Rohrer, M. 2020. "Lawsuits with Headless Foes: A Greek Incantation Motif." *Archiv Für Religionsgeschichte* 21–22 (1): 51–83. https://doi.org/10.1515/arege-2020-0004.

PART V

Expanding the Household

Dwelling Practices in Monastic and Military Contexts

11

Three Monks and a House

The Archaeology of Monastic Houses in Byzantine Egypt

DARLENE L. BROOKS HEDSTROM

Apa Zacharias, Apa Philotheus, and Apa Mena were granted a house in Jeme in 734 CE by a woman named Anna (*P.KRU* 106).[1] The house was found within the bustling town of Jeme, located within the walls of Medinet Habu, the old mortuary complex for Ramesses III.[2] The house and its contents were to become the legal property of the monastic community of Apa Paul, located in the hills of Dra' Abu el-Naga.[3]

Late antique Thebes, where the three monks lived, reflects an integrated Christian landscape with monastic and nonmonastic families living in complex households. Each owned property either as an individual or as part of a community, relied on builders and masons to make repairs, and used legal bequeaths to ensure houses moved into the appropriate hands. Yet this portrait of monastic houses seems at odds with the description of monasticism found in the earliest histories and hagiographies, in which Egyptian monks were cast as individuals severed from their homes, familial ties, and all forms of ownership. What interest could three monks have in acquiring property in a nonmonastic town? Were their interests purely financial for the benefit of their monastery, or something else? How did this house and its contents compare with the archaeological record of earlier monastic housing found elsewhere in Roman and Byzantine Egypt?

Defining Monastic Households: Methods and Theories

To begin, we need to consider what it means to study the history of monastic living in terms of concepts shaped by shelter, home, and community. In the earliest sources on monastic living, the cell or room is the physical focal point for monastic spiritual living. In the *Sayings of the Desert Fathers,* monks struggled with ownership and community. A young monk was told to stay in his cell, for this would be the path to becoming a monk. But he wanted to repair the door and roof, for they were old.

He was not satisfied with the conditions of his living quarters. His desire for a new door and roof reflected his spiritual immaturity.[4] On the one hand, the monk was encouraged to separate himself from the world by living in a cell alone, and on the other hand, he was admonished for his desire to improve his dwelling despite the cell's ability to "teach you everything."[5] Others, such as Abba Bessarion, who did not have a desire for a place to live or a house and lived more like an animal content in the natural world, did not have much difficulty leaving his previous life behind and sought the sand of the desert and the caves of the cliffs as his natural home.[6]

If we rely on the earliest presentation of monastic living, we might be left with the impression that monks only sought shelter because their bodies required it. Monastic literature is littered with stories of senior monks counseling younger colleagues to abandon the settled world: "He who flees from folk is like a bunch of ripe grapes, but he who is among folk is like an unripe grape."[7] The world, which often involved obligations of biological family and associated economic activities, impeded spiritual growth, withering a monk's spiritual state. The practical solution was physical separation that ostensibly limited, if not severed, familial and financial bonds.

Since monks moved into underutilized or abandoned landscapes to build their communities, they relied on their skills to build their spaces. John of Lycopolis was trained in carpentry and building and went to Mount Lycos to build his residence, which had a room for prayer, one for working and eating, and a third for the "needs of the flesh."[8] The spaces are not described in great detail, and in fact there was a general reticence about their built environments. Seeking pleasure in a building was discouraged: "If you have a cell with only just enough space for your head, do not under any circumstances build another one to have plenty of room in it."[9] Physical comfort paved a path toward temptations, which led to a lack of commitment to God. Such stories create one narrative of space and place, but that narrative does not reflect the complex story of how monks created a sense of place by building new monastic houses.

For example, there are far more occurrences of monks directing each other to see the anthropogenic landscape as a tool for successful ascetic living. "Unless an athlete spar with many, he cannot learn the skill of winning. . . . So, too, the monk; unless he be trained with brothers . . . he cannot live alone nor can he withstand his bad thoughts."[10] Staying physically within the cell was the real challenge, for it was in this new space, dedicated exclusively to a life for God, that monks experienced separation from the world and desired to flee *back* to the land of entanglements.

Therefore, it is not surprising when we find monks encouraging, or even admonishing, each other to remain within their dwellings or cells. For remaining within the cell was necessary in order to enhance spiritual progress.[11] Paul of Tamma, writing in the fourth century, equated the monastic dwelling with the embodiment of holiness in which the monk may internalize the fact of dwelling. His treatise *On the Cell* encourages monks to value the built environment: "Be wise and remain in your dwelling, which is your delight, and your cell will remain with you in your heart as you seek its blessing, and the labor of your cell will go with you to God."[12] The wise monk knows that his room, his cell, is the one place all monks share as the secure arena for spiritual work: "You shall be a wise man in your cell, building up your soul as you sit in your cell . . . while your soul and your thoughts watch God in astonishment, gazing at him all the days of your life."[13] The cell was a space that cultivated a spiritual mindset: "The person who learns the sweetness of the cell does not dishonor his neighbor in avoiding him."[14] These statements elucidate the importance of the house of monks as a performative space imbued with meaning that signals its difference or otherness from the houses found in their old communities.

Thomas Barrie explains the distinction between house and home as follows: the house is architectural or "material and instrumental" to one's physical and bodily existence, whereas the home is a "placeless idea, cultural construct, and historical object."[15] The intersection of instrumentality and cultural construct aids us in thinking about how we might reread monastic literature as it presents the monastic household. Viewing the monastic cell and the larger monastic community from an emic perspective allows for the "multiple realities" and "differing perceptions of reality" that are exhibited in monastic literature for a broader late antique Christian community.[16] Monastic authors fused the functionality or materiality of a dwelling to the concept of a "placeless" place, in which a monk internalized the architecture in a way that transcended the material world. We read of the complex and sometimes conflicting perceptions of what the monastic house is, what is used for, and whether a monk should treat it as a home.

Archaeological evidence of monastic settlements and individual houses or dwellings provides a unique collection of "big artifacts" for crafting a more nuanced history of the monastic house within a postprocessual view of buildings as unique expressions of the communities that built them. I find the concept of *emic* archaeology to be particularly useful in that it requires archaeologists to draw on literary and documentary sources as the "community's ideas," thus engendering a more culturally specific understanding of the built environment.[17] While I am limited in my ability to discuss monastic structures with the builders of the late antique monasteries, I read monastic letters and histories just as I "read" archaeological material to build a thicker interpretation of things as reflections of a community.[18] Tracing the historical path of monks without houses to the bequest of a house in an eighth century town is a fascinating story that will weave together the threads of monastic mythmaking, the brick and stone remains of monastic settlements, and faint whispers of monastic building activities found in documentary sources. In order to better understand how the three strands twist together, it is necessary to consider how the theoretical insights of household archaeology, together with a focus on "things," enhance our understanding of the various pieces of evidence.[19] The following analysis is not focused specifically on the features of monastic houses or their rooms—an attempt which would be more characteristic of the first decade of household archaeology[20]—but rather on exploring the monastic houses themselves as "big artifacts," as they inform us about the lived experience of individual monks and the relationship of houses to monastic inhabitants.[21]

There is a tension in the field of archaeology between archeologists working on materials as "a means to reach something else,"[22] such as to reconstruct the experience of monks or other individuals living in their houses, and those who focus on the "material non-human other," a perspective which ascribes agency to monastic houses as things worthy of study in their own right.[23] Put another way, archaeologists such as Ian Hodder, Bjørnar Olsen, and Timothy Webmoor outline the importance for the field to turn away from an anthropocentric view of materials[24] and to "turn to things" in which one "explore[s] how the objectness of things contributes to the ways things assemble *us*" and not vice versa.[25] Certainly, late antique Christian authors regarded monastic housing as a thing that could organize monks and create an order to living that was not possible in other environments. The call to take "things" seriously is not just a phenomenological or semantic exercise; the objective is an engaging path forward to reevaluate how we understand the relationship between materials and humans with the aim to treat them equally or at least symmetrically.[26] This means that we can also consider how even language found both in documentary and literary sources brings us closer to an emic archaeology of the monastic house by granting more value to the voices that describe homes, building, and living in a monastic community.

For example, late antique monastic communities referred to their houses with the Coptic term, *ma nshōpe*, which means "the place of dwelling," or more commonly "the dwelling place."[27] The monastic term replaces the usual secular terms for house found in our sources such as Greek *oikos* or Coptic *ēi*. It is also important to note that I do not use *monastery* or *cell* unless that is found in the original document. I also avoid *hermitage*, as this term is applied loosely to anything that is not clearly an enclosed monastery. *Hermitage* also does not reflect the reality of the appellations selected by monastic authors. The shift in nomenclature is significant, as the monastic *dwelling place* or the monastic *house* were, until recently, described in numerous ways by historians and archaeologists without much explanation. The choice to impart later medieval monastic terms onto the East, often from Western monasticism, obscured the identification of the living space as the space in which monks dwelt. Considering that household archaeology and the theoretical treatment of dwelling are at the heart of this discussion, it is even more appropriate to use *dwelling place* as the name given to the monastic houses found in the archaeological record.

Monastic Settlements and Houses

Kellia, or The Cells, is the most recognized site of early Egyptian monasticism. Located in the Delta, the monastic site is well known in late antique and medieval monastic literature, both in the East and the West, as one of the homes for the Desert Fathers, whose lives and spiritual accomplishments are recounted in the *Sayings of the Desert Fathers*. The popularity of the *Sayings* and the writings of residents from Kellia, in particular, formed the foundation for subsequent monastic communities in the East and the West.[28] Famous monastic authors, such as John Cassian and Evagrius, who lived at Kellia, presented the site as a nexus of spiritual and ascetic achievements without much attention to the physical world they inhabited.[29] In fact, it is difficult to recover the emic perspective of the monastic dwellings from their writings, which focus more on a monk's interior, spiritual work rather than one's interactions with the built environments more broadly. The landscape was essentially a canvas and did not merit much discussion or description. Recent scholarship draws our attention to how the writers crafted Egyptian monasticism for Christian readers who resided outside of Egypt and therefore presented a somewhat artificial portrait of monasticism that was not based on the reality of the lived experience.[30]

The disconnect between the *realia* of monastic life at Kellia and the words of monastic authors was evident with the first archaeological seasons of work at the site in the 1960s.[31] While the texts may present a story of a desert dotted with monks living with one or two others in modest homes, the identification of more than 1,500 monastic complexes, sometimes with sixty to eighty rooms, significantly undermines the mythologized and solitary landscape that might emerge from the words of Evagrius. In many ways, the spatial layout of the residences, with kitchens, latrines, courtyards, and reception areas, is similar to that of a Romano-Egyptian house or villa. Both the secular villa and the monastic residence provided comfortable living quarters and domestic areas for food preparation and storage, in addition to spaces for meeting or entertaining guests.

Documentary evidence from the rooms and complexes at Kellia in the form of dipinti serves as the main body of evidence of those who lived and moved within the houses at the site. The majority of the inscriptions were written in Boharic Coptic and in Greek, with a few in Arabic.[32] The painted inscriptions include references to a monk's name, his title, and occasionally his place of origin or his skill. In a complex identified as QR 306, monks used the walls to petition prayers and intercession by those who could read the walls.[33] This practice indicates an awareness that the spaces in which words were painted or inscribed could be part of performative, paraliturgical actions that were part of daily life.[34] In one dipinto, we read of a curse on anyone who removed items from the monastic dwelling, for such actions would result in total separation from God.[35] Other dipinti directly address readers with the expectation that Christian readers, presumably members of the community, would participate in actions that further created bonds between those living in other buildings.[36] The fact that no monastic archive survives from Kellia also impedes our ability to construct a nuanced narrative of how the monastic household interacted with each other or their physical residence. In contrast, the extensive Coptic corpus produced by Shenoute of Atripe (c. 347–465 CE), a prolific abbot of the White Monastery Federation in southern Egypt, and his successor Besa (r. 466–late 5th c. CE) describes the intersection between space, place, and the monk's spiritual being.[37] At Kellia we must rely on the documentary evidence of prayers painted or inscribed on walls to build a sense of place and dwelling.[38]

To illustrate the great diversity of monastic settlements and the status of Kellia as just one of many communities, I will examine four different sites that represent various forms of monastic building and house construction, thereby indicating the individuality of monastic households in Egypt. My selection of these sites serves as a counterbalance to the general perception that monasticism can be divided only into two categories: solitary dwellings, following the model of Antony, or communal monasteries, following the household model of Pachomius. For scholars of monasticism, this binary has been shown to be false, largely crafted by later authors and not based on experiences with actual monastic communities. Indeed, the monastic communities that I discuss exhibit monastic site designs and the construction of a household that could vary greatly, and these variations may allow us to infer that specific sites were known for their version of ascetic practice. Unlike later Western monastic communities, such as the Cistercians or Augustinians, where each monastery followed a similar spatial plan, Egyptian monastic sites did not follow a predictable, architectural plan.[39]

The four sites, moving from north to south, include the Monastery of Apa Jeremias at Saqqara, the Mountain of Cells at Jabal Nalqun, the Monastery of Apa Thomas at Wadi Sarga, and the semisubterranean dwellings at Esna in Upper Egypt. The four communities represent the diversity of the anthropogenic landscape of monasticism in terms of the spatial configuration of the community. In addition, each site differs from the others, with unique architectural design elements. The execution and placement of houses for construction of a monastic community and landscape permit us to examine the structures not only as windows onto monastic life, but also as reflections of how houses and their very components of brick, stone, and plaster responded to the natural environment and assembled monks.[40] The mutability of the built environment itself, as a thing made of smaller things from the surrounding area, such as stones, mud bricks, plaster, wood, and reeds, is an essential element for reconstructing how monastic communities were built anew or remodeled from abandoned spaces.

The four sites also serve as examples of communities of practice, which can be read in two ways—the practice of monasticism and the practice of building. Monastic letters and even the highly structured monastic rules and hagiographies point to the ways in which monks "negotiate with one another."[41] The houses create the locus in which "important relations and interactions are not just between people but also between people and the places they inhabit and the material culture they deploy."[42] The role of monks as makers in a fluctuating community of senior and junior members may inform how we read phases of buildings and even phases of expansion and construction as monastic sites.[43]

The first monastic site that I consider is the Monastery of Apa Thomas at Wadi Sarga, excavated in 1913 and 1914 in Middle Egypt (figure 11.1). The site includes a complex domestic settlement with a variety of houses with several rooms of at least one story. Previously known only through the 1922 publication of the ostraka from Wadi Sarga, the extensive evidence of the Monastery of Apa Thomas is being published for the first time by the British Museum.[44] The site was occupied in the late fifth or early sixth century, and the monks at Apa Thomas lived in apartments built along a steep hillside with seven terraces until the eighth century.[45] The settlement is located 11.5 kilometers inland from the Nile, and a monk could have reached the monastery on foot just under three hours or by animal in one and half hours. The presence of a large stable and numerous references to camel and donkey herders suggest transportation to and from the monastery was frequent and relatively easy, should one come by the Nile.

One cluster of domestic housing is known as the North Houses, with thirty-three individual rooms divided along seven terraces cut into the bedrock of the wadi (figure 11.2). One way to approach the household nature of the domestic quarter

Figure 11.1. Mud-brick buildings of the Monastery of Apa Thomas at Wadi Sarga. View east shows agricultural fields and the Nile beyond. (AES. Ar. 719. Courtesy of the Trustees of the British Museum.)

of the monastic site is to ascertain which rooms were part of a house or if the entire structure on its seven terraces was considered a single house. The extensive documentary sources recovered from the various middens at Wadi Sarga do not discuss the built environment at Apa Thomas in ways that allow us to ascribe particular ownership of one space to any one monk, although the sources do allow for a prosopography of those living at the site and serving in leadership positions.[46] Therefore, the houses as things themselves become the subject of analysis. Much as with houses from Neolithic and Protoliterate sites, we must consider the material remains as our sole guide in examining the boundaries of the households as defined by the architecture and the environment.

The nature of the wadi required builders to cut into the hill face and use stone boulders to create a stable foundation for the various rooms. Mud bricks were used to build the walls of the rooms, which were later plastered and painted, sometimes with images of saints, animals, and even dipinti.[47] In many cases, the builders took advantage of the limestone cliff to carve a bench along the north end of the building so that the room was equipped with a natural bench for sitting and sleeping. The remaining components of the room were then built around the geofeature. The adaptation and incorporation of the natural environment into the very fabric of the rooms demonstrate the notion that physical space had agency—space, itself, could

Figure 11.2. Excavation and clearing at the North Houses of the Monastery of Apa Thomas at Wadi Sarga. The photo illustrates the use of plaster, mortar, thin limestone chips, and mud brick in the design of the various rooms. (AES Ar. 719. Courtesy of the Trustees of the British Museum.)

organize individuals into specific activities for sleeping or daily crafts. Similarly, the location of small ovens and stoves in only four of the seven terraces suggests that activities, such as cooking and baking, took place in private kitchen spaces rather than communal kitchens shared by the entire monastic community.[48]

By reading the Apa Thomas ostraka and buildings together, we can see that monks identified with their houses, their belongings, and felt the need to keep order in a space in which houses were built against each other. In one letter (*O.Sarga* 169), Apa Enoch asks his son, Apa Mena, to bring wine to Apa Peter, who will then deliver the jugs to the dwelling place (*ma nshōpe*) of Apa Macarius in the community.[49] The letters are not just instructions, but also signs of permissions needed within the community to allow access to go into and out of houses to retrieve or deliver items. Such actions illustrate how moving through houses, or dwelling places, required testaments of communication. In another letter (*O.Sarga* 100), Patermoute tells another monk to "go into the dwelling place (*ma nshōpe*)" and into the church to retrieve rope and fishing nets in exchange for twelve loaves of bread.[50] One monk received a letter (*O.Sarga* 101) stating, "As soon as you shall receive this potsherd, go to the dwelling place (*ma nshōpe*)" and take a balance, a ball of netting, and a length of rope to Papa Pihew, who had told Apa Apollo he wished for these things.[51]

Where did these things—nets, rope, a balance, bread, and wine—rest within the various dwellings in the North Houses? The monastic houses held such items on the various built-in shelves and on bone or horn hooks embedded into the very fabric of the walls. We can observe the presence of thresholds, door jambs, and the remains of framing for wooden doors to determine whether some rooms were closed and locked while others were not. We can even place objects within rooms, but can we place people within the rooms? If we return to the spatial and environmental setting of the houses as expressed in the letters from Apa Thomas, we may observe who is asked to travel between houses and who is not. The instructions reflect the social status of particular monks and bring us closer to consider a social archaeology of the site, which demonstrates that Papa Pihew, Apa Phoebmmon, Apa Macarius, and Apa Petermoute do *not* travel, but Apa Mena and Apa Peter must. The letters and the physical remains of monastic houses offer us clues as to how monks interacted at the Monastery of Apa Thomas. By focusing on the houses, and their contents, as material, nonhuman others, we can begin to look past the individual monks and consider what the materials of Wadi Sarga may have required of the builders seeking to create a new community for monastic habitation.

When we compare Apa Thomas to the near contemporaneous monastic sites in Upper Egypt of Esna and ʻAdaima, we have less material to work with, as the latter sites do not have extensive written sources to give voice to the material remains. While Wadi Sarga is roughly a one-hectare site, Esna covers an area of 1,150 hectares with two clusters of buildings. Known for their unusual architecture as geotectures, meaning they are architectural features comprised of the natural environment—in this case, the desert floor, Esna and ʻAdaima housed monks physically below ground. Esna is the better known of the two sites, as information about it was published by the French Institute in an extensive, four-volume publication.[52] But both sites are similar in design and in execution. ʻAdaima shares the same features, spatial design, and contemporary ceramic remains and was likely occupied at the same time as Esna.[53] Monastic builders carved their dwellings so that the houses were hidden, literally, in the desert.[54] Was this decision made intentionally to align with monastic myths of asceticism and separation from the world? Or could the reason relate more to the natural environment, whose cooling properties would have created a more appropriate living space that was cool in the summer and warm in the winter? What can the houses at Esna tell us?

As semisubterranean dwellings, the kitchen and other rooms at Esna and ʻAdaima are accessed by a staircase which leads from ground level to a courtyard cut into the natural shale. Each residence contains a kitchen.[55] The nine buildings reflect uniform planning, with a clear design with a ground-level staircase, which leads down to a subsurface, open-air courtyard. Three or four additional rooms extend from the courtyard, creating interior spaces for the residents. At least two of the doorways led to very different kinds of rooms: a private kitchen and a room with a central east niche with walls painted and inscribed with prayers and images of saints. Excavators interpreted the additional rooms as either storage areas or sleeping quarters, based on the fact that the rooms were undecorated and lacking windows. In three cases, houses numbered 4, 7, and 9 had two decorated rooms with a central niche and accompanying annexes. The designs are consistent in layout, reflecting a conscious choice to employ architectural features, such as the semisubterranean plan that includes a descending staircase to an open-air courtyard; a large prayer room with painted niches; smaller, secondary rooms; and a kitchen with ovens and stoves.

The identity of the community is unknown, although we do have the names of male monks such as Apa Mena, Phib, Victor, Touan, John, Philox, Abraham, and Paphnoute. At Esna, as a male, homosocial community, there is much that we can discern from the houses themselves about the nature of the monastic life of its residents. They had private kitchens, cisterns, and extensive storage rooms, complete with large amphorae. They painted prayers of intercession on the walls of central rooms and provided Christian genealogies of saints. The multiroomed residences are quite elaborate, if not luxurious, for only two individuals, if we assume one person slept in each of the windowless rooms. They also took most of their belongings with them when they left this community. The residences at Esna bear no sign of conflagration, but only the natural erosion that would be expected for any building left unprotected for centuries in the desert. The sparse documentary sources from the site consist entirely of dipinti. The epigraphic and ceramic evidence suggests that occupation of the site was short-lived, from the early sixth century until the middle of the seventh century.

The layout of each house and the individual features of windows, alignment of air shafts, placement of kitchens and sand barriers, and niches reflect how the natural environment and the raw materials of the houses acted on the builders of this monastic community.[56] The execution of the construction and replicated layout reveals a conscious response to build a kitchen underground and to provide a reliable source of water in the middle of the desert plain (figure 11.3). Each room's placement around an open courtyard also demonstrates an attunement to the movement of air, light, and even people in and out of the spaces. But, in comparison to other monastic settlements from the sixth century, the choices of arrangements are a departure from more normative forms of monastic habitation and construction.

The community's monastic identity is most evident in the architectural plan and the way that the structures became a part of the desertscape (figure 11.4). As semisubterranean buildings, the structures are submerged in the landscape, revealing a keen awareness of environmental factors for building in the desert. Windowsills were designed to provide the most effective indirect light to rooms accessed from the open-air courtyard throughout the day. Ventilation shafts were positioned in corners of walls to facilitate the movement of fresh air into rooms not directly accessed from the courtyard, making the most of the natural winds across the desert. Even though all the doorways were equipped with socket doors to be closed as needed, half a meter-high revetment walls were built outside the doors, in the courtyard, to alleviate the constant need to move sand away from entrances. The marking of doorways with painted crosses, Christian dipinti, images of saints and monks (in a few cases), and painted architectural accents provided the physical markers of a living religious practice within a domestic setting.

The only epigraphic evidence that specifically references the houses is found in house number 4. The dipinto is written on the east wall of the north oratory. Here

Figure 11.3. A kitchen in a semisubterranean house at the monastic site of 'Adaima. (Courtesy of IFAO. Photo by J.-Fr. Gout in 1974.)

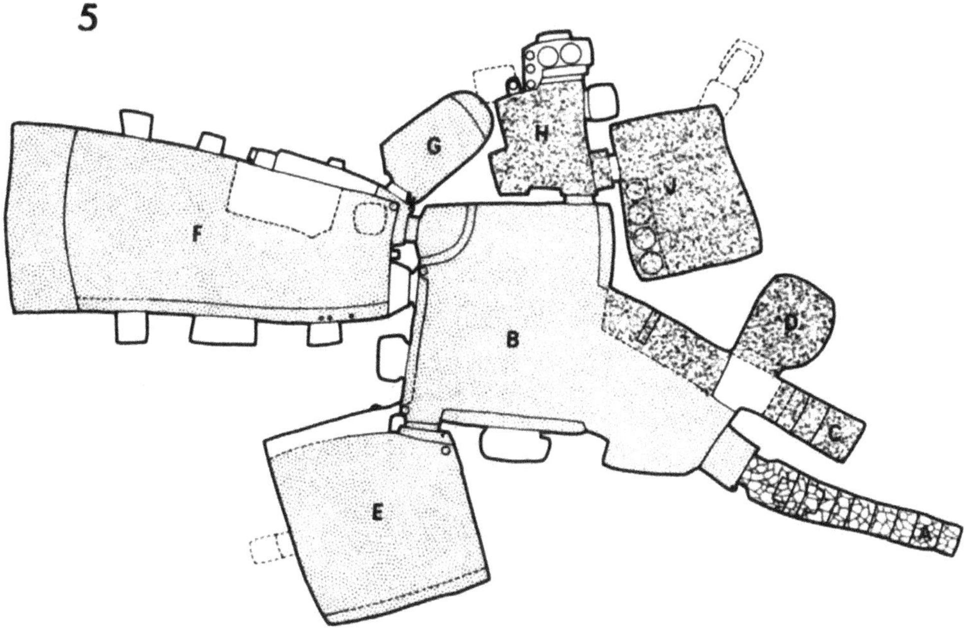

Figure 11.4. Plan of dwelling number 5 at Esna. (After S. Sauneron and J. Jacquet, *Les ermitage chrétiens du desert d'Esna* I. [Cairo : IFAO, 1972], plate XII.)

the author wrote a prayer, which was fairly illegible, but he included the phrase for "dwelling place" (*ma nshōpe*).[57] The same phrase is used to describe the terraced, monastic housing at the Monastery of Apa Thomas. Is the "dwelling place" a common name for smaller monastic residences? Does it appear at larger monastic sites? And does its usage persist after the seventh century?

Perhaps one of the best-known monastic sites from late antique Egypt is the Monastery of Apa Jeremias, located south of the Step Pyramid of Djoser at Saqqara. It was excavated from 1906–10 and the findings of this excavation were published immediately. Several pieces from this massive monastic settlement found their way into museum collections around the world and came to be considered hallmarks of what a Coptic monastery looked like. Subsequent analysis of the earlier excavated remains by Peter Grossmann places the development of the community around a large basilica church in the mid-sixth century.[58] After three centuries of expansion, the site was abandoned by the ninth century and never occupied again, although nonmonastic, Christian villages did continue into the ninth century.[59]

The archaeological excavation of the Monastery of Apa Jeremias provided the first opportunity to examine spatial relationships across a complex monastic settlement plan. The plan shows streets, footpaths, alleys, and seemingly planned spatial divisions of domestic quarters, which were separated from the more communal areas of church, infirmary, and refectory (figure 11.5). Like Apa Thomas, the Monastery of Apa Jeremias housed numerous letters, graffiti, and dipinti, which can augment the rich material remains recovered from the site. One of the significant challenges to analyzing the household nature of the material from Apa Jeremias is the fact that the archaeologist, James Quibell, failed to document any phases in his plans or discussions of various buildings. His plan of the site, enhanced later by Grossmann, therefore reflects all the excavated areas of the settlement without any differentiation between additions, modifications, or restructuring that might alter our perception of how monks occupied the various houses. The plan is not a plan of the monastery at any given phase, but is rather a plan that reflects all the spaces that Quibell excavated, and thus does not necessarily help us understand how dwellers experienced monastic houses in late antiquity.

One of the claims of the material turn is that modern archaeologists did and do constrain our understanding of the past by what they value, select, draw, catalogue, and ascribe meaning to. There is not necessarily a way around this problem, but I would argue that in the case of Apa Jeremias, we see the monastic site of Apa Jeremias through the eyes of Quibell. He was quick to call each room a chapel and to divide houses into single roomed spaces that severed the spatial relationships the rooms once had to each other. Therefore, our sense of a monastic house was immediately shaped by Quibell's inferences. Because he was prejudiced by monastic myths of separation and privacy, he envisioned the spaces to be chapels, not sites of daily activities. He also neglected to discuss any rooms that were devoid of wall paintings or containing significant finds that would interest him or potential collectors or museums. In fact, he dismissed large swaths of the site as of little interest because of their domestic nature.[60] Therefore, while we can ascribe particular meaning to various spaces as monastic houses in the large communal settlement at the Monastery of

Figure 11.5. Plan of the Monastery of Apa Jeremias showing all the spaces excavated by James Quibell. The map does not reflect any phasing of rooms or areas of the settlement. (Plan by Peter Grossmann.)

Jeremias, we must recognize that our current understanding of the houses is largely shaped by, and also limited by, Quibell's reading of the evidence and not the full extent of the preserved remains of the houses.

The last site is a contemporary of Apa Jeremias but located in the southeast edge of the Fayum at the site of Dayr al-Naqlun. It is a monastic settlement comprised of three distinct residential areas, including a cluster of eighty monastic residences in the hills of Jabal Naqlun, a multiperiod site on the desert plateau with medieval Christian buildings, and a smaller, monastic community located by a canal. The Mountain of the Cells, as it was called in documentary sources, was first occupied as early as the fifth century, with its last residents living in the ninth century.[61] In the documentary papyri from the dwellings, each complex was called a monastery, *monastērion*, and not a dwelling place, *ma nshōpe*. It was only later, in the eighth and ninth centuries, that the monks adopted Coptic and then shifted to use the "dwelling place" to refer to their homes.

Figure 11.6. Monastic dwelling at Naqlun made of mud bricks, natural shale caves, and plaster. (Photo by author.)

The Polish excavations, led by Włodzimierz Godlewski, have explored residences with a central courtyard, enclosed by a wall, which gave access to a footpath along the cliffs (figure 11.6). Six of the residences have been fully excavated.[62] The residence of Phibamo, which was occupied in the late fifth century and was abandoned during the sixth century, is the largest of the residences in the cliffs, with eighteen rooms divided into six clusters connected by two courtyards.[63] Only two monks apparently lived here, with the apartments creating two separate homes connected by an open courtyard.[64]

Like the dwelling at Esna, each of the homes in the hills of Naqlun included a private kitchen complete with a least a stove and, less frequently, a bread oven. The monks living in these cliffs had homes that provided physical distance from the more communal and mixed community of nonmonastic and monastic persons at the main church. However, as at Esna, the houses here were carved from the shale cliffs, sealed with walls of plaster and mud bricks mixed with numerous straw inclusions. The various rooms were less refined in comparison to what is found at Apa Thomas and Apa Jeremias. Few dipinti and only the simplest wall paintings of crosses grace the walls of these homes. What are we to make of the Naqlun homes, the residents, and the nature of monastic houses in the Fayum? As found elsewhere, the locally available materials play a significant role in the shape of the homes. The coarse shale did not make the same quality of mud bricks seen elsewhere in the

Nile Valley or the Delta. This fact resulted in plastered walls that were cruder and rougher than those found elsewhere. The raw materials played a significant role in the shape of the houses at Naqlun, and decisions about the quality of the walls or the paintings adorning the surfaces may have nothing to do with the actual builders or the monastic preferences of the residents. We know from the excavated letters that visitors went to the monasteries in the hills, and all referred to the settlement as the Mountain of the Cells, rather than the Mountain of the Monasteries. In looking at the houses at Naqlun, we can observe similar patterns of house designs, with kitchens, courtyards, communal spaces for guests, prayer, and labor along with the undecorated rooms.

Read together, the four monastic sites reflect the diversity of monastic houses in late antique Egypt and encourage us to see how houses, made of bricks, stones, plaster, and unique features, helped create their own configurations. Stella Souvatzi reminds us that "households are in a constant state of transitions and it is in the continually shifting relationships within and between households that wider societal changes can be best understood."[65]

Things and Monastic Houses

Household archaeology offers engaging paths of inquiry for examining hitherto unsuspected nuances and multiple facets of monastic construction. While it is tempting to consider all monastic material culture as steeped in religious meaning and therefore sacred, this myopic view of the evidence erases the very nature of monastic living, which was structured around new, but fictive, kinship groups that were based in very earthly associations. Indeed, monastic bodies were often troubled by implications of sexual impropriety.[66] Thus physical spaces with locking doors or private rooms or even structured seating arrangements at meals could be places to transgress forbidden boundaries. Monks who violated such boundaries were accused of pursuing "friendship" with another, which was understood as a euphemism for same-sex desire.[67] The physical space of one's place at the monastic table or the privacy of one's own dwelling place, as defined by the locking door, could engender questions about one's celibacy and purity. A monk's door could hide or protect his ascetic purity inside. Or it could protect the transmission of one's desires from watchful eyes.

Doors, tables, and dwelling places are elements of architecture. As objects, they are, as Cynthia Baker states, discursive things that require analysis. They are not merely transparent or objective facts that only require description. Baker persuasively articulates how "material objects . . . participate in the organization and contestation of meaning in a society."[68] The active intervention of monastic houses particularly takes effect in creating order between a father, or senior monk, his sons or his protégées, and even his servants. The need to create social order is mirrored in the need to create spatial order. By building new settlements, monks organized spaces to fulfill the practical needs of daily living alongside the needs for a new society in which place making was a dynamic activity in the sixth century and later.

Just as domestic settlements were long ignored by Egyptologists until now, the study of monastic settlements is demonstrating how important settlement archaeology is for building a more nuanced portrait of the ancient world. For example, we learn from monastic literature that the Delta was home to numerous monasteries, but very few have been found. Penelope Wilson acknowledges the limited physical remains of monastic settlements in the Delta. She outlines the practical, environmental factors that account for the dearth of archaeological material, including the challenges of floodplain archaeology, the reclamation of farmlands, and the lack of regulation to protect archaeological sites.[69] However, even with an incomplete picture of monastic houses, we still can use the existing evidence to draw important conclusions about monastic dwellings.

The act of dwelling was essential to making a space a house. This concept is at the heart of Martin Heidegger's belief that thresholds are boundaries that dissolve the lines that separate inner and outer spheres of living and make the home a space for emotions.[70] By stepping into the dwelling place, monks were making a house a home, and thereby transforming rooms into different kinds of spaces that are engendered with expectations for how space may foster spiritual growth and intimacy with the divine. German philosopher Otto Friedrich Bollnow considered dwelling as a "means to have a fixed place in space, to belong to this place and be rooted in it."[71] For Sarah Schlanger, the continuous dwelling is the idea of a community's "persistent places," and for Wendy Ashmore, the buildings and settlements evolve to become "life histories of place(s)."[72] Monastic houses, just like their secular counterparts, became persistent places with unique life histories.

Both the Pachomian and Shenoutean monastic communities were divided into houses as a way to manage the various communities. The houses included cells, or individual rooms, and in these more intimate spaces a monk was not allowed to hide secret food or to possess prohibited items such as woolen tunics, mantles, "soft sheepskin with unshorn wool," coins, pillows, or "various other conveniences."[73] For Shenoute, it was important to inspect the monastic houses once a month to ensure that all members of the community abided by the structures of the community: "The father superior shall enter all the houses [*ēi*] of the congregation [*synagōgē*] and inspect all the cells or rooms [*ri*] that are within them and all alcoves and all vessels that are holding their portion that they have put there, so that he may know whether they have an excess beyond the ordnance that is laid down, or whether someone has committed impiety by taking anything into his cell against the edifying rule that is laid down."[74] Shenoute's surveillance, by way of regular inspections, reveals that despite the community's goals for semi-independent, ascetic living, it was necessary to provide a mechanism for more structure within the houses. The house inspections reinforced the ideals of ascetic living and the importance of communal identity.[75] Without such inspections, it appears that conformity to particular habits would break down, especially when one was in the privacy of one's own room. Therefore, it was necessary to cross the boundary of the locked door and see inside the monk's dwelling place.

The idea that the monk's dwelling place, or home, was also the home of God is explicit in monastic literature. In late antique Thebes, for example, Jacob, the superior of the *topos* of Apa Phoibammon, names his heir as Victor (*P.KRU* 65) and describes the "the holy topos and all its dwelling places, namely its caves which are set for us up in the same mountain by those who came before us, by our fathers according to God, through documents drawn up for use, our fathers to be commemorated for all time."[76] The dwelling places were part of a larger, spiritual topography of the holy, or sacred, topos. To ensure a house's holiness required that a dwelling space be pure as well as its owners—the monks. The only way to guarantee this quality was to monitor the spiritual health of the monks who resided within the community. The monk was equated with the space in which he lived and practiced his asceticism. For it was within the monk's dwelling place that God might reside and the space itself was also imbued with the spiritual health of the resident.

Initially, the very sense of rootedness to a specific place seemed antithetical to the monastic movement, at least as it appears in the writings of its most ardent, late antique admirers.[77] One of the prominent themes in early monastic literature is a disdain for community and interaction with others outside of the immediate monastic community. Modern historians accepted this account until the discovery of monastic sites, with complex settlements and in close proximity to nonmonastic communities, caused a reconsideration of the late antique sources.[78] In fact, the lax enforcement of building codes during the late Roman and early Byzantine Periods provided an opportunity for new communities to repurpose, adapt, restore, and build in spaces not currently owned by either landowners or the church.[79] Monks adopted underutilized landscapes for building their homes. The new settlements were often visible from the Nile and accessible by foot.

If we dig deeper into the literary sources intended to serve as guides for monastic communities, we do see the importance of houses as places for monastic living. In fact, buildings, houses, and even God's house appear as major characters in monastic teachings. The houses serve as illustrations of the importance of places for spiritual development in that personal attachment fostered a sense of a persistent place. For example, Abba Isaiah of Sketis, writing in the late fifth to early sixth century, recognized that monks moved between different locations and modified buildings to make them their own. But he warned that an affection for a place could be dangerous: "If you go and live in a place where you are given a cell (or room) and you spend money to construct something in the cell (or room), then, if you leave it and another brother takes it over, do not remove him should you later wish to return."[80] Similarly, monks were told not to take anything useful from the space, so that those who became new residents could benefit from what was inside.[81] Being a guest in someone else's house required the warning not to "destroy, tear down, nor construct anything" without first seeking the blessing and permission of the monastic owner.[82]

Monastic houses are by their very nature new houses for a new household based on new spiritual kinship groups. While monks regarded themselves on the best of days as members of a heavenly household, the reality of monastic life is that they built homes, personalized those spaces, and held both legal and emotional attachments to their residences. Amos Rapoport described that for some group-specific institutions, "environments, even apparently humble dwellings, are more than material objects or structures: they are institutions, basic cultural phenomena"[83] and their "social networks, whether intensive or extensive, are usually centered on the dwelling."[84] Monastic houses are spaces, in Rapoport's reading of architecture, that provide cues "which trigger appropriate behavior" of those who reside within the houses.[85] We might return now to Shenoute and Pachomius as two leaders who knew that the dwelling was an important locus for creating community identity within the house and that if difficulties were to arise, they might come from what was happening within the private rooms of the monks. By bringing together archaeological, documentary, and historical evidence, we can observe how important monastic places were in reinforcing monastic identity and communities. This insight reflects the value of household archaeology in rereading monastic evidence with an eye toward finding the relationship between the built environment and the monk, not simply accepting the patristic tradition that monks shunned attachments to the material world.

To return to the opening questions, I propose the following answers. First, what interest could three monks have in acquiring property in a nonmonastic town? By the eighth century, monastics were well integrated into the economic and social affairs of nonmonastic communities to such a degree that even portions of buildings would be welcomed endowments. Second, were monks interested in property purely for the financial benefit for their monasteries? The material remains of monastic communities and their correspondence make clear that individual needs and desires played an essential role in the owning of big things, such as dwelling places or secular homes, and in small things, such as curtains, books, and bedding. Third, how did the later eighth-century house compare with earlier monastic housing? The earliest monastic houses are not attested in the archaeological record, but the earliest monastic manuals and guides do point to houses and rooms with personal things and suggest the practice of remodeling to suit individual monks' needs. By the sixth century, we can see a wide variety of monastic settlements as well as great diversity in their design, both of which suggest that monks could be selective about what type of monastic housing they adopted. It is perhaps this great variation and the ownership that monks had over their houses *within* a monastery that led to even greater participation in home ownership in spaces outside of the monastic community.

Notes

1 MacCoull 2009, 166–73.
2 Hölscher 1954; Wilfong 2002b, 1–22.
3 Eichner 2016, 159–70; Eichner and Polz 2022.
4 N.17. Trans. Wortley 2013, 16–17.
5 Moses 6. Trans. Wortley 2014, 195.
6 Bessarion 12. Trans. Wortley 2014, 80–81.
7 Moses 7. Trans. Wortley 2014, 195.
8 Palladius, *Lausiac History*, 35.1. Trans. Wortley 2015, 81.
9 N. 592.7. Trans. Wortley 2013, 405.
10 N. 624. Trans. Wortley 2013, 507.
11 Brooks Hedstrom 2009.
12 Paul of Tamma, *On the Cell* 1. Trans. Vivian and Pearson 1998.

13 Paul of Tamma, *On the Cell* 77. Trans. Vivian and Pearson 1998.
14 Theodore of Pherme 14. Trans. Wortley 2014, 120.
15 Barrie 2017, xxvii.
16 Fetterman 1998, 20–22.
17 For an application of an emic archaeological reading of Mayan material, see Sharer and Traxler 2006, 66–67; Ewen 2003, 69.
18 Emic archaeology was questioned in the mid-twentieth century by archaeologists, who embraced processual archaeology for its unbiased and scientific approach to archaeological material. In contrast, postprocessual archaeologists see benefits to emic archaeology, which seeks the uniqueness of each community, and its material remains through reading historical sources to build a richer understanding of the human past. For explorations of emic readings of the premodern, material world, see Baker 2013 and Elsner and Meyer 2014.
19 The archaeology of things will be discussed in greater detail, but the first major proponent of a focus on things is Brown 2001.
20 See Deetz 1982; Wilk and Rathje 1982; and compare the historical discussion of household archaeology in Barrett, introduction, this volume.
21 I follow the shift in household archaeology espoused in recent years to move away from the descriptive approach toward one that draws more on anthropological and sociological interpretations of the built environment. See Ashmore 2002; Robin 2003; Nash 2009.
22 Introna 2014.
23 Latour 2005.
24 For the discussion see Webmoor and Witmore 2008; Olsen 2010; Nativ 2014.
25 Hodder 2012, 14.
26 Webmoor 2007.
27 Brooks Hedstrom 2017b, 125–26.
28 Brunert 1994; Leyser 2006; Rapp 2006; Saak 2006.
29 For a detailed discussion of monastic communities and an overview of the archaeological evidence, see Wipszycka 2009; Brooks Hedstrom 2019.
30 Goehring 1999; Rapp 2006; Krawiec 2012.
31 Kasser et al. 1967; Kasser et al. 1972; Nenein and Wuttmann 2000; Grossmann 2002, 262–66, 491–99.
32 Vycichl 1994; Fournet 1997; Borel 2013.
33 van der Vliet 2017a.
34 Davis 2013; van der Vliet 2017b.
35 No. 23 in Room 2 of QR 306. On the role of the supernatural within the house, see further Frankfurter, chapter 10, this volume.
36 Bridel 1984.
37 Leipoldt 1913; Kuhn 1956; Layton 2014.
38 Schroeder 2004; Brooks Hedstrom 2009, 759–60.
39 Horn 1973; Kinder 2004.
40 Kemp 2000; Barnard et al. 2016.
41 Wenger 1998, 73.
42 Hendon 2009, 60.
43 Asylums, orphanages, workhouses, labor camps, reform establishments, leprosaria, and even monasteries are all institutions that were specifically designed to serve a select population. Recent work in confinement archaeology may provide new avenues for examining the design and function of monastic settlements as spaces intended to protect and control the body of a monk. See Casella 2011; Kay 2013.
44 I wish to thank Elisabeth O'Connell for access to the Wadi Sarga material on behalf of the Trustees for the British Museum.
45 Brooks Hedstrom 2017b, 33–36, 245–52.
46 Dekker 2013.
47 Brooks Hedstrom 2017b, 248.
48 Brooks Hedstrom 2017a.
49 O.Sarga 169. Trans. Crum and Bell, 1922, 139.
50 O.Sarga 100. Trans. Crum and Bell, 1922, 93–94.

51 O.Sarga 101. Trans. Crum and Bell, 1922, 94–95.
52 Sauneron and Jacquet 1972.
53 Sauneron 1974.
54 Brooks Hedstrom 2017b, 50–53, 263–65.
55 Sauneron and Jacquet, vol. 1, 1972, 18–24 and Pl. VIII.
56 Compare Davoli (chapter 1, this volume) for an analogous perspective on the environment's effects on dwelling construction.
57 Sauneron and Jacquet, vol. 1, 1972, 100. No. 49.
58 Grossmann and Severin 1982.
59 Brooks Hedstrom 2017b, 28–31, 225–37.
60 Quibell referred to the "poverty" of some rooms and poor workmanship in construction. Quibell 1912, 18, 28.
61 Brooks Hedstrom 2017b, 269–70.
62 Hermitages 1, 2, 25, 44 and 89; Godlewski 2008.
63 Godlewski 1998; 2000; 2008; Leclant and Minault-Gout 1999, 369.
64 Godlewski and Parandowska 1997.
65 Souvatzi 2012, 15.
66 McQuire 2010, 5–6.
67 Wilfong 2002a; Schroeder 2009; Krueger 2011.
68 Baker 2002, 25.
69 Wilson (2014, 43) describes it this way: "Towns must have seemed to be islands floating high above the inundation at one moment and above fields of yellow grain or blue flax at another. . . . Even islands in the lagoons and swamps were occupied, maximizing the resource potential of the north of Egypt to an extent that not even the pharaohs had achieved."
70 Heidegger 1993.
71 Bollnow 2011, 124.
72 Schlanger 1992, 92; Ashmore 2002, 1177–78.
73 *Pachomian Rule* 78 & 80–81. Trans. Veilleux 1981, 159.
74 See Shenoute, *Canons*, vol. 9, MONB.XS 336, in Leipoldt, 1913, 58; Trans. Layton, 2014, 167.
75 Jezierski 2006.
76 O'Connell 2007, 268; Schiller 1926, 26–32.
77 The writings of monastic authors John Cassian, Palladius, and historians, such as Socrates and Sozomen, reflect the mythmaking narrative of early monastics as wonder-working saints living with very little food or comfort. See Goehring 2003.
78 A similar observation of the disconnect between material remains and ancient texts is outlined in Goldberg 1999.
79 Brooks Hedstrom 2017b, 104–9.
80 Abba Isaiah, *Discourse* 4. Trans. Chryssavgis, 2002, 59.
81 Abba Isaiah, *Discourse* 4. Trans. Chryssavgis, 2002, 59.
82 Abba Isaiah, *Discourse* 5. Trans. Chryssavgis, 2002, 74.
83 Rapoport 1980, 159.
84 Rapoport 2005, 116.
85 Rapoport 1982, 60.

Works Cited

Ashmore, W. 2002. "'Decisions and Dispositions:' Socializing Spatial Archaeology." *American Anthropologist* 104: 1172–83.

Baker, C.M. 2002. *Rebuilding the House of Israel: Architectures of Gender in Jewish Antiquity*. Stanford: Stanford University Press.

Baker, P.A. 2013. *The Archaeology of Medicine in the Greco-Roman World*. Cambridge: Cambridge University Press.

Barnard, H., et al. 2016. "The Preservation of Exposed Mudbrick Architecture in Karanis (Kom Aushim), Egypt." *Journal of Field Archaeology* 41 (1): 84–100.

Barrie, T. 2017. *House and Home: Cultural Contexts, Ontological Roles*. New York: Routledge.

Bollnow, O.F. 2011. *Human Space*. Translated by C. Shuttleworth. London: Hyphen Press.

Borel, F.B. 2013. "Graffiti et tituli picti EK." In *Kellia: Kôm Qouçoûr 'Îsâ I: Fouilles de 1965 à 1978*, edited by D. Weidmann, 359–63. Louvain: Peeters.

Bridel, P. 1984. "La dialectique de l'isolement et de l'ouverture dans les monastères kelliotes: Espaces réserves-espace d'accueil." In *Le site monastique des Kellia (Basse-Égypte)*, edited by R. Kasser, 145–61. Louvain: Peeters.

Brooks Hedstrom, D.L. 2009. "The Geography of the Monastic Cell in Early Egyptian Monastic Literature." *Church History* 78 (4): 756–91.

Brooks Hedstrom, D.L. 2017a. "Baking Bread and Salting Fish: The Archaeology of Egyptian Monastic Kitchens and Ascetic Taste." In *Knowing Bodies, Passionate Souls: Sense Perceptions in Byzantium*, edited by M. Mullett, S.A. Harvey, and M. Mass, 183–206. Washington, DC: Dumbarton Oaks.

Brooks Hedstrom, D.L. 2017b. *The Monastic Landscape of Late Antique Egypt: An Archaeological Reconstruction*. Cambridge: Cambridge University Press.

Brooks Hedstrom, D.L. 2019. "The Archaeology of Early Monastic Communities." In *The Oxford Handbook of Early Christian Archaeology*, edited by D.K. Pettegrew, W.R. Caraher, and T.W. Davis, 147–65. Oxford: Oxford University Press.

Brown, B. 2001. "Thing Theory." *Critical Inquiry* 28 (1): 1–22.

Brunert, M.-E. 1994. *Das Ideal der Wüstenaskese und seine Rezeption in Gallien bis zum Ende des 6. Jahrhunderts*. Munster: Aschendorff.

Casella, E.C. 2011. "Lockdown: On the Materiality of Confinement." In *Archaeologies of Internment*, edited by A. Myers and G. Moshenksa, 285–95. New York: Springer.

Chryssavgis, J., trans. 2002. *Abba Isaiah of Scetis. Ascetic Discourses*. Kalamazoo, MI: Cistercian Publications.

Crum, W.E., and H.I. Bell, eds. 1922. *Wadi Sarga. Coptic and Greek Texts from the Excavations Undertaken by the Byzantine Research Account*. Hauniae: Glydendalske Boghandel-Nordisk Forlag.

Davis, S.J. 2013. "Completing the Race and Receiving the Crown: 2 Timothy 4:7–8 in Early Christian Monastic Epitaphs at Kellia and Pherme." In *Asceticism and Exegesis in Early Christianity: The Reception of New Testament Texts in Ancient Ascetic Discourse*, edited by H.-U. Weidemann, 334–73. Göttingen: Vandenhoeck & Ruprecht.

Deetz, J.J.F. 1982. "Households: A Structural Key to Archaeological Explanation." *American Behavioral Scientist* 25 (6): 717–24.

Dekker, R. 2013. "The Monastery of Apa Thomas at Wadi Sarga: Points of Departure for a Relative Chronology." In *Christianity and Monasticism in Middle Egypt: Al-Minya and Asyut*, edited by G. Gabra and H.N. Takla, 1–14. Cairo: AUC Press.

Eichner, I. 2016. "Aspekte des Alltagslebens im Pauloskloster (Deir el-Bachît) von Theben-West/Oberägypten anhand archäologischer Belege." In *Hinter Den Mauern Und Auf Dem Offenen Land. Leben Im Byzantinischen Reich*, edited by F. Daim and J. Drauschke, 159–70. Mainz: Verlag des Römisch-Germanischen Zentralmuseums.

Eichner, I., and D. Polz, eds. 2022. *Das Pauloskloster (Deir el-Bachît) in den Bergen von Djeme/Oberägypten: Eine Mönchsgemeinschaft am Rande der Wüste. Internationaler Workshop an der Österreichischen Akademie der Wissenschaften, Wien, 20.-21. Mai 2019*. Wiesbaden: Harrassowitz Verlag.

Elsner, J., and M. Meyer, eds. 2014. *Art and Rhetoric in Roman Culture*. Cambridge: Cambridge University Press.

Ewen, C.R. 2003. *Artifacts*. Walnut Creek, CA: AltaMira Press.

Fetterman, D.M. 1998. *Ethnography: Step-by-Step*. Thousand Oaks, CA: Sage.

Fournet, J.-L. 1997. "Quelques remarqes zur des inscriptions grecques des Kellia (Égypte) récemment éditées." *Zeitschrift für Papyrologie und Epigraphik* 117: 163–66.

Godlewski, W. 1998. "Excavations 1997." *Polish Archaeology in the Mediterranean* 9: 77–86.

Godlewski, W. 2000. "Naqlun: The Hermitage of Phibamo." In *Les civilisations du bassin méditerranéen: Hommages à Joachim Śliwa*, edited by K.M. Cialwicz and J.A. Ostrowski, 93–98. Krakow: Uniwersytet Jagielloński.

Godlewski, W. 2008. "Naqlun (Nekloni): The Hermitages, Cemetery and the Keep in the early 6th Century." In *Graeco-Roman Fayum: Texts and Archaeology: Proceedings of the Third*

International Fayum Symposion, Freudenstadt, May 29-June 1, 2007, edited by S.L. Lippert and M. Schentuleit, 101–12. Wiesbaden: Harrassowitz.

Godlewski, W., and E. Parandowska. 1997. "Excavations 1996." *Polish Archaeology in the Mediterranean* 8: 88–97.

Goehring, J.E. 1999. "The Encroaching Desert: Literary Production and Ascetic Space in Early Christian Egypt." In *Ascetics, Society, and the Desert: Studies in Early Egyptian Monasticism*, 73–88. Harrisburg, PA: Trinity Press International.

Goehring, J.E. 2003. "The Dark Side of Landscape: Ideology and Power in the Christian Myth of the Desert." *Journal of Medieval and Early Modern Studies* 33 (3): 437–51.

Goldberg, M.Y. 1999. "Spatial and Behavioural Negotiations in Classical Athenian City Houses." In *The Archaeology of Household Activities*, edited by P.M. Allison, 142–61. London: Routledge.

Grossmann, P. 2002. *Christliche Architektur in Ägypten*. Leiden: Brill.

Grossmann, P., and H.-G. Severin. 1982. "Reinigungsarbeiten im Jeremiakloster bei Saqqara: Vierter vorläufiger Bericht." *Mitteilungen des Deutschen Archäologischen Instituts Abteilung Kairo* 38: 155–93.

Heidegger, M. 1993. "Building Dwelling Thinking." In *Basic Writings*, edited by D. Farrell Krell, 348–51. Revised and expanded edition. San Francisco: Harper San Francisco.

Hendon, J.A. 2009. *Houses in Landscape: Memory and Everyday Life in Mesoamerica*. Durham, NC: Duke University Press.

Hodder, I. 2012. *Entangled: An Archaeology of the Relationships between Human and Things*. Oxford: Wiley-Blackwell.

Hölscher, U. 1954. *The Excavation of Medinet Habu*. Vol. 5. *Post Ramessid Remains*. Chicago: University of Chicago Press.

Horn, W. 1973. "On the Origins of the Medieval Cloister." *Gesta* 12: 13–52.

Introna, L.D. 2014. "Ethic and Flesh: Being Touched by the Otherness of Things." In *Ruin Memories: Materiality, Aesthetics, and the Archaeology of the Recent Past*, edited by B. Olsen and Þ. Pétursdóttir, 41–61. London: Routledge.

Jezierski, W. 2006. "Monasterium Panopticum: On Surveillance in a Medieval Closter: The Case of St. Gall." *Frühmittelalterliche Studien* 40: 167–82.

Kasser, R., et al. 1967. *Kellia 1965 I. Topographie générale, mensurations et fouilles aux Qouçour 'Isa et aux Qouçour el-'Abid, mensurations aux Qouçour el 'Izeila*. Genève: Georg.

Kasser, R., S. Favre, and D. Weidmann. 1972. *Kellia. Topographie. Recherches suisses d'archéologie copte*. Vol. 2. Genève: Georg.

Kay, E. 2013. "The Archaeology of Institutions: Exploring the Abbotsford Convent Site through Legislation." *Australasian Historical Archaeology* 31: 68–77.

Kemp, B.J. 2000. "Soil (Including Mud-Brick Architecture)." In *Ancient Egyptian Materials and Technology*, edited by P.T. Nicholson and I. Shaw, 78–103. Cambridge: Cambridge University Press.

Kinder, T.N., ed. 2004. *Perspectives for an Architecture of Solitude: Essays on Cistercians, Art, and Architecture in Honour of Peter Fergusson*. Turnhout: Brepols.

Krawiec, R. 2012. "Monastic Literacy in John Cassian: Toward a New Sublimity." *Church History* 81 (4): 765–95.

Krueger, D. 2011. "Between Monks: Tales of Monastic Companionship in Early Byzantium." *Journal of the History of Sexuality* 20: 28–61.

Kuhn, K.H., ed. 1956. *Letters and Sermons of Besa*. 2 vols. Louvain: Peeters.

Latour, B. 2005. *Reassembling the Social: An Introduction to Actor-Network-Theory*. Oxford: Oxford University Press.

Layton, B., trans. 2014. *The Canons of Our Fathers: Monastic Rules of Shenoute*. Oxford: Oxford University Press.

Leclant, J., and A. Minault-Gout. 1999. "Fouilles et travaux en Égypte et au Soudan, 1997–1998." *Orientalia* 68 (4): 349–476.

Leipoldt, J., trans. 1913. *Sinuthii Archimandritae: Vita et Opera Omnia*. Vol. 4. Paris: Imprimerie Nationale.

Leyser, C. 2006. "The Uses of the Desert in the Sixth-Century West." *Church History and Religious Culture* 86: 113–34.

MacCoull, L.S.B. 2009. *Coptic Legal Documents: Law as Vernacular Text and Experience in Late Antique Egypt*. Tempe, AZ: Arizona Center for Medieval and Renaissance Studies, in collaboration with Brepols.

McQuire, B.P. 2010. *Friendship and Community: The Monastic Experience, 350–1250*. Ithaca, NY: Cornell University Press.

Nash, D.J. 2009. "Household Archaeology in the Andes." *Journal of Archaeological Research* 17: 205–61.

Nativ, A. 2014. "Anthropocentricity and the Archaeological Record: Towards a Sociology of Things." *Norwegian Archaeological Review* 47 (2): 180–95.

Nenein, N.H., and M. Wuttmann. 2000. *Kellia II. L'ermitage copte QR 195.1. Archéologie et architecture*. Cairo: Institut français d'archéologie orientale.

O'Connell, E. 2007. "Transforming Monumental Landscapes in Late Antique Egypt: Monastic Dwellings in Legal Documents from Western Thebes." *Journal of Early Christian Studies* 15 (2): 239–73.

Olsen, B. 2010. *In Defense of Things: Archaeology and the Ontology of Objects*. Landham, MD: Alta Mira Press.

Quibell, J.E. 1912. *Excavations at Saqqara. 1908–9, 1909–10. The Monastery of Apa Jeremias*. Cairo: Institut français d'archéologie orientale.

Rapoport, A. 1980. "Vernacular Architecture and the Cultural Determinants of Form." In *Buildings and Society: Essays on the Social Development of the Built Environment*, edited by A.D. King, 158–69. London: Routledge.

Rapoport, A. 1982. *The Meaning of the Built Environment: A Nonverbal Communication Approach*. Tucson: University of Arizona Press.

Rapoport, A. 2005. *Culture, Architecture, and Design*. Chicago: Locke Science Publishing.

Rapp, C. 2006. "Desert, City, and Countryside in the Early Christian Imagination." *Church History and Religious Culture* 86: 93–112.

Robin, C. 2003. "New Directions in Classical Maya Household Archaeology." *Journal of Archaeological Research* 11 (4): 307–56.

Saak, E.L. 2006. "'Ex vita partum formatur vita fratrum': The Appropriation of the Desert Fathers in the Augustinian Monasticism of the Later Middle Ages." *Church History and Religious Culture* 86: 191–228.

Sauneron, S. 1974. "Adaïma." *Bulletin de l'Institut Français d'Archéologie Orientale* 74: 186–93.

Sauneron, S., and J. Jacquet. 1972. *Les ermitages chrétiens du désert d'Esna*, I–IV. Cairo: Institut français d'archéologie orientale.

Schiller, A.A., trans. 1926. "Coptic Wills, Translation and Commentary." JD diss., University of California, Berkeley.

Schlanger, S. 1992. "Recognizing Persistent Places in Anasazi Settlement Systems." In *Space, Time, and Archaeological Landscapes*, edited by J. Rossignol and L.-A. Wandsnider, 91–112. New York: Plenum Press.

Schroeder, C.T. 2004. "'A Suitable Abode for Christ': The Church Building as Symbol of Ascetic Renunciation in Early Monasticism." *Church History* 73 (3): 472–521.

Schroeder, C.T. 2009. "Queer Eye for the Ascetic Guy? Homoeroticism, Children, and the Making of Monks in Late Antique Egypt." *Journal of the American Academy of Religion* 77 (2): 333–47.

Sharer, R.J., with L.P. Traxler. 2006. *The Ancient Maya*. Stanford: Stanford University Press.

Souvatzi, S. 2012. "Between the Individual and the Collective: Household as a Social Process in Neolithic Greece." In *New Perspectives on Household Archaeology*, edited by B.J. Parker and C.P. Foster, 15–44. Winona Lake, IN: Eisenbrauns.

Veilleux, A., trans. 1981. *Pachomain Koinoia*. Vol. 2. *Pachomian Chronicles and Rules*. Kalamazoo, MI: Cistercian Publications.

Vivian, T., and B. Pearson, trans. 1998. "Saint Paul of Tamma on the Monastic Cell (de Cella)." *Hallel* 23 (2): 86–107.

van der Vliet, J. 2017a. "Kellia and Monastic Epigraphy." In *Christianity and Monasticism in Northern Egypt: Beni Suef, Giza, Cairo, and the Nile Delta*, edited by G. Gabra and H. Takla, 193–200. Cairo: AUC Press.

van der Vliet, J. 2017b. "The Wisdom of the Wall: Innovation in Monastic Epigraphy." In *Writing and Communication in Early Egyptian Monasticism*, edited by M. Choat and M.C. Giorda, 151–64. Leiden: Brill.

Vycichl, W. 1994. "Partie II : Les inscriptions arabes de l'ermitage QR 306." In *Explorations aux Qouçoûr er-Roubâ'îyât: Rapport des campagnes 1982 et 1983*, edited by R. Kasser, 315–20. Louvain: Peeters.

Ward, B., trans. 1975. *The Sayings of the Desert Fathers: The Alphabetical Collection*. Kalamazoo, MI: Cistercian Press.

Webmoor, T. 2007. "What About 'One More Turn After the Social' in Archaeological Reasoning? Taking Things Seriously." *World Archaeology* 39: 563–78.

Webmoor, T., and C.L. Witmore. 2008. "Things Are Us! A Commentary on Human/Things Relations under the Banner of a 'Social' Archaeology." *Norwegian Archaeological Review* 41 (1): 53–70.

Wenger, E. 1998. *Communities of Practice: Learning, Meaning, and Identity*. Cambridge: Cambridge University Press.

Wilfong, T. 2002a. "'Friendship and Physical Desire': The Discourse of Female Homoeroticism in Fifth-Century CE Egypt." In *Among Women*, edited by N.S. Rabinowitz and L. Auanger, 304–30. Austin: University of Texas Press.

Wilfong, T. 2002b. *Women of Jeme: Lives in a Coptic Town in Late Antique Egypt*. Ann Arbor: University of Michigan Press.

Wilk, R.R., and W.L. Rathje. 1982. "Household Archaeology." *American Behavioral Scientist* 25 (6): 617–39.

Wilson, P. 2014. "Living the High Life: Late Antique Archaeology in the Delta." In *Egypt in the First Millennium AD*, edited by E.R. O'Connell, 43–58. Louvain: Peeters.

Wipszycka, E. 2009. *Moines et communautés monastiques en Égypte (IVe-VIIIe siècles)*. Warsaw: Faculty of Law and Administration and Institute of Archaeology.

Wortley, J., trans. 2013. *The Anonymous Sayings of the Desert Fathers: A Select Edition and Complete English Translation*. Cambridge: Cambridge University Press.

Wortley, J., trans. 2014. *Give Me A Word: The Alphabetical Sayings of the Desert Fathers*. Yonkers, NY: St. Vladimir's Seminary Press.

Wortley, J., trans. 2015. *Palladius of Aspuna: The Lausiac History*. Kalamazoo, MI: Cistercian Publications.

12

Domestic Activities in Alternative Settings

The Ptolemaic Fort at Bi'r Samut, Egypt

JENNIFER GATES-FOSTER, BÉRANGÈRE REDON, AND MELANIE GODSEY

Households and dwellings are defined not only by the spatial locus of activities but also by the social matrix that brings members into relationships with one another. These communal and material dimensions of households are intertwined, so that spaces and places that would not ordinarily fit into standard definitions of "dwellings" can become vital laboratories for considering the range of structures and activities encompassed by an archaeology of domestic happenings.

How, and to what degree, can a structure not traditionally conceptualized as relating to a "household" as usually defined (e.g., a military fortification) be assessed in terms of its intrinsically domestic arrangements? The fortress at Bi'r Samut in Egypt's Eastern Desert (figure 12.1) presents a rare opportunity to observe the architecture and contents of a largely intact Hellenistic fortification abandoned in the last decade of the third century BCE. Excavated in 2014–16 by the Mission Archéologique Française du Désert Oriental,[1] the fortress comprised more than fifty architecturally defined spaces, almost all of which included intact floors and deposits dating to the last occupation phase of the fort.

Although this site was not based on a kinship unit, many types of activities documented at Bi'r Samut fit with the range of activities found in houses elsewhere in Egypt. However, an attempt to compare Samut with "typical" contemporary households elsewhere in Egypt has proven difficult. This is primarily because no standard house type or household configuration has been identified for Ptolemaic Upper Egypt, and indeed it is unclear if such an exercise would have value in any case, given the diversity of practices documented in households of the later Roman era.[2] Even so, examination of the architectural and depositional patterns indicates that Bi'r Samut was characterized by flexible and duplicative use of architectural space, while the artifact assemblage highlights an unusually large range of vessel forms and fabrics when compared with houses of the same era.

Figure 12.1. Overview of the fortification at Bi'r Samut, 2015. (© Gaël Pollin, IFAO, MAFDO.)

For example, the pottery assemblage from Bi'r Samut is marked by a surprising diversity of functional vessel types sourced from a broad range of production contexts, including the coastal Mediterranean and Delta, as well as Nubia. This variety highlights the diversity of supply sources available to the fort's inhabitants, some of whom were members of the Ptolemaic army or assigned to units of *Phylakites*. The population of the fort is difficult to characterize, but the ostraka recovered at the site make clear that it was mixed in terms of gender, ethnicity, and the roles fulfilled by the various occupants. Greek and demotic Egyptian languages are documented, while the onomastics of the site include Egyptian, Greek, Jewish, and Arab names.[3] Most of the people present were involved in the logistics of the fort, but they also include the soldiers and policemen mentioned above, as well as others whose jobs likely included camel drivers, elephant hunters, and so on.

The variety of vessel types, along with other artifacts, demonstrates that the fort fulfilled a range of diverse needs for these inhabitants, including the production of cloth, metalworking, animal husbandry, and—above all—the distribution and storage of food and water resources. These activities were crowded into the fort's interior spaces, reflecting the constraints imposed by the desert environment and the security concerns presented by the fort's location along a frontier zone.

Many of the fort's rooms and annexes were also flexible and multifunctional, serving as locations for food preparation and storage, along with other more specialized activities such as weaving. Even more illuminating, the duplication of zones for cooking and food preparation at many scales suggests a spatial configuration designed to accommodate multiple smaller social units with their own discrete activity spaces. At the same time, the fort's larger kitchens and grain storage facilities served as the principal storage point for foodstuffs and its cisterns for the centralized distribution of water. The flexibility of spatial use within the fort's walls suggests an open and dynamic social configuration, with only loosely defined functional divisions and little hierarchy of access. The distribution of pottery consumed at the site also suggests little differentiation of activity areas, beyond a few spaces clearly devoted to large-scale grain storage and some potentially used as strong rooms.

The duplication of activities and the diversity of storage and production spaces are hardly unique to the "forthold," highlighting the difficulty in locating archaeologically the special social dimensions of the family that are central to traditional definitions of the "household." This ambiguity is intriguing and raises the question of whether or not this pattern results from the way that a fort, as opposed to a house, functioned as a receptacle for a diverse and disconnected network of social actors, or indeed whether or not the flexible and multiple uses of the fort's rooms mirror broader practices in houses of Upper Egypt in the Ptolemaic era.

In either case, Bi'r Samut offers a rich and exciting opportunity to set the forthold alongside the household as a spatial and cultural unit. Here we compare several of the fort's rooms, which can be characterized as housing (at least in part) domestic activities, and with assemblages from Hellenistic house deposits from Egypt, especially at Syene (Aswan), and as further basis for comparative contextualization, assemblages from the Late Period Fortification at Tell el-Herr.

Architectural and Stratigraphic Overview

The fortification at Bi'r Samut is part of an archaeological zone that lies approximately 130 kilometers by road from the city of Edfu in the Nile Valley and almost an equal distance to the Red Sea coast, as the crow flies. Difficult to reach today and presumably even more so in antiquity, the Samut area lies deep in the remote heart of the Eastern, or Arabian, Desert. This hyper-arid region was intensively explored and exploited from the late fourth century BCE until the fifth century CE.[4]

The Ptolemaic kings, like their Pharaonic predecessors, were interested in the desert's abundant mineral resources—particularly its rich veins of gold-bearing quartz and precious stones—and exploited it as a source of wealth and as a conduit to distant lands. Beginning in the late fourth century BCE, an archipelago of mining installations,[5] fortified wells, subsidiary settlements, and small shelters were constructed along the route from Edfu, ancient Apollonopolis Magna, to Berenike Troglodytika on the coast, where a fortified outpost and harbor were constructed to facilitate the transport of battle elephants from East Africa under the supervision of the Ptolemaic army.[6]

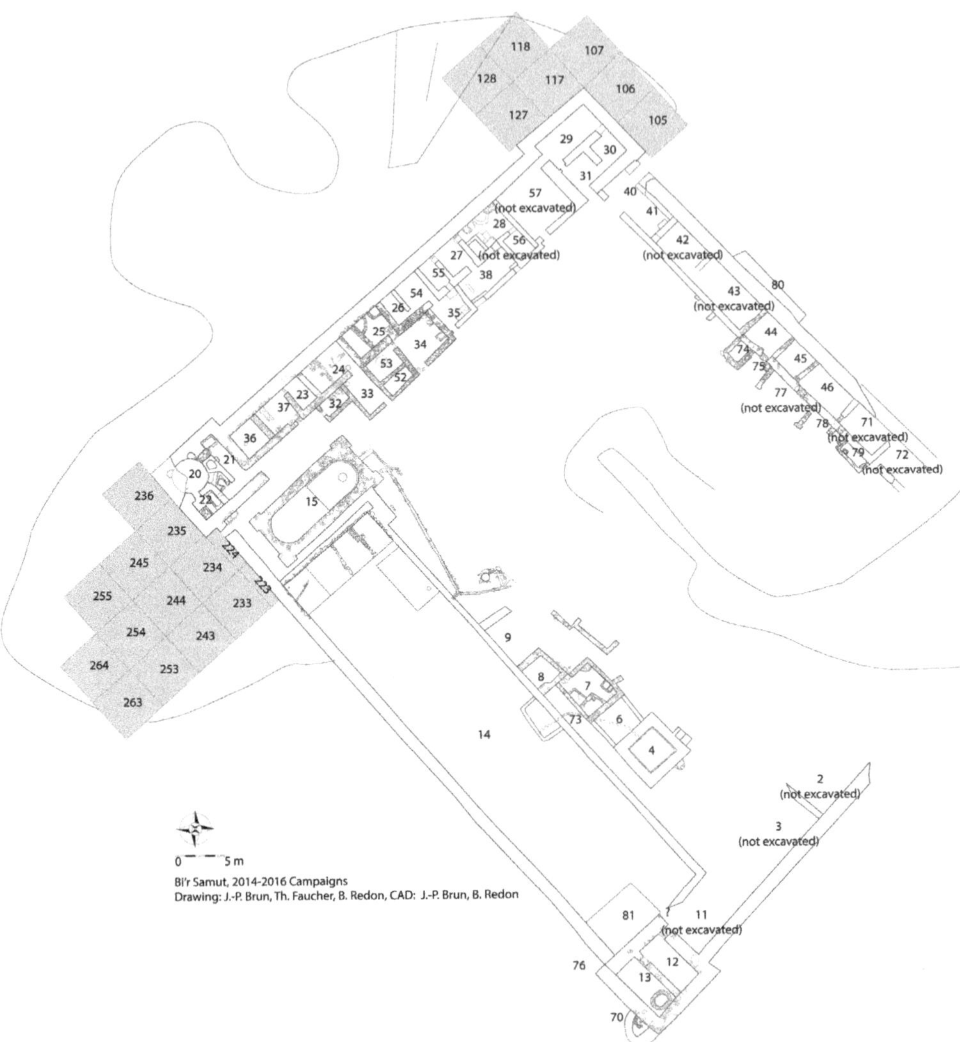

Figure 12.2. Plan of the fortification at Bi'r Samut. (© J.-P. Brun, Th. Faucher, B. Redon, MAFDO.)

Bi'r Samut is one of the largest Ptolemaic fortifications (with El-Kanaïs) along this road and indeed in all of Egypt, and the best documented (figure 12.2). As mentioned above, excavations at Bi'r Samut took place between 2014 and 2016 under the auspices of the Mission Archéologique Française du Désert Oriental and uncovered a large and well-preserved stone-built fortress surrounding a cistern and a destroyed well.[7] Two large middens were also excavated outside the main gate and postern gate, which produced some thirteen hundred Greek and demotic Egyptian ostraka dating to the third century BCE.[8] From these documents and other remains, we have learned the fort's likely foundation date is sometime in the last years of the first half of the third century BCE, probably during the 250s BCE, like other forts or fortified wells of the area.[9]

There are not many well-documented houses in Upper Egypt that date securely to the third century BCE and can therefore offer direct comparanda for Bi'r Samut's architectural plan (although see below for discussion of a second-century example). However, well-excavated examples of third-century domestic architecture are known from Tebtynis.[10] No two houses at Tebtynis are identical, but the excavators have noticed a few patterns in the house plans. Houses in this period were generally square or slightly rectangular, with one or two rooms incorporating purpose-built installations for various stages of food preparation and storage.[11] All had a second story, but it is unclear how the upper spaces of the house were used. Not every house had an unroofed space incorporated into the architectural block of the house, but if there was outdoor space, it was located at one end (see, for example, house 5200-I). Marouard has suggested that some cooking and household production activities occurred outside the architectural frame of the house in communal exterior spaces.[12] The lower floor required linear movement through the house since, unlike at Bi'r Samut, there was no central space from which to access many rooms.

At Bi'r Samut, we see a vastly different type of spatial configuration. The overall plan of the fort was largely visible on the surface before work began in January 2014 (figure 12.2). Exterior walls were clearly defined in most areas, indicating a large, almost square fortification with three intact square corner towers and a series of rooms built against the fort's original outer wall. Damage to the eastern half of the fort was due to wadi wash over the centuries, as well as damage to the site by looters in 2012 and 2013.

The fortress had two gates: a central gate in the northern wall and a postern gate in the southern wall. Large middens were visible outside the two gates of the fort—a main gate in the north (North Midden) and a postern gate in the West (West Midden). Midden deposits were also documented inside the fort's postern gate (especially in rooms 20 and 21), overlying some architectural features; these suggest that trips outside the fort to deposit refuse were no longer practical in the years or months immediately prior to the fort's abandonment sometime in the last decade of the third century BCE.

The fortress itself comprised more than fifty interior spaces. Excavations in 2015 and 2016 revealed that the outer walls and series of rooms were original to the fort's construction, and a series of additional rooms abutting the outer line of chambers was added later to provide smaller rooms in the fort's interior. A large cistern was also uncovered, along with the outline of a damaged well and several other ambiguous features. Much of the functional space of the courtyard was absorbed into these large water features. Although third century BCE houses in the Fayum took full advantage of outdoor spaces, the lack of preserved activity outside of the fort and the limited available workspace in the central courtyard indicate that outdoor work areas would have been at a premium in the fort, particularly after the construction of the smaller courtyard rooms.

At a minimum, the small courtyard rooms, each of which was provided with a cooking and storage installation, increased the number of lodgings available for the fort's occupants. This increase suggests that there was pressure on the fort to accommodate more people and to do so in semiprivate rooms with individual facilities.

It also indicates that shelter and security were of more importance than the open courtyard space that might be required for communal cooking, assembly, or other activities.

Distribution of Activities at Bi'r Samut

Another aspect of Bi'r Samut is the diversity of functions attested both within and between rooms. In January 2015, excavation began on the southwestern corner of the fort, which had been damaged by a glancing blow from a bulldozer. This round corner tower contained a largely intact Ptolemaic bathing complex (figure 12.3), including a central round plastered room with small basins for the first ablutions, a second room with a hip bathtub and an immersion bathtub for the cleansing operations, and an intact heating system with a furnace still retaining evidence of its last use.[13] The inclusion of a bathing facility in the fortification is not unprecedented,[14] although this is the first documented instance of such a facility in a Hellenistic fortification in Egypt. The suite of tubs and the heating system are integral to the fort's design, indicating that the provision of this facility was part of the fort's original rationale, despite the water-poor environment. These baths likely served only a select few in the fort—for example, high-ranking soldiers or privileged travelers; only two people could bathe at the same time.

The function of certain other rooms in the fort were also suggested by purpose-built installations. For example, Rooms 12 and 13 in the southeastern tower appear

Figure 12.3. Overhead view of the bath at Bi'r Samut. (© J.-P. Brun, MAFDO.)

Figure 12.4. Orthophotographic aerial view of Room 12 at Bi'r Samut. (© Bérangère Redon, MAFDO.)

to have functioned as storage facilities (figure 12.4). Room 12 contained twelve unusually large Egyptian amphorae with their necks removed; these amphorae were embedded in the floor for reuse as storage containers.[15] Analysis of the sediment in these vessels indicates that at least two of them stored charcoal, while others contained organic debris, although it is unclear whether this debris was introduced after the room's abandonment.[16] Small groups of storage containers were embedded in floors elsewhere in the fort, but this is the most condensed large-scale storage area. Room 13, adjacent to 12, had two small stone-lined, somewhat shallow storage pits dug into the floor.

Other items recovered from the floors of these rooms include a handmade cook pot, likely originating outside of Egypt—perhaps from somewhere in East Africa—and an iron pick head, along with many discarded and fragmentary ceramic vessel fragments. In addition, a faience amulet was also found on the floor of Room 12, alongside several grindstones and installations that likely served as work surfaces. A complete lamp and several coarsely formed alluvial lids for closing the reused amphorae round out the assemblage of materials abandoned on the floor of these adjoining rooms. The mixture of different functional artifact types—iron tools, storage vessels, lamps, cooking pots—is entirely typical of the floor groups from Bi'r Samut and suggests that spaces were not strictly divided into zones dedicated to specific activities.[17] In other words, there was no strict division into spaces dedicated simply to "storage" or food preparation, for example.

This conclusion is supported by the presence of artifacts suggesting specialized activities alongside more mundane tasks, such as cooking or the sheltering of animals. In Room 45, twenty-seven loom weights were found spread on the floor in groups of one, two, and five, probably where the loom stood when it was abandoned (figure 12.5). On the same floor, a fragment of gaming board in limestone and two sets of seven stone gaming pieces lay together; these were probably used by the inhabitants to pass the time. Although only fragmentary traces of wood among the weights suggest the loom itself, these objects are clearly associated with cloth production, and they appear alongside traces of leisure activities.

Adjacent to this room, Room 28 seems to have functioned exclusively as a venue for food preparation and storage. The room contains several stone-built basins and

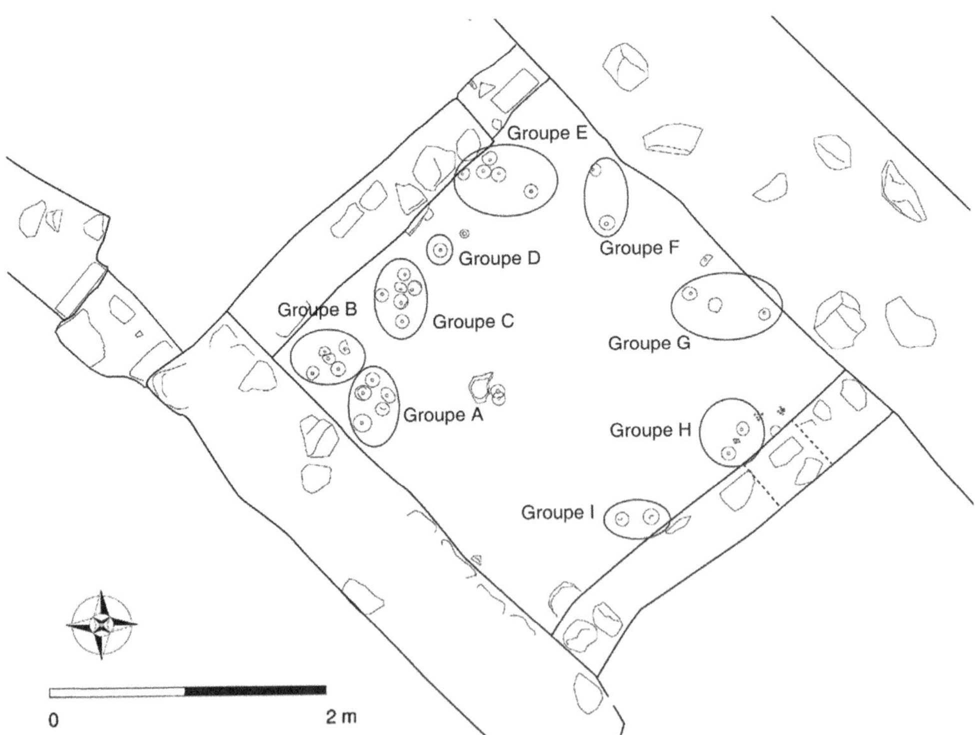

Figure 12.5. Plan of Room 45 at Bi'r Samut with position of the loom weights. (© B. Redon, MAFDO.)

Figure 12.6. Bread stamp with Silenus from Room 28 at Bi'r Samut. (© A. Bülow-Jacobsen, MAFDO.)

grain-grinding installations, as well as two ovens constructed from repurposed storage jars. The ceramic vessels from the floor include a mix of amphorae, jars, bowls, and cooking vessels, along with several specialized objects related to food preparation. These include three Egyptian-made bread stamps, two with geometric sunburst motifs and the third with a Silenus face (figure 12.6).

Room 25, in the same suite of rooms, produced a remarkable floor assemblage containing more than thirty-five complete or restorable vessels. These lay in no discernible order, jumbled among Greek and demotic Egyptian ostraka, writing implements, and organic remains. All lay beneath the carbonized remains of the fort's palm frond roofing.[18] This group of vessels exhibits several of the key characteristics of the third-century ceramic assemblage as a whole; the vessels from this room are very diverse in terms of their function (figure 12.7). There are jars, cook pots, perfume vessels, *alabastra*, *lekythoi*, *aryballoi*, flasks, *amphoriskoi,* and several types derived from older Egyptian forms, including high-shouldered jars and pomegranate-shaped vessels. The room also contained several large utilitarian vessels, including *dinoi* and kraters, as well as at least nine complete Egyptian Type 1 bead-rim amphorae.

In addition to this functional diversity, the vessels from Room 25 represent a wide range of production sources from within Egypt. Ptolemaic black ware, likely produced

Figure 12.7. Assemblage from Room 25 at Bi'r Samut. (© A. Bülow-Jacobsen, MAFDO.)

in the Delta, and vessels from the Mediterranean coast and the Theban region are all represented. Nubian eggshell wares, handmade desert wares, and Aswan-produced wares are also part of the fort's third-century assemblage. Given the fort's isolation and restricted access to supply routes—presumably, all materials coming to Bi'r Samut would have been carried by donkey or camel via the Edfu road—the range of supply sources represented is remarkable. It is tempting to see this as evidence for the centralized network of suppliers involved in provisioning Bi'r Samut. Perhaps the state's network of suppliers reached beyond the Thebaid because of the infrastructure chain that supported the state's expanding economic power over the third century. In any case, this diversity of resources is atypical for contemporary household assemblages, which are primarily regional even when small numbers of foreign imports are present.[19]

Many of the smaller rooms in the fort's interior (for example, Room 34) also yielded floor deposits that included plates, bowls, and jars containing the remains of foodstuffs (figure 12.8). Sheep/goat bone, antelope horn, fish bones, and murex shells appeared in several rooms, as did personal utensils fashioned from mollusks.[20] In situ cooking installations made of repurposed jars or amphorae were also present in most rooms, usually in pairs. Many rooms provided a place for individuals or small groups to prepare food, a consideration that might suggest that groups of travelers or other residents of the fort were assigned space within its walls and expected to prepare their own food during their tenure at the site.

In any case, the division of the fort's interior into many small rooms, most of which appear to have duplicate functions, supports this view. The densely packed arrangement of these spaces, and the lack of any subsidiary constructions outside the fort, also suggest that security issues constrained the availability of areas outside the fort for these activities. This constraint resulted in an intensity of use that is reflected in the distribution of materials within the fort's abandonment levels. The repetition of functional spaces, especially for cooking, grain processing, and animal husbandry, at a large and small scale indicates that differences in inclusivity were part of the system of social membership in the fort. The small "studio" units, such as Rooms 33 and 34, which were equipped with a kitchenette and small living space, provide a setting for a different scale of activity from the large-scale food preparation and storage areas in Rooms 25 and 28, and presumably also afford different kinds of social groupings.

Figure 12.8. Overhead photo of Room 34 at Bi'r Samut. (© J.-P. Brun, MAFDO.)

These spatial and artifactual patterns beg the question of exactly who was in residence in the fort. The ostraka (especially those written in demotic Egyptian) indicate that members of the Ptolemaic military, *phylakites*, and even women lived at and passed through Bi'r Samut.[21] Although gender roles are a central topic within household archaeology, the role of women at Bi'r Samut remains to be studied. The ostraka also record a range of purposes for people who lived at the fort. Most of them were traveling through to other locations in the desert or along the Red Sea coast, sometimes accompanied by companions, and were involved in the logistics of the desert trade and provisioning.[22]

The material evidence on its own points to a spectrum of activities that were appropriate to any domestic settlement, but here they were organized rather differently, because they were housed in spaces embedded in an architectural frame that was inherently supradomestic and defensive in purpose. Given these differences and similarities, what concept of a forthold can we outline at Bi'r Samut given the domestic character of the fort's remains, architecture notwithstanding? How do the patterns briefly outlined here synchronize with what is known about third century houses in Egypt, for example? Do they represent a completely different way of utilizing space for activities that can, when viewed on their own, broadly be characterized as domestic? How do these patterns compare to another fortification, albeit of a slightly earlier period and in a different environment?

A Comparative View: Houses in Syene (Aswan)

Examples of second century BCE domestic architecture at Syene (Aswan) in Upper Egypt provide a general basis for comparison with Bi'r Samut, alongside Tebtynis. In Area 15 at Syene, the relationship between activity spaces and types of socioeconomic connectivity reflects activity patterns and spatial organizations of households that go beyond the architectural configuration of a fortification, presenting a view of Upper Egyptian domestic structures and deposits in the city. A comparison between Bi'r Samut and the households of Ptolemaic Syene demonstrates a much different pattern of spatial organization and domestic activity at the two sites.

Late Period Syene is characterized by an internally oriented set of buildings on a highly regulated plan, which conforms to the historical evidence for its organization as a military settlement at this time. During these Late Period phases, the standard house types represented are typical tower houses.[23] The area was reconfigured in the early Ptolemaic Period, most notably with the addition of a relatively luxurious bathhouse in the second century BCE. This addition suggests that new connections with the Mediterranean *koine* of social practice reached Upper Egypt at this time.[24] The architectural remains also reveal that by the early second century BCE, the population of Syene had shifted from a military community to a domestic one, since houses were built and modified in a more organic way than in previous centuries.

By the late second century BCE, houses in Area 15 were being adapted into smaller, self-sufficient units that were likely more private and increasingly densely packed (figure 12.9). For example, the previously shared courtyard of Houses 1 and 2 shrank and seems to have only been accessible to the occupants of House 2.[25] The incomplete preservation of Houses 1, 2, and 5 in this period make it difficult to fully assess the relationship between households, but the nature of the structures and their continual modification and subdivision suggest a premium on space in the urban landscape of the town. The excavators characterize these houses as "typically Egyptian" and see them as evidence for continuity of traditional domestic practices even into the early Roman Period (Stratum C).[26]

Over this same period, the capacity for food production also increased. Two ovens in the courtyard continued to be the main location of food production for House 2. Sometime after, however, two additional bread ovens were installed in Room 2 of this house, and Room 10 acted as an indoor kitchen.[27] Based on comparanda from the Fayum, Delta, and Sinai, units with more than one bread oven usually provided bread for individuals who were not household members.[28] Could House 2 have provided the necessary bread beyond the immediate household, while other houses in the area were responsible for the production of different products? Or is the increase in capacity simply a reflection of the increasing density of occupation in the insula?

Partially finished faience vessels and large quantities of faience beads in Stratum D in House 5 at Syene suggest that specialized craft production was also a component of domestic life at Syene. Certain specialized activity spaces were also sometimes duplicated between households. For example, House 2 and House 5 both contained a dedicated dining room (*andron*). The increase in duplicated activity spaces suggests that households could operate independently.

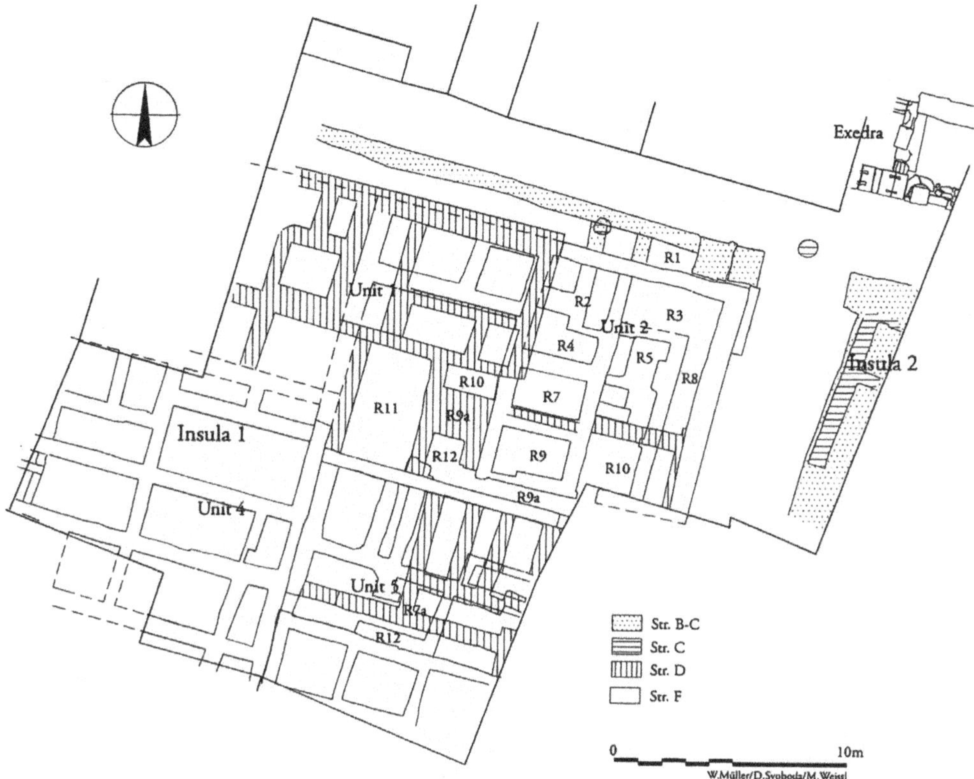

Figure 12.9. Plan of Insula 1 in Area 15 at Aswan (Syene). (After Müller 2010, fig. 14.)

The published ceramic assemblage from this domestic group consists primarily of vessels associated with Greco-Macedonian feasting practices.[29] One deposit from the substructures of House 1 reveals a valuable cross-section of ceramic vessels employed in this period. Tablewares suggest that even in Upper Egypt, the Mediterranean koine dictated drinking and dining habits. Red-slipped silt echinus bowls, plates with thickened rims, and cups with vertical rims imitate similar forms in the contemporary Mediterranean. Pouring vessels include a miniature amphora, a double-handled jug, and a fragment decorated with vegetal decoration similar to contemporary Hadra vases.[30] The cooking wares, however, are local Egyptian products and types; the angled-rim cookpot and the tall ledge rim cookpot are most common here, as they are at Bi'r Samut.

Although most ceramic vessels found at the site were produced in Egypt, a small number of the vessels found in domestic contexts at Syene were produced elsewhere in the Mediterranean. Fourth- to third-century imports include an Attic plate with incurving rim,[31] Attic west slope or Gnathian amphorae, two fragments of the ivy-platter group, *skyphoi,* and three lamps.[32] These vessels indicate connections with the Eastern Mediterranean, Greece, and southern Italy, though the vessels are not evident in large quantities, and their relative rarity could suggest that they arrived via individuals rather than through an established trade route. Sabine Ladstätter argues that these vessels demonstrate a connection to the Delta, rather than to long-distance locales, and Müller likewise sees these patterns as evidence for a light footprint left by foreign influence in the town.[33]

In the domestic contexts, the number of imports declines by the late third century BCE, but tableware and cooking wares still engage with the Mediterranean koine. The biconical cookpots and casseroles at Syene are part of the contemporary widespread adoption of Aegean and eastern Mediterranean cooking forms, if not practices, in Egypt at this time. Imported transport amphorae are still found in the second century, but Egyptian amphorae in Nile silt represent most of the assemblage. These patterns are broadly similar to those of the vessels recovered at Bi'r Samut.

The similarities in the ceramic assemblages at Syene and Bi'r Samut suggests that both sites are integrated into the Upper Egyptian economic sphere—hardly a surprise—but that Bi'r Samut benefits from a broader range of supply sources in the third century BCE than Syene. The differences in the architectural configuration of the domestic zone at Syene, when compared with Bi'r Samut, are also much more striking. The duplication of functional spaces and installations at Bi'r Samut is notably different, and the overall configuration of space is also radically dissimilar. This comparison supports a view of the fort at Bi'r Samut as something qualitatively different from a compact house with many rooms, inhabited by permanent residents; it is instead a completely different spatial animal designed to house multiple, transient social units that shared certain spaces but also maintained discrete, semiprivate quarters. The setting of Bi'r Samut in an expansive wadi rather than the confines of a walled settlement must also be considered.

A Forthold in the Delta: Tell el-Herr

In order to understand the nature of the forthold at Bi'r Samut, an examination of the Late Period fortification at Tell el-Herr in the Sinai is also highly useful, since it contextualizes the patterns observed at Bi'r Samut through comparison with another complex that nominally shares the same functional designation. The types of architectural integration, permanent installations, and extant ceramic assemblages from the late fifth century to the second quarter of the fourth century BCE at Tell el-Herr provide comparanda for the replication of domestic activity spaces, food production areas, and industrial installations at Bi'r Samut.

The discrete occupation from the end of the fifth century through the first quarter of the fourth century is historically defined by a change in control in Egypt from Persian kings to the Thirtieth Dynasty. Unlike at Bi'r Samut, no definitive answer can be given for who controlled Tell el-Herr in this period. The fortification was most likely constructed in the fifth century BCE to protect trade routes and the territorial power of either the Saite or Persian rulers.[34] The metal vessels, transport amphorae, and imported mortars preserved at Tell el-Herr illustrate exchange connections with Greece, Cyprus, the Persian heartland, and elsewhere in the Levant. Homes typically included cylindrical cups and Achaemenid-style bowls made in local fabrics.

An increase in population in the third quarter of the fifth century BCE led to an expansion and restructuring of the Iron Age fortification and settlement at Tell el-Herr. The following three decades (period VA) were years of (primarily, but not exclusively) military occupation at Tell el-Herr, associated with a centralized power structure and standardized, replicated domestic and industrial units in the fort and its associated structures. The settlement at the site was much larger in scale and longer in duration than at Bi'r Samut, but it nevertheless provides a calibrated measure for assessing qualitative differences between the household and the forthold.

The western and northern sectors of the site are well-preserved for this phase of its history. Orthogonal roadways shaped the residential blocks and created connections between domestic neighborhoods and the garrison buildings. Houses were arranged around major places of assembly, such as gateways, administrative buildings, and sanctuaries.[35] The structures of the northern sector cluster around the "palatial building." The houses in this area were strictly residential, with small installations or archaeological deposits that indicate food production. One building (47) was identified as a storage hub because of the enclosed floor plan and the presence of storage vessels. This building might have stored supplies used by the one extant tower house (44) or the insula of houses to the south.[36]

The western sector is composed of many regularly arranged insulae. These complexes incorporated not only tripartite houses (described below) of identical form, but also religious spaces.[37] Several mixed units (79 and 81–83), in which craft production and domestic activities occurred, were more accessible from the fort's gateway, but tripartite houses used for strictly domestic activities (including dwelling, food production, and storage) were part of the same insula.[38]

Bathing facilities and cisterns were not found in Tell el-Herr, but Séverine Marchi suggests that rainwater could have been collected through gutters or in unpreserved receptacles.[39] A centralized system might require the population to use one cistern, but in the case of Tell el-Herr, individual occupants or neighborhood representatives would likely need to make their own journeys outside the fortification to collect water.

The most common configuration of dwellings at Tell el-Herr was a tripartite structure, which was the most frequent residential unit in the fort (figure 12.10).[40] Replication of the overall form, shared dividing walls, and compact agglomeration into insulae throughout the fortification suggest centralized planning that required long-term cooperation among the occupants.[41] There is little evidence for utility spaces within these houses, suggesting that only small-scale food preparation and cooking would occur. The entry vestibule (A), in most instances,[42] served as the kitchen, such as it was, with a masonry bread oven opposite the door; but this zone could be also used for craft production (as in Houses 68 and 69) or as the location for a staircase to an upper floor (House 48). The larger main room (B) was always the center of domestic life, evidenced by the presence of serving vessels, tablewares, and lamps, and was generally not used for cooking and only rarely for the processing of grain. The back room (C) was not well-ventilated or lit, and it was used as storage for items such as weaving implements, jewelry, tools, ceramic and stone vessels, and foodstuffs.[43]

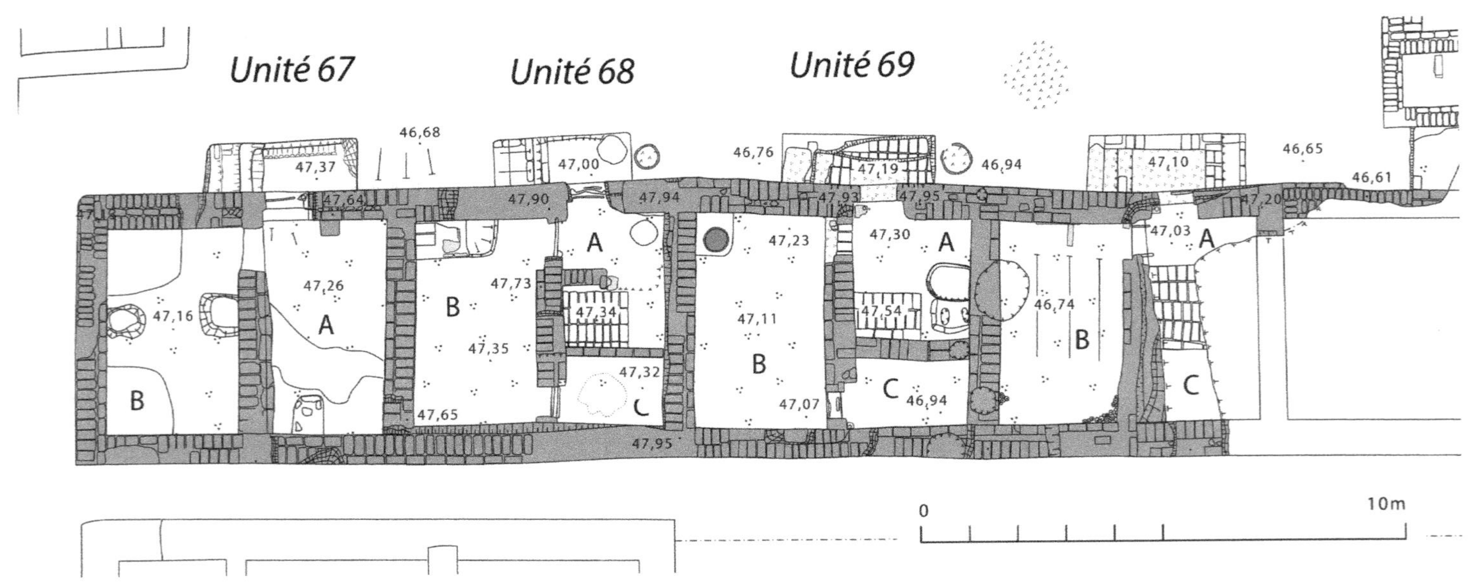

Figure 12.10. Tripartite houses (Unité 67–69) at Tell el-Herr. (After Marchi 2014, Pl. XXI.)

House 78 illustrates another variation on this house type, characterized by an open or covered courtyard (figure 12.11).[44] In this particular example, the location for domestic activities is not restricted in the same way. A courtyard (A), equipped with a large oven and hearth, a basin, and a storage area, was situated at the front of the house, while a second round bread oven was located at the back of the house (C), and these two areas were separated by a storage unit (B). Aside from these installations, very little material of daily domestic life was recovered from House 78. Did House 78 serve as a bakery, with its operators living elsewhere in the fort? This type of building suggests that some structures housed food production outside the household, an arrangement that would complement the smaller food production installations in some of the tripartite homes. At Bi'r Samut there were also both small and larger-scale bread production spheres operating simultaneously.

Larger structures like House 78 were not the only spaces at Tell el-Herr for large-scale or specialized production. Many tripartite homes also accommodated craft production, such as metallurgy (Houses 72 and 79–83). These smaller houses sometimes also had internally or externally attached bread ovens (Houses 77, 78, 84, and 93). Other tripartite houses included duplicate spaces for food production, such as House 94, which featured a food production space in the entry room but also a grinding installation in the main room.[45] Overall, there is no clear or consistent pattern of zones of food production at Tell el-Herr, but as at Bi'r Samut, there is duplication of production across a range of spaces and house types in the community, with some larger than others.

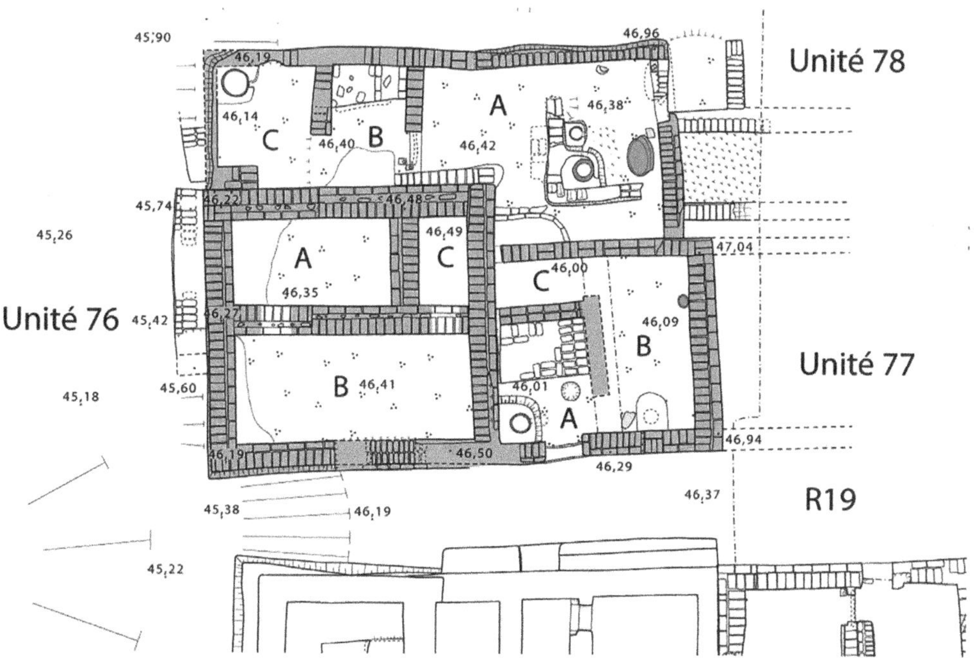

Figure 12.11. Courtyard house (Unité 78) at Tell el-Herr. (After Marchi 2014, Pl. XVI.)

The division of codependent activity spaces into smaller units is again demonstrated by the distribution of bread ovens. Not every home had a bread oven, but every insula had at least one or more.[46] Pooling of necessities for everyday life, therefore, did not need to extend beyond the neighborhood. It is possible, however, that other tasks without archaeological traces required access to centralized facilities. The wide thoroughfares leading to the administrative hubs of the fortification suggest that these spaces were frequented, perhaps to purchase or retrieve goods from storage facilities. The presence of weights and measures in craft-producing houses suggests that consumers could access goods in more localized settings as well. Occupants of the northern, eastern, and southeastern sectors would need to visit the western Sector, where both craft production and imported vessels were clustered, or the administrative storage hubs, to purchase products. The distinct zones for activities other than food production suggests that these communities still potentially participated in a centralized system that facilitated access to necessary goods.

The sharing of production space and household integration, either throughout the fort or within smaller communities, does not necessarily reveal connections via kinship groups. Marchi rightly points to the difficulty in assigning certain tasks to specific ethnicities or genders.[47] The duplication of house types at two different sizes suggests heterarchically dependent groups within a larger hierarchical social system. An insula or groups of insulae contributed to the larger community of the forthold, but smaller communities within an insula could operate independently. The members of the forthold at Tell el-Herr represent a contingent of individual households engaged in craft production, trade, and domestic necessities at a scale and range that were atypical for domestic settings elsewhere. In this respect, Tell el-Herr is a clear precursor for Bi'r Samut, which has many of the same conceptual features, but a radically different plan, smaller overall scale, and much shorter lifespan.

Transience and Domesticity at Bi'r Samut

The types of activities taking place at Bi'r Samut in the third century BCE, including the production of cloth, metalworking, animal husbandry, and—above all—the distribution and storage of food and water resources, transcend a mere military function for the site, and in fact, are comparable to or even exceed the range of activities within contemporary houses. These activities were packed into the fort's interior spaces, which seemingly necessitated close contact between, and regulation of, the occupants of the fort. The abandonment assemblages from the fortification of Bi'r Samut are also marked by a range of functional vessel types sourced from within Egypt, including the coastal Mediterranean and Delta, as well as Nubia. This finding highlights the diversity of supply sources available to the fort's inhabitants and also suggests a different economic network than that typical of a contemporary household, especially in Upper Egypt. The presence of imported amphorae in relatively small quantities is similar to import patterns in Syene, as discussed above.

The archaeological evidence, in the end, allows for a few conclusions about the social relationships among the transient population of the fort and its shared system of membership. The differentiation in the size of functional space, especially cooking and grain processing, suggests that occupants did not have equal access to methods of food preparation. This inequality could extend to variation in dwelling arrangements more broadly (i.e., sleeping spaces), but the archaeological evidence does not confirm this. As we might expect from a kinship-based household, shared space in the courtyard was available, with a communal water supply and workspace. However, in this context, some of the communal arrangements might reflect the isolated desert environment, in which exclusivity of the water supply would be practically infeasible. Although most rooms incorporated a range of functions, and it is unclear who had access to more specialized spaces, the bathing installations and weaving equipment each occupied separate spaces, suggesting that these were not activities in which the general population of the fort would expect to take part.

It is also possible that certain aspects of the fort's spaces and provisions were centralized or partitioned in service of permanent or semipermanent residents, while other facilities were geared toward the needs (and different social configurations) of itinerant travelers. The fort certainly served both groups simultaneously. Since part of the fort's architecture was lost to the wadi, and part of the eastern wing remains unexcavated (and now destroyed), it is possible that some of the common facilities were simply not documented. Travelers may have camped outside the fort, as they did at 'Abbad, another fort in the Eastern Desert, thereby leaving no archaeological traces.[48]

So how should we understand these patterns? Is the fort a household on a grand scale, organized around a hierarchy determined by military (or other) role and status? Is it an agglomeration of spaces designed to house subsidiary, discrete social units, each with its own provisioned space? In the end, given the scale and specificity of the site's overarching function, how useful is the analogy of the household when interrogating the material world of Bi'r Samut or other extradomestic spaces? At this stage of our analysis, the fragmentation of space and repetition of functions seems to be the most marked pattern in Bi'r Samut's architecture and abandonment assemblages. This finding suggests that we might approach the fort not as a single household, but as many smaller social units housed in a single, complex structure. We might draw an analogy to a ship's crew and passengers to help us conceptualize a space that is both domestic and transient, and designed to offer temporary quarter to social units whose relationships are multiscalar.

Notes

1 The French mission is funded by the French Institute of Oriental Archaeology, the French Ministry of Foreign Affairs, and the French National Center for Scientific Research. The fort of Bi'r Samut was excavated under the direction of Jean-Pierre Brun in 2014 and 2015, and by Jean-Pierre Brun, Thomas Faucher, and Bérangère Redon in 2016. Annual reports are published in the Supplement to the BIFAO, accessible online (https://www.ifao.egnet.net/recherche/rapports-activites/). For the three campaigns at Bi'r Samut, see Redon and Faucher 2015; 2016; 2017. A first overview of the results of the excavations is published in Redon 2016; 2018. Gates-Foster and Redon are members of the ERC Desert Networks project, and this project has received funding from the European Research Council (ERC) under the European Union's Horizon 2020 research and innovation program (grant agreement no. 759078).

2 See Boozer, chapter 8, this volume.
3 Cuvigny 2020, 2022; Chaufray 2023.
4 Gates-Foster 2012a; Brun et al. 2018; Sidebotham and Gates-Foster 2019.
5 Faucher 2018.
6 Gates-Foster 2012b; Redon 2018.
7 For an overview of bibliography related to the site of Bi'r Samut, see Sidebotham and Gates-Foster 2019, 194–99; and Redon and Faucher 2014, 2015, 2016.
8 Chaufray and Redon 2020; Cuvigny 2022; Chaufray 2022, 2023. The Greek ostraka are being studied by Hélène Cuvigny, with Laura Aguer and the participation of Bérangère Redon; Marie-Pierre Chaufray is in charge of the publication of the demotic ostraka.
9 Redon 2018; Sidebotham and Gates-Foster 2019.
10 Hadji-Minaglou 2007.
11 See Marouard, chapter 3, this volume.
12 Marouard 2008.
13 Brun et al. 2018.
14 In Egypt, mainly for the Roman Period, see Redon 2010.
15 They are all inscribed with jar labels, except one; see Chaufray 2019; Chaufray and Redon 2020. For discussion of the amphora assemblage at Bi'r Samut, see Gates-Foster 2022.
16 The archaeobotanical study is conducted by Charlène Bouchaud.
17 An obvious difficulty lies in whether or not the materials from the various floors and fills of these rooms constitute a representative sample of the actual *activities* housed in these rooms. The relationship between abandonment deposits and actual use deposits is complex and not to be assumed. In the case of Bi'r Samut, the fort was abandoned in the last decade of the third century BCE and only selectively reoccupied in the Roman Period. The rooms discussed in this article were not reoccupied, with the exception of the bath.
18 The roofing system of the fort was likely composed of a mix of materials, probably including rough cloth and palm frond ceilings.
19 See, for example, the domestic deposits at Tebtynis, discussed below, which show a reliance on locally produced products for table and coarseware types. See also Gill 2016 for comparable patterns from Dakhla and the Western Desert, where ceramic production was well established.
20 The faunal remains are studied by Martine Leguilloux.
21 Inv. nos. 990, 1101, 1102, 1186; Chaufray 2023. The mentions of soldiers are notably variable in the ostraka. The demotic ostraka mention members of the military and policemen, while in the Greek ostraka the army is almost entirely absent. See Cuvigny 2020; and Chaufray 2023 for the first published discussion of the ostraka from this point of view.
22 Chaufray 2019, 2022, 2023; Cuvigny 2020, 2022.
23 See Marouard, chapter 3, this volume; Müller 2008, 2010; Hepa 2021.
24 Berlin 2013; Müller and Hepa 2017.
25 Müller 2010, 435–36.
26 Müller (2010) dates the abandonment of the bath to the early Imperial Period. The relationship between the later Ptolemaic houses and the early Imperial iterations of these structures is not at all clear. Müller sees the area as developing from a more open plan in the Ptolemaic Period to one more densely packed, with increasingly subdivided and smaller living units.
27 Müller 2010, see discussion on 436.
28 Hadji-Minaglou 2007; Marchand 2011; Marchi 2014, especially 190; Hudson 2016.
29 See Lynch 2018 for a discussion of these vessel types and their functions in that setting.
30 Ladstätter 2010, 451.
31 Ladstätter 2015, 138, no. 15. For fourth-century parallels found elsewhere in Egypt and the Levant see Ladstätter 2015, nn. 38–41.
32 Ladstätter 2015, 139, nos. 19–20 (Gnathian amphorae); Ladstätter 2015, 142, no. 26 (ivy-platter group); Ladstätter 2015, 139–40, nos. 21–25 (*skyphoi*). Stratigraphically, vessel 22 (*skyphos*) originates from a deposit dated to the first half of the third century BCE. For discussion of the lamps, see Ladstätter 2015, 142–43, nos. 27–29.
33 Ladstätter 2010, 452; Müller 2010, 438.
34 Marchi 2014, 5.
35 Marchi 2014, 169.

36 Marchi 2014, 182.
37 The absence of religious spaces at Bi'r Samut is surprising, given that most comparable structures either of the Late Period or the Roman Period included religious facilities.
38 Marchi 2014, 163–64.
39 Marchi 2014, 186. Other Late Period military sites include bathing facilities, such as Elephantine (Kaiser et al. 1990, 214–21) and Syene (Müller 2008, 315, fig. 3).
40 Marchi 2014, 40.
41 Marchi 2014, 186.
42 Tell el-Herr Type III houses with food preparation installations in the entry room include Houses 55 and 67–70 in the North Sector, 77, 84, and 93 in the West Sector, and 28 in the East Sector.
43 Marchi 2014, 169–71.
44 Marchi 2014, 41, 170–71. This category of house (Type V) does not present a standard plan, but always includes a covered or open courtyard at either the front and/or rear of the unit.
45 Marchi 2014, 170.
46 Marchi 2014, 190.
47 Marchi 2014, 204–5.
48 Cuvigny 2017.

Works Cited

Berlin, A. 2013. "Something Old, Something New: Native Cultures under Ptolemaic Rule." In *Networks in the Hellenistic World: According to the Pottery in the Eastern Mediterranean and Beyond, BAR International Series 2539*, edited by N. Fenn and C. Römer-Strehl, 229–37. Oxford: Archaeopress.

Brun, J.-P., T. Faucher, and B. Redon. 2017. "An Early Ptolemaic Bath in the Fortress of Bi'r Samut (Eastern Desert)." In *Collective Baths in Egypt 2: New Discoveries and Perspectives, EtUrb* 10, edited by B. Redon, 13–23. Le Caire: Institut français d'archéologie orientale.

Brun, J.-P., T. Faucher, B. Redon, and S.E. Sidebotham, eds. 2018. *The Eastern Desert of Egypt during the Graeco-Roman Periods: Archaeological Reports*. Paris: College de France. doi:10.4000/books.cdf.5230.

Chaufray, M.-P. 2019. "Tituli ptolémaïques du désert oriental égyptien." In *New Approaches in Demotic Studies. Acts of the 13th International Conference of Demotic Studies in Leipzig, 4–8 September 2017*, edited by F. Naether, 39–92. Beihefte zur Zeitschrift für Ägyptische Sprache und Altertumskunde No. 10. Berlin: De Gruyter.

Chaufray, M.-P. 2022. "Les Blemmyes dans le désert Oriental égyptien à l'époque ptolémaïque (O.Blem. 1-16)." In *Blemmyes. New Documents and New Perspectives*, edited by H. Cuvigny, 75–103. Le Caire: Institut français d'archéologie orientale.

Chaufray, M.-P. 2023. "Multilinguisme à Samut." In *Le multilinguisme dans la Méditerranée antique*, edited by R. Roure. Pessac, Ausonius éditions, collection PrimaLun@. https://una-editions.fr/multilinguisme-a-samut/

Chaufray M.-P., and B. Redon. 2020. "Ostraka and Tituli Picti of Samut North and Bi'r Samut (Eastern Desert of Egypt). Some Reflections on Find Location." In *Using Ostraca in the Ancient World: New Discoveries and Methodologies*, edited by C. Caputo and J. Lougovaya, 165–82. Berlin: De Gruyter.

Cuvigny, H. 2017. "Quand Lichas plantait sa tente à Abbad. Un dossier de distribution d'eau sur la route d'Edfou à Bérénice (c. 240–210a)." *Chronique d'Égypte* 92 : 111–28.

Cuvigny, H. 2020. "L'élevage des chameaux sur la route d'Edfou à Bérénice d'après une lettre trouvée à Bi'r Samut (IIIe siècle av. J.-C.)." In *Les aisseaux du désert et des steppes: Les camélidés dans l'Antiquité* (Camelus dromedarius *et* Camelus bactrianus), edited by D. Agut-Labordère and B. Redon, 171–80. Lyon: Presses de la MOM.

Cuvigny, H., ed. 2022. *Blemmyes. New Documents and New Perspectives*. Le Caire: Institut français d'archéologie orientale.

Faucher, T. 2018. "Ptolemaic Gold: The Exploitation of Gold in the Eastern Desert." In *The Eastern Desert of Egypt during the Graeco-Roman Periods: Archaeological Reports*, edited by J.-P. Brun, T. Faucher, B. Redon, and S.E. Sidebotham, 1–16. Paris: College de France. doi:10.4000/books.cdf.5230.

Gates-Foster, J. 2012a. "The Eastern Desert." In *The Oxford Handbook of Roman Egypt*, edited by C. Riggs, 736–47. Oxford: Oxford University Press.

Gates-Foster, J. 2012b. "The Eastern Desert in the Ptolemaic Period: A Developing Picture." In *The Peoples of the Eastern Desert*, edited by H. Barnard and K. Duistermaat, 190–203. Los Angeles: University of California Press.

Gates-Foster, J. 2022. "Third Century BCE Supply Networks and Ptolemaic Transport Amphoras from 'Abbad and Bi'r Samut in Egypt's Eastern Desert." In *Networked Spaces: The Spatiality of Networks in the Red Sea and the Western Indian Ocean*, edited by B. Redon, 347–63. Lyon: Maison de l'Orient et de la Méditerranée.

Gill, J.C.R. 2016. *Dakhleh Oasis and the Western Desert of Egypt Under the Ptolemies*. Oxford: Oxbow.

Hadji-Minaglou, G. 2007. *Tebtynis IV. Les habitations à l'est du temple de Soknebtynis*. FIFAO 56. Le Caire: Institut français d'archéologie orientale.

Hepa, M. 2021. *Syene V. Zwei Rettungsgrabungen im Norden der antiken Stadt (Areal 62 und 90). Keramik und Befunde*. Beiträge zur ägyptischen Bauforschung und Altertumskunde, Band 23. Darmstadt: Philipp von Zabern.

Hudson, N. 2016. "A Hellenistic Household Ceramic Assemblage from Tell el-Timai (Thmuis), Egypt: A Contextual View." *Bulletin of the American Schools of Oriental Research* 376: 199–244.

Kaiser, W., et al. 1990. *Stadt und Tempel von Elephantine. 17./18. Grabungsbericht*. Mitteilungendes Deutschen Archäologischen Instituts Kairo 46. Mainz am Rhein: Philipp von Zabern.

Ladstätter, S. 2010. "Keramische Fundkomplexe aus Areal 15 der Stadtgrabung in Syene/Aswan." In *Städtisches Wohnen im östlichen Mittelmeerraum 4. Jh. v. Chr.—1. Jh. n. Chr.*, edited by S. Ladstätter and V. Scheiblreiter, 449–73. Wien: Österreicheschen Akademie der Wissenschaften.

Ladstätter, S. 2015. "Greek Pottery from Syene." In *From the Delta to the Cataract: Studies Dedicated to Mohamed El-Bialy*, edited by A. Jiménez-Serrano and C. von Pilgrim, 132–49. Leiden: Brill.

Lynch, K. 2018. "The Hellenistic Symposium as Feast." In *Feasting and Polis Institutions*, edited by F. van den Eijnde, J.H. Blok, and R. Strootman, 233–56. Leiden: Brill.

Marchand, S. 2011. "La dernière occupation d'une maison d'époque ptolémaïque du village de Tebtynis (Fayoum). Une céramique de transition tardo-hellénistique." *Cahiers de la céramique égyptienne* 9: 269–310.

Marchi, S. 2014. *L'habitat dans les forteresses de Migdol (Tell el-Herr) durant les Ve et IVe siècles av. J.-C. Étude archéologique*. Paris: Presses de l'Université Paris-Sorbonne.

Marouard, G. 2008. "Rues et habitats dans les villages de la chora égyptienne à la période gréco-romaine (IIIe s. av.–IVe s. apr. J.-C.): Quelques exemples du Fayoum (nome arsinoïte)." In *La rue dans l'Antiquité: Définition, aménagement et devenir de l'Orient méditerranéen à la Gaule*, edited by P. Ballet, N. Dieudonné-Glad, and C. Saliou, 117–28. Rennes: Presses universitaires de Rennes.

Müller, W. 2008. "Excavations in the Town Centre from the Late Period to Late Roman Times (Area 15)." In *The Town of Syene: Report on the 5th and 6th Season in Aswan*, edited by C. Von Pilgrim et al., 314–38. Mitteilungen des Deutschen Archaologischen Instituts Abteilung Kairo 64. Mainz am Rhein: Philipp von Zabern.

Müller, W. 2010. "Domestic Structures in Graeco-Roman Syene (Modern Aswan)." In *Städtisches Wohnen im östlichen Mittelmeerraum 4. Jh. v. Chr.—1. Jh. n. Chr.*, edited by S. Ladstätter and V. Scheiblreiter, 429–48. Wien: Österreicheschen Akademie der Wissenschaften.

Müller, W., and M. Hepa. 2017. "Two Baths from Syene." In *Collective Baths in Egypt 2: New Discoveries and Perspectives, EtUrb* 10, edited by B. Redon, 13–23. Le Caire: Institut français d'archéologie orientale.

Redon, B. 2010. "Les bains et l'armée en Égypte ptolémaïque et romaine." *Le Bulletin de l'Institut français d'archéologie orientale* 109: 407–50.

Redon, B. 2018. "The Control of the Eastern Desert by the Ptolemies: New Archaeological Data." In *The Eastern Desert of Egypt during the Graeco-Roman Periods: Archaeological Reports*, edited by J.-P. Brun, T. Faucher, B. Redon, and S.E. Sidebotham, 1–21. Paris: College de France. doi:10.4000/books.cdf.5230.

Redon, B., and T. Faucher. 2014. "Désert Oriental, district minier de Samut." *Rapport d'activité de l'IFAO 2013–2014, Le Bulletin de l'Institut français d'archéologie orientale* 113: 12–22.

Redon, B., and T. Faucher. 2015. "Désert Oriental, district minier de Samut." *Rapport d'activité de l'IFAO* 2014–2015, *Le Bulletin de l'Institut français d'archéologie orientale* 114: 24–33.

Redon, B., and T. Faucher. 2016. "Désert Oriental, district minier de Samut." *Rapport d'activité de l'IFAO 2015–2016, Le Bulletin de l'Institut français d'archéologie orientale* 115: 10–24.

Sidebotham, S.E., and J. Gates-Foster, eds. 2019. *The Archaeological Survey of the Desert Roads Between Berenike and the Nile Valley: Expeditions by the University of Michigan and the University of Delaware to the Eastern Desert of Egypt, 1987–2015*. Archaeological Reports Series Vol. 26. Boston: American Schools of Oriental Research.

Afterwords: Perspectives from Pharaonic Egypt and the Greco-Roman World

Afterword 1: Greco-Roman Households in Pharaonic Perspective

MIRIAM MÜLLER

Given my own research focus on Pharaonic-period households, the chapters presented in this volume have been a revelation of the fantastic work my colleagues undertake for the later periods of Egyptian history. This volume confirms the importance of studying and understanding houses, households, and homes, not only in ancient Egypt, but also throughout the wider Mediterranean and Near East. Simultaneously, the diverse research in the different chapters showcases a development over time, in that we are no longer concerned with the same issues that characterized the beginnings of household archaeology in the Mediterranean, such as what a household is and which physical space it occupies.[1] The study of Ptolemaic and Roman-period households in Egypt emphasizes that we need to overcome the often too narrowly defined approach of only looking at the actual house. The preceding chapters provide a broader perspective, as well as a great deal of new information about the identity and self-awareness of the inhabitants of Ptolemaic and Roman Egypt. Specifically, this volume brings together a great selection of case studies, presenting an integration of archaeology, texts, and material culture that expand our understanding of "houses" and "households" to include (among other things): the immediate surroundings of the physical frame of the house, such as the courtyards and street areas; the presence of extended families and different forms of cohabitation, spanning sometimes multiple houses; the study of violence and its location within the physical space of the household; the significance of textual records in combination with the archaeological record; the role of gender and women (an aspect of household studies that was for a long time neglected); the integration of bioarchaeological evidence in a focus on ancient diet; or use patterns and discard activity in household space.[2] Many contributions furthermore make use of ethnographic data, closely linking the study of contemporary societies and their material remains to the past society under scrutiny. The chapters further showcase new approaches in dealing with old excavation records and the ways that we can integrate and expand them into new research designs by implementing new archaeological techniques.

Many of the themes stated above have also played, and continue to play, an important role in research on Pharaonic households—with one major exception: the ubiquity of texts dealing with Ptolemaic and Roman-period households in Egypt. The study of Pharaonic-period households struggles with a lack of written evidence that could, for example, inform about the composition and size of households throughout Pharaonic history, or the evidence for owners and their social standing. Elite housing, at least, often reveals its occupants through inscriptions on fixed architectural elements, furniture, and objects, but the middle and lower classes are extremely difficult to detect archaeologically, and their households appear only rarely in records that were mostly found dissociated from the described circumstances and locations.[3] It is very promising to see that many of the chapters in this volume implement a combination of textual and archaeological records and further explore the potential of this material for the study of households in Egypt from the Greco-Roman Period.

Cross-Cutting Themes

The interactions between households constitute a leitmotif in all the case studies presented in this volume. Space and rights of access within the settlement structure were negotiated on all different levels. Bethany Simpson's examination of access patterns and thoroughfares in the different neighborhoods of ancient Karanis in chapter 2 and Darlene Brooks Hedstrom's discussion of the living quarters in the Monastery of Apa Thomas in chapter 11 both reveal an intricate cooperation on issues of space and passage that is confirmed by contemporary written documentation on agreements between neighbors.

In the same way, Sabine Huebner's work in chapter 5 on legal arrangements between family members and with creditors in the form of the *habitatio* (or the right of residence) illustrates complex interactions among house owners and dependents. Since the property was inherited in equal shares by male and female children, the widow would have to return to her natal house if no such arrangement existed. This division but also consolidation of property plays out on the ground in the form of multiple house contracts between extended families about the sharing and combining of one estate or neighboring properties, as discussed in chapter 2 by Bethany Simpson, chapter 4 by Dorothy Thompson, and chapter 7 by Richard Alston.

Other case studies remind us of less convivial community culture, as in Youssri Abdelwahed's vivid narrative (chapter 5) on complaints about verbal and physical abuse and trespassing, as well as in David Frankfurter's account (chapter 10) of apotropaic measures against the vulnerability of a domestic space that was constantly threatened by outside demonic forces. These studies remind us of the negative aspects of cohabitation, such as the resentment and quarrels over property that accompany the increasing urban pressure documented in Gregory Marouard's discussion (chapter 3) of settlement data from multiple Ptolemaic sites. Specifically, the vertical expansion of the tower houses reveals the challenge of finding new forms of coresidence in a community without losing too much space or accessibility. Similarly, the compact form of the Ptolemaic and Roman-period houses, with only limited uncovered courtyard space and no views into the interior of the houses, also responds to the arid environment and windy and dusty climate of Egypt, as Paola Davoli clearly outlines in chapter 1. Furthermore, the theme of domestic discard and possible solutions for the disposal of everyday debris, as Anna Boozer describes in chapter 8 for the Roman-period town of Trimithis, very much ties into this emphasis on pressing issues experienced in settlements and among households of Greco-Roman Egypt.

The comparison of activity areas and the evidence for shared facilities, such as ovens, in the Ptolemaic fort at Bi'r Samut in chapter 12 by Jennifer Gates-Foster, Bérangère Redon, and Melanie Godsey reveals close interaction among the fortress population, similar to that also evidenced in other settlements such as Karanis. These findings raise questions about whether individual households were present, with potential family structures, or whether such a fortress has to be seen as one big household for a community with exclusively military functions. Finally, Ross Thomas's account of domestic cults in the Greco-Roman Period in chapter 9 (as evidenced by figurines with different cultural influences) displays the realities of life on the periphery of empires where multiple cultural zones overlapped.

Taken together, all of these case studies reveal different forms of household agency, and in particular diverse individual decisions, modifications, and adjustments that can only be revealed by a thorough analysis of all the available lines of evidence. Looking back in time, and considering Ptolemaic and Roman-period households together with their Pharaonic predecessors, enables us to relate this theme of personal agency to a longstanding bias in Egyptological research. Scholars working on the prevalent settlement types of Pharaonic Egypt have questioned the very existence of household agency and the expression of different forms of household evolution, development, and growth.[4] One recent publication claims that model settlements, such as those that have been excavated from all different periods of Pharaonic Egypt, forced the population into ghettolike living circumstances that for a long time did not leave much room for individual or community agency.[5] Only recently has this dataset been studied for potential insights into a more detailed understanding of households' everyday dealings, and in particular household interactions and identity.[6]

Related Studies from a Pharaonic Perspective

Perspectives on households and daily life in ancient Egypt have considerably changed over the last two decades. Formerly, analysis focused on the pictorial and limited textual record, with archaeological data solely drawn from two well-documented settlement sites, Deir el-Medina and Amarna. More recently, there has been an enormous increase in information from long-term settlement excavations during the second half of the twentieth and beginning of the twenty-first century, as well as a new, integrated approach to the analysis of data on everyday life in Egypt. Although much can be gained from examining daily life as depicted in paintings and models, or from descriptions in letters or census lists, the material evidence from settlements presents the clearest and most reliable account of a society's everyday dealings. Already, sites such as Elephantine, Tell el-Dab'a, South Abydos, Amarna, and Amara West have been explored with a new perspective and have revealed novel information. Furthermore, with the implementation of new technologies such as microarchaeology, it is possible to grasp the lived experience of people in cities in different parts of the Egyptian empire, from the core to the periphery.

Scholars working in Pharaonic Egypt have similarly become aware of neighborhood interactions and the constant negotiation of space, the taking over of adjacent open and public areas such as streets and alleys, the incorporation of neighboring properties, or the splitting of houses and estates and reorganization of access. Similar phenomena can be seen in the late Middle Kingdom/early Second Intermediate Period neighborhood at Tell el-Dab'a[7] or the New Kingdom examples in the Main City of Amarna[8] and inside the city walls of Amara West.[9]

Household lifecycles, and the passing on of household property and management from father to son, have been documented in census records from the Middle Kingdom town of Kahun and also verified in the archaeological record of the site.[10] The theme of urban pressure, trash, and trespassing has been explored for the long-lived settlement of Elephantine at the traditional southern border of Egypt.[11] In the period of the Middle Kingdom, domestic waste management and an attempt to keep the houses and adjacent surroundings clean reveal an individual, but maybe also community, strategy to secure space in the valuable courtyard areas and passage of the streets and alleys on this narrowly confined island.

The question of how to deal with a special-purpose settlement, such as a fort or a monastery, and whether we are dealing with one big household organized under certain conditions and with only one specific group of members, such as soldiers or monks, is also being discussed for the many Pharaonic towns and villages that were built for a particular task. Workmen's settlements, such as the Walled Village in the eastern desert of Amarna, and fortresses like the Middle Kingdom strongholds in Nubia, have been examined for their potential inhabitants and for the interactions among residents who are assumed to be exclusively soldiers and officials[12] or families.[13] By analyzing the distribution of seal impressions and revealing their owners at Uronarti, or investigating the number and arrangement of bread-making facilities at Amarna, researchers have revealed individual households and properties, but at the same time documented a close-knit community that collaborated on a daily basis. We furthermore see a much closer intermingling of work and living space, to the extent that offices cannot really be differentiated from domestic space.[14] Most of the spaces inside smaller units in those uniform settlements were thus probably multifunctional.[15]

Additionally, new studies on domestic cults from the Pharaonic heartland and the alleged type sites of Egyptian urbanism, Deir el-Medina[16] and Amarna,[17] challenge long-held views of religious life in the New Kingdom by challenging the exclusivity of the veneration of the Aten and the resulting trend of a strong expression of personal piety. Rituals and performances, including certain objects pertaining to the realm of magic, were dedicated to protecting the Pharaonic house and are expressed in the material record, revealing the intricate nature of the perceived and expressed identities of individuals, households, and communities.[18] With so much information already to offer in the Egyptian "core," it will also be important to take a new look at analogous dynamics in the borderlands, with their potential exchange, adoption, and creation of new cultural expressions.

Trends in Pharaonic and Greco-Roman Household Studies

As noted in the preceding chapters, texts comprise a major component in the analysis of domestic space and household composition in Greco-Roman archaeology and also for the study of households in Greco-Roman Egypt. However, an equally extensive textual record does not exist for the examination of domestic space in the Pharaonic Period. While this discrepancy robs Egyptology of an important source and insight into household dealings in the third and second millennia BCE, the reliance on texts has also created a major bias in the perception of domestic arrangements in ancient Greece, Italy, and equally Greco-Roman Egypt. In particular, the supposed use of various rooms by different genders (*andron, gynaikon*) became a common reading of domestic space.[19] The gendered use of space was similarly addressed in household studies of the Pharaonic Period, based on depictions and related built features found in the two best-preserved settlements in Egypt, Deir el-Medina and Amarna, which seemed to delineate male and female spaces in typical Egyptian houses from the New Kingdom.[20] In Greco-Roman archaeology, it was only in the 1990s and early 2000s that thorough studies of artifact distribution reevaluated the picture derived from the texts.[21] Similar approaches followed in Egyptian archaeology of the Pharaonic Period.[22] With a new awareness of the validity of different sources, we cannot afford to neglect either one or the other. As this volume shows, a combination of archaeology, texts, and material culture will lead to a better understanding of the patchy remains that archaeologists and philologists encounter.

Therefore, bringing together the Greco-Roman and Egyptian worlds creates a fortunate and worthwhile opportunity. In Egypt, favorable conditions of preservation for both archaeological and textual sources allow for the combination and comparison of numerous family archives of papyri found in the vestiges of ancient houses and neighborhoods of the Greco-Roman Period.[23] Because of the perturbations and formation processes of the archaeological record, some have expressed pessimism regarding the clear association of texts with particular domestic spaces, and thus the possibility of assigning owners to the different buildings and retracing their family histories in the ancient remains of their properties.[24] Still, it has become clear that this approach bears enormous potential.[25]

Future Perspectives

Located on the imperial frontiers, Egypt naturally lends itself as a case study for investigating borderland interactions in the Greco-Roman Period. At first an outpost on the other side of the Mediterranean, Egypt hosted Greek immigrants from the seventh century BCE onward, before becoming the heart of the Ptolemaic

Empire and subsequently being relegated to a province at the periphery of the vast Roman Empire. From the Greco-Roman perspective, Egypt certainly constituted a contact zone, with foreign customs and beliefs that were quickly adapted and merged with traditional Greek and Roman motifs but also respected and admired.[26] In the same way, certain regions of northeast Africa, such as the western oases and parts of Nubia, constitute borderlands if viewed from the core of the Ptolemaic or Roman empires.[27] These areas have brought to light a naturally mixed material culture that stresses certain markers of identity and ethnicity, displaying various strategies for living in these border zones. Especially for the Pharaonic Period, areas at the periphery of the empire's sphere of influence and contact zones with neighboring regions, such as the eastern Nile Delta and Nubia, reveal a different picture from that gained from official records, which are mostly distorted by the representation of the ruler and shaped by territorial interests. A closer look at the archaeological evidence from settlements and a detailed study of households help to uncover multifaceted levels of cultural interaction and the creation of new identities through cultural exchange.[28]

Applications from the field of microarchaeology have contributed considerably to our understanding of certain practices in and around domestic space. It is the area of modern-day northern Sudan, Egyptian-occupied Nubia during the Middle and New Kingdoms, where micro- and ethnoarchaeological research coupled with experimental studies accompany the excavations at a number of sites such as Amara West and Sai Island.[29] Micromorphology has revealed insights into different techniques of constructing floors in house types of Egyptian and Nubian origin. These have been confirmed by observations of traditional building in the modern villages nearby. Different types of Egyptian and Nubian cooking pots and their imitations, as evidenced by petrology, inform about varying diet. The reconstruction of an area for the preparation of food and cooking has revealed how the different types of pots were employed. In Egypt, the implementation of different microarchaeological methods in settlement excavations is considerably hampered by the fact that the Egyptian authorities currently still do not allow exportation of archaeological samples for this kind of analysis, and facilities for on-site analysis and local laboratories have only recently been developed.[30] As a result, contributions with this focus were rare in the different chapters presented in this volume.[31]

Taken together, these studies demonstrate that there is still much to learn about ancient households. With every new angle, we can get a little closer to the lived experience of past societies, in the core and periphery of empires and in the constant exchange and negotiation between individuals and communities. As discussed in the introduction to this volume, households are clearly not passive bystanders, but influence and change societies from the bottom up. This volume showcases this theme in a very innovative way, and I look forward to exciting new avenues of research in the future!

Notes

1 Cf. Parker and Foster 2012.
2 Hendon 2004.

3 Cf. the Heqanakht letters, which give a vivid account of a wealthy middle-class farmer's household dealings, but were found in the debris of the entrance shaft of the tomb of Ibi, where Heqanakht was fulfilling his duty as mortuary priest (Allen 2002).
4 E.g., Kemp 2018, 194–244, for Middle Kingdom communities.
5 Mazzone 2017.
6 Müller 2015a. A recent conference on the occasion of the fiftieth anniversary of the excavations on Elephantine has expanded on the study of households and settlements in pharaonic Egypt and firmly established the field of household archaeology in Egyptology (Sigl 2022).
7 Müller 2015b; 2015c.
8 Kemp and Stevens 2010.
9 Spencer 2014a; 2014b; 2015.
10 Kemp 2018, 219–21; Kóthay 2001, 353–55; Muhs 2015, 326–29.
11 Arnold 2015.
12 Penacho 2015.
13 Samuel 1999.
14 Picardo 2015.
15 Spence 2015; Moeller 2015. This was also stressed by Gates-Foster, Redon, and Godsey in their study of the Ptolemaic fort at Bi'r Samut in chapter 12, this volume.
16 Weiss 2015.
17 Stevens 2006.
18 Jankuhn 1972.
19 E.g., Hoepfner and Schwandner 1994.
20 E.g., Ricke 1932; Meskell 2002. Cf. Kleinke 2007.
21 E.g., Nevett 1999; Allison 2004.
22 e.g., publications in the Tell el-Dab'a series; Von Pilgrim 1996.
23 Van Minnen 1994.
24 E.g., Landvatter 2016.
25 Muhs 2008; Nevett 2011.
26 Cf. Boozer 2012, 2013; Masson-Berghoff and Thomas 2019.
27 Boozer 2018.
28 Müller 2015d; 2019.
29 Dalton 2017; Budka 2017.
30 E.g., Sigl and Kopp 2020.
31 Cf. Thomas, chapter 9, this volume; Boozer, chapter 8, this volume.

Works Cited

Allen, J.P. 2002. *The Heqanakht Papyri*. Metropolitan Museum of Art Egyptian Expedition 27. New York: Metropolitan Museum of Art.

Allison, P.M. 2004. *Pompeian Households. An Analysis of the Material Culture*. Cotsen Institute of Archaeology Monographs 42. Los Angeles: University of California.

Arnold, F. 2015. "Clean and Unclean Space: Domestic Waste Management at Elephantine." In *Household Studies in Complex Societies. (Micro) Archaeological and Textual Approaches*, Oriental Institute Series 10, edited by M. Müller, 151–68. Chicago: The Oriental Institute of the University of Chicago Press.

Boozer, A.L. 2012. "Globalizing Mediterranean Identities: The Overlapping Spheres of Egyptian, Greek and Roman Worlds at Trimithis." *Journal of Mediterranean Archaeology* 25 (2): 219–42.

Boozer, A.L. 2013. "Frontiers and Borderlands in Imperial Perspectives: Exploring Rome's Egyptian Frontier." *American Journal of Archaeology* 117 (2): 275–92.

Boozer, A.L. 2018. "The Archaeology of Imperial Borderlands: A View from Roman Egypt and Sudan." In *The Archaeology of Imperial Borderlands. A Comparative Study of Empires in the Ancient Near East and Mediterranean World*, edited by B.S. Düring and T.D. Stek, 206–39. Cambridge: Cambridge University Press.

Budka, J. 2017. "Life in the New Kingdom Town of Sai Island: Some New Perspectives." In *Nubia in the New Kingdom: Lived Experience, Pharaonic Control, and Indigenous Traditions*, edited by N. Spencer, A. Stevens, and M. Binder, 429–48. Leuven: Peeters.

Dalton, M. 2017. "Reconstructing Lived Experiences of Domestic Space at Amara West: Some Preliminary Interpretations of Ancient Floor Deposits Using Ethnoarchaeological and Micromorphological Analyses." In *Nubia in the New Kingdom: Lived Experience, Pharaonic Control and Indigenous Traditions*, edited by N. Spencer, A. Stevens, and M. Binder, 357–88. Leuven: Peeters.

Hendon, J.A. 2004. "Living and Working at Home: The Social Archaeology of Household Production and Social Relations." In *A Companion to Social Archaeology*, edited by R.W. Preucel and L. Meskell, 272–86. Malden, MA: Blackwell.

Hoepfner, W., and E.-L. Schwandner. 1994. *Haus und Stadt im klassischen Griechenland*. Neubearbeitung, Wohnen in der klassischen Polis, Bd.1. München: Deutscher Kunstverlag.

Jankuhn, D. 1972. *Das Buch zum "Schutz des Hauses" (sA-pr)*. Bonn: Rudolf Habelt.

Kemp, B.J. 2018. *Ancient Egypt. Anatomy of a Civilization*. 3rd ed. Abingdon, UK: Routledge.

Kemp, B.J., and A. Stevens. 2010. *Busy Lives at Amarna. Excavations in the Main City (Grid 12 and the House of Ranefer, N49,18)*. Memoirs of the Egypt Exploration Society 90–91. London: Egypt Exploration Society.

Kleinke, N. 2007. *Female Spaces: Untersuchungen zu Gender und Archäologie im pharaonischen Ägypten*. Göttinger Miszellen, Beihefte 1. Göttingen: Seminar für Ägyptologie und Koptologie der Universität Göttingen.

Kóthay, K.A. 2001. "Houses and Households at Kahun: Bureaucratic and Domestic Aspects of Social Organization During the Middle Kingdom." In *"le lotus qui sort de terre": Mélanges offerts à Edith Varga*, edited by H. Györy. 349–68. Bulletin du Musée Hongrois des Beaux-Arts—Supplément. Budapest: Musée Hongrois des Beaux-Arts.

Landvatter, T. 2016. "Archaeological and Papyrological Inquiry at Karanis: Problems and Potentialities." In *Proceedings of the 27th International Congress of Papyrology, Warsaw, 29 July–3 August 2013*, edited by T. Derda, A. Łajtar, and J. Urbanik, 1493–518. The Journal of Juristic Papyrology, Supplement 28. Warsaw: University of Warsaw.

Masson-Berghoff, A., and R. Thomas, eds. 2019. "Naukratis in Context." *British Museum Studies in Ancient Egypt and Sudan* 24. https://webarchive.nationalarchives.gov.uk/20190801105854/https://www.britishmuseum.org/research/publications/online_journals/bmsaes/issue_24.aspx.

Mazzone, D. 2017. "The Dark Side of a Model Community: The 'Ghetto' of el-Lahun." *Journal of Ancient Egyptian Architecture* 2: 19–54.

Meskell, L. 2002. *Private Life in New Kingdom Egypt*. Princeton: Princeton University Press.

Moeller, N. 2015. "Multifunctionality and Hybrid Households: The Case of Ancient Egypt." In *Household Studies in Complex Societies: (Micro) Archaeological and Textual Approaches*, edited by M. Müller, 474–62. Oriental Institute Series 10. Chicago: Oriental Institute of the University of Chicago Press.

Muhs, B.P. 2008. "Fractions of Houses in Ptolemaic Hawara." In *Graeco-Roman Fayum—Texts and Archaeology. Proceedings of the Third International Fayum Symposion, Freudenstadt, May 29–June 1, 2007*, edited by S. Lippert and M. Schentuleit, 187–97. Wiesbaden: Harrassowitz.

Muhs, B.P. 2015. "Property Title, Domestic Architecture, and Household Lifecycles in Egypt." In *Household Studies in Complex Societies: (Micro) Archaeological and Textual Approaches*, edited by M. Müller, 321–37. Oriental Institute Series 10. Chicago: Oriental Institute of the University of Chicago Press.

Müller, M. 2015a. *Household Studies in Complex Societies: (Micro) Archaeological and Textual Approaches*. Oriental Institute Series 10. Chicago: Oriental Institute of the University of Chicago Press.

Müller, M. 2015b. "Late Middle Kingdom Society in a Neighborhood of Tell el-Dab^ca/Avaris." In *Household Studies in Complex Societies. (Micro) Archaeological and Textual Approaches*, edited by M. Müller, 339–70. Oriental Institute Series 10. Chicago: Oriental Institute of the University of Chicago Press.

Müller, M. 2015c. "New Approaches to the Study of Households in Middle Kingdom and Second Intermediate Period Egypt." In *From Archetype to Fragmented—New Studies on Middle Bronze Age Egypt (2000–1500 BC)*, edited by W. Grajetzki and G. Miniaci, 237–55. London: Golden House.

Müller. M. 2015d. "Modelling Household Identity in a Multi-ethnic Society." *Archaeological Review from Cambridge* 30 (1): 102–12.

Müller, M. 2019. "Appropriation of Territory Through Migrant Ritual Practices in Egypt's Eastern Delta." In *Perspectives on Lived Religion. Practices, Transmission, Landscape*, edited by H. Twiston Davies, N. Staring and L. Weiss, 27–38. Leiden: Sidestone Press.

Nevett, L.C. 1999. *House and Society in the Ancient Greek World*. Cambridge: Cambridge University Press.

Nevett, L.C. 2011. "Family and Household, Ancient History and Archeology: A Case Study from Roman Egypt." In *A Companion to Families in the Greek and Roman Worlds*, edited by B. Rawson, 15–31. Oxford: Blackwell.

Parker, B.J., and C.P. Foster. 2012. *New Perspectives on Household Archaeology*. Winona Lake, IN: Eisenbrauns.

Penacho, S. 2015. "Deciphering Sealing Practices at Uronarti and Askut: A Spatial Analysis of the Built Environment and Individual Sealers." PhD diss., University of Chicago.

Picardo, N. 2015. "Hybrid Households: Institutional Affiliations and Household Identity in the Town of Wah-sut (South Abydos)." In *Household Studies in Complex Societies: (Micro) Archaeological and Textual Approaches*, edited by M. Müller, 243–87. Oriental Institute Series 10. Chicago: Oriental Institute of the University of Chicago Press.

Ricke, H. 1932. *Der Grundriss des Amarna-Wohnhauses*. Wissenschaftliche Veröffentlichungen der Deutschen Orient-Gesellschaft 56. Leipzig: J.C.Hinrichs.

Samuel, D. 1999. "Bread Making and Social Interactions at the Amarna Workmen's Village, Egypt." *World Archaeology* 31 (1): 121–44.

Sigl, J., and P. Kopp. 2020. "Working from Home: Middle Kingdom Daily Life on Elephantine Island, Egypt." In *Approaches to the Analysis of Production Activity at Archaeological Sites*, edited by A.K. Hodgkinson and C. Lelek Tvetmarken, 8–24. Oxford: Archaeopress.

Sigl, J., ed. 2022. *Daily Life in Ancient Egyptian Settlements*. Sonderschriften des Deutschen Archäologischen Instituts Kairo 47. Wiesbaden: Harrassowitz.

Spence, K. 2015. "Ancient Egyptian Houses and Households: Architecture, Artifacts, Conceptualization, and Interpretation." In *Household Studies in Complex Societies: (Micro) Archaeological and Textual Approaches*, edited by M. Müller, 83–99. Oriental Institute Series 10. Chicago: Oriental Institute of the University of Chicago Press.

Spencer, N. 2014a. "Creating and Re-shaping Egypt in Kush: Responses at Amara West." *Journal of Ancient Egyptian Interconnections* 6 (1): 42–61.

Spencer, N. 2014b. "Amara West: Considerations on Urban Life in Occupied Kush." In *Proceedings of the 12th International Conference for Nubian Studies*, edited by D.A. Welsby and J.R. Anderson, 457–86. Leuven: Peeters.

Spencer, N. 2015. "Creating a Neighborhood within a Changing Town: Household and Other Agencies at Amara West in Nubia." In *Household Studies in Complex Societies: (Micro) Archaeological and Textual Approaches*, edited by M. Müller, 169–210. Oriental Institute Series 10. Chicago: Oriental Institute of the University of Chicago Press.

Stevens, A. 2006. *Private Religion at Amarna. The Material Evidence*. British Archaeological Reports International Series 1587. Oxford: Archaeopress.

Van Minnen, P. 1994. "House-to-House Enquiries: An Interdisciplinary Approach to Roman Karanis." *Zeitschrift für Papyrologie und Epigraphik* 100: 227–51.

Von Pilgrim, C. 1996. *Elephantine XVIII. Untersuchungen in der Stadt des Mittleren Reiches und der Zweiten Zwischenzeit*, Archäologische Veröffentlichungen 91. Mainz: Von Zabern.

Weiss, L. 2015. *Religious Practice at Deir el-Medina*. Egyptologische Uitgaven 29. Leiden: Nederlands Instituut voor het Nabije Oosten.

Afterword 2: Contextualizing Houses, Households, and Homes in the Classical World and Beyond

LISA NEVETT

The spatiality of the house, both in general and in the particular case of Ptolemaic to late antique Egypt, invites consideration of both practical and socially focused questions, and fosters dialogue on a wide range of issues. The richness and variety of the sources available from Egypt on houses and households offer an incomparable opportunity for study from both material and textual perspectives. Exceptional preservation of structures and texts, precision of chronology, and sheer volume of the available evidence create a database that scholars working in most other parts of the ancient world (such as classical Greece—my own specialism) can only admire. It is therefore surely in this Egyptian material, if anywhere in the ancient world, that the full potential of the house as a window onto the past can be realized. If that is so, then are there any points emerging from the preceding chapters that might be useful in other, less well-documented contexts in the ancient world, or even beyond?

Defining the Household

Perhaps most strikingly, the reader is treated to wonderfully vivid pictures. For example, Dorothy Thompson's portrait of a Ptolemaic village in the South Fayum in chapter 4 sets the physical structures of the houses among the other amenities of the village and identifies the inhabitants of this village by their names, ages, family relationships, occupations, and sometimes ethnicities. Such details show how houses (and the individuals dwelling within them) lay enmeshed within wider physical and social networks. Other textual sources, such as those drawn on by Youssri Abdelwahed in chapter 6, offer more specific information about various locations around and within the house: in this case, where violent assaults were alleged to have taken place. Although the layout of the domestic environment is more in evidence here in the pinpointing of the settings for these incidents, it still constitutes a backdrop, and as such its organization is not described in detail. By contrast, the material remains of the houses themselves provide vivid detail of a different kind, as Bethany Simpson demonstrates in chapter 2. Specifically, one of the strengths of the archaeological record is that it enables us to reconstruct physical relationships between spaces: relationships which must have both shaped, and been shaped by, the lives of the inhabitants of these villages and towns. Thus, two fundamentally different sources of evidence (texts and archaeology) offer the opportunity to reach an understanding of Egyptian society that encompasses an unusually wide variety of dimensions.

The immense quantity of evidence not only offers the possibility of telling the unique story of an individual household, as attested through a single document or archive, or through a specific domestic building, it also offers the prospect of constructing a more generalized picture of continuities and discontinuities across settlements and regions, or between social groups. In chapter 7, Richard Alston describes a few of the difficulties involved in making this kind of leap in scale, in relation to Bourdieu's famous interpretation of the Kabyle house as a macrocosm of Kabyle society.[1] But such a step can arguably be taken by aggregating evidence, as a number of the chapters here demonstrate. A rigorous theoretical framework can assist in this process, helping to frame questions and to order the information that might help to address them. In chapter 8, Anna Boozer's use of Lynn Meskell's concept of "material habitus" shows nicely how such theoretical perspectives can be crucial aids in this process.[2] Frameworks like these enable us to move systematically beyond simply reconstructing the physical settings of a single house or group of houses, and toward understanding the more general patterns of social interactions. At the same time, they facilitate a reorientation away from culture-historical observation toward a more analytical perspective.

Together, the case studies gathered in this volume ask a fundamental question: How should the household be defined, both physically and socially, in research on the Egyptian context? Discussions of the "household" in archaeological studies have tended to focus on its collective productive, reproductive, and symbolic activities.[3] Thompson adopts a somewhat more inclusive definition in chapter 4, encompassing also those who "lived, ate, and slept together . . . or joined in daily activities." The degree of specificity about household membership that the evidence affords is also illustrated by a number of the other chapters, including the very particular contexts of the creditor-debtor arrangements discussed in chapter 5 by Sabine Huebner. Then, in chapter 7, Alston challenges the validity of the standard anthropological terminology to describe the relationships between household members, because that terminology is not calibrated to the specific Egyptian situation. Overall, the scholarship on this material needs to move beyond the urge to build normative models of the household and instead to take advantage of the unique character of the available evidence in order to embrace, investigate, and understand diversity.

Several chapters address this challenge and collectively nuance the definition of "household" in interesting and complex ways. Although there is a common assumption in household archaeology that the physical house and social household are coterminous, such a one-to-one relationship does not always actually exist. This assumption of a direct correspondence between architectural space and social unit has therefore been criticized as imposing modern Western cultural expectations.[4]

Documentary evidence presented in chapter 7 (Alston) suggests that these expectations certainly do not hold true in Roman Egypt; instead, Alston identifies a range of potential arrangements, from individual houses that were split between several households, to a single household that had interests in multiple properties. At the same time, the evidence presented in chapters 11 (Brooks Hedstrom) and 12 (Gates-Foster, Redon, and Godsey) shows that a household (defined in terms of residence and/or economic cooperation) did not necessarily always consist of a nuclear or extended family, or indeed rely on any other kind of blood relationship. On the contrary, a household could also consist of individuals whose relationships were created and sustained by a shared system of values (in chapter 11, religious ones) or by a shared occupation or mission (like the military one in chapter 12). Untangling the social significance of a single structure identified in an archaeological context is thus very challenging, but what this evidence does show is that in the context of any research project on households, it is important to build up a culturally specific set of assumptions about who the occupants of a structure may have been, how they may or may not have been related, and in what sense (if at all) they may have constituted a single household.

The Roles of Houses and Households

Related to the definition of the household is the role played by the house itself. As a structure, the house was obviously of key importance in providing shelter for the household to perform some of its functions, such as production and reproduction (as Alston points out in chapter 7). But it is clear from a number of the different chapters that it had major significance in other respects, too. One of these was as an economic asset—an aspect that emerges clearly from Huebner's study of the legal right of *habitatio* (chapter 5). This framework effectively separated the economic value of a house from the right to reside in it, enabling different individuals to benefit from each. The law further complicates an already complex situation in which a single house seems not infrequently to have been split between multiple owners and/or households (as mentioned by Alston). For archaeologists working in this and other cultural contexts, it is a sobering fact that the physical structures of such buildings rarely offer any indication of modification or subdivision that might correspond with such intricate ownership situations.[5] We are faced, then, with the fact that an excavated house can be a poor guide to some of the realities of its occupants' social lives.

The practical role played by domestic space may have outweighed its symbolic importance, but the two may have also been closely linked. Perhaps partly as a result of their economic significance, Egyptian houses did have a variety of powerful symbolic valences. In particular, David Frankfurter focuses on this aspect of the house in chapter 10. At one level, the building materialized the success of its owner, because the ability to possess a house depended on economic prosperity. At another, less tangible, level, it was also viewed as a place of refuge and safety which contrasted with an outside world fraught with dangers. Some of these were literal, physical threats, and the possibility that they could result in actual violations underlies the documents discussed by Abdelwahed in chapter 6. The power of these acts may have stemmed in part from the fact that they broke the illusion that a house was a safe place. Besides such immediate dangers from other humans, Frankfurter focuses on a second realm in chapter 10: that of jealous and malevolent spirits—perhaps envisioned as resentful of the prosperity embodied in the house and conjured through the insecurities of owners aware of their own good fortune and how rapidly their luck could change. Whatever the precise explanation, Frankfurter's evidence shows the seriousness of the residents' concerns through the elaborate rituals that were apparently devised in order to keep such forces at bay. The remains of domestic ritual, found both in Egyptian contexts and elsewhere in the ancient world, provide independent witness to the reality of such practices.[6]

In chapter 9, Ross Thomas touches on a different aspect of the symbolic role of housing: its ability to express identity, including (in this case) ethnic and cultural affiliations. Such use of domestic buildings has been well attested by cross-cultural anthropological studies[7] and has also been a focus of scholarship on households both in prehistory and in the classical world.[8] While the compiler of Thompson's village survey in chapter 4 sometimes labels the occupants of a particular house as "Jew" or "Arab," Thomas's analysis of the use of terracottas shows that from the perspective of the house's occupants, the realities were likely to have been more complicated. Identity was contextual and multifaceted; a single household used material culture to express a range of different intersecting (and potentially even contradictory) affiliations. Remarkably, this kind of intersectionality is an area in which the material culture, rather than the texts, gives much of the insight into some of the subtleties involved.[9] The material culture offers multiple different strands of evidence that provide insight into a range of cultural practices that may have been used to create complementary—or even apparently conflicting—facets of a household's identity. It also provides an opportunity to explore the identities that households were creating for themselves, rather than—as in Thompson's examples—an identity perceived (or possibly imposed) by an outsider.

The Context of Houses and Households

Another important discussion emerging from several chapters relates to notions of "public" and "private." These terms are sometimes applied uncritically to ancient domestic contexts.[10] Nevertheless, it must be recognized that, like the definition of "household," the relevance and significance of these terms are determined by the cultural context in which they are deployed.[11] We must also ask whether they map onto emic concepts and/or are justifiable in an etic sense. In relation to our Egyptian material, Abdelwahed emphasizes in chapter 6 the importance of the house frontage as a common location for domestic violence and suggests that a violation of this area may have been particularly heinous, because it combined an assault on the household and its members with an open display of that assault to outsiders (that is, an action that was in some way "public"). The importance of the threshold as both a physical boundary (as demonstrated by Brooks Hedstrom in chapter 11) and a symbolic one (as shown by Frankfurter in chapter 10) reinforces the view that there was indeed an important distinction made between the interior and exterior of the house. While this evidence implies that there were contrasting public and private spheres in the Egyptian context, Alston in chapter 7 presents an argument that the two were conceptualized in an imprecise manner, owing to the fuzzy boundaries applied in Egyptian thought to both house and household. This understanding is supported and further unpacked by Paola Davoli's analysis in chapter 1, in which she describes ways that households may have controlled accessways and gates lying beyond the walls of their individual properties—again blurring the distinction between the property of individual households and that of their communities. In chapter 2, Simpson's discussion of the sharing of facilities such as courtyards and ovens, which apparently lay within the confines of individual houses, supports a similar conclusion, suggesting communal use of areas and structures that might otherwise have been considered as restricted to use by a single household. Therefore, while some degree of public and private distinction existed, the spheres may not have been as sharply divided as one might expect. Conceptual boundaries may not have always corresponded to physical ones, and the right places and the right cues are key to interpreting the evidence in these terms.

Consideration of the dichotomy between public and private in literal, physical terms, as a distinction between the exterior and interior spaces of a house, raises the question of how the household related to the wider community, both as a collective and through its members as individuals. The corollary of an emphasis on the importance of the physical house as the location of production and reproduction in a material sense is an awareness of how these roles play out in the social realm, with economic ties and kinship bonds that stretch outward, binding the household to the wider community. Nevertheless, the example of monastic households in chapter 11 (Brooks Hedstrom) shows that the extent of such contacts varied according to context. In some of these communities, she shows that active measures discouraged interactions between the inhabitants and the outside world, such as sinking the residential space below ground out of sight of the occupants of nearby settlements. It is unclear to what extent contact with the wider world may have been perceived as undesirable for some of the same reasons as those identified by Frankfurter in chapter 10 in the case of nonmonastic households.

The Dynamics of Houses and Households

A criticism sometimes leveled at household archaeology in general is that the vision of domestic life that it presents is too static.[12] The extensive Egyptian database offers an opportunity to move beyond such models to a more dynamic understanding of continuity and change across time and space—the potential to explore what Thompson refers to in chapter 4 as the "changing lives . . . of dwellings." How is such change made visible here, then? As Davoli suggests in chapter 1, the material record has much to contribute, even at a small scale. For example, mud-brick buildings are fairly undemanding to construct and modify, but offer great flexibility in terms of the house forms that can be made with them, and their potential to adapt to changing social and practical requirements. Alterations to the physical structure of the house thus potentially offer clues about changing household sizes and relationships. On the textual side, while Alston remarks on the difficulty of capturing change from the available sources, as Thompson points out, there are ways in which this can be done by adjusting the scale of the inquiry: for example, by thinking about such change on a longer time frame between the Ptolemaic and Roman Periods. The material evidence can be useful at this kind of broader scale, too. For example, regarding regional patterns of organization, as discussed by Davoli in chapter 1, on the one hand, there is evidence for a relative uniformity in the available building materials and the construction techniques applied to them, but on the other hand, archaeologists could still do more to understand the localized effects of geographical, geomorphological, and environmental contexts as sources of variability. An additional scale to consider is an intermediate spatial one: the neighborhood. This features anecdotally in some of the documents, such as Thompson's village survey, but both the neighborhood and the larger regional unit (the district) can potentially serve as units of analysis that are intermediate between the individual household and the settlement as a whole.[13] Such an approach would build on the observations already made in chapters 1 and 2 (by Davoli and Simpson), but shifting the focus more explicitly to this scale might open up new questions about urban structure. To what extent did kinship, occupation, socioeconomic factors, or ethnic-cultural identities influence the spatial clustering of households? Similarly, what factors may have determined ease of access to community facilities like temples?

As noted above, the Egyptian evidence explored in the present volume is uniquely detailed because of the unparalleled preservation of both the remains of the houses themselves, and also the texts relating to houses and households. However, the approaches are in some ways comparable with those being taken to ancient housing in other regions and periods. Drawing explicit parallels highlights some of the strengths and weaknesses of the trajectories of research in different subfields, and at the same time reveals new avenues of research that may already have been explored in other contexts. A key question underlying research on all ancient housing is how best to relate our textual and material sources. The authors in this volume generally adopt a balanced approach in which the two are evaluated independently. In the study of both ancient Greek and Roman housing, the situation was historically very different, with texts playing a dominant role. In the context of Classical Greece, the few texts mentioning aspects of domestic organization were used actively to shape interpretations of archaeological finds. For example, the fourteen volumes of David Robinson's *Excavations at Olynthus* (published between 1929 and 1952) include, alongside description of the excavated remains of large numbers of houses, appendices listing words from ancient Greek texts considered relevant to the description of the house.[14] Literary testimonia are also quoted in translation through brief, three-line excerpts that excise the wider literary context and ignore the subtleties of the original language.[15] In many cases, transliterated terms from these texts were confidently applied to the physical remains of the excavated houses.[16] Such a move entails a series of assumptions that today appear questionable, including that the world of the elite, male, Athenian authors of texts of various genres was similar to the lived experience of members of typical households in the city of Olynthos, some 250 miles to the north. In the context of work on Roman Italy, texts were comparably dominant: for example, early excavators at Pompeii sometimes seem to have moved the furnishings of the houses they were excavating, in order to make their finds resemble more closely those houses they had read about in the works of Latin authors (especially Vitruvius).[17]

Subsequent pioneering work focused on the underlying principles of spatial organization suggested by the texts, rather than on the architectural and other details. In the context of the Greek world, a binary separation of the two sexes was singled out as being the most significant social expectation articulated by Classical Attic writers and was argued to have influenced house layout.[18] In Roman contexts, the writings of Apuleius and Vitruvius were used as lenses through which to understand ways in which the architecture of elite houses may have supported elite social life.[19] By the mid-1980s, however, it became apparent that such text-based approaches gave access only to a rather narrow perspective and that the discussion needed to be broadened to include other types of structure as well as a wider range of social groups.[20] At the same time, re-examination of the archaeological evidence of a variety of Classical Greek houses indicated that a binary spatial pattern, which one might expect from direct application of the gendering of space articulated in the texts, was not obviously discernable in most archaeological evidence. In fact, there is a startling disjunction between the norms articulated in the texts and the layouts of the houses themselves: the plans of excavated structures at Olynthos, Athens, and elsewhere consist largely of rooms clustered around a single space.[21] Finding that, superficially at least, archaeological and textual evidence suggest differing interpretations of ancient social life should prompt us to reflect on a methodology that implicitly assumes the primacy of one type of source over another. But perhaps more interestingly, this discrepancy between archaeological and textual evidence also raises complex questions about the reasons why the two are seemingly in conflict, inviting more nuanced approaches to understanding how authors, builders, and inhabitants manipulated the impressions that texts, architecture, and furnishings made on their readers or viewers.

The Future of Household Archaeology

With reference to our Egyptian examples, some of the chapters of this volume already use several types of sources together to good effect, especially where one source on its own is insufficient (as, for example, with Marouard's study of Ptolemaic tower houses in chapter 3). In other instances, juxtaposition of a wider range of types of evidence might prompt further reflection. For instance, to what extent and in what ways might the importance of the house façade and entrance, highlighted by Abdelwahed based on texts, have been signaled physically through the architecture and/or decoration of this area in the houses themselves? In Greek and Roman contexts, the liminality of entrances is sometimes marked symbolically with a decorative motif, such as a protective Herakles or other painted or relief carved motif.[22] Interestingly, in some of his other work, Abdelwahed has shown that, both in Pharaonic and in later times, the entrances to Egyptian houses were sometimes a location for religious ritual.[23]

Other methodological issues of interest to those working on households across a range of cultural contexts might also benefit from examination through the Egyptian evidence. From an archaeological perspective, it is tempting to wonder how the often excellent preservation of houses and other structures might help with the development of conceptual frameworks for thinking about the use of domestic space in ancient contexts. For example, Boozer importantly details in chapter 8 a range of post-abandonment factors that can affect the state of the architectural remains of houses, as well as the range and locations of artifacts found in the houses, at Amheida. In chapter 12, Gates-Foster, Redon, and Godsey raise similar questions about whether the artifacts associated with the floors of the fort at B'ir Samut can be interpreted as evidence of the activities carried out in the spaces in which they were found. Thus, understanding depositional and post-depositional processes is important for the reconstruction of activity areas in any context, and the modeling of the cultural processes that lie behind artifact distributions at well-preserved historical (as opposed to prehistoric) sites is in many ways underdeveloped in comparison with discussions of the kinds of post-abandonment processes that Boozer discusses.

Moving forward, can the exceptionally well-preserved deposits at any of these sites help us to clarify how we can identify the range of activities carried out in multifunctional spaces? Or, for that matter, how might we differentiate multifunctional spaces from those that played a single role at any one time, but whose role changed over time—whether in a linear fashion, or following a cyclical pattern over a period of, say, a day or a year? Careful examination (microscopic as well as macroscopic) of the deposits in which artifacts were found might enable us to model some of the signatures of these different scenarios, in order to look for them in other parts of the ancient world. There is, however, a limit to the extent of possible comparison between cultures, sites, or even different houses at a single site, as both the activities of the inhabitants and the abandonment/post-abandonment processes can vary significantly. Therefore, although the Egyptian evidence is "good to think with" because of the wide range of types of material that survive and their typically good preservation, conclusions drawn from it will not always be generalizable to other parts of the ancient world. (This point is familiar in the context of other types of study, such as demography.)[24]

In conclusion, the case studies here reveal a number of common themes that relate to wider debates taking place in the analysis of households in the ancient world and beyond. The authors show that the Egyptian evidence has enormous potential to contribute to those debates but also to nuance them in unique ways, through the quantity and detail of the material available. This work creates the potential for a major synthesis in the future: by blending archaeological and textual evidence and structuring that evidence by period and area, we may hope to draw out patterns of continuity and change across time and space.

Notes

1 Bourdieu 1960.
2 Meskell 2005.
3 For a recent discussion, see, for example, Beaudry 2015.

4 Respectively, Douglass and Gonlin 2012, 2; and Briz i Godino and Madella 2013, 2, with earlier references.
5 See Muhs 2008.
6 In the Greek context, for example, see Rotroff 2013.
7 For a classic example, see Blanton 1994.
8 See, for example, Nanoglou 2008 and Hales 2003, respectively.
9 On intersectionality, see the work of Kimberlé Crenshaw, for example Crenshaw 2017.
10 For example, Morgan 2010, *passim*, in relation to Classical Greek society.
11 The case is made in detail for the Roman world by Andrew Riggsby 1997; for a more recent example, see Tuori 2015, esp. 10–11.
12 For example, Souvatzi 2008, 21–46.
13 In relation to archaeological contexts generally, see for example Smith and Novic 2012; and Smith et al. 2015.
14 Robinson 1946, 453–71.
15 Robinson, 1946, 359–462.
16 For example, Robinson 1938.
17 See, for example, Allison 1997.
18 Walker 1993 (first published in 1983).
19 Thébert 1987, with respect to Roman Africa; on Roman Italy, Wallace-Hadrill 1988; 1994, 3–61.
20 For example, Pirson 1999; Wallace-Hadrill 1996.
21 Nevett 1999.
22 See, for example, Bruneau 1964; Coralini 2001.
23 Abdelwahed 2016, 17–25 (I thank Caitlín Barrett for drawing this book to my attention).
24 See for example Scheidel 2001, 16.

Works Cited

Abdelwahed, Y. 2016. *Houses in Graeco-Roman Egypt: Arenas for Ritual Activity*. Oxford: Archaeopress.

Allison, P. 1997. "Artefact Distribution and Spatial Function in Pompeian Houses." In *The Roman Family in Italy*, edited by P. Weaver and B. Rawson, 321–54. Oxford: Oxford University Press.

Beaudry, M. 2015. "Households Beyond the House: On the Archaeology and Materiality of Historical Households." In *Beyond the Walls: New Perspectives on the Archaeology of Historical Households*, edited by M. Beadry and J. A. Nyman, 1–22. Gainesville: University of Florida Press.

Blanton, R. 1994. *Houses and Households: A Comparative Study*. New York: Plenum.

Bourdieu, P. 1960. "The Kabyle House or the World Reversed." *Algeria 1960: Essays by Pierre Bourdieu*. Translated by R. Nice. Cambridge: Cambridge University Press.

Briz i Godino, I., and M. Madella. 2013. "The Archaeology of Household—An Introduction." In *The Archaeology of Household*, edited by M. Madella, G. Kovács, B. Kulcsarne-Berzsenyi, and I. Briz i Godino, 1–5. Oxford: Oxbow.

Bruneau, P. 1964. "Apotropaia déliens. La massue d'Héraclès." *Bulletin de Correspondance Hellenique* 88: 159–68.

Coralini, A. 2001. *Hercules domesticus*. Naples: Electa.

Crenshaw, K. 2017. *On Intersectionality: Essential Writings of Kimberlé Crenshaw*. New York: The New Press.

Douglass, J.G., and N. Gonlin. 2012. "The Household as Analytical Unit: Case Studies from the Americas." In *Ancient Households of the Americas*, edited by J. G. Douglass and N. Gonlin, 1–46. Boulder: University Press of Colorado.

Hales, S. 2003. *The Roman House and Social Identity*. Cambridge: Cambridge University Press.

Meskell, L. 2005. "Introduction: Object Orientations." In *Archaeologies of Materiality*, edited by L. Meskell, 1–17. Oxford: Blackwell.

Morgan, J. 2010. *The Classical Greek House*. Exeter, UK: Bristol Phoenix Press.

Muhs, B. 2008. "Fractions of Houses in Ptolemaic Hawara." In *Graeco-Roman Fayum—Texts and Archaeology*, edited by S. Schentuleit and M. Lippert, 187–98. Wiesbaden: Harrassowitz Verlag.

Nanoglou, S. 2008. "Building Biographies and Households: Aspects of Community Life in Neolithic Northern Greece." *Journal of Social Archaeology* 8 (1): 139–60.

Nevett, L. 1999. *House and Society in the Ancient Greek World*. Cambridge: Cambridge University Press.

Pirson, F. 1999. *Mietwohnungen in Pompeji und Herkulaneum*. Munich: Verlag Dr. F. Pfeil.

Riggsby, A. 1997. " 'Public' and 'Private' in Roman Culture: The Case of the *Cubiculum*." *Journal of Roman Archaeology* 10: 36–56.

Robinson, D.M. 1938. *Excavations at Olynthus*, Vol. 8. *The Hellenic House*. Baltimore: Johns Hopkins University Press.

Robinson, D.M. 1946. *Excavations at Olynthus*. Vol. 12. *Public and Private Architecture*. Baltimore: Johns Hopkins University Press.

Rotroff, S.I. 2013. *Industrial Religion: The Saucer Pyres of the Athenian Agora*. Hesperia Supplement 47. Princeton, NJ: American School of Classical Studies at Athens.

Scheidel, W. 2001. "Progress and Problems in Roman Demography." In *Debating Roman Demography*, edited by W. Scheidel, 1–82. Leiden: Brill.

Smith, M.E., A. Engquist, C. Carvajal, K. Johnston-Zimmerman, M. Algara, B. Gilliland, Y. Kuznetsov, and A. Young. 2015. "Neighborhood Formation in Semi-urban Settlements." *Journal of Urbanism* 8 (2): 173–98.

Smith, M.E., and J. Novic. 2012. "Neighborhoods and Districts in Ancient Mesoamerica." In *The Neighborhood as a Social and Spatial Unit in Mesoamerican Cities*, edited by M.C. Arnauld, L. Manzanilla, and M.E. Smith, 1–26. Tucson: University of Arizona Press.

Souvatzi, S. 2008. *A Social Archaeology of Households in Neolithic Greece: An Anthropological Approach*. Cambridge: Cambridge University Press.

Thébert, Y. 1987. "Private Life and Domestic Architecture in Roman Africa." In *A History of Private Life: From Pagan Rome to Byzantium*, edited by P. Veyne, 313–409. Translated by A. Goldhammer. Cambridge, MA: Harvard University Press.

Tuori, K. 2015. "Introduction: Investigating Public and Private in the Roman House." In *Public and Private in the Roman House and Beyond*, edited by K. Tuori and L. Nissin, 1–15. Portsmouth, RI: Journal of Roman Archaeology Supplement.

Walker, S. 1993. "Women and Housing in Classical Greece." In *Images of Women in Classical Antiquity*, edited by A. Cameron and A. Kuhrt, 81–91. 2nd ed. London: Routledge.

Wallace-Hadrill, A. 1988. "The Social Structure of the Roman House." *Proceedings of the British School at Rome* 56: 43–97.

Wallace-Hadrill, A. 1994. *Houses and Society in Pompeii and Herculaneum*. Princeton: Princeton University Press.

Wallace-Hadrill, A. 1996. "Engendering the Roman House." In *I Claudia: Women in Ancient Rome*, edited by S. Mattheson and D. Kleiner, 104–15. New Haven: Yale University Art Gallery.

Index